The Constitution of Conflict

How the Supreme Court Undermines the Separation of Powers

Thomas Rives Bell

UNIVERSITY PRESS OF KANSAS

Published by the University Press of Kansas (Lawrence, Kansas 66045), which was organized by the Kansas Board of Regents and is operated and funded by Emporia State University, Fort Hays State University, Kansas State University, Pittsburg State University, the University of Kansas, and Wichita State University.

Library of Congress Cataloging-in-Publication Data

Names: Bell, Thomas Rives, author.
Title: The constitution of conflict : how the Supreme Court undermines the separation of powers / Thomas Rives Bell.
Description: Lawrence : University Press of Kansas, 2025. | Series: Constitutional thinking | Includes bibliographical references and index.
Identifiers: LCCN 2025016637 (print) | LCCN 2025016638 (ebook)
ISBN 9780700640386 (cloth)
ISBN 9780700640393 (ebook)
Subjects: LCSH: United States. Supreme Court. | Separation of powers—United States. | Constitutional law—United States. | BISAC: LAW / Constitutional | POLITICAL SCIENCE / History & Theory
Classification: LCC KF4565 .B45 2025 (print) | LCC KF4565 (ebook) | DDC 342.73/044—dc23/eng/20250414
LC record available at https://lccn.loc.gov/2025016637.
LC ebook record available at https://lccn.loc.gov/2025016638.

British Library Cataloguing-in-Publication Data is available.
Authorised Representative Details: Easy Access System Europe
Mustamäe tee 50, 10621 Tallinn, Estonia | gpsr.requests@easproject.com

Jacket design by Karl Janssen
Cover photograph: Sergii Figurnyi/Shutterstock.com.

For three teachers who have most inspired my vocation as a scholar and teacher
Jeffrey Tulis, David Crockett, and Lane Sunderland

And for my students
Who enrich my life and give joy to each day

CONTENTS

FOREWORD

This book is the result of a long-gestating and now impressively mature project. Readers will quickly discover a lucid argument—that the judiciary should stay out of most separation of powers disputes between the Congress and president—nested within a nuanced and complex constitutional theory.

Had this book been published a decade ago, it would have been a timely account of constitutional decay layered on top of an unnoticed continuing constitutional logic. That conjunction would have been illuminating. The Constitution continued to operate in ways not understood by its legal interpreters—but worked poorly because its ongoing unnoticed logic was at odds with the massive misunderstandings that dominated legal discourse and practice that Thomas Bell depicts so well. With the second election of Donald Trump as president, Bell's study offers readers something even more profound and timely, though unplanned and beyond the specific foci of the book. Bell's findings offer resources for a diagnosis of regime demise that is becoming visible in the first months of Trump 2.0.

As many citizens are coming to realize, Congress has abdicated its core responsibilities and "caved" to President Trump's anti-constitutional actions. All that seems to remain as a bulwark against his constitutional transgressions is an attentive judiciary. But the judiciary is ill-equipped to discipline or tether a president who decides to ignore adverse rulings and to attack the judges who issue them. Behind this constitutional crisis is the evacuation of power, understanding, and duty within the legislative branch. This result can be explained by the principal findings of Bell's book—that legal resolution has displaced political contestation between the Congress and president, that the judiciary is ill-suited to resolve disputes that had previously been deemed matters of high politics, and that the vacuum of institutional ambition and constitutional argumentation within the legislature as it abdicated its responsibilities to courts has been filled by a new form of factionalism—hyperpartisanship or tribalism—a topic Bell takes up toward the end of his book.

Thomas Bell labels this kind of constitutional theory "architectonic." That is an excellent descriptor that situates his kind of thinking within the ambit of theorizing that the Constitutional Thinking series is intended to foster. Indeed, while all the books in the series contribute to an architectonic enterprise in some way, of the books we have published thus far only those by Thomas Bell, John Finn, and Sotirios Barber treat architectonic constitutional theory as an explicit theme.

Bell mentions that his theory develops ideas published elsewhere by my fellow coeditor of this series Mariah Zeisberg, by George Thomas, and by me. Bell develops his argument in two ways that stamp his own distinctive mark on this way of thinking. First, he engages the best recent work within the legal academy that touches on this point of view but does not fully express it. Bell takes recent constitutional theorizing by legal academics seriously, and hopefully this book will generate conversation between political science and the very talented new generation of scholars in law schools. Second, he selects perfect cases to probe the dilemmas of constitutionalism over time—the need to remain faithful to a firm Constitution while at the same time justifying some kinds of institutional change to contend with socioeconomic change. These cases are superbly chosen political sites to better articulate architectonic theory as much as they are occasions to apply it.

I will say more about these remarkable cases and the basic features of an "architectonic" constitutional theory below. But first it is important to stress how different Bell's account is from the best resources we have on separation of powers in political science—resources that often share Bell's overall conclusion. Perhaps the "dean" of studies of constitutional conflict, or the lack of needed conflict, is Louis Fisher, whose enormous corpus of writing and years of work on the staff of the Congressional Research Service have generated a rich trove of historical material that all students of this subject find indispensable. This tradition has been carried on by his protege Jasmine Farrier and by Josh Chafetz, a political scientist and legal academic, whose recent book is the best of this genre. For all their merits, none of these scholars develops a theory. All offer descriptive material with which to contest or support claims made by the Supreme Court and resources for Congress to recover its voice and position in the constitutional order—but these are historical or empirical claims, not accounts of the overall design of the American constitutional order. None of these scholars distinguish the fundamental from the peripheral attributes of the Constitution, none discuss the philosophic presuppositions of the fundamental features, and none discuss the institutional, economic, and cultural implications of fundamental commitments over time as do scholars who take an architectonic point of view.

An architectonic approach takes the vantage point of an imagined founder—a person responsible for the design of a whole polity. It can be informed by study of the actual American founders—but it is not their specific intentions that are key. It is not an appeal to founding authority. Rather, it is the point of view of the problems that any founder seeks to solve that define this perspective. Constitution-makers seek to build polities intended to advance political purposes over time. This kind of project includes defining and assigning "power" and "rights" and "offices," but it is not principally an arrangement of offices and powers or a settlement of political conflict at the time a constitution is made. Instead, it is an attempt to build a way of life and to shape a future to better realize the aspirations of that way of life. The character and consequences of a future way of life—a large commercial republic—animated the debate between federalists and anti-federalists, for example. This future socioeconomic and cultural order was one not just predicted by the smartest "founders" but was, more importantly, induced by the new Constitution.

Anti-federalists rightly pointed out that the proposed Constitution did not make "separation of powers" one of its central design principles. One sign of this was that there is no "separation of powers" clause in the Constitution as there was in some previous state constitutions. Another indicator was that legislative, executive, and judicial power were not defined by their natures and cleanly assigned to distinct institutions. Instead, institutional structures were given pride of place and powers were mixed and assigned in ways to enable competing institutions to vindicate competing desiderata of democratic governance—popular will, rights, and security.

Following those of us who have developed this idea, Thomas Bell argues that conflict between the branches was thought to be fructifying to the extent that it provided a way to balance competing purposes of democratic governance. This is an inherently political task and is the reason courts are ill-suited to arbitrate disputes of this sort, except when vindicating the powers and duties of their own institution.

Bell's fascinating cases—regarding the legislative veto, recess appointments, executive agreements, and impeachment—all profoundly elaborate and illustrate an additional feature of this architectonic point of view. The conventional and common legalist perspective treats the Constitution as a horizontal project, with powers and procedures specified clearly enough that courts attempt to vindicate the design by insisting on adherence to its literal form. Thus, the legislative veto is unconstitutional because the Constitution specifies that the president must sign every order or resolution of the Congress that becomes law. Or, Congress only goes on "recess" when it formally adjourns. Or, abuses that are impeachable must offend the criminal code because "crimes" are mentioned. Or, only "treaties" count as international agreements.

One way to summarize the most important insight of this book is to suggest that Thomas Bell views the Constitution as a vertical design. The whole Constitution is a project in service of positive ends—forming a more perfect union, establishing justice, insuring domestic tranquility, providing for the common defense, promoting the general welfare, and securing the blessings of liberty. Legalists tend to ignore those ends—the preamble has no legal effect, for example, and many legalists treat the document as mainly a charter of negative rights—rights against the government. The architectonic perspective foregrounds the positive purposes of constitution making.

Bell shows that the whole Constitution—the complicated arrangements of structures and powers—can be understood hierarchically, as a cascade of means and ends subsidiary to the document's primary purposes. On this architectonic view, adherence to the literal processes of the Constitution may sometimes subvert the Constitution to the extent that such "fidelity" frustrates the purpose or point of the power or the process. Bell describes this judicial mistake as insisting on literal forms "for their own sake" rather than inquiring what the powers and processes were designed to achieve.

His chapter on the legislative veto is an excellent example of how fidelity to literal form can subvert higher order purposes. The legislative veto was an invention of Congress and the presidency together, intended to solve the problem that delegation of power to the president to make "rules" to enable the president to "take care" that the laws are faithfully executed seemed to abdicate Congress's most basic job. As the nation expanded and its problems became complex, administrative expertise became more necessary to identify and address the nation's challenges. Because rules can be enforced as law, the question obviously arose about how the legislature could give away its lawmaking power to the president and the executive branch in a way that did not ignore the reasons it had such power in the first place, namely representative and deliberative capacity. The bipartisan and bi-institutional solution was to render delegation accountable by requiring that expert-designed rules be returned to the legislature for approval in some cases, and for disapproval in others, before the rules were finalized.

The legislative veto was challenged and all statutes that contained legislative vetoes—more than three hundred laws—were struck down by the Supreme Court in a case called *INS v. Chadha*. The court found that the Constitution requires that "Every Order, Resolution, or Vote to which the Concurrence of the Senate and House of Representatives may be necessary shall be presented to the President of the United States . . . " and be either approved, vetoed, or repassed by a two-thirds vote of both houses. The court held that the legislative veto was a "vote" and that it required "presentment" to the president. Bell points out that the legislative veto device creatively served the purposes of the presentment clause. After all, it was the president and his subordinates that proposed the rule that was subject to the veto. In Bell's telling this arrangement simply reversed the order in which the two institutions acted. This new device made rulemaking more efficient *and* preserved legislatively accountability.

Bell's cases are all interesting because they illustrate how and why the migration of power between institutions can be justified if the purposes for which the power is assigned are enhanced. When one combines this insight about verticality with the earlier observation that arbitrating the relative weights of congressional and presidential power is an inherently political task, one sees how Bell mounts such a compelling case that prevailing practice of legalizing institutional conflict marks a profound decay of the American constitutional order.

Jeffrey K. Tulis
Coeditor, Constitutional Thinking series

ACKNOWLEDGMENTS

This book would not be possible without the support of a great many people. I am especially grateful to my teacher and mentor Jeffrey Tulis, whose support and guidance proved indispensable at all stages of the project. Many thanks also to George Thomas and Jasmine Farrier, each of whom read the full manuscript and provided invaluable feedback that greatly improved the final version.

I am grateful to several colleagues in the discipline for many conversations and for feedback at various stages, including Alec Arellano, Christina Bambrick, Jordan Cash, Joey Cozza, Michael Gibbs, Tara Ginnane, Alex Hindmann, Alex Hudson, Anthony Ives, Ben Kleinerman, Rich Lizardo, Maggie Moslander, Curt Nichols, Mark Rosen, Kyle Shen, Andrew Spiropoulos, Allen Sumrall, Mariah Zeisberg, and especially David Crockett, Connor Ewing, and Charles Zug. In particular, I would like to thank Josh Chafetz, Gary Jacobsohn, and H. W. Perry, each of whom served on my dissertation committee and offered substantial feedback that helped transform the dissertation into book form. Thanks also to the University Press of Kansas for publishing this book, to Senior Editor David Congdon for shepherding it through the review process, and to the editors of the Constitutional Thinking Series for their support of the project: Sanford Levinson, Jeffrey Tulis, Emily Zackin, and Mariah Zeisberg.

I could not have finished the book without the support of wonderful colleagues and friends at Knox College. I consider myself fortunate to teach in a remarkable political science department alongside talented and supportive colleagues: Andy Civettini, Sue Hulett, Karen Kampwirth, Yu Bin Kim, Duane Oldfield, and Katie Stewart. Lane and Jacklyn Sunderland have been especially welcoming as I made the move from Texas to the prairie of Illinois, inviting me into their lives and supporting me in every aspect of my life and work. Lane was my predecessor in my role at Knox for forty-seven years and has become a valuable mentor and dear friend.

Two friends in particular, Ron Belgau and Ashleen Menchaca-Bagnulo, have supported me throughout the book-writing process, engaging in countless conversations, reading drafts, editing, and shouldering the burden of my excessive anxiety. I can't imagine writing this book without their friendship, which has been a sustaining bulwark in my life.

Finally, words cannot express how grateful I am to my family, especially my parents Robert and Cheryl Bell, for their unconditional love and support that has made my life and vocation possible.

A condensed version of chapter 4 on recess appointments was previously published as "Perverse Politics: Recess Appointments, Noel Canning, and the Limits of Law" in *Presidential Studies Quarterly* 48, no. 2 (2018). A shortened version of the legislative veto chapter will appear in *Beyond Checks and Balances*, edited by Ben Kleinerman, Connor Ewing, and Charles Zug (University of Pennsylvania Press).

Introduction

According to a prominent narrative among critics of the US Constitution, the concept of separation of powers is in a state of crisis, suffering "through an enfeebled old age."[1] The static legal framework the separation of powers principle embodies, with its strict separation of different types of powers and checks and balances, is viewed as *a* (if not *the*) fundamental problem of American government today. The Constitution's governmental framework, the narrative goes, was designed for the relatively simple agrarian society of the eighteenth and nineteenth centuries but has proven unworkable in addressing the demands of modern government in the contemporary world.[2] Perhaps the most striking recent indictment of the American constitutional order's institutional arrangement—reminiscent of Woodrow Wilson's critique a century earlier—comes from prominent political scientists William G. Howell and Terry M. Moe. In their book aptly titled *Relic: How Our Constitution Undermines Effective Government*, Howell and Moe criticize the separation of powers framework—and especially what they characterize as the parochial Congress at its center—as ultimately creating an ineffective government due to its emphasis on constraint:

> If government is to address the myriad problems that arise in the modern world, it must be able to act, and act effectively. But it literally wasn't designed for that. It was designed for a different, pre-modern world. It is folly to think that what may have worked quite well in that world will also work in ours. Why would it? The founders had no idea what a modern society would look like, no idea what demands and problems it would generate, no idea what governmental effectiveness would require in such a context. They could not provide us with a government suitable for modern times even if they intended to.[3]

This indictment of the Constitution's inability to provide for effective governance should perhaps come as no surprise given the extent to which the separation of powers itself has, throughout American history, been characterized by its restraining purposes. Justice Louis Brandeis famously wrote that "the doctrine of the separation of powers was adopted by the Convention of 1787, not to promote efficiency but to preclude the exercise of arbitrary power."[4] Brandeis's dictum that the separation of powers doctrine favors safety over and against efficiency and effectiveness, moreover, represents the predominant view of constitutional theorists that the primary purpose of a constitution is to provide clear-cut rules to coordinate action, thereby creating the conditions for stability and predictability.[5] Given the emphasis on constraint, it is not necessarily even important how power is specifically allocated so long as the Constitution effectively coordinates action through a settled understanding of the law and its requirements. For example, John F. Manning argues that the Constitution's separation of powers represents nothing more than various practical compromises made at the Constitutional Convention. The Constitution's various clause-bound assignments of power, therefore, must be interpreted specifically to enforce the rules of the road, so to speak, and not as reflecting a comprehensive separation of powers theory underlying the Constitution.[6] Although there are some exceptions to the view that the primary purpose of separation of powers is to constrain and limit governmental action, such exceptions, as Jeremy Waldron observes, go "against the general trend."[7] According to Waldron, separation of powers constitutionalism has been so discredited by the focus on constraint that we may only be able to speak "elegiacally" about it as a positive concept.[8]

If the separation of powers is not inherently out of date, another prominent diagnosis posits that Madisonian political science has been rendered obsolete by the introduction of political parties. As Daryl Levinson and Richard Pildes argue, political parties have undermined the central assumption of the founders that the ambition of the office holder would be attached to the institution she inhabits.[9] Today, political parties bridge the separation of powers under conditions of unified partisan control of Congress and the presidency, thus undermining checks and balances. In other words, the separation of powers only works under certain partisan configurations. Even then, however, interbranch conflict is merely epiphenomenal, the result of a larger partisan conflict. This critique certainly makes sense of American politics today. Indeed, one does not need to look diligently to find examples of members of Congress, in particular, placing partisan advantage above the institutional prerogatives of their own branch. However, as will be discussed in the book's concluding chapter, this critique is often based on a misunderstanding of Madisonian political science, which contains within itself ways to think about the problem of excessive partisanship.

This book is about the complex relationship between the law and politics of the Constitution. While I develop a normative account of the proper working of the separation of powers, I ultimately do so by articulating an understanding of the logic and dynamic of the Constitution as a whole. Central to the book's inquiry is an exploration of how to understand the legal boundaries between Congress and the president, and how they are to be maintained. The diagnosis it makes, however, is different from those described. The main argument is that the Constitution is fundamental law, but not in the way envisioned by the judicialized or legalistic Constitution. According to the legalistic conception of the separation of powers, the Constitution is law in the sense that it is primarily a legal text that assigns powers that must be enforced, presumably by the judiciary. The Constitution is thus flattened and reduced to its textual limits understood in purely literalist terms. Given that the Constitution is conceived primarily, even purely, as a legal document, the judiciary is given supreme status as its ultimate interpreter and enforcer. To put it in spatial terms, the judiciary sits above the separation of powers, enforcing the textual limits of the Constitution. While the Supreme Court has never embraced a consistent methodology for enforcing the separation of powers—alternating inconsistently between formalist and functionalist approaches—it is broadly, if not almost unanimously, assumed that it should superintend the separation of powers to enforce the legal boundaries between the branches. While the purported animating principle of its competing approaches is liberty protection, this emphasis is more rhetorical than substantive.[10] Whether the court ensures strict textual separation or maintains the relative balance between the branches, the goods (primarily liberty) generated in the abstract by judicial superintendence are merely derivative consequences of enforcing the separation of powers itself. In short, in the hands of the judiciary, the separation of powers has been transformed into legalistic doctrines that emphasize textual limits at the expense of governmental ends.

As Sotirios Barber has argued, however, it is philosophically incoherent to establish a Constitution primarily to limit itself.[11] And, in fact, the framers did not understand constitutionalism in such terms. The Constitution, as Chief Justice John Marshall once wrote, was "intended to endure for ages to come, and consequently to be adapted to the various crises of human affairs."[12] To legally script answers to all the questions that would confront the polity in advance of the political circumstances that give rise to them would require that the Constitution "partake of the prolixity of a legal code," rendering it incomprehensible. A constitution, therefore, "requires that only its great outlines should be marked, its important objects designated, and the minor ingredients which compose those objects be deduced from the nature of the objects themselves."[13] If the Constitution is meant to endure for the ages, and to be adaptable to the "various crises of human affairs," then this suggests that the Constitution is not primarily about limits but about the achievement of the polity's unlimited ends.

Contrary to the dominant overly legalistic conception, this book argues that the Constitution establishes a legally indeterminate political architecture of differently designed institutions brought into political conflict with each other to advance the competing and politically contingent ends of the constitutional order. I thus integrate and build upon the work of scholars who advance an ends-oriented or political understanding of the Constitution's separation of powers, such as Jeffrey K. Tulis, George Thomas, and Mariah Zeisberg.[14] According to the architectonic view, the Constitution is fundamental law not primarily in the sense that it is a legal text to be decoded and enforced by the judiciary utilizing ordinary tools of legal analysis. Rather, it is fundamental law because it establishes an entire polity and its institutional forms, and a central feature of the Constitution's design is its self-enforcing nature through political conflict between the branches.[15] The framers understood that legal limits on governmental power enervate the government of its capacity to meet the unlimited needs of the polity, especially since unforeseen contingencies are endemic to political life. The Constitution thus set into motion a dynamic system of government to achieve these unlimited ends. Separation of powers and checks and balances are therefore properly understood as subordinate features of a political architecture that channels politics within and through differentiated political structures.[16] As *The Federalist* demonstrates, design ingredients such as mode of election, length of term, number of officeholders, competent powers, and reeligibility create structures of powers that induce or make more likely essential functional qualities necessary for good governance. These differentiated structures also make provision for competing institutional perspectives on political questions that confront the polity.[17] In this way, the separation of powers, rather than being primarily a textual principle to enforce through the courts, is the institutional means to the polity's unlimited and politically contingent ends. Political conflict between the branches—rather than legal determinacy—is a fundamental feature of the constitutional design, especially because the ends or aspirations of the polity are themselves both politically contingent and in considerable tension with each other.

Understood as a political architecture, the Constitution tames and subordinates judicial power. To return to spatial terms, judicial power exists within the Constitution's political framework rather than above the separation of powers as the sole interpreter of a legal text. Consequently, a core argument of the book, following Jesse Choper, is that separation of powers disputes between Congress and the president concerning their respective legal boundaries should be considered nonjusticiable political questions.[18] The judicial role should be limited to the protection of its own institutional prerogatives and to the safeguarding of rights. Interbranch disputes between Congress and the president concerning their respective legal boundaries only implicate rights in a derivative sense and should not serve as the basis for judicial resolution of the political question.[19] The scope of the judicial role in interbranch disputes is articulated in chapter 1. From a practical perspective, judicial review is superfluous given that both political branches have determinate tools to press their judgments against the other in politics, tools that are more powerful than judicial judgment. Moreover, while it is commonplace to assume that the judiciary can serve as an impartial arbiter of legal disputes between Congress and the president, turning to the courts can cause more problems than it solves. As Jasmine Farrier has demonstrated in her comprehensive overview of separation of powers litigation and its efficacy, such lawsuits are a symptom of constitutional dysfunction rather than its cure and thus cannot serve as a substitute for political contestation between the branches.[20] This is all the more true as the Supreme Court itself has become increasingly polarized along partisan lines.[21] I conclude with a discussion of a major source of constitutional dysfunction (hyperpartisanship) that makes it hard for Congress to exercise independent will and demonstrates how the architectonic conception points to pathways for reform that could mitigate the problem.

The book illuminates the logic and dynamic of the separation of powers system through an explication of case studies concerning the legislative veto, executive agreements, the appointments process, and congressional oversight of the executive branch. These case studies demonstrate that political and constitutional conflict between Congress and the president is an essential feature of the constitutional design, which calls for a dynamic interaction between the two branches to work out disputes in a political manner. The conception of separation of powers conflict showcased in these case studies is not simply reducible to a departmentalist account of constitutional interpretation outside the judiciary (though certainly that is an essential component of constitutional politics).[22] Rather, the case studies demonstrate the ways in which legal analysis cannot fully capture the dynamism of the political system as the branches respond to each other in politics across constitutional domains. Legal analysis is inadequate because what the branches need in any given circumstance cannot be determined in advance of the contextual factors that give rise to interbranch disputes. The framers thus established a legally indeterminate political architecture that could be responsive to the unforeseen exigencies that are endemic to political life precisely because it is both theoretically and practically impossible to legally script the answers to questions that themselves cannot be predicted in advance. In other words, the Constitution responds to the ineradicable problem of uncertainty not by drafting a Constitution with a code-like character but by creating institutions that can respond to new crises through their dynamic interaction. The separation of powers is thus not an end in itself to be maintained for legal reasons unrelated to the ends the Constitution seeks to achieve by way of institutional design. While conventional accounts of the separation of powers view settlement as an important feature of the constitutional system, laying the predicate for judicial superintendence of interbranch boundaries, this legalistic conception, as Daphna Renan argues, misses the ways in which the Constitution's provisionality—its fundamentally *unsettled* nature—is at the heart of the political project it established.[23] The separation of powers system allows for the ongoing contestation over the distribution of power as the polity seeks to accomplish new objectives in response to unforeseen problems, a dynamic process that is short-circuited when the court intervenes to settle separation of powers disputes concerning the legal boundaries between the political branches.

In the case studies, I take an analytical and empirical approach, contrasting the political conception of separation of powers articulated in chapter 1 with the conventional legalistic account that regards the separation of powers as primarily a textual principle (presumably to be enforced in a legalistic manner by the judiciary). Ultimately, the case studies demonstrate that the problem is not that the Constitution established a static legal order unadaptable to the needs of contemporary circumstances. Rather, the problem is that the separation of powers has been wrongly conceived in such terms. To put it in John Finn's helpful formulation, there are two constitutions: the juridic (or legalistic) Constitution and the civic (or political) Constitution.[24] These two constitutional understandings exist both simultaneously and in significant tension with each other. The political conception is more faithful to the founding design and political science of the framers. The legalistic conception, however, has been layered on top of the founding design, subverting it and muting its effectiveness as a governing system without actually displacing it. Put simply, political actors engage in constitutional politics within the established institutional system of the Constitution's political order (the actual polity as designed), but they do so on terms fundamentally reshaped by the legalistic gloss of the juridic constitution (imposed understandings that mischaracterize and thus undermine or subvert the constitutional order in practice). As the case studies demonstrate, many of the dilemmas or problems of contemporary governance arise in the space between these two constitutional understandings.

The case studies provide a few lessons that can be briefly introduced here before they are developed more fully in subsequent chapters. First, from the architectonic perspective described in chapter 1, the focus on the separation of powers as the institutional means to the polity's ends allows for a great deal of dynamism as the Constitution's legal limits are stretched, though not broken, to meet the needs of new developments and as the political branches work together to find functional solutions to new issues, such as the administrative state. Congress, for example, might need to delegate legislative power to the executive branch departments or agencies if the nation is to effectively govern a nationalized and industrial economy in a globalized world. The question is not whether Congress should be prohibited from delegating by a judicially-enforced nondelegation doctrine. Rather, what matters, if it chooses to delegate, is *how* it does so to ensure that it does not abdicate its own functions. Prior to the court's invalidation of the legislative veto, Congress and the president had negotiated a way to harness executive energy through delegation while ensuring democratic accountability by making such delegation ultimately subject to congressional approval or disapproval. In this way, judicial involvement—based on a flawed conception of the separation of powers—actually undermined the constitutional system, making it both less functional and less accountable. By disrupting the political branches' hard-fought compromise to balance competing constitutional goods through new institutional arrangements, the court also lent considerable credence to the notion that the Constitution is not up to the task of contemporary government.

Second, even in constitutional domains where the court hasn't intervened—such as in executive agreements—many think the Constitution has no bearing on contemporary practice and thus have a hard time employing meaningful constitutional standards for evaluation of governmental practice. The executive agreements case study demonstrates how the constitutional system works in ways that the legalistic conception misses or fails to understand. A narrow focus on the literal strictures of the text, in other words, misses the dynamism of the actual workings of the Constitution's political institutions. This does not mean that any arrangement the branches develop satisfies constitutional standards as well as others. But insofar as particular arrangements do not work well, they are open to criticism, contestation, and revision over time by politically accountable and responsive institutions. Constitutional construction is part of a long-term dynamic process of trial and error not easily subject to brightline rules and standards announced by the judiciary. Howell and Moe perhaps inadvertently provide another example of the separation of powers' dynamism while not seeing the Constitution as its source. In their book *Relic*, quoted at the outset, they argue that the Constitution should be amended to enhance executive power by giving the president the power to propose legislation to Congress that then must be fast-tracked to an up or down vote by Congress without amendment.[25] Leaving aside the question of whether this is a good proposal, it is worth noting that it is taken from an actual arrangement whereby Congress promised to fast-track approval of trade agreements negotiated by the president for an up-or-down vote without amendment so long as Congress was kept informed and its views considered throughout the negotiations.[26] The separation of powers, in other words, generated the very proposal that Howell and Moe argue would modernize the Constitution if adopted as a constitutional amendment. While it is easy to see the value of such an arrangement in some circumstances, it could be negotiated between Congress and the president without codifying it as a constitutional amendment. Indeed, such codification would deprive the branches of the political flexibility needed to reach workable compromises appropriate to different circumstances. The point here is that the separation of powers system is able to meet new needs while controlling itself through the interior structure of the government, to put it in Madison's formulation from *Federalist* 51. A narrow focus on the literal strictures of the Constitution misses the dynamism of interbranch politics, dynamism instantiated by the constitutional text but not fully reducible to it.

Third, the legalistic conception distorts political discourse, substituting political judgments and prudential arguments with the language and standards of law. Legal analysis often exclusively (and rightly) focuses on factors such as text, history, and precedent without any attention to the contextual factors that give rise to political disputes in the first place. The move to legal standards, therefore, means that politics take on the specialized language of law, making it less accessible to ordinary citizens while also ridding discourse of the contextual factors that are essential to resolving disputes. The problem, then, is that while political discourse shifts to a legal register that is inattentive to political circumstances, the politics animating interbranch disputes do not disappear. Rather, political context is merely viewed as irrelevant to the ultimate resolution of political disputes. This has the unintended effect of distorting how citizens understand and evaluate interbranch disputes. These points are borne out and elaborated upon in the case study chapters on recess appointments and congressional oversight of the executive branch.

An orienting principle of this book is the notion that the Constitution is not self-sustaining. Rather, it requires certain civic understandings and practices to make it work over time.[27] The burden is to demonstrate that the conventional account of the separation of powers is inadequate to meet the needs of the polity because it seeks to maintain the separation of powers as an end in itself rather than understanding the institutional system as the conduit through which citizens seek the politically contingent ends of the polity. This is an inescapably normative argument, but one derived from the Constitution itself and what I argue is the best version of its political science.[28] Recovering the conception of the separation of powers as a political architecture—and thus reorienting ourselves to the type of politics such a conception can foster and sustain—is essential to the ongoing task of constitutional maintenance.

Plan of the Book

The book is divided into two parts: a theoretical chapter and four case studies chapters that apply its framework. Chapter 1 juxtaposes the political conception of separation of powers with the conventional legalistic account. On the conventionalist account, the separation of powers—whether understood in formalist or functionalist terms—must be enforced as an end in itself. Any constitutional goods that flow from the enforcement of the separation of powers are merely derivative benefits. The legalistic conception of separation of powers thus reveals an inversion of means and ends. This chapter lays out the main argument that the separation of powers is more than a legal doctrine, that the differentiated institutional structures provide essential institutional competencies and induce competing perspectives on politics, and that disputes between Congress and the president concerning their legal boundaries should be considered nonjusticiable political questions. Judicial superintendence of the boundaries between Congress and the president extracts the Supreme Court from within the separation of powers, placing it above a legal text rather than within a system of government, which misunderstands the nature of the Madisonian system.

The next four chapters apply the theoretical framework of chapter 1 to case studies, the purpose of which is to showcase how to think politically about the Constitution in different contexts and how recourse to narrowly legalistic reasoning about the Constitution's assignments of power can undermine constitutional purposes. Specifically, I examine four cases: the legislative veto, executive agreements, recess appointments, and contemporary problems of congressional oversight. The cases selected reflect a broad array of constitutional phenomena and are thus able to demonstrate the analytical framework of the book across constitutional domains.

Chapter 2, on the legislative veto, considers the extent to which the Constitution's governing framework is adequate to the demands of modern governance. The legislative veto was a political invention that enabled congressional delegation to the executive branch and independent agencies while protecting democratic accountability. The Supreme Court invalidated the legislative veto in *INS v. Chadha* (1984), a decision that had sweeping impacts on the functions of government through its invalidation of more than three hundred statutes. The court's decision, however, was premised on a flawed, legalistic conception of the Constitution's separation of powers. The decision in *Chadha* thus subverted a healthy working relationship between the branches in which Congress was able to harness the efficiency and expertise of the executive branch while ensuring that the laws that govern citizens retain the consent of Congress. In this way, the legislative veto, far from undermining the separation of powers, was a healthy example of the governing framework adapting itself to the problems of modern government.

Chapter 3 evaluates the contemporary use of executive agreements in light of the Constitution's political architecture. The Constitution recognizes only one form of international agreement, the treaty, which may be negotiated by the executive but must be ratified by a two-thirds majority in the Senate. In contemporary practice, executive agreements vastly outnumber treaties. Can these agreements be reconciled with the Constitution? Although not without significant problems, the use of executive agreements and related congressional oversight of the executive branch, largely suggests a healthy working relationship between the branches perfectly consistent with the Constitution's separation of powers framework. This chapter explores the ways in which the political branches have engaged each other to develop this principled division of labor. Notably, because the court usually does not intervene in foreign affairs, understanding how the political branches have developed their approach to executive agreements over time provides a useful lens for understanding how Congress and the president can work together to develop new frameworks that make use of their institutional strengths while protecting their prerogatives. This case study is therefore important for understanding what constitutional politics can look like without judicial superintendence.

Chapter 4 examines the Supreme Court's intervention in the recess appointments controversy during the Obama administration in *National Labor Relations Board v. Noel Canning* (2014). The Supreme Court ruled unanimously that the recess appointments were unconstitutional even as it split five to four on how narrowly to construe the recess appointments clause. This chapter argues that the underlying purpose of the recess appointments clause—its principled commitment—is that the government ought to continue functioning absent democratic choice to the contrary. The clause, of course, originally had a technological function and was adopted because Congress only convened for parts of the year, and difficulties of travel and communication at the time meant that the president needed a mechanism to keep the government staffed. The formalistic line drawing by the court, without attention to larger constitutional objectives, not only legitimized partisan obstruction of the Senate by Republicans but also interfered with President Obama's ability to staff the offices and programs created by Congress. This chapter argues that political contestation between the branches—structured by constitutional arguments attentive to the actual political circumstances animating the dispute—could have restarted a stalled deliberative process whereas legal resolution distorted the political dynamics at play, giving the illusion of an imperial presidency while providing legal cover for congressional abdication. The chapter argues that the controversy posed a nonjusticiable political question and should have been left to the realm of politics.

Chapter 5 demonstrates how congressional oversight of the executive branch has been enervated by narrowly legal reasoning about congressional powers, especially regarding executive privilege and impeachment. This chapter is especially important in the scheme of the book because the presidency looms large in contemporary politics, the result of its institutional logic and comparative institutional advantages. As executive power grows, so must Congress's oversight capacities. The chapter concludes with the pitfalls of using a blunt weapon like criminal prosecution rather than the politically accountable power of impeachment.

The concluding chapter addresses the problem of partisanship and the separation of powers, asking whether the Madisonian system is workable in light of hyperpartisanship. Some scholars, most notably Daryl Levinson and Richard Pildes, conclude that the separation of powers has been replaced by a separation of parties. I argue that this analysis is too simplistic because there are a number of examples of the political branches defending institutional prerogatives regardless of larger partisan dynamics (and in fact this is demonstrated in at least two of the case study chapters). Moreover, it should not be terribly surprising that congressional and presidential interactions vary according to the partisan breakdown between the branches, as this is simply the logical outcome of a system responsive to outside political demands. Even so, it is true that hyperpartisanship, in many instances, undermines the effective functioning of the separation of powers, as indicated by congressional Republican behavior during the first Trump administration, especially during the impeachment proceedings. But to locate the problem fundamentally with the separation of powers itself is misplaced even as this diagnosis recognizes a deeply concerning feature of modern politics. Again, the architectonic view provides a way to think about, and to propose solutions to, the problem of excessive partisanship. As argued earlier, the separation of powers is not merely the legal relationship between the branches but is a feature of a larger political architecture based on an interrelated set of design choices, including mode of election, length of term, number of officeholders, competent powers, and reeligibility. Modern political innovations grafted onto the constitutional order, such as partisan primaries, exacerbate partisan polarization by misdirecting electoral ambition away from majoritarian constituencies, and undermine the effective functioning of governing institutions. The problem is not with separation of powers per se, but with contingent, extraconstitutional features of the present order.

1

Separation of Powers and the Problem of Ends and Means

There is widespread concern today that the court's handling of separation of powers issues has been, at best, inconsistent. Aziz Z. Huq and John D. Michaels, for example, describe the court's separation of powers jurisprudence as "a puzzle," noting that besides general acceptance of the basic premises that the separation of powers "promotes governmental accountability" and "secures individual rights," the court's attempt to translate the separation of powers into a workable legal doctrine "seems unmoored and unprincipled."[1] Such charges, moreover, are not merely of recent vintage. Rather, commentators on the court's separation of powers jurisprudence have sounded the alarm about the court's inconsistent and unprincipled jurisprudence going back at least thirty years. As one scholar put it in the early 1990s, "The Supreme Court's treatment of the constitutional separation of powers is an incoherent muddle."[2] The court has embraced inconsistent methodologies, often referred to as formalism and functionalism, and has applied them in an ad hoc manner.[3] Moreover, the court has at times looked to long-standing historical practice when abstract methodologies fail to yield clear decisions.[4] The inconsistent application of these divergent methodologies, moreover, cannot be blamed on the court's changing personnel given that individual justices have at times alternated between inconsistent approaches. Even in the absence of a consistent judicial approach to separation of powers cases, however, there is little question today that such questions should be decided by the Supreme Court. As Nikolas Bowie and Daphna Renan write, "Debates over the separation of powers have become debates over which lawyerly method courts should use to establish the Constitution's true limits. Although participants disagree whether those limits should be defined formally or functionally, or with reference to original public meaning, liquidation, or the gloss of historical practice, they agree that it is the Supreme Court—using the tools of legalism—that should decide them."[5]

The purpose here is not to show why one of these methodological approaches is better than the other. Rather, it is to show the logic and limitations of these approaches and how they ultimately attempt to reach the same goal, albeit by different means: the maintenance of the Constitution's separation of powers as an end in itself. The discussion here is brief and, of course, cannot do justice to all the various nuances and intricacies of the scholarly work on competing approaches to adjudicating separation of powers disputes. The purpose is to draw out in broad strokes the animating principles of each approach and to discuss the implications of these approaches for political practice more generally.

Formal Separation Account

The view of separation of powers most at odds with the perspective advocated here is the pure separation account, which is often associated with what is referred to as formalism in Supreme Court jurisprudence.[6] According to this view, the substantive natures of different types of powers—legislative, executive, and judicial—are discerned and assigned to the appropriate institution such that "Congress's grants of legislative power must enable it to legislate, the President's grant of executive power must enable him to execute all federal laws, and the federal judiciary's grant of judicial power must enable the federal courts to decide certain cases and controversies."[7] The branches, moreover, are prohibited from exercising powers appropriately assigned to the other branches. This separation of powers theory or doctrine is clearly summarized by M. C. Vile in his canonical treatment of the separation of powers:

> It is essential for the establishment and maintenance of political liberty that the government be divided into three branches or departments, the legislature, the executive, and the judiciary. To each of these three branches there is a corresponding identifiable function of government, legislative, executive, or judicial. Each branch of government must be confined to the exercise of its own function and not allowed to encroach upon the functions of the other branches. Furthermore, the persons who compose these three agencies of government must be kept separate and distinct, no individual being allowed to be at the same time a member of more than one branch.[8]

Constitutional formalists thus ensure that the exercise of any governmental power "comports strictly with the original blueprint laid down in Articles I, II, and III of the Constitution."[9] For example, when the court invalidated the legislative veto as an unconstitutional legislative usurpation of executive power it did so based on the presumption, noted by Chief Justice Burger, that the "Constitution sought to divide the delegated powers of the new federal government into three defined categories, legislative, executive, and judicial, to assure, as nearly as possible, that each Branch of government would confine itself to its assigned responsibility."[10] The court acknowledged that the branches are not "'hermetically' sealed off from one another" but still concluded that when any branch acts, it presumptively exercises the kinds of power granted to it by the Constitution. Similarly, when the Supreme Court ruled against the Truman administration's seizure of the steel mills during the Korean War, it did so because it could not find any express powers in Article II, narrowly construed, authorizing such action absent an explicit grant of power from Congress. President Truman's seizure of the steel mills, therefore, amounted to an unconstitutional usurpation of Congress's legislative power. As Justice Black wrote in his majority opinion:

> In the framework of our Constitution, the President's power to see that the laws are faithfully executed refutes the idea that he is to be a lawmaker. The Constitution limits his functions in the lawmaking process to the recommending of laws he thinks wise and the vetoing of laws he thinks bad. And the Constitution is neither silent nor equivocal about who shall make laws which the President is to execute.[11]

Defending Justice Black's opinion in the *Youngstown* case, David J. Siemers writes, "If politicians are allowed to crash through constitutional barriers when they are inconvenient, then there is no point to having a Constitution. If policy preferences would be considered more important than proper constitutional process, it would be an invitation for all the branches to be involved in every issue before government, because there would no longer be functional barriers between the branches."[12] While the founders "did anticipate that the branches would sometimes come into conflict with each other," Siemers argues, "they did not enshrine interbranch conflict as a governing norm." Rather, the Constitution ensures that such conflict does not become a governing norm by "clarifying which branch possessed what power."[13] While Justice Jackson's more flexible concurring opinion laying out a tripartite scheme for understanding the fluctuations of power between the political branches has carried the day in subsequent constitutional history, Jackson's concurrence still viewed presidential power as ultimately legally dependent upon Congress's exercise of its own power. If Congress has passed a law specifying a policy, the president's power to act unilaterally, even in the midst of a crisis, is greatly curtailed.

The formalist account of separation of powers thus empowers an active judiciary to police the constitutional and legal boundaries between the branches to ensure that each stays within its textually confined sphere of action.[14] The literal strictures of the constitutional text interpreted in light of original intent or original public meaning are of the utmost importance, and the court gives little to no weight to governmental needs induced by changed circumstances or to "broad objectives such as good or efficient government."[15] What matters is the scheme of government set out explicitly by the constitutional text. Given the importance of defining with legal precision the powers of the different branches, formalist legal scholars and practitioners utilize textual and historical analysis to determine the extent and limitations of the various clause-bound powers appropriately exercised by the different branches.[16] Michael W. McConnell's 2020 book on presidential power is emblematic of this approach. McConnell relies on a "close examination of the constitutional text bearing on presidential power" as well as its "historical context" to discern the "meaning and internal logic" of article II's grant of executive power.[17] McConnell thus reconstructs "the framers' design for the presidency based on the text they wrote, their experience of royal authority during colonial times, and the interpretive battles in the early years of the republic."[18] Through this textual and historical analysis, McConnell purports to aid the judiciary by determining what powers ought to be subject to exclusive presidential discretion as opposed to those powers that Congress can rightfully control or supervise. In sum, of central importance to the separationist model is that the Constitution clearly sets out a scheme of government that can be clearly ascertained using appropriate tools of legal analysis (textual and historical) and that the Constitution's textual allocation of power should be enforced as fundamental law by the judiciary.

This separationist approach, moreover, has been central for unitary executive theorists who advance a theory of hierarchical control of personnel decisions within the executive branch. According to this theory, members of the executive branch and governmental agencies must be subject to the "direct control" of the president, who alone can hire and fire subordinates throughout the executive branch without congressional oversight.[19] Advocates of the unitary executive theory marshal textual arguments in favor of exclusive presidential control of the executive branch, as well as historical and functional arguments.[20] The unitary executive, Calabresi and Yoo argue, was a response to the deficient executive power under the Articles of Confederation and the clearly perceived need for a vigorous and unitary executive branch.[21] Such arguments, however, generally neglect the extent to which the exclusive presidential removal power over executive branch officials has been deeply contested throughout American history.[22] Moreover, as Aziz Huq argues, while the arguments of unitary executive theorists have a great deal of historical depth and rhetorical sophistication, the arguments ultimately seem to indicate an "a priori commitment to robust presidential control": "Given that they are works that purport to be backward looking and historical, their contemporary relevance and harmony with positions in current political debates is rather hard to ignore."[23] Stephen Skowronek similarly argues that the unitary executive theory is the product of a conservative insurgency movement and that its textual and historical claims can best be understood as a formalistic attempt to bring the administrative state under the control of the president when consolidation of a national majority in Congress seemed unlikely.[24]

It is hard to overstate the implications of the separationist approach for contemporary political practice. Given the extent to which modern governmental practice departs significantly from the formalistic account of strict separation of powers, formalists "recognize the root and branch nature of their preferred reforms."[25] As Aziz Huq writes, "Congress exercises influence over the content of regulation and the operation of administrative agencies through its oversight process," and the "agencies themselves blend together the specification of first-order conduct rules, the investigation of past violations, and (at times) adjudication of such acts."[26] To name just one such reform that would have dramatic impacts on the scale of modern government, formal separationists support the revival of the long-dormant nondelegation doctrine, and would significantly curtail Congress's delegation of legislative power to the executive branch and administrative agencies.[27] The nondelegation doctrine is based on a purely formalistic understanding of the separation of powers. As Gary Lawson writes in his defense of the doctrine, "However difficult it may be to distinguish the legislative, executive, and judicial powers at the margins, the Constitution of 1788–89 clearly places such a distinction at the center of its structure. There are constitutional lines that the executive and judicial powers may not cross."[28] Citing Lawson, Justice Gorsuch argued in his dissenting opinion in *Gundy v. United States* (2018), that "if Congress could pass off its legislative power to the executive branch, the '[v]esting [c]lauses, and indeed the entire structure of the Constitution,' would 'make no sense.'"[29] Gorsuch continued:

> The framers warned us against permitting consequences like these. As Madison explained, "[t]here can be no liberty where the legislative and executive powers are united in the same person, or body of

> magistrates." The framers knew, too, that the job of keeping the legislative power confined to the legislative branch couldn't be trusted to self-policing by Congress; often enough, legislators will face rational incentives to pass problems to the executive branch. Besides, enforcing the separation of powers isn't about protecting institutional prerogatives or governmental turf. It's about respecting the people's sovereign choice to vest the legislative power in Congress alone. And it's about safeguarding a structure designed to protect their liberties, minority rights, fair notice, and the rule of law. So when a case or controversy comes within the judicial competence, the Constitution does not permit judges to look the other way; we must call foul when the constitutional lines are crossed. Indeed, the framers afforded us independence from the political branches in large part to encourage exactly this kind of "fortitude . . . to do [our] duty as faithful guardians of the Constitution."[30]

The Supreme Court recently introduced a version of the nondelegation doctrine called the "major questions doctrine."[31] This new doctrine essentially requires that Congress clearly state its intention to delegate statutory discretion to agencies on questions that a majority of the court deems "major." Given the vast array of federal regulations affecting nearly every facet of American life, requiring Congress to legislate every issue it determines to be of national significance would be impossible, and the practical impact would be to grind modern government to a halt. The questions concerning delegation and the separation of powers will be addressed in depth in chapter 2. Delegation poses problems precisely in the way Justice Gorsuch and other defenders of a judicially enforced nondelegation doctrine suggest. However, interbranch conflict between Congress and the president is a better safeguard than judicial enforcement, as evidenced by the legislative veto, which the court invalidated based on a formalistic understanding of the Constitution. Given this larger historical context, the court's formalistic invalidation of the legislative veto created the conditions for its contemporary formalistic policing of delegations. While the court has asserted that its recent delegation decisions are meant to empower Congress—to incentivize it to perform its democratic function better—the larger historical context reveals these opinions to be a form of "congressional gaslighting," as Beau Baumann has argued.[32] Such decisions, in other words, are better understood as a long-term project of judicial aggrandizement at the expense of both political branches.[33]

It is particularly striking how such an emphasis on enforcing textual boundaries between the branches does not make sense of the ways in which constitutional practice has departed significantly from the literal strictures of the constitutional text, for example, in the areas of war powers or international agreements. Given the foreign affairs context, the judiciary has been reticent to intervene in interbranch disputes regarding the boundaries of the branches due to a purported lack of judicially manageable standards (even though to enforce boundaries, say, with regard to treaties and executive agreements would only require the judiciary to make the branches abide by the specific constitutional procedure for international agreements rather than to engage the substance of agreements).[34] Moreover, very few, if any, scholars or practitioners today would argue in favor of treaty exclusivity, given the extent to which executive agreements have superseded the use of the treaty since at least World War II and are viewed as an essential mechanism by which the United States binds itself internationally. Given this discrepancy between modern constitutional practice and the strictures of the text, some, while accepting modern practice as legitimate, see such innovations as instances of major constitutional change.[35] The Constitution's static legal framework, in this telling, has been overcome or "updated" (sometimes by the People based on a theory of higher lawmaking) to make it workable in the modern world.[36] What is noteworthy about the idea that the Constitution has to be overcome or updated is the premise upon which the claim is based: that the Constitution's legal framework provides static limits based on the literal meaning of the text.

Given the dramatic implications of the pure separation model, especially in the domestic context, what is its animating logic? In other words, what is the fundamental purpose of the separation of powers enforced in this way? As the Vile quotation at the outset of this section suggests, the primary purpose of a strict separation of powers is "the establishment and maintenance of political liberty."[37] Indeed, the Supreme Court has often invoked the importance of protecting liberty when it intervenes to ensure that the Constitution's legal strictures are followed by the political branches. For example, Justice Gorsuch wrote in the conclusion to his concurring opinion in *National Federation of Business v. Occupational Safety and Health Administration* (2022) that constitutional limits must be enforced or "the liberties our Constitution's separation of powers seeks to preserve would amount to little."[38] Similarly, Justice Scalia wrote in his formalist dissent in *Morrison v. Olson* that the separation of powers operates to "ensure that we do not lose liberty."[39] And in *INS v. Chadha*, Chief Justice Burger wrote that "we have not found a better way to preserve freedom than by making the exercise of power subject to the carefully crafted restraints spelled out in the Constitution."[40]

Even so, such gestures toward liberty have often been more rhetorical than substantive. Writing in a widely cited critique of the court's separation of powers jurisprudence, Rebecca L. Brown argues that "the means has become too important and the end not important enough to the formalist school, so that the 'forest' of individual liberty is often lost in the 'trees' of absolute fealty to the Framers' words."[41] Rather than focusing on individual liberty, the court has more often emphasized bright-line rules deduced from the literal strictures of the Constitution to ensure "predictability and restraint in judging."[42] In short, invocations of the liberty-protecting purpose of the separation of powers are the rhetorical highlights of judicial opinions whose substantive focus is the enforcement of textual provisions in ways that do not seem to have any appreciable impact on liberty. Moreover, given that good and effective government is a necessary concomitant to protecting liberty, the enforcement of the literal strictures of the text, especially insofar as such textual enforcement at times thwarts innovations deemed necessary to good and effective government in the contemporary world, can undermine liberty rather than protect it.

This purely textual emphasis comes clearly to the fore in John F. Manning's argument that the Constitution does not contain a freestanding separation of powers principle.[43] Indeed, Manning writes that the Constitution contains no separation of powers clause, and, moreover, that it violates strict separation by blending power throughout the document. According to Manning, the Constitution is best understood as a series or bundle of discrete and disconnected compromises rather than containing a coherent theory of separation of powers that pervades the document. As Manning puts it,

> the Constitution adopts *no freestanding principle of separation of powers*. The idea of separated powers unmistakably lies behind the Constitution, but it was not adopted wholesale. The Constitution contains no Separation of Powers Clause. The historical record, moreover, reveals no one baseline for inferring what a reasonable constitution maker would have understood "the separation of powers" to mean in the abstract. Rather, in the Constitution, the idea of separation of powers, properly understood, reflects many particular decisions about how to allocate and condition the exercise of federal power. Indeed, the document not only separates powers, but also blends them in many ways

> in order to ensure that the branches have the means and motives to check one another. Viewed in isolation from the constitution makers' many discrete choices, the concept of separation of powers as such can tell us little, if anything, about where, how, or to what degree the various powers were, in fact, separated (and blended) in the Philadelphia Convention's countless compromises.[44]

Absent a background principle of separation of powers, Manning argues that the judiciary should enforce textual boundaries between the branches in those instances where the Constitution is specific. The adoption of a specific, rule-like provision, by the rule of negative implication, suggests that other mechanisms are appropriately ruled out: "If a parent tells a young child who has asked for a drink, 'you may have orange juice,' it almost surely means that the child may not grab a Mountain Dew from the refrigerator."[45] If, therefore, the Constitution provides a specific mechanism for lawmaking—bicameralism and presentment—the judiciary should enforce the specific provision chosen by the constitutional framers based on the plain meaning of the text. Hence, the legislative veto is unconstitutional according to Manning—and the court—because it was a mechanism by which Congress (or subsidiary parts of Congress) exercised lawmaking power outside of the Constitution's textually prescribed procedures for lawmaking.[46] Similarly, and as the court ruled in *Noel Canning v NLRB* (2014), there are clear textual limits to what counts as a valid recess appointment based on the specific meaning of the recess appointments clause (even based upon the majority's broad construction of the clause in *Noel Canning* based in part on historical usage). According to the clear terms of the clause, if the Senate is in session, at least in a technical sense, then there is no recess available for a recess appointment. While Manning presents himself as offering an alternative option to the formalist and functional models on offer, his clause-bound textual interpretation shares much in common with constitutional formalists.

What should be clear from the preceding discussion is that in the separationist account, the literal strictures of the constitutional text should be enforced by the judiciary. While the court often invokes the protection of liberty, at least rhetorically, to justify the safeguarding of constitutional structure, any appreciable gains for liberty are merely secondary or derivative consequences of enforcing the separation powers itself. This narrowly formalist and textual focus, moreover, makes it appear that much of the apparatus and practice of American constitutional government today is inconsistent with the founding design.

Checks and Balances

The other dominant strand of the court's inconsistent oscillations is referred to as functionalism, a methodology that emphasizes checks and balances more than rigid adherence to the constitutional text understood in its more literal sense. According to the functionalist approach, what is important is not rigid adherence to the constitutional text to ensure strict separation between the branches. Rather, the goal is to maintain the relative balance between the branches of government so that none of the branches encroach upon the core functions of the others.[47] As Justice White put it in his dissenting opinion in *Bowsher v. Synar* (1986), "The role of this Court should be limited to determining whether the [act in issue] so alters the balance of authority among the branches of government as to pose a genuine threat to the basic division between the lawmaking power and the power to execute the law."[48]

The essential difference between the separationists and the functionalists is the latter's skepticism that the powers of the different branches of government are easily subject to precise definition.[49] Rather, imprecision and indeterminacy are "inherent in the definition and separation" of the powers between the branches.[50] As Martin S. Flaherty writes, "The complex, messy, and at times contradictory ferment in constitutional thinking renders it unlikely at best that, by 1787, Americans had reached a consensus on the doctrine in anything like the precise, thoroughgoing manner that modern formalists prescribe."[51] Rather, balance, according to Flaherty, is the Constitution's preeminent separation of powers value bequeathed by the founders.[52] Of course, reasoning from structural features like balance that have no explicit basis in the constitutional text allows for a great deal of judicial discretion. As Elizabeth Brown notes, "In order for the functionalist system to work, someone must determine what values or functions are central to the constitutional structure, and must define the extent to which changed circumstances should be permitted to influence that determination."[53] This inevitably leads, in theory, to indeterminacy and ad hoc rulings as the criteria for judicial decision-making are far more subjective than on the formalist account. In practice, however, the functionalist approach has generally led the court to be far more deferential to the political branches than the separationist account allows so long as balance is maintained.[54] Ultimately, the emphasis on checks and balances is, like in the separationist account, justified with reference to the protection of liberty interests. Checks and balances are necessary to prevent the accumulation of power in any one institution to better protect liberty.[55] However, the primary fixation is on maintaining a constitutional principle—in this case, balance—that precedes liberty protection. In other words, legal resolution is not primarily oriented to liberty protection even if the enforcement of the separation of powers is understood to protect liberty.

The functionalist view that the separation of powers is too indeterminate to result in clear line drawing is a view that is often shared by political scientists who emphasize checking and balancing. Central to the concept of checks and balances is the idea that if an institution has a power, another institution must check that power. Moreover, exercises of power are particularly difficult given the many and varied veto points throughout the constitutional system. For example, a bill can only become a law after it has been passed by both houses of Congress and signed by the president—and even then, the legislation is subject to judicial review. Power, therefore, is easily frustrated, as any breakdown along the way means that the government cannot act.[56] The view that the varied veto points throughout the constitutional system are primarily geared toward making it more difficult for the government to act is a plausible reading of *The Federalist*, especially Madison's famous argument in *Federalist* 51 that the division of the government into "distinct and separate departments" (as well as division between the national and state governments) would serve as a "double security to the rights of the people."[57] Phillip Muñoz, citing Madison's famous line that "men are not angels," argues that "sometimes we forget the whole purpose of the separation of powers is to frustrate government action, to make it harder for government to act."[58] Madison further argues in *Federalist* 51 that the purpose of bicameralism is to provide an antidote to the overwhelming power of the legislature (which he referred to as an impetuous vortex earlier in *Federalist* 48) in republican forms of government. By dividing up the legislature into component parts, Congress will be less likely to abuse its power by passing improvident laws. It is better that it be difficult for Congress to pass good laws than for it to be too easy for it to pass bad laws.

The emphasis on checks and balances among political scientists, moreover, tends to emphasize constraint for its own sake. Woodrow Wilson's famous critique of the separation of powers framework, for example, was based on what he took to be its overly mechanistic Newtonian underpinnings:

> The makers of our federal constitution followed the scheme as they found it expounded in Montesquieu, followed it with genuine scientific enthusiasm. The admirable expositions of *The Federalist* read like thoughtful applications of Montesquieu to the political needs and circumstances of America. They are full of the theory of checks and

> balances. The president is balanced off against Congress, Congress against the President, and each against the courts. Our statesmen of the earlier generations quoted no one so often as Montesquieu, and they quoted him always as a scientific standard in the field of politics. Politics is turned into mechanics under his touch. The theory of gravitation is supreme.[59]

As Michael Zuckert notes, "According to Wilson's conception of separation of powers, how powers are divided and separated matters hardly or not at all; what matters is merely that they are separated and can check each other."[60] The Constitution, according to Wilson, needed to be reinterpreted and updated with Darwinian underpinnings so that it could overcome the inertia of ambition counteracting ambition.

Wilson's diagnosis of the problems with mechanistic checking and balancing has proven enduring among constitutional critics and reform advocates. Today, for example, Howell and Moe, in ways largely reminiscent of Wilson and the Progressives, argue that the Constitution's checks and balances make it nearly impossible for the government to act, and, when it does, to produce good policy given the varied veto points that stymie effective governmental action.[61] Therefore, they advocate for a constitutional amendment that would give the president more agenda-setting power (similar to fast-track trade authority, by which Congress delegates to the president the power to negotiate trade agreements while ensuring a timely vote without amendments). The Madisonian system, in their view, must be updated with a formal amendment because it has proven incapable of being adapted to the contingencies of modern government. Checks and balances, in this view, are primarily geared toward preventing the government from acting. While the concern for balance can be justified with reference to the protection of individual rights, an overemphasis on checks and balances can undermine the capacity of the government to act, thus resulting in constitutional failure. Checking and balancing, therefore, can be emphasized at the expense of achieving essential governmental objectives.

A Means to Ends: The Constitution's Political Architecture

While conventional accounts of the purposes of separation of powers—regardless of whether they emphasize the strict enforcement of legal boundaries or checking and balancing—tend to focus on how the constitutional design is meant to make it more difficult for the government to act, constraint is not the primary focus of the purposes of separation of powers as explained by *The Federalist*. Indeed, Publius makes clear that the Constitution was not intended to be a static legal framework that cannot adapt to the needs of unforeseen circumstances. Time and again, Publius makes clear that the political world is full of contingencies that one can never fully plan for in advance. For example, Anti-Federalists worried about the dangers a standing army poses to republican forms of government during times of peace and opposed the Constitution on the grounds that there was no explicit constitutional prohibition on such a practice. The Federalists' response to Anti-Federalist fears was to argue that legal limitations on powers granted inhibit the ability of the government to respond to the unforeseen exigencies of changing circumstances, and, consequently, can undermine the purposes of the constitutional order rather than advance them. As Madison wrote in *Federalist* 41:

> How could a readiness for war in time of peace be safely prohibited, unless we could prohibit, in like manner, the preparations and establishments of every hostile nation? The means of security can only be regulated by the means and the danger of attack. They will, in fact, be ever determined by these rules, and by no others. It is in vain to oppose Constitutional barriers to the impulse of self-preservation. It is worse than in vain; because it plants in the Constitution itself necessary usurpations of power, every precedent of which is a germ of unnecessary and multiplied repetitions.[62]

In other words, legal limitations on the power of the government meant to make government safe can actually serve to do the opposite, undermining the effective capacity of the government to respond to unforeseen circumstances. While a standing army might, as the Anti-Federalists urged, prove dangerous to the people's liberty, the latter would be more imperiled without a government capable of effectively providing for the common defense. In fact, while separation of powers is often defended, at least rhetorically, as primarily ordered to the protection of rights, as indicated earlier, such rights are themselves best secured by a government with competent powers. As Hamilton argued in the first essay of *The Federalist*, "it will be equally forgotten that the vigor of government is essential to the security of liberty; that, in the contemplation of a sound and well-informed judgment, their interest can never be separated; and that a dangerous ambition more often lurks behind the specious mask of zeal for the rights of the people than under the forbidden appearance of zeal for the firmness and efficiency of government."[63] In other words, while securing the rights of citizens is an important objective, it is only achieved by securing other governmental ends, such as national security. Publius thus argues in *The Federalist* that the powers of the national government should not be legally limited by prohibitions. Rather, the powers granted "ought to exist without limitation, *because it is impossible to foresee or to define the extent of national exigencies, and the correspondent extent and the variety of the means which may be necessary to satisfy them.*"[64] The Constitution, in this sense, is not an end to be maintained in a legal sense, but is itself the means to the unlimited ends of the polity itself.

The question thus becomes how the framers attempted to construct a government with the capacity to achieve fundamental constitutional objectives while controlling the government. The answer to this question can be found in the ways in which the framers constructed a government that differed altogether from separation of powers as it had been traditionally understood and substituted in its place, as Jeffrey K. Tulis has argued, an altogether new political design meant to vindicate the competing aims of the constitutional order—expression of majoritarian will, vindication of national security aims and energetic administration of government, and the protection of individual rights—through differently configured institutions brought into conflict by their shared powers.[65] The Constitution is thus an attempt to secure certain positive goods through differentiated institutions brought into political conflict. As Mariah Zeisberg has written, "Constitutional fidelity starts with the effective pursuit of proper governmental purposes," and, therefore, "constitutional theories that emphasize constraint as a primary conceptual category are inadequate."[66] Functional separation and checks and balances, according to Tulis and Zeisberg, are about the pursuit of governmental ends in political practice through the Constitution's differentiated institutions of government brought into conflict through their shared powers.

What is the nature of this political design? As already noted, the Constitution does not have a freestanding separation of powers principle that can be easily invoked to settle interbranch disputes based on the type of power appropriately wielded by certain types of institutions, and, in fact, the Constitution violates the terms of what might be considered a pure separation of powers doctrine by mixing the different types of powers within and between the various branches. James Madison's answer to the charge that the Constitution violated strict separation of powers was to argue in *Federalist* 48 that separation of powers was an unworkable concept on its own terms. Parchment barrier distinctions, Madison argued, were not sufficient to prevent the encroachment of the branches on the powers of the others:

> Will it be sufficient to mark, with precision, the boundaries of these departments, in the constitution of the government, and to trust to these parchment barriers against the encroaching spirit of power? This is the security which appears to have been principally relied on by the compilers of most of the American constitutions. But experience assures us, that the efficacy of the provision has been greatly overrated; and that some more adequate defense is indispensably necessary for the more feeble, against the more powerful, members of the government.[67]

Given that power is of an "encroaching" nature, Madison asserts, it is to be expected that the most powerful branch will subsume the powers of the other branches irrespective of the strictures of the law.[68] In republican forms of government, he continues, the legislative power necessarily predominates, and is "everywhere extending the sphere of its activity, and drawing all power into its impetuous vortex."[69] Madison's argument, moreover, is not merely theoretical. Rather, Madison argues, after canvassing governmental practice in the states at the time, that separation of powers principles demarcated as law on paper had proven insufficient in the practice of the state governments, resulting in legislative despotism as the legislative branches usurped the functions of the other branches.[70]

The solution to this problem, first, was to make the legislative, executive, and judicial branches independent of each other by grants of power derived from the Constitution itself, thereby giving each branch an independent source of political authority. Secondly, the framers designed institutions to perform distinctive functions in the constitutional order, and gave each of the branches all the powers necessary to achieve their governmental objectives. Finally, each branch has "partial agency" in the powers of the other branches—checks meant to influence, though not to control, the judgments and actions of the other branches. These checks were ultimately made possible by relying upon the ambition of officeholders in each of the branches to advance and defend the prerogatives of their branches vis-à-vis the others. As Madison famously declared in *Federalist* 51, "ambition must be made to counteract ambition."[71]

What should be clear from the preceding discussion is the ways in which such a self-enforcing political design significantly blurs the legal boundaries between the branches, placing it at odds with the formalists' strict separation account. The boundaries between the branches are not enforced with legal precision, but through political conflict between them. In fact, Madison makes clear in *Federalist* 37 the theoretical and practical impossibility of demarcating interbranch boundaries with legal precision in the first place in a passage worth quoting at length:

> The faculties of the mind itself have never yet been distinguished and defined, with satisfactory precision, by all the efforts of the most acute and metaphysical philosophers. Sense, perception, judgment, desire, volition, memory, imagination, are found to be separated by such delicate shades and minute gradations that their boundaries have eluded the most subtle investigations, and remain a pregnant source of ingenious disquisition and controversy. The boundaries between the great kingdom of nature, and, still more, between the various provinces, and lesser portions, into which they are subdivided, afford another illustration of the same important truth. The most sagacious and laborious naturalists have never yet succeeded in tracing with certainty the line which separates the district of vegetable life from the neighboring region of unorganized matter, or which marks the termination of the former and the commencement of the animal empire. A still greater obscurity lies in the distinctive characters by which the objects in each of these great departments of nature have been arranged and assorted.
>
> When we pass from the works of nature, in which all the delineations are perfectly accurate, and appear to be otherwise only from the imperfection of the eye which surveys them, to the institutions of man, in which the obscurity arises as well from the object itself as from the organ by which it is contemplated, we must perceive the necessity of moderating still further our expectations and hopes from the efforts of human sagacity. Experience has instructed us that no skill in the science of government has yet been able to discriminate and define, with sufficient certainty, its three great provinces the legislative, executive, and judiciary; or even the privileges and powers of the different legislative branches. Questions daily occur in the course of practice, which prove the obscurity which reins in these subjects, and which puzzle the greatest adepts in political science.[72]

Madison continues by observing the difficulty of using words to set forth a government and its requisite partitions given both the fundamental indeterminacy of language and the limits of the human mind to comprehend it. Indeed, Madison concludes, "When the Almighty himself condescends to address mankind in their own language, his meaning, luminous as it must be, is rendered dim and doubtful by the cloudy medium through which it is communicated."[73] Given the impossibility of defining the boundaries between the branches with precision, Tulis and Mellow observe that *The Federalist* never attempts to define powers by their natures and to then assign those powers to the appropriate branch—as would be appropriate if the framers were merely concerned with maintaining strict legal division between the branches.[74] Rather, the latter half of *The Federalist* (52–85) describes the ways in which differently designed institutions can serve positive functions in the constitutional order by bringing to bear different functional qualities and competing perspectives on politics. Rather than legalistically defining powers and assigning them to the appropriate institution, the latter half of *The Federalist* is a long exposition of how an interrelated set of institutional design ingredients, including mode of election, length of term, number of officeholders, competent powers, and reeligibility, create this new political architecture (see table 1). The challenge the framers faced in designing a government, as Madison wrote in *Federalist* 37, was how to ensure essential qualities necessary for good government (stability, energy, and liberty), and the concomitant "difficulty of mingling them together in their due proportions" in a republican form of government.[75] The emphasis in *The Federalist* on the structural ingredients of the new political design is indicative of the framers' novel, and frequently misunderstood, approach to this challenge.

For example, Congress is the institution meant to reflect the views of a diverse citizenry, geographically dispersed across the nation, by bringing these voices into a plural body in such a way as to foster deliberation—or at least to make deliberation more likely.[76] The different sizes and term lengths of the House and Senate—as well as differing modes of election—are indicative, moreover, of the fact that public opinion is not some monolithic entity, but, rather, that there are short-term and long-term interests and that adequate provision should be made for the expression of these different majoritarian perspectives. In fact, Madison makes clear in *Federalist* 62–63 that the Senate is not merely a checking body, but a deliberative body meant to bring a different, more stable, perspective on issues of public importance. The Constitution thus makes provision for fluctuations of public opinion with the House of Representatives elected every two years. On the other hand, the smaller Senate with longer terms provides a more stable perspective on the public good, thus guarding against mutability of the laws, which Madison notes in *Federalist* 62 is one of the great dangers endemic to democratic governance.

The independence and unity of the executive branch—as well as a more open-ended grant of executive power—is meant to induce energy to ensure the effective administration of government and the ability to effectively

Table 1.1

Institution	*Objective*	*Quality*	*Structure*
Congress	Majoritarian will	Deliberation	Plural; proximity to the people; bicameralism
President	Regime preservation; national security; administration	Energy	Unity; duration; independence; reeligibility
Judiciary	Rights protection	Judgment	Small, collegial body; tenure during good behavior; power linked to argument

Adapted from Tulis, *Rhetorical Presidency*, 41–44.

wield the foreign affairs powers of the United States by structuring an institution to be able to move with great speed, secrecy, and dispatch. While deliberation on the merits of policy is no doubt an essential quality for democratic governance, so too is decisive action to administer the government and to employ "the common strength" in the foreign arena.[77] As Hamilton wrote in *Federalist* 70, "In the legislature, promptitude of decision is oftener an evil than a benefit. The differences of opinion, and the jarring of parties in that department of the government, though they may sometimes obstruct salutary plans, yet often promote deliberation and circumspection, and serve to check excesses in the majority."[78] Such delay—caused by plurality—is a dangerous quality in the executive, however, merely counteracting "those qualities in the executive which are the most necessary ingredients in its composition—vigor and exposition, and this without counterbalancing any good."[79] Providing for an energetic executive, moreover, was no small concern for the framers after the Articles of Confederation's failure to make adequate provision for effective executive power, leaving the administration of the government for both domestic and foreign affairs in the hands of Congress and executive officials fully responsible to it.[80] The creation of the presidency was thus an attempt to increase the overall capacity of the government, to make government better and more effective.[81] The structural dimensions of the executive branch—independence, unity, competent powers, and reeligibility—are the ingredients for securing the energy sufficient to achieve these ends.

Finally, the court is biased toward the protection of rights, and its mode of selection by the political branches (to ensure appropriately qualified people sit on the bench), life tenure, and a small, collegial body are meant to induce the quality of judgment in particular cases and controversies. Its insulation from public pressures and its lack of enforcement powers enables it, moreover, to rule in a disinterested manner even against the majoritarian impulses more likely to be expressed through a legislature closely connected to swings in public opinion.

The branches, therefore, based on their differing electoral constituencies and institutional designs, make provision for different perspectives on the public good, perspectives, moreover, that at times conflict. Majoritarian will, at times, comes into conflict with the need for decisive action outside of the parameters considered by Congress. Individual rights are often in deep conflict with both majoritarian will and the decisive actions of the president to vindicate the aims of national security. Because of these different institutionally induced perspectives, when confronted with the same question it is possible, even likely, that the branches will reach different conclusions.[82] As Zeisberg writes,

> Far from being simple platforms for expressing preferences, the structure of each branch can be expected to support the articulation of certain kinds of preferences and certain forms of reasoning over and above others. As each branch carries out its functions, it develops particular forms of expertise both organizationally (such as the executive branch bureaucracy, or Congress's reference service) and informally (i.e. the entrenchment of bargaining attitudes in the legislature versus hierarchical decisional qualities in the executive branch).[83]

For example, the president represents the people as a whole, and the unitary nature of his office and his role as commander in chief induce the president to think primarily in terms of national security. Congress, on the other hand, with its power of the purse and its conglomeration of viewpoints from local constituencies across the country might face a different set of criteria regarding, for example, the use of financial resources, which might place it at odds with the president's judgments about how to use the nation's resources to vindicate national security concerns. Buoyed by a sense of urgency during an international crisis, the political branches might adopt certain policies meant, at least ostensibly, to protect the nation, but do so in a way that infringes the rights of a particular minority group. The judiciary (hopefully) can intervene to ensure that laws are generally applicable and do not unfairly target minority groups.

While the distinct functions and organizational features of the different branches can lead to different political judgments, checks and balances are the mechanism by which each branch can defend its judgments vis-à-vis the other branches. For example, the president can veto legislation, and has a great deal of discretion to direct the administration of the laws with an eye toward the national interest. Similarly, Congress can maintain oversight of the executive's discretion, and can press its own judgments through the legislative process by refusing to fund presidential initiatives it disagrees with, or by impeaching a president who consistently flouts the deliberative will of Congress. What is important to note here is the dynamism of the constitutional framework as the branches engage in politics across time. The Constitution's political design transcends mere balance of power as the different branches perform distinct functions that empower them at different points in time.[84] Political power is thus far more dynamic and diffused than a particular snapshot in time could possibly reveal. The exigencies of political circumstances and the president's structural capacities to act energetically mean that the president might, at times, act in ways unanticipated by Congress based on the needs of the moment. Congress, however, has checks—for example, through regular appropriations and power over appointments, investigations, and even impeachment—it can use to oversee, influence, or contest presidential actions up to the point of removing the president from office. While the Constitution requires an executive branch that can act with sufficient discretion and dispatch based on his own perception of the needs of the moment, Congress can influence how the president uses that authority by, for example, limiting the types of weapons available to the military. As Josh Chafetz argues, a Congress that is concerned about the United States' assertions of power across the globe might refuse to fund new aircraft carriers or new weapons.[85] As Chafetz writes, "Future presidents' decisions about whether or not to initiate a conflict, and how to do so, would be made in the shadow of those past appropriations decisions."[86] Moreover, Congress might use its investigative powers and public hearings on presidential use of force abroad, and come to its own conclusions about what would be considered legitimate and under what conditions, thus creating what Zeisberg refers to as a "national security paradigm" that constrains presidential behavior in the future by clearly outlining the parameters for presidential action. As she explains, "A constitutionally responsible Congress will exercise its power to judge not because the reactive judge is necessarily more accurate than the contemporary judge, but because the prospect of judging can be a disciplining force for a president contemplating such scrutiny in the future, and because retrospective judgments are one way for Congress to contribute to the political construction of defensible constitutional interpretations."[87]

What should be clear from this picture is that legal assignments of power are more than just about restraint, but about creating institutions that think and act in different ways in the service of securing the positive goods of the constitutional order. Checks and balances are not just about thwarting action, but about bringing these different institutional perspectives on politics into productive contestation both in particular moments of conflict and across time. John Finn thus characterizes American separation of powers as essentially a "dialogic device, or a means of establishing constitutional conversation among the branches."[88] When it comes to conflicts between the branches regarding their respective legal boundaries, there is not a legal principle that can adjudicate the branches' competing political claims. For example, no legal rule can determine the scope of executive privilege in advance of the political circumstances that give rise to such claims, as will be discussed in chapter 5.[89] Rather, both branches have potentially legitimate claims in informational disputes—the president might need to withhold information from Congress for, say, national security reasons, and Congress might need information to perform its oversight functions and to legislate. There is no meaningful legal principle that can be invoked that could possibly balance the competing claims beyond the branches' own arguments in particular situations, ultimately subject to the public's subsequent evaluation.

If the Constitution's institutions are meant to perform distinctive functions, and if the structural dimensions of those institutions provide criteria with which we can evaluate their performance of their distinctive tasks, then the unit of analysis for constitutional fidelity transcends mere legal assertions of power. What matters is not merely text, history, and structure, or some legal rule derived in advance about the functional uses of power. Rather, the branches gain political and constitutional authority by the ways in which they use their determinate constitutional tools to advance competing political claims in particular circumstances. Political authority, as Chafetz argues, is endogenous to politics. In other words, it is "largely generated through politics and is therefore not knowable in advance of politics."[90] Similarly, Zeisberg argues that the branches derive their constitutional authority from how they mobilize their unique institutional capacities in service of constitutional ends, providing content-dependent reasons to obey rather than relying on mere assertions of legal power.[91] A narrow focus on legal assignments of power without regard to how those powers are used in particular political circumstances provides too narrow a frame for constitutional evaluation because it is inattentive to how the Constitution is the institutional framework meant to achieve politically contingent goods rather than a legal framework to be enforced for its own sake. Zeisberg thus argues that it is possible to derive standards from the structures of differentiated institutions that can be used to evaluate how the branches engage in politics.[92]

How well does Congress engage in deliberation, bringing different (even marginal) points of view into robust debate? How well does Congress wield its investigative powers, debating the uses of presidential exercises of power and thus constraining presidential discretion in the future by making clear what it would consider acceptable executive action? How well does the executive branch wield its unique intelligence and epistemic capacities? These are important questions given Zeisberg's topic of choice—war powers—insofar as many of the key definitions of the debate (such as what constitutes an act of war in the first place) require political construction and elaboration rather than stemming from clear-cut and determinate constitutional language. The *structures* of the branches, in other words, point to political *duties*. The branches do not share power merely to check or frustrate the other branch in the exercise of its power, but to bring certain positive goods to the table. Why else have differentiated institutions in the first place if the structural dimensions of different institutions cannot provide insight into how to evaluate the functions of those institutions in contestation over their constitutional roles?

Yuval Levin makes a similar point, arguing, counterintuitively, that anti-institutional sentiment is on the rise because we have lost the ability to think institutionally, by which he means the propensity to be disciplined and formed by the purposes of the institutions we inhabit in ways that govern our conduct within them.[93] Institutions, Levin argues, have been diminished by an anti-institutional deformation he terms "outsiderism." "Rather than constrain and shape individuals," Levin writes, "these institutions seem to exist to display individuals—to give them prominence and gain them notice without stamping them with a particular character, a distinct set of obligations or responsibilities, or an ethic that comes with constraints."[94] This, Levin further argues, is a fundamental transformation in the purpose of institutions. Instead of serving as "molds that shape people's characters and habits," institutions have become "platforms" that allow people to display themselves and build their own brands at the expense of their institution.[95] For example, in a 2024 op-ed, Levin notes how Congress has been undermined by this pathology:

> Anyone who has attended a high-profile congressional hearing in recent years can attest that hearings have become production sessions for YouTube clips and other social media posts rather than opportunities for collective deliberation or debate. The travails of House Republicans in this Congress have had much to do with the tendency

> of members to treat the House as a platform for commentary or performance art.
>
> These performances often use Congress not only as a stage but also as a foil, treating the bargaining and deal making that is the essence of legislative work as a form of corruption. Members who view their roles this way are less interested in winning substantive policy concessions than in positioning themselves as outside observers narrating a morality play in which their own ineffectiveness stands as proof of their purity.[96]

What is compelling about Levin's insight is that he locates the problem not fundamentally with institutions themselves (as many do today, which is why there is a pervasive anti-institutional sentiment), but with their collapse in contemporary politics. Recognizing that institutions serve positive purposes that should shape the conduct and perspectives of those who operate within them enables Levin to propose reforms to those institutions that would help them perform these functions well. For example, it is often assumed that Congress's democratic functions require it to be fully transparent. Hence, over time, nearly every aspect of congressional life, including committee deliberations, are live streamed. Levin argues, however, that this undermines the essential qualities that Congress needs to perform its constitutional function well: deliberation and compromise. Every institution, he argues, requires an interior life that enables it to perform its distinct function. As he writes, "When an institution becomes too thoroughly transparent, it becomes indistinguishable from the open public space around it, and so it is simply another platform for public speech rather than a structure for meaningful action."[97] Operating in executive sessions more frequently, especially in committees, would create better conditions for members of Congress to perform their governing tasks appropriate to their institution by providing members with fewer opportunities to use the institution as a platform for their own political purposes rather than to work within the institution as it fulfills its constitutional and political functions.[98]

In sum, while competing judicial approaches seek to enforce the separation of powers as an end in itself, the framers understood the constitutional system as a means to the various politically contingent ends of the polity. The separation of powers, therefore, is not primarily a legal principle. Rather, it is a political architecture of differently designed institutions that bring to bear competing functional qualities and perspectives on the political questions that confront the polity. Constraint-oriented understandings of the separation of powers provide insufficient criteria for assessing the health of the constitutional order.

Should the Supreme Court Superintend the Separation of Powers?

While scholars and jurists disagree about appropriate judicial methods, it is largely taken for granted today that the Supreme Court, using standard tools of legal analysis, should be the ultimate arbiter of interbranch disputes regarding the political branches' constitutional and legal powers vis-à-vis each other.[99] That this is the dominant view, however, does not mean it is correct given the type of system the Constitution set into motion. Contrary to the conventional view, the argument here is that separation of powers disputes between Congress and the president regarding their constitutional and legal powers should be considered nonjusticiable political questions. In this significant respect, I follow Jesse Choper, who compellingly argues that the judiciary's role should be narrowly confined to the protection of rights rather than more broadly to the superintendence of the separation of powers.[100] Insofar as the question in a dispute concerns which political branch has the constitutional or legal power to do something (as opposed to the other branch), rights are only impacted in a secondary or derivative fashion, and thus should not come within the purview of the court. The argument here is twofold. The first aspect turns on the nature of the constitutional order (largely explicated in the previous section) and how it governs, or is maintained, as fundamental law. The second part concerns the nature of law itself, how the constitutional text incorporates principles that at times come into conflict, and how the political branches should argue about the Constitution's textual principles in conflicts over their respective powers in particular conflicts. These additional steps in the argument are essential because one can accept the basic notion that the separation of powers system described in the previous section establishes institutions to provide differentiated functional qualities or perspectives on politics and still argue, as David J. Siemers does, that judicial enforcement of the separation of powers is essential to preserving these functions.[101]

THE LEGAL TEXT OR THE SYSTEM OF GOVERNMENT?

Turning to the first question, how does the Constitution govern? This question, moreover, turns on a more fundamental question: What *is* the Constitution? The Constitution certainly is fundamental law, but how? The Constitution's written character has led to its common reception as a legal text, and the conflation of the Constitution with law has led to the notion that it is primarily, if not exclusively, the property of lawyers and judges to maintain and to thus protect us from constitutional failure.[102] At its most extreme, the Constitution, understood primarily as a legal text, has led to the commonly accepted view, articulated by the court itself, that the Supreme Court is the ultimate and final arbiter of constitutional meaning.[103] In this view, the court's interpretations of the Constitution *are* the Constitution.[104] As Jonathan Gienapp argues, however, the twin assumptions that the Constitution is fundamentally a written text, in the first place, and, in the second, that it is a conventional species of law, are historically contingent phenomena.[105] Rather, Gienapp argues, "In 1787, the Constitution was more often imagined as a system that needed to be brought into equilibrium than as words on parchment that meted out judgments. The written Constitution was not a discrete, self-sufficient thing; embedded within a wider, dynamic, invisible field of action, it was a script awaiting enactment."[106] The legalization of the Constitution thus developed over time, a phenomenon that coincides largely with the development of the legal community.[107]

If the Constitution is primarily understood as a legal text, then it is no surprise that it has come to be understood primarily as a species of law to be decoded and enforced exclusively by the judiciary. And yet, this is not necessarily the best way to understand how the Constitution is fundamental law, or how it is to be enforced as such. In other words, the notion that the writtenness of the Constitution translates to its status as a species of law that should be primarily interpreted and enforced by the judiciary presumes too much by prioritizing the text over its "framework character," or the system of government it creates.[108] As George Thomas writes, "The act of writing itself is no guarantee that fundamental law would be translated from word to deed."[109] Indeed, one of the fundamental problems *The Federalist* addresses is *how* to bond the word of the Constitution with the polity it created.[110]

As explained in more detail in the previous section, Madison explicitly rejects the fully judicialized, or overly legalistic, version of the Constitution as fundamentally a text that is enforced as law. Instead, Madison argues that parchment barriers are insufficient to ensure constitutional fidelity.[111] Rather than rely on parchment barriers, the Constitution creates independent institutions, provides them with tools to resist encroachment (checks and balances), and, finally, relies on human ambition as the primary mechanism by which those checks and balances are utilized to protect or press institutional prerogatives vis-à-vis the other branches.[112] In this way, the Constitution is fundamental law not in the sense that it is a text enforced as law by the court. The Constitution is fundamental law in the sense that it establishes the institutional forms of the polity, and the central feature of the Constitution's design is its self-enforcing nature. As Madison writes,

> To what expedient, then, shall we finally resort, for maintaining in practice the necessary partition of power among the several departments, as laid down in the Constitution? The only answer that can be given is, that as all these exterior provisions are found to be inadequate, the defect must be supplied, by so contriving the interior structure of the government as that its several constituent parts may, by their mutual relations, be the means of keeping each other in their proper places.[113]

Moreover, it should be noted that in the most famous essay written on American separation of powers, *Federalist* 51, Madison does not mention judicial review at all. This does not mean that the court's power of constitutional interpretation as applied to specific cases and controversies does not flow logically from the constitutional design, as explained by Hamilton in *Federalist* 78 and implemented in practice by Chief Justice Marshall in *Marbury v. Madison* (1803). In this sense, the power of judicial review is the court's distinctive mechanism (its check) for pressing its own constitutional judgments. This power, however, is tempered by its placement within the larger separation of powers system of which it is merely a part. The placement of judicial review within the larger separation of powers system thus precludes the notion of judicial supremacy.[114] While the court is obligated in certain instances to pass constitutional judgment in particular cases that come before it, the court's judgments do not prevent citizens and officers of the other branches from making their own constitutional judgments and arguments, and to seek to overturn, by lawful means, the court's judgments through political engagement, engagement that includes the reconstitution of the judiciary over time through political processes.[115] In this sense, judicial review is one facet of a larger dialogical enterprise that includes the entire citizenry acting through the Constitution's varied, multifaceted, and interconnected institutional forms. To elevate judicial review to judicial supremacy or finality, as Lincoln argued in his First Inaugural, deprives the people of self-government through their institutions of government, resigning "their Government into the hands of that eminent tribunal."[116] In the case of judicial supremacy, the Constitution is reduced to a text whose meaning is fixed in law by the court rather than serving as the institutional means through which the people seek the ends or aspirations of the polity announced in the preamble.[117]

Even descriptively, the notion that the Constitution is fundamentally or exclusively what the Supreme Court says misses much of the dynamism of the actual working of the constitutional system, as Neal Devins and Louis Fisher have demonstrated.[118] Even when the court acts, it is often not the final word, especially when there is significant backlash to particular decisions. Other times, the court is merely responsive to mobilized changes in public opinion, and its decisions are best characterized as merely codifying a state of affairs.[119] This is no surprise given that it takes time for dominant political coalitions to reconstitute the judiciary so that its rulings align with the preferences of the newly constituted democratic majority.[120] In the absence of judicial action, the political branches can take the lead role in constructing constitutional meaning and engaging in statecraft, as Maggie Blackhawk has demonstrated with her compelling case study on federal Indian law and American colonialism.[121] Such construction of constitutional meaning can be more dynamic and constitutionally creative than what courts can offer because the modes of reasoning are less legalistically constrained. For her part, Blackhawk argues that her case study on Indian law is illustrative of what constitutional construction could look like if the reigning juristocracy could give way to a more pluralistic constitutional culture that centered Congress rather than the courts.

The purpose here is to determine the role of the Supreme Court in separation of powers disputes concerning the legal boundaries between Congress and the president rather than to define the extent of the judicial role more generally. The preceding discussion, however, illuminates the peculiar way in which the Constitution is fundamental law and thus how judicial power, generally speaking, must be situated within the larger political system established by the Constitution, and thus tempered by it. When it comes to separation of powers disputes that concern the powers of the political branches vis-à-vis each other, judicial review poses significant problems.

First, judicial review of interbranch boundary disputes is superfluous given the political branches' own powers vis-à-vis each other. Members of the political branches, like the members of the court, take oaths to preserve and defend the Constitution, thus imposing on all constitutional actors a requirement of constitutional interpretation and fidelity.[122] Moreover, the political branches each have determinate tools to enforce their own constitutional and political judgments vis-à-vis the other in view of the public, tools that are more powerful than mere judicial judgment. If the president encroaches on congressional prerogatives or defies its political judgments, Congress has immense institutional powers and tools at its disposal. For example, it can refuse to consider the president's legislative agenda, hold up appointments for key offices throughout the federal government, or use its power over appropriations to defund programs and offices.[123] It is true that as the first mover, presidents can set into motion courses of events that are difficult, if not impossible, for Congress to control or unwind. If the president unilaterally sends troops into combat, for example, Congress might find it politically difficult to defund a war effort. The difficulties of congressional action, however, are not necessarily indicative of powerlessness. In fact, Congress has defunded war efforts during hostilities, as it did when it passed the Case-Church Amendment in 1973, cutting off all funding, direct and indirect, to the war effort in Vietnam.[124] Even taking the most extreme examples, there is no reason to think that a branch fundamentally resolved to exceed constitutional or legal boundaries will heed judicial judgment any more than it will the judgment of the other political branch, especially since the judiciary has "neither force nor will."[125] The same concerns one could raise with regard to the difficulty of congressional containment of a lawless executive could be similarly and more powerfully leveled against the judiciary.[126] Unlike Congress, the judiciary has no enforcement mechanisms to bring the other branches to heel; all the courts can do is pronounce judgment. In fact, Congress has the ultimate check, one far more powerful than judicial review: the power to remove the president from office. This power, however, has been enervated over time due to the fundamental misunderstanding that it only applies to violations of the law, rather than abuse of office or the public good. This has undermined the proper functioning of the separation of powers system.[127] An effective impeachment power is an essential component of the Constitution's political architecture, as will be discussed in the final case study chapter.

Secondly, and more fundamentally, judicial superintendence of the boundaries between the political branches extracts the court from within the separation of powers framework, placing it above the separation of powers. In other words, it prioritizes the Constitution understood as law over its framework character. Rather than defending its own prerogatives (such as the protection of rights or safeguarding its own institutional processes), the court becomes the arbiter of the other branches' respective powers in a way that makes the enforcement of the Constitutional text (understood primarily as law) the end to be achieved rather than the regime's politically contingent ends sought through the institutions of government. Judicial enforcement of constitutional and legal boundaries thus represents a fundamental misunderstanding of the nature of the constitutional order instantiated by the text but not reducible to it in its most literal sense. This does not mean that the court should have no role in separation of powers disputes, but that role should be confined to issues that directly implicate its prerogatives or directly infringe upon individual rights. In this regard, I follow Choper, who has argued that questions concerning the legal boundaries between Congress and the president (i.e. if the legal question concerns which branch has the power to do something that the government as a whole has the power to do) should be considered nonjusticiable. This is a point that requires further elaboration. Before further specifying the narrow parameters of the judicial role, however, it is important to first turn to the next part of the argument concerning the nature of law itself as indeterminate and containing a multiplicity of competing and contingent principles. As will be evident, the judiciary suffers from a comparative institutional disadvantage when it comes to deciding interbranch disputes concerning the legal boundaries of the other branches.

DYNAMIC INDETERMINACY: CONSTITUTIONAL PRINCIPLES AND THE PUBLIC GOOD

If the Constitution is fundamental law in that it creates a self-enforcing political order rather than operating as a legal code to be applied by the judiciary, what role should the Constitution play in political contestation between the branches regarding their respective powers? In other words, does a political approach to separation of powers problems amount to the abandonment or degradation of law? The answer to this question turns on the nature of law itself as both indeterminate and containing a multiplicity of competing and contingent principles. Legal indeterminacy is key here, moreover, because it allows for the activation of the Constitution's principles to contend with each other within the political framework of the constitutional order. This, naturally, requires human agency (channeled through appropriate institutional forms) as it is not possible to legally script the correct responses to the unforeseen problems that are endemic to political life. Indeed, application of the Constitution's textual principles requires practical reasoning and prudential judgment, and right answers to questions that confront the polity and stretch its legal limits cannot be known in advance of politics.

The account developed here is highly stylized. By operating at the level of constitutional ideals, I lay out a normative constitutional framework for evaluating political actors, and thus can distinguish high politics from low politics. Political actors engaged in high politics justify their actions with reference to the constitutional text and its underlying principles as it pertains to the public good. The problem with judicial review of interbranch boundaries is that the court's distinctive mode of institutional reasoning is insufficiently tailored to the politics that animate such disputes in the first place. Judicial resolution, moreover, incentivizes the political branches to engage the text more literally, and thus precludes the kinds of political justifications necessary to achieve the public good.

Turning to the first point, indeterminacy is a problem in any legal order given the inherent limitations of law to speak to all unforeseen contingencies. Separation of powers is a response to this fundamental indeterminacy, not by resolving it by supplying greater legal specificity such that law takes on a code-like character (a practical impossibility), but by responding to it through the appropriate institutional frameworks. For Locke, the inadequacies of law give rise to the need for executive prerogative, which by definition is "power to act according to discretion, for the public good, without the prescription of the law, and sometimes against it."[128] Such discretion is necessary, moreover, because law can never foresee and thus cover all possible circumstances. In fact, rigid adherence to the law might do more harm than good, "as not to pull down an innocent man's house to stop the fire, when the next to it is burning."[129] As Locke explains:

> In some governments the lawmaking power is not always in being, and is usually too numerous, and so too slow, for the dispatch necessary for execution; and because also it is impossible to foresee, and so by law to provide for, all accidents and necessities that may concern the public, or to make such laws as will do no harm, if they are executed with an inflexible rigor, on all occasions, and upon all persons, that may come in their way.[130]

The Constitution embraces this view of executive power by vesting the president with an open-ended grant of executive power derived from the Constitution itself while harnessing that power with the concomitant "duty" to faithfully execute the laws. The president, in other words, is not dependent on the other branches for continuity in office and exercises power independently of them. The enforcement of law, however, is not an exact science, and the use of discretionary power, and its justifications, are appropriately evaluated by the people through Congress, which itself has power to enforce its own constitutional and political judgments when it deems executive discretion runs afoul of the Constitution and the law, including impeachment and removal from office. Such situations and judgments, however, are deeply political and context-dependent, and thus not easily subject to judicial settlement given their prudential nature.

As should be clear in the preceding paragraphs, leaving interbranch disputes to be resolved through the political process should not entail abandonment of the Constitution or law such that politics is reduced to whatever the branches can get away with. Rather, the political branches have a fundamentally different orientation to the law. This orientation is akin to Lockean prerogative insofar as it is directed to the common good and rooted in the constitutional duties of the branches in relation to each other. Departures from the literal strictures of the text (constitutional or statutory), moreover, should not abandon the law. Instead, departures require argument, justifying how uses of power realize the fundamental purposes of the law, or why a particular law must give way to other constitutional commitments given the relevant circumstances.

This orientation to the law thus recognizes that the law incorporates principles that are instantiated in the text (either expressed or implied) and transcend it.[131] As Leslie Goldstein writes, "Constitutions must not contain the detailed 'prolixity of a legal code.'" Rather, one must ask "what general principle of law is suggested in the language of the text as considered in light of the structure of the document."[132] Recognizing that the text incorporates principles enables the document to be more flexible, and thus able to adapt to changing circumstances while simultaneously maintaining its core commitments. For example, "A principle distinguishing 'unreasonable searches and seizures' by whether or not private homes are physically invaded by police must be adapted to the era of electronic surveillance."[133] How a law applies to a specific circumstance, or whether it should give way entirely in that circumstance, is thus regulated by the underlying textual principle embedded within that law, considered in light of the multiplicity of textual principles embodied in the Constitution (and its legal regime) taken all together. In short, principles are norms that have what Ronald Dworkin calls a "dimension of weight" that varies according to particular circumstances, and are thus not conclusive in themselves in reaching particular decisions or outcomes. They require practical reasoning and prudential judgments to apply in specific circumstances in light of how those circumstances affect the weight of competing principles relative to others.[134] As Jack Balkin explains:

> Principles are norms that are normally indeterminate in reach, that do not determine the scope of their own extension, that may apply differently given changing circumstances, and that can be balanced against other competing considerations. Although the persuasive power of principles may originate from how we expect they will apply when we argue for them, their jurisdiction, their scope, their weight, and the kinds of practices they regulate can shift over time.[135]

The Constitution and its legal regime are thus the literal instantiation of principled commitments in a text. The Constitution, however, is "disharmonic," to borrow a term from Gary Jacobsohn, insofar as it contains a multitude of constitutional commitments and tensions within the document itself.[136] As Justice David Souter argues, the Constitution "guarantees many good things, and good things that compete with each other and can never all be realized, all together, all at once." For example, the First Amendment of the Constitution states that "Congress shall make no law . . . abridging freedom of speech." And yet, Justice Souter continues, even the categorical prohibition of the First Amendment's freedom of speech clause, "expressing the value of speech and publication in the terms of a right as paramount as any fundamental right can be," does "not quite get to the point of an absolute prohibition." Rather, Justice Souter argues, it fails to express a categorical command

> because the Constitution has to be read as a whole, and when it is, other values crop up in potential conflict with an unfettered right to publish, the value of security for the nation and the value of the president's authority in matters foreign and military. The explicit terms of the Constitution, in other words, can create a conflict of approved values, and the explicit terms of the Constitution do not resolve that conflict when it arises. The guarantee of the right to publish is unconditional in its terms, and in its terms the power of the government to govern is plenary. A choice may have to be made, not because language is vague but because the Constitution embodies the desire of the American people, like most people, to have things both ways. We want order and security, and we want liberty. And we want not only liberty but equality as well. These paired desires of ours can clash, and when they do a court is forced to choose between them, between one constitutional good and another one.[137]

Chief Justice Vinson expressed this disharmonic conception of the Constitution's legal order in his trenchant dissent in the *Youngstown* case. The court, led by Justice Black, ruled that President Truman usurped Congress's lawmaking power through his seizure of the steel mills to secure the production of steel during the Korean conflict amid ongoing strikes by steelworkers. Congress, the court reasoned, had consciously ruled out governmental seizure of property under such circumstances when it passed the Taft-Hartley Act a few years prior; the president was thus bound by the law Congress passed when it made its policy determination. Chief Justice Vinson, however, reasoned that President Truman's actions might be justified under the circumstances, circumstances Congress had not anticipated when it legislated on the matter. In fact, President Truman sent a message to Congress explaining the reasons for his actions in light of the circumstances, stating, moreover, that he would abide by the will of Congress whether it approved or disapproved his actions. Chief Justice Vinson thus argued:

> The absence of a specific statute authorizing seizure of the steel mills as a mode of executing the laws—both the military procurement program and the anti inflation program—has not until today been thought to prevent the President from executing the law. Unlike an administrative commission confined to the enforcement of the statute under which it was created, or the head to a department when administering a particular statute, the President is a constitutional officer charged with taking care that a "mass of legislation" be executed. Flexibility as to mode of execution to meet critical situations is a matter of practical necessity.[138]

Chief Justice Vinson's dissent thus recognizes that unforeseen circumstances *might* justify action not anticipated by the law—and, in fact, prohibited by it—in an instance where its enforcement could both limit the president's ability to faithfully execute other laws also passed by Congress and imperil American soldiers abroad. Such a situation, therefore, was best left to the realm of politics given that the law could not itself speak to the contingencies that led to its exceptions. While President Truman openly invited the judgment of Congress and stated his willingness to abide by it, Congress could have enforced its contrary judgments, up to the point of impeachment and removal, absent such a willingness on the part of the president. What is striking in this account, then, is that the court intervened in the midst of a substantive political interaction where the branches engaged each other responsively to resolve a major question confronting the political order. It is worth pointing out that while Chief Justice Vinson rightly recognized the politically contingent justifications for President Truman's actions, the argument here is that the issue posed a nonjusticiable political question. As such, while the court was wrong to decide the case against Truman, it would also have been wrong to sanction that action by ruling the other way, as Chief Justice Vinson urged in his dissent.

Perhaps the most famous example of a departure from the strictures of the legal text that was subsequently generally accepted as justified is President Abraham Lincoln's defense of his order to suspend habeas corpus, along with several other wartime measures that exceeded his normal powers, at the outset of the Civil War. At the outbreak of the Civil War, Lincoln acted decisively to meet the needs of the nation, believing that his oath to "take care that the Laws be faithfully executed" and to "preserve, protect, and defend" the Constitution required actions that would, under normal circumstances, be considered unlawful. The importance of vigorous executive action without legal sanction, moreover, was made all the more necessary by the fact that Congress was out of session and could not be safely convened in time to exercise its powers. Given congressional absence, Lincoln subsequently argued to a special session of Congress, that "no choice was left but to call out the war power of the government," and that although some of the actions taken might not be "strictly legal," they were justified by "what appeared to be popular demand and public necessity, trusting then, as now, that Congress would readily ratify them."[139] Congress subsequently ratified most of the wartime measures Lincoln had already taken, but did not sanction the president's suspension of habeas corpus for another two years, in large part due to concerns that, to provide specific statutory authorization, could undermine the flexibility and discretion the president needed to wield the power effectively by suggesting that the president did not have the power in the first place.[140] The president and Congress thus negotiated the limits of their respective powers to ensure that the powers of the national government could be exercised as effectively as possible given the dire circumstances.

Chief Justice Taney, however, ruled in *Ex Parte Merryman* (1861) that Lincoln's suspension of habeas corpus was unconstitutional because only Congress could suspend habeas corpus, noting that the suspension clause is in Article I and that "[t]his article is devoted to the Legislative Department of the United States, and has not the slightest reference to the Executive Department."[141] Lincoln and Congress subsequently ignored the ruling. It is, of course, true that when Lincoln defended the suspension to Congress, he gave an exhaustive technical legal argument regarding the president's power to suspend habeas corpus. But beyond the technical, and potentially contestable, legal argument, Lincoln provided a constitutional justification for his actions animated by a concern for overarching constitutional purposes and the concomitant duties of his office, asserting that the actions taken, even if violating the strict letter of the law, were necessary to preserve the constitutional order:

> The whole of the laws which were required to be faithfully executed were being resisted and failing of execution in nearly one-third of the states. Must they be allowed to finally fail of execution, even had it been perfectly clear that by the use of the means necessary to their execution some single law, made in such extreme tenderness of the citizen's liberty that practically it relieves more of the guilty than of the innocent, should to a very limited extent be violated? To state the

> question more directly, Are all the laws but one to go unexecuted, and the government itself go to pieces lest that one be violated? Even in such a case, would not the official oath be broken if the Government should be overthrown when it was believed that disregarding the single law would tend to preserve it?[142]

Lincoln thus argued the constitutional merits of his case before Congress and the public, providing publicly accessible reasons for why a violation of the strict letter of the law, if it could be so construed that the law in fact had been violated, was justified by the particular circumstances that gave rise to the suspension. To put it another way, the fact that there is a habeas corpus suspension clause in the first place points to the fact that the framers recognized that there might be times when the government needs to effectively wield this power, especially when courts of law cannot properly function. After determining that such a power, in certain defined circumstances, is necessary, it is then important, as a second-order consideration, to decide which branch is best suited to exercise such a power. There are, of course, good reasons why the legislature, as the most broad-based, publicly accountable body, should have the power, making it less likely that such a power could be abused by executive discretion. But, as Lincoln queried, should the government be prevented from exercising an essential constitutional power if the branch formally granted the power cannot meet to exercise it to the detriment, even destruction, of the constitutional order itself?

The habeas corpus suspension case is instructive because it demonstrates how the branches can negotiate their respective boundaries, motivated by the constitutional principles at stake and constrained by the relevant circumstances. While the president exercised a power that he conceded he might not have under normal circumstances (even as he argued that, in a technical sense, he did, in fact, have that power), he subjected his actions, and his arguments on behalf of them, to post hoc congressional scrutiny. Congress, in its turn, after deliberating on the appropriate scope of the president's authority, recognized the legitimacy of those actions in light of the circumstances. Purely legal analysis concerning which branch appropriately has the power could not ultimately answer the question of whether the president's action was constitutionally legitimate. This is true regardless of how the court decided the case. Had the court provided judicial sanction of the president's action (finding that the president did, in fact, have the power in a legal sense), this could provide legal cover for a future president to wield the power in circumstances less appropriate or dire without having to similarly make constitutional justifications to Congress and to the public, relying instead on judicial precedent for support. By leaving the issue to politics (and in this case, refusing to defer to the judiciary's pronouncement on the matter), the political branches argued about the constitutional purposes undergirding the text, making politically contestable claims to each other that could be evaluated by each other, and, of course, ultimately by the public.

Recognizing that law is both indeterminate and contains a multiplicity of principles, however, does not in itself answer the question of why such resolution is best left to politics. Indeed, the court could attempt to resolve interbranch disputes while also being attentive to these features of the law. However, judicial resolution of the boundaries between Congress and the president, as argued in the previous section, misconceives the nature of the constitutional order, placing the court above rather than within the separation of powers. This is especially true, since both political branches have the powers to contest each other's use of authority, thus making judicial superintendence superfluous when it comes to separation of powers disputes.

Furthermore, and more pertinent to the analysis here, judicial intervention in interbranch boundary disputes would require the court to make political judgments for which it is neither equipped nor accountable. This is, therefore, a question of comparative institutional competence and constitutional efficacy. The judicial process is more about settling disputes based on bright-line rules that could apply across cases, and is thus less appropriately attuned to the departures that might require public justification based upon prudential factors.[143] This attentiveness to law, moreover, is appropriate for a legal institution that must apply the law to specific cases and controversies. Courts seek consistency, and thus often engage in precedential reasoning that is backward looking, attempting to draw bright-line rules that can govern cases across times.[144] As Gordon Silverstein notes, "Unlike a vote in Congress, which can be ad hoc and responsive to quick and unexpected changes, the structure and style of legal decision-making emphasize explanations for how and why legal decisions hew to or differ from a long line of established cases."[145] Superintendence by the court is thus justified with reference to the stability and consistency the judiciary brings to the constitutional order.[146] According to Larry Alexander and Frederick Schauer, "It is as much a function of a constitution as of law in general to settle authoritatively what ought to be done, and to coordinate for the common good the self-interested and strategic behavior of individual officials."[147] The Constitution and laws are thus treated by the judiciary as if they have the character of a legal code, and the judiciary's strength is that it can provide coherence and uniformity to the laws through what Mariah Zeisberg has referred to as its settlement function.

As it concerns the political branches' respective boundaries, however, the attempt to settle the Constitution's legal meaning, or to add greater determinacy to law, fails to recognize the extent to which interbranch disputes involve or require political judgment and justifications, and are thus not easily resolved with recourse to legal processes. This is especially true given the priority of precedential reasoning and bright-line rules in judicial proceedings. Given the precedential nature of law, especially as enforced by the court, interbranch disputes resolved by the court provide legal precedents that can be utilized by future political actors even in circumstances where such actions would be less justified, if at all. The problem with precedent (as alluded to in the Lincoln example) is that even good precedents later carry the force of law and can be used by constitutional officeholders to defend actions that are less justifiable given differing circumstances. The presence of judicial precedent makes it easier to invoke past judicial decisions as the justification for certain actions rather than a more substantive, or political, defense of departures from the strictures of the law. To put this in the words of Justice Jackson,

> The principle then lies about like a loaded weapon ready for the hand of any authority that can bring forward a plausible claim of an urgent need. Every repetition imbeds that principle more deeply in our law and thinking and expands it to new purposes. All who observe the work of courts are familiar with what Judge Cardozo described as "the tendency of a principle to expand itself to the limit of its logic."[148]

The extent to which departures from the strict letter of the law are justifiable is more easily determined through political processes in which the arguments are more contextual and circumstantially confined. For example, chapter 4 details the recess appointment controversy during the Obama administration, arguing that the Supreme Court, which ruled nine to zero that President Obama's recess appointments violated the Constitution, should not have decided the case given that it posed what should have been a nonjusticiable political question. The argument is not that the court should have broadly construed the Recess Appointments Clause to legitimize the appointments. Rather, President Obama plausibly argued that the behavior of congressional Republicans necessitated his unprecedented actions as a form of what David E. Pozen has characterized as constitutional self-help.[149] This was the kind of political judgment that is ill-suited to judicial resolution precisely because the unique circumstances that led to textual departures were circumstantially contingent, and a judicial decision sustaining recess appointments while the Senate was technically in session could have created a precedent easily abused by future presidents.

Perhaps even more problematic, from a practical perspective, is that while judicial action is often justified with regard to the stabilizing effect it can have on the constitutional order, such benefits might themselves be elusive given increasing levels of partisanship and polarization on the court today.[150] Are the Supreme Court's recent decisions with regard to delegation or the constitutional structure of agencies principled decisions, or are they better understood as partisan efforts to dismantle the administrative state? If the court had sanctioned President Obama's recess appointments in *Noel Canning* based on the nonmajoritarian obstruction by congressional Republicans, would that be seen as a nakedly partisan effort by the court's liberal majority to support the president? As Daphna Renan argues, "The reality of a polarized Supreme Court, increasingly on partisan grounds, challenges the idea that the Court can operate as an effective stabilizing agent preserving a political equilibrium that the political branches are too polarized to maintain."[151]

Finally, judicialization of interbranch disputes moves political discourse from the plane of high politics, wherein officeholders must justify their decisions with reference to the constitutional text and its underlying principles, to the judiciary's legalistic approach to the text. Such a move is problematic because it precludes, or at least gives far less weight to, the kinds of justifications for purported legal departures from the literal strictures of the law that could be politically and constitutionally justified given the relevant circumstances.[152] In other words, while the law still matters in interbranch disputes, such disputes are by their nature political. Judicial resolution, or narrow legal reasoning, is appropriately less attentive to these political dynamics, and it is this inattentiveness that makes the court comparatively less well-suited for such a task. This comparative disadvantage, taken together with the fact that the political branches each have determinate tools for pressing their arguments and judgments that are more powerful than judicial judgment, underscores the extent to which judicial review is inappropriate in this context.

To sum up, lengthy judicial processes and precedential reasoning appropriate to such processes are comparatively less suited to the types of interbranch conflicts concerning the legal boundaries between the political branches. Given that the political branches each have tools more powerful than judicial judgment, there is no reason for them to substitute judicial processes for their own. Partisanship and polarization on the Supreme Court, moreover, makes it unlikely that it can serve as a neutral, stabilizing influence on constitutional politics. Rather, the political branches should engage each other to determine the limits of their respective legal boundaries in specific contexts. In such disputes, they should justify their actions vis-à-vis each other with reference to how their actions vindicate the principles of the Constitution or law at issue with reference to the public good. In so doing, the Constitution's legal framework, in the hands of the political branches, becomes itself the means to the polity's politically contingent, competing, and unlimited ends.

CLARIFYING THE JUDICIAL ROLE IN SEPARATION OF POWERS DISPUTES

What should be evident from the foregoing is the extent to which judicial review of separation of powers questions concerning the legal boundaries between the political branches poses significant problems for the practice of constitutional government. First, judicial superintendence of the separation of powers is based on a philosophically inaccurate understanding of the nature of the constitutional order, and, moreover, is superfluous given the powers of the political branches with regard to each other. Secondly, the court suffers from a comparative institutional disadvantage given the types of political and prudential judgments raised by interbranch conflicts. What, then, should be the role of the judiciary in separation of powers disputes concerning disputes between the political branches?

The argument here is that the Supreme Court should not decide disputes between Congress and the president regarding their respective constitutional and legal boundaries and should dismiss such cases as nonjusticiable.[153] It is true that clashes between Congress and the president can implicate individual rights, which is perhaps the strongest objection to this position. In such cases, however, individual rights are only impacted in a secondary or derivative sense if the primary question relates to the interbranch dispute itself. For example, in the *Youngstown* case, due process rights were certainly implicated when President Truman seized the steel mills even though Congress had ruled out seizure as a legitimate solution to labor strikes when it passed the Taft-Hartley Act a few years prior. The court was asked to resolve the interbranch dispute: whether the president had usurped Congress's lawmaking power by acting unilaterally in the midst of a crisis. Similarly, the question in *Ex Parte Merryman* was not whether the government has the power to suspend the writ of habeas corpus, but whether that power could be exercised by the president rather than Congress.[154] As Choper argues, in such interbranch disputes, "'liberty' claims are merely derivative" of an "initial finding that one of the political branches has encroached on the power of the other."[155] Such liberty claims, in other words, are ultimately not "based on any direct governmental infringement of personal constitutional liberties conventionally defined."[156] Given that the primary question in such cases concerns the interbranch dispute and only implicates a rights question as a secondary consequence of that dispute, the fact that rights are implicated should not serve as the basis for judicial resolution of the interbranch dispute. This is especially true given that such disputes can be resolved through political contestation between Congress and the president without turning to a neutral arbiter. In fact, as demonstrated at length in the two previous sections (and in the case studies to follow), judicial review of such disputes is no panacea and might cause more problems than it solves.

This is not to say, however, that there is no appropriate role for the judiciary in such cases. For example, there is no question that President Truman's seizure of the steel mills amounted to a public seizure of private property, thus raising the question of whether the property was taken for public use with just compensation, as required by the Fifth Amendment. As Choper writes, if the court "agreed that a 'taking' had occurred, it should have ordered compensation if and when the claim was properly presented."[157] The court could do this without deciding the dispute between Congress and the president. In fact, as argued above, there might, at times, be good reasons for the president, as commander in chief, to take decisive action to protect the nation outside the specific parameters of existing law. To do this might implicate rights in the derivative fashion explained above. Failure to do so, on the other hand, could also undermine rights because their protection ultimately relies on the security of the constitutional order. To return to the Federalist argument, rights are not safeguarded by purely legal limits on power, but by creating a system of competing institutions that can meet the unlimited and politically contingent needs of the political order. In this way, as Hamilton observed in *Federalist* 84, "the Constitution is itself, in every rational sense, and to every useful purpose, A BILL OF RIGHTS."[158] A liberty justification for the judicial policing of interbranch boundaries, in other words, is inattentive to the ways in which the separation of powers itself safeguards rights through its complex structure of countervailing power.

In addition to treating legal disputes concerning the boundaries between Congress and the president as nonjusticiable, the account here also counsels for judicial deference to the political branches as they engage in the process of statecraft through legislation pursuant to the necessary and proper clause.[159] In recent years, the court has increasingly taken cases from private litigants challenging the constitutional structure of agencies in the abstract even when the structure of the agency has nothing to do with the substantive regulatory outcome sought by litigants. For example, the court invalidated two layers of for-cause removal protection from the president in *Free Enterprise Fund v. Public Co. Accounting Oversight Board* (2010).[160] Most recently, the court invalidated the single-director structure of the Consumer Financial Protection Bureau.[161] Such decisions are rooted in the notion that the constitutional structure is inherently fixed either by some overarching separation of powers doctrine or by historical convention, and that there is no room for the political branches to design new mechanisms to meet new and unanticipated challenges.[162] Such a notion, however, is inconsistent with the ways in which early congresses debated constitutional meaning, recognizing the provisional nature of their settlements on issues such as the removal power.[163] The point here is not that Congress and the president always get things perfectly right, or that there are no criteria for the evaluation of provisional settlements made through the political process. Rather, the point is that the political process is the proper venue for ongoing contestation and revision given that applying the Constitution's abstract principles to new situations requires prudential judgment. As Renan argues, "Institutional contestation and innovation have always been hallmarks of our system of partially differentiated, partially interdependent powers. There is no ideal or essential allocation of power between the political branches. Rather, how much or what types of accommodation, power-sharing, and institutional checking between the executive and Congress are legitimate or desirable is a set of questions that is inherently *un*fixed."[164] There is no reason, therefore, to turn over such decisions to a judicial process in which five jurists on the Supreme Court have the power to invalidate the provisional arrangements negotiated by Congress and the president. This is especially true given the increasingly partisan nature of such decisions, nearly always splitting the court into its partisan factions.

Conclusion

The argument up to this point should reveal the dynamism of the Constitution's governmental framework. The Constitution is not "living" in the sense that it is updated to meet the needs of modern society based on the enlightened views of members of the Supreme Court. Rather, it is a dynamic system of government that maintains its basic shape through conflict between the political branches. The needs of the polity might bend and stretch the Constitution's legal limits, but the political branches are hardwired to vindicate the Constitution's competing principles through political contestation. This contestation, properly understood, eludes settlement insofar as the needs of the political community, and how constitutional principles will apply to unforeseen circumstances, cannot be predicted in advance.

This political orientation to the Constitution can, of course, result in political or even constitutional failure, but this is the case with any human enterprise, including the courts. The burden of the book is to demonstrate the superiority of the political approach to constitutional politics to its legalistic counterpart (which is also prone to failure in perhaps more subtle and profound ways). This burden is borne by four case study chapters, which cover a wide range of constitutional phenomena: delegation and the judicially invalidated legislative veto, executive agreements and treaties, President Obama's judicially invalidated recess appointments, and contemporary questions concerning congressional oversight of the executive branch. Through these case studies, I demonstrate how understanding the separation of powers as a political architecture, not a purely legal doctrine, provides a better framework for constitutional evaluation while at the same time showcasing the dynamism of the constitutional order.

2

Legislative Veto

There is little doubt that the legislative veto was one of the most consequential constitutional innovations in the history of American government before it was invalidated by the Supreme Court in *INS v. Chadha* (1983). The legislative veto was a mechanism by which Congress delegated legislative power by statute to the executive branch or to bureaucratic agencies while retaining the ability to veto executive actions or proposed bureaucratic rules in particular instances. Congress used several variants of the legislative veto, including joint resolutions that required the president's signature (or veto). However, the most controversial legislative vetoes—the vetoes at issue in and invalidated by the court in *Chadha*—were those that did not meet the Constitution's requirements for lawmaking (bicameralism and presentment). For example, Congress could pass a concurrent resolution of approval, thus requiring that both houses approve a proposed rule before it could go into effect. Alternatively, Congress could allow proposed rules to go into effect after a specified period of time (usually sixty days) unless one or both houses disapproved by passing either a simple or concurrent resolution of disapproval, respectively.

Legislative vetoes were first passed in appropriations acts dealing with executive reorganization in 1933, granting the president wide discretion and latitude to reorganize the executive branch by executive order unless Congress passed a resolution of disapproval within sixty days. Presidents, of course, lobbied for reorganization authority so that such reorganizations would not be stymied by going through the full, and cumbersome, legislative process where such bills were often easily defeated. Congress, on the other hand, assuaged worries about congressional abdication by attaching legislative vetoes to this vast transfer of legislative power to the executive branch.

While the legislative veto was only used sporadically over the course of the next few decades, during the 1960s Congress began to use it frequently, especially as it increasingly delegated legislative power to the executive branch and to bureaucratic agencies. Legislative vetoes were included in a number of statutes that were part of the legislative response to fears of an "imperial presidency" during the Nixon era, including the War Powers Act of 1974, the Budget and Impoundment Act of 1974, and the Federal Trade Act of 1974, among many others. During the 1970s Congress enacted 353 legislative veto provisions, an increase of more than 300 percent from the previous decade.[1] This increased use of the legislative veto makes sense given the vast increase in regulatory authority and rulemaking that occurred during the same time period. For example, from 1955 to 1960, Congress enacted 37 regulatory statutes compared to 119 passed by Congress between 1966 and 1975.[2] As bureaucratic rulemaking skyrocketed in the 1970s, many government reformers called for a generic legislative veto by which all agency regulations would be subject to some form of the legislative veto.[3]

Given the expansion of the national government's prerogatives following the New Deal, and the huge growth of government in the decades after, supporters of the legislative veto viewed it as an essential mechanism for Congress to retain control of its delegated powers and ensure democratic accountability over the administrative state. Such delegation was regarded—as well as sanctioned and endorsed by the judiciary—as essential given the complexity of modern government and the vast array of issues that require national attention. Without such controls over delegation, many contended that Congress was committing "legiscide," surrendering democratic oversight by ceding power to unelected and unaccountable bureaucrats.[4] Others, however, viewed the increased use of the legislative veto as an assault on presidential power and an example of congressional overreach.[5]

The purpose of this chapter is to show that the legislative veto, while seemingly a departure from the literal strictures of the constitutional text, was actually an example of the dynamism of the Constitution's separation of powers, an attempt to realize the energy of the executive branch while balancing that efficiency with the aims of republican government.[6] That the legislative veto is a political invention meant to bring to bear separation of powers values on the problems of modern government is particularly evident given that it merely alters the order of interbranch action without changing the substantive involvement of the two branches when it comes to lawmaking. In other words, the legislative veto—itself authorized by a statute passed by both houses of Congress and signed by the president—merely reverses the sequence of interbranch action, allowing the executive branch to engage in the lawmaking function reserved to Congress by the Constitution while ensuring that such rules (which are themselves legally binding on citizens) only go into effect so long as both houses of Congress agree. The first part of this chapter traces the development of and rationale for the legislative veto in light of the need to delegate, noting, where relevant, how the mechanism worked in varying policy contexts, such as executive reorganization, budgets and impoundments, foreign policy, and administrative rulemaking. In short, this section demonstrates how the legislative veto was an essential mechanism for bringing to bear the competing desiderata of American constitutionalism on the complex problems of modern government. This, of course, is not to say that the legislative veto is devoid of problems, as amply noted by many political science critics of the veto.[7] The benefits of the veto, I argue, outweigh the costs.

The Supreme Court, however, ruled the legislative veto unconstitutional in *INS v. Chadha* (1983), claiming it violated separation of powers doctrine. The court's sweeping decision thus invalidated over three hundred laws—more laws in this one instance than in all other Supreme Court actions combined. According to the court, once Congress delegates to executive officials, any subsequent action it takes to exercise control over those delegations must meet the constitutional requirements for legislation—including bicameralism and presentment—outlined in Article I, section 7, clause 2. While the court conceded that the legislative veto is an efficient mechanism for adapting the government to modern circumstances, it was nevertheless struck down as an unconstitutional shortcut through the separation of powers framework because Congress acted in a nonlegislative way, meddling in the administration of government.

The court's decision in *Chadha*, however, was deeply problematic insofar as the court attempted to make tidy categorizations about types of powers based solely on who wields those powers—that is, when power is wielded by an executive official, it is presumptively executive. In this way, the court not only mischaracterized the fundamental nature of the constitutional design by overly emphasizing "parchment barrier" distinctions but also, ultimately, as Justice White argued in his trenchant dissent, led to the very phenomenon the court attempted to avoid with its formalistic reading of the Constitution: the concentration of legislative, executive, and judicial power in the same hands. Moreover, the scope of the court's decision was particularly troubling given that the legislative veto at issue in *Chadha* differed substantially from other contexts in which Congress implemented the veto because the particular veto in *Chadha* dealt with quasi-judicial power in an adjudicatory setting rather than the wielding of Congress's delegated legislative power. In this light, then, the court went well beyond the question at issue in the case, disrupting decades of interbranch negotiation and compromise.

Finally, this chapter concludes by considering the impact of the court's ruling on legislative vetoes. While Congress's ability to retain oversight of its delegated legislative power has been substantially curtailed—as evidenced by the failure of the Congressional Review Act's (CRA) joint resolution of disapproval mechanism—the legislative veto has survived in other forms.[8] Legislative veto surrogates, though not as powerful in a formal sense, operate much like the legislative vetoes invalidated by *Chadha*. The persistence of the legislative veto points to the vitality of the Constitution's political architecture.

The Problem (and the Necessity) of Delegation

Article I of the Constitution explicitly states that "all legislative Powers herein granted shall be vested in a Congress of the United States." Even so, legislative delegation of rulemaking and adjudicatory power to administrators emerged as a central feature of the national government almost as soon as the Constitution was ratified in 1789.[9] Congressional delegation skyrocketed in the twentieth century as Congress increasingly found itself incapable of legislating effectively given the vast array of complex issues on the national agenda. The national government's role expanded into complex and increasingly technical issues like transportation, communication, employment, wages and prices, labor relations, race relations, and the environment, among others.

From a practical perspective, of course, such delegations of legislative power are justifiable for a number of reasons, especially if the national government is to have the ability to deal effectively with issues of national concern.[10] First, given the number of issues on the legislative agenda, Congress can delegate to alleviate its workload, prioritizing and focusing on issues it deems especially important. This is particularly important given the number of federal regulations that reach into nearly all facets of American life. In 2016, for example, the Federal Register included 3,853 final rules, taking up 38,652 pages, exceeding the previous record set in 2013 by 46 percent.[11] While page counts provide an imperfect assessment of the number of annual regulations, they do underscore the great extent of federal regulation that has existed for much of the past century, at an ever-increasing pace. Without the ability to delegate, the national government would clearly be unable to deal with all the issues that Congress deems of national importance.

Secondly, many issues require expertise that average legislators are unlikely to have, especially given the wide range of issues confronting Congress in the modern world. Hence, while Congress can legislate with general goals in mind, it is often best to leave the specifics to those with the appropriate training and expertise. For example, it is not hard to imagine the difficulty with which Congress would write, say, nuclear power plant safety regulations (and perhaps even less difficult to imagine why most citizens would not want Congress to undertake such a task!). Delegation to entities that have resources in both time and expertise, therefore, allows Congress to ensure that federal regulations are adapted well to the various nuances and contingencies of specific problems, a task that surely exceeds the capabilities of a deliberative body of generalists.

However, such delegation has not come without significant controversy. Even if legislative delegation to the executive branch and administrative agencies is a necessity for modern government on the scale with which it has existed during the past century, this does not necessarily entail that widespread delegation is an unqualified good, its benefits for governmental capacity and efficiency notwithstanding. In fact, delegation is deeply problematic from the perspective of democracy and public accountability. Insofar as Congress delegates its legislative authority to other entities, it diminishes its own constitutional role, placing lawmaking power in the hands of less democratic and electorally accountable actors.[12] As the court argued in *Schechter Poultry Co. v. United States* (1935), the last case in which the court struck down a statute on nondelegation grounds, Congress can certainly delegate to others the responsibility for "the making of subordinate rules within prescribed limits," but the "necessity and validity of such provisions, and the wide range of administrative authority which has been developed by means of them, cannot be allowed to obscure the limitations of the authority to delegate, if our constitutional system is to be maintained."[13] In other words, delegation of legislative power to the president or administrative agencies in ways that allows Congress to avoid choosing between political alternatives (as opposed to merely administrative or logistical options) subverts the constitutional design by leaving lawmaking authority in entities that are not electorally accountable or representative of the range of diverse interests in the general public. The court's ruling in *Schecter*, however, proved to be an outlier in American constitutional history, one of only two instances where the court invalidated a law for violating the purported doctrine. In fact, while in the nineteenth and into the twentieth century the judiciary often at least rhetorically invoked a nondelegation principle, courts rarely if ever invalidated delegations on such grounds, leading two prominent scholars to characterize the notion of a judicially enforced nondelegation doctrine as a myth.[14]

While the current Supreme Court seems poised to reintroduce some version of a nondelegation doctrine, recent scholarship casts significant doubt on the constitutional pedigree of a judicially enforced nondelegation doctrine.[15] First, the mythic quality of the doctrine obscures the fact that delegation was widespread at the outset of American governance and provoked little, if any, controversy.[16] Given the extraordinary propensity of the first Congresses to extensively debate the Constitution's meaning and limitations on governmental action, its willingness to delegate without sparking even a hint of constitutional controversy is striking.[17] Secondly, the fundamental premise undergirding a nondelegation principle is unapologetically formalistic, resting on the notion that different types of power are easily differentiated by their natures and assigned to and exclusively exercised by the appropriate branch, so that only the legislature can wield legislative power, and so on.[18] This formalistic notion, as argued in chapter 1, hardly comports with founding era conceptions of power. As Mortenson and Bagley argue, echoing Madison in *Federalist* 37, "sophisticated discussions of the founding recognize that efforts to classify government action in the abstract are irreducibly indeterminate."[19] Finally, from a practical perspective, the judicial enforcement of a nondelegation doctrine suffers from many of the same pitfalls of subjectivity that animate the concerns of those who oppose open-ended grants of delegated legislative authority. As Adrian Vermeule put it, writing in the wake of the Supreme Court's ruling in *West Virginia v. EPA* (2022), "the doctrine displays the same vagueness of standards that the Court finds objectionable, under the nondelegation rubric, when authority is granted to agencies. What is constitutional overreach for unelected bureaucrats in the agencies is constitutional virtue for the unelected bureaucrats on the bench."[20] The inherent subjectivity in criteria, and the concomitant unpredictability of judicial action in enforcing such a doctrine, thus invites lawsuits targeting all aspects of the administrative state, easily frustrating the ability of the government to regulate key aspects of American life. Such judicial action, and its accompanying chaos, is a poor substitute for political choice made by the people's representatives.

To make the case against a *judicially* enforced nondelegation doctrine, however, is not to unqualifiedly dismiss the core tenets of its political insight. The key insight of the nondelegation doctrine is that delegations risk writing Congress, the most democratic and politically accountable institution in the government, out of the lawmaking process, leaving it in the hands of unelected and unaccountable administrators. While there are clear benefits to delegating to an expert administration for the sake of addressing particular policy questions with efficiency and the requisite expertise, expertise is no substitute for the political choices that a self-governing community must make. In other words, there is not necessarily a "correct" answer to many public policy questions that an expert administrator will be able to produce outside of the political process.[21] Nearly all the questions of political life are certainly aided by expertise, but expertise is no substitute for the balancing of the various commitments and political trade-offs that are inherent in a government run by popular opinion. For example, vague congressional mandates to the Environmental Protection Agency (EPA) to issue regulations that ensure "clean air" (which, assuredly a vast majority of Americans think is something worth having) do not answer the question of how to balance the need for clean air with, say, ensuring that businesses are not overly burdened by regulations to ensure a vibrant economy (also something that Americans surely want). Expertise cannot fully account for the political trade-offs inherent in any policy choice. As Russell Muirhead argues, the good of democratic government is not reducible to "getting things right." Rather, democracy is ultimately about "making things right."[22] In other words, the good of democratic government is, in many respects, procedural, providing a space in which people can regularly adjudicate their competing claims and then to enact laws in accordance with the deliberative will of the majority. However, if the various political choices and trade-offs that constitute democratic life are not clear, then citizens will have a difficult time holding their government accountable and ensuring that laws and governmental policies reflect democratic demands.

Many critics of open-ended delegation note that these political choices are exactly what delegation obscures. Theodore Lowi famously argued in his highly influential study on open-ended delegations that such delegations can result in governmental impotence in the face of democratic demands.[23] Because Congress often delegates with broad mandates that provide little, if any, guidance to administrators based on specific political decisions made by Congress, administrators thus have great freedom to make policy decisions that cater to the specific demands of the particular interest groups that are most impacted by regulations.[24] Hence, governmental policy is not the result of an overarching congressional plan wherein political trade-offs are made in light of general governmental objectives. Rather, policy is made piecemeal in response to different interest groups across the bureaucracy.

Congress can take advantage of the obscurity created by delegation. If administrators are making choices rather than Congress, members of Congress can pass the blame onto those administrators, praising or criticizing particular governmental decisions based on the particular audience.[25] Jonathan Adler demonstrates how this phenomenon worked with the EPA's decision to begin regulating greenhouse gasses under the Clean Air Act.[26] The Clean Air Act of 1970 (later amended in 1977 and 1990) authorized the EPA to regulate carbon emissions. During the Obama administration, however, the EPA began to extend its rulemaking to the regulation of greenhouse gasses. While the court sanctioned the EPA's regulation of greenhouse gasses under the Clean Air Act, Congress never passed a statute directing the agency to do this.[27] In fact, the EPA acknowledged that to regulate greenhouse gasses according to the same formula as carbon emissions would produce absurd results that would grind air pollution programs to a halt. Consequently, the EPA regulated greenhouse gasses on an entirely new formula based on what it deemed to be reasonable absent congressional legislation on the matter.[28] The result, of course, is that a bureaucratic agency essentially made law that affects millions of people without any public deliberation or political accountability by elected officials in Congress. It is even more notable, according to Adler, that members of both parties in Congress criticized the EPA for either being too lenient or too strict "as if the decision to regulate greenhouse gasses was the EPA's and the EPA's alone."[29]

In sum, while delegation might be necessary, it can only go so far before it undermines core constitutional values. The energy essential to good government must be held in tension with the need for public accountability. Although there is little basis in the constitutional text or founding-era history to support a judicially enforced nondelegation doctrine, a Congress motivated by its constitutional prerogatives should ensure that delegations comport with political principles deduced from the Constitution's allocation of power. Prior to its invalidation by the court, the legislative veto was a mechanism that performed this vital function.

The Legislative Veto and Constitutional Politics

The legislative veto was a political tool invented to bring the competing desiderata of American constitutionalism—majoritarian will and energy—to bear on the problem of big government by allowing Congress to approve or disapprove certain rules, regulations, or executive actions. What is important to note—and what should be clear from the previous section—is that the legislative veto was created in response to the fact of delegation of legislative power and the ways in which such delegation, without qualifications, can undermine core principles of separation of powers by placing the lawmaking function in entities other than Congress. While there is significant evidence to suggest that delegation occurred long before its general acceptance by the court during the New Deal—suggesting the practical impossibility of nondelegation given the demands of modern life—by the middle of the twentieth century, such delegation was sanctioned by the judiciary and since that time has been a firmly entrenched feature of the constitutional order. As Congressman Elliott Levitas (D-GA), a primary advocate of the legislative veto, put it, "If you ask the man on the street who makes the laws in this country, he would likely tell you that Congress does. But he would be wrong, because more edicts regulating his life are promulgated by unelected bureaucrats than are passed by the elected Congress." According to Levitas, the legislative veto was a mechanism meant to restore the political architecture of the Constitution by giving "the public, through their elected representatives, an input into and a control over the rules which govern their lives."[30] That Congress viewed the legislative veto as an essential mechanism to restore the Constitution's political architecture is evidenced by the increasing use of the legislative veto in all kinds of issue areas, including executive reorganization, budgets and impoundments, and bureaucratic rulemaking through the 1970s before *Chadha*.

What must be noted first is that legislative vetoes were included in laws passed by both houses of Congress and signed by the president. Legislative vetoes were thus part of a political arrangement between the two branches whereby Congress agreed to delegate its legislative power to the executive branch (or to independent agencies) while reserving the right to approve or disapprove specific exercises of that *legislative* power.[31] Often, presidents asked for this power, and Congress at times only begrudgingly acquiesced to presidential requests for delegated authority. Congress attached legislative vetoes to its delegations of legislative power, recognizing both the need for delegation and the importance of reconciling such delegations with Congress's constitutional role as the nation's lawmaker. Insofar as presidents opposed the inclusion of legislative vetoes in statutes, Congress could always refuse to delegate in the first place. Both branches often had good reasons to compromise.

For example, legislative vetoes were first included in laws granting the president the power to reorganize the executive branch by executive order rather than having to wait for Congress to legislate such plans. The legislative process is cumbersome and slow, and competing congressional pressures and compromises often stymie reorganization efforts rather than ensure that such reorganization efforts actually realize the overarching goal of efficient administration of the government. Such plans, therefore, are

Table 2.1: Types of Legislative Vetoes

Types of Legislative Vetoes	*Explanation*
Concurrent Resolution of Approval	Regulations only go into effect if both houses vote to approve
Concurrent Resolution of Disapproval	Regulations go into effect (usually after sixty days) unless both houses vote to disapprove
Simple Resolution of Disapproval	Regulations go into effect (usually after sixty days) unless one house votes to disapprove
Committee approval or disapproval	Regulations go into effect based on committee approval or disapproval

ultimately difficult to pass legislatively because opponents of the plan—perhaps agencies that will be discontinued or consolidated—can use all the procedural mechanisms and hurdles of the legislative process to ensure defeat of a bill.

When Congress debated whether to grant reorganization authority to President Roosevelt in 1938, one vocal senator at the time went so far as to say that the reorganization powers requested by President Roosevelt would result in "an absolute dictatorship," while another said that such grants of power to the president meant that "pretty soon, there will not be any use for Congress," and that lawmakers "might just as well stay at home and endorse Executive directives by mail."[32] When Congress finally granted the president reorganization authority in 1939, it only agreed to delegate power by also attaching a legislative veto provision. Reorganization plans automatically went into effect after sixty days unless Congress passed a concurrent resolution of disapproval.[33] The benefits of this political arrangement are clear. Granting the president legislative authority to reorganize the executive branch subject to a legislative veto allows the executive branch to craft a coherent plan in an efficient manner, and opponents of the plan have to convince a majority in both chambers to oppose the plan rather than just a majority in one chamber. While the balance of power is shifted greatly to the executive branch, Congress still maintains a deliberative role and can prevent reorganization plans with which it disagrees, as it did several times during the Truman administration when it vetoed the creation of several proposed executive agencies. Moreover, Congress's veto power gives it negotiating leverage—much like the president's veto power in a normal legislative process—to ensure that plans reflect Congress's own set of priorities. All in all, 102 executive reorganization plans were submitted to Congress from 1939 until *Chadha*; Congress disapproved 19 of them, demonstrating that Congress still had the final say even as it offered the president a more efficient alternative to the normal lawmaking process.[34]

The budget impoundment controversy during the Nixon administration similarly illuminates the logic of the legislative veto and how it was a vital component of healthy interbranch politics. Presidents since George Washington routinely impounded (or delayed the spending of) appropriated funds based on executive discretion, and this discretion makes sense given that changes in conditions on the ground might require adjustments to the actual spending of appropriated funds in ways not anticipated by Congress when it originally legislated. President Nixon, however, refused to spend money appropriated by Congress at an unprecedented level, at times attempting to change the policy choices made by Congress by refusing to spend money for certain programs that he disliked.[35] While President Nixon's motives were based on his policy disagreements, he translated his political motives into a sophisticated constitutional argument about the inability of Congress to develop coherent policy oriented to the national good because it was too beholden to parochial interests to make difficult decisions about budget cuts, continually increasing spending to satisfy various constituency groups. On the other hand, the president looked out for the national interest and, therefore, needed the ability to impound funds when Congress did not make difficult choices. Of course, from a legal perspective, the president either has the power to refuse to spend appropriated funds or he does not have that power. Even so, Congress responded to the president in the realm of politics, acknowledging the veracity of President Nixon's constitutional argument by admitting its own difficulties in crafting a coherent budget directed to the national good (especially since, at the time, the budgeting process was largely decentralized with overlapping jurisdiction among several committees), and recognizing both the legitimacy of the president's superior budget resources and national perspective. Hence, Congress passed the Budget Control and Impoundment Act of 1974, formally granting the president the power to impound or even to permanently refuse to spend appropriated funds subject to a legislative veto. In addition, Congress centralized its budgeting process and created the Congressional Budget Office to give itself a national perspective on the national budget comparable to the Office of Management and Budget (OMB) in the White House. In short, the legislative veto mechanism was central to the political conflict over budget issues, giving the president the power to refuse to spend money appropriated by Congress (and to make arguments defending executive branch judgments) while ultimately ensuring that the most popularly accountable branch of government retained oversight over the national budget.

As these two examples demonstrate, the legislative veto was a mechanism Congress used to ensure that, in delegating legislative power to outside entities, it did not abdicate its constitutional responsibilities to enact laws in accordance with the deliberative public will. Indeed, given the bending of constitutional structure with regard to delegation of legislative power from Congress to the executive branch, Edward S. Corwin explained the basic constitutional rationale for the legislative veto as follows:

> It is generally agreed that Congress, being free not to delegate, is free to do so on certain stipulated conditions, as, for example, that the delegation shall terminate by a certain date or on the occurrence of a specified event; the end of a war, for instance. Why then, should not one condition be that the delegation shall continue only as long as the two houses are of opinion that it is working beneficially? As we have seen, moreover, it is generally agreed that the maxim that the legislature may not *delegate* its powers signifies at the very least that the legislature may not *abdicate* its power. Yet how, in view of the scope that legislative delegations take nowadays, is the line between *delegation* and *abdication* to be maintained? Only, I urge, by rendering the delegated powers recoverable without the consent of the delegate.[36]

Yet, even if the utility of the legislative veto is manifest in these examples—as well as in areas such as bureaucratic rulemaking, as discussed in the previous section—the question becomes whether the legislative veto violates the stipulation in Article I, section 7, clause 2, which requires that

> every order, resolution, or vote to which the Concurrence of the Senate and the House of Representatives may be necessary (except on a question of adjournment) shall be presented to the President of the United States; and before the Same shall take Effect, shall be approved by him, or being disapproved by him, shall be repassed by two thirds of the Senate and House of Representatives, according to the Rules and Limitations prescribed in the Case of a Bill.

This clause suggests, at least ostensibly, that any action taken by Congress must meet the requirements for presentment to the president for his signature or veto, as well as bicameralism. However, the way the legislative veto worked in actual practice provides compelling evidence that the legislative veto fulfills the spirit of this clause even if it contravenes the literal letter of the law. The veto power, as Hamilton expressed in *Federalist* 73, is important both for protecting the president from unconstitutional congressional encroachments upon his constitutional prerogatives and to give the president the ability to press his different political views vis-à-vis the Congress. The president's veto power, therefore, is a primary mechanism by which interbranch conflict occurs.[37] By analyzing the records of the Constitutional Convention, however, it becomes clear that this further stipulation that "every order, resolution, or vote" that requires the consent of both houses must be presented to the president was an answer to Madison's concern that the Congress would attempt to circumvent the president's veto power by using semantic distinctions (like "orders," "resolutions," or "votes") to pass what, in actuality, are *bills* in order to circumvent the president's veto.[38]

If legislative vetoes, as already indicated, are part of political arrangements established by statutes that merely reverse the sequence of interbranch action without changing the major substantive involvement of the branches, then this concern is unwarranted. In other words, such statutes greatly empower the president (or subordinate executive officials), vesting the executive branch with the power to propose regulations or subsidiary laws pursuant to its authorizing legislation. The legislative veto merely ensures that such laws only go into effect if Congress assents to them. The veto power, therefore, is not implicated because legislative proposals come directly from the executive.[39] Presumably, the president would not veto his own legislative proposals. This was the position taken by Griffin Bell, attorney general for President Jimmy Carter, regarding executive reorganization. Such proposals were constitutional, according to Bell, because reorganization statutes permit the president to "submit to Congress only those plans which he approves."[40] While Bell distinguished executive reorganization vetoes from other types of legislative vetoes, executive control, however, would seemingly extend to legislative vetoes more generally. For example, presidential control extends to bureaucratic rulemaking as well—even if such rulemaking is not directly handled by the president or members of the Executive Office of the President in the White House—because the president has political control of the bureaucracy through his power to appoint (with advice and consent) and fire subordinates within the executive branch at pleasure. The Constitution also gives the president the power to request "the Opinion, in writing, of the principal Officer in each of the executive Departments, upon any Subject relating to the Duties of their respective offices."[41] This, as Javits and Klein argue, allows the president to require that any proposed policy action or subsidiary law be submitted to the president before prior review.[42] In fact, before the court invalidated the legislative veto in *Chadha*, the executive branch required that all proposed final rules be submitted to the OMB for review and approval before they were transmitted to Congress for its approval or disapproval.[43] Since that time, executive control over bureaucratic rulemaking has increased.[44] Hence, it is unlikely that presidents or their subordinates will allow rules to be submitted to Congress to approve or disapprove, with which they disagree. While the president certainly cannot micromanage all aspects of the bureaucracy, the potential for control is certainly there. Moreover, the president can train his attention on issues that are particularly important for the administration.

While some have contended that legislative vetoes are problematic in the case of Independent Regulatory Commissions because such commissions are politically insulated from the president (and, consequently, the president does not have the same kind of control over the substance of rules and regulations proposed), this view is unpersuasive.[45] Insofar as such commissions engage in rulemaking—which is in all its essentials substantive lawmaking—then it makes sense that Congress would use legislative vetoes to ensure that regulations emanating from these independent agencies reflect congressional intent. To disallow legislative vetoes in this instance would allow independent agencies to issue rules and regulations without *any* political oversight, even to ensure that such regulations ultimately accord with congressional mandates in the first place.

In addition to this, legislative vetoes are not instances of substantive legislation because Congress is merely approving or disapproving—without amendment—specific rules or regulations issued by those wielding the legislative power delegated by Congress.[46] If, on the other hand, Congress were to add amendments to legislative vetoes that altered the substance of the proposal coming from the executive branch, then those amendments would amount to substantive legislation that would require bicameralism and presentment. This, however, is not how legislative vetoes were designed or how they were used by Congress in practice. Hence, congressional invalidation of a proposed administrative action merely maintains the status quo. If Congress vetoes a proposed regulation before it goes into effect, the executive branch goes back to the drawing board and submits another rule. Similarly, if only one house votes to approve without agreement from the other chamber, this just means that both chambers do not agree to the legislation in question, and so it does not go into effect. Finally, because legislative vetoes were not themselves acts of substantive legislation, bicameralism does not pose any major problems. In fact, the different veto mechanisms (one house versus two houses) provide the national government with flexibility to address political questions between the branches appropriately.

Table 2.2 shows the various types of veto provisions used by Congress

Table 2.2: Veto Provisions Classified by Form, Pre-*Chadha*

Type of Veto	*1932–1983*
Concurrent Resolution of Disapproval	64
Concurrent Resolution of Approval	36
Simple Resolution of Disapproval	103
Simple Resolution of Approval	0
Committee Disapproval by both houses	2
Committee Disapproval by either house	12
Committee Approval by both houses	102
Committee Approval by either house	64

Source: Rogelio Garcia and Clark Norton, "Congressional Veto Legislation in the 98th Congress," Congressional Research Service, 1984, 4–19.

prior to the legislative veto's invalidation in *Chadha*. Several things are worth noting. First, the vast majority of legislative vetoes that took place using chamber resolutions adhered to the general constitutional principle of bicameralism. Concurrent resolutions of disapproval are the only veto mechanism in which rules, regulations, or administrative actions go into effect even if one of the two chambers disapproves (provided that the other house *does* approve). Murray Dry, however, notes that such arrangements were often beneficial to interbranch politics, adapting the power relationship between the branches in ways reflective of the type of political dispute at issue.[47]

For example, the Budget and Impoundment Act of 1974 included two different types of vetoes for each of the ways that presidents might refuse to spend funds (deferrals versus rescissions). For deferrals (wherein the president merely postpones the spending of appropriated funds), the president had to issue a report to Congress explaining the reasons for the deferral. The funds had to be made available for their stated purpose, however, if either house passed an "impoundment resolution" disapproving the proposed deferral. For rescissions (wherein the president refuses to spend certain appropriated funds permanently), such appropriations had to be spent as Congress originally legislated unless Congress passed a concurrent resolution of approval. In short, the legislative veto mechanisms in this instance were set up such that the burden of proof rested with the president when he proposed permanent alterations to the budget passed by Congress, whereas the burden of proof rested with Congress when the president merely tried to use discretion for when such funds should be spent. Similarly, the Arms Export Control Act put the burden of proof on Congress to disallow the sale of arms to foreign countries by a concurrent resolution of disapproval within thirty days of receiving notice of the pending sale. While this violates the principle of bicameralism (because the sale could go through if the two chambers disagree), Congress determined that this particular issue area required greater deference to presidential judgment. Hence, Congress adapted the legislative veto with a great degree of flexibility and attentiveness to the particularities of specific issue areas, departing from the principle of bicameralism when the issue area necessitated more deference to executive branch judgment.[48]

This still raises the issue of committee vetoes, which were the most dramatic departure from the principle of bicameralism. Such vetoes, however, are merely reflective of the way Congress divides its workload. Generally speaking, committees have a great deal of influence over their area of jurisdiction relative to the rest of the chamber and, therefore, have a great deal of freedom to shape policy. Committees are generally representative of the chamber as a whole both in terms of the partisan breakdown of the chamber as well as reflective of different geographies, and so forth. It is difficult to imagine a committee operating at odds with the rest of the chamber for a significant period of time without some sort of backlash from the chamber. Reflecting the ways in which Congress operates, committees have a great deal of power in developing the legislation that makes it to the floor. Barbara Hinkson Craig, for example, who is particularly critical of legislative vetoes—and especially committee level vetoes—demonstrates that even when Congress merely inserts report and wait provisions into bills, committees have a great deal of leverage to effectively veto administration proposals.

In sum, the legislative veto statutes merely reverse the sequence of interbranch action by delegating legislative power to the executive branch while retaining the right to approve or disapprove specific proposals. The president and his subordinates in bureaucratic agencies are granted vast amounts of power and discretion to make law for the sake of efficiency and the need for expertise, power that they would not ordinarily have absent congressional delegation. Such delegation is greatly beneficial for harnessing the efficiency and expertise of the administration. Such delegation, however, is also deeply problematic from the perspective of democratic government. The legislative veto, therefore, is the mechanism by which the national government harnesses the benefits that come with delegation while ensuring that the most democratically accountable branch of government maintains its status as lawmaker by reserving the right to veto exercises of its delegated power. While the need for energy in government often requires delegation given the scope and complexity of national concerns and issues, the need for responsiveness to the public will in a constitutional democracy, on the other hand, requires that Congress take responsibility for the laws that bind its citizens. From this perspective then, the larger purposes of the separation of powers, far from being undermined by the legislative veto, are actually realized by it.

Chadha and the Legal Undermining of Constitutional Politics

The legislative veto was a working political arrangement agreed upon by the political branches for several decades. This arrangement greatly empowered the executive branch by delegating to its lawmaking power to secure the benefits of efficiency and expertise while ensuring that the laws that govern citizens were only made in accordance with the deliberative will of the people expressed through Congress. The legislative veto, therefore, merely reversed the order of interbranch action while retaining the *substantive* political involvement of the two branches. The Supreme Court, however, invalidated the legislative veto in *INS v. Chadha* for its failure to abide by the Constitution's requirements for legislation: bicameralism and presentment. Writing for the court, Chief Justice Warren Burger declared that while the legislative veto was clearly a useful and efficient tool for congressional oversight of the executive branch, "the fact that a given law or procedure is efficient, convenient, and useful in facilitating functions of government, standing alone, will not save it if it is contrary to the Constitution."[49] The court went on to assert that "convenience and efficiency are not the primary objectives—or the hallmarks—of democratic governance."[50]

Much can be said about the court's decision in *Chadha*, but the discussion here will focus on two particular concerns. First, the court's analysis stemmed from an overly legalistic conception of separation of powers wherein the powers of government—legislative, executive, and judicial—are defined by their essences and then assigned to the appropriate branch. Starting from this premise led the court to miss the actual facts on the ground, ignoring the reality of delegation and, consequently, giving the illusion that the legislative veto enabled an imperial and tyrannical Congress to usurp all the powers of government in contravention of basic separation of powers values. Far from vindicating separation of powers values, however, the court's formalistic approach perversely generated precisely what it purported to curtail: the concentration of legislative, executive, and judicial power in the executive branch.

The second issue concerns the sweeping nature of the court's decision in *Chadha* and the court's failure to distinguish between different classes of legislative vetoes. The type of legislative veto implicated in *Chadha* concerned whether a house of Congress could pass a resolution overturning the attorney general's decision that a resident alien should not be deported due to certain hardship issues. The legislative veto in question did not concern oversight of Congress's delegated powers, but, rather, dealt with a quasi-judicial hearing and, therefore, the protection of individual liberties from arbitrary governmental action. Hence, the court's sweeping decision invalidated over three hundred statutes and upset four decades worth of political negotiation between Congress and the executive branch when the actual issue of the case did not require that the court reach the merits on all applications of the legislative veto.

THE COURT'S LEGALISTIC PREMISES

The court characterized the legislative veto as a mechanism by which Congress stepped out of its legislative role to usurp executive functions in violation of the basic purposes of the separation of powers. The legislative veto, therefore, proved problematic because it empowered Congress vis-à-vis the executive branch, flying in the face of the framers' "profound conviction" that the powers of the legislative branch needed to be the "most carefully circumscribed" lest Congress dominate the constitutional system.[51] As the court argued, the presentment and bicameralism clauses need to be preserved because they serve "essential constitutional functions" by safeguarding the president from Congress and protecting "the whole people from improvident laws."[52] As Justice White noted in his dissent, there is nothing wrong with the court's "truismatic exposition of these clauses."[53] The presentment and bicameralism clauses are essential to the lawmaking function for all the reasons the court cited in *The Federalist*.

The question, then, is why the court viewed the legislative veto as *legislation* such that the constitutionally prescribed mechanisms for legislation—presentment and bicameralism—applied. This is an especially important question given that the legislative veto—far from being an instance of congressional encroachment on executive prerogatives—was, in reality, a response to the need for congressional delegation of legislative authority to the executive branch. The legislative veto was a mechanism by which Congress retained its constitutional role, albeit in an attenuated sense, as it greatly expanded presidential power through delegation, transforming the president and executive subordinates into the nation's primary lawmakers. Congress could merely approve or disapprove substantive legislative proposals from the executive branch without amendment, ensuring that Congress's exercise of the legislative veto did not itself entail substantive legislation.

The court's legalistic premises about the separation of powers, however, led it to mischaracterize the power dynamics between the branches, and, ultimately, to undermine the robust constitutional politics sustained by the legislative veto. Indeed, the court asserted that the "Constitution sought to divide the delegated powers of the new federal government into three defined categories, legislative, executive, and judicial, to assure, as nearly as possible, that each Branch of government would confine itself to its assigned responsibility."[54] While not "'hermetically' sealed off from one another," the court contended that when any branch acts, it is "presumptively exercising the power the Constitution has delegated to it."[55] In other words, when an executive official acts, that action is presumptively "executive," and when Congress acts, it acts in a presumptively legislative way. This, of course, is a problematic presumption given that in *Federalist* 37, Madison noted the difficulty of theoretically disentangling the different types of governmental power. Rather, the political science of the framers departed from the classical separation of powers' emphasis on powers, focusing instead on bringing to bear competing perspectives on politics by inducing conflict between differently structured institutions—hence, the mixing of different types of power, such as the president's veto power (which is legislative in nature), and the Senate's role in treaty making (a power traditionally assigned solely to the executive branch). These examples of shared powers, moreover, are more than mere exceptions to a general principle of separation. On the contrary, they point to the complete transformation of separation of powers from legal doctrine to political architecture.

Beyond this problematic presumption, the court concluded that the legislative veto must be characterized as an act of lawmaking for two additional reasons. First, the legislative veto was "essentially legislative in purpose and effect" because it altered the "legal rights" of citizens outside the legislative branch in ways that would not have occurred absent congressional use of the veto.[56] As Justice White observed in his dissent, however, this ignores the fact that when the executive branch wields legislative power delegated to it by Congress—such as in bureaucratic rulemaking—the exercise of this legislative power by executive officeholders alters the legal rights of citizens, and this action is accomplished without the constitutional safeguards of bicameralism and presentment. While the court acknowledged this conundrum in a footnote, it brushed it aside by claiming that executive officials act in presumptively executive ways: "Executive action under legislatively delegated authority that might resemble 'legislative' action in some respects is not subject to the approval of both Houses of Congress and the President for the reason that the Constitution does not so require."[57] In short, legislative power delegated to the executive branch becomes executive—that is, nonlegislative—based merely on the fact that such power is wielded by executive branch officials, and, therefore, is not subject to the Constitution's requirements for lawmaking.

Secondly, the court asserted that the legislative veto had to be considered an act of lawmaking because there are only four constitutional provisions that allow one house of Congress to act outside of the legislative process.[58] But the question is not whether the Constitution specifically authorizes legislative vetoes, but whether Congress can enact a statute delegating legislative power subject to a legislative veto. If the legislative veto is derivative of a statute, then it does not matter that the Constitution does not explicitly provide for it. Since the early days of the republic, the court has recognized that the necessary and proper clause implies powers not explicitly stated in the Constitution that enable Congress to effectuate its will.[59] In *Chadha*, the court explained that the necessary and proper clause does not give Congress the power to review exercises of its delegated power with a legislative veto because the legislative veto was not a "constitutionally permissible means" of implementing its power.[60] This, of course, begs the question, especially given that one of the reasons the court asserted that the legislative veto was impermissible—and, therefore, could not be authorized by a statute under the necessary and proper clause—was that the Constitution did not directly sanction this type of congressional action as one of the four ways in which Congress could act nonlegislatively.

What is particularly peculiar about this, as Justice White pointed out in his dissent, is that the court was inconsistent on the question of whether Congress has the power to enact veto statutes based on its authority under the necessary and proper clause. In fact, the court had long upheld actions similar to the legislative veto so long as those vetoes were exercised by nongovernmental entities. For example, in *Currin v. Wallace* (1939), the court upheld a statute that allowed certain restrictions on agriculture commodities to go into effect once a prescribed majority of affected farmers voted for it. Similarly, in *United States v. Rock Royal Cooperative* (1939), the court upheld a statute that gave producers of certain commodities the right to veto marketing orders issued by the secretary of agriculture.[61] Hence, Congress could delegate legislative power subject to a veto from a specified interest group, but it could not reserve to *itself* the power to approve or disapprove exercises of its delegated legislative power. This discrepancy is telling. Evidently, the court believed that the framers were so fearful of a powerful Congress that Congress cannot even modify its own powers in response to the modern fact of *executive-dominated government*.[62] According to the court's logic, Congress can only act in a strictly legislative way and cannot take any action to oversee its delegated lawmaking functions outside of enacting a new statute. This, even as other entities are not subject to the same constraints for the mere fact that those entities are not Congress.

The court's formalism gave the illusion that Congress was stepping outside its constitutionally prescribed role in an attempt to encroach on executive prerogatives when, in fact, the legislative veto was a tool that allowed Congress to empower the executive branch to make law—so that the government could adequately address the myriad complex issues on the national agenda—while ultimately ensuring that laws governing citizens still retained the consent of Congress, the most broad-based, publicly accountable, and deliberative branch of government. The court's failure to consider the legislative veto in light of delegation (in fact, the majority opinion does not mention delegation or the administrative state except in a passing footnote) kept it from recognizing that the legislative veto, far from undermining constitutional structure, incorporated basic separation of powers values into the practice of modern government.

Hence, the court's reasoning in *Chadha*, beyond its departure from the political science of *The Federalist*, also fails on its own formalistic terms. A strictly formalistic interpretation of separation of powers, as ostensibly advanced by the court, would mean that Congress cannot delegate legislative power. It would seem to follow from the court's legalistic premises that the Congress legislates, and that the executive branch administers the government. To be consistent, therefore, the court should have revived the notion that Congress cannot delegate legislative power to the executive branch. Indeed, as Justice White wrote, the majority's holding represented "a profoundly different conception of the Constitution than that held by the courts which sanctioned the modern administrative state."[63] Although some prominent commentators at the time worried that the court's *Chadha* decision signaled a major shift in the court's jurisprudence for just this reason, the court has only recently begun to make moves in this direction.[64]

The court's ruling in *Chadha*, therefore, ultimately and perversely undermined separation of powers values, notwithstanding Justice Burger's purported intentions to safeguard constitutional structure and to vindicate the Constitution's separation of powers. Categorizing delegated legislative power as executive solely because it is wielded by an executive branch official, and then narrowly defining the powers of Congress, actually frees the executive branch and bureaucratic agencies from separation of powers constraints such that they end up wielding legislative, executive, and judicial powers—the very definition of tyranny according to Madison.[65] In sum, Congress enacted legislative vetoes to adapt the Constitution's institutional framework to account for the problem of delegation. The court's inconsistent and futile attempt to confine different types of power in the appropriate branch, on the other hand, led to the consolidation of power in the administrative state, unmoored from the political controls of the larger separation of powers framework.

LEGISLATIVE VERSUS ADJUDICATORY LEGISLATIVE VETOES

Also deeply troubling about the court's decision in *Chadha* is that it invalidated an entire class of legislative veto statutes based on a particularly problematic, and easily differentiated, legislative veto. Consequently, the court irresponsibly issued a ruling far more sweeping than the case necessitated, disrupting a decades-long working relationship agreed to by both political branches. The particular veto at issue in *Chadha* concerned whether one house of Congress could pass a resolution overturning an order of the attorney general to suspend a deportation over a finding of hardship.

Jagdish Rai Chadha was an immigrant from Kenya who lived in the United States on a student visa. Chadha was scheduled for deportation but requested that the Immigration and Naturalization Service (INS) suspend his deportation because he met the statutory criteria for residence in the United States because of the hardship he would face if deported.[66] INS granted Chadha's request after a hearing, and, as required by law, reported to Congress the names of 339 other persons, along with Chadha's, who also had their deportations suspended for meeting the statutory criteria. Congress thus had the opportunity to exercise its veto to overturn any of the INS decisions it deemed improper. After reviewing the list, the House Committee on the Judiciary determined that six of those people, including Chadha, did not meet the statutory criteria, and it introduced a resolution to the House floor, stating that "the House of Representatives does not approve the granting of permanent residence in the United States to the aliens hereinafter named."[67] The House then passed the resolution without further explanation and without a recorded vote.[68]

The problem with this application of the legislative veto in the immigration context is that it was adjudicatory, dealing with and altering the legal rights of particular individuals, rather than serving as a mechanism by which Congress oversaw its delegated, and generally applicable, legislative power. As Justice Powell argued in his concurring opinion, "the House did not enact a general rule; rather it made its own determination that six specific persons did not comply with certain statutory criteria."[69] Hence, the House of Representatives (acting like an appellate court) took on functions generally reserved to the judiciary without providing any of the safeguards normally afforded to citizens in judicial contexts, such as the right to counsel and the right to a hearing before taking legal action. While noting the imperfect parallel, Justice Powell argued that the "effect on Chadha's personal rights would not have been different in principle had he been acquitted of a federal crime and thereafter found by one House of Congress to have been guilty."[70] Such trial by legislature, Justice Powell observed, is anathema to separation of powers values: "[The bill of attainder clause], and the separation of powers doctrine generally, reflect the Framers' concern that trial by a legislature lacks the safeguards necessary to prevent the abuse of power."[71] Congress's job is to enact legislation that is generally applicable while leaving the adjudication of the rights of citizens in individual cases to those branches more appropriately structured to do so in ways that protect the rights of citizens from the whims and vicissitudes of the current political majority.[72]

Given the adjudicatory nature of the legislative veto at issue in *Chadha*, then, it is clearly easily distinguished from legislative vetoes as such. As Lawrence Tribe argues, "If exercise of the legislative veto is objectionable because it amounts to a trial by legislature, that objection persists even if bicameral action and presentment to the President are assured."[73] In other words, Congress could not have overturned the decision of the INS and deported Chadha even by going through the full legislative process. The court's holding with regard to Chadha was the right decision given that the application of law to specific individuals should only occur within adjudicatory settings that provide proper legal safeguards, safeguards that a legislature does not provide. The court erred, however, in failing to distinguish this particular congressional action from traditional forms of the legislative veto. The vast majority of legislative vetoes did not pertain to the application of law to specific individuals in adjudicatory settings but, rather, were merely mechanisms by which Congress ensured that the generally applicable laws that govern citizens retain the consent of their representatives in Congress.

Given this distinction, it is striking that the court used *Chadha* as its vehicle to strike down all legislative vetoes, applying *Chadha* without comment in eight cases handed down the next month.[74] The court did this in two ways. First, it misdiagnosed the actual problem in *Chadha* by failing to notice that no congressional action would have been constitutionally legitimate given the adjudicatory nature of the issue. Secondly, it elided the difference between the adjudicatory nature of that congressional action and legislative vetoes enacted to oversee Congress's delegated legislative functions. The court thus invalidated all legislative vetoes without having to substantively defend the expansiveness of its ruling. The adjudicatory nature of congressional action in *Chadha* no doubt shaped the court's perceptions about the problem of Congress altering legal rights, which, in the case at hand, was deeply problematic. Such assumptions, however, do not easily translate, if at all, to the legislative context where rights are altered by executive officials wielding delegated legislative power (and, this, without the constitutional constraints of bicameralism and presentment). In *Chadha*, congressional action altered the legal rights of individuals in specific situations without the safeguards necessary for the protection of individual rights required in adjudicatory settings. In the legislative context, however, Congress used legislative vetoes to oversee the use of its delegated, and generally applicable, legislative powers. In this way, legislative vetoes employed in the legislative context protected individual rights by ensuring that laws made in the executive branch and in bureaucratic agencies were reflective of the public will. The court's unnuanced and simplistic reasoning led it to miss this crucial and fundamental difference.

It is deeply unfortunate that the court invalidated over three hundred laws (more laws struck down in one decision than in all other Supreme Court decisions combined!) without any consideration of how the differences between the specific issue in *Chadha* and legislative vetoes more generally might affect the constitutionality of legislative vetoes in differing contexts. At best, the court's decision in *Chadha* was breathtakingly sloppy. At worst, the court was looking for a pretext to invalidate all legislative vetoes and used the particular veto in *Chadha* as a smoke screen, collapsing the issues to more easily indict all legislative vetoes. If the latter case, the sloppiness of the court's reasoning disguised its indefensible activism. Either way, the court went well beyond its constitutional role, policing the boundaries of the political branches and disrupting a working relationship meant to instill separation of powers values to the practice of modern government.

Political Criticisms of the Legislative Veto

Even if the legislative veto was intended to be a positive invention that reconciles the inevitable need to delegate in the modern world with the larger political purposes of the separation of powers framework, this does not necessarily mean that the legislative veto performed this function well. This section, therefore, considers plausible objections to the legislative veto from within the political perspective of separation of powers articulated in this book. While the critiques assessed here are plausible, they ultimately do not prove that the legislative veto undermines constitutional politics in the ways contended. Even so, such critiques provide useful criteria for assessing congressional use of the legislative veto.

THE EFFECTIVENESS OF THE LEGISLATIVE VETO GIVEN THE SCALE OF DELEGATION

The first critique is that the legislative veto was largely inconsequential and prevented Congress from using better institutional tools at its disposal. The most prominent proponent of this view is Jessica Korn, who, in an award-winning book, contends that the legislative veto, rather than serving as a tool that fosters substantive interbranch politics, merely gave the illusion of congressional power and engagement.[75] Korn argues that the veto was a Progressive Era shortcut through the separation of powers that allowed Congress to look powerful without actually mobilizing its institutional tools and capacities to engage in robust interbranch politics.[76] In Korn's account, legislative vetoes were inconsequential in practice, especially compared to other forms of legislative oversight. She develops her argument by examining case studies of policy areas before and after *Chadha* to show how Congress actually performed its oversight functions better without the veto.

This critique certainly has merit in some issue contexts. Take, for example, the War Powers Resolution of 1973, an example that Korn does not use. At the height of discontent over presidential war powers during the Vietnam Era, Congress passed the War Powers Resolution in order to "fulfill the intent of the framers of the Constitution" and to restore the constitutional balance between the branches with regard to the exercise of war authority by requiring that the United States only commit troops in the case of a "declaration of war," "statutory authorization," or in the case of "a national emergency created by attack upon the United States, its territories or possessions, or its armed forces."[77] In the absence of a formal declaration of war or statutory authorization, the president was required to submit a formal report notifying Congress within forty-eight hours of committing troops abroad. This formal notification would open a sixty-day window, after which the president was required to remove troops from hostilities unless Congress formally declared war or passed statutory authorization (or if Congress had not given the president a thirty-day extension). Moreover, the resolution provided a legislative veto mechanism that stipulated that Congress could force the president to end hostilities by passing a concurrent resolution.

As Gordon Silverstein notes, however, the War Powers Resolution has been an abject failure, freeing the president from constitutional constraints.[78] Before the War Powers Resolution, the president's ability to constitutionally commit troops abroad in the absence of congressional approval was on shakier constitutional ground, which had a constraining effect on presidential action. By allowing the president to commit troops up to ninety days without prior congressional sanction, on the other hand, the War Powers Resolution "removed any claim that the president lacked constitutional authority to use force without prior congressional authorization."[79] Presidents have taken great advantage of this newfound clarity where there was once constitutional ambiguity. Once troops are committed, Congress has a difficult time ending the hostilities. Silverstein concludes, therefore, that Congress "undercut its own constitutional position without gaining anything in terms of practical control on the use of force."[80] In this regard, then, the War Powers Resolution (with its attached legislative veto) made Congress *appear* powerful vis-à-vis the executive branch when it comes to the exercise of war powers. But this appearance has not been reality, as the president's position has only been strengthened.

But just because the legislative veto might be inconsequential in some policy areas (such as war powers), this does not mean that the legislative veto is inconsequential across the board. In fact, although Korn contends that the legislative veto merely symbolized congressional power rather than impacting policy outcomes in any meaningful sense, her case studies do not bear this out. In fact, at times they demonstrate the importance of the veto. For example, Korn examines the congressional oversight of educational policy.[81] Congress inserted a legislative veto into the Education Amendments of 1972 (which established the Pell Grant financial aid program) as well as the General Education Provisions Act of 1974. The legislative veto proved inconsequential in the education context, however, because Congress used other kinds of oversight mechanisms. Indeed, even before *Chadha*, Congress often chose to legislate the annual-based formulas for Pell Grants when it disagreed with the proposals coming from the executive branch rather than to exercise its veto power.[82] This makes intuitive sense given the particular disagreement with the Reagan administration at the time. The Reagan administration wanted to dramatically cut Pell Grant spending, and no funds would be spent until a plan was finalized. Pell Grant dispersal would therefore be delayed greatly if Congress had to keep vetoing plans with which it disagreed if the administration would not come into agreement with Congress's own policy preferences on the matter. Hence, Congress chose to legislate its preferences rather than to continually veto administration plans. After *Chadha*, however, Congress rescinded its delegation to propose the needs analysis formulas for Pell Grants, because it viewed the legislative veto as an essential mechanism by which administration proposals reflected congressional preferences. Without the veto, Congress began to legislate the needs analysis formulas every year. Thus,

Korn concludes that the court's invalidation of the legislative veto forced Congress to do a better job by encouraging "members to enact their policy convictions about the Pell Grant program into law." The Supreme Court, therefore, "made it easier for members to fulfill that aspect of their representative function that requires them to make Congress explicitly responsible for broadly supported public policies."[83]

While Korn effectively shows that the legislative veto was not always a decisive tool in this particular policy context, her case study is ultimately not convincing when considered against the full backdrop of delegation and the vast number of federal regulations issued each year (3,853 final rules in 2016 alone). Indeed, even if Congress was able to micromanage the needs analysis formula for Pell Grants, it certainly could not similarly micromanage *every* policy area it deemed important unless it was to do substantially less. Of course, many vocal opponents of the legislative veto, such as Antonin Scalia before he joined the Supreme Court, advocated just this type of return to a limited role for the national government with more specific legislation and more traditional oversight through hearings and the appropriations process.[84]

However, other scholars have demonstrated that the legislative veto was a more effective tool of congressional oversight than traditional methods. After reviewing five agency programs during the 1970s, Harold Bruff and Ernest Gellhorn concluded that the legislative veto significantly altered "the working relationship" between Congress and bureaucratic agencies, making those agencies far more responsive to congressional views than they would be absent a legislative veto provision.[85] Traditional forms of legislative oversight, such as authorization renewal and appropriations hearings, provided ad hoc and sporadic opportunities for oversight, whereas the legislative veto ensured "regular and systematic examination of the substantive details of an agency's program."[86] The legislative veto, by contrast, gave congressional committees negotiating power with agencies that helped bring final rules and regulations into alignment with congressional preferences.

Finally, it is worth noting that Korn's definition of legislative veto is limited solely to formal expressions of that power. Korn, however, argues that report-and-wait provisions—wherein federal administrators are required to publish proposed final rules in the Federal Register for a specified period of time before such rules can go into effect—were highly effective at bringing the Department of Education to heel.[87] Such report-and-wait provisions, however, work almost exactly like formal legislative vetoes—as I address in greater depth in the final section of this chapter—and, indeed, are subject to the same kind of critiques as formal legislative vetoes even as they are untouchable by the legal argument against legislative vetoes, as articulated by the court in *Chadha*.[88] Such report-and-wait provisions, as Korn acknowledges, can be quite successful at ensuring that federal regulations reflect congressional intent because agencies and administrators are incentivized to keep good relations with their oversight committees, lest they lose funding or policy flexibility. Even so, they are generally not as effective as formal vetoes because Congress has no formal mechanism outside of enacting a statute—which would require congressional supermajorities to overcome a presidential veto—should the executive branch persist in issuing regulations with which Congress disagrees. Hence, Korn's praise of report-and-wait provisions hardly makes the case that legislative vetoes are an ineffective policy tool. Rather, it suggests the opposite.

THE LEGISLATIVE VETO AND THE POLITICS OF NEGOTIATION AND COMPROMISE

Korn's case study with regard to foreign policy is similarly illuminating even as it also fails to convince that the legislative veto was merely a tool that allowed Congress to symbolize congressional power while, in reality, abdicating its political prerogatives vis-à-vis the executive branch. Korn examines how Congress attached the legislative veto to the Jackson–Vanik amendment to the Trade Act of 1974, tying human rights to trade policy, specifically to the extension of Most Favored Nation (MFN) trade status. However, Congress only once attempted, and lost by a wide margin, to exercise the veto regarding the extension of MFN to Romania in 1979.[89] After *Chadha*, however, Congress had a great deal of success in confronting the executive branch over its extension of MFN by passing conditions bills (passed by both houses and signed by the president) that required that nations meet certain human rights benchmarks before the United States extended MFN. For example, Congress successfully passed a conditions bill in 1990 that tied the extension of MFN to China to certain human rights benchmarks after public outcry regarding the Tiananmen Square massacre.[90] Korn concludes that these conditions bills were better than the legislative veto because it was a way to prod foreign nations to make human rights advances to receive MFN rather than for Congress to deny them MFN by exercising its veto.

This analysis also overstates the case against the legislative veto, in that it assumes that legislative vetoes were only effective if and when they were deployed by Congress. However, legislative vetoes, rather than merely serving as an outward expression of congressional power, might actually serve as a tool that fosters interbranch cooperation and compromise that precludes publicly visible interbranch conflict.[91] For example, when it came to foreign arms sales, Congress used the threat of the veto to force negotiation and accommodation of its views. After US arms sales hit an all-time high in 1974, Congress included the Nelson-Bingham Amendment in the Foreign Aid Authorization for fiscal year 1975, requiring the president to give Congress advance notice of arms sales exceeding twenty-five million dollars (reduced in 1981 to seven million dollars) and subjecting the proposed arms sale to a concurrent resolution of disapproval. Congress was particularly concerned that arms sales to the Middle East (both to Israel and its hostile neighbors) were creating an arms race in the region, and there was significant public concern about the issue. Congress only once threatened a veto regarding arms sales (pertaining to Hawk missiles to Jordan), but intense negotiation in the face of a legislative veto threat forced the administration to back down from its proposed arms sale and to compromise in light of congressional concerns.[92] As Martha L. Gibson notes, after this incident the viable threat of the legislative veto forced negotiation between the executive branch and Congress long before arms sale agreements were finalized and reported to Congress, thus ensuring that such deals accommodated congressional concerns during their formation. This cooperative spirit was undermined, however, by the legislative veto's invalidation. Without the legislative veto, Congress was left to engage in repeated high-profile conflicts regarding arms sales, including the introduction of joint resolutions of disapproval. In some instances, the president was forced to rescind arms agreements in ways that embarrassed both the United States and the recipients of arms sales.[93]

Similarly, the legislative veto protected the institutional concerns of Congress with regard to MFN trade policy and attendant human rights concerns. Unlike arms sales, MFN, generally speaking, was not an issue of high public concern. Hence, Congress could use the legislative veto to ensure interbranch compromise and negotiation, but, unlike with arms sales, Congress lacked the electoral incentives to engage in high-profile conflict with the executive branch after it lost the legislative veto. Tiananmen Square, however, sparked widespread outrage in the American public and made MFN trade status a politically salient issue, providing Congress the opportunity to engage in more high-profile conflict with the executive branch by holding public hearings and passing conditions bills. The point here is the legislative veto ensured compromise and accommodation with the executive branch before *Chadha*, while the high-profile interbranch conflict Korn documents with regard to China and MFN was, in many ways, due to external factors that empowered Congress vis-à-vis the executive branch in this particular context. It does not necessarily follow that the legislative veto was wholly inconsequential to MFN trade status or that conditions bills were always the best solution.

In short, Korn's case studies overstate the case that the legislative veto was merely symbolic of congressional power. By disregarding the extent of delegation (by asserting that Congress could just legislate more specifically and micromanage policy as it did with education policy) as well as by ignoring how the legislative veto fostered different types of interbranch conflict (negotiation and compromise versus high-profile conflict) across issues that varied in terms of public salience, Korn fails to account for the ways in which the legislative veto aids healthy interbranch politics. Korn's case studies, in other words, do not speak to the full benefits or imperfections of the legislative veto. However, it is valid to worry about using the legislative veto as an excuse not to do the hard work of actual interbranch politics, as demonstrated by the war powers example discussed earlier. Indeed, such concerns could potentially counsel against the pre-*Chadha* push to have a generic veto applied to all agency regulations rather than to use the veto where Congress most wanted the leverage. In sum, Korn's worries are ultimately worth taking seriously because she operates within the political framework of separation of powers, attempting to evaluate how well Congress performs oversight of its delegated legislative powers. The concern about inserting legislative vetoes merely to appear powerful is certainly a line of inquiry worth pursuing—and could certainly be the case at times—even if the evidence presented by Korn is ultimately unpersuasive.

THE LEGISLATIVE VETO AND THE PROBLEM OF INTEREST GROUPS POLITICS

The second line of critique against the legislative veto primarily concerns its application to bureaucratic rulemaking. Critics of the veto charged that it undermined the separation of powers values applied to bureaucratic rulemaking by the Administrative Procedure Act (APA).[94] The APA is a good example of Congress attempting to ensure that its delegated powers are exercised according to separation of powers principles by requiring agency rulemaking to be made in accordance with legislative values. As David Rosenbloom argues, the legislative history of the APA of 1946 reveals that Congress views agencies as extensions of itself—a much closer relationship than a principal-agent relationship—when they engage in legislative functions delegated to them by Congress.[95] Hence, Congress went to great lengths to shape the ways that those agencies engaged in the legislative process by requiring those agencies to hold public hearings and open-comment proceedings in addition to taking congressional views into account in the formulation of final rules.

Critics of the legislative veto argue that the veto undermines these open and democratic processes by allowing powerful interest groups to lobby congressional committees behind the scenes and get those committees to use the threat of a legislative veto to move regulations closer to their preferences.[96] A few points can be made in response to these criticisms. First, the kind of interest group pressure that critics of the legislative veto point to exists even for mechanisms that they concede are perfectly constitutional. In fact, one of Barbara Hinkson Craig's examples of this type of interest group subversion of democratic politics concerned a joint resolution, a type of legislative veto that meets all of the Constitution's procedural requirements for lawmaking (bicameralism and presentment).[97] Hence, if interest group lobbying disqualifies the legislative veto, then it also calls into question perfectly constitutional methods of congressional oversight, including the regular legislative process.

Secondly, such critiques overemphasize the democratic quality of decision-making in bureaucratic agencies (even when they operate according to congressionally prescribed APA procedures) while overly denigrating congressional oversight, characterizing congressional procedures as dominated by special interests at odds with the public good. In fact, there is no reason to conclude that bureaucratic agencies, on the whole, do a better job of making rules in accordance with the deliberative public will.[98] For example, open-comment proceedings are often dominated by those most impacted by forthcoming regulations. Indeed, as William West and Joseph Cooper note, given the massive bureaucratic apparatus, it can be difficult for less financed interest groups—or, for that matter, ordinary citizens—to find out basic information about when and where such proceedings take place.[99] Moreover, given the fact that the rulemaking process can take years, well-financed interest groups are better positioned to utilize the administrative process to their advantage.

In a democratic society, there is no substitute for a generalized and electorally accountable legislature tasked with weighing and balancing competing interests across policy areas. This is a job that only Congress can perform. While agencies bring expertise and single-minded focus to bear on complex problems—the reason for delegating to such agencies in the first place—agencies can also exist in a policy vacuum with attendant biases that do not reflect the general concerns of the public. This does not mean Congress will always do this job well, or that there will never be occasions where special interests rule the day. But none of these arguments prove that the legislative veto's problems outweighed its benefits, even as it points to an area of concern.

In short, while critics of the legislative veto argued that it undermined rather than served fundamental separation of powers values, closer examination points to the opposite conclusion. Given the vast number of issues of national concern, delegation empowers the executive branch and the bureaucracy to engage in Congress's legislative functions, while the legislative veto ensures that the deliberative will of the people is still expressed through their representatives in Congress. Even if some evidence points to problems with the legislative veto in practice, such examples, on the whole, cannot form a principled basis for rejecting the legislative veto entirely, even as such concerns are important to note and point to ways to evaluate interbranch politics in practice.

The Persistence of Separation of Powers

The court's decision in *Chadha* effectively invalidated any legislative veto that did not meet the legislative requirements of bicameralism and presentment.[100] This had dramatic effects on Congress's ability to formally oversee its delegated powers. Since 1983 Congress has not enacted veto statutes that give it the power to overturn rules and regulations by concurrent or simple resolutions of approval or disapproval. Consequently, if Congress disagrees with a particular executive action, or a rule or regulation issued from an agency, it has to mobilize and go through the full legislative process to overturn by law the specific rule or action at issue. In this situation, the interbranch dynamics greatly favor the executive branch. Given that Congress is seeking to overturn exercises of its delegated legislative power wielded by executive officials, such congressional action is far more susceptible to a presidential veto. Hence, supermajorities in both chambers are often necessary for Congress to substantively engage the executive branch to oversee its delegated legislative powers.

The cumbersome nature of the full legislative process to correct bureaucratic regulations has been on full display since Congress passed the CRA in 1996 as an attempt to provide oversight after the invalidation of the legislative veto. The CRA required that all final rules be presented to Congress sixty days before going into effect, thus providing Congress time to review and then possibly overturn agency regulations by passing a joint resolution of disapproval (subject to the president's veto, meaning that supermajorities in both chambers are generally necessary to disapprove). Between its enactment in 1996 and 2016, however, only one regulation was overturned, and only 5 percent of regulations promulgated by the executive branch have ever resulted in resolutions introduced on a chamber floor.[101] In recent years, the CRA has been used more vigorously. This use, however, has been contained to what might be termed "midnight rulemaking." Congressional Republicans and Republican President Donald Trump were able to use the CRA to subsequently overturn a number of last-minute rules promulgated during the last months of the Obama administration.[102] The CRA, however, is largely ineffective when the political branches disagree.

Due to the apparent failure of the CRA to give teeth to Congress's oversight of the bureaucratic rules and regulations issued in its name, Congress tried (and failed) to pass a new mechanism that, while still following the Constitution's lawmaking procedures, would greatly favor Congress rather than the president. The REINS Act (Regulations from the Executive in Need of Scrutiny) would require that any major rule with a significant effect on the national economy would be subject to a joint resolution of approval.[103] This would have the effect of turning bureaucratic rulemaking into mere legislative proposals—and agencies into study commissions—since such legislative proposals would only go into effect if Congress subsequently went through the full legislative process to enact them into law. While the REINS Act received the support of many commentators who hoped to see Congress regain its constitutional role in the legislative process, the legislation never passed the Senate.[104] If it had passed, the blanket rule it established to subject all economically significant major rules to congressional approval would undoubtedly create logistical problems for Congress by forcing it to deal legislatively with every issue at a certain threshold of economic significance, thus undercutting one of the rationales for delegating in the first place.[105] One of the practical benefits of the legislative veto before *Chadha* was its relative adaptability, giving Congress the flexibility to employ it in issue areas that most concerned it and in ways appropriate to the political dynamics of specific issues. With the invalidation of the legislative veto, Congress's options are severely limited. The failure of the CRA and the potential logistical nightmare of approving all major rules and regulations through the REINS Act points to the difficulties with which Congress used the joint resolution mechanisms to oversee its delegated lawmaking powers.

The effects of the *Chadha* ruling, however, have not only been detrimental to effective congressional oversight powers. Stripped of the legislative veto, Congress has, at times, chosen to rescind or change the mechanisms by which it oversees its delegated powers, at times in ways that greatly disadvantage the executive branch. For example, after *Chadha* Congress still granted the president the power to reorganize the executive branch, but rather than subject the president's proposals to a simple resolution of disapproval (meaning that the plan went into effect after a certain period of time *unless* one house mobilized to veto the plan), Congress subjected the reorganization plan to a joint resolution of approval (meaning that the plan did not go into effect unless both houses of Congress legislated it into law within a specified period of time). This is a far more onerous process, and one that made it far more difficult for the president to get his plans approved. Given this, presidents stopped requesting reorganization authority soon after *Chadha*, and Congress has rarely taken on reorganization efforts itself. When it does act, it does so generally only as a response to major crises rather than with the kind of proactiveness that came with executive leadership.[106]

However, it can be easy to overstate the impacts of the *Chadha* decision on the practice of interbranch politics by looking at formal exercises of the legislative veto. While the concurrent and simple resolutions have all but disappeared from the congressional arsenal, Congress has continued to attach legislative veto provisions to bills. Most often such legislative vetoes are included in appropriations bills, requiring, in fairly standard language, that specified actions may not be executed without the "prior approval of the Committees on Appropriations of both Houses," or that the appropriations committees for both houses must be notified (generally fifteen days) in advance.[107] The White House has often objected to the presence of such vetoes—claiming that they violate the court's *Chadha* decision. As Louis Fisher has noted, however, it is one thing for the president to condemn such legislative veto provisions as unconstitutional, but "agencies have a different attitude. They have to live with their review committees, year after year, and have a much greater incentive to make accommodations and stick by them. . . . Agencies cannot risk. . . . collisions with the committees that authorize their programs and provide funds."[108] Similarly, Congress can insert report-and-wait provisions in bills that require that agencies keep Congress informed of new rules and regulations. While report-and-wait provisions do not contain formal mechanisms to veto specific executive action or rulemaking, they make it more likely that executive actions or agency regulations comport with congressional views. If executive officials diverge too far from congressional preferences, they imperil important relationships with their oversight committees.

Critics of report-and-wait provisions hoped to see them invalidated because they perform the same function as formal legislative vetoes invalidated by the court.[109] At first, the US Court of Claims did just this, striking down the report-and-wait provisions as a violation of separation of powers. While it found report-and-wait provisions to be "facially inoffensive," it was evident "from congressional and agency practice" that such provisions operated as "a *de facto* . . . congressional veto."[110] On appeal, however, the appeals court upheld the distinction between formal and informal vetoes, even though informal legislative vetoes work just like formal ones. The court noted that "committee chairmen and members naturally develop interest and expertise in the subjects entrusted to their continuing surveillance. Officials in the executive branch have to take these committees into account and keep them informed, respond to their inquiries, and if may be, flatter and please them when necessary." Even so, "there is nothing unconstitutional about this: indeed, our separation of powers makes such informal cooperation much more necessary than it would be in a pure system of parliamentary government."[111]

The difference between these informal legislative vetoes and the formal ones invalidated by *Chadha* is that the latter mechanism, according to the court, violates the Constitution's procedural requirements for lawmaking. In most other respects, however, they largely foster the same kind of interbranch politics that opponents of the legislative veto found so objectionable in the first place. Indeed, the logic of the *Chadha* decision is that Congress can only act legislatively. The court went to great lengths to explain why the framers were so concerned with the powers of Congress that its powers were the most circumscribed. Therefore, Congress could not act to even oversee its delegated legislative functions unless it went through the entire legislative process. After Congress legislates, the executive branch administers the government. This artificial, and static, notion of separation of powers imposed by the court in *Chadha* has ultimately proven undesirable and unworkable for both branches. The framers constructed a separation of powers system in which the branches would negotiate the limits of their respective powers in ordinary political disputes rather than according to static legal rules. The legislative veto is a prime example of interbranch politics wherein both branches negotiated the limits of their powers and came up with a working relationship that, while changing the order of interbranch action when it comes to lawmaking, maintained the substantive involvement of the branches. The court's formalistic focus missed these larger political dynamics that, far from being contrary to the Constitution, are, rather, the product of it. Given this, it is hardly surprising that such interbranch negotiation has continued despite the court's intervention. The court's notion of separation of powers articulated in *Chadha* can thus best be understood as layered on top of a working political order, disrupting the practice of healthy politics, but not entirely displacing it. The fact that interbranch politics has persisted in much the same way points to the vitality of the Constitution's political architecture, albeit significantly diminished, in spite of the negative, and very real, effects of bad judicial reasoning.

It is worth noting in conclusion that in recent years the court has begun to more aggressively police delegations of legislative power to bureaucratic departments and agencies. The court has made two major moves relevant to this chapter. First, as indicated earlier, the court has begun to require that Congress clearly state its intention to delegate statutory authority on questions a majority of the court deems major (the major questions doctrine).[112] Secondly, in *Loper Bright Enterprises v. Raimondo* (2024), the court overturned Chevron deference. According to the court's prior standard, articulated in *Chevron U.S.A., Inc. v. Natural Resources Defense Council, Inc.* (1984), the judiciary would defer to agency interpretations of ambiguous statutes it was tasked to enforce so long as the agency interpretations were reasonable. Writing for the court in *Loper*, Chief Justice Roberts argued that the 1946 APA's requirement that courts reviewing agency actions "shall decide all relevant questions of law" requires that courts reviewing agency actions "must exercise independent judgment in determining the meaning of statutory provisions."[113] In so doing, the court has set itself up as the primary interpreter of statutes, giving itself immense power to decide challenges across the administrative state and to substitute judicial judgment for that of expert administrators. The implications of the court's decision are not yet clear as of this writing. However, it is worth pointing out that the court's recent decisions giving it more power to assess delegations have often been justified by the court as a corrective measure to encourage Congress to do a better job of performing its own democratic function to legislate clearly. Such decisions, however, neglect the court's kneecapping of Congress in *Chadha*, effectively cutting Congress off from its delegated powers. Before *Chadha*, the legislative veto was a mechanism that gave it *direct* oversight over the rules and regulations coming out of the administrative state with the ability to approve or disapprove regulations. Given this larger historical context, the court's recent decisions are better understood as a long-term project of judicial aggrandizement at the expense of both political branches.[114] The court's formalism in *Chadha* laid the predicate for its contemporary policing of delegations. Such decisions, however, are no substitute for political contestation between Congress and the president, a dynamic process that the court dramatically undermined in *Chadha*.

3

Executive Agreements

The Constitution specifies only one mechanism for entering into international agreements. Article II, section 2, clause 2 provides that "[the President] shall have Power, by and with the Advice and Consent of the Senate, to make Treaties, provided two-thirds of the Senators present concur." Today, however, the vast majority of international agreements entered into by the United States are concluded as executive agreements, not treaties. The president enters most of these agreements without subsequent congressional ratification. While such agreements have been used in limited contexts since the founding, the economic challenges of the Great Depression and the national government's unprecedented actions to deal with them—including the transnational dimensions of those issues—resulted in a significant increase in the use of executive agreements.[1] In addition, the United States' move away from isolationism to embrace its role as a superpower in an increasingly globalized world following World War II meant that the foreign affairs agenda of the United States dramatically increased.[2] The volume of the United States' global interactions following the New Deal and World War II, therefore, meant that it would be literally impossible to conduct international agreements through the cumbersome treaty ratification process. As Louis Fisher has argued, executive agreements are an essential feature of modern government due to the "sheer increase in volume of the amount of business and contacts between the United States and other countries."[3] Today, treaties comprise approximately only 5 percent of international agreements entered into by the United States, while the United States enters into approximately three hundred to four hundred executive agreements per year.[4] There is widespread consensus, moreover, that such executive agreements are legally interchangeable with treaties.[5]

The purpose of this chapter is to consider the use of executive agreements from a political understanding of the Constitution's separation of powers.

Given the executive branch's institutional advantages in the foreign affairs arena, it is no surprise that the vast majority of international agreements entered into by the United States are *executive* agreements. These advantages are based on a principled commitment to effectiveness in foreign affairs, a commitment made all the more obvious by contrast with the ineffectiveness of executive power under the Articles of Confederation.[6] Attention to the structural dimensions of the separation of powers framework, moreover, reveals that the rise of executive agreements is not merely the result of "rational actors" updating their institutions to meet the needs of foreign affairs.[7] This characterization is true as far as it goes, but it suggests that modern constructs are the result of adaptation disconnected from principled constitutional commitments. The rise of executive agreements is not an example of "updating" the Constitution. Their use, within certain limits, is the working out of the Constitution's political logic.

But, of course, the use of executive agreements cannot be endlessly malleable if the Constitution is to maintain its basic character. Even when the branches depart from the literal strictures of the Constitution, the treaty clause points to political criteria that should guide the branches in their deliberations about when an agreement is acceptably an executive agreement versus one requiring a stronger form of congressional authorization. As I will argue, the choice of the Senate—and the reasons underlying that choice—points to a concern that the House of Representatives is constructed to be too reflective of momentary, and at times fleeting, changes in public opinion. The framers signaled the need for significant international agreements to have sufficient buy-in from Congress to ensure a stable foreign policy and to safeguard the credibility of the nation in the foreign arena. While executive agreements are used frequently, historical practice demonstrates that there is a salient distinction between the types of agreements conducted as treaties versus those concluded without Senate authorization.

This chapter begins with a discussion of the positive purposes of a vigorous executive branch in foreign affairs, and how executive agreements can be understood in light of this commitment to vigorous executive power in the foreign arena. Here, I detail the ways in which Congress can use its institutional capacities to oversee executive agreements. It is difficult to imagine the president breaking completely free from separation of powers constraints given Congress's political controls, such as its power over appropriations, should Congress exercise its powers effectively. The major problem with executive agreements in recent history is not executive pre-predominance per se, but a lack of effective oversight by Congress through its failure to ensure transparency.[8] While the transparency regime for the past several decades has proven inadequate, Congress recently enacted significant reforms in this area.[9]

The second part of this chapter considers the criteria that should guide the branches (especially Congress) as they negotiate when an agreement is appropriately an executive agreement versus one requiring more congressional input. There is a great deal of evidence to suggest that Congress has often guarded its prerogatives over treaty-making, demanding that important agreements be submitted to the Senate as treaties (regardless of the partisan dynamics between the institutions) and that presidents have complied with congressional demands even when doing so has ensured defeat for particular treaties.[10] While these interbranch negotiations often have exhibited a great deal of constitutional health, Congress has at times failed to show sufficient political ambition, deferring to legal arguments about executive power rather than asserting its political prerogatives. I consider the interbranch negotiations concerning the Iran Agreement, arguing that although President Obama had the legal authority to enter into the agreement, Congress was insufficiently motivated by its own political prerogatives to ensure that important changes to American foreign policy receive sufficient support in Congress to be durable commitments regardless of the president's legal authority to enter into such an agreement. The lack of congressional buy-in, moreover, left the agreement politically vulnerable to the whims of the next president.

Foreign Affairs and the Limits of Constitutionalism

A discussion of treaties and executive agreements in the context of the Constitution's political architecture is illuminating because international agreements pose particular, and complicated, problems for the practice of constitutional government. Alexander Hamilton acknowledged as much when he answered the objections of those who argued that the treaty-making power ought to be lodged either exclusively with Congress or with the president. Indeed, when Hamilton took up the treaty clause in *Federalist* 75, he argued that treaty-making, in its essence, "does not seem strictly to fall within the definition of either one of them." In the ordinary practice of constitutional government, the purpose of the legislative branch, Hamilton asserts, is to "prescribe rules for the regulation of the society," while the purpose of the executive branch is to employ the common strength, "either for this purpose or for the common defense." Treaties, however, strain the constitutional enterprise because they do not fit neatly into either category. Rather, Hamilton argues, "Its objects are CONTRACTS with foreign nations, which have the force of law, but derive it from the obligations of good faith. They are not rules prescribed by the sovereign to the subject, but agreements between sovereign and sovereign. The power in question seems therefore to form a distinct department, and to belong, properly, neither to the legislative nor to the executive."[11]

The framers recognized, following classical separation of powers theorists such as John Locke and the Baron de Montesquieu, that the foreign arena is a realm that poses unique problems for constitutional government because law cannot bind foreign nations in the same way that it can bind citizens within a regime.[12] In the context of a specific regime, people leave the state of nature, forming a social contract by which individuals collectively transfer the power to enforce the law and protect natural rights to the community as a whole, setting up a government to serve as an impartial judge and enforcer of their own natural rights against the claims of others. Government thus serves a kind of settlement function, and law brings order and stability where there was once chaos. Such stability, however, is impossible to maintain in the international arena where no such overarching and impartial government regulates the constituent parts of the international order. The international arena, in other words, always exists in a state of nature, and potentially a state of war. Locke makes this clear in his discussion of the federative power. While it is typical to think of separation of powers as the division between three types of power—legislative, executive, and judicial—the federative power, according to Locke, is the power to "respond to actions of foreigners" rather than to direct the actions of those who live within the regime.[13] This power, moreover, is far more difficult for governments to exercise than the mere enforcement of their laws because the "plans and interests of foreigners vary so greatly that they cannot be anticipated by a set of standing laws for each eventuality."[14] Hence, it is particularly important that the power over foreign affairs "be left in great part to the prudence of those who have it, trusting them to do their best for the advantage of the commonwealth."[15] It is this unique nature of foreign affairs that led Hamilton to assert that treaties form a unique department for constitutional government, stretching the very limits of constitutional government itself as it seeks to preserve itself in its dealings with foreign nations.

The question thus becomes, how did the framers design an institutional framework to achieve the aims of the constitutional order in foreign affairs, and what does the nature of that design tell us about what we ought to expect with regard to a phenomenon such as executive agreements? Returning to *Federalist* 75, Hamilton supplies an answer by noting that it is important to consider the *qualities* the two branches bring to bear on foreign affairs: "The qualities elsewhere detailed as indispensable in the management of foreign negotiations, point out the Executive as the most fit agent in those transactions; while the vast importance of the trust, and the operation of treaties as laws, plead strongly for the participation of the whole or a portion of the legislative body in the office of making them."[16] It must be stressed that Hamilton emphasizes the positive contributions of differently structured institutions for the practice of foreign affairs. The branches do not share power in treaty-making merely to check each other. Rather, they share power because the nation's effectiveness in foreign affairs, and the purposes of republican government, require the involvement of these differently structured institutions. It makes sense, therefore, to take each of the two institutions—and their role in foreign affairs—in turn.

Executive Power in Foreign Affairs

It is important to note at the outset the extent to which the Constitution makes provision for the effective use of executive power in the context of foreign affairs. The executive branch is structured to meet the needs of the nation, both domestically and in foreign affairs, through its independent and unitary structure. In other words, the executive branch is structured to summon the nation's strength in foreign affairs because its powers are derived directly from the Constitution and are not dependent upon the powers of the other branches to implement them.

This conception of executive power—power derived from the Constitution itself and not formally dependent, at least in a legal sense, upon the will of Congress—differs substantially, however, from constitutional orthodoxy today wherein the powers of the executive branch are seen to be legally dependent, at least to some degree, upon congressional approval or sanction. Justice Jackson supplied this general framework when he famously wrote in *Youngstown Sheet and Tube Co. v. Sawyer* (1952) that "presidential powers are not fixed but fluctuate depending upon their disjunction or conjunction with those of Congress."[17] Indeed, Jackson asserted that the president's power is at the maximum when he acts "pursuant to an express or implied authorization of Congress," that the president's power is at its "lowest ebb" when he acts contrary to congressional authority," and that, finally, there is a "zone of twilight" when it is impossible to determine whether Congress supports particular actions.[18] This tripart schema has provided a paradigm for legal assessment and enforcement of interbranch boundaries by the judiciary.[19] Moreover, this framework has often been used to assess whether executive agreements are legal.[20] This legalistic notion of the president's powers vis-à-vis Congress, however, makes the president subordinate to Congress. As Joseph Bessette argues, according to the court's notion of separation of powers when the powers between the two branches conflict, "Congress retains all its authority, while the president loses all overlapping powers to Congress."[21]

The framers, however, recognized that a vigorous executive branch—wholly independent from Congress for the exercise of its own powers—is essential to success in foreign affairs. Writing about the importance of executive power to the effectiveness of government more generally in *Federalist* 70, Hamilton argued that executive vigor is essential to the maintenance of constitutional government because it supplies energy to the constitutional order. Indeed, Hamilton asserted that "energy in the executive is a leading character in the definition of good government."[22] A feeble executive, on the other hand, "implies a feeble execution of the government. A feeble execution is but another phrase for a bad execution; and a government ill executed, whatever it may be in theory, must be, in practice, a bad government."[23] Hamilton goes on to list the "ingredients" of executive energy: "unity; duration; and adequate provision for its support; and competent powers."[24] Unity is particularly important for the present discussion, especially as it pertains to the government's effectiveness in foreign affairs. Unity can be undermined in one of two ways. First, it can be destroyed by vesting the executive power in more than one individual. Secondly, and crucially, unity can be destroyed by vesting the executive power "ostensibly" in one person, but subjecting that person "in whole or in part to the control and cooperation of others, in the capacity of counselors to him."[25] The quality of energy so essential for effective governance is thus secured and induced by designing an executive branch that is wholly independent of Congress—with powers derived from the Constitution itself—and headed by a single individual. In the ordinary practice of governance, deliberation on the merits of public policy is essential, but it is no less essential to have an institution designed to implement and enforce the laws with vigor and efficiency, and to act quickly and decisively when the laws do not speak to certain contingencies or, perhaps more importantly, when emergencies require particularly decisive action to preserve the regime from both internal and external threats.

Such qualities are particularly important in the arena of foreign affairs where deliberation, perhaps even more than in a domestic context, is more often a liability than an asset. Experience under the Articles of Confederation confirmed the necessity of executive vigor for the effective practice of government generally, but especially for effectiveness in the foreign arena.

Under the Articles, there was no independent executive branch.[26] Rather, Congress retained for itself the executive tasks associated with foreign affairs by either dealing with such tasks as an entire body or by delegating certain executive tasks to committees or boards responsible to the whole.[27] This often proved to be a disaster, as deliberation often hampered the government's ability to act as quickly and effectively as circumstances required. By the time of the Constitutional Convention, Charles Thach notes, the Continental Congress "was a thoroughly discredited body," because it was so unable to perform executive and administrative tasks efficiently and effectively.[28] Indeed, Thach continues,

> [Congress] exercised the great nonlegislative powers of appointment, of determining financial policy, and of control of foreign affairs as well. Its incapacity in all three lines of endeavor is too well known to require demonstration. Factional differences kept important offices unfilled for long periods. Time and again purely personal considerations proved the governing factor in determination of foreign policy. The laborious efforts to draft instructions for the negotiations of the treaty of peace with the accompanying intrigues of the French faction against the English faction served to prove Congress as incompetent in this capacity as in its strictly administrative character.[29]

Hence, the structural qualities of the executive branch are meant to make the government more effective in foreign affairs in ways that a legislature is unlikely to be able to achieve given its plural structure. Given these structural advantages in foreign affairs, the framers placed the power to make treaties with the executive branch. As Gary Schmitt notes, the framers did not give the power to make treaties to the president (or, for that matter, make the president commander in chief) until the executive branch had been structured to be a safe repository of those powers by securing its independence from Congress and by vesting the power in a single head. As Schmitt writes, "If institutional independence was a critical requirement for both the effective and safe use of such a power, then the framers were sound in their determination to withhold those powers until a proper repository could be built."[30]

The advantages of the executive branch in foreign affairs in general and in the formation of international agreements are fairly obvious. The formation of treaties, "of whatever nature," according to Jay in *Federalist* 64, requires the virtues of the executive branch because their negotiation almost always requires "perfect *secrecy* and immediate *dispatch*."[31] A legislature is often not able to provide this, which, as evidenced by practice under the

Articles of Confederation, hinders the ability of the national government to negotiate treaties effectively.[32] Foreign adversaries, motivated by either "mercenary or friendly motives," are doubtless more likely to rely on the secrecy of the president than they are to confide in the Senate, "and still less in that of a large popular assembly."[33] Moreover, the tides and fortunes are constantly shifting in foreign affairs, and the government needs the ability to respond quickly to events that are seldom predictable and often defy the most carefully laid-out plans. According to Jay in *The Federalist*:

> The loss of a battle, the death of a prince, the removal of a minister, or other circumstances intervening to change the present posture and aspect of affairs may turn the most favorable tide into a course opposite to our wishes. As in the field, so in the cabinet, there are moments to be seized as they pass, and they who preside in either should be left in a capacity to improve them.[34]

Lodging the power to negotiate and make treaties with foreign nations in the executive branch thus ensures that secrecy and dispatch appropriate to the needs and contingencies of quickly changing circumstances in foreign affairs are met. It is for these functional reasons—the ability to act with vigor, decisiveness, and secrecy as the circumstances require—that led classical separation of powers theorists Locke and Montesquieu to place the federative power (which included the power to make treaties and to conduct war) solely with the executive branch, citing the inability of a deliberative body to adequately meet the exigencies of foreign affairs. As Montesquieu wrote, discussing the importance of giving the executive full control over the military, "when once an army is established, it ought not to depend immediately on the legislature, but on the executive power; and this from the very nature of the thing, its business consisting more in action than in deliberation."[35] Rather than involving the legislature in a formal sense in the negotiation and ratification of treaties, the legislature was to be given other powers, such as power over appropriations, meant to influence, though not directly control, the actions of the executive branch. The legislature can limit executive discretion by exercising its own political prerogatives over appropriations and its determinations about the size of the army and even the types of weapons that the legislature will fund. As Josh Chafetz notes, Congress's power over the purse gives it substantial power to limit presidential discretion with regard to the exercise of its foreign affairs powers by, for example, choosing to eliminate funding for new aircraft carriers or long-range bombers, thus making it more difficult for the president to "project American power overseas."[36]

The essential point for Locke and Montesquieu—and for the framers who experienced firsthand the problems associated with government absent an appropriately designed executive branch—was that foreign affairs requires the vigor and efficiency that comes from a unitary and independent executive branch, and that provision must be made to ensure the effective use of executive power. As Gary Schmitt has argued, "By separating executive power from legislative power the Constitution frees the executive to meet the exigencies of foreign affairs, thereby increasing the overall capacity of the government."[37] The Constitution vests the executive power in the president, providing the president all powers necessary to act to preserve the nation in its dealings with foreign nations. Given that the needs and exigencies of the nation in the foreign sphere are, by their nature, illimitable, the executive is granted power to meet these needs. The executive's power expands as the needs of the nation in the foreign sphere expand given the executive's distinct institutional advantages in foreign affairs. As Madison argued in *Federalist* 41, to place legal limitations on the government's ability to meet the needs of foreign affairs would shackle the government, preventing it from attaining legitimate constitutional ends, including, potentially, the very survival of the constitutional order:

> The means of security can only be regulated by the means and the danger of attack. They will, in fact, be ever determined by these rules and by no others. It is in vain to oppose constitutional barriers to the impulse of self-preservation. It is worse than in vain; because it plants in the Constitution itself necessary usurpations of power, every precedent of which is a germ of unnecessary and multiplied repetitions.[38]

There is thus an inherent tension, as Madison noted in *Federalist* 37, between the aims of republican government and the ability for the government to preserve itself in its dealings with foreign nations. In *Federalist* 70, Hamilton did not assuage the concerns of those who feared a "vigorous Executive is inconsistent with the genius of republican government." Rather, he argued, the "enlightened well-wishers to this species of government must at least *hope* that the supposition is destitute of foundation" given that vigorous executive power is an essential ingredient to good government, and, indeed, a necessary ingredient for the very survival of the constitutional order itself.[39] Republican government can only be maintained with a vigorous executive branch with the capacity to act to meet the needs of the nation, and this capacity can only be ensured by a grant of power directly from the Constitution to the president rather than by shackling the executive branch to the legislature. This is not to say that the president's power over foreign affairs is illimitable and that any action the president takes to preserve the nation in foreign affairs is constitutionally legitimate. To return to Jackson's concurrence in *Youngstown*, there is an element of truth to the notion that the president's power fluctuates according to the views of Congress. Contrary to Jackson, however, this power is constrained not by legal limitations (presumably enforceable by the judiciary) but by the exercise of Congress's own political prerogatives should it disapprove of exercises of executive discretion.

In short, if separation of powers is ultimately a principled division of labor meant to promote the efficient and effective use of power, then the executive's predominance in foreign affairs should come as no surprise, and neither should *executive* agreements. The rise of and use of executive agreements do not, at least in principle, mean that the executive branch has exceeded separation of powers constraints because Congress has political capacities (often retrospective) that it can mobilize to oversee, and constrain, the use of executive agreements.

The Use and Control of Executive Agreements

As should be clear at this point, the rise of executive agreements is, in many respects, the outworking of a principled division of labor. The executive branch has gained predominance not as the result of historical accident or the rational updating of institutions but because an independent and unitary executive branch is structured to be preeminent in foreign affairs because the nation's vitality in the foreign sphere requires it. This section considers how executive agreements are used and how they are reconciled with the constitutional structure (i.e., how does Congress maintain oversight of executive agreements?). Executive agreements are not uniformly controversial. Rather, how controversial an executive agreement is ultimately depends on whether an executive agreement is entered into pursuant to a statutory grant of power by Congress or whether it is based solely on the president's Article II powers.

EX ANTE CONGRESSIONAL-EXECUTIVE AGREEMENTS

The vast majority of executive agreements are concluded based on delegated power from Congress in what are known as ex ante congressional-executive agreements. Given transparency issues—which will be discussed at length later on—it is impossible to know the precise number or percentage of executive agreements entered into based on delegated statutory authority, although most scholars estimate that such agreements constitute roughly

80 to 85 percent of all executive agreements.[40] Congress makes these delegations, as it often does in a domestic context, because it cannot respond quickly to rapidly changing situations on the ground. The reasons for congressional delegation to the executive branch in the foreign sphere, however, are magnified compared to the reasons domestically given the volatility of foreign affairs.

The precedent for future ex ante congressional-executive agreements based on delegated statutory power was set when—at the height of the New Deal—President Roosevelt requested power to act quickly in negotiating reciprocal trade agreements without returning to Congress for approval.[41] Faced with an unprecedented economic collapse and the need to deal with the global implications of the Great Depression, Roosevelt asked Congress to grant the executive branch the power to negotiate reciprocal trade agreements that could change tariffs up to 50 percent of what Congress had established by law. As Roosevelt argued to Congress:

> Other governments are to an ever increasing extent winning their share of international trade by negotiated, reciprocal trade agreements. If American agricultural and industrial interests are to retain their deserved place in this trade, the American government must be in a position to bargain for that place with other governments. . . .
>
> If the American government is not in a position to make fair offers for fair opportunities, its trade will be superseded. If it is not in a position at a given moment rapidly to alter the terms on which it is willing to deal with other countries, it cannot adequately protect its trade against discriminations and against bargains injurious to its interests. Furthermore, a promise to which prompt effect cannot be given is not an inducement which can pass current at par in commercial negotiations.
>
> For this reason, any smaller degree of authority in the hands of the Executive would be ineffective. The executive branches of virtually all other important trading countries already possess some such power.[42]

In response, Congress voted overwhelmingly to grant President Roosevelt the authority he requested. In doing so, Congress acknowledged the president's concern that the United States would not be able to achieve its international objectives if the Senate were to convene to approve every such agreement. When Congress reauthorized the delegation to enter into executive agreements in 1937, the Senate Report asserted that "trade agreements should not be subjected to the cumbrous treaty-making procedure."[43] The House of Representatives' report further underscored the need for executive vigor if the United States was to accomplish its trade objectives, acknowledging that congressional procedures were not adequate to the needs of the moment: "The Senate and the House of Representatives are in session for only part of the year and in recent years the demands upon their time when in session have been enormous. Were either senatorial or congressional ratification to be required, the inevitable delay and the further uncertainty as to ratification would go far toward destroying the incentive of foreign governments to enter into any trade negotiations at all."[44] Congress and the president, therefore, negotiated their boundaries with respect to international trade, determining, through their deliberations, that the institutional advantages of the executive branch needed to be harnessed to ensure effectiveness in international commerce, especially at a moment of great crisis. Such discretion in this case, moreover, was not unlimited as Congress's delegations were limited and periodically renegotiated. In this way, Congress delegated power to the executive branch to perform an essential function that could not conceivably be accomplished through the treaty ratification process, but it also ensured that this executive discretion would be evaluated and subject to congressional oversight.

Ex ante congressional-executive agreements expanded dramatically over the course of the twentieth century, driven in large part by an expansive foreign aid program (foreign aid agreements constitute a significant percentage of ex ante congressional-executive agreements).[45] Executive agreements based on delegated statutory power are, at least in theory, hardly controversial insofar as Congress has the political tools necessary to influence executive discretion. Some scholars, however, worry that the president has too much power in foreign affairs given the widespread and, at times, overly broad delegations to the executive branch. As Oona Hathaway contends, such delegations essentially grant the executive branch unfettered discretion in foreign affairs, satisfying the form of interbranch cooperation without the substance.[46] Some delegations, often authorized decades ago, are so broad so as to provide very little meaningful guidance to the executive branch (though other provisions, discussed later, can restrict the scope of these delegations). For example, the Foreign Assistance Act of 1973 states that the president is "authorized to furnish . . . assistance, on such terms and conditions as he may determine."[47] Similarly, the Mutual Education and Cultural Exchange Act of 1961 granted the executive broad power to conclude "agreements with foreign governments and international organizations, in furtherance of the purposes of this Act."[48] These two examples are typical of the broad and vague delegations that serve as the basis for most executive agreements today.[49] Of course, the broadness of such delegations is arguably appropriate given that such delegations are meant to be flexible enough to enable the president to respond to events on the ground rather than to tie the president's hands through overly specific legislation (the reason for delegating in the first place). Moreover, open-ended delegations are at times essential for long-term planning and investment. For example, prior to the Foreign Assistance Act of 1961, Congress included sunset provisions in its foreign assistance legislation, and, therefore, had to reauthorize foreign aid every few years.[50] In requesting that Congress overhaul the foreign assistance program, President Kennedy argued that "uneven and undependable" short-term delegations undermined efficient long-term planning.[51] Congress thus overhauled the program with longer-term grants of power.

At the end of the day, Congress has substantial power to influence executive discretion through its control over appropriations. It is, of course, difficult for Congress to defund an executive agreement with which it disapproves in order to undercut the agreement. Moreover, to do so could undercut the United States' credibility in foreign affairs because the withholding of funds to implement a particular agreement could mean that the United States is noncompliant with its international obligations.[52] Even so, Congress can scrutinize executive use of delegated authority and alter its funding priorities—or perhaps end the delegation altogether—should the executive branch exercise its authority in ways that defy congressional priorities. This gives Congress substantial power to both harness the benefits of executive energy and discretion in foreign affairs while influencing (though not directly controlling) how that discretion is used in the long-term, and Congress has, at times, been fairly adept at using the appropriations process to constrain executive discretion with regard to executive agreements.

For example, Congress has often, to great effect, attached appropriation riders to its delegations for foreign aid. As Josh Chafetz notes, since 1986, Congress has attached appropriations riders prohibiting the payment of direct assistance to nations' whose elected head of state was deposed in a military coup.[53] A 2014 study, moreover, demonstrates that administrations have generally complied, albeit begrudgingly, with this congressional demand.[54] The existence of the appropriations rider, Chafetz contends, has created problems for administrations who do not want to comply. For example, when the Obama administration wanted to avoid cutting off aid to Egypt after the 2013 Egyptian coup, the administration simply refused to characterize the coup as such. Extensive, and negative, media coverage of the issue, however, eventually forced the administration to comply with congressional demands.[55] In addition to this, Congress (through the so-called Leahy amendment) has used appropriations riders barring foreign aid from groups known to commit human rights violations, generating substantial conflict between the executive branch and Congress.[56] In 2011, 1,766 individuals and units from 46 countries were denied assistance on human rights grounds.[57] Beyond appropriations riders, Congress can also alter its funding priorities, providing more strict guidance for the executive branch. Lisa L. Martin, for example, demonstrates how in the 1980s Congress substantially altered the Food Aid Program in response to disagreements with the executive branch. Broad delegations, Martin argues, signaled general interbranch agreement on the issue. When the executive branch used that discretion in ways that diverged from congressional expectations, Congress responded by narrowing the delegations.[58]

In short, Congress wields substantial powers to oversee the use of executive agreements—especially those executive agreements entered into based on its delegated power—should it choose to use its political capacities in response to the need to delegate. As Gary Schmitt observed in a study of military agreements from 1946 to 1973, presidential reporting requirements and annual appropriation hearings in each house indicated substantial congressional control of agreements entered into based on statutory delegation. Schmitt concluded that it was perhaps a "misnomer to refer to these accords as *executive* agreements" given the extent to which such agreements ultimately relied upon Congress for their substance.[59] The point here is that this type of executive agreements are not, in principle, problematic because Congress has all the tools necessary to ensure that the substance of executive agreements reflects its own political priorities and to contest presidential use of its delegated power when the president acts in ways that are inconsistent with those priorities. There are, however, reasons to believe that Congress has not sufficiently used these political capacities.

It should be mentioned that Congress's ability to oversee its delegated powers in foreign affairs has been substantially curtailed by the court's invalidation of the legislative veto. Given that the legislative veto is the subject of the previous chapter, there is no reason to dwell on this issue at length here. However, the rise of executive agreements and the legislative veto occurred in tandem (one of the original applications of the legislative veto, in fact, was in the Lend-Lease Act of 1941), with the legislative veto often serving as the price for broad and wide-ranging delegated powers in foreign affairs. While the legislative veto was never successfully used in the foreign sphere, the viable threat of the veto ensured that the executive branch consulted with Congress during the negotiation and formation of international agreements. For example, arms sales under the Arms Export Control Act of 1974 were subject to a legislative veto. Congress only once threatened to use the veto (regarding the sale of Hawk missiles to Jordan). The administration, under intense pressure from Congress, backed down from that particular agreement. The viable threat of the veto in that incident, however, resulted in much closer consultation with Congress long before such agreements were finalized.[60] Legislative veto provisions thus ensured that congressional delegations in the foreign affairs context—delegations that, to be successful, were often long-term and broad grants of power to enable sufficient flexibility and long-term planning—did not result in congressional abdication, providing Congress opportunities to assert its political perspective in particular circumstances. As Hathaway argues, many of Congress's long-term delegations in foreign affairs were made precisely because the legislative veto provided Congress with a viable mechanism for continued political influence. The long-term delegations made (often without sunset provisions) are hard to repeal by statute because repeal would likely require veto-proof majorities. The invalidation of the legislative veto thus significantly undercut congressional control of its delegated powers in foreign affairs, and the United States' expanded role in the global arena makes it difficult to walk back such delegations.[61] A strict reading of the branches' powers vis-à-vis each other in terms of lawmaking (in the case of the invalidation of the legislative veto) has thus undermined the political capacities of the branches in an area (international agreement making) where a more expansive notion of constitutional purposes has taken hold.

SOLE EXECUTIVE AGREEMENTS

Agreements entered into based solely on the president's constitutional powers are the most controversial international agreements because they are neither mentioned by the Constitution nor authorized in advance by Congress. Such agreements, however, have been upheld by the Supreme Court and retain a legal status on par with treaties.[62] Scholars estimate that sole executive agreements constitute around 5 to 10 percent of executive agreements (though, again, this is simply an estimate given data limitations and transparency issues discussed below).[63] While sole executive agreements are potentially the most controversial because Congress is not formally involved in making them, such agreements fit within the general constitutional framework specified in the previous section. A fundamental reason for constructing a vigorous executive branch with powers derived directly from the Constitution—and thus independent of Congress—was to ensure that the constitutional order would be able to meet the needs of the nation in foreign affairs. Hence, the president, at times, enters into sole executive agreements related to national security and defense. Sole executive agreements in this area deal with issues such as intelligence sharing, cross-servicing agreements, joint military missions, and training exercises, and, as such, fall squarely within the president's powers as commander in chief. All status of forces agreements (SOFAs), which deal with issues pertaining to the legal rights of US personnel stationed abroad, are entered into as sole executive agreements (with the sole exception of the treaty that established NATO, which is perhaps not a surprise given the significance of the commitment). Such agreements, while at times merely routine, can be highly consequential, such as the SOFA and the "Strategic Framework" for friendship and cooperation that President George W. Bush concluded with Iraq at the very end of his presidency, entering into force on January 1, 2009.[64] The agreement was particularly controversial because it was concluded after the 2008 election but before President Obama entered into office. The executive agreements included a withdrawal timeline that would significantly affect US and Iraqi relations related to the war effort well into the Obama administration.[65] The substantive nature of the two sole executive agreements concluded with Iraq at the end of the Bush administration led some members of Congress (for example, Senator Obama on the campaign trail) and some legal scholars to demand that the agreements be submitted to the Senate for ratification as a treaty.[66] The agreements were implemented without any congressional authorization.

While they are at times highly significant and controversial, it can be easy to overstate the problems associated with sole executive agreements. Like agreements based on delegated statutory power, sole executive agreements are unlikely to evade separation of powers constraints entirely should Congress exercise its own political prerogatives over foreign affairs. Military and basing agreements, for example, might be concluded as sole executive agreements, but at the end of the day, Congress controls the purse strings and can choose to fund or not to fund bases overseas. By keeping itself apprised of executive action, Congress can place itself in a position to contest presidential use of sole executive agreements. Indeed, all exercises of presidential power related to foreign affairs are ultimately subject to Congress's independent constitutional powers should Congress use its political capacities effectively. As Josh Chafetz notes, Congress's power over the purse gives it substantial power even to end wars when troops are already committed on the ground, a feat that Congress accomplished when it passed the Case-Church Amendment in 1973, effectively cutting off all funding, direct and indirect, to the war effort in Vietnam.[67] Sole executive agreements are but a subset of this larger constitutional picture and, as such, they are constrained by the larger separation of powers system.

TRANSPARENCY PROBLEMS: A FAILURE OF CONGRESSIONAL OVERSIGHT

The argument thus far has been fairly straightforward: Executive agreements do not, in principle, pose major constitutional concerns in light of the principled division of labor embodied by the Constitution's political architecture. Moreover, Congress has political capacities that enable it to exercise substantial control of executive agreements regardless of whether those agreements are entered into based on delegated power or solely on the president's own constitutional powers. Exercising those political prerogatives effectively, however, requires that Congress have accurate and up-to-date information about executive agreements. While it is certainly true that the president is the dominant actor in the negotiation and conclusion of the vast majority of international agreements (without subsequent approval by Congress), Congress has a great deal of power to influence the direction of American foreign policy through the exercise of its political prerogatives vis-à-vis the executive branch. Congress can alter statutory delegations, influence executive discretion through the appropriations process, and even use other political tools up to and including impeachment should the executive branch persist in actions that violate the deliberative will of Congress. Acquiring the relevant information regarding executive exercises of authority, however, is a necessary prerequisite to using these political capacities when the branches disagree. Indeed, it is impossible to have an argument about political differences between the branches if Congress does not know how the executive branch is using its power.

Transparency was the goal of the Case-Zablocki Act of 1972 (also known as the Case Act), which required that the secretary of state report all international agreements entered into by the United States through mechanisms other than treaties to Congress within sixty days after agreements entered into force.[68] Congress was rightly concerned that the massive uptick in executive agreements had left it in the dark on major international commitments. Of particular concern were secret agreements that committed the United States to serious international obligations without congressional knowledge or approval. Perhaps the most notable, and controversial, of such agreements was a secret annex to a basing agreement with Spain. In the context of the basing agreement, the United States and Spain noted their mutual security interests and pledged to work within their constitutional processes to take action to preserve their common security interests.[69] While basing agreements were generally concluded as executive agreements—and considered within the purview of the president's power as commander in chief—this agreement clearly committed the United States to a more substantive pact. Given this agreement, and others like it, Congress was concerned that the executive branch was essentially acting unfettered in the foreign arena. As the Senate Committee Report for the Case Act stated:

> As the committee has discovered, there have been numerous agreements contracted with foreign governments in recent years, particularly agreements of a military nature, which remain wholly unknown to Congress and the people. A number of agreements have been uncovered by the Symington subcommittee . . . including, for example, an agreement with Ethiopia in 1960, agreements with Laos in 1963, with Thailand in 1964 and again in 1967, with Korea in 1966 and certain secret annexes to the Spanish bases agreement.[70]

Given that such agreements could constitute significant commitments on the part of the United States, Congress asserted its need to know what those commitments could entail: "These agreements, which can in an instant commit or involve this country in possible hostilities, must be formally and systematically examined by the Congress before they are triggered by events."[71] Even so, Congress acknowledged that the executive branch had good reasons, at times, for keeping certain agreements secret, especially from the public, and, therefore, created mechanisms for specialized committees to review sensitive agreements rather than the whole of Congress. Under the provisions of the Case Act, the Senate Foreign Relations Committee and the House Foreign Affairs Committee receive the agreements and can then follow up with questions or criticisms, or hold closed-door hearings.[72] The need for secrecy, however important, could not be a pretext for keeping Congress completely in the dark about US commitments. As Senator Case (for whom the Act is named) argued:

> The most important purpose of this legislation is to make the American people aware of what our international relationships are on a continuing basis, for two reasons. First, so that the public, where those arrangements are sound and the direction of policy is wise, can support it. . . . Second, so that the administration from time to time is checked in its efforts to do things that are unwise by the force of public opinion on a continuing basis.[73]

Unfortunately, the accountability regime embodied by the Case Act has hardly lived up to its aspirations.[74] First, there are major problems regarding executive branch compliance with the terms of the Case Act. While agreements are supposed to be reported to Congress within sixty days after they enter into force, reporting is "often late and perpetually incomplete."[75] For example, in 2004 the House Committee on International Relations learned that more than six hundred classified and unclassified agreements dating back to 1997 had not been reported to Congress due to organizational failures at the State Department.[76] Many of the reporting failures are due to a lack of centralized planning resulting from, at least in part, the fact that the Federal Register Act has excluded the reporting for international agreements since its inception in 1934. Perhaps even more problematic is the fact that the State Department is not itself always aware of all the agreements concluded by other departments and agencies (especially since the reporting to the State Department is often late), and a great deal of confusion at times exists within the executive branch about the nature of American commitments. For example, in 1999 the General Accounting Office reported that "[t]he number of trade agreements to which the United States is currently a party is uncertain" and that "key agencies were unable to provide a definitive count of all U.S. trade agreements that are currently in force."[77] Moreover, a report from the International Security Advisory Board maintained as recently as 2015 that because there is no "comprehensive and readily accessible archival database of all existing agreements . . . there is a surprising degree of uncertainty about what status agreements are in force and their terms."[78] The report further asserted that "in some cases, different parts of the U.S. government disagree about whether agreements exist with a particular nation, whether agreements are still in force, and what their terms are."[79] While Congress amended the Case Act in 2004 to bring about greater executive branch compliance, major compliance issues persist, as Curtis Bradley and Jack Goldsmith recently noted, "and the result in practice is that Congress lacks a full picture of U.S. agreements, and the public (including those in the public who have the incentive and ability to monitor the government) has highly selective access to these agreements and little ability to perceive the overall agreement practices of the executive branch."[80]

Beyond the issues with executive branch reporting under the Case Act, Congress has not acted to ensure that information about executive agreements is made available to the public in easily accessible ways. Pursuant to the Case Act, a list of all nonclassified international agreements are supposed to be posted to the State Department website no later than 180 days after entering into force (although, as mentioned earlier, the reporting of these agreements is never up to date or complete).[81] Even when agreements are posted online, the State Department only posts the *texts* of agreements and does not cite the legal authority by which agreements were made. While the State Department, through its Circular 175 procedure, makes a determination about the legal basis for agreements when deciding whether an agreement is authorized by statute or needs to be concluded as a treaty (or with some form of congressional ratification), these determinations are never released to the public even though they are rarely classified.[82] Different types of executive agreements (ex ante congressional-executive agreements and sole executive agreements) are thus posted without distinction. Hence, it is nearly impossible for researchers—and, for that matter, average citizens—to determine whether the executive branch has exceeded its legal authority in the conclusion of executive agreements, or even whether executive agreements have any legal basis at all.[83]

It should be noted that this lack of governmental transparency has not always been the norm. For example, when Gary Schmitt conducted his research into executive agreements in the early 1980s, he relied upon a government source that listed all executive agreements with their legal citations through the 1960s (excluding classified agreements).[84] Determining the legal basis for executive agreements today (if one can find agreements in the first place), however, requires considerable guesswork. While scholars estimate, for example, that executive agreements based on statutory delegations comprise 80 to 85 percent of executive agreements, this estimate involves connecting executive agreements to statutes by conducting keyword searches in the Statutes at Large.[85] Obviously, this is a fraught and painstaking process. In one of the more recent comprehensive studies of executive agreements, Oona Hathaway and her research assistants searched the Statutes at Large database and connected executive agreements to statutes in nearly every issue area conceivable.[86] For example, by searching the Statutes at Large for "agriculture" or "agricultural commodities" in the same sentence as "agreements" Hathaway was able to find 167 agreements, most of which were pursuant to the Agricultural Trade and Development and Assistance Act of 1954.[87] Much of the work here, however, is speculative and is prone to error.

Moreover, the Case Act only requires the executive branch to report *legally binding* international commitments.[88] The United States, however, increasingly enters into "political" agreements, whereby both nations disclaim any intention to form a legally binding instrument, even as they commit to do certain things.[89] Such agreements are neither reported to Congress nor publicized, though such agreements can have significant consequences for the public. As Bradley and Goldsmith maintain, such political commitments have been used especially prominently in regulatory contexts in order to facilitate greater cooperation between US bureaucratic agencies and their foreign counterparts, and these agreements, although not legally binding, "can have an enormous impact on the everyday activities of U.S. firms and persons."[90] Moreover, such agreements are being used increasingly for important international commitments. Indeed, two of the most prominent international commitments concluded during the Obama administration—the nuclear deal with Iran and the Paris Climate agreement—were "political" agreements and thus did not impose legally binding commitments under international law. These types of "political" commitments, as Harold Koh argues, are increasingly becoming the norm in international lawmaking as international affairs becomes less about drafting static texts and more of "a process of building relationships to foster normative principles in new issue areas."[91] As such "political" agreements proliferate and have significant impacts on US foreign policy and the regulatory regimes that impact the daily lives of Americans, Congress has not acted to ensure that such commitments are publicly recorded and made known in any systematic way.

This transparency regime for executive agreements (to the extent that it exists) contrasts significantly with the administrative state, where both proposed and final rules and regulations—pursuant to the Administrative Procedure Act (APA) of 1946—are cataloged and listed in the *Federal Register*, allowing time for agencies to hold open proceedings where members of the public can comment on proposed rules and regulations prior to the finalization of rules. As David Rosenbloom argues, Congress, when debating the APA, recognized that bureaucratic departments and agencies operate as mere extensions of Congress when they issue rules and regulations based on delegated legislative power.[92] To address the constitutional and accountability problems associated with delegation of legislative power to the executive branch, Congress developed mechanisms meant to bring legislative values to the rulemaking process by requiring that information about rules and regulations—including their legal basis and general applicability—is public.[93] By requiring the publication of this information, Congress provides opportunities to take public views into account in the formation of rules and regulations. The Federal Register Act similarly requires that various executive actions, such as presidential proclamations and executive orders be published in the *Federal Register*. Perhaps most importantly, this record enables citizen and media watchdog groups to raise awareness when the executive branch acts in ways that are potentially problematic, giving Congress the opportunity to respond to executive actions with which it disagrees. Indeed, given the volume of administrative action today, it is impossible for Congress to oversee every executive or administrative action. Neither would such micromanagement necessarily lead to better oversight given that this would require Congress to spend a great deal of time addressing potential executive noncompliance that is not publicly salient, and, moreover, given the scale of the national agenda, would likely miss many instances of executive discretion with which it disagrees. By providing a record of executive branch action, on the other hand, Congress can engage in what Matthew D. McCubbins and Thomas Schwartz refer to as "fire-alarm" oversight.[94] An informational record available to the public, in short, enables concerned citizens and watchdog groups to bring potential abuses of executive discretion to the attention of Congress, giving it opportunities to respond.

International agreements have been excluded from publication in the *Federal Register* since publishing began in 1934. This is perhaps not surprising given that such agreements were used sparingly at the time. While Congress has enacted informational reforms with the Case Act since that time, these reforms have never been in any way comparable to the vast informational resources created by the APA and the Federal Register Act in the domestic sphere. The *Federal Register*, published daily, is voluminous. In 2016, it included 3,853 final rules constituting 38,652 pages.[95] This, of course, does not include the lists of proposed rules. By contrast, the United States enters approximately three hundred to four hundred international agreements per year, and yet the information regarding these commitments is difficult to find (given major reporting problems), and, when reported, is reported without relevant information (such as the legal authorization).

Events during the Obama administration highlighted why the current transparency regime for international agreements is inadequate. The Obama administration frequently employed a legal theory justifying executive agreements that were not directly authorized by a specific statute, but, nevertheless, the administration argued were consistent with the tapestry of existing law and, moreover, could be implemented, according to the administration, without subsequent legislation.[96] Some legal scholars have characterized such executive agreements as "executive agreements plus."[97] Perhaps most controversially, the Obama administration announced that it intended to ratify the Anti-Counterfeiting Trade Agreement (ACTA) without seeking ratification by Congress. The administration, however, only provided vague explanations for why it had the authority to enter the ACTA as a sole executive agreement.[98] While the administration argued that the agreement would not require any changes to existing law, many members of Congress and large swaths of the legal community objected to the administration's decision to ratify the ACTA without congressional approval, arguing that the administration did not have legal authority to conclude the agreement without Congress.[99] The administration ultimately argued that it had the authority to conclude the agreement based on the Trade Act of 1974, although this law did not delegate to the administration the power to conclude agreements without congressional approval.[100] While the administration never renounced its legal position, it never ratified the agreement in the face of political pressures.[101] This example highlights the extent to which the executive branch has, at times, seemed to stretch the limits of its authority in defense of the legal basis for certain agreements. The ACTA was a particularly controversial agreement and, as such, attracted the attention of Congress and the legal community. It is certainly possible that there are other examples of agreements made with tenuous legal authority. Absent a better transparency regime, however, it is difficult to know whether the executive branch is routinely exceeding its legal authority or entering agreements in ways that defy the political preferences of Congress.

While informational problems have posed significant challenges to congressional oversight of international agreements, Congress has recently enacted significant reforms in this area, pointing to signs of constitutional health and vitality. The transparency regime of the last several decades, as described previously, made it nearly impossible to evaluate executive branch conduct in foreign affairs. In December 2022, however, Congress passed sweeping reforms to this transparency regime in the National Defense Authorization Act for Fiscal Year 2023. As Jack Goldsmith, Curtis Bradley, and Oona Hathaway write, the reforms now require that the State Department transmit new agreements to Congress every month with a detailed explanation of their legal authorizations.[102] In addition to this, the State Department must publish all nonclassified agreements to its website within 120 days of the agreement entering into force, and these agreements must contain detailed information about the legal authority the executive branch used to enter into the agreement. The law also provides for better accountability and centralization within the executive branch by requiring departments and agencies to transmit agreements and their legal authority to the State Department within fifteen days after concluding the agreement. Pursuant to this requirement, each agency must appoint a Chief International Agreement Information Officer, and the Comptroller General is required to audit the State Department to monitor its compliance with the reporting and publishing requirements. Congress appropriated one million dollars annually for five years to cover the costs of compliance with the new requirements. Finally, the new reforms require that the executive branch also report legally nonbinding agreements. Goldsmith, Bradley, and Hathaway conclude that "this legislative enactment represents the most significant transparency reform for international agreements in a half century."[103]

In short, ensuring transparency by requiring that agreements be posted with legal justifications would better enable Congress to perform its oversight function while preserving the benefits of executive vigor and energy in foreign affairs. Given that the executive branch is designed to summon the nation's strength and effectiveness in foreign affairs, the rise of executive agreements does not in principle signal constitutional subversion. Rather, executive dominance is the outworking of a principled constitutional commitment. The major problem with executive agreements is not executive dominance, but, rather, the failure of Congress to effectively mobilize its political capacities. While political practice of the last several decades points to major problems in congressional oversight, recent reforms point to signs of constitutional health, as Congress has enacted significant reforms to supervise executive agreements.

Congressional Involvement in International Agreements

While executive agreements are to be expected given the structural advantages of the executive branch in foreign affairs, the use of executive agreements cannot be endlessly malleable if the constitutional order is to maintain its basic character. Under the Constitution, the Senate retains significant oversight of treaties with its power to ratify them by the consent of two-thirds of the senators present. Returning to *Federalist* 75, Hamilton notes the logic of this arrangement by pointing out the fact that treaties, while requiring the institutional capacities of the executive branch to ensure effectiveness in foreign affairs, also "plead strongly for the participation of the whole or a portion of the legislative body in the office of making them" because treaties operate as laws and are thus binding on citizens.[104] While the need for vigor and dispatch would seem to require placing the power to make treaties solely with the executive branch as Locke and Montesquieu had urged, the framers departed from these separation of powers theorists, recognizing the importance of enhanced congressional involvement in treaty-making to ensure that treaties, because of their status as law, reflect the deliberative will of the people expressed by their representatives in Congress.[105] The treaty clause, in this regard, ultimately brings the branches into a productive conflict over the nation's involvement in foreign affairs. Shared powers over treaty-making, in short, is both about creating an institutional framework that is effective in foreign affairs by harnessing the institutional advantages of the executive branch and about ensuring that the government's success in foreign affairs is made consistent with the aims of republican government.

Of course, given the scale of the nation's involvement in foreign affairs, it would be impossible for the Senate to ratify all international agreements as treaties. "Processing such a workload through the Article II process," as Glen

Krutz and Jeffrey Peake argue, "would grind the presidential-congressional system to a halt, at least in regard to foreign policy, at both ends of Pennsylvania Avenue."[106] Much of this chapter, therefore, has considered how the rise of *executive* agreements was anticipated by the Constitution's principled division of labor and how Congress can use its political capacities to constrain agreements. This section is concerned with a separate, albeit closely connected, question: What political criteria, deduced from the animating purposes of the treaty clause, should guide the branches' political negotiations about the level of congressional authorization certain agreements ought to take? This question is more fundamental than whether a particular agreement is legal. Indeed, Congress can assert its political prerogatives in ways that fail to achieve its constitutional purposes even as, legally speaking, it provides authorization for a particular agreement (as in the Iran Agreement, which will be discussed later). Understanding the treaty clause politically, in short, does not mean that any political resolution the branches come up with is rightly characterized as a healthy instance of constitutional politics.

In order to elucidate the underlying purposes of the Constitution's treaty-making architecture, it is necessary to examine the best reasons for placing the power to ratify treaties in the Senate rather than in the Congress as a whole. Highlighting this choice, and the framers' overarching purposes in making it, helps to clarify the kind of politics it was intended to inspire. In other words, the primary task is to understand what is signified by the logic of placing the power to ratify treaties in the Senate and how the purposes underlying this decision should inform how the branches negotiate their boundaries in a world where it would be impossible to conduct all agreements as treaties.

Although there was considerable disagreement about whether both houses should have a role in ratifying treaties—with notable members of the Convention such as James Madison and James Wilson, for example, both repeatedly arguing in favor of the involvement of the House—the convention ultimately chose to place the power to ratify treaties solely in the Senate. The Senate, as a smaller chamber of older, wiser statesmen elected by state legislatures, would serve longer terms than members of the House, giving senators, according to Jay in *The Federalist*, "sufficient time to become perfectly acquainted with our national concerns, and to form and introduce a system for the management of them."[107] Given that treaties can potentially take a long time to negotiate, and given the complexity of national affairs more generally, placing the power to ratify treaties in a more stable legislative body would thus enable members to take the long view in foreign affairs and, consequently, make it more likely that the good of the nation was met in foreign affairs. As Hamilton further explained in *Federalist* 75:

> The fluctuating and, taking its future increase into the account, the multitudinous composition of that body [the House of Representatives], forbid us to expect in it the qualities which are essential to the proper execution of such a trust. Accurate and comprehensive knowledge of foreign politics; a steady and systematic adherence to the same views; a nice and uniform sensibility to national character, decision, *secrecy*, and dispatch, are incompatible with the genius of a body so variable and so numerous.[108]

The framers' choice to place the power to ratify treaties in the Senate, therefore, points to an underlying concern that the United States enters into international agreements credibly because they enjoy widespread and stable public backing.

As is made clear in *The Federalist*, one of the great dangers of republican government is mutability of the laws. While it is good for the government to be responsive to public opinion, "a continual change even of good measures is inconsistent with every rule of prudence and every prospect of success."[109] The Senate, therefore, was intended to guard against mutability of the laws, ensuring that adequate provision is made for the long-term good of the nation, not just the short-term and elusive notions of the people more likely to be expressed by the House of Representatives given its proximity to the people because of its larger size and more frequent elections. The dangers of mutability of the laws, while problematic for republican government in general, are especially pronounced in the foreign arena, where a lack of constancy undermines the trust of foreign nations. As Madison argued in *Federalist* 62, commenting on the ways in which the Senate would buttress the credibility of the United States among foreign nations,

> An individual who is observed to be inconstant to his plans, or perhaps to carry on his affairs without any plan at all, is marked at once by all prudent people as a speedy victim to his own unsteadiness and folly. His more friendly neighbors may pity him, but all will decline to connect their fortunes with his; and not a few will seize the opportunity of making their fortunes out of his. One nation is to another what one individual is to another; with this melancholy distinction, perhaps, that the former, with fewer of the benevolent emotions than the latter, are under fewer restraints also from taking undue advantage of the indiscretions of each other. Every nation, consequently, whose

> affairs betray a want of wisdom and stability, may calculate on every loss which can be sustained from the more systematic policy of its wiser neighbors. But the best instruction on this subject is unhappily conveyed to America by the example of her own situation. She finds that she is held in no respect by her friends; that she is the derision of her enemies; and that she is a prey to every nation which has an interest in speculating on her fluctuating councils and embarrassed affairs.[110]

The ultimate choice to place the power to ratify treaties in the Senate, therefore, points to the importance that major foreign policy commitments enjoy widespread support of the public, buttressing the credibility of the United States in foreign affairs by making it less likely that the nation will abandon such agreements based on momentary, and at times fleeting, changes in public opinion. At least in theory, therefore, the high threshold required for Senate ratification is not primarily intended to make agreements more difficult to enter—a mere instance of checks and balances—but, rather, to ensure that the agreements entered into by the United States are done so in ways that have the backing of the public, and, consequently, are durable enough to win the respect of foreign nations. This, moreover, as alluded to by Madison in the aforementioned quotation, was a central concern of the Constitutional Convention. Indeed, one of the major problems of governmental practice under the Articles of Confederation was the inability of the United States to keep its treaty obligations because the national government could not enforce state compliance.[111] The trust of foreign nations was thus undermined, making it more likely that other nations would, in turn, fail to uphold their own obligations toward the United States. Part of the problem under the Articles of Confederation was that treaties were not considered supreme law of the land, and, perhaps more centrally, the national government did not have adequate enforcement mechanisms to ensure state compliance. The task for the constitutional framers, therefore, was to create the conditions for effectiveness in foreign affairs by unleashing the vigor of an adequately structured executive branch while also ensuring that there was sufficient public support for international agreements to make those commitments credible. Such public support, moreover, is especially important in a republican government, where the president, while originally perpetually eligible for reelection, would ultimately serve at the pleasure of the people. Because the Senate is better constituted to channel the long-term, deliberative will of the people, its support is thus particularly important to ensure the credibility of the nation without a hereditary monarch. The choice to have the backing of a supermajority of the Senate, therefore, was meant to ensure that the United States' important foreign policy commitments are not quickly and imprudently jettisoned when, for example, a president from a different political party takes office, or after a wave-election in the House of Representatives. The Senate's distance from the people thus allows, at least in theory, for more reflection, leading to more stable support for major international commitments.

While in modern practice lower forms of authorization are, at least legally speaking, considered to be constitutionally legitimate (such as ex post congressional-executive agreements that require authorization by a majority vote in both chambers rather than the supermajoritarian requirement in the Senate), presidents, following this logic, have routinely brought important international agreements to the Senate for ratification to signal the credibility of the agreement even though—or, rather, because—the Senate process is far more cumbersome than other post hoc approval mechanisms.[112] As Lisa L. Martin argues, presidents have to consider how the form an international agreement takes signals the durability of the agreement.[113] Foreign nations are going to be suspicious of the durability of an agreement if it appears that it is conducted with a lower form of authorization because it does not have sufficient support in Congress. This has been borne out in practice as foreign nations have, at times, publicly urged that agreements be concluded as treaties for the very reason that treaties, because they are concluded with a stronger form of authorization, are considered to represent a more durable commitment on the part of the United States.[114] For example, when the United States and Russia negotiated what became the Strategic Offensive Reduction Treaty (SORT) in 2002, there was some question about what form the new arms control agreement would take. President George W. Bush favored a more flexible "gentlemen's agreement" rather than a full-blown treaty. Russian President Vladimir Putin, on the other hand, wanted to ensure that any agreement reached would bind subsequent administrations and that, therefore, the accord needed to be concluded as a treaty. The Senate, moreover, concurred, asserting its prerogatives to ratify arms control agreements as treaties given the importance of such commitments for American foreign policy.[115]

The point here is that the logic undergirding the Senate's inclusion in the treaty clause points to a constitutional good that a stable and deliberative body brings to the practice of foreign affairs, ensuring both that the international commitments entered into by the United States enjoy the widespread support of the public, and, consequently, enable the United States to form credible commitments internationally. If such stability is a constitutional good, moreover, then executive agreements cannot be used for any agreement if the constitutional order is to maintain its basic character. In other words, there should be a qualitative difference between what is acceptably concluded as some form of executive agreement compared to those agreements that require more stringent congressional scrutiny and a higher form of congressional authorization based on the significance of the international commitment. There is, however, no way to deduce a specific line, in a legalistic sense, demarcating when an agreement should be concluded as one form or another, and the judiciary has been highly reticent to enter the fray, asserting lack of judicial competence to issue such a bright-line rule.[116] Such decisions, rather, are appropriately left to political negotiation between the branches.

There are many examples of Congress—and especially the Senate—protecting its institutional prerogatives, demanding that the president submit international agreements to the Senate to be ratified as treaties. The Senate has exercised its prerogatives regardless of the partisan dynamics between the branches. Indeed, the Senate considers some issue areas (such as arms control and human rights) to be sufficiently important and, consequently, demands that such agreements be concluded as treaties rather than agreements with a lower threshold of authorization. For example, since World War II presidents have submitted nearly every arms control treaty to the Senate for ratification. Such agreements are highly consequential because they have established the United States' nuclear deterrence strategy of "mutually assured destruction," sought to restrict the spread of nuclear weapons, and led to the demilitarization of Europe.[117] The one major exception to this general practice was the 1972 Strategic Arms Limitation Talks (SALT I) agreement, which was concluded as a congressional-executive agreement. This agreement, however, was considered a temporary agreement (only lasting for five years), and both sides understood that the agreement was a placeholder until a more substantive treaty could be concluded at a later date.[118] When SALT II faced considerable political opposition from Congress, President Carter considered submitting the agreement to both houses to be approved by majority vote rather than as a treaty but was forced to submit the agreement as a treaty after sustained Senate pressure.[119] Similarly, President George W. Bush attempted to conclude the Strategic Offensive Reduction Treaty (SORT) as a congressional-executive agreement but submitted the agreement as a treaty after considerable pressure from both Russian President Vladimir Putin and members of the Senate.[120] Finally, while the United States signed the Comprehensive Nuclear Test Ban Treaty during the Clinton administration, the treaty has not been ratified by the Senate. Although the treaty (which had majority support in Congress) stalled out in the Senate, neither President Clinton nor President Obama considered submitting the agreement to Congress as anything other than a treaty given congressional sentiment on the matter.

As the aforementioned examples indicate, the Senate has consistently asserted its political prerogatives over arms control agreements, attaching a declaration to arms control treaties in several instances stating that agreements "that would obligate the United States to reduce or limit the Armed Forces or armaments of the United States in a militarily significant manner [should be concluded] only pursuant to the Treaty Power as set forth in Article II, Section 2, Clause 2 of the Constitution."[121] The Senate has insisted that treaties be used in other areas as well, including human rights accords, political/military agreements, environmental agreements, and extradition. Such agreements are concluded as treaties because the Senate demands it. The Senate's demands are political demands, especially given that many contend that such agreements can and should be appropriately concluded as congressional-executive agreements given the difficulty of securing Senate ratification.[122] Moreover, the consensus of the legal community is that congressional-executive agreements are completely legally interchangeable with treaties.[123] It is beyond the scope of this chapter to wade into the interchangeability debate other than to note that the Senate's repeated demands that important agreements be submitted to the Senate for ratification contradict this general scholarly consensus. As Bradley and Morrison conclude, "Historical practice suggests a constitutionally salient distinction between 'major' and 'minor' agreements."[124]

It should be noted, moreover, that when the United States uses ex post congressional-executive agreements instead of treaties for major international commitments, it does so in limited contexts that with few exceptions lie within Congress's plenary powers pursuant to Article I, Section 8 to regulate trade and foreign commerce. For all the constitutional controversy surrounding ex post congressional-executive agreements, they are used sparingly (one per year on average).[125] Of course, such agreements can be highly consequential. Indeed, ex post congressional-executive agreements have been used for major economic agreements such as the World Trade Organization and the Bretton Woods Convention, which "did nothing less than create the foundations of the new world economic order."[126] Moreover, today all major trade agreements, such as the North American Free Trade Agreement (NAFTA), are concluded by congressional-executive agreement rather than as treaties. Even so, in areas such as trade, Congress could just as easily legislate the United States into compliance with the international obligations imposed by such agreements irrespective of whether the United States actually ratifies the agreements. As John Yoo argues, "If, for example, Congress were to adopt unilaterally the changes in tariffs, customs laws, or national treatment required by NAFTA or the WTO, in the absence of an international agreement, it would have ample authority to do so pursuant to Article I, Section 8."[127] In this way, such agreements still retain significant congressional buy-in and do not represent any subversion of constitutional principles.

In fact, when Congress has used congressional-executive agreements in the area of trade, it has developed mechanisms such as fast-track authority that give it substantial input during the negotiation and formation of agreements in exchange for fast-track approval post hoc. By requiring the executive branch to keep relevant congressional committees informed throughout negotiations (and even to have members of Congress on the negotiation delegation), Congress ensures that the final deal submitted to Congress for approval closely aligns with congressional views.[128] By fast-tracking approval (with strict time limits on a final vote and no floor amendments), Congress buttresses the United States' negotiating credibility by ensuring that the agreement will not languish in Congress or be subsequently amended in ways that substantially alter the carefully negotiated agreement, a perennial problem with treaties. Unlike the vast majority of treaties, moreover, such agreements involve Congress at the "advice" stage, leading some commentators like Ackerman and Golove to assert that the ex post congressional-executive agreement, as used with fast-track trade authority, approximate founding ideals better than does interbranch negotiation in treaty formation.[129] The fundamental point here is that when Congress has used ex post congressional-executive agreements instead of treaties, it has used them in areas where it has the plenary constitutional authority to legislate on the matter, and it has often used the agreements in ways that enhance, rather than diminish, its political control over the issues concerned.

Constitutional Versus Legal Claims

The claims of Congress vis-à-vis the president regarding its prerogatives over international agreements are ultimately political claims. Congress's role in foreign affairs is not merely about checking and balancing. Rather, Congress's shared powers over foreign affairs in general, and treaty-making in particular, is ultimately about bringing positive political goods to the practice of foreign affairs, making it more likely that the United States' foreign policy will be stable and its agreements credible. Congress, as demonstrated earlier, has often asserted its political prerogatives to ratify important agreements as treaties rather than to allow those agreements to be entered into at a lower level of authorization. Interbranch contestation surrounding the nuclear deal with Iran, however, reveals the ways that an overly legalistic focus on the powers of the branches can miss—and, consequently, undermine—the larger political purposes of the branches' shared powers over international agreements. Legal analysis provides an inadequate framework for evaluating interbranch behavior with regard to foreign affairs.

The Iran nuclear deal (known formally as the Joint Comprehensive Plan of Action or "JCPOA") was a political agreement signed by the P5+1 (the UN Security Council's five permanent members plus Germany) and Iran. According to the terms of the deal, Iran agreed to end key components of its nuclear development program. In exchange, the United States agreed to suspend its unilateral sanctions against Iran, and the United Nations agreed to lift the international sanctions it had imposed. The agreement was controversial, to say the least. When Congress learned that President Obama was attempting to broker a deal that would lift congressionally imposed sanctions on Iran, there was widespread, and bipartisan, opposition. Particularly controversial was the administration's decision to enter the agreement without subsequent approval from Congress, with the president claiming that he had sufficient authority to conclude the agreement without congressional authorization.[130] The administration's position on the issue resulted in Republican members of Congress writing a controversial open letter addressed to the "leaders of the Islamic Republic of Iran," informing them that any agreement entered into without legislative approval could be abandoned by the next president "with the stroke of a pen."[131]

The administration argued that the sanctions regime implemented by Congress delegated to the president the power to suspend sanctions against Iran if the president determined that to do so would be in the national interest.[132] The president, moreover, intended to complete the agreement as a "political" agreement, meaning that it would impose no legal obligations on the United States under international law. The administration believed that a legally nonbinding agreement would give it sufficient flexibility to reimpose sanctions should Iran fail to comply with its terms.[133] Harold Koh argues that political agreements, like the one brokered with Iran, are particularly important in contexts where regimes fundamentally distrust each other. As Koh argues, "The Iran Nuclear Deal" was "a confidence-building device designed to shift from a pattern of confrontation toward a pattern of cooperation with Iran."[134] The agreement would thus be successful if both nations, step by step, abided by the terms of the agreement, leading to greater compliance over time and, perhaps, paving the way to a legally binding arrangement. Given the "political" nature of the proposed accord—that it would not legally bind the United States or the next president—President Obama argued that he had sufficient legal authority to bring the nation into compliance with the terms of the agreement by waiving sanctions pursuant to his waiver authority.

Congress, however, rightly asserted its institutional prerogatives to review any agreement concluded with Iran before the agreement took effect, given the significance of the agreement for American foreign policy. Congress overwhelmingly passed the Iran Nuclear Agreement Review Act of 2015, requiring the president to submit the final negotiated agreement to Congress, and, moreover, prohibiting the president from waiving sanctions pursuant to the agreement during a sixty-day review period. According to the terms of the legislation, the agreement could go into effect if Congress voted to approve the deal during that window. Congress, however, reserved the right to disapprove the agreement by passing a joint resolution of disapproval. If Congress did not act, the agreement would go into effect at the end of the sixty-day period. Moreover, the legislation included significant oversight mechanisms meant to keep Congress informed of Iranian compliance with the agreement (should it go into effect), requiring the president to certify that Iran was in compliance with the terms of the agreement every ninety days. Congress could fast-track legislation to reimpose sanctions if Iran violated the terms of the agreement. Speaking about the merits of the legislation, Senator Jeff Flake (R-AZ) argued that "since this agreement is slated to last well beyond the President's term and even the next President's term, any effective, enduring agreement has to have congressional buy-in. Let me repeat. If this legislation fails, the President will be able to sign a final agreement and have a nice signing ceremony, but an effective, enduring agreement to prevent Iran from obtaining a nuclear weapon will require congressional buy-in."[135]

Congress was able to mobilize veto-proof majorities in both chambers to enact the legislation subjecting any proposed agreement to congressional review, a feat that took considerable negotiating skill by top congressional leaders.[136] Ultimately, President Obama acquiesced to congressional pressure and announced that he would sign the legislation. This was hardly a concession, however, given that under the terms of the legislation, it would take supermajorities in Congress to *disapprove* any agreement made with Iran, because any joint resolution of disapproval would be met with a veto. Given these dynamics, once the deal was negotiated, the president needed only to convince just over a third of one chamber to support the deal for it to go into effect. Members of Congress agreed that the Iran Deal ultimately constituted a major change in US foreign relations toward Iran, but Congress's rhetoric about the importance of congressional "buy-in" to ensure an "effective and enduring" agreement was not matched in the terms of the actual bill as passed. Congressional deliberations were inconsequential because members of Congress could enjoy the political benefits of voting against the agreement while knowing that a "no" vote would have no effect on the final outcome. It is hard to know how members of Congress would have voted had their choices mattered. The deal thus went into effect even though majorities in both houses of Congress opposed the bill.[137] While the deal was legal—and, as David Golove argues, there is no doubt about its legality after Congress passed the review act—it was left politically vulnerable because it was a major foreign policy commitment made not only without the imprimatur of Congress, but against its expressed will.[138]

This is not to say that the Iran Deal should have been concluded as a treaty. There are perhaps good arguments—along the lines of Koh's arguments earlier—for "political" agreements that help move states toward better relations with each other through more flexible arrangements. It is to say, however, that the treaty clause points to criteria that should guide how Congress asserts its political prerogatives against the president's claims, legal or otherwise. Whether the president has legal authority to take a certain action is beside the point. A Congress that is motivated by the overarching purposes of the treaty clause would demand to deliberate and vote on an agreement in a way that matters given the importance of such an agreement for American foreign policy, and, moreover, would wield its other political capacities, up and to impeachment, should the president persist in acting against the deliberative and majoritarian will of Congress. As argued in the previous section, one of the overarching goals of the treaty clause was to safeguard the stability of American foreign policy by ensuring that international commitments entered into by the United States had sufficient public support, thus buttressing the United States' credibility in the international arena. A constitutionally motivated Congress, irrespective of the president's legal claims, would advance and defend its prerogatives, asserting the need to ensure the credibility of the nation in foreign affairs by ensuring that any major agreement retained sufficient public support to be a durable commitment. Congress's substantive deliberations about a controversial and consequential foreign policy choice could help move public support toward the agreement. Faced with an actual choice—and the responsibility for the ultimate outcome—congressional deliberations could underscore the wisdom (or futility) of the agreement.

Of course, some, like Harold Koh and Jack Goldsmith, argue that such agreements, like the Iran Deal, entered into by the executive branch without robust congressional support are, in fact, durable because they are difficult for future presidents to unwind.[139] As Koh argued prior to the Trump administration's decision to "exit" the Iran Agreement, "[i]f the Iranians continue to keep their part of the bargain, legal or political, the new Administration will be hard-pressed to replace a working multilateral deal with nothing."[140] Indeed, according to Koh, "deals are sticky, regimes are path-dependent, and in complex political equations, the locus of domestic legal authority often plays a subsidiary role."[141] As the deal gained traction, moreover, all involved (national and business interests) started to rely on the new legal framework, as they began to invest their resources in Iran's increasingly globally connected economy.[142]

Koh and Goldsmith might be correct that most presidents would not exit the agreement absent Iranian noncompliance with its terms. Even so, this does not mean that the agreement was not left politically vulnerable should a president decide, even against what many perceive to be in the best interest of the nation, to exit the agreement, as President Trump ultimately decided.[143] It would have been far more difficult for President Trump to have exited the agreement had the agreement had the deliberative and affirmative consent of Congress at the outset. No doubt the United States' credibility on the international stage—and especially with Iran—has been seriously compromised. It is highly unlikely that the United States will be able to broker a better deal with Iran in the near future given that it cannot be trusted to keep the commitments that it makes.[144] As Wendy Sherman, the chief negotiator for the United States during the Iran Deal negotiations, wrote, the United States' exit from the deal "has given U.S. allies less reason to trust Washington on future deals or to take U.S. interests into account."[145]

It is perhaps no surprise that President Obama stretched the limits of his constitutional authority (given the absence of robust political support in Congress) to conclude an important multilateral agreement with Iran that the administration believed would be the best option for preventing Iran from developing nuclear weapons, taking a major risk in the hope that the next president would have every incentive to stick with the agreement to the extent that Iran continued to comply with its terms. It is also possible, perhaps even likely, that over time such a deal, if Iran complied, would gain the support of Congress and the American people. The problem, however, is that this was a high-stakes gamble. Given that the agreement was made in opposition to the expressed will of Congress—even though Congress buttressed its legality by passing the review act—it did not have the support necessary to survive if a president was determined to exit. And, moreover, both the fact that public sentiment was clearly against the agreement when it entered into effect and that nearly every Republican presidential candidate vowed in the primaries to exit the deal points to the fact that the agreement was built firmly on sand.[146]

The interbranch negotiation surrounding the Iran agreement is instructive because it demonstrates how the law—whether the president has the legal authority to do something or not—does not provide sufficient criteria for evaluating how the branches engage each other in politics to achieve the aims of the constitutional order in foreign affairs. Without Congressional buy-in, the Iran deal lacked the broad-based support needed for a durable commitment. And when President Trump withdrew from the deal, it undermined American credibility with important allies. While the Iran agreement might appear, at first glance, as an instance of presidential overreach, the real constitutional failure was Congress's inability (or unwillingness) to exercise its political capacities in a way that matched its rhetoric. Indeed, Congress expressed the importance of exercising its prerogatives over the agreement given the major change the deal represented for American foreign policy toward Iran. But, ultimately, it exercised its prerogatives in a way that was of no consequence (and, in fact, only further buttressed the president's legal position). The ultimate interbranch resolution, as far as the durability of the agreement was concerned, left the United States in the same position it would have been in had Congress abdicated entirely.

The point of this illustration is not to overstate the case about congressional abdication over international agreements. As demonstrated in the previous section, Congress has, at times, exercised its prerogatives over treaty-making even when to do so meant the failure of agreements that had majority support in both houses of Congress but could not reach the supermajority requirement of the Senate. In this case, President Obama was able to convince Congress—or at least enough members of his own party—that his legal position trumped Congress's political prerogatives. This case, therefore, illustrates both the promise of the political approach to separation of powers insofar as Congress demanded to play a role in the agreement's conclusion, and the residue of a legalistic notion of separation of powers to the extent that the political resolution was determined more by recourse to narrow legal reasoning than deep constitutional principles.

4

Recess Appointments

On the surface, there is nothing particularly interesting or even controversial about the US Constitution's recess appointments clause, which states that "the President shall have Power to fill all Vacancies that may happen during the Recess of the Senate, by granting Commissions which shall expire at the End of their next Session."[1] In fact, the clause was approved by the Constitutional Convention with little discussion and without any debate, signaling that the framers understood the clause merely as a necessary exception to the normal appointments procedures, which requires the advice and consent of the Senate for presidential appointments.[2]

"Uncontroversial," however, is not a term that describes the use of recess appointments in recent practice. On the contrary, recess appointments were one of the central points of contention between the Congress and the Obama administration, culminating in a showdown at the Supreme Court. At issue were several intrasession recess appointments made to the National Labor Relations Board (NLRB) and to the Consumer Financial Protection Bureau (CFPB) in January 2012 even as Congress maintained pro forma sessions—in which a single senator came in to gavel the Senate into session once every three days, but in which no business took place—precisely to prevent President Obama from making recess appointments. The court intervened in *NLRB v. Noel Canning*, declaring that the Senate, not the president, determines when it is in session, so long as it, at least technically, retains the capacity to conduct business.

Much of the current literature on recess appointments among legal scholars is an attempt to determine the specific meaning of the recess appointments clause and, consequently, to legally settle in some way the boundary between the branches when it comes to the appointments process.[3] This, moreover, is hardly surprising given that the legal meaning of the clause was the central question before the Supreme Court when it decided the case in *Noel Canning*. Political scientists, on the other hand, have largely been concerned with checks and balances and how recess appointments fit within the president's unilateral toolkit, and, therefore, how the ruling in *Noel Canning* affects those interbranch dynamics.[4] Among these scholars, the court's ruling is seen as an example of "powering down the presidency" by legally enforcing interbranch boundaries and buttressing Senate prerogatives vis-à-vis the president.[5]

The purpose of this chapter is to reframe the recent interbranch dispute surrounding recess appointments by considering how the modern use of recess appointments can be better understood and evaluated as part of the dynamic political order established by the Constitution. The Constitution, in this understanding, is more than a legal framework intended to settle disputes between the branches or to maintain legal balance through judicial oversight. Instead, the legal provisions of the Constitution rest on a set of normative commitments and substantive goals. From this larger constitutional perspective, the substantive goal of the recess appointments clause is that the government should continue running, absent democratic choice to the contrary. While the literal function of the clause was to ensure the proper functioning of government when the technological difficulties of travel and communication made long congressional recesses necessary, this literal function is better understood in terms of this higher-order constitutional principle. From this perspective, then, there might be other occasions wherein recess appointments are justifiable, even beyond the original intentions and expectations of the constitutional framers: in this case, the breakdown of governmental processes due to the sheer problem of unfettered partisanship.

Evaluating recess appointments from this larger constitutional perspective reveals judicial resolution of the issue actually subverted the Constitution's political processes, preventing the president from staffing the national government even as he faced unprecedented partisan obstruction from a minority faction in the Senate. The court's policing of constitutional boundaries based on a literal reading of the purposes of the recess appointments clause thus made it appear that the president had acted lawlessly even as he pressed legitimate constitutional claims to keep the government functioning absent the deliberative will of Congress to the contrary. Conversely, the legal resolution of the issue sanctioned constitutionally suspect congressional behavior, making unprecedented partisan obstruction of the institution appear high-minded compared to the president's purported "lawlessness." The recess appointments, therefore, were a response to the breakdown of interbranch politics, a problem that judicial resolution disguised rather than resolved.[6]

Political contestation between the branches, unencumbered by the legal arguments about the literal purposes of the recess appointments clause, would have provided opportunities for institutional actors in each of the branches to make arguments about their respective behavior that could then be judged and evaluated by the other branches and the public at large. The court's intervention in *Noel Canning*, however, precluded this interbranch deliberation. In other words, the recess appointments clause became a site for interbranch contestation, but the conflict itself was based on larger political dynamics between the branches that were then obscured by the focus on the literal meaning of the clause. The recess appointments controversy and its subsequent resolution by the court, therefore, illuminate the problems with an overly legalized conception of the Constitution's separation of powers.

Standard Legal Account of Recess Appointments

Article II, section 2, clause 2 of the US Constitution provides the president with the power to appoint with the "advice and consent" of the Senate "ambassadors, other public ministers and consuls, judges of the Supreme Court, and all other officers of the United States, whose appointments are not herein otherwise provided for, and which shall be established by law." The recess appointments clause—which states in Article II, section 2, clause 3 that "he president shall have power to fill up all vacancies that may happen during the recess of the Senate, by granting commissions which shall expire at the end of their next session"—is an ancillary clause, meant to ensure the functioning of government in the Senate's absence. Indeed, Alexander Hamilton wrote in *Federalist* 67 that "the relation in which [the recess appointments clause] stands to the [appointments clause], which declares the general mode of appointing officers of the United States, denotes it to be nothing more than a supplement to the other, for the purpose of establishing an auxiliary method of appointment, in cases to which the general method was inadequate."[7]

For most of American history, recess appointments were hardly controversial. In fact, they served a valuable function in an age where limited communication and long-distance travel meant that Congress met continuously for several months before recessing so that members could travel back to their states and districts. The practical necessities of the recess appointments clause in a time where significant portions of the year were marked by congressional absence help explain why the Constitutional Convention did not view the clause as controversial and saw no need to even debate its meaning.[8] The purpose of the clause was simple: The president needs the power to ensure the functioning of the federal government in the face of congressional absence. This power, moreover, was necessarily circumscribed by the temporary nature of such appointments as recess appointed officials merely serve until the end of the next Senate session. Recess appointments, in this way, cannot serve as a method by which the Senate is continually circumvented given that such appointments are merely temporary.

Moreover, recess appointments, as a supplement to the general appointment procedures, were considered better than the alternatives: an extended vacancy until the next session, recalling the Senate out of recess to consider a nomination, or keeping the Congress in perpetual session (which would conflict with the prevailing understanding of republican government and would be expensive and logistically challenging).[9] In fact, Justice Joseph Story, commenting on the clear logic of the recess appointments clause in his *Commentaries on the Constitution of the United States*, wrote that the decision to allow for recess appointments was "so obvious that it can require no elucidation," because without them, "the Senate should be perpetually in session, in order to provide for the appointment of officers."[10] The absence of such a clause, Justice Story asserted, "would have been at once burdensome to the Senate and expensive to the public," and so its insertion represented the need for "convenience, promptitude of action, and general security."[11]

Given the fundamental purpose of the recess appointments clause, it was interpreted narrowly at the outset of American government. President Washington had the first opportunity to construe it however broadly would fit his purposes. When presented with the opportunity to make a recess appointment for an office that had become vacant while the Senate had been in session, Washington deferred judgment to Attorney General Edmund Randolph, who wrote to President Washington that "the Spirit of the Constitution favors the participation of the Senate in all appointments. But as it may be necessary oftentimes to fill up vacancies, when it may be inconvenient to summon the senate a temporary commission may be granted by the President. This power then is to be considered as an exception to the general participation of the Senate. It ought too to be interpreted strictly."[12] Alexander Hamilton, perhaps one of the strongest defenders of executive power among the framers, also concluded that recess appointments were limited to vacancies that arise during a recess, not any vacancy that happens to exist:

"It is clear, that independent of the authority of a special law, the President cannot fill a vacancy which happens during a session of the Senate."[13]

Even so, the prevailing historical understanding of how widely the clause should be interpreted recognized that to construe it too strictly could undermine the purpose for which it was adopted in the first place. Attorney General William Wirt asserted in an 1823 opinion that while the text clearly demonstrates that recess appointments can only be made when a vacancy arises during a recess, such a construction could hinder the president's ability to make an appointment to a federal office far from the nation's capital should he not receive word that such a vacancy exists in time for him to make an appointment before the ensuing recess: "The substantial purpose of the Constitution was to keep these offices filled and powers adequate to this purpose were intended to be conveyed. But if the President shall not have the power to fill a vacancy thus circumstanced, the powers are inadequate to the purpose, and the substance of the Constitution will be sacrificed to a dubious construction of its letter."[14] Even so, Wirt maintained that such a construction would not give license to the president to circumvent Senate confirmation. While he asserted that the clause should be construed broadly enough to ensure "the substantial meaning of the instrument" and to avoid the "most embarrassing inconveniences," such a construction "cannot possibly produce mischief, without imputing to the president a degree of turpitude entirely inconsistent with the character which his office implies."[15] In short, in early practice recess appointments were understood as serving a practical and necessary purpose in the constitutional order. Insofar as the clause was construed beyond its specific textual instantiation, it was done so not to undermine the letter of the law but in service to the broader commitment of the clause.

In the twentieth century, however, recess appointments became increasingly controversial as presidents used them more frequently, even as Congress stayed in session far more regularly. Moreover, recess appointments, including within shorter intrasession recesses, became a mechanism by which presidents attempted to staff the executive branch in the face of Senate obstruction.[16] Table 4.1 shows the number of recess appointments made by each president starting with Ronald Reagan up until the court's ruling in *Noel Canning* in 2014. Given the proliferation of recess appointments at the expense of Congress's constitutional power to advise and consent to executive nominations, it is perhaps not surprising that this practice ultimately resulted in a showdown before the Supreme Court in 2013 in *National Labor Relations Board v. Noel Canning*. The controversy surrounding this case stemmed from the Senate's use of pro forma sessions to prevent recess

Table 4.1: Number of Recess Appointments per President

	Recess appointments	*Yearly average*	*Presidential total*
Ronald Reagan I	134	33.5	
Ronald Reagan II	98	24.5	232
George H. W. Bush	78	19.5	78
William Clinton I	35	8.75	
William Clinton II	104	26	139
George W. Bush I	106	26.5	
George W. Bush II	65	16.25	171
Barack Obama I	32	8	
Barack Obama II	0	0	32

Source: Henry B. Hogue et al., "The Noel Canning Decision and Recess Appointments Made from 1981–2013," Congressional Research Service, 2013.

appointments. Such sessions of the Senate were supposed to serve as a buffer to keep the president from making such nominations by keeping the Senate in perpetual session via having one senator gavel the chamber into session once every three days so that the legislature would not be in recess for longer than three days. This strategy was considered in the 1980s and 1990s but never used.[17]

When the Senate finally implemented pro forma sessions in 2007 to prevent President George W. Bush from making recess appointments, the president abided by the will of the Senate. President Bush was thus prevented from making recess appointments for the last fourteen months of his presidency because Congress, at least technically, did not recess.[18] Such pro forma sessions, according to some estimates, prevented President Bush from making dozens of appointments, diminishing presidential influence in a variety of policy areas.[19]

After Republicans regained the House in the 2010 midterm elections, the Senate once again began holding pro forma sessions to prevent President Obama from making recess appointments even though Democrats held a majority in the Senate. The Senate maintained pro forma sessions because the Republican-controlled House of Representatives would not agree to adjourn. The adjournments clause in the Constitution (Article I, section 5, clause 4) requires that both chambers agree to any adjournment longer than three days. Hence, the House was able to force the Senate to maintain pro forma sessions to prevent recess appointments, while, at the same time, the

Republican minority in the Senate obstructed appointments through the use of the filibuster.

In these circumstances, President Obama made three recess appointments to the NLRB, and also appointed Richard Cordray to the CFPB during a short three-day break between pro forma sessions. The recess appointments to the NLRB came after months of Senate delay and as NLRB vacancies kept it from reaching a quorum, thus preventing it from functioning. Appointments to the NLRB had become increasingly partisan over the years, and so recess appointments became a prime way for the president to ensure that the board could maintain a quorum, allowing labor groups and organizations to air grievances against employers and ensuring that business interests could face the threat of sanctions for unfair business practices.[20] Richard Cordray's appointment to the CFPB was similarly thwarted by a partisan filibuster by Senate Republicans, the minority party in the Senate, and this after the Republicans had blocked Elizabeth Warren's nomination to the post.

Given these circumstances, President Obama, under advice from the Office of Legal Counsel, declared "the President may determine that pro forma sessions at which no business is to be conducted do not interrupt a Senate recess for the purposes of the Recess Appointments Clause."[21] By not counting the pro forma sessions as legitimate interruptions to the Senate's recess, President Obama determined that the Senate had recessed from December 20, 2011, and would not reconvene until January 23, 2012, a recess of longer than a month. These appointments set off a partisan firestorm, with nearly forty Republican senators condemning the appointments and voicing their intention to file a "friend of the Court" brief, expressing their support for legal action in a letter to the president.[22] Senator John Cornyn (R-Texas) went so far as to say that "American democracy was born out of a rejection of the monarchies of Western Europe, anchored by limited government and separation of powers," and that "we refuse to stand by as this president arrogantly casts aside our Constitution and defies the will of the American people under the election-year guise of defending them."[23]

In its determination of the scope of the recess appointments clause in *NLRB v. Noel Canning* (2014), the court largely considered the original meaning of the text and looked to historical practice to fill in textual gaps. Hence, most of the debates focused on whether the president can make appointments for any vacancy in any recess or only those in which the particular vacancy arose. Moreover, the court considered the definition of recess, and whether the clause applied to both intersession and intrasession recesses. The court ruled unanimously that President Obama's recess appointments exceeded constitutional limits, though it split five to four on how widely the clause should be construed. While a minority on the court would restrict the use of recess appointments solely to intersession recesses and only for vacancies that arose in the particular recess, the majority construed the clause far more broadly.

Writing for the court, Justice Breyer argued that an examination of founding era dictionaries, common usage of the term "recess" during the founding era, and historical practice could not definitively answer the question of what types of recesses are appropriate.[24] Because presidents had made recess appointments for both types of recesses and because the distinction between the two types is largely inconsequential today, the court held that either type of recess is appropriate for recess appointments. Drawing upon historical precedent, however, the court drew a bright-line rule, declaring that recesses of less than ten days—regardless of what type of recess—would be constitutionally inappropriate. The court made this determination by looking to the adjournments clause, concluding that a recess of shorter than three days was constitutionally inappropriate.[25] According to the court's reasoning, a recess that is not long enough to require the consent of the other chamber is presumptively too short for recess appointments. The court also held that historical practice revealed that presidents had never, minus a few exceptions, made recess appointments during recesses lasting fewer than ten days. Moreover, the majority declared that reading the clause to only apply to vacancies that arise during a recess could prevent the president from making necessary appointments. Given that the very purpose of the recess appointments clause is to ensure that the president can "obtain the assistance of subordinate officers when the Senate, due to its recess, cannot confirm them," construing it too narrowly "would prevent the President from making any recess appointment that arose before a recess, no matter who the official, no matter how dire the need, no matter how uncontroversial the appointment, and no matter how late in the last session the office fell vacant."[26]

The crucial part of the ruling, however, concerned the legitimacy of pro forma sessions. Indeed, Justice Breyer asserted that "the Senate is in session when it says it is, provided that, under its own rules, it retains the capacity to transact Senate business."[27] The court, thus, placed great emphasis on the ability of each House to "determine the Rules of its Proceedings."[28] Perhaps ironically, the majority's broad interpretation of what would constitute an acceptable recess appointment, despite Justice Scalia's trenchant critique of the majority's decision as granting the president too much power vis-à-vis Congress, made it *easier* for the Senate to block recess appointments than the minority's strict construal of the clause in Justice Scalia's concurrence. The decision, therefore, was widely characterized as a "rebuke" of the president by the Supreme Court.[29]

The implications for the president have already been clearly exhibited in practice. President Obama was prevented from making any recess appointments during his second term in office.[30] After Senate Republicans refused to even conduct hearings for his Supreme Court nominee Merrick Garland, there was some speculation that the president could recess appoint him to the court.[31] Senate Majority Leader Mitch McConnell, however, moved to keep the Senate in pro forma sessions, thus preventing any such appointment. Hence, as Ian Ostrander aptly notes, the court's ruling in *Noel Canning*, even in its broad interpretation of the clause, is an example of "powering down the presidency," especially during periods of divided government.[32]

The Appointments Process and the Constitution's Political Architecture

The court's decision in *Noel Canning* clearly had the effect of diminishing the president's ability to make recess appointments. The main question of this chapter is whether the legal resolution of the issue missed key elements of the dispute and, therefore, subverted and ended a political struggle between the branches that would have been better left to the political process. Answering this question requires understanding the Constitution in light of its purposes and ends. If the Constitution is primarily understood as a legal document—in which the branches' powers are understood primarily in terms of the literal meaning of the constitutional text—then it makes sense that the court would enforce constitutional boundaries as it did in *Noel Canning*. The court's determination of the limits of the clause and its legal buttressing of Senate prerogatives ("The Senate is in session when it says it is") is thus a logical outgrowth of the type of project established by the Constitution. Constitutional fidelity, in this view, is best understood in terms of adherence to the legal text as interpreted and enforced by the judiciary. The Constitution, therefore, serves a settlement function in the constitutional order, and separation of powers is primarily understood in terms of constraint.

An alternative way to understand the recess appointments phenomenon, however, is to view it as situated within the dynamic political order created by the Constitution. From this perspective, the Constitution does more than assign powers to the branches in a strictly legal sense. Rather, the Constitution establishes congeries of structures, powers, and duties. The recess appointments controversy can best be evaluated by attention to the larger substantive ends of the appointments process in general and why the framers included both branches in that process. The choice to include the political branches in the process of staffing the executive branch and the judiciary was not an arbitrary choice, as made clear by the constitutional debates over the issue. Instead, both political branches bring specific capacities and perspectives that are important to the process.

Hamilton illustrates in *Federalist 76* how the different *structures* of the two elected branches of the government are both important to the selection and confirmation of nominees. For example, the unitary nature of the executive better enables the choice of a nominee because it avoids the "display of all the private and party likings and dislikes, partialities and antipathies, attachments and animosities, which are felt by those who compose the assembly."[33] Hamilton continued, "I proceed to lay it down as a rule that one man of discernment is better fitted to analyze and estimate the peculiar qualities adapted to particular offices than a body of men of equal or perhaps even of superior discernment."[34] Indeed, the "sole and undivided responsibility of one man will naturally beget a livelier sense of duty and a more exact regard to reputation. He will, on this account, feel himself under stronger obligations, and more interested to investigate with care the qualities requisite to the stations to be filled, and to prefer with impartiality the persons who may have the fairest pretensions to them."[35] Placing the power to appoint in the hands of the president, therefore, makes it more likely that a choice will be selected in a timely manner, avoiding the delay that would be caused by placing the choice in a deliberative assembly. Furthermore, by placing the power to appoint in the hands of one person, it increases the chances that the person will nominate good candidates for the post because blame for bad choices will reflect solely upon the president. In a legislature, however, blame could be diffused across the body.

Beyond the particular structural qualities that presumably foster better selection, the president is certainly motivated by political concerns as well. At least in theory, the president makes selections with an eye toward a nominee's character, competence, but also a nominee's particular views on the subject matter for which that nominee will exercise responsibility. The administration of the laws is not merely technical but involves discretion and political judgments. Hence, a nominee's particular policy views are important considerations for the president, who ultimately is tasked with overseeing the executive branch and administering the laws passed by Congress. The president thus has a vested role in nominating subordinates based on his own political preferences.

The deliberative capacities of the Senate, on the other hand, ensure that an appointment is only concluded after a public process. This deliberation, while extending to the character and competence of a nominee, certainly also pertains to larger questions of politics as well. This is especially true when it comes to staffing the judiciary. The president obviously makes his or her selection of jurists with regard to the particular constitutional views—not just the professionalism or legal competence—of a nominee. These questions, therefore, are certainly fair game for the Senate to consider given the contestability of the criteria involved in the selection process. Indeed, questions concerning what constitutes a qualified jurist or a good interpretation of the Constitution are political questions. The Constitution does not itself specify how it ought to be interpreted. Neither does it provide criteria as to what kind of person should appropriately serve. The political circumstances surrounding a particular vacancy, moreover, perhaps raise further considerations regarding what would constitute an appropriate choice. Should there be an ideological balance on the court and, consequently, should the Senate demand that the replacement for a swing vote have similarly moderate ideological leanings? Does the Senate believe that a recent case was wrongly decided (for example, cases dealing with abortion or campaign finance), and that the constitutional questions surrounding the case should be reconsidered—and, moreover, that any potential jurist should answer questions about how they would rule if the constitutional question was to be revisited in a similar case? Senate confirmation hearings and floor debate, therefore, are essential mechanisms for both advancing congressional preferences on the choice as well as engaging the wide range of issues that would constitute a valid choice, especially given the contestability of political criteria in the first place.

This is an important point to dwell on, especially given the ways in which Senate confirmation hearings have largely been marked by the absence of substantive deliberation in recent years, perhaps most strikingly in the Congress's refusal to hold hearings at all for Merrick Garland—or to even meet with him. The Senate Republicans declared that they would not hold confirmation hearings and would not consider the nomination because it was an election year and, consequently, the American people should rightly decide who the next Supreme Court justice should be by choosing the next president, who would then make the nomination.[36] This, of course, presumes that the American people can be trusted to make such an important choice in an election—an election, moreover, in which who the next Supreme Court jurist should be is but one issue among many—absent substantive Senate deliberations on the matter. As Joseph Bessette argues, "We should not be surprised if instantaneous opinion bears little resemblance to what would result from serious reasoning on the merits."[37] Indeed, if a polling company were to conduct a poll at the outset of the nomination, it would likely find public opinion to be shallow and uninformed, as most citizens can hardly be expected to have thought much about it or to know the relevant criteria for making an informed judgment on the matter. And yet, the poll results are generally seen as indicative of public preferences. Therefore, the people's voice in an election can hardly be viewed as a referendum on a Supreme Court nomination if there is no deliberation fostered by the political institutions that are meant to channel and refine public opinion through their deliberations. Why have a Congress at all if technological advancements have made it possible to make decisions based on public opinion surveys that presidents can consult?

While the blocking of Garland's appointment was perhaps one of the most extreme examples of Congressional failure to substantively deliberate on the merits of particular jurists, such confirmation hearings, as Jeffrey K. Tulis argues, have long been marked by the absence of robust deliberation. Potential jurists refuse to answer substantive questions about their relevant constitutional views on a number of publicly salient issues even as the political issues animating support or disapproval of a nominee are evident to anyone who watches the events unfold.[38] The one exception in the modern era, Tulis observes, is the infamous Robert Bork confirmation hearing, which is today generally viewed as the type of political event to be avoided.[39] While the Senate deliberations regarding Bork certainly had their fair share of nastiness—indeed, the verb "to bork," meaning to systematically defame or vilify, was added to the lexicon—the Senate asked substantive questions of Bork, and he answered the questions with a high degree of candor. As Nina Totenberg commented at the time,

> The Committee's hearings on the nomination of Judge Robert Bork were, in my view, the first time the process worked properly. Leaving aside for the moment the question of outside influences, the Senate, for a change, gave itself enough time, and the senators prepared themselves. They asked probing but, for the most part, respectful and proper questions, and they knew enough to follow up and find out what the nominee really meant in his answers.[40]

Given the substantive nature of the Senate deliberations, the public was greatly informed, moreover, about the specific nature of Bork's views on a number of highly consequential issues, especially as senators pressed him to clarify his views during their questioning:

> The senators' questioning was effective not because Bork's position was right or wrong, but because the nominee was not permitted simply to make a broad motherhood-and-apple-pie statement embracing free speech. His restricted view of what speech is protected by the Constitution became clear. In other areas—privacy, gender discrimination, race discrimination—Bork was similarly pressed so that his views emerged with some clarity, not in broad generalizations, but tested against what he had said in the past.[41]

As the public became more informed over the course of the confirmation process, public opinion changed dramatically, as shown in a series of *Washington Post*-ABC News polls.[42] A month after Bork was nominated, but before the hearings, a poll found that only about 45 percent of respondents had heard of Bork, and of these, 45 percent supported, while 40 percent opposed the nomination.[43] Public support began to change during the hearings, however, as revealed by a poll taken directly before and after the hearings, in which 70 percent of respondents had heard of Bork, and of those, 44 percent supported his nomination, while 48 percent opposed.[44] Ten days after the Senate rejected Bork's nomination, public opinion had decisively moved against Bork. Indeed, 78 percent of respondents had heard of Bork, and of those, only 38 percent supported his nomination, while 52 percent opposed.[45] What should be clear from this evidence is that the substantive nature of the confirmation hearings greatly impacted public opinion, thus demonstrating the ways in which the Senate's deliberations are essential to constructing public opinion by bringing the publicly salient issues to the fore in robust debate.

While some deference might be accorded to the president for the appointment of executive branch nominees, this does not mean that Congress should fully defer to the president in the staffing of departments and agencies. Indeed, the executive branch is largely tasked with implementing laws passed by Congress, laws over which Congress has a legitimate stake in maintaining oversight. Insofar as the administration of government requires discretion and political and policy judgments, Congress certainly has a role in deliberating on whether a particular nominee is appropriate. Given the move toward administrative governance dominated by the executive branch, the appointments process is a crucial way in which Congress maintains a role in the programs and offices it creates. Moreover, Congress can affect the administration of the laws by changing laws, eliminating or diminishing the power of particular departments or agencies. These, however, are all *affirmative* actions determined by the deliberative will of a majority in Congress.

From this perspective, the branches do not share power over appointments primarily in terms of a checking function, or merely to maintain a legal balance of power. Rather, the legal assignments of power point to affirmative duties, the exercise of which is meant to ensure the selection of good nominees through interbranch deliberation—and even conflict—about the direction of the government and the administration of the laws, areas in which both branches have a legitimate stake. The branches both bring a variety of concerns to that process, and the political engagement between the branches is thus meant to foster deliberation about the ends of government, structured by the different perspectives and concerns of differently constituted institutions.

Legal Resolution and the Subversion of Politics

With this account of the purposes of the branches' shared power over appointments in view, it becomes possible to see how the judicial resolution of the recess appointments controversy undermined a dynamic political process between the branches because it missed, or at least obscured, the underlying nature of the dispute in the first place. While President Obama made recess appointments during a three-day weekend between two pro forma sessions of the Senate, these appointments were not made to bypass the majoritarian will of the Senate. On the contrary, President Obama made the recess appointments because the deliberative process itself had broken down due to hyperpartisan obstruction of the Senate by a minority faction. The president's actions, therefore, were a response to congressional abdication in the appointments process rather than a willful attempt to ignore the affirmative decisions of the Senate majority.[46]

By the time President Obama made the recess appointments at issue in *Noel Canning*, Senate Republicans, as the minority party in the Senate, had held up nearly two hundred agency nominations, nearly half (43 percent) of all of President Obama's civilian nominees.[47] For a striking contrast, during the last two years of President George W. Bush's term—when he faced a unified Democratic Congress—75 percent of his civilian nominees were still confirmed. Moreover, by mid to late 2009, during the midst of the financial crisis—and as crucial decisions needed to be made regarding the implementation of the Troubled Asset Relief Program—the Senate had failed to confirm key Treasury Department officials, as well as key officials in other economic and banking-related departments and agencies.[48] The result was that the president and his administration were hampered in their ability to implement the very laws that Congress had passed and tasked him to implement, and this during the midst of an economic crisis that called for decisive action.

The obstruction of executive nominees extended beyond mere delay. The Republican minority obstructed some nominees through the filibuster because they disagreed with the laws to be implemented, or disliked the departments or agencies that needed to be staffed. In fact, in some instances, Republicans vowed to block *any* nomination, no matter how distinguished or qualified the individual. One striking example of such obstruction by Senate Republicans—especially as it relates to the recess appointments at issue in *Noel Canning*—was the filibuster of Richard Cordray to head the CFPB. The CFPB was established by Congress in the Dodd–Frank Wall Street Reform and Consumer Financial Protection Act, passed by Congress and signed by President Obama in 2010. The Republicans, who opposed key provisions of the law (including the structure of the CFPB), vowed not to confirm a director until aspects of the law were changed. Hence, Republicans, even while praising Cordray's background, qualifications, and character, refused to consider his nomination, and blocked it by filibuster.[49] In other words, while Congress had only recently passed the law, Republicans, from their minority position in the Senate, made its implementation impossible. Such tactics extended to other offices as well, including a filibuster of Donald Berwick, whom President Obama later recess appointed, to run the Centers for Medicare and Medicaid Services, because Republicans opposed, and sought to obstruct, the implementation of the health care law.[50] President Obama's invalidated recess appointments to the NLRB, moreover, were meant to give the board a quorum—after months of filibusters and delays—so that it could actually adjudicate pending claims. Criticizing Republican obstruction, Senator Chuck E. Schumer (D-NY) said, "The Republicans' goal here is not simply to object to people who have views they think are out of the mainstream, but to shut down parts of the government they don't like."[51] Having lost the debate on the laws they opposed, Senate Republicans, from their minority position in the Senate, attempted to keep those laws from being implemented by obstructing nominations.

The president, therefore, was not prevented from making appointments because the nominees were opposed by the deliberative will of Congress. Rather, the president was prevented from making appointments because of partisan obstruction at an unprecedented level, using delay tactics such as holds and filibusters, tools whose constitutional status are highly questionable themselves.[52] Of course, delay in the service of enhanced deliberation can be a good thing. Indeed, *The Federalist* makes clear that one of the benefits of having a Senate constituted as a smaller body than the House of

Representatives, and with significantly longer terms of office, was to add a more stable and deliberative perspective on politics than the House, given the House's closer proximity to the people. A legislative chamber so constituted would thus be less likely to give into the passions of the people through quick and shortsighted decision-making.[53]

The filibuster is often celebrated in the context of the Senate's tradition of unlimited debate and thus characterized as a tool that enhances the deliberative qualities of the Senate.[54] However, the problem with the filibuster, as Josh Chafetz argues, is that in actual practice, the "filibuster is not about unlimited debate—indeed, it is not about debate at all. It is simply about permanent minority obstruction."[55] Moreover, the historical record does not provide support for the way the filibuster is used today. In early constitutional practice, delay in Senate voting was in the service of majoritarianism, not in opposition to that principle. For example, in 1790, the House of Representatives voted to move Congress to Philadelphia, but the Senate voted down the measure. Samuel Johnston was so sick he had to be brought in his bed to participate in the vote.[56] Taking advantage of bad weather, the House of Representatives took up the issue again. Given that Johnston was not able to be brought to the Senate chamber due to the rain, other senators who opposed the motion spoke until the Senate adjourned for the day, thus ensuring that the minority could not win by taking advantage of bad circumstances.[57] While filibusters were used frequently throughout the nineteenth century—championed especially by John C. Calhoun—they did not prevent the majority from enacting its agenda. Indeed, given the smaller legislative agenda at the time, the majority could simply wait out the minority. In fact, every bill filibustered before 1880 eventually passed.[58] As the congressional agenda increased, the Senate introduced cloture rules in 1917 so that filibusters would not derail the entire Senate agenda. During the twentieth century, the mechanism was most prominently (and infamously) used against civil rights legislation.

Today filibusters are not deliberative at all, because they merely force supporters to muster sixty votes to pass a piece of legislation—or to confirm a nominee. Moreover, given the two-track system the Senate has developed, once the intention to filibuster is announced, the issue is moved off the calendar until the majority can muster sixty votes, ensuring that filibusters do not prevent the Senate from moving on to other issues. As Chafetz argues, this "significantly decreases the costs of filibustering—no longer must a filibusterer justify his tying up the entire business of the Senate to his constituents or colleagues, and no longer must the filibusterer summon the physical endurance to hold the Senate floor."[59] In practice, the increased use of the filibuster now means that almost any controversial legislation or nomination requires a sixty-vote supermajority to pass and that a minority can continually prevent the majority's preferences from being enacted into law without having to make substantive justifications for the obstruction.[60]

Article I, section 5, clause 2 of the Constitution—as noted by the court in *Noel Canning*—grants each chamber of Congress the power "to Determine the Rules of its Proceedings." From a purely legal perspective, then, there is nothing unconstitutional about the filibuster. However, its widespread use, especially for nominations to staff the government, undermines the governmental efficiency for which the Articles of Confederation were abandoned in the first place.[61] Criticizing supermajoritarian rule under the Articles, Alexander Hamilton wrote in *Federalist* 22 that the result of such rules, rather than being beneficial to good government, is to "destroy the energy of the government, and to substitute the pleasure, caprice, or artifices of an intransigent, turbulent, or corrupt junto to the regular deliberations and decisions of a respectable majority."[62] The filibuster, as practiced today, solidifies the power of the minority, basically changing the Constitution such that those provisions that merely require majority votes in Congress now require supermajority votes in the Senate. As Chafetz argues, the problematic nature of the filibuster, in its current form, is perhaps made most clear by analogy. The Constitution also gives both chambers the power to "Judge . . . the Elections . . . of its own members."[63] There would thus seemingly be no constitutional problem with the Senate adopting a rule stating that any member of the Senate seeking reelection would be deemed the winner of the election unless the challenger received at least 60 percent of the vote.[64] Indeed, the Seventeenth Amendment only provides that "the Senate . . . shall be composed of two Senators from each State, elected by the people thereof," and that "the electors in each State shall have the qualifications requisite for electors of the most numerous branch of the State legislatures," but does not state that the candidate with the most votes wins. But, as Chafetz notes, such a rule could not be constitutional because it would entrench officeholders and make it harder for the people to hold their government accountable: "Any use of the Senate's power under the Rules of Proceedings Clause that frustrates this principle must be unconstitutional."[65] No doubt, such a rule would be widely viewed as constitutionally inappropriate if a chamber of Congress were to adopt it, and this is true regardless of whether such a rule could be found unconstitutional by the judiciary. The way the filibuster works today entrenches the preferences of past majorities in the same manner as does the hypothetical presented earlier for legislators, making it difficult for new majorities to change governmental policy.[66]

Of course, the Senate is not meant to be a rubber stamp for the president's agenda, and, as noted earlier, there might be legitimate ways in which Congress opposes the president and his agenda. For example, the Senate can vote down individual nominees and force the president to submit a new nominee more favorable to the Senate. The Senate can also abolish departments or agencies, or diminish their influence within the federal government. The problem, however, with the appointments process as it has played out in recent years, though especially during the Obama administration, is the wholesale obstruction of the administration by a minority faction within the Senate rather than affirmative actions on behalf of the Senate majority after a deliberative process. Without affirmative choices made by the Congress, the president is left to administer a government without key subordinates. Congressional use of the filibuster to engage in wholesale obstruction of the will of the majority poses major constitutional problems even though there is no legal or judicial solution to it. The fact that constitutional norms are underenforced, however, does not mean that there is not a way to evaluate or to think constitutionally about such norms. As Paul Brest argues, the fact that the judiciary is deferential in such contexts does not "suggest that the legislature should exercise restraint in assessing the constitutionality of its own product."[67] What should be clear from the present discussion is the extent to which the filibuster as practiced today in no way advances constitutional aims, merely grinding the government to a halt without substantive engagement with the issues at stake.

In light of this breakdown of the appointments process due to partisan obstruction in the Senate, President Obama had a legitimate constitutional claim to make recess appointments in his attempt to fulfill his constitutional task to take care that the laws be faithfully executed. While the framers imagined instances wherein the Senate would be out of session due to the technological difficulties of travel and communication during the eighteenth and nineteenth centuries, the larger purpose of the clause—its animating principle—is the continuation of government absent congressional choice to the contrary. In other words, the president's job is to faithfully execute laws passed by Congress, and he requires subordinates to help him in this administrative function. Given this larger purpose, the president had a legitimate claim that his recess appointments were appropriate given that the deliberative process in the Senate had broken down due to the obstructionist tactics of a Senate minority, those tactics made possible by recourse to a Senate procedural rule that is constitutionally suspect. President Obama made precisely this type of argument in his "We Can't Wait" campaign.[68] As he argued in a statement upon recess appointing Richard Cordray to head the CFPB,

> The Constitution gives the President the authority to make temporary recess appointments to fill vacant positions when the Senate is in recess, a power all recent Presidents have exercised. The Senate has effectively been in recess for weeks, and is expected to remain in recess for weeks. In an overt attempt to prevent the President from exercising his authority during this period, Republican Senators insisted on using a gimmick called "pro forma" sessions, which are sessions during which no Senate business is conducted and instead one or two Senators simply gavel in and out of session in a matter of seconds. But gimmicks do not override the President's constitutional authority to make appointments to keep the government running. Legal experts agree. In fact, the lawyers who advised President Bush on recess appointments wrote that the Senate cannot use sham "pro forma" sessions to prevent the President from exercising a constitutional power.[69]

The president, therefore, was using his recess appointments power in order to keep the government functioning based on the choices a majority in Congress had already made, and in light of what the majority in the Senate would likely have approved absent such obstruction. While it is true that this is not a use of recess appointments imagined by the framers, neither did the framers intend a Senate so thoroughly enervated by hyperpartisanship that it was unable to function. The president was simply making temporary appointments to achieve the overarching purpose of the clause.

Ultimately, only political contestation between the branches could have settled these competing claims. Political contestation wherein the branches could justify their behavior to each other in front of the electorate—rather than legal determinacy—would perhaps structure a more robust deliberative space in which the political branches could have worked out the merits of differing constitutional and policy positions, a process that was abruptly ended by the court's intervention into the process. Leaving such a dispute to politics, moreover, would not necessarily give the president a free hand. Rather, the president ultimately has to make legitimate constitutional claims about the need for recess appointments given the relevant circumstances. Congress, of course, has political tools to combat the president's use of recess appointments should those appointments actually undermine the will of the deliberative majority of the Senate. Congress can censure the president, cut off funding for the offices in question, and even impeach a president who continues to defy the will of Congress.

In fact, it is not difficult to imagine different scenarios in which the Congress would strongly oppose and resist recess appointments. For example, there was some speculation that President Trump wanted to fire Attorney General Jeff Sessions so that he could appoint a new attorney general who could then fire Independent Counsel Robert Mueller, who was investigating potential collusion between Russia and the Trump campaign during the 2016 election, as well as potential obstruction of justice by President Trump for firing FBI Director James Comey after Comey allegedly refused to end the investigation. Senators from both parties made clear that they would oppose such a move and that there was no room in the Senate calendar to consider a replacement for Sessions should the president fire him.[70] Senator Lindsey Graham (R-SC) went so far as to say that "if Jeff Sessions is fired there will be holy hell to pay."[71] The Senate then held pro forma sessions to prevent President Trump from making such a move. Given the political circumstances surrounding President Trump and the Russia investigation, it is hard to imagine Congress allowing such an appointment to go unanswered. The difference between the two scenarios is clear: President Obama made recess appointments in order to fulfill his constitutional duty to enforce and administer the duly passed laws of the United States, whereas President Trump's hypothetical recess appointment would have been an attempt to obstruct an ongoing investigation.

On the other hand, the legal resolution in *Noel Canning* sanctioned the partisan obstruction of the appointments process by placing great emphasis on the Senate's ability to determine its own rules. This legitimation, therefore, gave the Senate a free hand to act however it pleases while providing the president little recourse to make valid constitutional claims regarding the staffing of the executive branch in the face of obstruction by a Senate minority. Hence, the legal resolution of the issue disguised—even subverted—the political dynamics at play. Perversely, the president's attempt to fulfill his constitutional duties was rendered an example of the imperial presidency while congressional abdication of its own prerogatives was elevated by the pretense of law.

Conclusion

The recess appointments controversy illuminates how certain understandings of the Constitution can undermine it in the long term. The court's policing of the Constitution's formal boundaries certainly seems like a good approach because it ostensibly removes the messiness of politics from constitutional practice. The problem with this approach is that the legal line drawing does not remove politics from interbranch disputes. On the contrary, legal resolution pathologizes politics, subordinating other constitutional goods for the sake of legal certainty.

In the case at hand, the court's protection of the Senate's power to advise and consent missed the fact that the deliberative process in the Senate had broken down due to partisan obstruction by a minority faction. The court's line drawing thus prevented the president from making a constitutional case that, absent the deliberative and majoritarian will of the Senate to the contrary, the government needed to continue running. Hence, a minority faction did not have to justify its own behavior because it hid behind the letter of the law. Political contestation between the branches, wherein each of the branches would be forced to make constitutional claims and justify their behavior to each other, would reopen a deliberative space that was foreclosed by the court's intervention into the matter. The court thus legitimized the partisan obstruction of the Senate's prerogatives while preventing the president from ensuring the faithful execution of the laws. The legal parsing of the text to find the literal meaning of the recess appointments clause, therefore, missed the underlying nature of the dispute and prevented the branches from engaging with each other politically.

This is not to say that a political understanding of the Constitution's separation of powers would solve the political problem of hyperpartisanship or would make politics less messy. But such an approach at least has the benefit of not doubling down on the pathologies associated with hyperpartisanship, especially in the Congress where members seem particularly unwedded to the outlook and prerogatives of their own institution. The burden of politics, at the very least, requires political actors to make actual arguments unobscured by the pretense of law. The problem with considering the Constitution solely on a legal dimension, therefore, is that it flattens the relevant criteria for constitutional evaluation, considering neither the constitutional ends nor how the Constitution establishes differing institutional structures to achieve those ends through conflict within and between competing institutions. In short, an overly legalized conception of separation of powers allows a letter-of-the-law reading of the Constitution to undermine the practice of constitutionalism.

5

Congressional Oversight and Impeachment

Presidential impeachment was once a rare phenomenon. Prior to the twenty-first century, only Presidents Andrew Johnson and Bill Clinton were impeached, and neither was convicted. As a result of the Watergate scandal, President Nixon resigned from office prior to his impending impeachment and certain Senate conviction. During the last two years of President Donald Trump's administration, however, the number of impeachments in American history doubled as he became the first president to be impeached twice.

President Trump was impeached for the first time in December 2019 for allegedly threatening to withhold foreign assistance to Ukraine unless the Ukrainian government agreed to open a corruption investigation into Hunter Biden, son of the then-frontrunner for the Democratic presidential nomination. The assistance was delivered to Ukraine after a whistleblower complaint. Congressional Democrats argued that President Trump's alleged quid pro quo arrangement was an attempt to seek foreign interference in the 2020 presidential election in order to discredit a likely rival.[1] While under ordinary circumstances this would have been deeply inappropriate, the allegations were even more serious given Russian interference in the 2016 election and serious concerns that the Trump campaign had been involved in some way in those efforts. While the Democratic Party was initially reluctant to pursue impeachment over Russian election interference, the Ukraine scandal seemed to provide a clear-cut, and easily provable, case of impeachable conduct. The House of Representatives also passed a second article of impeachment for obstruction of Congress. In an unprecedented act of executive defiance of Congress's oversight authority, President Trump's White House counsel, Pat Cipollone, sent a letter to House Speaker Nancy Pelosi, declaring that the administration would not cooperate with an impeachment inquiry that it regarded as "illegitimate" and constitutionally invalid."[2] The

White House thus refused to supply any witnesses or documents. Trump was acquitted in the Senate almost exclusively along party lines, falling short of the two-thirds threshold required for conviction. Only Republican Senator Mitt Romney crossed the aisle with his vote to convict President Trump on the first impeachment article. In acquitting President Trump, Republicans embraced a construction of the impeachment power that limited it to violations of statutory law, which they claimed the alleged quid pro quo was not. As for the second impeachment article, Republicans argued that the president could not be convicted for obstruction given that the House had not gone to court to enforce its subpoenas (even though long-standing Justice Department policy held that such subpoena disputes pose nonjusticiable political questions). Congress's failure to seek judicial enforcement of its subpoenas, according to Trump's Republican defenders, meant that impeachment for obstruction was premature.

Trump was impeached for a second time in response to his conduct following the 2020 presidential election. The January 6, 2021, breach of the Capitol building by a mob intent on disrupting the electoral vote count followed weeks of allegations by Trump that the election had been stolen from him. The president's conduct before, during, and after the attempted insurrection led lawmakers in the House to introduce and quickly pass a single article of impeachment charging incitement of insurrection. While the Senate vote garnered far more Republican support for conviction than in the first impeachment trial, Trump was again acquitted. While not absolving President Trump of responsibility for his conduct, Republicans embraced the view that he was not eligible for conviction because the Senate trial occurred after he left office. Despite the Senate's purported lack of power to convict Trump, Republicans—most notably Senator Mitch McConnell—argued that Trump should be held accountable for any criminal actions taken while in office. They argued that the proper remedy for such abuses of power resides in the criminal justice system rather than the Senate.

After President Trump's second acquittal, he became the Republican nominee for president while also coming under federal criminal indictment for taking and refusing to return classified documents and for his conduct in the events of the January 6 insurrection. These federal indictments were accompanied by thirty-four felony convictions in New York for allegedly paying hush money to a porn star in advance of the 2016 election, as well as indictments in Georgia for his attempt to overturn the election results in that state. These actions fueled Republican allegations that Democrats had weaponized the justice system to prevent President Trump's reelection. Despite all this, he won reelection in November 2024.

This brief recapitulation of events provides the context for this final case study chapter, which analyzes some of the enduring constitutional questions concerning the extent of Congress's oversight powers in light of the Trump impeachment controversies and their aftermath. While the Trump controversies provide essential context to the questions examined here, the chapter is not about Trump per se. Rather, the impeachments, acquittals, and subsequent criminal indictments of Trump raise fundamental questions about the proper functioning of the separation of powers system. In particular, I focus on three problems of congressional oversight and the ways in which legalistic understandings and practice undermine a healthy and robust interbranch politics. First, how should the branches resolve informational disputes? This is a difficult problem because of the potential for conflict between two constitutionally implied powers: the president's implied power of executive privilege and Congress's implied power of legislative oversight. These implied powers, however, can be hardened into legalistic conceptions that deny the constitutional prerogatives of the other branch and thus disrupt or forestall productive political negotiation and argumentation. In recent years, the political branches have increasingly turned to the judiciary to resolve such informational disputes. This turn to the courts, however, poses both practical and theoretical problems. Such disputes should be left to Congress and the president to work out, making arguments in politics about the need to have or withhold certain information. The Constitution provides Congress with tools, including impeachment, to give leverage when negotiating with a noncompliant president in oversight disputes.

The need for a viable impeachment power raises the second question of this chapter: What should be considered a high crime and misdemeanor for the purposes of impeachment? There is significant scholarly evidence that political misconduct and abuse of power can rise to the level of high crimes and misdemeanors and that impeachable conduct need not be confined to strictly legal violations. However, both historical and contemporary practice complicate, if not outright contradict, this theoretical consensus. This chapter outlines why a viable and politically capacious impeachment power is necessary for the proper functioning of the separation of powers and evaluates contemporary political practice accordingly. The legalistic and narrow construction of impeachment was fully on display in Republicans' embrace of the view that impeachable offenses require indictable crimes. While Democrats rejected this view, in theory, the main impeachment article passed by the House was narrowly legalistic, focusing exclusively on the purported quid pro quo, thus undercutting a larger political case against

President Trump for his general approach to the office, of which the quid pro quo was but an example.

Finally, this chapter highlights the need for a robust impeachment power by examining the challenges of using the criminal justice system against a former president. To be clear, the argument here is not that criminal indictments should not be pursued if a president violates the law, especially as brazenly as President Trump. Rather, the political dangers of indicting a former president further demonstrate the need for impeachment as the appropriate constitutional remedy for presidential abuse of power. In fact, the political problems of prosecuting a former president largely disappear if Congress exercises its own oversight powers because an impeachment conviction bars a president from running for federal office. Senate Republicans, therefore, were derelict in their duty when they argued that President Trump bore responsibility for the events of January 6, but that the criminal justice system, rather than Congress, was the proper venue for holding him to account. This fact is amplified by the fact that Donald Trump is, as of this writing, once again president even after the grave political crimes he committed against the state.

In the larger context of this book's core arguments, this case study on congressional oversight is especially important given the outsize role of the president in contemporary politics. While the presidency looms large in modern politics, the growth of presidential power is accounted for by the institutional and structural qualities of the executive branch. The development of the modern presidency, in other words, is prefigured in the founding design.[3] As the needs of the nation expand, presidential power grows to meet the needs of the contemporary world. The unity and independence of the executive branch, which induce the quality of energy, makes it more likely that the nation can meet the challenges of unforeseen exigencies. As argued at the outset, sometimes this requires the president to operate outside the confines of existing law, or even against the strict letter of the law. Such actions, akin to Lockean prerogative, require constitutional justifications that by their nature are both contextual and prudential, and, therefore, open to argument and contestation. This is a fundamental feature of a political system designed to be responsive to the demands of unforeseen problems. The separation of powers is thus the means to ends that can never be known in advance given that uncertainty is endemic to political life.

Even so, Congress's own institutional powers and capacities empower it to oversee and contest executive uses (or abuses) of power. Congress can use its power of the purse to withhold funding for programs that are implemented in ways that contradict congressional intent, or it can hold up key nominations until the president capitulates to congressional demands. To do any of these things, however, Congress needs information about the executive branch decisions or actions it wishes to regulate. Ultimately, Congress can use its power of oversight and impeachment, giving it the power of the final say in political contestations. The viable threat of impeachment is essential to give teeth to Congress's other powers. As will be evident in the three issue areas discussed in this chapter, contemporary practice and narrowly legalistic understandings of Congress's power significantly hobble it in its dealings with the executive branch, undermining the proper working of the Constitution's institutional architecture.

Informational Disputes

How should informational disputes between Congress and the president be resolved? This is a fundamental and enduring question, especially insofar as each branch potentially has legitimate needs for information both in order to fulfill its particular institutional functions and to serve the overarching needs of the polity.[4] The problem in contemporary practice is that the powers of the branches to obtain or to withhold information have hardened into legal or doctrinal conceptions of the branches' powers that deny the constitutional status and prerogatives of the other branch, and thus make information disputes nearly intractable. Such doctrinal understandings, especially as promoted by the White House Office of Legal Counsel (OLC), have developed in the shadow of the Supreme Court's limited rulings on executive privilege, rulings that while limited in scope have shaped the ways in which such disputes are understood and thus resolved.[5] This section discusses the implied powers of each of the branches: the power of Congress to obtain information to help it legislate and hold presidents accountable for abuse of power, and the power of the president to withhold information when its disclosure could damage the national interest, especially in terms of national security.

What should be clear in the following is the political valence of information disputes insofar as each branch potentially has valid claims to the need for information or secrecy. Far from representing a problem for the constitutional order, interbranch clashes over information are indicative of the ways in which the Constitution establishes countervailing structures and powers to determine the respective needs of a political community in any particular circumstance. Indeed, the polity both aspires to have democratic responsiveness and accountability (and so Congress needs the requisite information to legislate well) and the need to ensure the security and stability of the nation (which sometimes entails the need for executive branch secrecy). There is no legal principle that can be invoked in advance of any particular dispute given that the appropriate settlement in any one case is both contextual and requires prudential judgment.

Since Watergate, the political branches have increasingly turned to the courts to resolve such disputes. The judiciary, however, is ill-equipped to resolve them for both theoretical and practical reasons. This became a central point of contention during the first impeachment of President Trump. The second impeachment article in 2019 referred to Trump's total and unprecedented obstruction of Congress. For his part, President Trump and his defenders argued that he could not be impeached for obstruction of Congress given that the House had not gone to court to enforce its subpoenas, even as the Justice Department argued in related court proceedings that congressional subpoenas should be considered nonjusticiable political questions best left to resolution in the political sphere.

THE IMPLIED POWER OF CONGRESSIONAL OVERSIGHT

Article I of the Constitution grants Congress legislative power and lists the areas in which it may legislate, qualifying its specifically enumerated legislative powers with the provision that it also has all powers necessary and proper to effectuate its constitutional grants of authority. The Constitution does not explicitly grant Congress oversight or investigative powers. Even so, such powers have long been understood to be necessary concomitants to its legislative powers. As Josh Chafetz writes, "Gathering information is not a peripheral part of Congress's job; it is central to the legislature's identity and function."[6] Indeed, Congress needs information to accurately understand the complexities and nuances of the problems the nation faces so that it can appropriately tailor and enact legislation in response. It requires information in order to vet nominees appointed by the president to staff the departments and agencies created and funded by Congress. It requires information to ensure that departments and agencies implement legislative programs in accordance with congressional views, and to ensure the public monies are spent appropriately. It requires information so that it can make modifications to existing policy and appropriations over time as conditions change. Congress needs information about foreign affairs if the Senate is to exercise its power to advise and consent to treaties. And finally, in this non-exhaustive list, Congress needs information to ensure executive fidelity to the rule of law if it is to appropriately wield its sole power of impeachment.

A Congress that exercises its investigative powers well can have enormous benefits for the country. For example, during World War II, Senator Harry S. Truman led the bipartisan Special Committee to Investigate the National Defense Program (also known as the Truman Committee). Through its efforts, and spending less than one million dollars on its investigations, the Truman Committee is estimated to have saved the government $10–15 billion and saved the lives of US military personnel by uncovering defective equipment and materials.[7] This is rightly regarded as an instance where the US government worked exceedingly well.

The Supreme Court has consistently construed Congress's investigative powers broadly, stating in *Quinn v. United States* (1955) that its power to investigate is "coextensive with its power to legislate."[8] Indeed, as the court put in an earlier case, "a legislative body cannot legislate wisely or effectively in the absence of information respecting the conditions which the legislation is intended to affect or change; and where the legislative body does not itself possess the requisite information—which not infrequently is true—recourse must be had to others who do possess it."[9] This need for information has only grown as the needs of the nation have expanded during the past century. As discussed in other chapters, the growth of the national government has meant that Congress often must delegate legislative power to expert departments and agencies if the government is to accomplish the wide range of tasks deemed essential to modern government. Congress's expanded oversight and investigative functions, in light of delegation, ensure democratic accountability as contemporary governmental tasks have become centralized in the administrative state. As Keith Whittington notes, the expanded retrospective powers of the legislature were anticipated by liberal reformers in the nineteenth century.[10] John Stuart Mill, for example, argued that the investigative power would become the central function of legislatures as the complexity of modern life made proactive and nuanced legislation more difficult—the reason for expansive delegation in the first place. As Mill wrote,

> The proper office of a representative assembly is to watch and control the government: to throw the light of publicity on its acts; to compel a full exposition and justification of all of them which any one considers questionable; to censure them if found condemnable, and, if the men who compose the government abuse their trust, or fulfill it in a manner which conflicts with the deliberate sense of the nation, to expel them from office, and either expressly or virtually appoint their successors.

> This is surely ample power, and security enough for the liberty of the nation.[11]

Given that Congress requires information to effectively govern and effectuate its constitutional powers, it has long exercised the power to compel testimony and documents through its power to issue and enforce subpoenas, and to punish those who refused to comply with contempt. This power, as scholars such as James M. Landis, C. S. Potts, and Josh Chafetz have shown in painstaking detail, has historical roots in parliamentary practice in England dating back hundreds of years.[12] Colonial legislatures early on assumed the power to investigate and exercised the power to send for "persons, papers, and records."[13] Moreover, as states wrote new constitutions during the revolutionary period, many explicitly granted their legislatures contempt powers, and other state legislatures exercised such powers even in the absence of an explicit grant, recognizing the contempt power as an inherent power of the institution, derivative, in many cases, of the power to determine the rules of their own proceedings.[14] Beginning as early as its first session, Congress understood broadly its power to investigate and compel testimony, including from the executive branch. In 1792 the House voted to inquire into a specific military dispute. Rather than request that the president conduct an inquiry, members of Congress thought it was most appropriate to conduct the investigation themselves and voted forty-four to ten to create their own investigative committee.[15] James Madison, along with four other members of the Constitutional Convention then in Congress, voted in favor of the inquiry, a fact the Supreme Court later noted when sustaining Congress's broad investigative powers.[16]

Exercising its inherent contempt power, Congress can send its sergeant at arms to arrest those held in contempt and hold them until the end of the congressional term or until they comply, a power that has been sustained by the Supreme Court as essential to its investigative functions. While Congress has rarely exercised this power, choosing instead to pass a statute in 1857 criminalizing contempt and turning the matter over to the Justice Department to prosecute, this turn to criminal prosecution was meant to alleviate Congress's workload rather than to supplant the power of inherent contempt and to replace Congress's own enforcement powers.[17] This is especially true since the Justice Department is unlikely to prosecute a member of the executive branch in an interbranch dispute. In any event, Congress's ability to arrest those held in contempt is essential to reinforcing its ability to attain information to aid it in its governing tasks.

As should be evident from the preceding, it is generally uncontested that Congress requires information for the performance of its constitutional functions. The problem lies with those who would harden this congressional prerogative into a claim of congressional supremacy that would make the executive branch's withholding of information to Congress—what is referred to as executive privilege—constitutionally unjustifiable in *any* circumstance.[18] In this view, the executive branch is merely the clerk of Congress and thus fully subordinate to it. Raoul Berger is perhaps the most prominent advocate of this position, though his notion of congressional supremacy has contemporary adherents. In his magisterial treatment of the subject, he referred to "executive privilege" as a "constitutional myth."[19] For Berger, the constitutional framers were fearful of a powerful executive branch given their experience of royal power, and thus created an executive branch that was subordinate to Congress. As Berger writes, "The framers did not endow the President with more power than the King had, but with less; they removed notable powers formerly exercised under the Crown prerogative and lodged them in Congress, not the President."[20] Berger emphasizes Madison's statement in *Federalist* 51 that "in a republican form of government, the legislature necessarily predominates" as indicative of the fact that Congress "was to be the senior partner, from which it follows, no junior could conceal the state of the Union."[21] Indeed, Berger characterizes Madison's statement in *Federalist* 51 as "both an explanation and justification of the disproportionate distribution made by the Constitution between the legislative and executive branches."[22] "A close look at the Founders' conception of the executive power will disclose its meager scope," Berger writes, highlighting Roger Sherman's view of the presidency as "nothing more than an institution for carrying the will of the Legislature into effect."[23]

Berger's account of executive privilege has been disputed by a number of scholars.[24] However, the notion of congressional supremacy, which serves as the foundation of his concomitant rejection of executive privilege, has many contemporary advocates.[25] In their view, the Constitution establishes a republican form of government in which the legislative power predominates. The framers' desire to establish such a republican form of government, coupled with their deep-seated fear of tyrannical executive power, led them to subordinate the executive branch to Congress in all respects. Therefore, it is constitutionally inappropriate for the executive branch to ever withhold information from Congress. Yet, this notion of congressional supremacy misunderstands the nature of the American constitutional order, from which an implied power to executive branch secrecy in specific circumstances can be justified. Like Congress's implied power to investigate and compel information, the implied power of executive privilege can also be hardened in ways that undercut Congress's constitutional prerogatives by misconceiving executive privilege in doctrinal terms.

THE IMPLIED POWER OF EXECUTIVE SECRECY

Little explication at this point is necessary to demonstrate how a notion of congressional supremacy in the constitutional order that negates *any* assertion of executive privilege is inconsistent with the constitutional design. For starters, such an account is historically inaccurate. One of the great triumphs of the constitutional convention was the creation of a strong and vigorous executive branch, especially after the failures of the Articles of Confederation to provide for good and effective governance.[26] The independence of the executive from Congress, and its unitary nature, were deemed necessary for securing essential qualities of good government: energy, secrecy, and dispatch, as Hamilton noted in *Federalist* 70.

It is also worth noting Berger's misleading quotation of Madison when he writes in *Federalist* 51 that the "legislative power necessarily predominates."[27] Rather than making a normative statement about the superiority of legislative power, Madison is concerned with ensuring that the interior design of the government keeps the branches within their constitutional limits. He argues that the legislative power, given its proximity to the people, tends to be the most powerful branch in republican systems, "drawing all power into its impetuous vortex," as he writes in *Federalist* 48.[28] Therefore, he argues in *Federalist* 51 that since the legislative power necessarily predominates, the legislature needs internal checks, such as bicameralism, so that it does not overpower and thus undermine the constitutional system. The purpose of the constitutional design, in other words, was not to make Congress preeminent but to ensure that the branches would each be able to perform their functions in pursuit of essential constitutional ends, ends that are themselves in tension. The creation of a powerful executive branch, and the tempering of overwhelming legislative power, was necessary to achieve these aims.

Even so, Berger and others are correct to note the importance of majoritarian will and the protection of rights for republican government generally. However, it is philosophically inaccurate to understand majoritarian will and rights protection as the supreme values of American constitutionalism that must be safeguarded against executive abuse of power. Rather, majoritarian will and the protection of rights are constitutional goods held in tension both with each other and with other goals of the polity, such as security and regime preservation. A polity that cannot protect itself from external and internal threats, even if it has a legislature fully committed to its majoritarian function, is destined to fail. It is for this reason, as already alluded to in previous chapters, that Hamilton notes at the very outset of *Federalist* 70 that there are some who think that "vigorous executive power is inconsistent with the genius of republican government." Rather than resolve that tension, he writes that the "enlightened well-wishers to this species of government must at least hope that the supposition is destitute of foundation; since they can never admit its truth, without at the same time admitting the condemnation of their own principles."[29] In other words, republican government cannot survive without a vigorous executive.

From this general picture of separation of powers, it is possible to derive the need for governmental secrecy in particular circumstances for specific reasons. This is perhaps most clear in the area of national security, wherein the executive branch might want to keep specific military plans secret, protect vital intelligence sources, or delicately handle ongoing diplomatic negotiations, among countless other possible examples. As David Crockett writes, "There have been any number of specific examples in American history, and certainly the rapidity and lethality of modern warfare make the wise employment of secrecy and speed that much more imperative."[30] The president might also have potential claims to secrecy regarding internal deliberations so that he can enjoy the candid and frank advice of subordinates. Generally speaking, the publicity of internal discussions might undermine the president's ability to receive honest counsel. In this regard, Crockett continues, echoing Hamilton, secrecy aids the executive branch in the performance of its unique governmental tasks in ways that would not make sense in a legislative branch given the centrality of public deliberation in the enactment of laws. Claims to secrecy are thus context-dependent. While they might have particular force in the national security realm, they are hardly categorical. Claims to secrecy and privilege have perhaps less weight in other circumstances, such as in the implementation of legislative schemes, wherein Congress has a particular interest in ensuring that the execution of the law accords with congressional intent. In short, the need for secrecy in the executive branch in the performance of its constitutional functions juxtaposed against the need for information by Congress and the courts in the performance of theirs reflects an inherent tension of constitutional needs.

The Supreme Court recognized these constitutional tensions in *United States v. Nixon* (1974) when it gave its imprimatur to the notion of executive privilege even as it denied President Nixon's claim to an "absolute, unqualified presidential privilege of immunity from judicial process under all circumstances." The court acknowledged that executive privilege is essential for the president to rely on "complete candor and objectivity from advisors" and that this generally calls for "great deference" from the courts. However, the court asserted that "when the privilege depends solely on the broad, undifferentiated claim of public interest in the confidentiality of such conversations, a confrontation with other values arises." The court thus distinguished a broad and general interest from one in which the president sought to "protect military, diplomatic, or sensitive national security secrets."[31] Given that President Nixon's purported need to withhold information did not include a national security justification, the court weighed the competing institutional prerogatives between the judiciary and the president, finding that "the allowance of the privilege to withhold evidence that is demonstrably relevant in a criminal trial would cut deeply into the guarantee of due process of law and gravely impair the basic function of the courts."[32] In short, the court recognized that the national interest might require secrecy and thus the withholding of information. The extent to which secrecy would be allowed, however, turned on the nature of the specific claim made in the instant case. It is worth noting at this point that the *Nixon* case concerned an interbranch dispute between the president and the judiciary, justifying judicial involvement in a way that is not warranted in similar disputes between Congress and the president.

Space does not permit a detailed examination of historical examples of executive privilege and how such claims were resolved. Such examinations have been explored in detail elsewhere.[33] The purpose here is to show how this implied power to secrecy has been hardened into a legalistic doctrine that is inconsistent with the constitutional design. As the executive branch has developed doctrinal notions of executive privilege in the shadow of the judiciary's limited rulings on the subject, executive privilege has been transformed from the power to withhold specific information in certain contexts for justifiable reasons to a categorical power of the executive branch that itself must be protected.[34] Jonathan Shaub artfully refers to this development as "prophylactic" executive privilege.[35] As the practice of executive privilege has grown, according to Shaub, "it has transformed into an absolute, multifaceted, affirmative presidential authority to control the dissemination of a broad swath of information and to issue directives about the dissemination of that information."[36] This hardened, doctrinal notion of privilege has thus rendered Congress "virtually impotent" to compel disclosure of information.[37]

This hardened conception of executive privilege is largely the product of the executive branch OLC, given the paucity of judicial precedents in this area. Even so, the judiciary's limited forays have not been inconsequential insofar as its decisions have provided rhetorical tools for ever-expanding executive branch conceptions of its own power.[38] Returning to *Nixon*, it is worth noting that the Supreme Court's judgment in that case, in terms of larger interbranch relations, was actually quite narrow insofar as it was limited to a dispute between the president and the judiciary. The question before the court was whether the president had a compelling claim to withhold the tapes from a grand jury proceeding in a criminal case. The court weighed the competing institutional needs between itself and the president, recognizing the potential validity of executive privilege claims while finding Nixon's arguments unpersuasive in that case. Even so, the court gave rhetorical power to future presidents by acknowledging the existence of executive privilege and noting that such claims are "presumptively valid" and deserving of even greater deference in the area of national security. The court also gave its imprimatur to the candor rationale. As Kitrosser notes, pointing to an episode during the Obama administration, the candor rationale is "intrinsically expansive."[39] For example, after a social media star gained entrance to a White House state dinner without an invitation, the administration prevented the White House's social secretary from testifying before Congress, "based on the separation of powers," and the need for "the White House staff to provide advice to the president confidentially."[40]

It is certainly appropriate for the judiciary to protect its own processes as it did in *Nixon*. The judiciary, however, has been far less supportive of congressional claims to information than it has been to itself. For example, two months before *Nixon*, a federal appeals court denied the Senate Select Committee on Presidential Campaign Activities access to the same tapes at issue in *Nixon*.[41] In that case, the appellate court unanimously ruled that the congressional subpoena should only be enforced if the evidence were "demonstrably critical to the responsible fulfillment of the Committee's functions" and that Congress did not have a sufficient need for the tapes.[42] In doing so, the appeals court disparaged the political nature of Congress compared to the judiciary's impartiality. As Judge David Bazelon wrote for a unanimous court, "While fact-finding by a legislative committee is undeniably a part of its task, legislative judgments normally depend more on the predicted consequences of proposed legislative actions and their political acceptability, than on precise reconstruction of past events."[43] Unlike in a grand jury, which needs "precise evidence," there was "no comparable need in the legislative process."[44] This, of course, was an absurd contention given the central role the Senate Select Committee played in uncovering the existence of the tapes in the first place, breaking the Watergate Scandal wide into the open. As Josh Chafetz writes,

> The combination of the Supreme Court's decision in the trial subpoena case and the lower courts' decisions in the Senate Committee case make a clear statement about the courts' view of whether Congress or the judiciary was best equipped to oversee a lawless president. Unsurprisingly, the judges thought that courts were the right institution for the job, and they used rhetoric that not only elevated their own branch, but also simultaneously belittled its rival for the role.[45]

The "demonstrably critical" test established by the appeals court sets an onerous standard for Congress to meet in disputes with the executive branch.[46] The executive branch has thus deployed this standard to deny information to Congress in a wide range of settings, and, in fact, it views it as the only applicable balancing test in informational disputes.[47]

The roots of what Shaub terms "prophylactic" privilege can be traced to the Supreme Court's 2004 ruling in *Cheney v. United States*. In that case, the court found that Vice President Cheney did not need to formally invoke executive privilege or comb through information to determine areas in which he would make specific objections. Rather, he could object to the entire discovery process as burdening the executive branch by forcing it to specifically invoke executive privilege. As the ruling put it, "Contrary to the District Court's and the Court of Appeals' conclusions, *Nixon* does not leave them the sole option of inviting the Executive Branch to invoke executive privilege while remaining otherwise powerless to modify a party's overly broad discovery requests. Executive privilege is an extraordinary assertion of power 'not to be lightly invoked.'"[48] The court thus purported to protect the executive branch from "vexatious litigation that might distract it from the energetic performance of its constitutional duties."[49] While this ruling was construed narrowly in *House Judiciary Committee v. Miers* (2008) to not encompass an absolute testimonial immunity for high-level advisors, Kitrosser notes that *Cheney* offers a "tantalizing tool" to administrations that seek to gain "executive privilege's benefits without incurring the potential political, legal, or practical hassles of actually invoking it."[50]

While the judiciary's rulings on executive privilege have been rare, they have provided tools for the development of a legalistic doctrine of executive privilege within the executive branch that it has deployed to the detriment of Congress's ability to attain information. The judiciary's precedents, along with the OLC's expansive interpretation of political branch precedents, have led to an expansive, even comprehensive, conception of its privilege powers. Shaub's characterization of this phenomenon is worth quoting at length:

> What was formerly a doctrine about the president's authority to prevent the disclosure of specific pieces of information has become a doctrine almost entirely about prophylaxis. The new prophylactic executive privilege prohibits, as a constitutional matter, the release of any information potentially covered by the executive branch's view of executive privilege. And the executive branch has added an additional layer of protection for the prophylaxis itself, concluding that the privilege prohibits not just disclosure itself but also any burden on the executive branch's authority to monitor the release of such information. Accordingly, executive branch officials claim the authority to direct all current and former employees and officials not to disclose any information in response to a congressional subpoena and, in some circumstances, to refuse to appear altogether in response to a congressional subpoena.[51]

While broader and more legalistic conceptions of executive privilege have been in development for some time, the first Trump administration deployed them in unprecedented and maximal ways. This included exercising a prophylactic privilege in which administration officials refused to answer questions on the grounds that they needed to protect the president's right to invoke privilege at a later date while then never following up with a formal assertion.[52] The administration's obstruction of Congress, however, culminated in a letter from White House Counsel Pat A. Cipollone sent to House Speaker Nancy Pelosi and three committee chairs conducting investigations, declaring the White House's refusal to cooperate in any way with an impeachment inquiry it regarded as "illegitimate" and "constitutionally invalid."[53] The White House thus refused to cooperate with congressional investigations entirely.[54] The administration's blanket refusal to comply with any congressional subpoenas was based on three grounds, articulated in its Senate trial memorandum. First, the administration asserted blanket testimonial immunity for administration officials. Citing *Nixon*, the president argued that "the privilege protecting the confidentiality of presidential communications 'is fundamental to the operation of Government and inextricably rooted in the separation of powers under the Constitution.'"[55] However, the court in *Nixon* did not characterize executive privilege as a categorical and inviolable right of the presidency. In fact, the court ruled against Nixon in that case, finding that its own institutional prerogatives trumped those of the president. Secondly, the administration argued that the congressional subpoenas were constitutionally invalid and that there was no legitimate legislative purpose for the subpoenas until the

House passed an impeachment inquiry.[56] This was an absurd contention given that nothing in the constitutional text even remotely suggests that the House has no power over impeachments unless it authorizes an inquiry. As Whittington argues, the Constitution grants the House the sole power of impeachment, and grants each chamber the power to determine the rules of its own proceedings. While the House could adopt rules requiring an impeachment inquiry vote, no such rule exists.[57] Finally, the administration objected to a prohibition on agency counsel (though not private counsel) in impeachment-related depositions. The Trump administration never formally invoked executive privilege in either the House or Senate proceedings and thus never specified particular information that needed to be protected for the public good. Rather, it used the combination of these three rationales to refuse *any* cooperation with a congressional investigation it characterized as constitutionally improper. Its constitutional justifications, in other words, called into question Congress's constitutional powers while construing its own powers as categorical and inviolable.

The House responded to this unprecedented level of obstruction by impeaching the president for obstruction of Congress in addition to the abuse of power article related to the Ukrainian quid pro quo. The House's obstruction article was not based on any specific refusal but, rather, was related to the totality of the obstruction. As the impeachment article states, President Trump directed the "unprecedented, categorical, and indiscriminate defiance of subpoenas issued by the House of Representatives pursuant to its 'sole Power of Impeachment,'" and in doing so, "sought to arrogate to himself the right to determine the propriety, scope, and nature of an impeachment inquiry into his own conduct, as well as the unilateral prerogative to deny any and all information to the House of Representatives."[58]

This thus raises an important question: How should interbranch disputes regarding congressional subpoenas be resolved? Many defenders of President Trump argued that the impeachment article for obstruction was at least premature because Congress did not turn to the judiciary to enforce its subpoenas. Before turning to that question, however, it should be clear at this point that executive privilege—understood as the power to withhold information from Congress or the public for specified reasons—is an implied power of the presidency. Over time, however, this power has hardened into a legalistic doctrine wielded by the executive branch. Rather than make justifications for privilege in specific instances, the executive branch protects its inherent power of executive privilege. In doing so, it denies Congress's legitimate oversight powers.

SHOULD THE JUDICIARY DECIDE INFORMATIONAL DISPUTES?

The second impeachment article in 2019 for obstruction of Congress met considerable resistance because the House did not go to court to seek the enforcement of its subpoenas prior to impeaching for obstruction. As the dissenting voices in the House Impeachment Report put it, President Trump was impeached for his "assertion of valid constitutional privileges."[59] Underlying this contention was the notion that the administration's refusal to cooperate should be regarded as legitimate until the judiciary ruled otherwise. As House Republicans further put it, the majority's decision to impeach showed "the American people disdain for working within the constitutional framework."[60] The decision to impeach prior to going to court represented "a strategic choice by the Majority" and was "not an appropriate justification for impeachment."[61] Jonathan Turley echoed this argument in his congressional testimony: "A President cannot 'substitute[] his judgment' for Congress on what they are entitled to see and likewise Congress cannot substitute its judgment as to what a President can withhold. The balance of those interests is performed by the third branch that is constitutionally invested with the authority to review and resolve such disputes."[62] Turley further characterized the House of Representatives' obstruction article as "perfectly Nixonian" insofar as the House "asserted the same 'absolute, unqualified' authority of Congress to demand evidence while insisting that a president has no authority to refuse it."[63] Impeaching the president for obstruction without going to the courts, Turley continued, "would itself be an abuse of power . . . by Congress."[64] Hence, according to Turley and House Republicans, only the judiciary has an "absolute, unqualified" authority to "substitute [its] judgment" for the judgment of the other branches.

Before disputing the substance of this view, it is first worth pointing out the Trump administration's complete inconsistency on this point. While the Trump administration and its defenders contended in public and before Congress that impeachment was an inappropriate remedy for subpoena enforcement, they argued the opposite in court, reflecting a long-term and bipartisan view by the Justice Department that such disputes raise nonjusticiable political questions. As the House managers wrote in their impeachment brief:

> President Trump is telling one story to Congress while spinning a different tale in the courts. He is saying to Congress that the Committees should have sued the Executive Branch in court to enforce their subpoenas. But he has argued to that court that Congressional Committees cannot sue the Executive Branch to enforce their subpoenas.

> President Trump cannot tell Congress that it must pursue him in court, while simultaneously telling the courts that they are powerless to enforce Congressional subpoenas.[65]

In fact, in a judicial proceeding that occurred on January 30, 2020 (at the same time the Senate was in session as a court of impeachment), Justice Department lawyers argued that judicial enforcement of congressional subpoenas was inappropriate. The case in question concerned congressional subpoenas related to the Trump administration's inclusion of a citizenship question on the 2020 Census. Justice Department officials argued that congressional powers, such as appropriations and even impeachment, were the proper remedy for subpoena enforcement.[66] Head Impeachment Manager Adam Schiff (D-CA) was incredulous on the Senate Floor:

> Today, while we have been debating whether a President can be impeached for essentially bogus claims of privilege for attempting to use the courts to cover up misconduct, the Justice Department, in resisting House subpoenas, is in court today and was asked: Well, if the Congress can't come to the court to enforce subpoenas because, as we know, they are in here arguing, Congress must go to court to enforce its subpoenas, but they are in the court saying: Congress, thou shall not do that, so the judge says: If the Congress can't enforce its subpoenas in court, then what remedy is there? And the Justice Department lawyers' response is impeachment—impeachment. You can't make this up. I mean, what more evidence do we need of the bad faith of this effort to cover up?[67]

Putting aside these inconsistencies (and the bad faith motives they suggest), the notion that the courts should be relied on to enforce congressional subpoenas in interbranch disputes has been generally accepted since Watergate when the political branches first turned to the courts as ostensibly neutral arbiters. The extent to which this view has taken hold is perhaps encapsulated by an episode that occurred during the Trump impeachment trial. One of the major debates that took place during the trial concerned whether the Senate should subpoena witnesses. The debate centered on whether the Senate should subpoena the testimony of former national security advisor John Bolton, especially after *The New York Times* broke a story concerning his claim, made in his then-forthcoming book, that Trump had told him in August that he was withholding Ukraine aid to force an investigation into Biden.[68] McConnell and his top legal aides developed a strategy to convince fellow Republicans that a court fight to compel witnesses would take too long, especially after Cipollone confirmed to McConnell that the administration would invoke executive privilege to prevent Bolton's testimony.[69] The decisive vote against calling witnesses came from Lisa Murkowski after McConnell convinced her that her vote against calling witnesses was necessary to save the courts.[70] As Murkowski put it in her statement, "It has also become clear some of my colleagues intend to further politicize this process, and drag the Supreme Court into the fray, while attacking the Chief Justice. I will not stand for nor support that effort. We have already degraded this institution for partisan political benefit, and I will not enable those who wish to pull down another."[71]

The point here is that the notion that Congress should have gone to court to enforce its subpoenas, rather than resorting to impeachment, represents a fairly entrenched view that the courts are the proper venue to settle such disputes. At least since Watergate, information disputes between the branches have been conducted with recourse to the courts as a backstop. This view, however, is problematic for a number of reasons. First, recourse to the courts takes too long. This was the reason why the House decided not to pursue litigation to enforce its subpoenas in the lead up to the impeachment, choosing instead to add an article for obstruction.[72] Such lengthy delays, no doubt, were also the reason why President Trump argued that the House needed to exhaust judicial remedies prior to impeachment. Take, for example, litigation concerning former White House counsel, Don McGahn. The House judiciary committee subpoenaed McGahn because he was a key witness to several episodes detailed in the Mueller Report on Russian interference in the 2016 election. After the White House ordered McGahn not to comply, the House filed suit on August 7, 2019. McGahn, represented by the Department of Justice, argued that the House did not have standing to sue the executive branch to enforce subpoenas. The litigation continued until the parties reached an agreement in July 2021, nearly two years later (and long after Trump left the White House). In some cases, litigation takes so long that by the time it ends, the issue is moot either because a new administration has taken office or because the congressional term ends and a new Congress is seated. The House Impeachment Report cited a number of recent examples where this was the case. For example, in *Committee on the Judiciary v. Miers*, the Judiciary Committee sought to enforce subpoenas issued in 2007 to obtain testimony from Harriet Miers regarding the firing of several US attorneys. Even though the case was ultimately resolved in the committee's favor, it did not receive testimony until June 2009 (after President Bush had left office). Similarly, in *Committee on Oversight and Reform v. Holder*, the House Committee on Oversight and Reform sought documents and testimony related to Operation Fast and Furious. The committee first issued subpoenas in October 2011, and the case was not successfully resolved until August 2014.[73] In both of those cases, litigation dragged on well past Congress's timely need for the information. As the House put it in its impeachment report, "It would be unwise, indeed dangerous, to allow Presidents to defy all subpoenas in an impeachment inquiry and then assert that the House cannot impeach without exhausting judicial remedies."[74]

Secondly, there is no reason for Congress to substitute the judiciary's judgment for its own, especially when its own constitutional processes are called into question. It was one thing for the court in *Nixon* to decide that judicial processes trumped the administration's need to keep certain presidential communications secret. In that case, the court decided an interbranch dispute between its own branch and the president rather than serve as an impartial umpire between the other two branches. There is no comparable reason, however, for the courts to weigh and balance competing institutional needs between Congress and the president. As detailed already, the court in *Nixon* was far more generous to its own institutional prerogatives than the appeals court was to Congress in a companion case dealing with the same tapes, even going so far as to disparage Congress compared to the courts. This trend of judicial aggrandizement at the expense of Congress in information disputes has only continued. For example, in *Trump v. Mazars*, the Supreme Court denied Congress's access to President Trump's financial information even as it granted the same information to a New York state prosecutor in *Trump v. Vance*. Josh Chafetz characterizes the court's companion cases in *Vance* and *Mazers* as of a piece with *Nixon* and *Senate Select Committee*. In both of those cases, contends Chafetz, the judiciary applauded its own impartiality compared to Congress's base political motivations.[75]

Given the judiciary's disparagement of Congressional prerogatives, and the delays of the judicial process, there is no reason for Congress to defer to the courts in the enforcement of its own powers. This is especially true because Congress has immense political weapons to press its judgments against the executive branch. These can range from holding up the president's political agenda, refusing to confirm nominees, or defunding offices and programs. It can even exercise its inherent contempt power, and arrest those held in contempt. Indeed, the courts' mechanisms for enforcing subpoenas (contempt of court) is no stronger than Congress's own enforcement mechanisms other than the fact that respect for Congress's own powers has waned as they have grown dormant. Resisting arrest by officers of the court when held in contempt of court would no doubt be a serious offense perhaps worthy of impeachment. But there is no reason that resisting a congressional subpoena and Congress's sergeant at arms should be considered any less of an offense. Congress and the judiciary are coequal branches, each holding the power to compel information and testimony essential to their institutional functions. Congress thus signals its weakness by going to the courts to enforce its prerogatives, giving an illusion that, unlike the courts, it should not have the final say over the extent of its powers.

Finally, and most fundamentally, judicial intervention makes it seem like there is a neutral legal principle that can be used to decide any informational dispute apart from the arguments the political branches make in particular contestations. As we have seen, both branches have inherent needs for information (or for secrecy) to perform their constitutional functions. The extent to which the president needs to withhold information, and the concomitant need of Congress to have that information, can only be resolved based on arguments circumscribed by the particular circumstances that give rise to specific disputes. For example, the president might compromise and allow the intelligence committees of each chamber to see certain state secrets rather than the entire Congress. If Congress is engaged in inquiries that seem intended more to harass the president than to acquire information conducive to the public interest, it might very well lose the battle of public opinion with the president and therefore decide not to ratchet up the conflict in that particular situation. Given the inherent delays of judicial processes, and the zero-sum results of litigation, legalizing conflicts is less attuned to the particular political dynamics undergirding specific disputes and thus less suitable to providing the types of flexible compromises necessary.

Recourse to the judiciary shrouds executive privilege claims in doctrinal and precedential reasoning appropriate to courts, but less attuned to the dynamics of politics and to the types of arguments appropriate to the political domain. Executive privilege is an implied power of the presidency to withhold information and to justify that refusal with reference to the public good in specific circumstances. The move to think more legalistically about privilege has led to the transformation of this power into a categorical power or right of the presidency to protect any information it does not wish to disclose without making particular justifications. This is the vision of presidential power that the House of Representatives challenged with its obstruction charge because such a posture from the executive branch sought to shield it from any political accountability. The power to withhold information for justifiable reasons exists because the polity aspires to ends that sometimes justify secrecy. If secrecy becomes a right inherent in the executive branch that is itself necessary to protect, then we have prioritized the means of the constitutional order and substituted them for the ends.

The Enervation of the Impeachment Power

If Congress's oversight disputes with the executive branch are best left to politics, then this raises the question of the appropriate scope of the impeachment power. While informational disputes are directly implicated by this question, the scope of the impeachment power is relevant to any interbranch dispute and to presidential accountability more generally. An overly legalistic construction of the impeachment power as applying only to indictable offenses has enervated Congress's ability to hold presidents accountable for misconduct while in office, rendering the impeachment power obsolete in practice. Narrow constructions of the impeachment power persist even though there is broad scholarly consensus that the power extends beyond criminal misconduct to political abuses of power more generally.[76] The move in practice to strictly legal standards for impeachment, moreover, focuses political discourse on narrow violations of law that distract attention away from the political issues actually animating interbranch disputes in the first place.[77] Narrow construction of the impeachment power distorts and narrows the public's view, substituting the standards and language of criminal law for the political judgments and prudential arguments necessary for political accountability.

Before demonstrating the ways in which the impeachment power in practice has taken on a legalistic frame that deprives the polity of a healthy interbranch politics, it is first important to demonstrate how the impeachment power should be understood within the constitutional system. It is against this backdrop that contemporary practice can best be evaluated. Impeachment procedures are clearly, though succinctly, laid out in the Constitution. Article II, section 4 states that "the President, Vice President and all civil Officers of the United States, shall be removed from Office on Impeachment for, and Conviction of, Treason, Bribery, or other high Crimes and Misdemeanors." The House of Representatives has the sole power of impeachment by majority vote.[78] Impeachment by the House amounts to a charge of misconduct similar to an indictment in the criminal context. The House thus has the power to allege impeachable misconduct and to pass articles of impeachment detailing one or more offenses. Beyond granting the House the sole power of impeachment, the text is silent about how the House is to exercise this power. In the lead up to the first impeachment of President Trump, the administration and its defenders argued that the House needed to formally authorize an impeachment inquiry, and that its oversight powers, such as committee subpoenas, would not be valid until the House took this step. However, neither the Constitution nor congressional rules require it. And, in fact, one can imagine a scenario in which members of Congress would be direct witnesses to an impeachable offense (as on January 6, 2021) and move immediately to impeach. While there might be good political reasons to take additional steps to ensure that a case against a president is ironclad, and that it rises above the passions of political factionalism, these, as Keith Whittington argues, are political judgments, not constitutional requirements.[79]

The Senate has the sole power to try all impeachments, which is to say that the Senate determines both whether the alleged conduct in fact occurred, and, if so, whether such conduct ought to result in conviction and removal from office.[80] When it holds an impeachment trial, the Senate is transformed into a fundamentally different institution akin to a jury. The chief justice of the Supreme Court presides and administers an oath in which the senators swear "to do justice impartially." At the conclusion of a Senate impeachment trial, a two-thirds vote is needed to convict and remove a president from office. The Senate may also disqualify the convicted individual from holding any future office by a majority vote. The two-chamber process is indicative of the framers' concern that political passions often motivate the drive to impeach. The Senate is a smaller chamber further removed from the momentary swings in public opinion due to its longer terms of office. These structural qualities thus make it a safer repository for the power to ultimately convict and remove a president from office. The two-thirds threshold for conviction, furthermore, makes the protection of innocence more secure because the supermajoritarian threshold requires significant consensus. Finally, it is worth emphasizing that the only punishments for an impeachment conviction are removal from office and possible disqualification. Once the individual is removed from office, however, the Constitution stipulates that he or she remains liable to be tried in criminal court.

The power and scope of the impeachment clause ultimately turns on the types of offenses it encompasses. Does the scope of the impeachment power extend to political abuses of power, or should it be limited solely to indictable crimes? Presidents are eligible for impeachment for "Treason, Bribery, or other high Crimes and Misdemeanors." The Constitution explicitly, and narrowly, defines treason as "levying War against [the United States], or adhering to their enemies, giving them Aid and Comfort." Bribery might involve either taking or giving bribes. While bribery suggests a legal violation, it was merely a common law violation at the time of ratification, and Congress did not make it an indictable offense until 1790.[81] The most difficult interpretive question, therefore, concerns what constitutes "high crimes and misdemeanors." This is an especially important question given that in practice the phrase has been used to narrowly construe the impeachment clauses to indictable offenses based on a plain reading of the constitutional text, which, on face value, does seem to suggest criminality.

Debates at the Constitutional Convention shed some light on the proper scope of the impeachment power. The proceedings of the convention give the impression that impeachable offenses require a higher threshold than mere partisan differences. A September 4 draft of the Constitution listed impeachable offenses as limited solely to treason and bribery. When, on September 8, the convention took up the question of impeachable offenses, George Mason objected to limiting them to treason and bribery, arguing that a great many offenses were not encompassed by those narrow categories. He moved to add "maladministration" to the list of impeachable offenses, seconded by Elbridge Gerry. Madison, however, argued that "so vague a term" as maladministration would be "equivalent to a tenure during the pleasure of the Senate," thereby suggesting that impeachment required a higher threshold. Gouverneur Morris agreed with Madison, asserting that elections every four years is a sufficient guard against maladministration. The phrase "high crimes and misdemeanors" was thus substituted for "maladministration."[82]

While the framers were clearly concerned that maladministration would be too loose and malleable as a standard for impeachment, there is compelling evidence that the phrase "high crimes and misdemeanors" was meant to encompass political offenses. The evidence for the more capaciously political interpretation of "high crimes and misdemeanors" can be traced through English impeachment precedents. As Raoul Berger notes in his careful and detailed study of impeachment, "To understand what the framers had in mind we must begin with English law, for nowhere did they more evidently take off from that law than in drafting the impeachment provisions."[83] English history, dating back more than four hundred years prior to the Constitutional Convention, is replete with examples of impeachments for "high crimes and misdemeanors," and the types of offenses for which officials were impeached (even if not ultimately convicted) were wide-ranging and broadly political. In fact, the phrase "high crimes and misdemeanors" is a composite phrase well known in English impeachment practice that is wholly separate from criminal law. Berger dates the first usage of the phrase "high crimes and misdemeanors" to proceedings against the Earl of Suffolk in 1386. At that time, "misdemeanors" were not a known criminal offense. Rather, what today would be a "misdemeanor" would have then been prosecuted as a "trespass." And it wasn't until well into the sixteenth century that "trespasses" were "supplanted by 'misdemeanors' as a category of ordinary crimes."[84] Impeachment, Berger concludes, was conceived "because the objects of impeachment, for one reason or another, were beyond the reach of ordinary criminal redress."[85] "High crimes and misdemeanors" were thus "a category of *political* crimes against the state."[86] Such political crimes were understood to embrace maladministration. As William Blackstone wrote in his *Commentaries on the Laws of England*, "the first and principle [high misdemeanor] is the *mal-administration* of such high officers, as are in the public trust and employment. This is usually punished by the method of parliamentary impeachment."[87]

The constitutional drafters would have been well aware of English impeachment precedents, especially since the impeachment trial of Warren Hastings in England began just a few weeks before the start of the Constitutional Convention of 1787. In fact, Mason referred to the Hastings trial when he objected that limiting impeachable offenses to "treason" and "bribery" would not reach a great many offenses against the political community: "Why is the provision restrained to Treason & bribery only? Treason as defined in the Constitution will not reach many great and dangerous offences (sic). Hastings is not guilty of Treason. Attempts to subvert the Constitution may not be Treason as above defined. As bills of attainder which have saved the British Constitution are forbidden, it is the more necessary to extend the power of impeachments."[88] Hastings was impeached for "high crimes and misdemeanors" for oppressive and corrupt use of governmental power during his time in office as governor-general of Calcutta, not for an indictable crime. The fact that "high crimes and misdemeanors" were used for political offenses in a trial that clearly caught the attention of the constitutional drafters is evidence that the framers understood that the standard they adopted for impeachable offenses encompassed political, not strictly illegal, offenses. The phrase ultimately adopted—high crimes and misdemeanors—was a known category of impeachable offenses with a precise meaning that encompassed a broad range of offenses against the state. Whereas Madison objected to the vagueness of "maladministration," "high crimes and misdemeanors" as a known category of impeachable offense arguably encompassed maladministration within its scope. As Michael Stokes Paulsen concludes,

> It is thus a slight overstatement to say, as some commentators have said, that "mal-administration" was rejected as a ground for impeachment.

> It is more accurate to say that concerns over the possible vagueness of the word were redressed by repairing to the familiar, general term-of-art "high Crimes and Misdemeanors," a term probably nearly as capacious but at least somewhat more precise, and arguably importing a sense that the officer must be found to have behaved in a way that can be judged wrongful (in some sense) and not properly permitting removal over ordinary disagreements "at the pleasure" of the legislature.[89]

The Federalist gives further and explicit support to the notion that impeachment is a political power of Congress meant to punish misconduct and violations of the public's trust. Writing in *Federalist* 65 about why the Senate is the proper repository of the power to try impeachments, Hamilton argued that

> a well-constituted court for the trial of impeachments is an object not more to be desired than difficult to be obtained in a government wholly elective. The subjects of its jurisdiction are those offenses which proceed from the misconduct of public men, or, in other words, from the abuse or violation of some public trust. They are of a nature which may with peculiar propriety be denominated POLITICAL, as they relate chiefly to injuries done immediately to the society itself.[90]

Hamilton further asserted that the Senate, operating as an impeachment court, could not be "tied down" by "strict rules, either in the delineation of the offense by the prosecutors, or in the construction of it by the judges." Commenting on Hamilton's argument in *Federalist* 65, Michael Gerhardt explains that impeachable offenses comprise "a unique set of transgressions" that defy "neat delineation."[91] Joseph Story also voiced this view in his *Commentaries on the Constitution*, writing that impeachable offenses are "various in their character" and too "indefinable" to be captured solely by positive law. Rather, they must be "examined upon very broad and comprehensive principles of public policy and duty."[92]

Leaving these historical and contextual arguments to the side, there are also practical and theoretical reasons for a more politically capacious construction of impeachable offenses. From a practical perspective, the notion that impeachable offenses should be limited solely to indictable crimes misunderstands the nature of constitutional office and duty. Presidents are bound by their oath of office, swearing during their inauguration to "faithfully execute the Office of President of the United States," and "to the best of [their] ability," to "preserve, protect and defend the Constitution of the United States." The oath of office thus places on presidents additional responsibilities and obligations to the political community that ordinary citizens do not share. That the oath distinguishes constitutional officers from private citizens is underscored by the Fourteenth Amendment's disqualification clause in section 3, barring from office those who previously swore an oath to the Constitution and then waged insurrection against the United States. The disqualification does not extend to private citizens, but only applies to those who took on constitutional obligations by swearing an oath to defend the Constitution.

Charles Black highlights the ways in which presidents can violate the Constitution in a manner that could be clearly impeachable even if a private citizen could not be indicted for the action in question. For example, a president who says he will refuse to nominate any Roman Catholic to his cabinet might well be impeached for violating Article VI's prohibition on religious tests as a "Qualification to any Office or public Trust under the United States," even though such a violation could not result in a criminal indictment or conviction.[93] It would be well within a private citizen's First Amendment right to advocate for such a qualification for office as a matter of free speech, but a president who commits to such an action, and follows through, would explicitly violate the Constitution even if a private citizen could not be held criminally liable for such an action. Similarly, Black suggests the possibility of a president abusing the pardon power, "granting full pardons, in advance of indictment or trial, to all federal agents or police who killed someone in the line of duty, in the District of Columbia, whatever the circumstances and however unnecessary the killing."[94] It stretches the imagination to think that the impeachment power could not reach such willful contempt for the rule of law. Black's point here is similar to the objection made by George Mason at the Constitutional Convention to limiting impeachable offenses to treason and bribery: that the scope of impeachable offenses would not reach a great deal of conduct that amounts to abuse of power or violations of the oath of office. Limiting the impeachment power in this way enervates the impeachment power of its ability to reach offenses against the political community, thus diminishing political accountability.

What should be clear from the preceding is that the historical and theoretical evidence clearly demonstrates that impeachment was intended for political offenses that extended beyond mere criminality. While scholars disagree about the precise scope of the impeachment power, there is clear consensus on two points. First, there is widespread consensus today that the impeachment power is less politically capacious than, as Gerald Ford once controversially put it, "whatever a majority of the House of Representatives considers [it] to be at a given moment in history."[95] The framers' concern that maladministration as a standard was too malleable and would thus make the president too dependent on Congress is clear evidence that impeachment was intended to be a more elevated process than mere partisan disagreement. Secondly, there is also broad consensus that the power extends beyond indictable offenses to abuses of power more generally. This consensus was clear in the lead up to the first Trump impeachment when the House Judiciary Committee held hearings in December 2019 on the appropriate scope of the impeachment power. While they disagreed on the precise scope of impeachable offenses, each of the four witnesses (Noah Feldman, Michael J. Gerhardt, Pamela S. Karlan, and Jonathan Turley) argued that they do not require violations of the law.[96] Turley's position was perhaps the most congenial to Republican defenders of President Trump insofar as he argued that impeachable offenses, even if not violations of the law in the strict sense, should be as serious as legal violations. Explaining the Constitution's provision concerning "other high crimes and misdemeanors," Turley argued, "the word 'other' reflects an obvious intent to convey that the impeachable acts other than bribery and treason were meant to reach a similar level of gravity and seriousness (even if they are not technically criminal acts)."[97]

Despite the historical and practical evidence that impeachable offenses extend beyond indictable offenses to political abuses of power and violations of the Constitution, political practice has largely followed a much narrower, legalistic conception of the purposes of impeachment, thus muting its effects in practice.[98] This trend continued during the Trump impeachments. In 2019, President Trump was impeached for allegedly withholding essential foreign assistance to Ukraine unless the Ukrainian government agreed to open a corruption investigation into Hunter Biden, son of the then-frontrunner for the Democratic presidential nomination. The assistance was delivered to Ukraine after a whistleblower complaint. During the Senate trial, Republicans, following the lead of Harvard Law professor Alan Dershowitz, adopted a remarkably narrow construction of impeachable offenses. Serving as part of President Trump's defense team during the Senate trial, Dershowitz argued that impeachable offenses require an actual crime or "crime-like conduct." Dershowitz further claimed that "purely noncriminal conduct including abuse of power and obstruction of Congress are outside the range of impeachable offenses."[99] In fact, Dershowitz went so far as to argue that if President Trump had committed the alleged quid pro quo, that it would, as a matter of law, be unimpeachable if he had done it with the public good in mind: "If a president does something which he believes will help him get elected, in the public interest, that cannot be the kind of quid pro quo that results in impeachment."[100] Even Republican senators were incensed by how far Dershowitz took the argument. Senator Roy Blunt (R-MO), a top McConnell ally, reportedly walked up to Pat Cipollone afterward, demanding that he fire Dershowitz on the spot.[101]

To make his argument, Dershowitz relied heavily on the political precedents set during the Johnson impeachment. While Congressional Republicans were incensed at President Andrew Johnson's total obstruction of their Reconstruction agenda and his demagogic disparagement of Congress, the president's defenders insisted that he could only be impeached for violating the law. Anticipating that Johnson would fire the holdover Secretary of War Edwin Stanton, Congress passed the Tenure of Office Act, thus supplying the predicate for impeachment when Johnson followed through on firing Stanton. Nine out of the eleven articles of impeachment dealt with violations of the Tenure of Office Act, reflecting this narrow construction. The other two articles charged Johnson with attempting "to bring into disgrace, ridicule, hatred, contempt and reproach, the Congress of the United States," and with denying that "the legislation of said Congress was obligatory upon him." In the impeachment trial, former justice Benjamin Curtis, whom Dershowitz heavily relied upon in 2020, argued that the two political articles of impeachment were constitutionally improper:

> My first position is, that when the Constitution speaks of treason, bribery, and other crimes and misdemeanors, it refers to, and includes only, high criminal offenses against the United States, made so by some law of the United States existing when the acts complained of were done, and I say that this is plainly to be inferred from each and every provision of the Constitution on the subject of impeachment.[102]

Johnson was ultimately acquitted in the Senate, falling one vote shy of a conviction. The acquittal, however, was more the result of pragmatic political calculations and thus does not necessarily represent an ironclad vindication for the narrow view that impeachable offenses are reserved to violations of the statutory law. By the time of the Senate trial, some Republicans worried about a Wade presidency if Johnson were removed. Moreover, Johnson finally pledged to stop obstructing Congress's Reconstruction agenda, and this proved sufficient to garner enough votes to acquit. That the impeachment effort ended with Johnson's political surrender underscores the extent to which the articles of impeachment themselves, focusing almost exclusively on legal violations, masked Congress's true discontent with Johnson. Even so, the Johnson impeachment created an enduring political precedent useful to presidents. As Keith Whittington puts it, "It is the familiar strategy of the defense attorney that when the facts are against you, argue the law, and when the law is against you, argue the facts."[103] This has often meant that presidents, relying on historical examples such as the Johnson impeachment, argue to Congress that they can only be impeached for violations of the law.[104]

Dershowitz's arguments suggested that the Senate did not need to establish a record of the facts because even if President Trump had committed the alleged offense, it would not rise to the level of an impeachable offense meriting removal from office. This was a decisive point in the debate over whether the Senate should call witnesses, especially John Bolton. Worried that they would lose the vote to call witnesses, Republican senators, including Mitch McConnell, Ted Cruz, and Lindsey Graham, colluded with the Trump defense team, insisting that they make the argument that the quid pro quo was not impeachable because it was not a crime.[105] The Trump lawyers were hesitant to make this argument because Trump was insistent that there was no quid pro quo, that it was a "perfect" phone call. Even so, Republican senators finally convinced the president's lawyers to embrace Dershowitz's arguments. In response to a question asking whether the alleged conduct would amount to an impeachable offense even if John Bolton were to "testify in the light most favorable to the allegations," Trump's lawyers responded that it would not.[106]

All told, seventeen Republican senators adopted this position as justification for voting to acquit President Trump, enough votes for an acquittal. That so many Senate Republicans were willing to embrace such an extraordinarily narrow interpretation of the impeachment power—abandoning the consensus view—underscores the power of partisanship. A year later, when President Trump was impeached a second time for inciting the mob that stormed the Capitol to prevent the certification of Joe Biden as the winner of the election, many Republicans once again embraced a narrowly legalistic construction of the impeachment power, arguing that Trump's action were protected by the First Amendment because they did not meet the Supreme Court's strict legal criteria for criminal incitement. As Senator Mike Lee (R-UT) put it:

> No one can condone . . . President Trump's words, actions, and omissions on that day . . . The fact is that the word "incitement" has a very specific meaning in the law, and Donald Trump's words and actions on January 6, 2021, fell short of that standard. The House rushed its impeachment without an investigation, charged President Trump with

a crime it failed properly to allege, and then sat on its poorly worded Article until after he left office.[107]

Returning to the first impeachment, while enough Republicans explicitly argued that impeachment is reserved solely for criminal misconduct, Democrats were perhaps also constrained by legalistic conceptions of the impeachment power, albeit more subtly. By limiting the grounds of impeachment to the quid pro quo incident (which an Inspector General report determined was illegal) and the president's subsequent obstruction of the impeachment investigation, the House of Representatives missed its opportunity to show how President Trump's behavior was not an isolated incident but, rather, indicative of his general approach to the office. The impeachment over Ukraine sidelined all the other congressional investigations into Trump's misconduct. Congressman Jamie Raskin (D-MD) tried to persuade Speaker Pelosi to pursue a larger impeachment case against the president to demonstrate to the public how the Ukraine incident was part of a pattern of presidential misconduct. He worried that the focus on the Ukraine incident made it seem like it was an aberration rather than a mere example of the president's style. Instead, he urged Speaker Pelosi to broaden the probe. As Rachael Bade and Karoun Demirjian write in their detailed reporting of the Trump impeachments, "Broadening their probe to include things like the president's emoluments clause violations, Raskin argued, could let Democrats weave a narrative that centered on corruption and self-enrichment."[108] Once the public saw how the president was using his office for corrupt gain, it would be easy to show how the Ukrainian quid pro quo was just another instance of abuse of power, and it would be easier for the public to understand why the president needed to be removed. The House's case, on the other hand, focused on whether the quid pro quo took place and whether it warranted removal from office. Ripped from context, the quid pro quo was not as thoroughly damning as it could have been otherwise. The narrow focus, free of the larger context Raskin hoped would be persuasive to the public, also made it harder to make the case that the president posed such a grave danger to the nation that he needed to be removed from office. This is not to say that the impeachment case was not damning in its own right, but it was too narrow to convey the larger political concerns that motivated the impeachment efforts in the first place. The Democrats found an open-and-shut instance of an abuse of power—and potential violation of the law—and focused all their attention on that.

Even so, the Democrats might have been right strategically to wait for such a clear constitutional abuse. The impeachment power is ultimately tempered and constrained by public opinion. Given the limited historical examples, and the impeachment power's legalistic gloss in practice (impeachments have only ever occurred for clear violations of the law), it is not clear that the public would have had the constitutional imagination or patience for the kind of impeachment case Raskin would have mounted. If that is the case, the problem is the deep and entrenched public understanding of the impeachment power that enervates it in practice. Considering the extraordinary powers that contemporary presidents exercise, it is striking that Congress understands its powers of oversight as limited to executive violations of the law. As Gene Healy provocatively writes,

> Consider that most jobs in this country are employment-at-will; absent membership in a legally protected class, most of us can be fired for good reason, bad reason, or no reason at all. At the top of the corporate hierarchy, for-cause termination is the norm—CEOs can be cashiered for "moral turpitude," "unprofessional conduct," and the like. Yet we've somehow managed to convince ourselves that the one job in America where you have to commit a felony to get fired is the one where you actually get nuclear weapons.[109]

From the larger perspective of the separation of powers, the enervation of the impeachment power makes it nearly impossible for Congress to push its political judgments against the president. As I have argued in this book, much of contemporary government is dominated by the executive branch, and this is to be expected given the constitutional design. If the impeachment power is understood only to apply to narrow violations of the law, Congress is virtually impotent in its dealings with the executive branch. Take the example of informational disputes. As William H. Rehnquist recognized in 1971 when he served as assistant attorney general, "the Executive Branch has a head start in any controversy with the Legislative Branch, since the Legislative Branch wants something the Executive Branch has, and therefore the initiative lies with the former. All the Executive has to do is maintain the status quo, and he prevails."[110] While Congress certainly has lesser tools available to it—from defunding offices, holding up key appointments, and derailing the president's legislative agenda—ultimately the viable threat of impeachment empowers Congress long before actual impeachments ramp up. In other words, a viable impeachment power would perhaps force political compromise and accommodation that would make it less likely that impeachment would actually need to be used. Given the executive branch's inherent institutional advantages, impeachment is the tool that gives Congress leverage in political disputes because it can ultimately remove a president from office. For these reasons, Tulis has identified the impeachment power as "a vital attribute of the theoretical architecture of a well-functioning separation of powers regime."[111] An enervated impeachment power disempowers Congress, undermining the separation of powers system.

The Dangers of Substituting Criminal Prosecution for Impeachment and Conviction

How should presidents be held accountable for their actions while in office? The previous section detailed the ways in which impeachable offenses should be construed broadly enough to encompass political offenses. A narrowly legalistic frame enervates Congress of its power to hold presidents accountable. Indeed, limiting impeachable offenses to strictly illegal actions excludes broad swaths of presidential misconduct from the purview of Congress and makes it difficult for Congress to press its political disagreements with the executive branch. Furthermore, a narrowly legalistic frame focuses the public's attention on narrow slices of law that often obscures larger, and perhaps more important, reasons for why impeachment could be necessary. This final section focuses on a related issue: the problems of using the legal system to combat presidential misconduct as a substitute for Congress's impeachment powers. As will be evident, the deterioration of Congress's constitutional powers, and the subsequent need for law enforcement to fill the void, can have long-lasting and deleterious effects on the constitutional order.

Following the breach of the Capitol building on January 6 by a mob intent on overturning the results of the 2020 election, Republican support for President Trump seemingly evaporated. When the Senate finally reconvened late in the evening to certify the election, Senator Lindsay Graham, one of President Trump's most ardent supporters, spoke at length, declaring that he and Trump "had one hell of a ride," but "enough is enough."[112] Although House Republican Leader Kevin McCarthy denounced the impeachment efforts against Trump for the insurrection, he took to the House Floor to proclaim that President Trump bore responsibility for the events of January 6 and that he should "accept his share of responsibility."[113] While McCarthy argued that a congressional censure, rather than impeachment, was the appropriate punishment, one cannot overstate the significance of his condemnation at the time, especially in light of his usual subservience to Trump. Many of President Trump's cabinet members also resigned in protest, including Attorney General Bill Barr and Secretary of Transportation Elaine Chao (wife of Senate Majority Leader Mitch McConnell).[114]

The House quickly impeached President Trump on January 13, 2021, on a single article for inciting the insurrection.[115] The entire Democratic Caucus, along with ten Republicans, voted to impeach the president, making it the most bipartisan presidential impeachment ever conducted. Members of Congress had endured the Capitol riot, running and hiding for their lives as rioters attacked and brutally assaulted Capitol Police and as they yelled about hanging Vice President Mike Pence (even building a gallows). Given that members of Congress were direct witnesses to, and victims of, the impeachable conduct, the House was able to impeach almost immediately without a thorough investigation. In fact, Democratic members of Congress began drafting Articles of Impeachment on January 6. While subsequent investigations by the bipartisan Congressional January 6th Committee (which held public hearings in the summer of 2022) and criminal investigations by state and federal authorities have continued to supply information further demonstrating the extent of President Trump's culpability for the insurrection, these subsequent developments have mostly supplied a more detailed picture of what was already known in January 2021.

The impeachment managers, led by Congressman Jamie Raskin (D-MD), a former law professor, laid out in incredible detail how Trump incited the events of that day (the account here is a summary of the events as presented by House impeachment managers). Indeed, the assault on the Capitol was not merely the result of President Trump's speech, in which he urged his followers to march to the Capitol and to "fight like hell" if they wanted to have a country. Rather, President Trump's speech, and the violent assault that transpired immediately afterward, was the culmination of a monthslong campaign to cast doubt on the election results, a campaign that began even before the election. Prior to the election, not only did President Trump refuse to say whether he would accept the election results if he lost; he repeatedly asserted that he could only lose if there was massive fraud.[116] President Trump thus primed his supporters to be suspicious of the election results if he lost. After in fact losing the election, he refused to concede, and his allegations of massive election fraud proliferated. As the impeachment managers put it, "President Trump told his supporters over and over again, nearly every day, in dozens of tweets, speeches, and rallies, that their most precious right in our democracy—their voice, their vote—was being stripped away, and they had to fight to stop that. They believed him, and so they fought."[117] At President Trump's request, the Justice Department investigated his allegations of voter fraud and found no support for such claims.[118] Even so, the president and his lawyers continued to amplify unsubstantiated claims of voter fraud, claims that courts across the country dismissed for lack of evidence.

While President Trump propagated the Big Lie about election fraud, he and his lawyers mounted a pressure campaign to get state election officials in Georgia, Michigan, Pennsylvania, and Arizona to decertify their elections based on unsubstantiated allegations of fraud propagated by the president and his allies. He even asked election officials to change the results—to literally find him votes—so that he could win the election, and he threatened them with criminal penalties if they refused.[119] As January 6 neared, the date of the proceeding when Congress would officially count electoral votes and certify Joe Biden as the winner of the election, President Trump and his associates pressured Vice President Mike Pence to refuse to accept electoral votes from highly contested states and send the votes back to the states to be recertified.[120] Pence steadfastly refused to do this, stating that he did not have the constitutional power to do anything but open and count the votes. President Trump thus took to Twitter to pressure the vice president and told his supporters that it was up to Pence to do his duty and stop the steal.[121]

As all this was taking place, President Trump planned a rally on January 6 in front of the White House, scheduled to coincide with the congressional certification of the election. At the rally, Trump again recounted unsubstantiated (and false) allegations of voter fraud and told his supporters, "If you don't fight like hell, you're not going to have a country anymore."[122] He then urged the crowd to march down Pennsylvania Avenue toward the Capitol to give the "weak" Republicans "the kind of pride and boldness that they need to take back our country."[123]

As the rally broke up, thousands of people surged toward the Capitol. The mob swiftly overwhelmed the Capitol Police and forced its way into the building. Outside, some erected a gallows and began to chant "Hang Mike Pence!" Senior members of Congress were evacuated as the mob ransacked the Capitol, and as other members of Congress hid and barricaded themselves in offices. Back at the White House, President Trump was reportedly gleeful and surprised that his staff were not also excited. He took no action to call in the National Guard and made no public statements condemning the violence or calling his supporters off even as members of his staff and his daughter Ivanka Trump begged him to call for an end to the violence. In fact, even Republican House Minority Leader Kevin McCarthy pleaded with President Trump to intervene or to release a statement denouncing the attack, to which Trump responded, "Well, Kevin, I guess these people are more upset about the election than you are."[124] Rather than taking any action to end the assault on the Capitol, President Trump used the delay in the congressional proceedings to call senators, lobbying them to continue to delay the certification of electoral votes. Moreover, as his supporters chanted "Hang Mike Pence!" he took to Twitter to inflame them further, declaring that "Mike Pence didn't have the courage to do what should have been done to protect our Country and our Constitution."[125]

As the Capitol riot raged on, and as Trump supporters violently assaulted Capitol Police (at least one died) and ransacked the building, senior congressional leaders who had been evacuated to Fort McNair pleaded with the Pentagon to send in the National Guard to end the insurrection; they were, however, stymied in their efforts and told that it would take the Pentagon four hours to formulate a plan and to respond. Unsatisfied, congressional leaders finally turned to Vice President Mike Pence.[126] At 4:08, three hours after the assault on the Capitol began, the vice president called the acting defense secretary and the chairman of the Joints Chief of Staff and ordered them to clear the Capitol at once, an order that was not technically his to give.[127] President Trump, in short, sat by watching with excitement as the mob he instigated through weeks of misinformation about a stolen election attacked the Capitol on his command to prevent the certification of the election. More than three hours after the insurrection began, President Trump finally released a video in which he urged his supporters to leave the Capitol in peace. Even in this communication, however, Trump referred to the "fraudulent election," and rather than condemn any of the violence of that day, said to his supporters (the mob), "We love you. You're very special."[128] He later wrote on Twitter that "these are the things and events that happen when a sacred landslide election victory is so unceremoniously & viciously stripped away from great patriots who have been badly & unfairly treated for so long. Go home with love & in peace. Remember this day forever!"[129]

The events of January 6 amounted to the greatest assault on the Capitol since the British ransacked it during the War of 1812, striking at the heart of American constitutional democracy. Emphasizing the significance of the insurrection, William Baude and Michael Stokes Paulsen write:

> To be sure, the events of January 6 itself—the attack on Congress and the Capitol—did not remotely rival in overall magnitude, or in sheer carnage, the experience of the U.S. Civil War, where more than 600,000 people died. Still, considered as discrete events, it is notable that more people died, and many more were injured, as a result of the January 6, 2021 attack on the Capitol than died or suffered injuries as a result

> of the attack on Fort Sumter. The events of January 6 match, in their essential elements—concerted resistance to federal authority, serious attempts to frustrate execution of national law, attacks on government officials and facilities, intimidation and violence—and arguably exceeded in their seriousness, the events of the Whiskey Rebellion, Fries' Rebellion, and other more limited historical insurrections.[130]

As damning and as accurate as Baude and Paulson's indictment of President Trump is, it does not spell out the full measure of the threat the nation faced on January 6. In fact, much of the potential damage from the January 6 insurrection was blunted by its failure. It is well within the realm of possibility that the siege of the Capitol could have led to the murder of Vice President Pence, House Speaker Pelosi, Senator Romney, and others who would have opposed Trump's plans (and, in fact, anyone the mob encountered). Had Pence been killed, it would have taken longer to deploy the military. It is also possible that had security been more fully breached, enough members of Congress could have been captured to continue the session under threat from the forces holding the Capitol. If Trump held the presidency under those circumstances, it is likely that there would have been enormous opposition from blue state governors to Trump's legitimacy, and considerable conflict within the military as to where their loyalties were supposed to lie. That would potentially be a recipe for a much wider civil war, using weapons capable of inflicting far more damage than those used in the Civil War. Even without that level of violence, Acting Attorney General for the Civil Division Jeffrey Clark contemplated using the Insurrection Act to impose martial law to control protesters in the event the coup succeeded. And perhaps most importantly, this was the only insurrection in US history where the commander in chief was fomenting the insurrection in order to hold power unlawfully. This created the potential for violent conflict between divided federal forces, a far more serious threat than a small group of armed insurrectionists standing up to the unified power of the federal government.

The seriousness of the insurrection was clear to members of Congress, which explains why the House so quickly impeached the president for inciting insurrection. Given the proximity to the inauguration, however, the Senate did not take up the impeachment trial until after President Joe Biden took office. The fact that the Senate impeachment trial occurred after President Trump left office became a significant point of contention for Republicans, especially after conservative former judge J. Michael Luttig penned an op-ed arguing that the Senate trial of a former president would be unconstitutional.[131] Soon afterward, forty-five Republicans voted preemptively on January 26 to declare the impeachment trial unconstitutional on that basis.[132] Although the motion failed fifty-five to forty-five, the vote suggested the difficulty of securing the seventeen Republican votes that would be necessary to reach the two-thirds vote necessary for conviction. For Republicans, a jurisdictional hurdle to the impeachment trial could allow them to acquit the president while still criticizing his conduct (and thus avoiding political blowback from Trump supporters who constituted a significant segment of their Republican primary electorates). Judge Luttig's argument purported to be based on a plain reading of the constitutional text and structure. As he wrote:

> The very concept of constitutional impeachment presupposes the impeachment, conviction and removal of a president who is, at the time of his impeachment, an incumbent in the office from which he is removed. Indeed, that was the purpose of the impeachment power, to remove from office a president or other "civil official" before he could further harm the nation from the office he then occupies.
>
> The plain text of the Constitution's several Impeachment Clauses confirms this understanding of this limit on Congress' impeachment power. For example, Article II, Section 4 of the Constitution reads, "The President, Vice President and all civil officers of the United States, shall be removed from Office on Impeachment for, and Conviction of, Treason, Bribery, or other high Crimes and Misdemeanors." In the same constitutional vein, Article I, Section 3 provides in relevant part: "Judgment in Cases of Impeachment shall not extend further than to removal from Office, and disqualification to hold and enjoy any Office of honor, Trust or Profit under the United States."[133]

As impeachment managers pointed out, however, the plain language of the constitutional text is capacious enough to include impeachment trials for former presidents. Article I, section 3 states that "when the President of the United States is tried, the Chief Justice shall preside: And no *Person* shall be convicted without the Concurrence of two thirds of the Members present."[134] The Constitution further stipulates that "Judgment in Cases of Impeachment shall not extend further than to removal from Office, and disqualification to hold and enjoy any Office of honor, Trust or Profit under the United States: but the *Party* convicted shall nevertheless be liable and subject to Indictment, Trial, Judgment and Punishment, according to Law."[135] As Raskin emphasized, the Constitution states that no *person* shall be convicted without the concurrence of two-thirds members present and that the constitutional punishments (removal and disqualification) pertain to the *party* convicted. The use of these terms makes the provision clearly apply to former officials who have become private citizens after committing impeachable offenses while in office. This plain reading of the text, moreover, becomes fully persuasive when placed in historical context. As Raskin noted in his opening remarks, every English impeachment trial that occurred during the framers' lifetime concerned a former official. This is important given the influence of English law and practice on the US Constitution. In fact, the framers designed the impeachment power in the midst of the Warren Hastings impeachment trial in England, which took place four years after Hastings left his role as governor-general of Bengal. Many states also conducted impeachment trials for former officials, and some state constitutions even required that impeachment trials only occur after officials left office.

After ratification, on at least two occasions, the Senate spent considerable time debating whether a former official could be tried by the Senate.[136] The first instance came after the Senate expelled Senator William Blount of Tennessee for conspiring with the British to sell Florida and Louisiana.[137] The Senate expelled him four days after the House impeached him. It then decided to hold an impeachment trial so that it could convict and disqualify him from future office. Given the proximity of that case to the framing and ratification of the Constitution, members of Congress would have been thoroughly familiar with the intended reach of the impeachment clauses. The second instance came after the Civil War when Secretary of War William Belknap resigned from office immediately after the release of a House Report detailing his involvement in a corruption scheme.[138] His resignation was timed to avoid further investigation and to prevent his disqualification from future office. The House proceeded to impeach him anyway. At the impeachment trial, Belknap argued that he could not be tried and convicted as a former official, an argument that enraged members of the Senate. The Senate debated the jurisdictional question for two weeks before deciding to proceed. Ultimately, the Senate concluded that it would set a dangerous precedent if it decided it did not have authority to try impeachments of former officials, as it would allow officials to commit gross acts of misconduct and to avoid political sanctions for them.

The plain language of the constitutional text and historical precedent has led the vast majority of scholars who have considered the question, including conservative legal scholars such as Michael McConnell and Steven Calabresi, to conclude that the Senate's power to try impeachment cases extends to former officials.[139] While Professor Jonathan Turley argued in 2021 that the Senate did not have the power to try a former official, twenty years prior he argued in a 146-page study that the Senate did have such a power, since one of the punishments for an impeachment conviction is disqualification from office.[140] As Turley put it then, commenting on the Belknap impeachment, "If impeachment was simply a matter of removal, the argument for jurisdiction in the Belknap case would be easily resolved against hearing the matter. The Senate majority, however, was correct in its view that impeachments historically had extended to former officials, such as Warren Hastings."[141]

The Trump impeachment managers drew on these textual and historical arguments to make a more powerful normative constitutional argument: that a so-called January Exception to the impeachment powers of Congress would enable presidents to commit gross misconduct during their last months in office and to then face no political repercussions. As Congressman Raskin argued,

> Their argument is that if you commit an impeachable offense in your last few weeks in office, you do it with constitutional impunity; you get away with it. In other words, conduct that would be a high crime and misdemeanor in your first year as President and your second year as President and your third year as President and for the vast majority of your fourth year as President you can suddenly do in your last few weeks in office without facing any constitutional accountability at all.
>
> This would create a brand new January exception to the Constitution of the United States of America—a January exception. And everyone can see immediately why this is so dangerous. It is an invitation to the President to take his best shot at anything he may want to do on his way out the door, including using violent means to lock that door, to hang on to the Oval Office at all costs, and to block the peaceful transfer of power.[142]

Even with these compelling arguments for the Senate's jurisdiction in the case, former President Trump was ultimately acquitted by a vote of fifty-seven to forty-three, far short of the two-thirds vote required to convict. At least eight senators voted to acquit based solely on procedural grounds while acknowledging that House managers had proven the substance of their case.[143] Had not so many Republicans latched onto the procedural argument as a way to avoid reaching the merits of the impeachment case, it is highly possible that Trump would have been convicted. The procedural loophole was a mechanism used by Republican senators to acquit Trump while simultaneously condemning his actions. His actions, they contended, were reprehensible, worthy of the highest reproach. The Senate, however, was an improper venue for accountability given that it did not have the power to try a former official. Republican Senate Minority Leader Mitch McConnell perhaps stated this position most strongly. Acknowledging that President Trump was "practically and morally responsible for provoking the events of the day," he concluded that the Senate lacked the power to convict. As he stated on the Senate floor immediately following the acquittal, "If President Trump were still in office, I would have carefully considered whether the House managers proved their specific charge."[144] McConnell further argued that "if this provision does not limit impeachment and conviction powers [to sitting officials], then it has no limits at all. The House's 'sole power of Impeachment' and the Senate's 'sole Power to try all Impeachments' would create an unlimited circular logic, empowering Congress to ban any private citizen from Federal office."[145] This, of course, is an absurd contention. The limiting principle to the impeachment power is that impeachment applies to officials and former officials for impeachable conduct committed by them while in office. The notion that to convict former President Trump for gross misconduct while in office would give license to Congress to use its impeachment power for any private citizen—private citizens who have not taken the oath of office—is to suggest that rational distinctions are impossible.

Even so, Senator McConnell did not argue that Trump should get off scot-free. Rather, he asserted that even though the Senate, unlike President Trump, "put our constitutional duty first" by not improperly extending the impeachment power to a former official, Trump could still be held liable for his conduct while in office: "He didn't get away with anything yet—yet. We have a criminal justice system in this country. We have civil litigation, and former Presidents are not immune from being accountable by either one."[146] In other words, while the Senate could not (or would not) bar Trump from office for conduct McConnell and several other Republican senators acknowledged to be worthy of impeachment and removal on the merits, law enforcement could fill in the void, finally providing legal consequences for a lawless president.

Hopes that law enforcement could serve as an adequate substitute for the constitutional powers of Congress in holding President Trump accountable, however, have proven to be elusive, as criminal prosecution raises as many problems for the constitutional order as it solves. This is not to say that President Trump should not be tried and punished for criminal actions associated with his conduct while in office. The federal criminal indictments brought against President Trump for his actions related to January 6 are serious and substantial. Subsequent investigations by the congressional January 6

Committee and by federal investigators have revealed the extent of misconduct unknown at the time of the impeachment trial (although House managers presented the big picture with startling accuracy even then). In Georgia, Trump's indictment, along with eighteen allies and associates of the former president, on racketeering charges reveals attempts at election subversion that are serious and worthy of criminal prosecution.

Even if Trump's conduct warrants criminal prosecution, such legal action, absent impeachment and conviction, raises serious problems for the constitutional order. If the Senate had done its job, rather than claiming that the criminal justice system was the proper (and only) forum for accountability, it would be far easier to pursue Trump for criminal misconduct because the political stakes would be far lower. Absent political accountability, the options on offer represent a Hobson's choice: "Damned if you do, damned if you don't." If Trump violated the law, criminal prosecution is warranted. Failure to prosecute, even for good prudential reasons, would underscore the notion that citizens are not equal before the law, because presidents are above the law. Choosing to forego prosecution would be an invitation to future misconduct and would no doubt be a lesson well-learned that it is possible to act with impunity as president and to face no legal consequences.

While the choice not to prosecute raises the challenges discussed, prosecution poses challenges just as perilous. As Damon Linker persuasively argues, the boundary between law and politics is far more permeable than many recognize:

> Politicians make the laws and sometimes appoint the prosecutors responsible for enforcing them. Moreover, a prosecutor's decision about whether to seek an indictment is far from automatic. It's a judgment call, and politics is one of the factors influencing it. This is especially so when the prosecutor is the Attorney General appointed by the currently serving Democratic president and the alleged criminal is the Republican former president of the United States.[147]

All these political factors are exacerbated by the fact that Donald Trump was the Republican nominee for president during the ongoing criminal prosecutions and subsequently won reelection. This political dynamic naturally raises the charge of politicized prosecution (no matter how well-supported the allegations against Trump may be). The charge that the Justice Department has been weaponized against Trump and the Republican Party has become a rallying cry on the right, embraced by members of Congress and contenders for the Republican presidential nomination.[148] Trump, moreover, used his candidacy as an argument that prosecution should be delayed because of the political difficulties of prosecuting a presidential candidate, and he has consistently referred to prosecutions as election interference. The discrediting of legal institutions, of course, was always to be expected. Trump delegitimizes any rule or system that ever calls him to account. He knows no authority but his own feelings and impulses, and he demagogically calls into question the professional integrity of journalists, politicians, and legal authorities. Such demagoguery is rhetorically powerful even if such charges are wholly inaccurate. The Senate's failure to punish Trump politically through the impeachment process, therefore, has forced the legal system into the political fray, thus discrediting, in the eyes of many, the rule of law. This discrediting of legal institutions no doubt lays the predicate for their actual weaponization under the second Trump administration, using the Justice Department for reprisals against political opponents. As Trump told supporters at a rally in Waco, Texas, "I am your warrior, I am your justice . . . For those who have been wronged and betrayed . . . I am your retribution."[149]

There are also inherent challenges in any trial. It is difficult even to define what a truly impartial jury would look like when 47 percent of the electorate voted for Trump in the 2020 election and many believe his claims of election interference. Once the trial begins, Trump's lawyers need to only convince one juror to avoid conviction, regardless of the strength of the evidence presented. Trump, of course, would treat any outcome other than a conviction as vindication (even if not actually acquitted), and he would thus be fully unleashed. While Trump might feel vindicated by a decision not to prosecute for violations of the law, a failure to convict after pursuing prosecution would make Trump even more dangerous. Even if the result of these prosecutions is successful convictions, it will have been a gamble and done great damage to the credibility of legal institutions, even if the process is conducted with complete fairness to Trump.

Any hopes that the judiciary could serve as the proper venue for presidential accountability, moreover, have been dashed by the Supreme Court's lawless decision in *Trump v. United States*, declaring that the president is absolutely immune from prosecution so long as he uses his core constitutional powers to engage in the conduct at issue.[150] The court's six conservative justices invented a new constitutional standard inconsistent with the constitutional text, history, and precedent. The practical result is an exceedingly high standard for criminal prosecution of former presidents no matter how egregious the conduct in question so long as the president uses core constitutional powers or engages in official acts. The problem is that the constitutional text explicitly imagines criminal prosecution for presidential misconduct when it limits the punishment of impeachable offenses to removal from office, stating that "the Party convicted shall nevertheless be liable and subject to Indictment, Trial, Judgement and Punishment, according to Law."[151] Additionally, the carve-outs for core constitutional powers and for official acts would seemingly make it impossible to prosecute presidents for accepting bribes given that bribes are generally made in exchange for official acts. Could a president accept a bribe in exchange for a pardon (an official act)? The court's opinion is, at best, unclear on this point, and, at worst, creates a new constitutional immunity for presidents ex nihilo. As Justice Sotomayor wrote in dissent, joined by Justices Kagan and Jackson,

> The Court effectively creates a law-free zone around the President . . . When he uses his official powers in any way, under the majority's reasoning, he will now be insulated from criminal prosecution. Orders the Navy's Seal Team 6 to assassinate a political rival? Immune. Organizes a military coup to hold onto power? Immune. Takes a bribe in exchange for a pardon? Immune. Immune, immune, immune.
>
> Let the President violate the law, let him exploit the trappings of his office for personal gain, let him use his official power for evil ends. Because if he knew that he may one day face liability for breaking the law, he might not be as bold and fearless as we would like him to be. That is the majority's message today.
>
> Even if these nightmare scenarios never play out, and I pray they never do, the damage has been done. The relationship between the President and the people he serves has shifted irrevocably. In every use of official power, the President is now a king above the law.[152]

The full implications of the court's decision are not yet clear, and it likely would have heard challenges to the application of its new standards by the trial court. Such questions, however, are moot given that Trump has returned to the presidency and the charges against him have been dropped.

All the preceding underscores why criminal justice proceedings are poor substitutes for political accountability, and why Congress should not have shirked its constitutional duty to punish official abuses of power. The criminal justice system, in short, is a blunt instrument. The risks to the political community are high, and favorable outcomes are far from assured, even unlikely. Perhaps most importantly, the crimes associated with Trump's conduct capture but a narrow slice of his abuses of power. Even if one cannot prove criminal culpability for the events of January 6, it is another thing entirely to conclude that Trump bore no responsibility for the events of that day, or that his actions did not constitute a gross abuse of power and dereliction of duty that rise to the level of high crimes and misdemeanors. McConnell suggested as much when he argued that "by the strict criminal standard, the President's speech probably was not incitement. However—however—in the context of impeachment, the Senate might have decided this was acceptable shorthand for the reckless actions that preceded the riot."[153]

Relying on law enforcement to keep political officials in line thus shrouds political abuses of power in the language and standards of law, standards that require far higher burdens of proof. This makes it all the more difficult to punish misconduct by political leaders, making them less accountable. The failure to convict and disqualify from office also limits the available options to forego criminal prosecutions and to even pardon. If Congress uses its own processes of impeachment and conviction, it opens up space for prudential judgment to determine whether it would be better for the political community to move on rather than to endure the national trauma of criminal prosecutions, as President Ford ultimately decided with regard to Richard Nixon. Absent congressional action, on the other hand, criminal proceedings become the only mechanism for accountability and the case for foregoing them is greatly diminished. Congress's shirking of its constitutional authority—based on a tenuous, if not wholly frivolous, argument about its jurisdiction—thus represents a major failure of the constitutional order, one with continuing and possibly deleterious consequences. Given the reelection of a lawless demagogue to the office he once thoroughly tarnished, the long-term consequences are perhaps more severe than can be imagined.

Conclusion

The executive branch has immense constitutional powers and dominates contemporary governance. In this context, Congress must exercise its oversight powers. As we have seen, these oversight powers are necessary to adequately obtain information to perform its legislative functions and to ensure executive fidelity to the rule of law. What should be evident from the preceding is the extent to which legalized understandings of the separation of powers have rendered Congress impotent. Significantly, Congress's own conceptions of its powers are often the problem. Indeed, members of Congress routinely turn to the courts to enforce their subpoenas and have routinely embraced narrow conceptions of the impeachment power that have made it impossible to oversee lawless presidents or to press political judgments against the executive branch.

Looming over this entire chapter—and much of this book—is the problem of partisanship. The embrace of narrowly legalistic impeachment constructions, for example, were induced by partisanship as Republicans sought to shield a president of their own party from accountability. Moreover, it is hard to imagine Republicans enforcing congressional prerogatives, such as its subpoenas, against the unprecedented assault on their own institution's constitutional powers. This chapter perhaps more than any of the other case studies points to a serious problem for the constitutional order. Has the kind of partisanship on display in the oversight disputes detailed above rendered the separation of powers unworkable today? This is the question to which I turn in the book's concluding chapter.

Conclusion
Does Hyperpartisanship Undermine the Separation of Powers?

The main argument of this book is that Congress and the president should resolve separation of powers disputes between themselves without intervention by the judiciary. In other words, disputes that concern the legal boundaries of the two political branches should be considered nonjusticiable political questions. This view exists well outside of the scholarly mainstream. Indeed, while there is considerable disagreement about which interpretive methodologies should be utilized, it is hardly a contested proposition that the Supreme Court, utilizing the ordinary tools of legalism, should superintend the Constitution's separation of powers.[1]

The argument against judicial resolution of interbranch disputes relies on both practical and theoretical justifications that should be briefly restated here before considering a major objection to the argument of the book. First, both Congress and the president have determinate tools to advance their positions vis-à-vis the other branch that are more powerful than mere judicial judgment. For example, while the president has immense power as the first mover in American politics (based on the executive's structural advantages, induced by unity and independence), Congress has a number of powerful tools at its disposal that can both limit executive discretion (budgetary power, for example), and it has the power of the final word through investigations and ultimately impeachment and removal from office. In other words, both political branches have the means to enforce their prerogatives and political judgments against the other. In fact, while it is largely taken for granted today that disputes between Congress and the president should be taken to the judiciary for resolution, *Federalist* 51, the essay largely recognized as the preeminent commentary on the Constitution's separation of powers, does not mention the court at all. Rather, the separation of powers system is self-enforcing through political contestation, not bound by judicial enforcement. Indeed, in earlier essays Publius decried the insufficiency of parchment barriers to maintain the branches in their proper spheres, and subsequent development of the argument in later papers demonstrates that the answer to the inadequacies (and, indeed, the impossibility) of legal certainty is the creation of a self-sustaining political system wherein each of the political branches have the means and motives to defend themselves and to push their own judgments in politics.

More fundamentally, judicial resolution of interbranch boundaries represents a fundamental misunderstanding of the nature of the constitutional system, treating the Constitution primarily as a text to be interpreted and enforced by the judiciary rather than the instantiation of a system of government.[2] Judicial superintendence of the separation of powers extracts the court from within the separation of powers, placing it above the other branches. Such judicial enforcement, moreover, reveals a problem of ends and means. For legalists, the goal is the maintenance of the separation of powers itself, and constitutional goals, such as the protection of liberty, are merely secondary benefits derived from enforcing the Constitution's textual limits. In the account offered here, the separation of powers is not an end in itself but is itself the means to the Constitution's politically contingent and at times conflicting ends or aspirations. Hence, political contestation between the branches is not a pathology to be avoided through judicial settlement. Rather, such conflict is productive because the different structures of the Constitution's competing institutions induce competing perspectives on politics and allow for a great deal of flexibility and dynamism.

The dynamism of the constitutional order should be clear from the preceding. As Hamilton argued in *Federalist* 23, legal limitations on power only hamper the ability of the government to meet unforeseen exigencies. Law cannot anticipate and respond to every future circumstance. Instead, the government must have "unlimited" power to meet the needs of the political community, and so the interior structure of the government (the separation of powers system) was the solution to the problem of the uncertainties that are endemic to political life. The dynamism of the constitutional order's institutional apparatus, and its ability to respond to the challenges of contemporary life, was demonstrated in two of the case study chapters.

The legislative veto was a response to the need to delegate legislative authority to the executive branch or administrative agencies both for the sake of efficiency and the need for expertise. Such delegation, however, poses problems for constitutional government by placing legislative power in the hands of less democratically accountable actors. The legislative veto was a congressional response to this problem, enabling Congress to harness the energy of the executive branch while ensuring that it did not abdicate its own constitutional function. While the current court is highly skeptical of congressional delegations of power, the invention of the legislative veto was a political response to this concern. In other words, the legislative veto is an example of the political branches engaging each other to meet the needs of the political community while ensuring democratic accountability in the operation of government. Judicial intervention, however, thwarted this healthy development. By cutting Congress off from its delegated powers, the court forced it to choose between doing less, or delegating without accountability. It is of course true that some critics of the legislative veto—such as the late Antonin Scalia, prior to his appointment to the court—viewed its invalidation as a first step towards rolling back widespread delegation, especially insofar as the legislative veto made it easier for Congress to delegate.[3] While there might be good reasons for Congress to take more ownership of its legislative prerogatives—as Jessica Korn, for example, has argued—this is a prudential objection rather than a principled constitutional one.[4] Indeed, if the branches in their political negotiations determine that the only way to effectively accomplish some governmental objective is through delegation, then it is incumbent upon the branches to determine how to accomplish that goal while also ensuring that such delegation is reconciled to constitutional structure. The legislative veto, in this way, is a primary example of the ways in which the constitutional order is adaptable to the various crises and exigencies of unforeseen circumstances while maintaining its structure through the political negotiation of the political branches. Judicial invalidation of the legislative veto, based on flawed premises and shoddy legal reasoning, fed the view that the Constitution is the enemy of good and effective government because it is too static and, therefore, unadaptable to the needs of contemporary government.

Similarly, the case study on executive agreements demonstrated that while the vast majority of international agreements made by the United States do not comply with the Constitution's explicit textual mechanism (the treaty), executive agreements do not, in themselves, suggest a major departure from constitutional principles. This case is especially instructive because the court's reticence to rule on interbranch issues related to foreign powers means that governing authority in this arena has largely been left to the political process. Even so, the evidence is clear that there is a qualitative difference between treaties and agreements that are conducted at lower levels of authorization, and that Congress, regardless of partisan dynamics between the branches, has consistently demanded that international agreements dealing with certain subject matters (such as arms treaties) be conducted as treaties. In fact, even as most legal scholars view executive agreements, congressional-executive agreements, and treaties to be legally interchangeable, political practice suggests the opposite. The vast majority of executive agreements (in excess of 95 percent) are pursuant to statutory grants of power such as foreign aid. Congress maintains significant oversight of these agreements through its ordinary legislative powers such as the appropriations power. While sole executive agreements (those entered into based on the president's independent constitutional powers) pose the most difficult constitutional questions, even these agreements can never be conducted fully outside of the purview of Congress. Agreements related to the military, for example, still come before Congress in other ways, including appropriations and oversight hearings. Finally, for all the controversy around congressional-executive agreements, in which both houses of Congress approve international agreements by majority vote, such agreements are very rare and have generally dealt with issues that are fully within Congress's plenary authority to legislate, such as trade agreements.[5] Such agreements, moreover, have often been designed to get extensive congressional buy-in throughout the negotiation process (including members of Congress on the negotiations team) in exchange for fast-track approval. In this way, such agreements hardly represent a departure from separation of powers principles but are an example of a healthy political order. While there are certainly political problems with executive agreements, especially related to transparency and reporting, these indicate a failure of congressional oversight that by itself does not mean that the separation of powers does not govern contemporary practice; this is especially true since Congress has recently undertaken reform efforts in this area.[6] In short, the case studies on the legislative veto and executive agreements demonstrate the vitality of the Constitution's governing institutions, their ability to stretch to meet new circumstances while maintaining the basic shape of the constitutional order.

The idea of judicial resolution of interbranch conflict is so ingrained in many people's thinking that they might assume that allowing the political branches to resolve disputes means that the Constitution has no bearing on political discourse. On the contrary, the constitutional text contains and incorporates competing and contingent principles, and these textual and structural principles have weights that vary according to the political circumstances that give rise to disputes.[7] Given that departures from the text are often a response to political circumstances, they require political justification to explain why such actions vindicate the purposes of the law and the common good (akin to Lockean prerogative).

The case study in recess appointments illustrated this point.[8] While the court's resolution of the recess appointment controversy during the Obama administration focused on the historical meaning of the recess appointments clause and how historical usage or "gloss" ought to inform the court's interpretation of the clause, the divergent opinions on the court (while having no practical difference on the particular case) settled the meaning of the constitutional text in ways that were inattentive to the political circumstances that gave rise to the controversy in the first place. The court's focus on the literal meaning of the constitutional text precluded President Obama from arguing that congressional behavior justified such recess appointments because a Senate partisan minority, using the filibuster, was preventing the confirmation of key governmental roles not by voting them down but by endlessly obstructing. In other words, President Obama could have argued that the fundamental purpose of the recess appointments clause is that the government should continue to function absent democratic choice to the contrary, and that his recess appointments were thus justified in the face of unprecedented partisan obstruction by a minority faction of one chamber of Congress. Instead, the court's intervention made Republican obstruction look high-minded and principled (which it was not), while the president's attempts to staff the departments and offices of the government appeared lawless. Judicial resolution of interbranch conflicts, given the nature of judicial action, precludes the types of politically contingent constitutional arguments available to political actors and has the potential to distort the political dynamics at play. This is not a bug of judicial decision-making; rather, judicial resolution of political contestations between the branches is inappropriate precisely because the judiciary is comparatively less well-suited to the types of constitutional arguments appropriate to such contestations. The turn to strictly legal arguments, moreover, makes politics the province of lawyers and legal experts, depriving ordinary citizens of an accessible political discourse. In this way, the judicialized separation of powers, while appearing to be more closely connected to the text of the Constitution, can actually subvert constitutional purposes.

Finally, none of the foregoing suggests that the Supreme Court should not play a distinctive function in separation of powers disputes. However, the court's role should be narrowly confined to governmental action that directly infringes upon individual rights, and not merely as a secondary or derivative consequence of an interbranch dispute. In other words, the recess appointments controversy should not have presented a justiciable controversy because the legal question concerned the limits of the political branches' power with respect to each other. Here, the legal rights of individuals were only indirectly affected by such a boundary dispute. Similarly, the legislative veto controversy demonstrates what would have been a more narrowly constrained and thus appropriate ruling. Insofar as the legislative veto in question in *Chadha* pertained to what amounted to a deportation proceeding conducted by the House of Representatives, such an exercise was more akin to a bill of attainder and thus constitutionally impermissible. In other words, such a procedure would have been constitutionally impermissible had it been conducted by both houses of Congress and the president through the Constitution's formal lawmaking process, as Justice Powell argued in his concurring opinion. Therefore, the action at issue and invalidated in *Chadha* is easily distinguished from legislative vetoes concerning delegated legislative power. Confining the court to the narrower role of protecting individuals against direct violations of their rights, as opposed to policing the textual boundaries of Congress and the president, keeps the court within and a part of the Constitution's separation of power system rather than above it as a superintending outside entity.

Does Hyperpartisanship Undermine the Separation of Powers?

The purpose of this concluding chapter is to consider a potentially powerful challenge to my main argument—that separation of powers disputes between Congress and the president should be resolved between them without recourse to the judiciary—and to propose a tentative answer to that objection. The core of the objection is that a political solution to separation of powers disputes between Congress and the president is unworkable today given levels of partisan polarization. According to this view, the unanticipated introduction of political parties immediately following the founding has undermined the Madisonian system, rendering its political science obsolete.[9] This phenomenon has only been exacerbated by increasing political polarization. As Daryl Levinson and Richard Pildes put it, "Few aspects of the founding generation's political theory are now more clearly anachronistic than their vision of legislative-executive separation of powers."[10] Rather, they argue, the "law and theory" described in *Federalist* 51 perfectly represent the government the framers designed only if one ignores the reality of parties, the existence of which are a crucial element in the way government actually functions. Levinson and Pildes maintain that the Madisonian system of government relied on a "personalization" of institutions, in which those institutions would have wills of their own. In other words, members of the coordinate departments would care more about the "intrinsic" interests of their branches than their own political motivations. Regardless of whether this assumption ever held true, they assert, it certainly is not true in contemporary political life. Indeed, they write,

"Political competition and cooperation along relatively stable lines of policy and ideological disagreement quickly came to be channeled not through the branches of government" but through the political parties they "despised" and sought to prevent.[11] In this way, the distinction between unified government (when the same party controls both the presidency and both chambers of Congress) and divided government is the main factor that determines whether the branches will have opposed wills. Hence, only under conditions of divided government will Congress and the president have distinct wills from each other. Under unified control, the separation between the branches will be bridged or overcome, thus essentially transforming the separation of powers into a kind of parliamentary system that relegates the minority party to irrelevance. Even when there is interbranch contestation under conditions of divided government, however, it is not the Madisonian system doing the work per se. Rather, such interbranch contestation is epiphenomenal: The institutions are merely the site of a larger partisan conflict playing out. This is a particularly dangerous situation, according to Levinson and Pildes, because Congress can only fulfill its constitutional role of checking the president under contingent political circumstances.

There is certainly much that is true about Levinson and Pildes' analysis, as any observer of contemporary politics would have to admit. For example, congressional Republicans refused to criticize or punish even the most lawless actions of President Trump during his tenure in office. This required them to interpret "impeachable offenses" in ways that would essentially enervate congressional oversight of the executive. They also refused to publicly condemn and refute the election conspiracies peddled by former President Trump after President Biden took office. This extreme form of partisanship corrodes the proper functioning of the constitutional order as partisan advantage trumps the public good. Even so, while Levinson and Pildes' argument and descriptions of contemporary American politics are worth taking seriously, there are significant ways in which their analysis misses key features of the Constitution's political science, causing them to question the contemporary efficacy of the entire Madisonian scheme, which they deem a failure.

Before critiquing Levinson and Pildes's analysis on the theoretical level, it is worth noting that their description of American politics is overly simplistic in a number of ways, which distorts their analysis.[12] For example, Josh Chafetz has noted that what constitutes unified government is itself far more complicated and rare than Levinson and Pildes acknowledge. Rather than a unified/divided government dichotomy, Chafetz maintains that unified government is very much a matter of degree. In contemporary politics, for example, the use of the filibuster in the Senate essentially means that unified party control only fully occurs when a party can control a supermajority of the Senate. This, however, is an increasingly rare phenomenon. The filibuster, moreover, has become a powerful tool by which partisan minorities in the Senate can check the agenda of the majority party. The notion of unified government is even further complicated when one considers the power of the Supreme Court in contemporary politics, even if, as argued here, such power is, in normative terms, outsized. Given the power that the court has to thwart governing majorities, unified government can technically only be achieved once partisans have also captured the Supreme Court. In short, the conditions for unified government are much more stringent than Levinson and Pildes acknowledge, making it much less likely that one party can totally erode or overcome separation of powers constraints.

Secondly, Chafetz maintains that Levinson and Pildes overstate party discipline, which is a necessary concomitant for their theory of unified government. While parties have grown more ideologically homogeneous and distinct from each other over time, this does not mean that party discipline always holds true. Rather, even under unified government, the president's co-partisans in Congress cannot be fully relied upon to push the president's agenda, and, in fact, congressional support for presidential initiatives is very much a function of presidential support in the electorate. Even after he had won reelection, and with Republican control of both houses of Congress, President George W. Bush's social security reform effort was essentially dead on arrival even with his own party. President Obama struggled to pass health care reform even with majorities in both the House and Senate. President Trump failed to get the Republicans in Congress to fund his border wall before the new Democratic majority took over the House, leading to an extended government shutdown. And President Biden's struggles with Joe Manchin and Kyrsten Sinema during the first two years of his administration also forced interbranch negotiations in order to find acceptable solutions to both branches.

Finally, it is worth noting that there are times when Congress, regardless of broader partisan dynamics, stands for congressional prerogatives against the executive branch. This was amply demonstrated in the case study chapter on executive agreements. Congress has regularly required that substantial agreements in particular issue areas be conducted as treaties rather than executive agreements with lower thresholds of congressional authorization, and it has enforced that judgment against the executive branch regardless of the partisan dynamics between the branches. Even though executive agreements are considered legally interchangeable with treaties as a matter of international law, political practice makes clear that Congress has not fully acquiesced to that view. If political parties fully undermined the Madisonian scheme, as Levinson and Pildes maintain, then one would not expect this to be the case.

Putting these descriptive complications aside, more problematically, Levinson and Pildes misconceive the nature of the separation of powers system, overemphasizing checks and balances. In Levinson and Pildes's characterization of separation of powers, the primary function or purpose of the Madisonian scheme of competing institutions is that they would thwart each other. This is perhaps understandable if *Federalist* 51 is read by itself, especially since that essay does emphasize how the branches will keep each other in their proper places through checking and balancing. Read as a whole, however, the overarching emphasis in *The Federalist* is not balance per se. Rather, the branches each perform distinctive functions in the pursuit of important governmental objectives. The executive branch is structured to induce energy to better enable it to vindicate the needs of the political order, especially when times of emergency require quick and decisive action—even outside the existing parameters of law. The legislative branch, on the other hand, is structured to induce the quality of deliberation so that it can be responsive to democratic demands with regard to the public good. In this way, the system is not about checking and balancing so much as it is about the achievement of politically contingent constitutional goods through functional differentiation and inducing competing institutional perspectives on difficult political problems. The constitutional system is meant to shape, channel, and be responsive to politics.

By overemphasizing the checking and balancing function of the separation of powers, however, Levinson and Pildes are primed to see constitutional failure when there is political agreement between the branches that is induced by unified government. Their emphasis on checks and balances as the preeminent goal of Madisonian political science represents a depoliticized view of the political order. While there are certainly reasons to be concerned with the impact of hyperpartisanship on the proper functioning of the governing apparatus, unified control of the government and the ways in which that can lead to efficient outcomes can be indicative of a government responsive to politics rather than proof of constitutional failure. This is especially the case given that the sequencing of staggered elections in American politics means that it often takes several elections to build a political coalition that culminates in a unified government. While political parties can corrode constitutional politics, their existence, and the fact that contemporary interbranch politics is largely structured by them, is only

small and particular constituencies. While there is certainly not a direct parallel between founding choices and the contemporary problem of hyperpartisanship, attention to the founding insight that electoral structures shape the behavior of officeholders points the way to institutional improvements that could mitigate the contemporary problem. Insofar as Congress seems insufficiently motivated to pursue the public interest ahead of narrow and base forms of partisanship, this is less a failure of the constitutional system itself and more a failure to think within the confines of its political science and its assumptions about human motivation.

In particular, consider how modern partisan primaries drive polarization in Congress, creating perverse electoral incentives that make it harder to deliberate, bargain, and compromise, lest one face an ideological challenger in the party primary.[21] Partisan primary electorates tend to be much smaller than in the general election—only about 20 to 25 percent of voters. More crucially, this narrow slice of the electorate tends to consist of strong partisans who are more ideologically extreme than the average American voter.[22] While this is true for both parties, the polarization is asymmetric as Republican primary voters tend to be more ideologically extreme than in the Democratic party, which has more moderates within its ranks.[23]

Because partisan primary electorates tend to be more ideologically extreme, members of Congress face intense pressure to appease them. This is especially true because most congressional seats are safe, meaning the winner of the primary is likely the winner of the general election. For most congressional seats, then, there are only incentives to appease an extreme partisan base rather than a majority of the district. The frequency of ideological challenges in primaries has increased in recent years as party activists have weaponized primaries to move parties in their preferred ideological direction.[24] One does not have to look far to find examples of popular general election candidates who were "primaried" from the ideological flank of their party. In rare instances, well-known incumbents, such as Senator Joe Lieberman, were subsequently able to run and win reelection as independents. Senator Lisa Murkowski was able to win a write-in campaign after a "sore loser" law prevented her from running as an independent after losing a Republican primary. Both of these examples underscore the extent to which partisan primaries can pull the parties away from popular general election candidates. Partisan primaries can also be perversely weaponized by members of the opposing party who cross over to vote for the most extreme candidates in the hopes that this will give their own party a better chance in the general election.[25] Such strategic voting by partisans across the aisle can also have the effect of further entrenching partisan polarization.

The practical impact of partisan primaries on the government has been substantial. Today, there is no ideological overlap between the parties in Congress, and moderates in both parties have been largely eliminated. The Pew Research Center notes that there are now only two dozen moderate lawmakers across both parties compared to nearly 140 in 1970.[26] This trend has occurred even as the electorate's political preferences have remained relatively stable during the past several decades. Morris Fiorina has shown that there is a discrepancy between the ideological composition of the public at large and that of elected officials. In a series of works, Fiorina argues that the American public is far more ideologically heterogeneous and centrist than our sorted, ideologically distinct, and polarized parties in government.[27] Insofar as electoral outcomes are polarized, this is a function of the general election choices on offer to the public (candidates chosen by extreme partisan primary electorates). In other words, American politics *is* polarized today. This polarization, however, is the product of electoral incentive structures that leave the public with general election candidates (and then governing officials) that are more extreme than average American voters. As Fiorina concludes,

> All in all, the data compiled by academic and commercial survey organizations indicate that in broad outline the American public has changed little in the past four decades. In the aggregate, the public today looks much the same as the one that chose between Jimmy Carter and Gerald Ford in 1976, well before the polarization era. This inconvenient fact makes it hard to argue—as some pundits and a few political scientists continue to do so—that polarization in Congress and state legislatures, and among party activists and donors has been driven by the polarization of the vast majority of Americans who do not belong to the political class.[28]

Electoral incentive structures have a dramatic impact on the ability of members of Congress to break from their partisan tribe on any issue lest they be punished in a primary election, thus making compromise and political negotiation all but impossible if members of Congress want to be reelected. As Yuval Levin writes, this means that members of Congress "find it politically dangerous to do the job Congress exists to do."[29] In a healthy democracy, elected officials would strive to build majoritarian coalitions to win elections. Appealing to majoritarian constituencies, moreover, would allow members of Congress to build coalitions across different issues in the give-and-take of the legislative process. This dynamic, however, is undermined by the incentives of partisan primaries, which pull elected officials toward the fringes. As an example of the perverse incentives of partisan primaries, consider the dramatic disconnect between the vociferous criticism of Trump by congressional Republicans in private compared to their vocal and ardent support in public because their ever-extreme base of support in the primaries held the keys to their political futures.[30] Such political behavior, given the hyperpartisan incentive structure, would be unsurprising to the framers who recognized that ambition and interest are some of the most powerful motivations in political life and thus sought ways to appropriately channel or mitigate such interests to orient officeholders to the public good. The framers' assumption, moreover, has been borne out by contemporary political science research that suggests that the desire for reelection is a powerful, if not the most important, driver of congressional behavior.[31]

It does not have to be this way. In fact, there are a number of reforms on offer that could better orient members of Congress to more majoritarian constituencies. For example, Katherine M. Gehl and Michael E. Porter recommend final-five ranked-choice voting.[32] In this scenario, states hold open primaries, and the top five candidates go to a ranked-choice general election. This is similar to the electoral system in Alaska. In Alaska, anyone can run in an open primary in which voters choose one candidate. The top four advance to a ranked-choice general election. Unlike in partisan primaries, ranked-choice general elections require candidates to appeal to as broad a constituency as possible, including trying to earn people's second and third choice vote. The practical value of such an approach is that it beats partisan primaries on their own purported rationale: that they are democratic. Insofar as partisan primary voters choose general election candidates, voters in general elections are often forced to choose between candidates who would not be their top choice (or even perhaps their second or third). Ranked-choice voting is a solution to that problem and could thus be an antidote to the kind of corrosive hyperpartisanship on display in contemporary politics.

In another variant, used in California and Washington state, there is an open primary in which candidates from all parties run on a single ballot. The top two candidates advance to the general election regardless of their partisan affiliation, meaning that a general election could have two candidates from the same party. Researchers have found that this type of electoral system leads to more moderate legislators compared to closed primary systems.[33] This is borne out by the records of the ten Republican members of the House who voted to impeach Donald Trump in January, 2021. Only two, Rep. Dan Newhouse of Washington and Rep. David Valadao of California, were able to win reelection; neither faced a partisan primary. Rep.

Jaime Herrera Beutler of Washington was defeated in her open primary but came only .5 percent behind Joe Kent, the Trump-backed challenger who advanced to the general election and lost to Democrat Marie Gluesenkamp Perez. The remaining three Republican members of the House who voted to impeach Trump and sought reelection faced partisan primaries and were defeated by much larger margins than Rep. Herrera Beutler. In addition, all four of those who chose not to run for reelection would have faced a partisan primary.

Of course, moving to open primaries and ranked-choice general election runoffs (or similar variants) can also cause problems, especially by weakening political parties. Strong political parties can be good for democracy, especially if the parties are incentivized to capture the middle rather than trying to win elections by merely mobilizing the base. Partisan primaries incentivize base maximization rather than majoritarian coalition building. Moving to purely open primaries, however, can remove partisan cues and informational shortcuts that make democracy possible, especially for those who only occasionally pay attention to politics.[34] In this telling, open primaries attempt to depoliticize politics by ridding it of partisanship. There are, however, real partisan and ideological disagreements in the country that cannot be masked over by an appeal to centrism. What is needed is not centrism—as if there is some ideal policy point between ideological positions—but moderation, which is to say that members of Congress should be incentivized to deliberate and compromise across a range of issues without the immediate threat of losing their jobs. This is why some, like Yuval Levin, advocate for ranked-choice voting *within* partisan primaries with the hope that this would result in party nominees with broader appeal.[35] This would both strengthen parties and help them to build stronger coalitions that seek to capture as many votes as possible.

This discussion of electoral design is not meant to suggest that reform in this area would be a panacea. Rather, the point here is that parties are not necessarily corrosive of the separation of powers. The political science assumptions underlying the Madisonian system provide insights into how electoral mechanisms can shape institutional performance both internally and in relation to each other. Insofar as contemporary electoral mechanisms are more likely to foster tribal attachments, tinkering with electoral incentive structures could have a salutary impact by reorienting members of Congress to more majoritarian (and less ideologically extreme) constituencies. The point here is not to recommend a particular mechanism but to demonstrate a way to think about the contemporary problem of hyperpartisanship and how assumptions about human ambition underlying the Constitution's political science provide criteria for evaluation and reform. American federalism, moreover, allows electoral reformers space for experimentation and trial and error with different approaches.

Constitutional reform and maintenance requires attentiveness to the political science of the constitutional framers and their understanding of human motivation. As noted at the outset of the book, the Constitution is not self-sustaining. Rather, it requires certain civic understandings that make it work over time. I have argued that many of the problems in contemporary political life result from distorted civic understandings. Recovering the Constitution's political architecture and the ways in which politics is channeled through a dynamic system of institutions, makes it possible for the polity to be responsive to the unforeseen challenges that are endemic to political life. The Constitution is not a static legal text to be enforced by the court as an end in itself. Rather, the separation of powers system of competing institutions is itself the means to the Constitution's multiple, competing, and politically contingent ends. Political conflict between the institutions is thus an essential element of constitutional health, and the source of the constitutional order's vitality and dynamism. Failure to understand this fundamental dimension of the Constitution, however, can have serious and deleterious consequences, as demonstrated in the case studies. Indeed, as the legalistic conception erodes civic capacities over time, it can transform the Constitution from an ongoing and dynamic institutional political practice into a mere lawyer's brief, resulting in constitutional failure. A recovery of the notion that the Constitution establishes a political architecture, along with all of the features attendant to that more capacious and dynamic conception, retrains our evaluative capacities, enabling us to reform our politics in ways that can restore constitutional health.

NOTES

INTRODUCTION

1. Eric A. Posner and Adrian Vermeule, *The Executive Unbound: After the Madisonian Republic* (Oxford University Press, 2010), 208.
2. Woodrow Wilson, *Constitutional Government in the United States* (Columbia University Press, 1908); Stephen M. Griffin, *Broken Trust: Dysfunctional Government and Constitutional Reform* (University Press of Kansas, 2015).
3. William G. Howell and Terry M. Moe, *Relic: How Our Constitution Undermines Effective Government—and Why We Need a More Powerful Presidency* (Basic Books, 2016), 23.
4. Myers v. United States, 272 US 52 (1926), 293.
5. Larry Alexander and Frederick Schauer, "On Extrajudicial Constitutional Interpretation," *Harvard Law Review* 110, no. 7 (1997): 1359–1387; Jon Elster, *Ulysses Unbound: Studies in Rationality, Precommitment, and Constraints* (Cambridge University Press, 2000), 100; Giovanni Sartori, *Comparative Constitutional Engineering: An Inquiry into Structures, Incentives and Outcomes* (Macmillan, 1994), 196.
6. John F. Manning, "Separation of Powers as Ordinary Interpretation," *Harvard Law Review* 124, no. 8 (2011): 1939–2040.
7. Jeremy Waldron, *Political Political Theory: Essays on Institutions* (Harvard University Press, 2016), 30.
8. Waldron, *Political Political Theory*, 71.
9. Daryl J. Levinson and Richard H. Pildes, "Separation of Parties, Not Powers," *Harvard Law Review* 119, no. 8 (2006): 2311–2386.
10. Rebecca L. Brown, "Separated Powers and Ordered Liberty," *University of Pennsylvania Law Review* 139 (1991): 1513–1566.
11. Sotirios A. Barber, *On What the Constitution Means* (Johns Hopkins University Press, 1984).
12. McCulloch v. Maryland 17 U.S. 316 (1819), 415.
13. *McCulloch v. Maryland*, 407.
14. Jeffrey K. Tulis, *The Rhetorical Presidency* (Princeton University Press, 1987), 41–45; Jeffrey K. Tulis and Nicole Mellow, *Legacies of Losing in American Politics* (University of Chicago Press, 2018), 54–59; George Thomas, *The Madisonian Constitution* (Johns Hopkins University Press, 2008); Mariah Zeisberg, *War Powers: The Politics of Constitutional Authority* (Princeton University Press, 2013).
15. Thomas, *Madisonian Constitution.*
16. Tulis, *Rhetorical Presidency*, 41–44; Zeisberg, *War Powers.*
17. Jeffrey K. Tulis, "Deliberation Between Institutions," in *Debating Deliberative Democracy*, ed. James S. Fishkin and Peter Laslett (Blackwell, 2003).
18. Jesse H. Choper, *Judicial Review and the National Political Process: A Functional Reconsideration of the Role of the Supreme Court* (University of Chicago Press, 1980).

19. The argument of this book is limited to separation of powers disputes concerning the legal boundaries between the branches. Certainly, other areas of the constitutional text more readily lend themselves to judicial review, especially rights provisions. I do not advance a theory of judicial review with regard to these other questions.
20. Jasmine Farrier, *Constitutional Dysfunction on Trial: Congressional Lawsuits and the Separation of Powers* (Cornell University Press, 2019).
21. Lee Epstein, "Partisanship 'All the Way Down' on the U.S. Supreme Court," *Pepperdine Law Review* 51, no. 3 (2024): 489–514; Neal Devins and Lawrence Baum, "Split Definitive: How Party Polarization Turned the Supreme Court into a Partisan Court," *Supreme Court Review* 2016 (2016): 301–365.
22. John Agresto, *The Supreme Court and Constitutional Democracy* (Cornell University Press, 1984); Neal Devins and Keith E. Whittington, eds., *Congress and the Constitution* (Duke University Press, 2005); J. Mitchell Pickerill, *Constitutional Deliberation in Congress: The Impact of Judicial Review in a Separated System* (Duke University Press, 2004).
23. Daphna Renan, "'Institutional Settlement' in a Provisional Constitutional Order," *California Law Review* 108 (2020): 1995–2005; Nikolas Bowie and Daphna Renan, "The Separation of Powers Counterrevolution," *Yale Law Journal* 131, no. 7 (2022): 2020–2125; Daphna Renan, "Presidential Norms and Article II," *Harvard Law Review* 131, no. 8 (2018): 2187–2282; Jonathan Gienapp, *The Second Creation: Fixing the American Constitution in the Founding Era* (Belknap Press, 2018).
24. John E. Finn, *Peopling the Constitution* (University Press of Kansas, 2014).
25. Howell and Moe, *Relic*, 143–180.
26. Bruce A. Ackerman and David Golove, *Is NAFTA Constitutional?* (Harvard University Press, 1995), 904–908; Sharyn O'Halloran, *Politics, Process, and American Trade Policy* (University of Michigan Press, 1994), 139–175; Jasmine Farrier, *Congressional Ambivalence: The Political Burdens of Constitutional Authority* (University Press of Kentucky, 2010), 81–114.
27. George Thomas, *The Founders and the Idea of a National University: Constituting the American Mind* (Cambridge University Press, 2014).
28. James W. Ceaser, *Liberal Democracy and Political Science* (Johns Hopkins University Press, 1992), 41–69.

CHAPTER 1: SEPARATION OF POWERS AND THE PROBLEM OF ENDS AND MEANS

1. Aziz Huq and Jon Michaels, "The Cycles of Separation-of-Powers Jurisprudence," *Yale Law Journal* 126, no. 2 (2016): 349.
2. Rebecca L. Brown, "Separated Powers and Ordered Liberty," *University of Pennsylvania Law Review* 139, no. 6 (1991): 1517.
3. Peter L. Strauss, "Formal and Functional Approaches to Separation of Powers Questions—A Foolish Inconsistency?" *Cornell Law Review* 72, no. 3 (1987): 488–526.
4. Curtis A. Bradley and Trevor W. Morrison, "Historical Gloss and the Separation of Powers," *Harvard Law Review* 126, no. 2 (2012): 411–485.

5. Nikolas Bowie and Daphna Renan, "The Separation of Powers Counterrevolution," *Yale Law Journal* 131, no. 7 (2022): 2024–2025.
6. Strauss, "Formal and Functional Approaches."
7. Steven G. Calabresi and Saikrishna B. Prakash, "The President's Power to Execute the Laws," *Yale Law Journal* 104, no. 3 (1994): 544.
8. M.J.C. Vile, *Constitutionalism and the Separation of Powers*, 2nd ed. (Liberty Fund, 1998), 11.
9. Brown, "Separated Powers and Ordered Liberty," 1524.
10. INS v. Chadha, 462 US 919 (1983), 951.
11. Youngstown Sheet & Tube Co. v. Sawyer 343 U.S. 579 (1952), 587.
12. David J. Siemers, *The Myth of Coequal Branches: Restoring the Constitution's Separation of Functions* (University of Missouri Press, 2018), 29–30.
13. Siemers, *Myth of Coequal Branches*, 30.
14. See, for example, Martin H. Redish, *The Constitution as Political Structure* (Oxford University Press, 1995), 101: The "Court's role in separation of powers cases is to be limited to determining whether the challenged branch action falls within the definition of that branch's constitutionally derived powers."
15. Brown, "Separated Powers and Ordered Liberty," 1523.
16. See, for example, Calabresi and Prakash, "President's Power to Execute the Laws"; Saikrishna Prakash, "The Essential Meaning of Executive Power," *University of Illinois Law Review* no. 3 (2003): 701–820; Saikrishna B. Prakash and Michael D. Ramsey, "The Executive Power over Foreign Affairs," *Yale Law Journal* 111, no. 2 (2001): 231–356; Saikrishna Prakash, "The Sweeping Domestic War Powers of Congress," *Michigan Law Review* 113, no. 8 (2015): 1337–1396.
17. Michael W. McConnell, *The President Who Would Not Be King* (Princeton University Press, 2020), 6.
18. McConnell, *President Who Would Not Be King*, 7.
19. Steven G. Calabresi and Kevin H. Rhodes, "The Structural Constitution: Unitary Executive, Plural Judiciary," *Harvard Law Review* 105, no. 6 (1992): 1158.
20. Steven G. Calabresi and Christopher S. Yoo, *The Unitary Executive: Presidential Power from Washington to Bush* (Yale University Press, 2008), 30–38.
21. Calabresi and Yoo, *Unitary Executive*, 39–41.
22. J. David Alvis, Jeremy D. Bailey, and F. Flagg Taylor IV, *The Contested Removal Power, 1789–2010* (University Press of Kansas, 2013); Jonathan Gienapp, "Removal and the Changing Debate over Executive Power at the Founding," *American Journal of Legal History* 63, no. 3 (2023): 229–250; Jonathan Gienapp, "Making Constitutional Meaning: The Removal Debate and the Birth of Constitutional Essentialism," *Journal of the Early Republic* 35, no. 2 (2015): 375–418; Aziz Z. Huq, "Removal as a Political Question," *Stanford Law Review* 64, no. 1 (2013): 1–76.
23. Aziz Z. Huq, "Separation of Powers Metatheory," *Columbia Law Review* 118, no. 5 (2018): 1529.
24. Stephen Skowronek, "The Conservative Insurgency and Presidential Power: A Developmental Perspective on the Unitary Executive," *Harvard Law Review* 122, no. 8 (2009): 2070–2103.

25. Huq, "Separation of Powers Metatheory," 1530.
26. Huq, "Separation of Powers Metatheory," 1529–1530.
27. Ilan Wurman, "Nondelegation at the Founding," *Yale Law Journal* 130, no. 4 (2021): 1490–1556; Martin H. Redish, "Pragmatic Formalism, Separation of Powers, and the Need to Revisit the Nondelegation Doctrine," *Loyola University Chicago Law Journal* 51, no. 2 (2019): 363–418; McConnell, *President Who Would Not Be King*, 326–335; Philip Hamburger, *Is Administrative Law Unlawful?* (University of Chicago Press, 2015).
28. Gary Lawson, "Delegation and Original Meaning," *Virginia Law Review* 88, no. 2 (2002): 342–343.
29. Gundy v. United States 139 S. Ct. 2116 (2019), Gorsuch dissenting at 2135, citing Lawson, "Delegation and Original Meaning," 327, 340.
30. *United States v. Gundy* (2018), Gorsuch dissenting, 2135
31. EPA v. West Virginia 597 U.S. 697 (2022); Biden v. Nebraska 600 U.S. 477 (2023).
32. Beau J. Baumann, "Americana Administrative Law," *Georgetown Law Journal* 111 (2023): 470.
33. Baumann, "Americana Administrative Law," 470; Allen C. Sumrall and Beau J. Baumann, "Clarifying Judicial Aggrandizement," *University of Pennsylvania Law Review* 172 (2023): 24–42.
34. Jide Nzelibe, "The Uniqueness of Foreign Affairs," *Iowa Law Review* 89, no. 3 (March 2004): 941–1010; "Nondelegation's Unprincipled Foreign Affairs Exceptionalism," *Harvard Law Review* 134 (2021): 1132–1161.
35. Bruce A. Ackerman and David Golove, *Is NAFTA Constitutional?* (Harvard University Press, 1995).
36. Bruce A. Ackerman, *We the People* (Belknap Press of Harvard University Press, 1991).
37. Vile, *Constitutionalism and the Separation of Powers*, 11.
38. National Federation of Business v. Occupational Safety and Health Administration 595 U. S. ____ (2022), Gorsuch, J., concurring, Slip Opinion at 7.
39. Morrison v. Olson, 487 U.S. 654 (1988), 710–711.
40. INS v. Chadha, 462 U.S. 919 (1983), 959.
41. Brown, "Separated Powers and Ordered Liberty," 1525.
42. Brown, "Separated Powers and Ordered Liberty," 1525.
43. John F. Manning, "Separation of Powers as Ordinary Interpretation," *Harvard Law Review* 124, no. 8 (2011): 1939–2040.
44. Manning, "Separation of Powers," 1944–1945.
45. Manning, "Separation of Powers," 2010; Harold Koh, "The President Versus the Senate in Treaty Interpretation: What's All the Fuss About?" *Yale Journal of International Law* 15, no. 2 (1990): 335.
46. However, as I demonstrate in my chapter on the legislative veto, the only way to characterize the legislative veto as an independent act of lawmaking is to invoke a background principle of separation of powers and to add to that background principle the unargued presumption that, when any branch acts, it wields the type of power granted to it by the Constitution.
47. Manning, "Separation of Powers," 1952.
48. Bowsher v. Synar 478 U.S. 714 (1986), 776.

49. Huq, "Separation of Powers Metatheory," 1530.
50. Peter L. Strauss, "The Place of Agencies in Government: Separation of Powers and the Fourth Branch," *Columbia Law Review* 84, no. 3 (1984): 603; Huq, "Separation of Powers Metatheory," 1530.
51. Martin S. Flaherty, "The Most Dangerous Branch," *Yale Law Journal* 105, no. 7 (1996): 1755; Huq, "Separation of Powers Metatheory," 1530.
52. Flaherty, "Most Dangerous Branch," 1816.
53. Brown, "Separated Powers and Ordered Liberty," 1528.
54. Strauss, "Formal and Functional Approaches," 489; Manning, "Separation of Powers," 1950–1958.
55. Huq, "Separation of Powers Metatheory," 1532; Abner S. Greene, "Checks and Balances in an Era of Presidential Lawmaking," *University of Chicago Law Review* 61, no. 1 (1994): 176; Cass R. Sunstein, "Constitutionalism After the New Deal," *Harvard Law Review* 101, no. 2 (1987): 443; David H. Moore, "Taking Cues from Congress: Judicial Review, Congressional Authorization, and the Expansion of Presidential Power," *Notre Dame Law Review* 90, no. 3 (2015): 1028.
56. The veto point is a common unit of analysis in political science studies of the separation of powers. For example, see: Keith Krehbiel, *Pivotal Politics: A Theory of U.S. Lawmaking* (University of Chicago Press, 1998).
57. Alexander Hamilton et al., *The Federalist Papers*, ed. Clinton Rossiter (Signet, 2003), #51, 320.
58. Vincent Phillip Muñoz, "Constitutional Principles: Separation of Powers," YouTube video, August 24, 2012, The Bill of Rights Institute and Jack Miller Center, https://www.youtube.com/watch?v=Nnqk-yGzYYg.
59. Woodrow Wilson, *Constitutional Government in the United States* (Columbia University Press, 1908).
60. Michael Zuckert, "On the Separation of Powers: Liberal and Progressive Constitutionalism," *Social Philosophy and Policy* 29, no. 2 (2012): 359.
61. William G. Howell and Terry M. Moe, *Relic: How Our Constitution Undermines Effective Government—And Why We Need a More Powerful Presidency* (Basic Books, 2016).
62. Hamilton et al., *Federalist Papers*, #41, 253.
63. Hamilton et al., *Federalist Papers*, #1, 29.
64. Hamilton et al., *Federalist Papers*, #23, 149. Emphasis in original.
65. Jeffrey K. Tulis, *The Rhetorical Presidency* (Princeton University Press, 1987), 41–45; Jeffrey K. Tulis, "Impeachment in the Constitutional Order," in *The Constitutional Presidency*, ed. Jeffrey K. Tulis and Joseph M. Bessette (John Hopkins University Press, 2009), 241–245; Jeffrey K. Tulis and Nicole Mellow, *Legacies of Losing in American Politics* (University of Chicago Press, 2018); Mariah Zeisberg, *War Powers: The Politics of Constitutional Authority* (Princeton University Press, 2013), 20–50.
66. Mariah Zeisberg, "Constitutional Fidelity and Interbranch Conflict," *Good Society* 13, no. 3 (2004): 24.
67. Hamilton et al., *Federalist Papers*, #48, 305.
68. Hamilton et al., *Federalist Papers*, #48, 305.
69. Hamilton et al., *Federalist Papers*, #48, 306.
70. Hamilton et al., *Federalist Papers*, #48, 306–310.

71. Hamilton et al., *Federalist Papers*, #51, 319.
72. Hamilton et al., *Federalist Papers*, #37, 224.
73. Hamilton et al., *Federalist Papers*, #37, 225.
74. Tulis and Mellow, *Legacies of Losing*, 57.
75. Hamilton et al., *Federalist Papers*, #37, 223.
76. Joseph M. Bessette, *The Mild Voice of Reason: Deliberative Democracy and American National Government* (University of Chicago Press, 1994).
77. Hamilton et al., *Federalist Papers*, #75, 449.
78. Hamilton et al., *Federalist Papers*, #70, 427.
79. Hamilton et al., *Federalist Papers*, #70, 425.
80. Charles C. Thach Jr., *The Creation of the Presidency, 1775–1789: A Study in Constitutional History* (Johns Hopkins Press, 1969); Max M. Edling, *A Revolution in Favor of Government: Origins of the U.S. Constitution and the Making of the American State* (Oxford University Press, 2008); Michael J. Klarman, *The Framers' Coup: The Making of the United States Constitution* (Oxford University Press, 2016), 11–72; Louis Fisher, "The Efficiency Side of Separated Powers," *Journal of American Studies* 5, no. 2 (1971): 113–131.
81. Thach, *Creation of the Presidency*; Fisher, "Efficiency Side of Separated Powers"; David K. Nichols, *The Myth of the Modern Presidency* (Pennsylvania State University Press, 1994).
82. Jeffrey K. Tulis, "Deliberation Between Institutions," in *Debating Deliberative Democracy*, ed. James S. Fishkin and Peter Laslett (Blackwell, 2003); Zeisberg, *War Powers*, 27–28.
83. Zeisberg, *War Powers*, 27.
84. Siemers, *Myth of Coequal Branches*.
85. Josh Chafetz, *Congress's Constitution: Legislative Authority and the Separation of Powers* (Yale University Press, 2017), 74–77.
86. Chafetz, *Congress's Constitution*, 74.
87. Mariah Zeisberg, "Relational Conception of War Powers," in *The Limits of Constitutional Democracy*, ed. Jeffrey K. Tulis and Stephen Macedo (Princeton University Press, 2010), 188.
88. John E. Finn, *Peopling the Constitution* (University Press of Kansas, 2014), 57.
89. David A. Crockett, "Executive Privilege," in Tulis and Bessette, *Constitutional Presidency*; Mark J. Rozell and Mitchel A. Sollenberger, *Executive Privilege: Presidential Power, Secrecy, and Accountability*, updated ed. (University Press of Kansas, 2020); Gary J. Schmitt, "Executive Privilege: Presidential Power to Withhold Information from Congress," in *The Presidency in the Constitutional Order*, ed. Jeffrey K. Tulis and Joseph M. Bessette (Louisiana State University Press, 1981).
90. Chafetz, *Congress's Constitution*, 18.
91. Zeisberg, *War Powers*, 45–50.
92. Zeisberg, *War Powers*, 31–40.
93. Yuval Levin, *A Time to Build: From Family and Community to Congress and the Campus, How Recommitting to Our Institutions Can Revive the American Dream* (Basic Books, 2020).
94. Levin, *Time to Build*, 33.
95. Levin, *Time to Build*, 33–34.

96. Yuval Levin, "This Is Why Americans Are So Cynical About Politics," *New York Times*, January 21, 2024, https://www.nytimes.com/2024/01/21/opinion/america-politics-cynical-dysfunctional.html.
97. Levin, *Time to Build*, 52–53.
98. Yuval Levin, "Building a More Civil and Collaborative Culture in Congress: Some Diagnostic and Prescriptive Reflections," statement before the House Select Committee on the Modernization of Congress, June 17, 2021, 9–10.
99. Bowie and Renan, "Separation of Powers Counterrevolution," 2024–2025.
100. Jesse H. Choper, *Judicial Review and the National Political Process: A Functional Reconsideration of the Role of the Supreme Court* (University of Chicago Press, 1980). Choper is the lone dissenter in the legal academy of the view that separation of powers disputes should be decided by the Supreme Court. I agree with Choper's argument, as will be evident, though we differ in our ultimate rationales for arguing that separation of powers disputes should be nonjusticiable. For Choper, given that each of the branches has determinate tools they can use to press their judgments, the court should preserve its legitimacy for rights cases. This is ultimately a prudential justification for judicial deference in separation of powers cases. I agree with Choper that the political branches' powers are sufficient to resolve political disputes between the branches. The account I develop in what follows, however, provides a principled justification for why the court should abstain from such disputes based on a notion of what the Constitution fundamentally is, and how judicial review of separation of powers disputes regarding the respective boundaries of the political branches represents a fundamental perversion of the Constitution's political design. I think this is implicit in Choper's account. His descriptions of separation of powers and the branches' powers with regard to each other demonstrate his understanding of the systemic and dynamic nature of the constitutional order. I attempt to spell this out by considering how the Constitution is often understood as a text rather than a system of government in ways that give the court preeminent status in interpreting it, including defining the respective legal boundaries of the other two branches.
101. Siemers, *Myth of Coequal Branches*.
102. Finn, *Peopling the Constitution*, 2.
103. Erwin Chemerinsky, "In Defense of Judicial Supremacy," *William & Mary Law Review* 58, no. 5 (2017): 1459–1494; Larry Alexander and Frederick Schauer, "On Extrajudicial Constitutional Interpretation," *Harvard Law Review* 110, no. 7 (1997): 1359–1387; Larry Alexander and Frederick Schauer, "Defending Judicial Supremacy: A Reply," *Constitutional Commentary* 17 (2000): 455–482; Robert C. Post and Reva B. Siegel, "Protecting the Constitution from the People: Juricentric Restrictions on Section Five Power," *Indiana Law Journal* 78, no. 1 (2003): 1–45.
104. See Cooper v. Aaron 358 U.S. 1 (1958); and City of Boerne v. Flores 521 U.S. 507 (1997).
105. Jonathan Gienapp, *The Second Creation: Fixing the American Constitution in the Founding Era* (Belknap Press, 2018).
106. Gienapp, *Second Creation*, 7.
107. John Brigham, *The Cult of the Court* (Temple University Press, 1991), 35;

David Ray Papke, *Heretics in the Temple: Americans Who Reject the Nation's Legal Faith* (NYU Press, 1998), 3–13; Finn, *Peopling the Constitution*, 2.

108. George Thomas, *The Madisonian Constitution* (Johns Hopkins University Press, 2008), 21–23; Stephen M. Griffin, *American Constitutionalism: From Theory to Politics* (Princeton University Press, 1996), 59–87; John Agresto, *The Supreme Court and Constitutional Democracy* (Cornell University Press, 1984), 71.
109. Thomas, *Madisonian Constitution*, 14.
110. William F. Harris, *The Interpretable Constitution* (Johns Hopkins University Press, 1993).
111. Hamilton et al., *Federalist Papers*, #48.
112. Hamilton et al., *Federalist Papers*, #51.
113. Hamilton et al., *Federalist Papers*, #51, 317–318.
114. Thomas, *Madisonian Constitution*, 14–38; Agresto, *Supreme Court and Constitutional Democracy*; Lane V. Sunderland, *Popular Government and the Supreme Court* (University Press of Kansas, 1996); Greg Weiner, *The Political Constitution: The Case Against Judicial Supremacy* (University Press of Kansas, 2019).
115. Gary J. Jacobsohn, *The Supreme Court and the Decline of Constitutional Aspiration* (Rowman & Littlefield, 1986), 95–137; Jack M. Balkin, *Constitutional Redemption: Political Faith in an Unjust World* (Harvard University Press, 2011).
116. Abraham Lincoln, "Inaugural Address," March 4, 1861, found at https://teachingamericanhistory.org/document/first-inaugural-address/.
117. Jacobsohn, *Supreme Court and the Decline of Constitutional Aspiration*; Sotirios A. Barber, *On What the Constitution Means* (Johns Hopkins University Press, 1984).
118. Neal Devins and Louis Fisher, *The Democratic Constitution* (Oxford University Press, 2015); Louis Fisher, *Constitutional Dialogues: Interpretation as Political Process* (Princeton University Press, 2016); Keith E. Whittington, *Constitutional Construction: Divided Powers and Constitutional Meaning* (Harvard University Press, 1999).
119. Gerald N. Rosenberg, *The Hollow Hope: Can Courts Bring About Social Change?* 2nd ed. (University of Chicago Press, 2008).
120. Robert A. Dahl, "Decision-Making in a Democracy: The Supreme Court as a National Policy-Maker," *Journal of Public Law* 6, no. 2 (1957): 279–295.
121. Maggie Blackhawk, "Legislative Constitutionalism and Federal Indian Law," *Yale Law Journal* 132 (2023): 2205–2303.
122. Corey Brettschneider, *The Oath and the Office: A Guide to the Constitution for Future Presidents* (W. W. Norton, 2018); J. Mitchell Pickerill, *Constitutional Deliberation in Congress: The Impact of Judicial Review in a Separated System*, Constitutional Conflicts (Duke University Press, 2004).
123. Choper, *Judicial Review and the National Political Process*, 281–86; Chafetz, *Congress's Constitution*, 45–200.
124. Chafetz, *Congress's Constitution*, 74–75.
125. Hamilton et al., *Federalist Papers*, #78, 464.
126. For example, if Congress impeaches a president after he refuses to spend appropriated funds in the manner specified by Congress (or refuses to allow any member of his staff to testify before Congress), what is to keep the president

from dispatching troops to surround Congress, thus ending the argument? This is perhaps an extreme example, but the answer to this objection is that a president who refuses to submit to the political judgment of Congress—backed up by the viable threat of impeachment—has no more incentive to abide by a ruling of the Supreme Court curtailing the president's power.

127. Charles L. Black and Akhil Reed Amar, *Impeachment: A Handbook* (Yale University Press, 1998); Josh Chafetz, "Impeachment and Assassination," *Minnesota Law Review* 95 (2010): 347–423; Michael J. Gerhardt, *The Federal Impeachment Process*, 3rd ed. (University of Chicago Press, 2019); Tulis, "Impeachment in the Constitutional Order"; Gene Healy, *Indispensable Remedy: The Broad Scope of the Constitution's Impeachment Power* (Cato Institute, 2018).
128. John Locke, *Second Treatise of Government*, ed. C. B. Macpherson (Hackett, 1980), 84.
129. Locke, *Second Treatise of Government*, 84.
130. Locke, *Second Treatise of Government*, 84.
131. Ronald Dworkin, *Taking Rights Seriously* (Harvard University Press, 1978), 22–28; Jack M. Balkin, *Living Originalism* (Harvard University Press, 2011), 44, 349–352; Leslie Friedman Goldstein, *In Defense of the Text: Democracy and Constitutional Theory* (Rowman & Littlefield, 1991); Robert Alexy, *A Theory of Constitutional Rights*, trans. Julian Rivers (Oxford University Press, 2002).
132. Goldstein, *In Defense of the Text*, 3–4. Goldstein's account thus differs from Ronald Dworkin's insofar as the text itself incorporates or points to principles incorporated by it rather than a judge's moral philosophy. The account here prioritizes the text. Departures from the literal meaning of the text should be justified according to how actions realize the purposes of the law itself or other constitutional provisions it comes into conflict with.
133. Goldstein, *In Defense of the Text*, 4.
134. Dworkin, *Taking Rights Seriously*, 26.
135. Balkin, *Living Originalism*, 44.
136. Gary Jeffrey Jacobsohn, "The Disharmonic Constitution," in Tulis and Macedo, *Limits of Constitutional Democracy*; Gary Jeffrey Jacobsohn, *Constitutional Identity* (Harvard University Press, 2010).
137. Justice David H. Souter, "Text of Justice David Souter's Speech," *Harvard Gazette*, May 27, 2010, https://news.harvard.edu/gazette/story/2010/05/text-of-justice-david-souters-speech/.
138. Youngstown Sheet & Tube Co. v. Sawyer, 343 U.S. 579 (1952), 701–702.
139. Abraham Lincoln, "Message to Congress in Special Session," July 4, 1861, available at https://teachingamericanhistory.org/library/document/message-to-congress-in-special-session/
140. George C. Sellery, "Lincoln's Suspension of Habeas Corpus as Viewed by Congress," *Bulletin of the University of Wisconsin* 149 History series, 1, no. 3 (1907): 239–245; James A. Dueholm, "Lincoln's Suspension of the Writ of Habeas Corpus: An Historical and Constitutional Analysis," *Journal of the Abraham Lincoln Association* 29, no. 2 (2008): 49–55.
141. Ex Parte Merryman, 17 F. Cas. 144 (1861), 148, available at https://law.resource.org/pub/us/case/reporter/F.Cas/0017.f.cas/0017.f.cas.0144.3.html.
142. Lincoln, "Message to Congress in Special Session."

143. Herbert Wechsler, "Toward Neutral Principles of Constitutional Law," *Harvard Law Review* 73, no. 1 (1959): 1–35.
144. Zeisberg, *War Powers*, 250–253; Mark Tushnet, "How Courts Implement Social Policy," *Tulsa Law Review* 45, no. 4 (2010): 855–862.
145. Gordon Silverstein, *Law's Allure: How Law Shapes, Constrains, Saves, and Kills Politics* (Cambridge University Press, 2009), 64.
146. Alexander and Schauer, "On Extrajudicial Constitutional Interpretation," 1371–1381.
147. Alexander and Schauer, "On Extrajudicial Constitutional Interpretation," 1376.
148. Korematsu v. United States (1944), 323 U.S. 214, 246.
149. David E. Pozen, "Self-Help and the Separation of Powers," *Yale Law Journal* 124, no. 1 (2014): 2–90.
150. Lee Epstein, "Partisanship 'All the Way Down' on the U.S. Supreme Court," *Pepperdine Law Review* 51, no. 3 (2024): 489–514; Neal Devins and Lawrence Baum, "Split Definitive: How Party Polarization Turned the Supreme Court into a Partisan Court," *Supreme Court Review* 2016 (2016): 301–366.
151. Daphna Renan, "Presidential Norms and Article II," *Harvard Law Review* 131 (2018): 2253.
152. Thomas R. Bell, "Perverse Politics: Recess Appointments, Noel Canning, and the Limits of Law," *Presidential Studies Quarterly* 48, no. 2 (2018): 373–386.
153. While I am talking about justiciability here, I am not working within the court's contemporary political questions doctrine with criteria announced in *Baker v. Carr*. It does not matter if the court thinks that it can resolve the case with judicially manageable standards. As I demonstrated in the previous section, the political branches are well-equipped to handle such disputes themselves.
154. The question in *Ex Parte Merryman* is different from a claim that the writ was improperly suspended because a state of emergency does not exist or because the public safety does not require it. If the conditions for the suspension do not pertain, then the writ would be impermissibly suspended no matter the governmental process. Even in this instance, however, judicial deference is wise, since such a determination would require second-guessing the political branches. If the president suspends habeas corpus inappropriately, Congress has the power to reimpose it. If Congress chooses not to, then it is unlikely that courts would have any real impact.
155. Choper, *Judicial Review and the National Political Process*, 273.
156. Choper, *Judicial Review and the National Political Process*, 273.
157. Choper, *Judicial Review and the National Political Process*, 327.
158. Hamilton et al., *Federalist Papers*, #84, 514. Emphasis in original.
159. Bowie and Renan, "Separation of Powers Counterrevolution."
160. *561 U.S. 477* (2010).
161. Seila Law LLC. v. Consumer Financial Protection Bureau, 591 U.S. 197 (2019).
162. Daphna Renan, "'Institutional Settlement' in a Provisional Constitutional Order," *California Law Review* 108 (2020): 1998.
163. Gienapp, "Removal and the Changing Debate over Executive Power"; Bowie and Renan, "Separation of Powers Counterrevolution," 2041–2047; Alvis, Bailey, and Taylor, *Contested Removal Power*; Huq, "Removal as a Political Question."
164. Renan, "'Institutional Settlement'," 1999.

CHAPTER 2: LEGISLATIVE VETO

1. Michael J. Berry, *The Modern Legislative Veto: Macropolitical Conflict and the Legacy of Chadha* (University of Michigan Press, 2017), 8.
2. Joseph Cooper, "The Legislative Veto in the 1980s," in *Congress Reconsidered*, ed. Lawrence C. Dodd and Bruce I. Oppenheimer, 3rd ed. (CQ Press, 1985), 377.
3. Berry, *Modern Legislative Veto*, 41–45.
4. Theodore J. Lowi, *The End of Liberalism: The Second Republic of the United States*, 2nd ed. (Norton, 1979).
5. L. Gordon Crovitz and Jeremy A. Rabkin, eds., *The Fettered Presidency: Legal Constraints on the Executive Branch* (American Enterprise Institute, 1989); John R. Bolton, *The Legislative Veto: Unseparating the Powers* (American Enterprise Institute, 1977).
6. Murray Dry, "The Congressional Veto and the Constitutional Separation of Powers," in *The Presidency in the Constitutional Order*, ed. Jeffrey K. Tulis and Joseph M. Bessette (Louisiana State University Press, 1981).
7. Jessica Korn, *The Power of Separation: American Constitutionalism and the Myth of the Legislative Veto* (Princeton University Press, 1996); Barbara Hinkson Craig, *The Legislative Veto: Congressional Control of Regulation* (Westview Press, 1984); Harold H. Bruff and Ernest Gellhorn, "Congressional Control of Administrative Regulation: A Study of Legislative Vetoes," *Harvard Law Review* 90, no. 7 (1977): 1369–1440.
8. Louis Fisher, "The Legislative Veto: Invalidated, It Survives," *Law and Contemporary Problems* 56, no. 4 (1993): 273–292; Berry, *Modern Legislative Veto*, 84–107.
9. Jerry L. Mashaw, *Creating the Administrative Constitution: The Lost One Hundred Years of American Administrative Law* (Yale University Press, 2012); Julian Davis Mortenson and Nicholas Bagley, "Delegation at the Founding," *Columbia Law Review* 121, no. 2 (2021): 277–368.
10. James M. Landis, *The Administrative Process*, Storrs Lectures on Jurisprudence 1938 (Yale University Press, 1966); Jonathan H. Adler, "Placing Reins on Regulations: Assessing the Proposed Reins Act," *New York University Journal of Legislation and Public Policy* 16 (2013): 9–10; David H. Rosenbloom, *Building a Legislative-Centered Public Administration: Congress and the Administrative State, 1946–1999* (University of Alabama Press, 2000), 133–134.
11. Clyde Wayne Crews Jr., "Ten Thousand Commandments: An Annual Snapshot of the Federal Regulatory State," Competitive Enterprise Institute, 2017, 3, https://cei.org/sites/default/files/Ten%20Thousand%20Commandments%202017.pdf. When one includes all proposed rules—not just final rules—the page count for 2016 was 95,894.
12. Gary Lawson, "Delegation and Original Meaning," *Virginia Law Review* 88, no. 2 (2002): 327–404.
13. Schechter Poultry Corp. v. United States, 295 US 495 (1935), 530.
14. Keith Whittington and Jason Iuliano, "The Myth of the Nondelegation Doctrine," *University of Pennsylvania Law Review* 165, no. 2 (2017): 379–431.
15. Eric A. Posner and Adrian Vermeule, "Interring the Nondelegation Doctrine," *University of Chicago Law Review* 69 (2002): 1721–1762; Mortenson and Bagley, "Delegation at the Founding."

16. Mashaw, *Creating the Administrative Constitution*; Mortenson and Bagley, "Delegation at the Founding," 332–366.
17. David P. Currie, *The Constitution in Congress: The Federalist Period, 1789–1801* (University of Chicago Press, 1999); Mortenson and Bagley, "Delegation at the Founding," 333–334.
18. Lawson, "Delegation and Original Meaning," 342–343. "However difficult it may be to distinguish the legislative, executive, and judicial powers at the margins, the Constitution of 1788–89 clearly places such a distinction at the center of its structure. There are constitutional lines that the executive and judicial powers may not cross."
19. Mortenson and Bagley, "Delegation at the Founding," 315.
20. Adrian Vermeule, "There Is No Conservative Legal Movement," *Washington Post,* July 6, 2022, https://www.washingtonpost.com/outlook/2022/07/06/epa-roberts-conservative-court-libertarian/.
21. Roger A. Pielke, *The Honest Broker: Making Sense of Science in Policy and Politics* (Cambridge University Press, 2007).
22. Russell Muirhead, "The Politics of Getting It Right," *Critical Review* 26, no. 1–2 (2014): 115–128.
23. Lowi, *End of Liberalism*.
24. David Schoenbrod, *Power Without Responsibility: How Congress Abuses the People Through Delegation* (Yale University Press, 1995), 86.
25. Schoenbrod, *Power Without Responsibility*, 88–94.
26. Adler, "Placing Reins on Regulations," 13–16; Jonathan H. Adler, "Heat Expands All Things: The Proliferation of Greenhouse Gas Regulation Under the Obama Administration," *Harvard Journal of Law and Public Policy* 34, no. 2 (2011): 421–452.
27. Massachusetts v. EPA 449 U.S. 497 (2007).
28. Adler, "Heat Expands All Things," 422; idem, "Placing Reins on Regulations," 15.
29. Adler, "Placing Reins on Regulations," 15.
30. 129 Cong. Rec. H931–43 (daily ed., March 8, 1983) (Statement of Rep. Levitas).
31. Joint resolutions are resolutions that are passed by both houses of Congress and presented to the president for his signature or veto. At issue here are concurrent and simple resolutions, which are resolutions that do not require the president's signature and, consequently, cannot be vetoed by him.
32. Richard Polenberg, *Reorganizing Roosevelt's Government: The Controversy over Executive Reorganization, 1936–1939* (Harvard University Press, 1966), 129, 166; Berry, *Modern Legislative Veto*, 32.
33. Subsequent reorganization authorizations in later years used different variations of the legislative veto that shifted the balance between the two branches. For example, at times, plans went into effect unless one house passed a resolution of disapproval.
34. Berry, *Modern Legislative Veto*, 34–35. Congress stopped granting the president reorganization authority after the court's invalidation of the legislative veto in *Chadha*. Since that time, Congress has rarely undertaken the task of reorganizing the executive branch. Moreover, when Congress has acted in this regard, it has generally acted in response to major crises instead of acting proactively.

For example, Congress established the Department of Homeland Security after 9/11. Similarly, Congress established the Consumer Financial Protection Bureau *after* the economic crisis of 2008. Even so, much congressional action in this regard has been to add to the existing administrative apparatus rather than to reorganize or streamline. This, of course, further suggests the difficulty with which Congress can accomplish this important task without delegation. See: John W. York and Rachel Greszler, "A Model for Executive Reorganization," Heritage Foundation, November 3, 2017, 2, https://www.heritage.org/political-process/report/model-executive-reorganization.

35. Louis Fisher, *Congressional Abdication on War and Spending* (Texas A&M University Press, 2000), 115–127; Keith E. Whittington, *Constitutional Construction: Divided Powers and Constitutional Meaning* (Harvard University Press, 1999), 162–173.
36. Edward S. Corwin, *The President, Office and Powers* (New York University Press, 1940), 130.
37. Matthew N. Beckmann, *Pushing the Agenda: Presidential Leadership in U.S. Lawmaking, 1953–2004* (Cambridge University Press, 2010); Keith Krehbiel, *Pivotal Politics: A Theory of U.S. Lawmaking* (University of Chicago Press, 1998).
38. James Madison reportedly argued that "if the negative of the President was confined to *bills*, it would be evaded by acts under the form and name of Resolutions, votes &c." (emphasis in original). Max Farrand, ed., *The Records of the Federal Convention of 1787* (Yale University Press, 1923), 301; Dry, "Congressional Veto," 205; Jacob K. Javits and Gary J. Klein, "Congressional Oversight and the Legislative Veto: A Constitutional Analysis," *New York University Law Review* 52 (1977): 480.
39. Javits and Klein, "Congressional Oversight and the Legislative Veto."
40. Letter of the attorney general to the president, in response to an inquiry on the constitutionality of section 906(a) of the executive reorganization statute, 5 U.S. Code, Sect. 901ff.: 43 Opins. A.G. 10 (1977), quoted in Dry, "Congressional Veto," 209.
41. US Constitution, Article II, section 2, clause 1.
42. Javits and Klein, "Congressional Oversight and the Legislative Veto," 487.
43. Javits and Klein, "Congressional Oversight and the Legislative Veto," 487–490.
44. Steven Croley, "White House Review of Agency Rulemaking: An Empirical Investigation," *University of Chicago Law Review* 70 (2003): 821–886; Elena Kagan, "Presidential Administration," *Harvard Law Review* 114, no. 8 (2001): 2245–2385.
45. Javits and Klein, "Congressional Oversight and the Legislative Veto," 490.
46. Javits and Klein, "Congressional Oversight and the Legislative Veto," 486.
47. Dry, "Congressional Veto," 212–213.
48. Dry, "Congressional Veto," 212–213.
49. INS v. Chadha, 462 US 919 (1983), 944.
50. *INS v. Chadha*, 944.
51. *INS v. Chadha*, 951.
52. *INS v. Chadha*, 948. The court quoted Alexander Hamilton's discussion of the importance of the president's veto power in *Federalist* 73: "It establishes a

salutary check upon the legislative body, calculated to guard the community against the effects of faction, precipitancy, or of any impulse unfriendly to the public good which may happen to influence a majority of that body. . . . The primary inducement to conferring the power in question upon the Executive is to enable him to defend himself; the secondary one is to increase the chances in favor of the community against the passing of bad laws through haste, inadvertence, or design." Moreover, the court quoted James Wilson who argued at the Constitutional Convention that dividing the legislative power into two distinct houses was ultimately an attempt to make it difficult for Congress to act. In a unicameral legislature, there are few checks to prevent arbitrary and unjust legislative action other than merely relying on the "virtue and good sense" of those who compose the legislature.

53. *INS v. Chadha*, 979 (White, J., Dissenting).
54. *INS v. Chadha*, 951.
55. *INS v. Chadha*, 951.
56. *INS v. Chadha*, 952.
57. *INS v. Chadha*, 952n16.
58. The House of Representatives alone was given the power to initiate impeachments (art. I, sec. 2, cl. 2); the Senate alone was given the power to conduct trials following impeachment on charges initiated by the House and to convict following trial (art. I, sec. 3, cl. 5); the Senate alone was given final unreviewable power to approve or disapprove presidential appointments (art. II, sec. 2, cl. 2); and the Senate alone was given the unreviewable power to ratify treaties negotiated by the president (art. II, sec. 2, cl. 2).
59. McCulloch v. Maryland 17 U.S. 316 (1819).
60. *INS v. Chadha*, 940–941.
61. *INS v. Chadha*, 987 (White, J. Dissenting).
62. H. Lee Watson, "Congress Steps Out: A Look at Congressional Control of the Executive," *California Law Review* 63, no. 4 (1975): 983–1094. Watson similarly argues that the framers were so fearful of a too-powerful Congress that Congress cannot act outside of enacting laws.
63. *INS v. Chadha*, 1002 (White, J., Dissenting).
64. Laurence H. Tribe, "The Legislative Veto Decision: A Law by Any Other Name," *Harvard Journal on Legislation* 21 (1984): 17.
65. Alexander Hamilton et al., *The Federalist Papers*, ed. Clinton Rossiter (Signet, 2003), #47, 298.
66. Barbara Hinkson Craig, Chadha: *The Story of an Epic Constitutional Struggle* (University of California Press, 1990), 3–35; Berry, *Modern Legislative Veto*, 61–65. After Kenya won its independence from the United Kingdom, it decided that those born in Kenya prior to independence would be granted citizenship unless their parents had immigrated to Kenya themselves. Chadha's parents were both immigrants. Children of immigrants, however, were entitled to apply for citizenship. Alternatively, many Kenyan Asians were also able to apply for passports from Great Britain because Kenya was a former colony. However, given the vast influx in applicants, Great Britain cracked down on immigration, setting new quotas. Chadha applied for a student visa and earned a degree in business administration from Bowling Green State Univer-

sity in Ohio in 1966 before going on to earn a master's degree in political science and economics in 1971. When Chadha's student visa expired, however, he faced deportation, but with no country or citizenship outside the United States.

67. *INS v. Chadha*, 963–964 (Powell, J., Concurring).
68. *INS v. Chadha*, 963–964.
69. *INS v. Chadha*, 964–965.
70. *INS v. Chadha*, 965n8.
71. *INS v. Chadha*, 962.
72. *INS v. Chadha*, 967 (Powell, J., Concurring). Justice Powell quoted Chief Justice John Marshall: "It is the peculiar province of the legislature to prescribe general rules for the government of society; the application of those rules would seem to be the duty of other departments." *Fletcher v. Peck* (1810).
73. Tribe, "Legislative Veto Decision," 16.
74. Berry, *Modern Legislative Veto*, 73.
75. Korn, *Power of Separation.*
76. Korn starts from the premise that the legislative veto—not the widespread delegation of modern government—was the real break with constitutional structure. However, delegation was the break with constitutional structure, and, as I previously demonstrated, was a part of constitutional practice long before the New Deal. The legislative veto, therefore, was an attempt to bring interbranch politics back in, albeit in a modified fashion, to ensure that congressional delegation did not amount to abdication. Even so, Korn's concerns regarding the politics the legislative veto fosters are well worth considering because she is ultimately concerned with the Constitution's political architecture and how well the branches perform their different political functions in the constitutional order.
77. H.J.Res.542—War Powers Resolution.
78. Gordon Silverstein, *Law's Allure: How Law Shapes, Constrains, Saves, and Kills Politics* (Cambridge University Press, 2009), 209–243.
79. Silverstein, *Law's Allure*, 220.
80. Silverstein, *Law's Allure*, 220.
81. Korn, *Power of Separation*, 69–90.
82. Korn, *Power of Separation*, 77–78.
83. Korn, *Power of Separation*, 90.
84. Antonin Scalia, "The Legislative Veto: A False Remedy for System Overload," *Regulation: AEI Journal on Government and Society* (1979): 19–26.
85. Bruff and Gellhorn, "Congressional Control," 1420.
86. Bruff and Gellhorn, "Congressional Control," 1423.
87. Korn, *Power of Separation*, 74.
88. For example, Barbara Hinkson Craig's first case study in her book criticizing the legislative veto is about report and wait provisions, wherein she shows that such provisions gave Congress (and its committees) a great deal of power to negotiate and ensure that regulations come into alignment with congressional preferences. Craig, *Legislative Veto*, 58–82; Fisher, "Legislative Veto"; Berry, *Modern Legislative Veto*, 90–99.
89. Korn, *Power of Separation*, 99.
90. Korn, *Power of Separation*, 104.

91. Martha Liebler Gibson, "Managing Conflict: The Role of the Legislative Veto in American Foreign Policy," *Polity* 26, no. 3 (1994): 441–472.
92. Gibson, "Managing Conflict," 454.
93. Gibson, "Managing Conflict," 455.
94. Bruff and Gellhorn, "Congressional Control"; Craig, *Legislative Veto.*
95. Rosenbloom, *Building a Legislative-Centered Public Administration.*
96. Bruff and Gellhorn, "Congressional Control"; Craig, *Legislative Veto.*
97. Craig, *Legislative Veto*, 57–82.
98. John Chubb, for example, examined energy policymaking during the 1970s (an issue area with several legislative veto provisions) and concluded that bureaucratic policymaking was "generally biased in favor of concentrated interests," while legislative participation was more inclusive. John E. Chubb, *Interest Groups and the Bureaucracy: The Politics of Energy* (Stanford University Press, 1983), 258–264; Cooper, "Legislative Veto in the 1980s," 373.
99. William West and Joseph Cooper, "The Congressional Veto and Administrative Rulemaking," *Political Science Quarterly* 98, no. 2 (1983): 292–293.
100. Berry, *Modern Legislative Veto*, 92–93; Korn, *Power of Separation*, 34–36.
101. Morton Rosenberg, "Congressional Review of Agency Rulemaking: An Update and Assessment of the Congressional Review Act after a Decade," report, Congressional Research Service, May 8, 2008; idem, "Whatever Happened to Congressional Review of Agency Rulemaking: A Brief Overview, Assessment, and Proposal for Reform," *Administrative Law Review* 51, no. 4 (1999): 1051–1092.
102. Paul J. Larkin Jr., "Reawakening the Congressional Review Act," *Harvard Journal of Law and Public Policy* 41, no. 1 (2018): 187–252.
103. Berry, *Modern Legislative Veto*, 102–104.
104. Adler, "Placing Reins on Regulations"; George F. Will, "A Check on the Regulatory State," *Washington Post*, June 6, 2012, https://www.washingtonpost.com/opinions/a-check-on-the-regulatory-state/2012/06/06/gJQAjmabJV_story.html?utm_term=.60d7d653f350.
105. Ronald M. Levin, "The REINS Act, Unbridled Impediment to Regulation," *George Washington Law Review* 83 (2015): 1453–1463; Tribe, "Legislative Veto Decision," 19.
106. York and Greszler, "Model for Executive Reorganization," 2.
107. Berry, *Modern Legislative Veto*, 97.
108. Fisher, "Legislative Veto," 288.
109. Morton Rosenberg and Jack H. Maskell, "Congressional Intervention in the Administrative Process: Legal and Ethical Considerations," Congressional Research Service, 1990, 30; Brett G. Kappel, "Judicial Restrictions on Improper Congressional Influence in Administrative Decision-Making: A Defense of the Pillsbury Doctrine Note," *Journal of Law & Politics* 6 (1989): 137.
110. City of Alexandria v. United States, 3 CL.Ct 667, 683 (1983).
111. City of Alexandria v. United States, 737 F2d 1022, 1025 (Fed. Cir. 1984).
112. West Virginia v. EPA, 597 U.S. 697 (2022); Biden v. Nebraska, 600 U.S. 477 (2023).
113. Loper Bright Enterprises v. Raimondo, 603 U.S. ___ (2024), 16 (slip opinion).
114. Beau J. Baumann, "Americana Administrative Law," *Georgetown Law Journal* 111 (2023): 465–527; Allen C. Sumrall and Beau J. Baumann, "Clarifying

Judicial Aggrandizement," *University of Pennsylvania Law Review* 172 (2023): 24–42.

CHAPTER 3: EXECUTIVE AGREEMENTS

1. Oona A. Hathaway, "Treaties' End: The Past, Present, and Future of International Lawmaking in the United States," *Yale Law Journal* 117, no. 7 (2008): 1236–1372. For example, at the outset of American government, Congress authorized the executive branch to enter executive agreements to establish postal service with foreign nations, 1286.
2. Hathaway, "Treaties' End," 1286–1306.
3. *Treaties and Other International Agreements: The Role of the United States Senate. A Report by the Congressional Research Service*, 2001, 40.
4. Hathaway, "Treaties' End," 1286–1306; Curtis A. Bradley and Jack L. Goldsmith, "Presidential Control over International Law," *Harvard Law Review* 131, no. 5 (2018): 1201–1297. Such executive agreements are concluded in a number of forms. Perhaps the most controversial are those agreements concluded as sole executive agreements, which are concluded based solely on the president's independent constitutional powers in Article II related to his diplomatic prerogatives and his independent powers as commander in chief. Other executive agreements are made pursuant to a treaty obligation, intended to bring the United States into compliance with its treaty obligations. The vast majority of executive agreements are congressional-executive agreements, which can be broken down into two categories. Ex post congressional-executive agreements are similar to treaties in that such agreements entered into by the executive branch are subsequently approved by Congress. However, rather than ratification by a supermajority of the Senate, such agreements are authorized by majority vote in both chambers. Such ex post congressional-executive agreements have been used for international agreements of major consequence, such as the World Bank and the Bretton Woods Convention. They have also been used for major trade agreements such as the World Trade Organization and NAFTA. With a few exceptions, however, such agreements have been limited to areas (international trade and commerce) that Congress can govern based on its Article I powers. Moreover, such agreements are rare, constituting less than 1 percent of all international agreements entered into by the United States. The vast majority of executive agreements—approximately 80 to 85 percent are based on delegated authority to the executive branch to enter into agreements (ex ante congressional-executive agreements). Foreign aid agreements, for example, constitute a large percentage of such agreements.
5. See Restatement (Third) of Foreign Relations Law § 303 (1987).
6. Charles C. Thach Jr., *The Creation of the Presidency, 1775–1789*, new ed. (Liberty Fund, 2010); Louis Fisher, "The Efficiency Side of Separated Powers," *Journal of American Studies* 5, no. 2 (1971): 113–131; Gary J. Schmitt, "Separation of Powers: Introduction to the Study of Executive Agreements," *American Journal of Jurisprudence* 27 (1982): 113–138.
7. Glen S. Krutz and Jeffrey S. Peake, *Treaty Politics and the Rise of Executive Agreements: International Commitments in a System of Shared Powers* (University of Michigan Press, 2009).

8. Jack L. Goldsmith, Curtis A. Bradley, and Oona A. Hathaway, "The Failed Transparency Regime for Executive Agreements: An Empirical and Normative Analysis," *Harvard Law Review* 134, no. 2 (2020): 629–725.
9. Curtis A. Bradley, Jack Goldsmith, and Oona Hathaway, "Congress Mandates Sweeping Transparency Reforms for International Agreements," *Lawfare* (blog), December 23, 2022, https://www.lawfareblog.com/congress-mandates-sweeping-transparency-reforms-international-agreements.
10. Krutz and Peake, *Treaty Politics*, 71–95; Curtis A. Bradley and Trevor W. Morrison, "Historical Gloss and the Separation of Powers," *Harvard Law Review* 126, no. 2 (2012): 468–476.
11. Alexander Hamilton et al., *The Federalist Papers*, ed. Clinton Rossiter (Signet, 2003), #75, 499.
12. For a more in-depth discussion of the thought of Locke and Montesquieu on foreign affairs, see Schmitt, "Separation of Powers."
13. John Locke, *Second Treatise of Government*, Early Modern Texts, 47, available at https://www.earlymoderntexts.com/assets/pdfs/locke1689a.pdf.
14. Locke, *Second Treatise of Government*, 47.
15. Locke, *Second Treatise of Government*, 47.
16. Hamilton et al., *Federalist Papers*, #75, 499.
17. Youngstown Sheet & Tube Co. v. Sawyer 343 U.S. 579 (1952), 635 (Jackson, J., Concurring).
18. *Youngstown v. Sawyer*, 635, 637 (Jackson, J., Concurring).
19. See Dames & Moore v. Regan, 453 U.S. 654 (1981).
20. Harold Hongju Koh, "Triptych's End: A Better Framework to Evaluate 21st Century International Lawmaking," *Yale Law Journal*, 126 (2018): 345–349.
21. Joseph M. Bessette, "Confronting War: Rethinking Jackson's Concurrence in Youngstown v. Sawyer," in *The Limits of Constitutional Democracy*, ed. Jeffrey K. Tulis and Stephen Macedo (Princeton University Press, 2010), 206.
22. Hamilton et al., *Federalist Papers*, #70, 421.
23. Hamilton et al., *Federalist Papers*, #70, 422.
24. Hamilton et al., *Federalist Papers*, #70, 422.
25. Hamilton et al., *Federalist Papers*, #70, 423.
26. Fisher, "Efficiency Side of Separated Powers"; Thach, *Creation of the Presidency*, 115–129; Schmitt, "Separation of Powers," 121–125.
27. Thach, *Creation of the Presidency*, 45–64.
28. Thach, *Creation of the Presidency*, 64.
29. Thach, *Creation of the Presidency*, 63–64.
30. Schmitt, "Separation of Powers," 129.
31. Hamilton et al., *Federalist Papers*, #64, 390.
32. Early practice under the Constitution also confirmed the inability of Congress (as a plural body) to deal well in the foreign affairs arena. During the negotiation of the Jay Treaty of 1795 (a crucial treaty with England to resolve issues remaining after the revolution), a senator involved in the negotiations leaked information regarding the negotiations to a local newspaper. This reinforced President Washington's view that the Senate was not "a safe repository for diplomatic secrets." See Joseph Ralston Hayden, *The Senate and Treaties, 1789–1817: The Development of the Treaty-Making Functions of the United States*

Senate During Their Formative Period, University of Michigan Publications, Humanistic Papers (Macmillan, 1920), 90–93.

33. Hamilton et al., *Federalist Papers*, #64, 390–391.
34. Hamilton et al., *Federalist Papers*, #64, 391.
35. Montesquieu, *The Spirit of the Laws*, trans. Thomas Nugent (Hafner, 1949), 161.
36. Josh Chafetz, *Congress's Constitution: Legislative Authority and the Separation of Powers* (Yale University Press, 2017), 74.
37. Schmitt, "Separation of Powers," 115.
38. Alexander Hamilton et al., *Federalist Papers*, #41, 253.
39. Herbert J. Storing, "Introduction," in Thach, *Creation of the Presidency*.
40. Hathaway, "Treaties' End"; Ryan Harrington, "Understanding the 'Other' International Agreements," *Law Library Journal* 108, no. 3 (2016): 343–359. This estimate is taken from Oona Hathaway's exhaustive empirical study on executive agreements. Hathaway estimates that nearly 80 to 85 percent of executive agreements are authorized by statute after searching the Statutes at Large for keywords that could match the substance executive agreements concluded between 1980 and 2000. Given the guesswork involved, of course, this is only an estimate. The latter, moreover, is in keeping with Loch Johnson's 1984 study, in which he estimated that around 87 percent of executive agreements were based on statutory authority. See Loch K. Johnson, *The Making of International Agreements: Congress Confronts the Executive* (New York University Press, 1984). Similarly, Gary Schmitt, in his 1983 study of military agreements, found that 85 percent of all such agreements from 1946 to 1973 were authorized (at least in some way) by statute. See Gary J. Schmitt, "Executive Agreements and Separation of Powers: A Reconsideration," *American Journal of Jurisprudence* 28 (1983): 189–230.
41. Such agreements were not entirely unprecedented. The McKinley Tariff Act of 1896, for example, enabled the president to enter into certain reciprocal trade agreements on certain specified commodities.
42. Franklin D. Roosevelt, Message from the President of the United States Transmitting a Request to Authorize the Executive to Enter into Executive Commercial Agreements with Foreign Nations, H.R. Doc. no. 273, 73rd Cong., Sess. 2 (1934), quoted in Bruce A. Ackerman and David Golove, *Is NAFTA Constitutional?* (Harvard University Press, 1995), 847.
43. Senate Report no. 111 75th Cong 1st Sess. (1937), 3; Ackerman and Golove, *Is NAFTA Constitutional?* 851.
44. H.R. Report no. 166, 75th Cong. 1st Sess. (1937), 114; Ackerman and Golove, *Is NAFTA Constitutional?* 851.
45. Oona Hathaway, "Presidential Power over International Law: Restoring the Balance," *Yale Law Journal* 119, no. 2 (2009): 155–166.
46. Hathaway, "Presidential Power over International Law," 212–215.
47. Foreign Assistance Act of 1973, Pub. L. No. 93–189, sec. 12(b)(1), S. 503 (a), 87 Stat. 714, 720 (codified at 22 U.S.C. S 2311(a)).
48. Pub. L. no. 87–256, S 103, 75 Stat. 527, 529 (codified as amended at U.S.C. S 2453 (2012)).
49. Harrington, "Understanding the 'Other' International Agreements," 348–349.

50. Dianne E. Rennack and Susan G. Chesser, "Foreign Assistance Act of 1961: Authorizations and Corresponding Appropriations" (Congressional Research Service, July 29, 2011).
51. Rennack and Chesser, "Foreign Assistance Act of 1961," 1.
52. Hathaway argues that the Congress's power over appropriations is not a sufficient check on the use of such agreements because it is difficult to defund agreements. Asking this particular question, however, obscures the long-term influence the appropriations power can have over the use of executive agreements. Hathaway, "Presidential Power over International Law," 225–230.
53. Chafetz, *Congress's Constitution*, 74.
54. "Congressional Control of Foreign Assistance to Post-Coup States: Assessing Executive Compliance from Honduras to Egypt," *Harvard Law Review* 127, no. 8 (2014): 2503–2509.
55. "Congressional Control of Foreign Assistance to Post-Coup States," 2503–2509; Chafetz, *Congress's Constitution*, 74.
56. Eric Schmitt, "Military Says Law Barring U.S. Aid to Rights Violators Hurts Training Mission," *New York Times*, June 20, 2013.
57. Schmitt, "Military Says Law Barring U.S. Aid."
58. Lisa L. Martin, *Democratic Commitments: Legislatures and International Cooperation* (Princeton University Press, 2000), 112–146.
59. Schmitt, "Executive Agreements," 218.
60. Martha Liebler Gibson, "Managing Conflict: The Role of the Legislative Veto in American Foreign Policy," *Polity* 26, no. 3 (1994): 454–455.
61. Hathaway, "Presidential Power over International Law," 194–205.
62. Belmont v. United States, 301 U.S. 324 (1937); Pink v. United States, 315 U.S. 203 (1942).
63. Bradley and Goldsmith, "Presidential Control over International Law," 1214–1215.
64. R. Chuck Mason, "U.S.-Iraq Withdrawal/Status of Forces Agreement: Issues for Congressional Oversight," Congressional Research Service, July 13, 2009.
65. Bradley and Goldsmith, "Presidential Control over International Law," 1248.
66. Bruce Ackerman and Oona Hathaway, "An Agreement Without Agreement," *Washington Post*, February 15, 2008, http://www.washingtonpost.com/wp-dyn/content/article/2008/02/15/AR2008021502539.html.
67. Chafetz, *Congress's Constitution*, 74–75.
68. S. Rep. No. 92–591, 3 (1972) ("The bill does not undertake to resolve fundamental questions relating to the treaty power of the Senate and the frequently countervailing claim—or simple use—of executive authority to enter into binding agreements with foreign countries without the consent of Congress. S. 596 undertakes only to deal with the prior, simpler, but nonetheless crucial question of secrecy.")
69. Schmitt, "Executive Agreements," 203–206.
70. "Executive Agreements," in *CQ Almanac 1972*, 28th ed., 05–619–05–621, Washington, DC, *Congressional Quarterly*, 1973, http://library.cqpress.com/cqalmanac/cqal72–1251460.
71. "Executive Agreements."
72. One scholar has estimated that the United States is a party to 1000–1800 secret (classified) agreements. See Ashley S. Deeks, "A (Qualified) Defense of Secret Agreements," *Arizona State Law Journal* 49 (2017): 713–794.

73. Quoted in Deeks, "(Qualified) Defense of Secret Agreements," 775n273.
74. Much of the information reported in this section comes from Bradley and Goldsmith, "Presidential Control over International Law," 1270–1297; Jack L. Goldsmith, Curtis A. Bradley, and Oona A. Hathaway, "The Failed Transparency Regime for Executive Agreements: An Empirical and Normative Analysis," *Harvard Law Review* 134, no. 2 (2020): 629–725; Curtis A. Bradley, Jack L. Goldsmith, and Oona Hathaway, "Executive Agreements: International Lawmaking Without Accountability?" *Lawfare* (blog), January 9, 2019, https://www.lawfareblog.com/executive-agreements-international-law making-without-accountability; Harrington, "Understanding the 'Other' International Agreements," 352–353.
75. Bradley and Goldsmith, "Presidential Control over International Law," 1274; Harrington, "Understanding the 'Other' International Agreements," 352–353.
76. CONG. REC. H11026 (daily ed. Dec. 7, 2004); Bradley and Goldsmith, "Presidential Control over International Law," 1274n343.
77. "International Trade: Improvements Needed to Track and Archive Trade Agreements," United States General Accounting Office, December 1999, p. 4, https://www.gao.gov/assets/230/228531.pdf; Bradley and Goldsmith, "Presidential Control over International Law," 1274n345.
78. "Report on Status of Forces Agreements," International Security Advisory Board, January 16, 2015, p. 39, https://www.state.gov/documents/organization /236456.pdf; Bradley and Goldsmith, "Presidential Control over International Law," 1274n346.
79. "Report on Status of Forces Agreements," 39.
80. Bradley and Goldsmith, "Presidential Control over International Law," 1274–1275.
81. See, for example, a list of international agreements concluded in 2018: "2018 Treaties and Agreements," accessed February 16, 2019, https://www.state.gov /s/l/treaty/tias/c78676.htm.
82. Harrington, "Understanding the 'Other' International Agreements," 352.
83. Harrington, "Understanding the 'Other' International Agreements," 352–353. Harrington discusses the dilemmas for researchers attempting to determine the legal basis for executive agreements.
84. United States Department of State Office of the Legal Adviser for Treaty Affairs, *International Agreements Other Than Treaties 1946–1968: A List Noting Their Legal Bases and Their Possible Effect on Internal Law in the United States* (Department of State, 1969); Schmitt, "Executive Agreements," 197n32.
85. Harrington, "Understanding the 'Other' International Agreements," 357–358.
86. Hathaway, "Treaties' End," 1260 (finding statutory authorizations for agreements ranging from agriculture to space cooperation).
87. Hathaway, 1268n76; Harrington, "Understanding the 'Other' International Agreements," 358.
88. Harrington, "Understanding the 'Other' International Agreements," 353.
89. Harrington, "Understanding the 'Other' International Agreements," 353; Duncan B. Hollis and Joshua J. Newcomer, "'Political' Commitments and the Constitution," *Virginia Journal of International Law* 49, no. 3 (2009): 507–584.
90. Bradley and Goldsmith, "Presidential Control over International Law," 1218–1219. Bradley and Goldsmith cite several examples. The Federal Reserve Board

uses political commitments to coordinate capital requirements and other banking rules with foreign bank regulators. Similarly, the Federal Trade Commission uses political commitments for a variety of issues such as bilateral trust cooperation and multilateral commitments to fight spam. The Food and Drug Administration makes political commitments on issues such as the safety of medical products and the opening of markets to US food manufacturers. Examples such as these could be multiplied.

91. Koh, "Triptych's End," 367.
92. David H. Rosenbloom, *Building a Legislative-Centered Public Administration: Congress and the Administrative State, 1946–1999* (University of Alabama Press, 2000).
93. Under the APA, agencies provide notices of proposed rulemaking, substantive rules and interpretations of general applicability, statements of general policy, rules of practice and procedure, descriptions of agency forms, rules of organization, descriptions of an agency's central and field organization, and amendments or revisions to the foregoing. See 5 U.S.C. S. 552(a)(1).
94. Mathew D. McCubbins and Thomas Schwartz, "Congressional Oversight Overlooked: Police Patrols versus Fire Alarms," *American Journal of Political Science* 28, no. 1 (1984): 165–179; Bradley and Goldsmith, "Presidential Control Over International Law," 1284–1285.
95. Clyde Wayne Crews Jr., "Ten Thousand Commandments: An Annual Snapshot of the Federal Regulatory State," Competitive Enterprise Institute, 2017, 3, https://cei.org/sites/default/files/Ten%20Thousand%20Commandments%20 2017.pdf.
96. As legal advisor for the State Department from 2009 to 2013, Harold Koh has been the most prominent advocate for this approach. See Harold Koh, "Address: Twenty-First-Century International Lawmaking," *Georgetown Law Journal* 101, no. 3 (2013): 725–748; Koh, "Triptych's End."
97. Peter Spiro and Daniel Bodanski, "Executive Agreements +," *Vanderbilt Journal of Transnational Law* 49, no. 4 (2016): 885–929. For example, the Obama administration ratified the Minamata Convention on Mercury even though the law that it cited for the agreement's legal basis did not expressly authorize the administration to make international agreements based on the law.
98. Jean Galbraith, "International Law and the Domestic Separation of Powers," *Virginia Law Review* 99, no. 5 (2013): 1040.
99. Jack Goldsmith and Lawrence Lessig, "Anti-Counterfeiting Agreement Raises Constitutional Concerns," *Washington Post*, March 26, 2010, http://www.washingtonpost.com/wp-dyn/content/article/2010/03/25/AR2010032502403.html; Oona Hathaway and Amy Kapczynski, "Going It Alone: The Anti-Counterfeiting Trade Agreement as a Sole Executive Agreement," *American Society of International Law: Insights* 15, no. 23 (2011), /insights/volume/15/issue/23/going-it-alone-anti-counterfeiting-trade-agreement-sole-executive.
100. Sean Flynn, "ACTA's Constitutional Problem: The Treaty Is Not a Treaty," *American University International Law Review* 26, no. 3 (2011): 922; Harrington, "Understanding the 'Other' International Agreements," 352.
101. Spiro and Bodanski, "Executive Agreements +," 910.
102. Bradley, Goldsmith, and Hathaway, "Congress Mandates Sweeping Transparency Reforms."

103. Bradley, Goldsmith, and Hathaway, "Congress Mandates Sweeping Transparency Reforms."
104. Hamilton et al., *Federalist Papers*, #75, 499.
105. Madison makes a similar argument in the Pacificus-Helvidius Debates. While Locke and Montesquieu viewed the treaty-making power as an executive power, the republican theory of the Constitution required significant legislative involvement.
106. Krutz and Peake, *Treaty Politics*, 14.
107. Hamilton et al., *Federalist Papers*, #64, 390.
108. Hamilton et al., *Federalist Papers*, #75, 451.
109. Hamilton et al., *Federalist Papers*, #62, 378. In *Federalist* 62, Madison provides several reasons for why mutability of the laws is bad in general. First, mutability of the laws, due to a constantly changing legislature, will make laws too voluminous and incoherent to be known and understood by the public. Secondly, such mutability gives the rich and enterprising an unfair advantage because they have the resources to know the law and to consider its long-term effects. Third, mutability of the laws undermines efficient business and commerce that relies on stability in the laws that determine taxes, interest rates, and economic conditions. Finally, mutability destroys reverence for the law in general.
110. Hamilton et al., *Federalist Papers*, #62, 378–379.
111. Frederick W. Marks, *Independence on Trial: Foreign Affairs and the Making of the Constitution* (Louisiana State University Press, 1973), 3–15.
112. See Restatement (Third) Foreign Affairs Law of the United States § 303 (1987).
113. Lisa L. Martin, "The President and International Commitments: Treaties as Signaling Devices," *Presidential Studies Quarterly* 35, no. 3 (2005): 440–465; similarly, Julian Nyarko demonstrates that treaties generally last longer than executive agreements. See Julian Nyarko, "Giving the Treaty a Purpose: Comparing the Durability of Treaties and Executive Agreements," *American Journal of International Law* 113, no. 1 (2019): 54–89.
114. Hathaway, "Treaties' End." Some scholars, like Oona Hathaway, argue that it is wrong to assume that treaties—because of their supermajoritarian requirement in the Senate—create better and more durable international agreements. Hathaway argues that it is impossible to know whether the consensus required for majority votes in both houses (as is done with ex post congressional-executive agreements) is really less durable than what is required for treaties. Hathaway assumes that majority support in both houses requires significant consensus. Moreover, such agreements, she argues, are self-executing, since they are enacted as federal laws; whereas treaties, according to the Supreme Court, are not necessarily self-executing and often require subsequent legislation to implement their terms. Ex post congressional-executive agreements, therefore, have the added advantage of bringing the United States fully into compliance with international obligations. Moreover, because it is generally understood that presidents can exit treaties without congressional consent, Hathaway argues that ex post congressional-executive agreements are more durable because they are essentially passed as statutes, which, consequently, require both branches to abrogate. My purpose here is not to dispute Hathaway, whose arguments I find generally compelling, but to point to the constitutional concern that important foreign policy decisions have sufficient congressional buy-in to be

durable. While Hathaway thinks that mechanisms other than treaties—in all instances where she believes such instruments are constitutionally appropriate—better accomplish this goal, she is ultimately motivated by a concern for durable commitments.

115. David E. Sanger, "Nuclear Arms Treaty: The Accord; Bush and Putin to Sign Pact to Cut Nuclear Warheads; Weapons Can Be Stockpiled," *New York Times*, May 14, 2002, https://www.nytimes.com/2002/05/14/world/nuclear-arms-treaty-accord-bush-putin-sign-pact-cut-nuclear-warheads-weapons-can.html; Martin, "President and International Commitments."
116. See *Made in USA Foundation Inc. v. United States* (2001).
117. John C. Yoo, "Laws as Treaties?: The Constitutionality of Congressional-Executive Agreements," *Michigan Law Review* 99, no. 4 (2001): 804–805.
118. Yoo, "Laws as Treaties," 805.
119. Bradley and Morrison, "Historical Gloss and the Separation of Powers," 474; Phillip R. Trimble and Jack S. Weiss, "The Role of the President, the Senate and the Congress with Respect to Arms Control Treaties Concluded by the United States," *Chicago-Kent Law Review* 67, no. 2 (1991): 661–662.
120. Krutz and Peake, *Treaty Politics*, 71–73.
121. Bradley, Goldsmith, and Hathaway, "Executive Agreements," 474, quoting Senate Executive Report no. 102–22 (1991).
122. See, generally, Edward S. Corwin, *The Constitution and World Organization*, American Civilization Program Series (Princeton University Press, 1944); Hathaway, "Treaties' End."
123. See Restatement (Third) of Foreign Relations Law § 303 (1987): "The prevailing view is that the congressional-executive agreement can be used as an alternative to the treaty in every instance." See also: Louis Henkin, *Foreign Affairs and the United States Constitution*, 2nd ed. (Oxford University Press, 1996), 217: "It is now widely accepted that the congressional-executive agreement is available for wide use, even general use, and is a complete alternative to a treaty." See, generally, Hathaway, "Treaties' End"; Myres S. McDougal and Asher Lans, "Treaties and Congressional-Executive or Presidential Agreements: Interchangeable Instruments of National Policy: II," *Yale Law Journal* 54, no. 3 (1945): 534–615.
124. Bradley and Morrison, "Historical Gloss and the Separation of Powers," 476.
125. Bradley and Goldsmith, "Presidential Control Over International Law," 1212. Bradley and Goldsmith were able to locate nineteen such agreements dating back to 1980, mostly dealing with trade and commerce. Hathaway, "Treaties' End," argued that such agreements were used in every conceivable issue area. Her claim is problematic insofar as her claim conflates ex ante and ex post congressional-executive agreements. For major agreements, ex post congressional-executive agreements are used sparingly.
126. Ackerman and Golove, *Is NAFTA Constitutional?* 891.
127. Yoo, "Laws as Treaties?" 822–823.
128. See, generally, Sharyn O'Halloran, *Politics, Process, and American Trade Policy* (University of Michigan Press, 1994), 139–175; Jasmine Farrier, *Congressional Ambivalence: The Political Burdens of Constitutional Authority* (University Press of Kentucky, 2010), 81–114.

129. Ackerman and Golove, *Is NAFTA Constitutional?* 904–908.
130. David E. Sanger, "Obama Sees an Iran Deal That Could Avoid Congress," *New York Times*, October 19, 2014, https://www.nytimes.com/2014/10/20/us/politics/obama-sees-an-iran-deal-that-could-avoid-congress-.html.
131. Peter Baker, "G.O.P. Senators' Letter to Iran About Nuclear Deal Angers White House—The New York Times," *New York Times*, March 9, 2015, https://www.nytimes.com/2015/03/10/world/asia/white-house-faults-gop-senators-letter-to-irans-leaders.html.
132. Dianne E. Rennack, "Iran: U.S. Economic Sanctions and the Authority to Lift Restrictions," Congressional Research Service, 2016.
133. Wendy Sherman, "How We Got the Iran Deal and Why We'll Miss It," *Foreign Affairs*, August 13, 2018, https://www.foreignaffairs.com/articles/2018-08-13/how-we-got-iran-deal. The United States' lead negotiator with Iran, Wendy Sherman, noted that "the deal would require constant reviews of Iran's compliance and it had to allow enough flexibility to quickly restore sanctions if Iran didn't keep its promises. It would have been very difficult to build such flexibility into a formal treaty."
134. Koh, "Triptych's End," 354.
135. Congressional Record 114th Cong. 1st Sess. April 29, 2015, vol. 161, no. 63, 2493.
136. Manu Raju and Burgess Everett, "How Cardin and Corker Clinched the Iran Deal: An Indicted Senator and Democratic Disagreements Made for a Tough Assignment," *Politico*, April 14, 2015, http://www.politico.com/story/2015/04/ben-cardin-bob-corker-iran-deal-116979.
137. Jennifer Steinhauer, "Democrats Hand Victory to Obama on Iran Nuclear Deal—The New York Times," *New York Times*, September 10, 2015, https://www.nytimes.com/2015/09/11/us/politics/iran-nuclear-deal-senate.html. Senate Democrats filibustered a resolution of disapproval in the Senate. The House of Representatives did not pass a resolution of disapproval, although it would have easily passed the House.
138. David Golove, "Congress Just Gave the President Power to Adopt a Binding Legal Agreement with Iran," *Just Security*, May 14, 2015, https://www.justsecurity.org/23018/congress-gave-president-power-adopt-binding-legal-agreement-iran/.
139. Koh, "Triptych's End," 355–66; Jack Goldsmith, "The Contributions of the Obama Administration to the Practice and Theory of International Law," *Harvard International Law Journal* 57, no. 2 (2016): 471.
140. Koh, "Triptych's End," 362.
141. Koh, "Triptych's End," 364.
142. Dominic Gates, "Boeing's $9.5 Billion Iran Deals, Always Uncertain, Are Now Effectively Dead," *Seattle Times*, May 8, 2018, https://www.seattletimes.com/business/boeing-aerospace/boeings-8-billion-iran-deal-always-uncertain-is-now-effectively-dead/.
143. Mark Landler, "Trump Abandons Iran Nuclear Deal He Long Scorned," *New York Times*, May 8, 2018, https://www.nytimes.com/2018/05/08/world/middleeast/trump-iran-nuclear-deal.html.
144. Kay Armin Serjoie, "'The Americans Cannot Be Trusted.' How Iran Is Reacting

to Trump's Decision to Quit Nuclear Deal," *Time*, May 9, 2018, http://time.com/5270821/iran-nuclear-deal-trump-ayatollah-khameini-hassan-rouhani/.

145. Sherman, "How We Got the Iran Deal."
146. Nick Gass and Adam B. Lerner, "GOP Candidates Vow to Roll Back Iran Deal," *Politico*, July 14, 2015, https://www.politico.com/story/2015/07/gop-candidates-vow-to-roll-back-iran-deal-120081.html.

CHAPTER 4: RECESS APPOINTMENTS

1. Article II, section 2, clause 3.
2. Michael A. Carrier, "When Is the Senate in Recess for Purposes of the Recess Appointments Clause?" *Michigan Law Review* 92, no. 7 (1994): 2224.
3. Michael B. Rappoport, ""The Original Meaning of the Recess Appointments Clause," *UCLA Law Review* 52 (2005): 1487–1578.
4. Ryan C. Black et al., "Adding Recess Appointments to the President's 'Tool Chest' of Unilateral Powers," *Political Research Quarterly* 60, no. 4 (2007): 645–654; Ryan C. Black et al., "Assessing Congressional Responses to Growing Presidential Powers: The Case of Recess Appointments," *Presidential Studies Quarterly* 41, no. 3 (2011): 570–589; Pamela C. Corley, "Avoiding Advice and Consent: Recess Appointments and Presidential Power," *Presidential Studies Quarterly* 36, no. 4 (2006): 670–680; Ian Ostrander, "Powering Down the Presidency: The Rise and Fall of Recess Appointments," *Presidential Studies Quarterly* 45, no. 3 (2015): 558–572.
5. Ostrander, "Powering Down the Presidency."
6. David E. Pozen, "Self-Help and the Separation of Powers," *Yale Law Journal* 124, no. 1 (2014): 2–90.
7. Alexander Hamilton et al., *The Federalist Papers*, ed. Clinton Rossiter (Signet, 2003), #67, 408.
8. Carrier, "When Is the Senate in Recess?" 2224.
9. Rappoport, "Original Meaning of the Recess Appointments Clause," 1498.
10. Joseph Story, *Commentaries on the Constitution of the United States* (Hilliard, Gray, 1833), 573–574.
11. Story, *Commentaries on the Constitution of the United States*, 574.
12. Edmund Randolph, "Opinion on Recess Appointments," July 7, 1792, Founders Online, http://founders.archives.gov/documents/Jefferson/01-24-02-0176.
13. See letter from Alexander Hamilton to James McHenry, May 3, 1799, in Harold C. Syrett, *Papers of Alexander Hamilton*, vol. 23 (Columbia University Press, 1979), 94; Rappoport, "Original Meaning of the Recess Appointments Clause," 1520.
14. 1 Opinion of the Attorney General 631 (1833), 632. (Hereinafter, Wirt Opinion).
15. Wirt Opinion, 634.
16. Black et al., "Adding Recess Appointments"; Corley, "Avoiding Advice and Consent"; Ostrander, "Powering Down the Presidency."
17. Henry B. Hogue, "Recess Appointments: Frequently Asked Questions," Congressional Research Service, 2013, 11.
18. Henry B. Hogue, "Recess Appointments Made by Barack Obama," Congressional Research Service, 2017, 12.
19. Ostrander, "Powering Down the Presidency," 563; Black et al., "Assessing Congressional Responses."

20. Joan Flynn, "A Quiet Revolution at the Labor Board: The Transformation of the NLRB 1935–2000," *Ohio State Law Journal* 61 (2000): 1361–1455; Ostrander, "Powering Down the Presidency."
21. Hogue, "Recess Appointments Made by Barack Obama," 14.
22. Seung Min Kim, "Republicans Join Challenge of Recess Appointments," *Politico*, February 3, 2012, https://www.politico.com/news/stories/0212/72422.html.
23. Kim, "Republicans Join Challenge."
24. National Labor Relations Board v. Noel Canning, 573 U.S. 513 (2014), 9–21 (Slip opinion).
25. Art. I, sec. 5, cl. 4.
26. *National Labor Relations Board v. Noel Canning*, 23, 26. (Slip opinion).
27. *National Labor Relations Board v. Noel Canning*, 34.
28. Art. I, sec. 5, cl. 2.
29. Adam Liptak, "Supreme Court Rebukes Obama on Right of Appointment," *New York Times*, June 26, 2014, https://www.nytimes.com/2014/06/27/us/supreme-court-president-recess-appointments.html.
30. Hogue, "Recess Appointments Made by Barack Obama."
31. Amber Phillips, "How Obama Could Appoint Merrick Garland to the Supreme Court, and Why It'll Never Happen," *Washington Post*, March 21, 2016, https://www.washingtonpost.com/news/the-fix/wp/2016/03/21/how-obama-could-appoint-merrick-garland-to-the-supreme-court-and-why-itll-never-happen/.
32. Ostrander, "Powering Down the Presidency."
33. Hamilton et al., *Federalist Papers*, #76, 454.
34. Hamilton et al., *Federalist Papers*, #76, 454.
35. Hamilton et al., *Federalist Papers*, #76, 454.
36. Mike DeBonis and Paul Kane, "Republicans Vow No Hearings and No Votes for Obama's Supreme Court Pick," *Washington Post*, February 23, 2016, https://www.washingtonpost.com/news/powerpost/wp/2016/02/23/key-senate-republicans-say-no-hearings-for-supreme-court-nominee/.
37. Joseph M. Bessette, *The Mild Voice of Reason: Deliberative Democracy and American National Government*, American Politics and Political Economy Series (University of Chicago Press, 1994), 213.
38. Jeffrey K. Tulis, "Constitutional Abdication: The Senate, the President, and Appointments to the Supreme Court," *Case Western Reserve Law Review* 47 (1996): 1331–1357.
39. Tulis, "Constitutional Abdication," 1353–1357.
40. Nina Totenberg, "The Confirmation Process and the Public: To Know or Not to Know," *Harvard Law Review* 101, no. 6 (1988): 1220.
41. Totenberg, "Confirmation Process and the Public," 1220–1221.
42. Josh Chafetz, *Congress's Constitution: Legislative Authority and the Separation of Powers* (Yale University Press, 2017), 23.
43. Al Kamen, "Bork Fails to Catch Public's Eye: Opinion Is Split Among the Informed," *Washington Post*, August 7, 1987.
44. Edward Walsh, "Public Opposition to Bork Grows: In Shift, Plurality Objects to Confirmation, Post-ABC Poll Finds," *Washington Post*, September 25, 1987.

45. Edward Walsh and Richard Morin, "Majority Opposes Bork, Poll Shows," *Washington Post*, October 16, 1987.
46. Pozen, "Self-Help and the Separation of Powers."
47. Jonathan Weisman, "Experts Say Obama's Recess Appointments Could Signify End to a Senate Role," *New York Times*, January 7, 2012, https://www.nytimes.com/2012/01/08/us/politics/experts-say-obamas-recess-appointments-could-signify-end-to-a-senate-role.html.
48. Thomas E. Mann and Norman J. Ornstein, *It's Even Worse Than It Looks: How the American Constitutional System Collided with the New Politics of Extremism*, rev. and expanded ed. (Basic Books, 2016), 97.
49. Mann and Ornstein, *It's Even Worse Than It Looks*, 100.
50. Mann and Ornstein, *It's Even Worse Than It Looks*, 99.
51. Weisman, "Experts Say Obama's Recess Appointments Could Signify."
52. Josh Chafetz, "The Unconstitutionality of the Filibuster," *Connecticut Law Review* 43, no. 4 (2011): 1003–1040; David A. Crockett, "The Contemporary President: Should the Senate Take a Floor Vote on a Presidential Judicial Nominee?" *Presidential Studies Quarterly* 37, no. 2 (2007): 313–330.
53. See *Federalist Papers*, #62–63.
54. Michael J. Gerhardt, "The Constitutionality of the Filibuster," *Constitutional Commentary* 21, no. 1 (2004): 445–451.
55. Josh Chafetz and Michael J. Gerhardt, "Debate, Is the Filibuster Constitutional," *University of Pennsylvania Law Review PENNumbra* 158 (2010): 250.
56. Chafetz, "Unconstitutionality of the Filibuster," 1221; Catherine Fisk and Erwin Chemerinsky, "The Filibuster," *Stanford Law Review* 49, no. 2 (1997): 187–188.
57. Chafetz, "Unconstitutionality of the Filibuster," 1023–1024.
58. Fisk and Chemerinsky, "Filibuster," 195.
59. Chafetz, "Unconstitutionality of the Filibuster," 1010; Fisk and Chemerinsky, "Filibuster," 203. ("The stealth filibuster is easier, both physically and politically. . . . ").
60. Given rule changes in the Senate, however, filibusters now cannot be used for executive appointments, and Senate Republicans also changed the rules to prohibit filibusters for judicial nominations as well. These rule changes now mean that filibusters are no longer used to hold up executive nominations. Even so, the point of this chapter is to show how the court's legalistic conception of the recess appointments clause and its subsequent invalidation of President Obama's recess appointments was not attentive to the political dynamics involved in that particular instance. The rule changes that would have made such recess appointments no longer necessary, in other words, does not bear on the specific critique made in this chapter.
61. Sarah A. Binder and Steven S. Smith, *Politics or Principle: Filibustering in the United States Senate* (Brookings Institution Press, 1996), 31–33.
62. Hamilton et al., *Federalist Papers*, #22, 143.
63. Art. I, sec. 5, cl. 1.
64. Chafetz, "Unconstitutionality of the Filibuster," 1010–1011.
65. Chafetz, "Unconstitutionality of the Filibuster," 1013.
66. Chafetz, "Unconstitutionality of the Filibuster," 1013.

67. Paul Brest, "The Conscientious Legislator's Guide to Constitutional Interpretation," *Stanford Law Review* 27, no. 3 (1975): 586.
68. "We Can't Wait," The White House, accessed January 31, 2024, https://obamawhitehouse.archives.gov/node/111049.
69. "America's Consumer Watchdog," whitehouse.gov, January 4, 2012, https://obamawhitehouse.archives.gov/blog/2012/01/04/americas-consumer-watchdog.
70. Amber Phillips, "How Trump Could Replace Jeff Sessions in a Recess Appointment," *Washington Post*, July 27, 2017, https://www.washingtonpost.com/news/the-fix/wp/2017/07/27/how-trump-could-replace-jeff-sessions-in-a-recess-appointment-and-how-republicans-can-prevent-that/.
71. Phillips, "How Trump Could Replace Jeff Sessions."

CHAPTER 5: CONGRESSIONAL OVERSIGHT AND IMPEACHMENT

1. See Impeaching Donald John Trump, President of the United States, for High Crimes and Misdemeanors ("Articles of Impeachment"), H.R. Res. 755, 116th Cong. (2019).
2. Letter from Pat A. Cipollone, Counsel for President Trump, to Nancy Pelosi, House Speaker; Eliot L. Engel, Chairman of Foreign Affairs Comm.; Adam B. Schiff, Chairman of Permanent Select Comm. on Intelligence; and Elijah E. Cummings, Chairman of Comm. on Oversight and Reform 7 (Oct. 8, 2019) [hereinafter Cipollone Letter].
3. David K. Nichols, *The Myth of the Modern Presidency* (Pennsylvania State University Press, 1994); Charles C. Thach Jr., *The Creation of the Presidency, 1775–1789* (Liberty Fund, 2010); Jeffrey K. Tulis, "The Constitutional Presidency in American Constitutional Development," in *The Constitution and the American Presidency*, ed. Martin L. Fausold and Alan Shank (SUNY Press, 1991).
4. David A. Crockett, "Executive Privilege," in *The Constitutional Presidency*, ed. Jeffrey K. Tulis and Joseph M. Bessette (John Hopkins University Press, 2009); Mark J. Rozell and Mitchel A. Sollenberger, *Executive Privilege: Presidential Power, Secrecy, and Accountability*, updated ed. (University Press of Kansas, 2020); Gary J. Schmitt, "Executive Privilege: Presidential Power to Withhold Information from Congress," in *The Presidency in the Constitutional Order*, ed. Jeffrey K. Tulis and Joseph M. Bessette (Louisiana State University Press, 1981).
5. Heidi Kitrosser, "The Shadow of Executive Privilege," *Minnesota Law Review* 15, no. 3 (2017): 547–566; idem, "Like 'Nobody Has Ever Seen Before': Precedent and Privilege in the Trump Era," *Chicago-Kent Law Review* 95, no. 2 (2021): 519–536; Jonathan Shaub, "The Executive's Privilege," *Duke Law Journal* 70, no. 1 (2020): 1–91.
6. Josh Chafetz, *Congress's Constitution: Legislative Authority and the Separation of Powers* (Yale University Press, 2017), 152.
7. Steve Drummond, *The Watchdog: How the Truman Committee Battled Corruption and Helped Win World War Two* (Hanover Square Press, 2023).
8. Quinn v. United States, 349 U.S. 155 (1955), 160.
9. McGrain v. Daugherty, 273 U.S. 135 (1927), 175.
10. Keith E. Whittington, "Trump's Defiance Is Destroying Congress's Power,"

Atlantic (blog), October 14, 2019, https://www.theatlantic.com/ideas/archive/2019/10/trumps-defiance-destroying-congress/599923/.

11. John Stuart Mill, *Considerations on Representative Government* (Parker, Son, and Bourn, 1861), 104. Quoted in Whittington, "Trump's Defiance Is Destroying Congress's Power."
12. Chafetz, *Congress's Constitution*; James M. Landis, "Constitutional Limitations on the Congressional Power of Investigation," *Harvard Law Review* 40, no. 2 (1926): 153–221; C. S. Potts, "Power of Legislative Bodies to Punish for Contempt," *University of Pennsylvania Law Review* 74 (1926): 691–725; Brianne J. Gorod, Brian R. Frazelle, and Ashwin P. Phatak, "The Historical and Legal Basis for the Exercise of Congressional Oversight Authority," Constitutional Accountability Center, January 2019, https://www.theusconstitution.org/wp-content/uploads/2019/01/Congressional-Oversight-Issue-Brief.pdf.
13. Potts, "Power of Legislative Bodies," 708.
14. Chafetz, *Congress's Constitution*, 170–171.
15. Gorod, Frazelle, and Phatak, "Congressional Oversight Authority," 4.
16. McGrain v. Daugherty, 273 U.S. 135 (1927), 161 (citing 3 Cong. Ann. 494).
17. An Act More Effectually to Enforce the Attendance of Witnesses on the Summons of Either House of Congress, and to Compel Them to Discover Testimony, chap. 19, sec. 1, 11 Stat 155, 155 (1857); Chafetz, *Congress's Constitution*, 175.
18. I use the term "executive privilege" loosely to refer to any withholding of information from Congress regardless of whether a formal legal claim to privilege is made. As will be evident in the next section, executive privilege has taken on a legalistic framework that I contest, and I do not fully embrace the legal categories in my own description of the phenomenon here. I thus refer to executive privilege as the general withholding of information.
19. Raoul Berger, *Executive Privilege: A Constitutional Myth* (Harvard University Press, 1974), 3.
20. Berger, *Executive Privilege*, 13.
21. Berger, *Executive Privilege*, 13.
22. Berger, *Executive Privilege*, 50.
23. Berger, *Executive Privilege*, 52.
24. Crockett, "Executive Privilege"; Rozell and Sollenberger, *Executive Privilege*; Schmitt, "Executive Privilege."
25. David Gray Adler, "Con: A Broad Executive Privilege Is Essential to the Successful Functioning of the Presidency," in *Debating the Presidency: Conflicting Perspectives on the American Executive*, ed. Richard J. Ellis and Michael Nelson (CQ Press, 2006); Louis Fisher, *The Politics of Executive Privilege* (Carolina Academic Press, 2003).
26. Thach, *Creation of the Presidency*.
27. Alexander Hamilton et al., *The Federalist Papers*, ed. Clinton Rossiter (Signet, 2003), #51, 319.
28. Hamilton et al., *Federalist Papers*, #48, 306.
29. Hamilton et al., *Federalist Papers*, #70, 421.
30. Crockett, "Executive Privilege," 220.
31. United States v. Nixon, 418 U.S. 683 (1974), 706.

32. *United States v. Nixon*, 712.
33. Rozell and Sollenberger, *Executive Privilege.*
34. Kitrosser, "Shadow of Executive Privilege"; Shaub, "Executive's Privilege."
35. Shaub, "Executive's Privilege," 55–70.
36. Shaub, "Executive's Privilege," 10.
37. Shaub, "Executive's Privilege," 10.
38. Kitrosser, "Shadow of Executive Privilege"; idem, "Like 'Nobody Has Ever Seen Before'."
39. Kitrosser, "Like 'Nobody Has Ever Seen Before'," 522.
40. Kitrosser, "Like 'Nobody Has Ever Seen Before'," 522.
41. Senate Select Committee. v. Nixon, 498 F.2d 725 (D.C. Cir. 1974) (en banc).
42. *Senate Select Committee. v. Nixon*, 731.
43. *Senate Select Committee. v. Nixon*, 732.
44. *Senate Select Committee. v. Nixon*, 732.
45. Josh Chafetz, "Nixon/Trump: Strategies of Judicial Aggrandizement," *Georgetown Law Journal* 110, no. 1 (2021): 135.
46. Kitrosser, "Like 'Nobody Has Ever Seen Before'," 523.
47. Kitrosser, "Like 'Nobody Has Ever Seen Before'," 522; Shaub, "Executive's Privilege," 11.
48. Cheney v. United States District Court 542 U.S.367 (2004), 389.
49. *Cheney v. United States District Court*, 382.
50. Kitrosser, "Like 'Nobody Has Ever Seen Before'," 522–523.
51. Shaub, "Executive's Privilege," 57.
52. Kitrosser, "Shadow of Executive Privilege," 547–548; "In Refusal to Answer Questions, Sessions Denies Claiming Executive Privilege," *All Things Considered*, National Public Radio, June 13, 2017, https://www.npr.org/2017/06/13/532816894/in-refusal-to-answer-questions-sessions-denies-claiming-executive-privilege.
53. Cipollone Letter, 8, 2.
54. Michael Stern, "Why Officials Keep Testifying Despite White House Counsel's Letter on Impeachment Inquiry," *Just Security*, October 28, 2019, https://www.justsecurity.org/66742/why-officials-keep-testifying-despite-white-house-counsels-letter-on-impeachment-inquiry/.
55. Trial Memorandum of President Donald J. Trump (for Senate Impeachment Proceedings), 36.
56. Trial Memorandum of President Donald J. Trump (for Senate Impeachment Proceedings), 37.
57. Keith Whittington, "Must the House Vote to Authorize an Impeachment Inquiry?" *Lawfare*, October 9, 2019, https://www.lawfaremedia.org/article/must-house-vote-authorize-impeachment-inquiry.
58. Articles of Impeachment Against Donald J. Trump, Article II: Obstruction of Congress.
59. US House of Representatives, *Impeachment of Donald J. Trump, President of the United States: Report of the Committee on the Judiciary* (with dissenting views), 116th Cong., 1st sess., December 16, 2019, H. Rept. 116–346 [hereinafter House Impeachment Report], 197.
60. House Impeachment Report, Dissenting Views, 197.

61. House Impeachment Report, Dissenting Views, 197.
62. Jonathan Turley, "The Impeachment Inquiry into President Donald J. Trump: The Constitutional Basis for Presidential Impeachment," written statement, December 4, 2019, 40.
63. Turley, "Impeachment Inquiry into President Donald J. Trump," 40.
64. Turley, "Impeachment Inquiry into President Donald J. Trump," 42.
65. House Impeachment Brief in the Impeachment of Donald J. Trump, at 39n228 (citing Brief for Def-Appellant at 2, 32–33; Committee on the Judiciary v. McGahn, no. 19–5331 (D.C. Cir. Dec. 9, 2019); Def.'s Mot. to Dismiss or in the Alternative, for Summ. J. at 19–20; Kupperman v. U.S. House of Representatives, no. 19–3224 (D.D.C. Nov. 14, 2019)).
66. Marshall Cohen and Katelyn Polantz, "In Contrast with Trump Legal Team, Justice Department Lawyer Says House Can Impeach over Defied Subpoenas," CNN, January 30, 2020, https://www.cnn.com/2020/01/30/politics/trump-impeachment-subpoena-hearing/index.html.
67. Congressional Record, 117th Cong., 1st sess., January 30, 2021, vol. 166, no. 20, statement of Rep. Adam Schiff, S701.
68. Maggie Haberman and Michael S. Schmidt, "Trump Tied Ukraine Aid to Inquiries He Sought, Bolton Book Says," *New York Times*, January 26, 2020, https://www.nytimes.com/2020/01/26/us/politics/trump-bolton-book-ukraine.html; Rachael Bade and Karoun Demirjian, *Unchecked: The Untold Story Behind Congress's Botched Impeachments of Donald Trump* (William Morrow, 2022), 392–423.
69. Bade and Demirjian, *Unchecked*, 404.
70. Bade and Demirjian, *Unchecked*, 414.
71. Senator Lisa Murkowski, "Murkowski's Statement on Senate Impeachment Process Vote," January 31, 2020, https://www.murkowski.senate.gov/press/release/murkowskis-statement-on-senate-impeachment-process-vote.
72. House Impeachment Report, 161–164.
73. House Impeachment Report, 163.
74. House Impeachment Report, 164.
75. Chafetz, "Nixon/Trump."
76. Raoul Berger, *Impeachment: The Constitutional Problems* (Harvard University Press, 1973); Charles L. Black Jr. and Philip Bobbitt, *Impeachment: A Handbook* (Yale University Press, 2018); Michael J. Gerhardt, *The Federal Impeachment Process*, 3rd ed. (University of Chicago Press, 2019); Gene Healy, *Indispensable Remedy: The Broad Scope of the Constitution's Impeachment Power* (Cato Institute, 2018); Michael Stokes Paulsen, "Taking Impeachment Seriously—Michael Stokes Paulsen," *Law & Liberty* (blog), June 28, 2018, https://lawliberty.org/taking-impeachment-seriously/; Jeffrey K. Tulis, "Impeachment in the Constitutional Order," in Tulis and Bessette, *Constitutional Presidency*; Keith E. Whittington, "A Formidable Weapon of Faction? The Law and Politics of Impeachment," *Wake Forest Law Review* 55, no. 2 (2020): 381–414.
77. Tulis, "Impeachment in the Constitutional Order."
78. US Constitution, Art. I, sec. 2, cl. 5.
79. Whittington, "Must the House Vote?"

80. US Constitution, Art. I, sec. 3.
81. Berger, *Impeachment*, 76; Gerhardt, *Federal Impeachment Process*, 105.
82. Max Farrand, ed., *The Records of the Federal Convention of 1787*, vol. 2 (Yale University Press 1967), 550.
83. Berger, *Impeachment*, 54.
84. Berger, *Impeachment*, 61.
85. Berger, *Impeachment*, 59.
86. Berger, *Impeachment*, 61. Emphasis in original.
87. Berger, *Impeachment*, 61–62.
88. Farrand, *Records of the Federal Convention of 1787*, vol. 2, 550.
89. Michael Stokes Paulsen, "The Original Meaning of 'High Crimes and Misdemeanors,' Part II—Michael Stokes Paulsen," *Law & Liberty* (blog), August 9, 2018, https://lawliberty.org/the-original-meaning-of-high-crimes-and-misdemeanors-part-2/.
90. Hamilton et al., *Federalist Papers*, #65, 394–395.
91. Gerhardt, *Federal Impeachment Process*, 107.
92. Joseph Story, *Commentaries on the Constitution of the United States*, ed. Thomas Cooley, 4th ed. (Lawbook Exchange, 2005), 541.
93. Black and Bobbitt, *Impeachment*, 31.
94. Black and Bobbitt, *Impeachment*, 31.
95. David E. Kyvig, *The Age of Impeachment: American Constitutional Culture Since 1960* (University Press of Kansas, 2008), 96; Whittington, "Formidable Weapon of Faction?" 403.
96. Adam Liptak, "Key Excerpts from Legal Scholars' Arguments on Impeachment," *New York Times*, December 4, 2019, https://www.nytimes.com/2019/12/04/us/politics/karlan-feldman-turley-gerhardt.html.
97. Turley, "Impeachment Inquiry into President Donald J. Trump," 10.
98. Tulis, "Impeachment in the Constitutional Order."
99. Congressional Record, 116th Cong., 2nd sess., January 27, 2020, vol. 166, no. 17, statement of Alan Dershowitz, S611.
100. Congressional Record, 116th Cong., 2nd sess., January 29, 2020, vol 166, no. 19, statement of Alan Dershowitz, S650.
101. Bade and Demirjian, *Unchecked*, 415.
102. Quoted in Congressional Record, 116th Cong., 2nd sess., January 27, 2020, vol. 166, no. 17, statement of Alan Dershowitz, S610.
103. Whittington, "Formidable Weapon of Faction?" 403.
104. Allen C. Sumrall, "Incongruous Ideas of Impeachment: 'Impeachable Offenses' and the Constitutional Order," *Presidential Studies Quarterly* 50, no. 4 (2020): 948–967.
105. Bade and Demirjian, *Unchecked*, 414–418.
106. US Senate, *Senate Trial Transcript*, 116th Cong., 2nd sess., January 30, 2020, vol. 166, no. 20, S735.
107. "Sen. Lee Statement on Acquittal of Former President Trump," Mike Lee US Senator for Utah, February 13, 2021, https://www.lee.senate.gov/2021/2/sen-lee-statement-on-acquittal-of-former-president-trump.
108. Bade and Demirjian, *Unchecked*, 260.
109. Healy, *Indispensable Remedy*, 84–85.

110. Memorandum from William H. Rehnquist, Assistant Att'y Gen., Off. of Legal Couns., U.S. Dep't of Just., to John D. Ehrlichman, Assistant to the President for Domestic Affs., Power of Congressional Committee to Compel Appearance or Testimony of "White House Staff," 6–7 (Feb. 5, 1971) [hereinafter Rehnquist Memorandum] (emphasis omitted), https:// www.justice.gov/olc/page/file/1225961/download [https://perma.cc/TX6S-VS56].
111. Tulis, "Impeachment in the Constitutional Order," 229.
112. Congressional Record, 117th Cong., 1st sess., January 6, 2021, vol. 167, no. 4, S31.
113. Congressional Record, 117th Cong., 1st sess., January 13, 2021, vol. 167, no. 8, H172.
114. "The Trump Administration Officials Who Resigned over Capitol Violence," *New York Times*, January 17, 2021, https://www.nytimes.com/article/trump-resignations.html.
115. See Impeaching Donald John Trump, President of the United States, for High Crimes and Misdemeanors ("Articles of Impeachment"), H.R. Res. 24, 117th Cong. (2021).
116. "A List of the Times Trump Has Said He Won't Accept the Election Results or Leave Office If He Loses," CNN, September 24, 2020, https://www.cnn.com/2020/09/24/politics/trump-election-warnings-leaving-office/index.html.
117. Congressional Record, 117th Cong., 1st sess., vol. 167, no. 25. February 10, 2021, S621.
118. "Barr Says No Evidence of Widespread Voter Fraud in Election," *Wall Street Journal*, December 1, 2020, https://www.wsj.com/articles/trump-campaign-files-more-election-challenges-in-wisconsin-michigan-11606849219.
119. Congressional Record, 117th Cong., 1st sess., February 10, 2021, vol. 167, no. 25, S624–S626.
120. Congressional Record, 117th Cong., 1st sess., February 10, 2021, vol. 167, no. 25, S627.
121. Congressional Record, 117th Cong., 1st sess., February 10, 2021, vol. 167, no. 25, S627.
122. Brian Naylor, "Read Trump's Jan. 6 Speech, a Key Part of Impeachment Trial," National Public Radio, February 10, 2021, https://www.npr.org/2021/02/10/966396848/read-trumps-jan-6-speech-a-key-part-of-impeachment-trial.
123. Naylor, "Read Trump's Jan. 6 Speech."
124. Bade and Demirjian, *Unchecked*, 468.
125. Congressional Record, 117th Cong., 1st sess., February 10, 2021, vol. 167, no. 25, S643.
126. Bade and Demirjian, *Unchecked*, 475–485.
127. Bade and Demirjian, *Unchecked*, 485.
128. Congressional Record, 117th Cong., 1st sess., February 10, 2021, vol. 167, no. 25, S643.
129. Congressional Record, 117th Cong., 1st sess., February 10, 2021, vol. 167, no. 25, S643.
130. William Baude and Michael Stokes Paulsen, "The Sweep and Force of Section 3," *University of Pennsylvania Law Review*, 172, no. 3 (2024): 732.
131. J. Michael Luttig, "A Senate Impeachment Trial After Trump Leaves Office

Would Be Unconstitutional," *Washington Post*, January 12, 2021, https://www.washingtonpost.com/opinions/2021/01/12/once-trump-leaves-office-senate-cant-hold-an-impeachment-trial/.

132. Sahil Kapur, "Most Senate Republicans Declare Trump's Trial Unconstitutional. Here's What That Means for Conviction," *NBC News*, January 26, 2021, https://www.nbcnews.com/politics/congress/most-republicans-declare-trump-s-trial-unconstitutional-here-s-what-n1255704.
133. Luttig, "Senate Impeachment Trial After Trump Leaves Office."
134. Emphasis mine.
135. Emphasis mine.
136. Brian C. Kalt, "The Constitutional Case for the Impeachability of Former Federal Officials: An Analysis of the Law, History, and Practice of Late Impeachment," *Texas Review of Law & Politics* 6, no. 2 (2001): 13–135.
137. Kalt, "Impeachability of Former Federal Officials," 86–89.
138. Kalt, "Impeachability of Former Federal Officials," 94–102.
139. Michael McConnell and Ken Gormley, "Yes, the Senate Has the Power to Try Trump. He Was Impeached in Office," *Washington Post*, February 4, 2021, https://www.washingtonpost.com/opinions/2021/02/04/yes-senate-has-power-try-trump-he-was-impeached-office/; Steven G. Calabresi and Norman Eisen, "We Disagree on a Lot. But We Both Think Trump Should Be Convicted," *New York Times*, January 13, 2021, https://www.nytimes.com/2021/01/13/opinion/trump-impeachment-bipartisan.html.
140. Jonathan Turley, "Trump Impeachment Trial—Why His Best Defense May Be No Defense," *Fox News*, January 17, 2021, https://www.foxnews.com/opinion/trump-impeachment-trial-defense-strategy-jonathan-turley.
141. Jonathan Turley, "Senate Trials and Factional Disputes: Impeachment as a Madisonian Device," *Duke Law Journal* 49, no. 1 (1999): 56.
142. Congressional Record, 117th Cong., 1st Sess. February 9, 2021, vol. 167, no. 24, S590.
143. Ryan Goodman and Josh Asabor, "In Their Own Words: The 43 Republicans' Explanations of Their Votes Not to Convict Trump in Impeachment Trial," *Just Security*, February 15, 2021, https://www.justsecurity.org/74725/in-their-own-words-the-43-republicans-explanations-of-their-votes-not-to-convict-trump-in-impeachment-trial/.
144. Congressional Record 117th Cong. 1st Sess. February 13, 2021, vol. 167, no. 28, S736.
145. Congressional Record 117th Cong. 1st Sess. February 13, 2021 Vol. 167, no. 28, S736.
146. Congressional Record 117th Cong. 1st Sess. February 13, 2021, vol. 167, no. 28, S736.
147. Damon Linker, "The Case Against Prosecuting Donald Trump," *Persuasion*, September 2, 2022, https://www.persuasion.community/p/the-case-against-prosecuting-donald.
148. Jennifer Medina, "G.O.P. Contenders Feed Voter Distrust in Courts, Schools and Military," *New York Times*, August 7, 2023, https://www.nytimes.com/2023/08/07/us/politics/trump-republican-primary-candidate-trust.html.
149. Robert Downen and William Melhado, "Trump Vows Retribution at Waco

Rally: 'I Am Your Warrior, I Am Your Justice,'" *Texas Tribune*, March 26, 2023, https://www.texastribune.org/2023/03/25/donald-trump-waco-rally-retribution-justice/.

150. Trump v. United States, 603 U.S. ___ (2024).
151. Art. I, sec. 3, cl. 7.
152. Trump v. United States, 603 U.S. ___ (2024) (Sotomayor, J., dissenting), 30–31.
153. Congressional Record 117th Cong. 1st Sess. February 13, 2021, vol. 167, no. 28, S736.

CONCLUSION: DOES HYPERPARTISANSHIP UNDERMINE THE SEPARATION OF POWERS?

1. Nikolas Bowie and Daphna Renan, "The Separation of Powers Counterrevolution," *Yale Law Journal* 131, no. 7 (2022): 2024–2025.
2. George Thomas, *The Madisonian Constitution* (Johns Hopkins University Press, 2008).
3. Antonin Scalia, "The Legislative Veto: A False Remedy for System Overload," *Regulation: AEI Journal on Government and Society* (1979): 19–26.
4. Jessica Korn, *The Power of Separation: American Constitutionalism and the Myth of the Legislative Veto*, Princeton Studies in American Politics (Princeton University Press, 1996).
5. John C. Yoo, "Laws as Treaties?: The Constitutionality of Congressional-Executive Agreements," *Michigan Law Review* 99, no. 4 (2001): 757–852.
6. Curtis A. Bradley, Jack Goldsmith, and Oona Hathaway, "Congress Mandates Sweeping Transparency Reforms for International Agreements," *Lawfare* (blog), December 23, 2022, https://www.lawfareblog.com/congress-mandates-sweeping-transparency-reforms-international-agreements.
7. Leslie Friedman Goldstein, *In Defense of the Text: Democracy and Constitutional Theory* (Rowman & Littlefield, 1991); Ronald Dworkin, *Taking Rights Seriously*, 5th ed. (Harvard University Press, 1978), 22–28; Jack M. Balkin, *Living Originalism* (Harvard University Press, 2011), 44, 349–352.
8. Thomas R. Bell, "Perverse Politics: Recess Appointments, Noel Canning, and the Limits of Law," *Presidential Studies Quarterly* 48, no. 2 (2018): 373–386.
9. Daryl J. Levinson and Richard H. Pildes, "Separation of Parties, Not Powers," *Harvard Law Review* 119, no. 8 (2006): 2311–2386.
10. Levinson and Pildes, "Separation of Parties," 2314.
11. Levinson and Pildes, "Separation of Parties," 2313.
12. Josh Chafetz, *Congress's Constitution: Legislative Authority and the Separation of Powers* (Yale University Press, 2017), 28–35.
13. Russell Muirhead, *The Promise of Party in a Polarized Age* (Harvard University Press, 2014).
14. Thomas E. Mann and Norman J. Ornstein, *It's Even Worse Than It Looks: How the American Constitutional System Collided with the New Politics of Extremism*, rev. and expanded ed. (Basic Books, 2016), xiv.
15. Mann and Ornstein, *It's Even Worse Than It Looks*, xix.
16. Jeffrey K. Tulis, "On the State of Constitutional Theory," *Law and Social Inquiry* 16 (1991): 716.

17. James W. Ceaser, *Presidential Selection* (Princeton University Press, 1979); Jeffrey Tulis, *The Rhetorical Presidency* (Princeton University Press, 1987).
18. Herbert J. Storing, "In Defense of the Electoral College: Statement on Proposals for Direct Popular Election of the President of the United States, July 22, 1977," repr. in *Toward a More Perfect Union: Writings of Herbert J. Storing*, ed. Joseph Bessette (AEI Press, 1995).
19. Alexander Hamilton et al., *The Federalist Papers*, ed. Clinton Rossiter (Signet, 2003), #10, 77.
20. Hamilton et al., *Federalist Papers*, #10, 77.
21. Nick Troiano, *The Primary Solution: Rescuing Our Democracy from the Fringes* (Simon & Schuster, 2024); Kevin R. Kosar, "Conservatives Should Look More Closely at Systemic Election Reforms," American Enterprise Institute, https://www.aei.org/research-products/report/conservatives-should-look-more-closely-at-systemic-election-reforms/, October 3, 2023; Yuval Levin, "What We Can Do to Make American Politics Less Dysfunctional," *New York Times*, October 9, 2023, https://www.nytimes.com/2023/10/09/opinion/american-politics-congress-reform.html.
22. David W. Brady, Hahrie Han, and Jeremy C. Pope, "Primary Elections and Candidate Ideology: Out of Step with the Primary Electorate?" *Legislative Studies Quarterly* 32, no. 1 (2011): 79–105; Elaine Karmarck and Alexander R. Podkul, "The 2018 Primaries Project: The Ideology of Primary Voters," Brookings Institution, October 23, 2018, https://www.brookings.edu/articles/the-2018-primaries-project-the-ideology-of-primary-voters/.
23. Norm Ornstein, "Yes, Polarization Is Asymmetric—and Conservatives Are Worse," *Atlantic* (blog), June 19, 2014, https://www.theatlantic.com/politics/archive/2014/06/yes-polarization-is-asymmetric-and-conservatives-are-worse/373044/; Mann and Ornstein, *It's Even Worse Than It Looks.*
24. Troiano, *Primary Solution*, 40–57.
25. Annie Linskey, "Democrats Spend Tens of Millions Amplifying Far-Right Candidates in Nine States," *Washington Post*, September 12, 2022, https://www.washingtonpost.com/politics/2022/09/12/democrats-interfere-republican-primaries/; Savannah Kuchar, "Democrats Spent Millions Boosting Ultra Right Candidates in Midterms. The Strategy Worked," *USA Today*, November 15, 2022, https://www.usatoday.com/story/news/politics/2022/11/15/democrats-boosted-trump-gop-primaries-helping-midterms/10670042002/.
26. Drew DeSilver, "The Polarization in Today's Congress Has Roots That Go Back Decades," *Pew Research Center* (blog), March 10, 2022, https://www.pewresearch.org/short-reads/2022/03/10/the-polarization-in-todays-congress-has-roots-that-go-back-decades/.
27. Morris P. Fiorina, *Unstable Majorities: Polarization, Party Sorting, and Political Stalemate* (Hoover Institution Press, 2017); Morris P. Fiorina, Samuel J. Abrams, and Jeremy C. Pope, *Culture War? The Myth of a Polarized America*, 3rd ed. (Longman, 2010).
28. Fiorina, *Unstable Majorities*, 29.
29. Levin, "What We Can Do to Make American Politics Less Dysfunctional."
30. Martin Pengelly, "Bernstein Names 21 Republican Senators Who Privately

Expressed Contempt for Trump," *Guardian*, November 23, 2020, https://www.theguardian.com/us-news/2020/nov/23/carl-bernstein-21-republican-senators-expressed-contempt-for-trump; Gino Spocchia, "Kinzinger Reveals Why Republicans Are Scared to Criticize Trump," *Independent*, October 20, 2021, https://www.independent.co.uk/news/world/americas/us-politics/adam-kinsinger-trump-marjorie-greene-b1941855.html; Rachael Bade, Ryan Lizza, and Eugene Daniels, "Playbook: The Republicans Secretly Rooting for a Trump Loss," *Politico*, September 5, 2024, https://www.politico.com/newsletters/playbook/2024/09/04/the-republicans-secretly-rooting-for-a-trump-loss-00177272.

31. David R. Mayhew, *Congress: The Electoral Connection*, 2nd ed. (Yale University Press, 2004).
32. Katherine M. Gehl et al., *The Politics Industry: How Political Innovation Can Break Partisan Gridlock and Save Our Democracy* (Harvard Business Review Press, 2020).
33. Christian R. Grose, "Reducing Legislative Polarization: Top-Two and Open Primaries Are Associated with More Moderate Legislators," *Journal of Political Institutions and Political Economy* 1, no. 2 (2020): 267–287.
34. Muirhead, *Promise of Party in a Polarized Age*, 147.
35. Levin, "What We Can Do to Make American Politics Less Dysfunctional."

BIBLIOGRAPHY

Ackerman, Bruce, and Oona Hathaway. "An Agreement Without Agreement." *Washington Post*, February 15, 2008. http://www.washingtonpost.com/wpdyn/content/article/2008/02/15/AR2008021502539.html.

Ackerman, Bruce A. *We the People*. Belknap Press of Harvard University Press, 1991.

Ackerman, Bruce A., and David Golove. *Is NAFTA Constitutional?* Harvard University Press, 1995.

Adler, David Gray. "Con: A Broad Executive Privilege Is Essential to the Successful Functioning of the Presidency." In *Debating the Presidency: Conflicting Perspectives on the American Executive*, edited by Richard J. Ellis and Michael Nelson. CQ Press, 2006.

Adler, Jonathan H. "Heat Expands All Things: The Proliferation of Greenhouse Gas Regulation Under the Obama Administration." *Harvard Journal of Law and Public Policy* 34, no. 2 (2011): 421–452.

Adler, Jonathan H. "Placing Reins on Regulations: Assessing the Proposed Reins Act." *New York University Journal of Legislation and Public Policy* 16 (2013): 1–37.

Agresto, John. *The Supreme Court and Constitutional Democracy*. Cornell University Press, 1984.

Alexander, Larry, and Frederick Schauer. "Defending Judicial Supremacy: A Reply." *Constitutional Commentary* 17 (2000): 455–482.

Alexander, Larry, and Frederick Schauer. "On Extrajudicial Constitutional Interpretation." *Harvard Law Review* 110, no. 7 (1997): 1359–1387.

Alexy, Robert. *A Theory of Constitutional Rights*. Translated by Julian Rivers. Oxford University Press, 2002.

Alvis, J. David, Jeremy D. Bailey, and F. Flagg Taylor IV. *The Contested Removal Power, 1789–2010*. University Press of Kansas, 2013.

"America's Consumer Watchdog." The White House, January 4, 2012. https://obamawhitehouse.archives.gov/blog/2012/01/04/americas-consumer-watchdog.

Bade, Rachael, and Karoun Demirjian. *Unchecked: The Untold Story Behind Congress's Botched Impeachments of Donald Trump*. William Morrow, 2022.

Bade, Rachael, Ryan Lizza, and Eugene Daniels. "Playbook: The Republicans Secretly Rooting for a Trump Loss." *Politico*, September 5, 2024. https://www.politico.com/newsletters/playbook/2024/09/04/the-republicans-secretly-rooting-for-a-trump-loss-00177272.

Baker, Peter. "G.O.P. Senators' Letter to Iran About Nuclear Deal Angers White House." *New York Times*, March 9, 2015. https://www.nytimes.com/2015/03/10/world/asia/white-house-faults-gop-senators-letter-to-irans-leaders.html.

Balkin, Jack M. *Constitutional Redemption: Political Faith in an Unjust World*. Harvard University Press, 2011.

Balkin, Jack M. *Living Originalism*. Harvard University Press, 2011.

Barber, Sotirios A. *On What the Constitution Means*. Johns Hopkins University Press, 1984.

"Barr Says No Evidence of Widespread Voter Fraud in Election." *Wall Street Journal*, updated December 1, 2020. https://www.wsj.com/articles/trump-campaign-files-more-election-challenges-in-wisconsin-michigan-11606849219.

Baude, William, and Michael Stokes Paulsen. "The Sweep and Force of Section 3." *University of Pennsylvania Law Review* 172 (2024): 605–745.

Baumann, Beau J. "Americana Administrative Law." *Georgetown Law Journal* 111 (2023): 465–527.

Beckmann, Matthew N. *Pushing the Agenda: Presidential Leadership in U.S. Lawmaking, 1953–2004*. Cambridge University Press, 2010.

Bell, Thomas R. "Perverse Politics: Recess Appointments, Noel Canning, and the Limits of Law." *Presidential Studies Quarterly* 48, no. 2 (2018): 373–386.

Belmont v. United States, 301 U.S. 324 (1937).

Berger, Raoul. *Executive Privilege: A Constitutional Myth*. Harvard University Press, 1974.

Berger, Raoul. *Impeachment: The Constitutional Problems*. Harvard University Press, 1973.

Berry, Michael J. *The Modern Legislative Veto: Macropolitical Conflict and the Legacy of Chadha*. University of Michigan Press, 2017.

Bessette, Joseph M. "Confronting War: Rethinking Jackson's Concurrence in Youngstown v. Sawyer." In Tulis and Macedo, *Limits of Constitutional Democracy*.

Bessette, Joseph M. *The Mild Voice of Reason: Deliberative Democracy and American National Government*. American Politics and Political Economy Series. University of Chicago Press, 1994.

Biden v. Nebraska, 600 U.S. 477 (2023).

Binder, Sarah A., and Steven S. Smith. *Politics or Principle: Filibustering in the United States Senate*. Brookings Institution Press, 1996.

Black, Charles L., Jr., and Akhil Reed Amar. *Impeachment: A Handbook*. Reissue edition. Yale University Press, 1998.

Black, Charles L., Jr., and Philip Bobbitt. *Impeachment: A Handbook*. Yale University Press, 2018.

Black, Ryan C., Anthony J. Madonna, Ryan J. Owens, and Michael S. Lynch. "Adding Recess Appointments to the President's 'Tool Chest' of Unilateral Powers." *Political Research Quarterly* 60, no. 4 (2007): 645–654.

Black, Ryan C., Anthony J. Madonna, Ryan J. Owens, and Michael S. Lynch. "Assessing Congressional Responses to Growing Presidential Powers: The Case of Recess Appointments." *Presidential Studies Quarterly* 41, no. 3 (2011): 570–589.

Blackhawk, Maggie. "Legislative Constitutionalism and Federal Indian Law." *Yale Law Journal* 132 (2023): 2205–2303.

Bolton, John R. *The Legislative Veto: Unseparating the Powers*. Studies in Legal Policy 148. American Enterprise Institute for Public Policy Research, 1977.

Bowie, Nikolas, and Daphna Renan. "The Separation of Powers Counterrevolution." *Yale Law Journal* 131, no. 7 (2022): 2020–2125.

Bowsher v. Synar 478 U.S. 714 (1986).

Bradley, Curtis A., and Jack L. Goldsmith. "Presidential Control over International Law." *Harvard Law Review* 131, no. 5 (2018): 1201–1297.

Bradley, Curtis A., Jack Goldsmith, and Oona Hathaway. "Congress Mandates Sweeping Transparency Reforms for International Agreements." *Lawfare* (blog), December 23, 2022, https://www.lawfareblog.com/congress-mandates-sweeping-transparency-reforms-international-agreements.

Bradley, Curtis A., Jack L. Goldsmith, and Oona Hathaway. "Executive Agreements: International Lawmaking Without Accountability?" *Lawfare* (blog), January 9, 2019, https://www.lawfareblog.com/executive-agreements-international-lawmaking-without-accountability.

Bradley, Curtis A., and Trevor W. Morrison. "Historical Gloss and the Separation of Powers." *Harvard Law Review* 126, no. 2 (2012): 411–845.

Brady, David W., Hahrie Han, and Jeremy C. Pope. "Primary Elections and Candidate Ideology: Out of Step with the Primary Electorate?" *Legislative Studies Quarterly* 32, no. 1 (2011): 79–105.

Brest, Paul. "The Conscientious Legislator's Guide to Constitutional Interpretation." *Stanford Law Review* 27, no. 3 (1975): 585–601.

Brettschneider, Corey. *The Oath and the Office: A Guide to the Constitution for Future Presidents*. W. W. Norton, 2018.

Brigham, John. *The Cult of the Court*. Temple University Press, 1991.

Brown, Rebecca L. "Separated Powers and Ordered Liberty." *University of Pennsylvania Law Review* 139 (1991): 1513–1566.

Bruff, Harold H., and Ernest Gellhorn. "Congressional Control of Administrative Regulation: A Study of Legislative Vetoes." *Harvard Law Review* 90, no. 7 (1977): 1369–1440.

Calabresi, Steven G., and Norman Eisen. "We Disagree on a Lot. But We Both Think Trump Should Be Convicted." *New York Times*, January 13, 2021. https://www.nytimes.com/2021/01/13/opinion/trump-impeachment-bipartisan.html.

Calabresi, Steven G., and Saikrishna B. Prakash. "The President's Power to Execute the Laws." *Yale Law Journal* 104, no. 3 (1994): 541–665.

Calabresi, Steven G., and Kevin H. Rhodes. "The Structural Constitution: Unitary Executive, Plural Judiciary." *Harvard Law Review* 105, no. 6 (1992): 1153–1216.

Calabresi, Steven G., and Christopher S. Yoo. *The Unitary Executive: Presidential Power from Washington to Bush*. Yale University Press, 2008.

Carrier, Michael A. "When Is the Senate in Recess for Purposes of the Recess Appointments Clause?" *Michigan Law Review* 92, no. 7 (1994): 2204–2247.

Ceaser, James W. *Liberal Democracy and Political Science*. Johns Hopkins University Press, 1992.

Ceaser, James W. *Presidential Selection*. Princeton University Press, 1979.

Chafetz, Josh. *Congress's Constitution: Legislative Authority and the Separation of Powers*. Yale University Press, 2017.

Chafetz, Josh. "Impeachment and Assassination." *Minnesota Law Review* 95 (2010): 347–423.

Chafetz, Josh. "Nixon/Trump: Strategies of Judicial Aggrandizement." *Georgetown Law Journal* 110, no. 1 (2021): 125–150.

Chafetz, Josh. "The Unconstitutionality of the Filibuster." *Connecticut Law Review* 43, no. 4 (2011): 1005–1040.

Chafetz, Josh, and Michael J. Gerhardt. "Debate, Is the Filibuster Constitutional?" *University of Pennsylvania Law Review PENNumbra* 158 (2010): 245–267.

Chemerinsky, Erwin. "In Defense of Judicial Supremacy." *William & Mary Law Review* 58, no. 5 (2017): 1459–1494.

Cheney v. United States District Court 542 U.S.367 (2004)

Choper, Jesse H. *Judicial Review and the National Political Process: A Functional Reconsideration of the Role of the Supreme Court*. University of Chicago Press, 1980.

Chubb, John E. *Interest Groups and the Bureaucracy: The Politics of Energy*. Stanford University Press, 1983.

City of Alexandria v. United States, 737 F2d 1022, 1025 (Fed. Cir. 1984).

City of Alexandria v. United States 3 CL.Ct 667, 683 (1983).

Cohen, Marshall, and Katelyn Polantz. "In Contrast with Trump Legal Team, Justice Department Lawyer Says House Can Impeach over Defied Subpoenas." CNN, January 30, 2020. https://www.cnn.com/2020/01/30/politics/trump-impeachment-subpoena-hearing/index.html.

"Congressional Control of Foreign Assistance to Post-Coup States: Assessing Executive Compliance from Honduras to Egypt." *Harvard Law Review* 127, no. 8 (2014): 2499–2520.

Cooper, Joseph. "The Legislative Veto in the 1980s." In *Congress Reconsidered*, ed. Lawrence C. Dodd and Bruce I. Oppenheimer, 3rd ed. CQ Press, 1985.

Corley, Pamela C. "Avoiding Advice and Consent: Recess Appointments and Presidential Power." *Presidential Studies Quarterly* 36, no. 4 (2006): 670–680.

Corwin, Edward S. *The Constitution and World Organization*. American Civilization Program Series. Princeton University Press, 1944.

Corwin, Edward S. *The President, Office and Powers*. New York University Press, 1940.

Craig, Barbara Hinkson. Chadha: *The Story of an Epic Constitutional Struggle*. University of California Press, 1990.

Craig, Barbara Hinkson. *The Legislative Veto: Congressional Control of Regulation*. Westview Press, 1984.

Crews, Clyde Wayne, Jr. "Ten Thousand Commandments: An Annual Snapshot of the Federal Regulatory State." Competitive Enterprise Institute, 2017. https://cei.org/sites/default/files/Ten%20Thousand%20Commandments%202017.pdf.

Crockett, David A. "The Contemporary President: Should the Senate Take a Floor Vote on a Presidential Judicial Nominee?" *Presidential Studies Quarterly* 37, no. 2 (2007): 313–330.

Crockett, David A. "Executive Privilege." In Tulis and Bessette, *Constitutional Presidency*.

Croley, Steven, "White House Review of Agency Rulemaking: An Empirical Investigation." *University of Chicago Law Review* 70 (2003): 821–886.

Crovitz, L. Gordon, and Jeremy A. Rabkin, eds. *The Fettered Presidency: Legal Constraints on the Executive Branch*. AEI Studies 485. American Enterprise Institute, 1989.

Currie, David P. *The Constitution in Congress: The Federalist Period, 1789–1801*. University of Chicago Press, 1999.

Dahl, Robert A. "Decision-Making in a Democracy: The Supreme Court as a National Policy-Maker." *Journal of Public Law* 6, no. 2 (1957): 279–295.

Dames & Moore v. Regan, 453 U.S. 654 (1981).

DeBonis, Mike, and Paul Kane. "Republicans Vow No Hearings and No Votes for Obama's Supreme Court Pick." *Washington Post*, February 23, 2016. https://www.washingtonpost.com/news/powerpost/wp/2016/02/23/key-senate-republicans-say-no-hearings-for-supreme-court-nominee/.

Deeks, Ashley S. "A (Qualified) Defense of Secret Agreements." *Arizona State Law Journal* 49 (2017): 713–794.

DeSilver, Drew. "The Polarization in Today's Congress Has Roots That Go Back Decades." *Pew Research Center* (blog), March 10, 2022. https://www.pewresearch.org/short-reads/2022/03/10/the-polarization-in-todays-congress-has-roots-that-go-back-decades/.

Devins, Neal, and Lawrence Baum. "Split Definitive: How Party Polarization Turned the Supreme Court into a Partisan Court." *e Supreme Court Review* 2016 (2016): 301–366.

Devins, Neal, and Louis Fisher. *The Democratic Constitution*. Oxford University Press, 2015.

Devins, Neal, and Keith E. Whittington, eds. *Congress and the Constitution*. Constitutional Conflicts. Duke University Press, 2005.

Downen, Robert, and William Melhado. "Trump Vows Retribution at Waco Rally: 'I Am Your Warrior, I Am Your Justice.'" *Texas Tribune*, March 26, 2023. https://www.texastribune.org/2023/03/25/donald-trump-waco-rally-retribution-justice/.

Drummond, Steve. *The Watchdog: How the Truman Committee Battled Corruption and Helped Win World War Two*. Hanover Square Press, 2023.

Dry, Murray. "The Congressional Veto and the Constitutional Separation of Powers." In Tulis and Bessette, *Presidency in the Constitutional Order*.

Dueholm, James A. "Lincoln's Suspension of the Writ of Habeas Corpus: An Historical and Constitutional Analysis." *Journal of the Abraham Lincoln Association* 29, no. 2 (2008): 47–66.

Dworkin, Ronald. *Taking Rights Seriously*. 5th ed. Harvard University Press, 1978.

Edling, Max M. *A Revolution in Favor of Government: Origins of the U.S. Constitution and the Making of the American State*. Oxford University Press, 2008.

Elster, Jon. *Ulysses Unbound: Studies in Rationality, Precommitment, and Constraints*. Cambridge University Press, 2000.

Epstein, Lee. "Partisanship 'All the Way Down' on the U.S. Supreme Court." *Pepperdine Law Review* 51, no. 3 (2024): 489–514.

Ex Parte Merryman, 17 F. Cas. 144 (1861).

"Executive Agreements." In *CQ Almanac* 1972, 28th ed., 05–619–05–621. Washington, DC, *Congressional Quarterly*, 1973. http://library.cqpress.com/cqalmanac/cqal72-1251460.

Farrand, Max, ed. *The Records of the Federal Convention of 1787*. Yale University Press, 1923.

Farrier, Jasmine. *Congressional Ambivalence: The Political Burdens of Constitutional Authority*. University Press of Kentucky, 2010.

Farrier, Jasmine. *Constitutional Dysfunction on Trial: Congressional Lawsuits and the Separation of Powers*. Cornell University Press, 2019.

Finn, John E. *Peopling the Constitution*. Constitutional Thinking. University Press of Kansas, 2014.

Fiorina, Morris P. *Unstable Majorities: Polarization, Party Sorting, and Political Stalemate*. Hoover Institution Press, 2017.

Fiorina, Morris P., Samuel J. Abrams, and Jeremy C. Pope. *Culture War? The Myth of a Polarized America*. 3rd ed. Longman, 2010.

Fisher, Louis. *Congressional Abdication on War and Spending*. Texas A&M University Press, 2000.
Fisher, Louis. *Constitutional Dialogues: Interpretation as Political Process*. Princeton University Press, 2016.
Fisher, Louis. "The Efficiency Side of Separated Powers." *Journal of American Studies* 5, no. 2 (1971): 113–131.
Fisher, Louis. "The Legislative Veto: Invalidated, It Survives." *Law and Contemporary Problems* 56, no. 4 (1993): 273–292.
Fisher, Louis. *The Politics of Executive Privilege*. Carolina Academic Press, 2003.
Fisk, Catherine, and Erwin Chemerinsky. "The Filibuster." *Stanford Law Review* 49, no. 2 (1997): 181–254.
Flaherty, Martin S. "The Most Dangerous Branch." *Yale Law Journal* 105, no. 7 (1996): 1725–1839.
Flynn, Joan. "A Quiet Revolution at the Labor Board: The Transformation of the NLRB 1935–2000." *Ohio State Law Journal* 61 (2000): 1361–1455.
Flynn, Sean. "ACTA's Constitutional Problem: The Treaty Is Not a Treaty." *American University International Law Review* 26, no. 3 (2011): 903–926.
Galbraith, Jean. "International Law and the Domestic Separation of Powers." *Virginia Law Review* 99, no. 5 (2013): 987–1048.
Garcia, Rogelio, and Clark Norton, "Congressional Veto Legislation in the 98th Congress." Congressional Research Service, 1984.
Gass, Nick, and Adam B. Lerner. "GOP Candidates Vow to Roll Back Iran Deal." *Politico*, July 14, 2015. https://www.politico.com/story/2015/07/gop-candidates-vow-to-roll-back-iran-deal-120081.html.
Gates, Dominic. "Boeing's $9.5 Billion Iran Deals, Always Uncertain, Are Now Effectively Dead." *Seattle Times*, May 8, 2018. https://www.seattletimes.com/business/boeing-aerospace/boeings-8-billion-iran-deal-always-uncertain-is-now-effectively-dead/.
Gehl, Katherine M., Michael E. Porter, Mike Gallagher, and Chrissy Houlahan. *The Politics Industry: How Political Innovation Can Break Partisan Gridlock and Save Our Democracy*. Harvard Business Review Press, 2020.
Gerhardt, Michael J. "The Constitutionality of the Filibuster." *Constitutional Commentary* 21, no. 1 (2004): 445–451.
Gerhardt, Michael J. *The Federal Impeachment Process*. 3rd ed. University of Chicago Press, 2019.
Gibson, Martha Liebler. "Managing Conflict: The Role of the Legislative Veto in American Foreign Policy." *Polity* 26, no. 3 (1994): 441–472.
Gienapp, Jonathan. "Making Constitutional Meaning: The Removal Debate and the Birth of Constitutional Essentialism." *Journal of the Early Republic* 35, no. 2 (2015): 375–418.
Gienapp, Jonathan. "Removal and the Changing Debate over Executive Power at the Founding." *American Journal of Legal History* 63, no. 3 (2023): 229–250.
Gienapp, Jonathan. *The Second Creation: Fixing the American Constitution in the Founding Era*. Belknap Press, 2018.
Goldsmith, Jack. "The Contributions of the Obama Administration to the Practice and Theory of International Law." *Harvard International Law Journal* 57, no. 2 (2016): 455–473.

Goldsmith, Jack L., Curtis A. Bradley, and Oona A. Hathaway. "The Failed Transparency Regime for Executive Agreements: An Empirical and Normative Analysis." *Harvard Law Review* 134, no. 2 (2020): 629–725.

Goldsmith, Jack, and Lawrence Lessig. "Anti-Counterfeiting Agreement Raises Constitutional Concerns." *Washington Post*, March 26, 2010. http://www.washingtonpost.com/wp-dyn/content/article/2010/03/25/AR2010032502403.html.

Goldstein, Leslie Friedman. *In Defense of the Text: Democracy and Constitutional Theory*. Rowman & Littlefield, 1991.

Golove, David. "Congress Just Gave the President Power to Adopt a Binding Legal Agreement with Iran." *Just Security*, May 14, 2015. https://www.justsecurity.org/23018/congress-gave-president-power-adopt-binding-legal-agreement-iran/.

Goodman, Ryan, and Josh Asabor. "In Their Own Words: The 43 Republicans' Explanations of Their Votes Not to Convict Trump in Impeachment Trial." *Just Security*, February 15, 2021. https://www.justsecurity.org/74725/in-their-own-words-the-43-republicans-explanations-of-their-votes-not-to-convict-trump-in-impeachment-trial/.

Gorod, Brianne J., Brian R. Frazelle, and Ashwin P. Phatak. "The Historical and Legal Basis for the Exercise of Congressional Oversight Authority." Washington, DC, Constitutional Accountability Center, January 2019. https://www.theusconstitution.org/wp-content/uploads/2019/01/Congressional-Oversight-Issue-Brief.pdf.

Greene, Abner S. "Checks and Balances in an Era of Presidential Lawmaking." *University of Chicago Law Review* 61, no. 1 (1994): 123–196.

Griffin, Stephen M. *American Constitutionalism: From Theory to Politics*. Princeton University Press, 1996.

Griffin, Stephen M. *Broken Trust: Dysfunctional Government and Constitutional Reform*. University Press of Kansas, 2015.

Grose, Christian R. "Reducing Legislative Polarization: Top-Two and Open Primaries Are Associated with More Moderate Legislators." *Journal of Political Institutions and Political Economy* 1, no. 2 (2020): 267–287.

Gundy v. United States 139 S. Ct. 2116 (2019).

Haberman, Maggie, and Michael S. Schmidt. "Trump Tied Ukraine Aid to Inquiries He Sought, Bolton Book Says." *New York Times*, January 26, 2020. https://www.nytimes.com/2020/01/26/us/politics/trump-bolton-book-ukraine.html.

Hamburger, Philip. *Is Administrative Law Unlawful?* Repr., University of Chicago Press, 2015.

Hamilton, Alexander, James Madison, John Jay, and Charles R. Kessler. *The Federalist Papers*. Edited by Clinton Rossiter. Signet, 2003.

Harrington, Ryan. "Understanding the 'Other' International Agreements." *Law Library Journal* 108, no. 3 (2016): 343–359.

Harris, William F. *The Interpretable Constitution*. Johns Hopkins Series in Constitutional Thought. Johns Hopkins University Press, 1993.

Hathaway, Oona A. "Presidential Power over International Law: Restoring the Balance." *Yale Law Journal* 119, no. 2 (2009): 140–268.

Hathaway, Oona A. "Treaties' End: The Past, Present, and Future of International Lawmaking in the United States." *Yale Law Journal* 117, no. 7 (2008): 1236–1372.

Hathaway, Oona, A., Curtis A. Bradley, and Jack L. Goldsmith. "Presidential Control Over International Law." *Harvard Law Review* 131, no. 5 (March 2018): 1203–1297.

Hathaway, Oona A., and Amy Kapczynski. "Going It Alone: The Anti-Counterfeiting Trade Agreement as a Sole Executive Agreement." *American Society of International Law: Insights* 15, no. 23 (2011).

Hayden, Joseph Ralston. *The Senate and Treaties, 1789–1817: The Development of the Treaty-Making Functions of the United States Senate during Their Formative Period.* University of Michigan Press, 1969. Originally published in 1920 by Macmillan.

Healy, Gene. *Indispensable Remedy: The Broad Scope of the Constitution's Impeachment Power.* Cato Institute, 2018.

Henkin, Louis. *Foreign Affairs and the United States Constitution.* 2nd ed. Oxford University Press, 1996.

Hogue, Henry B. "Recess Appointments: Frequently Asked Questions." Congressional Research Service, 2013.

Hogue, Henry B. "Recess Appointments Made by Barack Obama." Congressional Research Service, 2017.

Hogue, Henry B., Maeve P. Carey, Michael W. Greene, and Maureen Bearden. "The Noel Canning Decision and Recess Appointments Made from 1981–2013." Congressional Research Service, 2013.

Hollis, Duncan B., and Joshua J. Newcomer. "'Political' Commitments and the Constitution." *Virginia Journal of International Law* 49, no. 3 (2009): 507–584.

Howell, William G., and Terry M. Moe. *Relic: How Our Constitution Undermines Effective Government—And Why We Need a More Powerful Presidency.* Basic Books, 2016.

Huq, Aziz Z. "Removal as a Political Question." *Stanford Law Review* 64, no. 1 (2013): 1–76.

Huq, Aziz Z. "Separation of Powers Metatheory." *Columbia Law Review* 118 (2018): 1517–1582.

Huq, Aziz Z., and Jon Michaels. "The Cycles of Separation-of-Powers Jurisprudence." *Yale Law Journal* 126, no. 2 (2016): 346–437.

"In Refusal to Answer Questions, Sessions Denies Claiming Executive Privilege." *All Things Considered*, National Public Radio, June 13, 2017. https://www.npr.org/2017/06/13/532816894/in-refusal-to-answer-questions-sessions-denies-claiming-executive-privilege.

INS v. Chadha, 462 US 919 (1983).

"International Trade: Improvements Needed to Track and Archive Trade Agreements." United States General Accounting Office, December 1999.

Jacobsohn, Gary Jeffrey. *Constitutional Identity.* Harvard University Press, 2010.

Jacobsohn, Gary Jeffrey. "The Disharmonic Constitution." In Tulis and Macedo, *Limits of Constitutional Democracy.*

Jacobsohn, Gary Jeffrey. *The Supreme Court and the Decline of Constitutional Aspiration.* Rowman & Littlefield, 1986.

Javits, Jacob K., and Gary J. Klein. "Congressional Oversight and the Legislative Veto: A Constitutional Analysis." *New York University Law Review* 52 (1977): 455–497.

Johnson, Loch K. *The Making of International Agreements: Congress Confronts the Executive*. New York University Press, 1984.

Kagan, Elena. "Presidential Administration." *Harvard Law Review* 114, no. 8 (2001): 2245–2385.

Kalt, Brian C. "The Constitutional Case for the Impeachability of Former Federal Officials: An Analysis of the Law, History, and Practice of Late Impeachment." *Texas Review of Law & Politics* 6, no. 2 (2001): 13–135.

Kamen, Al. "Bork Fails to Catch Public's Eye: Opinion Is Split Among the Informed." *Washington Post*, August 7, 1987.

Kappel, Brett G. "Judicial Restrictions on Improper Congressional Influence in Administrative Decision-Making: A Defense of the Pillsbury Doctrine Note." *Journal of Law & Politics* 6 (1989): 135–171.

Kapur, Sahil. "Most Senate Republicans Declare Trump's Trial Unconstitutional. Here's What That Means for Conviction." *NBC News*, January 26, 2021. https://www.nbcnews.com/politics/congress/most-republicans-declare-trump-s-trial-unconstitutional-here-s-what-n1255704.

Karmarck, Elaine and Alexander R. Podkul. "The 2018 Primaries Project: The Ideology of Primary Voters." Brookings Institution, October 23, 2018. https://www.brookings.edu/articles/the-2018-primaries-project-the-ideology-of-primary-voters/.

Kim, Seung Min. "Republicans Join Challenge of Recess Appointments." *Politico*, February 3, 2012. https://www.politico.com/news/stories/0212/72422.html.

Kitrosser, Heidi. "Like 'Nobody Has Ever Seen Before': Precedent and Privilege in the Trump Era." *Chicago-Kent Law Review* 95, no. 2 (2021): 519–536.

Kitrosser, Heidi. "The Shadow of Executive Privilege." *Minnesota Law Review* 15, no. 3 (2017): 547–566.

Klarman, Michael J. *The Framers' Coup: The Making of the United States Constitution*. Illustrated ed. Oxford University Press, 2016.

Koh, Harold. "Address: Twenty-First-Century International Lawmaking." *Georgetown Law Journal* 101, no. 3 (2013): 725–748.

Koh, Harold. "The President Versus the Senate in Treaty Interpretation: What's All the Fuss About?" *Yale Journal of International Law* 15, no. 2 (1990): 331–344.

Koh, Harold Hongju. "Triptych's End: A Better Framework to Evaluate 21st Century International Lawmaking." *Yale Law Journal* 126 (2018): 338–368.

Korn, Jessica. *The Power of Separation: American Constitutionalism and the Myth of the Legislative Veto*. Princeton Studies in American Politics. Princeton University Press, 1996.

Kosar, Kevin R. "Conservatives Should Look More Closely at Systemic Election Reforms." American Enterprise Institute, October 3, 2023. https://www.aei.org/research-products/report/conservatives-should-look-more-closely-at-systemic-election-reforms/.

Krehbiel, Keith. *Pivotal Politics: A Theory of U.S. Lawmaking*. University of Chicago Press, 1998.

Krutz, Glen S., and Jeffrey S. Peake. *Treaty Politics and the Rise of Executive Agreements: International Commitments in a System of Shared Powers*. University of Michigan Press, 2009.

Kuchar, Savannah. "Democrats Spent Millions Boosting Ultra Right Candidates in Midterms. The Strategy Worked." *USA Today*, November 15, 2022. https://www.usatoday.com/story/news/politics/2022/11/15/democrats-boosted-trump-gop-primaries-helping-midterms/10670042002.

Kyvig, David E. *The Age of Impeachment: American Constitutional Culture Since 1960*. University Press of Kansas, 2008.

Landis, James M. *The Administrative Process*. Storrs Lectures on Jurisprudence 1938. Yale University Press, 1966.

Landis, James M. "Constitutional Limitations on the Congressional Power of Investigation." *Harvard Law Review* 40, no. 2 (1926): 153–221.

Landler, Mark. "Trump Abandons Iran Nuclear Deal He Long Scorned." *New York Times*, May 8, 2018. https://www.nytimes.com/2018/05/08/world/middleeast/trump-iran-nuclear-deal.html.

Larkin, Paul J., Jr. "Reawakening the Congressional Review Act." *Harvard Journal of Law and Public Policy* 41, no. 1 (2018): 187–252.

Lawson, Gary. "Delegation and Original Meaning." *Virginia Law Review* 88, no. 2 (2002): 327–404.

Levin, Ronald M. "The REINS Act: Unbridled Impediment to Regulation Fiftieth Anniversary of the Administrative Conference of the United States." *George Washington Law Review* 83 (2015): 1446–1486.

Levin, Yuval. "Building a More Civil and Collaborative Culture in Congress: Some Diagnostic and Prescriptive Reflections." Statement before the House Select Committee on the Modernization of Congress, June 17, 2021.

Levin, Yuval. "This Is Why Americans Are So Cynical About Politics." *New York Times*, January 21, 2024. https://www.nytimes.com/2024/01/21/opinion/america-politics-cynical-dysfunctional.html.

Levin, Yuval. *A Time to Build: From Family and Community to Congress and the Campus, How Recommitting to Our Institutions Can Revive the American Dream*. Basic Books, 2020.

Levin, Yuval. "What We Can Do to Make American Politics Less Dysfunctional." *New York Times*, October 9, 2023. https://www.nytimes.com/2023/10/09/opinion/american-politics-congress-reform.html.

Levinson, Daryl J., and Richard H. Pildes. "Separation of Parties, Not Powers." *Harvard Law Review* 119, no. 8 (2006): 2311–2386.

Lincoln, Abraham. "Inaugural Address." March 4, 1861. Available at https://teachingamericanhistory.org/document/first-inaugural-address/.

Lincoln, Abraham. "Message to Congress in Special Session." July 4, 1861. Available at https://teachingamericanhistory.org/library/document/message-to-congress-in-special-session/.

Linker, Damon. "The Case Against Prosecuting Donald Trump." *Persuasion*, September 2, 2022. https://www.persuasion.community/p/the-case-against-prosecuting-donald.

Linskey, Annie. "Democrats Spend Tens of Millions Amplifying Far-Right Candidates in Nine States." *Washington Post*, September 12, 2022. https://www.washingtonpost.com/politics/2022/09/12/democrats-interfere-republican-primaries/.

Liptak, Adam. "Key Excerpts from Legal Scholars' Arguments on Impeachment." *New York Times*, December 4, 2019. https://www.nytimes.com/2019/12/04/us/politics/karlan-feldman-turley-gerhardt.html.

Liptak, Adam. "Supreme Court Rebukes Obama on Right of Appointment." *New York Times*, June 26, 2014. https://www.nytimes.com/2014/06/27/us/supreme-court-president-recess-appointments.html.

"A List of the Times Trump Has Said He Won't Accept the Election Results or Leave Office If He Loses." CNN, September 24, 20202. https://www.cnn.com/2020/09/24/politics/trump-election-warnings-leaving-office/index.html.

Locke, John. *Second Treatise of Government*. Edited by C. B. Macpherson. Hackett, 1980.

Locke, John. *Second Treatise of Government*. Early Modern Texts. Available at https://www.earlymoderntexts.com/assets/pdfs/locke1689a.pdf.

Loper Bright Enterprises v. Raimondo, 603 U.S. ___ (2024),

Lowi, Theodore J. *The End of Liberalism: The Second Republic of the United States*. 2nd ed. Norton, 1979.

Luttig, J. Michael. "A Senate Impeachment Trial After Trump Leaves Office Would Be Unconstitutional." *Washington Post*, January 12, 2021. https://www.washingtonpost.com/opinions/2021/01/12/once-trump-leaves-office-senate-cant-hold-an-impeachment-trial/.

Mann, Thomas E., and Norman J. Ornstein. *It's Even Worse Than It Looks: How the American Constitutional System Collided with the New Politics of Extremism*. Rev. and expanded ed. Basic Books, 2016.

Manning, John F. "Separation of Powers as Ordinary Interpretation." *Harvard Law Review* 124, no. 8 (2011): 1939–2040.

Marks, Frederick W. *Independence on Trial: Foreign Affairs and the Making of the Constitution*. Louisiana State University Press, 1973.

Martin, Lisa L. *Democratic Commitments: Legislatures and International Cooperation*. Princeton University Press, 2000.

Martin, Lisa L. "The President and International Commitments: Treaties as Signaling Devices." *Presidential Studies Quarterly* 35, no. 3 (2005): 440–465.

Mashaw, Jerry L. *Creating the Administrative Constitution: The Lost One Hundred Years of American Administrative Law*. Yale University Press, 2012.

Mason, R. Chuck. "U.S.-Iraq Withdrawal/Status of Forces Agreement: Issues for Congressional Oversight." Congressional Research Service, July 13, 2009.

Massachusetts v. EPA 449 U.S. 497 (2007).

Mayhew, David R. *Congress: The Electoral Connection*. 2nd ed. Yale University Press, 2004.

McConnell, Michael W. *The President Who Would Not Be King*. Princeton University Press, 2020.

McConnell, Michael, and Ken Gormley. "Yes, the Senate Has the Power to Try Trump. He Was Impeached in Office." *Washington Post*, February 4, 2021. https://www.washingtonpost.com/opinions/2021/02/04/yes-senate-has-power-try-trump-he-was-impeached-office/.

McCubbins, Mathew D., and Thomas Schwartz. "Congressional Oversight Overlooked: Police Patrols versus Fire Alarms." *American Journal of Political Science* 28, no. 1 (1984): 165–179.

McCulloch v. Maryland, 17 U.S. 316 (1819).

McDougal, Myres S., and Asher Lans. "Treaties and Congressional-Executive or Presidential Agreements: Interchangeable Instruments of National Policy: II." *Yale Law Journal* 54, no. 3 (1945): 534–615.

McGrain v. Daugherty, 273 U.S. 135 (1927)

Medina, Jennifer. "G.O.P. Contenders Feed Voter Distrust in Courts, Schools and Military." *New York Times*, August 7, 2023. https://www.nytimes.com/2023/08/07/us/politics/trump-republican-primary-candidate-trust.html.

Mill, John Stuart. *Considerations on Representative Government*. Parker, Son, and Bourn, 1861.

Montesquieu, *The Spirit of the Laws*. Translated by Thomas Nugent. Hafner, 1949.

Moore, David H. "Taking Cues from Congress: Judicial Review, Congressional Authorization, and the Expansion of Presidential Power." *Notre Dame Law Review* 90, no. 3 (2015): 1019–1053.

Morrison v. Olson, 487 U.S. 654 (1988).

Mortenson, Julian Davis, and Nicholas Bagley. "Delegation at the Founding." *Columbia Law Review* 121, no. 2 (2021): 277–368.

Muirhead, Russell. "The Politics of Getting It Right." *Critical Review* 26, no. 1–2 (2014): 115–128.

Muirhead, Russell. *The Promise of Party in a Polarized Age*. Harvard University Press, 2014.

Muñoz, Vincent Phillip. "Constitutional Principles: Separation of Powers." YouTube video, August 24, 2012, The Bill of Rights Institute and Jack Miller Center. https://www.youtube.com/watch?v=Nnqk-yGzYYg.

Myers v. United States, 272 US 52, 293 (1926).

National Federation of Business v. Occupational Safety and Health Administration 595 U. S. ____ (2022).

National Labor Relations Board v. Noel Canning, 573 U.S. 513 (2014).

Naylor, Brian. "Read Trump's Jan. 6 Speech, A Key Part Of Impeachment Trial." National Public Radio, February 10, 2021. https://www.npr.org/2021/02/10/966396848/read-trumps-jan-6-speech-a-key-part-of-impeachment-trial.

Nichols, David K. *The Myth of the Modern Presidency*. Pennsylvania State University Press, 1994.

"Nondelegation's Unprincipled Foreign Affairs Exceptionalism." *Harvard Law Review* 134 (2021): 1132–1161.

Nyarko, Julian. "Giving the Treaty a Purpose: Comparing the Durability of Treaties and Executive Agreements." *American Journal of International Law* 113, no. 1 (2019): 54–89.

Nzelibe, Jide. "The Uniqueness of Foreign Affairs." *Iowa Law Review* 89, no. 3 (2004): 941–1010.

Ornstein, Norm. "Yes, Polarization Is Asymmetric—and Conservatives Are Worse." *Atlantic* (blog), June 19, 2014. https://www.theatlantic.com/politics/archive/2014/06/yes-polarization-is-asymmetric-and-conservatives-are-worse/373044/.

Ostrander, Ian. "Powering Down the Presidency: The Rise and Fall of Recess Appointments." *Presidential Studies Quarterly* 45, no. 3 (2015): 558–572.

O'Halloran, Sharyn. *Politics, Process, and American Trade Policy*. University of Michigan Press, 1994.

Papke, David Ray. *Heretics in the Temple: Americans Who Reject the Nation's Legal Faith*. NYU Press, 1998.

Paulsen, Michael Stokes. "The Original Meaning of 'High Crimes and

Misdemeanors,' Part II." *Law & Liberty* (blog), August 9, 2018. https://lawliberty.org/the-original-meaning-of-high-crimes-and-misdemeanors-part-2/.

Paulsen, Michael Stokes. "Taking Impeachment Seriously." *Law & Liberty* (blog), June 28, 2018. https://lawliberty.org/taking-impeachment-seriously/.

Pengelly, Martin. "Bernstein Names 21 Republican Senators Who Privately Expressed Contempt for Trump." *Guardian*, November 23, 2020. https://www.theguardian.com/us-news/2020/nov/23/carl-bernstein-21-republican-senators-expressed-contempt-for-trump.

Phillips, Amber. "How Obama Could Appoint Merrick Garland to the Supreme Court, and Why It'll Never Happen." *Washington Post*, March 21, 2016. https://www.washingtonpost.com/news/the-fix/wp/2016/03/21/how-obama-could-appoint-merrick-garland-to-the-supreme-court-and-why-itll-never-happen/.

Phillips, Amber. "How Trump Could Replace Jeff Sessions in a Recess Appointment." *Washington Post*, July 27, 2017. https://www.washingtonpost.com/news/the-fix/wp/2017/07/27/how-trump-could-replace-jeff-sessions-in-a-recess-appointment-and-how-republicans-can-prevent-that/.

Pickerill, J. Mitchell. *Constitutional Deliberation in Congress: The Impact of Judicial Review in a Separated System*. Constitutional Conflicts. Duke University Press, 2004.

Pielke, Roger A. *The Honest Broker: Making Sense of Science in Policy and Politics*. Cambridge University Press, 2007.

Pink v. United States, 315 U.S. 203 (1942).

Polenberg, Richard. *Reorganizing Roosevelt's Government: The Controversy over Executive Reorganization, 1936–1939*. Harvard University Press, 1966.

Posner, Eric A., and Adrian Vermeule. *The Executive Unbound: After the Madisonian Republic*. Oxford University Press, 2010.

Posner, Eric A., and Adrian Vermeule. "Interring the Nondelegation Doctrine." *University of Chicago Law Review* 69 (2002): 1721–1762.

Post, Robert C., and Reva B. Siegel. "Protecting the Constitution from the People: Juricentric Restrictions on Section Five Power." *Indiana Law Journal* 78, no. 1 (2003): 1–45.

Potts, C. S. "Power of Legislative Bodies to Punish for Contempt." *University of Pennsylvania Law Review* 74 (1926): 691–725.

Pozen, David E. "Self-Help and the Separation of Powers." *Yale Law Journal* 124, no. 1 (2014): 2–90.

Prakash, Saikrishna. "The Essential Meaning of Executive Power." *University of Illinois Law Review* 3 (2003): 701–820.

Prakash, Saikrishna. "The Sweeping Domestic War Powers of Congress." *Michigan Law Review* 113, no. 8 (2015): 1337–1396.

Prakash, Saikrishna B., and Michael D. Ramsey. "The Executive Power over Foreign Affairs." *Yale Law Journal* 111 (2001): 231–356.

Quinn v. United States, 349 U.S. 155 (1955).

Raju, Manu, and Burgess Everett. "How Cardin and Corker Clinched the Iran Deal: An Indicted Senator and Democratic Disagreements Made for a Tough Assignment." *Politico*, April 14, 2015. http://www.politico.com/story/2015/04/ben-cardin-bob-corker-iran-deal-116979.

Randolph, Edmund. "Opinion on Recess Appointments." July 7, 1792. Founders Online. http://founders.archives.gov/documents/Jefferson/01-24-02-0176.

Rappoport, Michael B. "The Original Meaning of the Recess Appointments Clause." *UCLA Law Review* 52 (2005): 1487–1578.

Redish, Martin H. *The Constitution as Political Structure*. Oxford University Press, 1995.

Redish, Martin H. "Pragmatic Formalism, Separation of Powers, and the Need to Revisit the Nondelegation Doctrine." *Loyola University Chicago Law Journal* 51, no. 2 (2019): 363–418.

Renan, Daphna. "'Institutional Settlement' in a Provisional Constitutional Order." *California Law Review* 108 (2020): 1905–2005.

Renan, Daphna. "Presidential Norms and Article II." *Harvard Law Review* 131 (2018): 2187–2282.

Rennack, Dianne E. "Iran: U.S. Economic Sanctions and the Authority to Lift Restrictions." Congressional Research Service, 2016.

Rennack, Dianne E., and Susan G. Chesser. "Foreign Assistance Act of 1961: Authorizations and Corresponding Appropriations." Congressional Research Service, 2011.

"Report on Status of Forces Agreements." International Security Advisory Board, January 16, 2015, 39. https://www.state.gov/documents/organization/236456.pdf.

Restatement (Third) Foreign Affairs Law of the United States § 303 (1987).

Rosenberg, Gerald N. *The Hollow Hope: Can Courts Bring About Social Change?* 2nd ed. University of Chicago Press, 2008.

Rosenberg, Morton. "Congressional Review of Agency Rulemaking: An Update and Assessment of the Congressional Review Act after a Decade." Report, Congressional Research Service, May 8, 2008.

Rosenberg, Morton. "Whatever Happened to Congressional Review of Agency Rulemaking: A Brief Overview, Assessment, and Proposal for Reform." *Administrative Law Review* 51, no. 4 (1999): 1051–1092.

Rosenberg, Morton, and Jack H. Maskell. "Congressional Intervention in the Administrative Process: Legal and Ethical Considerations." Congressional Research Service, 1990.

Rosenbloom, David H. *Building a Legislative-Centered Public Administration: Congress and the Administrative State, 1946–1999*. University of Alabama Press, 2000.

Rozell, Mark J., and Mitchel A. Sollenberger. *Executive Privilege: Presidential Power, Secrecy, and Accountability*. Updated ed. University Press of Kansas, 2020.

Sanger, David E. "Nuclear Arms Treaty: The Accord; Bush and Putin to Sign Pact to Cut Nuclear Warheads; Weapons Can Be Stockpiled." *New York Times*, May 14, 2002. https://www.nytimes.com/2002/05/14/world/nuclear-arms-treaty-accord-bush-putin-sign-pact-cut-nuclear-warheads-weapons-can.html.

Sanger, David E. "Obama Sees an Iran Deal That Could Avoid Congress." *New York Times*, October 19, 2014. https://www.nytimes.com/2014/10/20/us/politics/obama-sees-an-iran-deal-that-could-avoid-congress-.html.

Sartori, Giovanni. *Comparative Constitutional Engineering: An Inquiry into Structures, Incentives and Outcomes*. Macmillan, 1994.

Scalia, Antonin. "The Legislative Veto: A False Remedy for System Overload." *Regulation: AEI Journal on Government and Society* (1979).

Schechter Poultry Corp. v. United States, 295 US 495 (1935).

Schmitt, Gary J. "Executive Agreements and Separation of Powers: A Reconsideration." *American Journal of Jurisprudence* 28 (1983): 189–230.

Schmitt, Gary J. "Executive Privilege: Presidential Power to Withhold Information from Congress." In Tulis and Bessette, *Presidency in the Constitutional Order*.

Schmitt, Gary J. "Separation of Powers: Introduction to the Study of Executive Agreements." *American Journal of Jurisprudence* 27 (1982): 114–138.

Schoenbrod, David. *Power Without Responsibility: How Congress Abuses the People Through Delegation*. Yale University Press, 1995.

Sellery, George C. "Lincoln's Suspension of Habeas Corpus as Viewed by Congress." *Bulletin of the University of Wisconsin* 149. History series, 1, no. 3 (1907): 213–285.

Senate Select Comm. v. Nixon, 498 F.2d 725 (D.C. Cir. 1974)

Serjoie, Kay Armin. "'The Americans Cannot Be Trusted.' How Iran Is Reacting to Trump's Decision to Quit Nuclear Deal." *Time*, May 9, 2018. http://time.com/5270821/iran-nuclear-deal-trump-ayatollah-khameini-hassan-rouhani/.

Shaub, Jonathan. "The Executive's Privilege." *Duke Law Journal* 70, no. 1 (2020): 1–91.

Sherman, Wendy. "How We Got the Iran Deal and Why We'll Miss It." *Foreign Affairs*, August 13, 2018. https://www.foreignaffairs.com/articles/2018-08-13/how-we-got-iran-deal.

Siemers, David J. *The Myth of Coequal Branches: Restoring the Constitution's Separation of Functions*. University of Missouri Press, 2018.

Silverstein, Gordon. *Law's Allure: How Law Shapes, Constrains, Saves, and Kills Politics*. Cambridge University Press, 2009.

Skowronek, Stephen. "The Conservative Insurgency and Presidential Power: A Developmental Perspective on the Unitary Executive." *Harvard Law Review* 122 (2009): 2070–2103.

Souter, Justice David H. "Text of Justice David Souter's Speech." *Harvard Gazette*, May 27, 2010. https://news.harvard.edu/gazette/story/2010/05/text-of-justice-david-souters-speech/.

Spiro, Peter, and Daniel Bodanski, "Executive Agreements +." *Vanderbilt Journal of Transnational Law* 49, no. 4 (2016): 885–929.

Spocchia, Gino. "Kinzinger Reveals Why Republicans Are Scared to Criticise Trump." *Independent*, October 20, 2021. https://www.independent.co.uk/news/world/americas/us-politics/adam-kinsinger-trump-marjorie-greene-b1941855.html.

Steinhauer, Jennifer. "Democrats Hand Victory to Obama on Iran Nuclear Deal." *New York Times*, September 10, 2015. https://www.nytimes.com/2015/09/11/us/politics/iran-nuclear-deal-senate.html.

Stern, Michael. "Why Officials Keep Testifying Despite White House Counsel's Letter on Impeachment Inquiry." *Just Security*, October 28, 2019. https://www.justsecurity.org/66742/why-officials-keep-testifying-despite-white-house-counsels-letter-on-impeachment-inquiry/.

Storing, Herbert J. "In Defense of the Electoral College: Statement on Proposals for Direct Popular Election of the President of the United States, July 22, 1977." Reprinted in Joseph Bessette, ed. *Toward a More Perfect Union: Writings of Herbert J. Storing*. AEI Press, 1995.

Story, Joseph. *Commentaries on the Constitution of the United States*. Hilliard, Gray, 1833.

Story, Joseph. *Commentaries on the Constitution of the United States*. Edited by Thomas Cooley. 4th ed. Lawbook Exchange, 2005.

Strauss, Peter L. "Formal and Functional Approaches to Separation of Powers Questions—A Foolish Inconsistency?" *Cornell Law Review* 72, no. 3 (1987): 488–526.

Strauss, Peter L. "The Place of Agencies in Government: Separation of Powers and the Fourth Branch." *Columbia Law Review* 84, no. 3 (1984): 573–669.

Sumrall, Allen C. "Incongruous Ideas of Impeachment: 'Impeachable Offenses' and the Constitutional Order." *Presidential Studies Quarterly* 50, no. 4 (2020): 948–967.

Sumrall, Allen C., and Beau J. Baumann. "Clarifying Judicial Aggrandizement." *University of Pennsylvania Law Review* 172 (2023): 24–42.

Sunderland, Lane V. *Popular Government and the Supreme Court*. University Press of Kansas, 1996.

Sunstein, Cass R. "Constitutionalism After the New Deal." *Harvard Law Review* 101, no. 2 (1987): 421–510.

Thach, Charles C., Jr. *The Creation of the Presidency, 1775–1789*. Liberty Fund, 2010.

Thomas, George. *The Founders and the Idea of a National University: Constituting the American Mind*. Cambridge University Press, 2014.

Thomas, George. *The Madisonian Constitution*. Johns Hopkins Series in Constitutional Thought. Johns Hopkins University Press, 2008.

Totenberg, Nina. "The Confirmation Process and the Public: To Know or Not to Know." *Harvard Law Review* 101, no. 6 (1988): 1213–1229.

Treaties and Other International Agreements: The Role of the United States Senate. A Report by the Congressional Research Service. 2001.

Tribe, Laurence H. "The Legislative Veto Decision: A Law by Any Other Name." *Harvard Journal on Legislation* 21 (1984): 1–27.

Trimble, Phillip R., and Jack S. Weiss. "The Role of the President, the Senate and the Congress with Respect to Arms Control Treaties Concluded by the United States." *Chicago-Kent Law Review* 67, no. 2 (1991): 645–704.

Troiano, Nick. *The Primary Solution: Rescuing Our Democracy from the Fringes*. Simon & Schuster, 2024.

Trump v. United States, 603 U.S. ___ (2024).

"The Trump Administration Officials Who Resigned over Capitol Violence." *New York Times*, January 17, 2021. https://www.nytimes.com/article/trump-resignations.html.

Tulis, Jeffrey K. "Constitutional Abdication: The Senate, the President, and Appointments to the Supreme Court." *Case Western Reserve Law Review* 47 (1996): 1331–1357.

Tulis, Jeffrey K. "The Constitutional Presidency in American Constitutional Development." In *The Constitution and the American Presidency*, edited by Martin L. Fausold and Alan Shank. SUNY Press, 1991.

Tulis, Jeffrey K. "Deliberation Between Institutions." In *Debating Deliberative Democracy*, edited by James S. Fishkin and Peter Laslett. Blackwell, 2003.

Tulis, Jeffrey K. "Impeachment in the Constitutional Order." In Tulis and Bessette, *Constitutional Presidency*.

Tulis, Jeffrey K. "On the State of Constitutional Theory." *Law and Social Inquiry* 16 (1991): 711–716.

Tulis, Jeffrey K. *The Rhetorical Presidency*. Princeton University Press, 1987.

Tulis, Jeffrey K., and Joseph Bessette, eds. *The Constitutional Presidency*. John Hopkins University Press, 2009.

Tulis, Jeffrey K., and Joseph Bessette, eds. *The Presidency in the Constitutional Order*. Louisiana State University Press, 1981.

Tulis, Jeffrey K., and Stephen Macedo, eds. *The Limits of Constitutional Democracy*. Princeton University Press, 2010.

Tulis, Jeffrey K., and Nicole Mellow. *Legacies of Losing in American Politics*. University of Chicago Press, 2018.

Turley, Jonathan. "Senate Trials and Factional Disputes: Impeachment as a Madisonian Device." *Duke Law Journal* 49, no. 1 (1999): 1–146.

Turley, Jonathan. "Trump Impeachment Trial—Why His Best Defense May Be No Defense." *Fox News*, January 17, 2021. https://www.foxnews.com/opinion/trump-impeachment-trial-defense-strategy-jonathan-turley.

Tushnet, Mark. "How Courts Implement Social Policy." *Tulsa Law Review* 45, no. 4 (2010): 855–862.

United States v. Nixon, 418 U.S. 683 (1974).

United States Department of State Office of the Legal Adviser for Treaty Affairs. International Agreements Other Than Treaties 1946–1968: A List Noting Their Legal Bases and Their Possible Effect on Internal Law in the United States. The Department of State, 1969.

Vermeule, Adrian. "There Is No Conservative Legal Movement." *Washington Post*, July 6, 2022. https://www.washingtonpost.com/outlook/2022/07/06/epa-roberts-conservative-court-libertarian/.

Vile, M.J.C. *Constitutionalism and the Separation of Powers*. Liberty Fund, 1998.

Waldron, Jeremy. *Political Political Theory: Essays on Institutions*. Harvard University Press, 2016.

Walsh, Edward. "Public Opposition to Bork Grows: In Shift, Plurality Objects to Confirmation, Post-ABC Poll Finds." *Washington Post*, September 25, 1987.

Walsh, Edward, and Richard Morin. "Majority Opposes Bork, Poll Shows." *Washington Post*, October 16, 1987.

Watson, H. Lee. "Congress Steps out: A Look at Congressional Control of the Executive." *California Law Review* 63, no. 4 (1975): 983–1094.

"We Can't Wait." The White House. Accessed January 31, 2024. https://obamawhitehouse.archives.gov/node/111049.

Wechsler, Herbert. "Toward Neutral Principles of Constitutional Law." *Harvard Law Review* 73, no. 1 (1959): 1–35.

Weiner, Greg. *The Political Constitution: The Case Against Judicial Supremacy*. University Press of Kansas, 2019.

Weisman, Jonathan. "Experts Say Obama's Recess Appointments Could Signify End to a Senate Role." *New York Times*, January 7, 2012. https://www.nytimes.com/2012/01/08/us/politics/experts-say-obamas-recess-appointments-could-signify-end-to-a-senate-role.html.

West, William, and Joseph Cooper. "The Congressional Veto and Administrative Rulemaking." *Political Science Quarterly* 98, no. 2 (1983): 285–304.
West Virginia v. EPA, 597 U.S. 697 (2022).
Whittington, Keith. "Must the House Vote to Authorize an Impeachment Inquiry?" *Lawfare*, October 9, 2019. https://www.lawfaremedia.org/article/must-house-vote-authorize-impeachment-inquiry.
Whittington, Keith, and Jason Iuliano. "The Myth of the Nondelegation Doctrine." *University of Pennsylvania Law Review* 165, no. 2 (2017): 379–431.
Whittington, Keith E. *Constitutional Construction: Divided Powers and Constitutional Meaning*. Harvard University Press, 1999.
Whittington, Keith E. "A Formidable Weapon of Faction? The Law and Politics of Impeachment." *Wake Forest Law Review* 55, no. 2 (2020): 381–414.
Whittington, Keith E. "Trump's Defiance Is Destroying Congress's Power." *Atlantic* (blog), October 14, 2019. https://www.theatlantic.com/ideas/archive/2019/10/trumps-defiance-destroying-congress/599923/.
Will, George F. "A Check on the Regulatory State." *Washington Post*, June 6, 2012. https://www.washingtonpost.com/opinions/a-check-on-the-regulatory-state/2012/06/06/gJQAjmabJV_story.html?utm_term=.60d7d653f350.
Wilson, Woodrow. *Constitutional Government in the United States*. Columbia University Press, 1908.
Wurman, Ilan. "Nondelegation at the Founding." *Yale Law Journal* 130, no. 4 (2021): 1490–1556.
Yoo, John C. "Laws as Treaties?: The Constitutionality of Congressional-Executive Agreements." *Michigan Law Review* 99, no. 4 (2001): 757–852.
York, John W., and Rachel Greszler. "A Model for Executive Reorganization." Heritage Foundation, November 3, 2017. https://www.heritage.org/political-process/report/model-executive-reorganization.
Youngstown Sheet & Tube Co. v. Sawyer 343 U.S. 579 (1952),
Zeisberg, Mariah. "Constitutional Fidelity and Interbranch Conflict." *Good Society* 13, no. 3 (2004): 24–30.
Zeisberg, Mariah. "Relational Conception of War Powers." In Tulis and Macedo, *Limits of Constitutional Democracy*.
Zeisberg, Mariah. *War Powers: The Politics of Constitutional Authority*. Princeton University Press, 2013.
Zuckert, Michael. "On the Separation of Powers: Liberal and Progressive Constitutionalism." *Social Philosophy and Policy* 29, no. 2 (2012): 335–364.

INDEX

www.ingramcontent.com/pod-product-compliance
Lightning Source LLC
Chambersburg PA
CBHW030714171125
35525CB00018B/158/J
* 9 7 8 0 7 0 0 6 4 0 3 8 6 *

THINKING LIKE A LAWYER

ESSAYS ON LEGAL HISTORY AND GENERAL HISTORY FOR JOHN CROOK ON HIS EIGHTIETH BIRTHDAY

EDITED BY

PAUL MCKECHNIE

BRILL
LEIDEN · BOSTON · KÖLN
2002

This book is printed on acid-free paper.

Library of Congress Cataloging-in-Publication Data

McKechnie, Paul.
Thinking like a lawyer : essays on legal history and general history for John Crook on his eightieth birthday / edited by Paul McKechnie.
p. cm. — (Mnemosyne. Supplements, ISSN 0169-8958 ; v. 231. History and archaeology of classical antiquity)
Includes bibliographical references and index.
ISBN 9004124748 (hb : acid-free paper)
1. Roman law. 2. Rome—History. I. Crook, J.A. (John Anthony) II. McKechnie, Paul, 1957- III. Mnemosyne, bibliotheca classica Batava. Supplementum ; 231. IV. Mnemosyne, bibliotheca classica Batava. Supplementum. History and archaeology of classical antiquity

KJA147 .T48 2002
340.5'4—dc21 2001059241

Die Deutsche Bibliothek - CIP-Einheitsaufnahme

[Mnemosyne / Supplementum]
Mnemosyne : bibliotheca classica Batava. Supplementum. – Leiden ; Boston ; Köln : Brill
Früher Schriftenreihe
Teilw. u.d.T.: Mnemosyne / Supplements
Reihe Supplementum zu: Mnemosyne
231. McKechnie Paul : Thinking like a lawyer.

Thinking like a lawyer : essays on legal history and general history for John Crook on his eightieth birthday / ed. by Paul McKechnie.
– Leiden ; Boston ; Köln : Brill, 2002
(Mnemosyne : Supplementum ; 231)
ISBN 90-04-12474-8

ISSN 0169-8958
ISBN 90 04 12474 8

PRINTED IN THE NETHERLANDS

NONIS NOUEMBRIBUS MMI*

Iure peritus adest; linguis faueatis, amici:
  natalem ex animo commemorare decet.
Crucquius est nomen; Ioannes saepius audit:
  mense sub undecimo lustra bis octo feret.
principio iuuenis sese inuenit inter Amicos
  Principis ignotus Consiliumque petit.
scrutatur fontes; Comitum comes euenit ipse:
  nomina Amicorum cuncta coronis habet.
postmodo de prelo paret *Ius Vitaque Romae.*
  qui labor auctori! lectio laeta tamen.
historiis docet ille; sapit placuisse docendo;
  consulto causas enucleare libet.
deinde *Vicaria Vox* auditur causidicorum
  uendibili lingua proficiente reis.
en, tria doctrinae monumenta carentia morte:
  Rhetor, Ius Uiuum, Consiliumque Ducis.
uiuas et valeas, Ioannes care, precamur,
  consultus iuris iustitiaeque simul.

ON JOHN CROOK'S EIGHTIETH BIRTHDAY (5.11.2001)

The lawyer's clock is running, so pray silence, friends.
The form is: the lawyer's own birthday honours.

Surname: CROOK. Usual appellation: JOHN.
Age in years: 80. D.O.B.: O5 NOV 1921.
1st Publ.: CONSILIUM PRINCIPIS, IMPERIAL COUNCIL AND COUNCIL-LORS
FROM AUGUSTUS TO DIOCLETIAN (CAMBRIDGE, 1955)
Junior then, he found himself dealing with Emperors' Friends;
New boy in town, he went in search of the Counselling;
In focussed work on the sources, there emerges a Councillor's Counsel;
Appended, the catalogue of all known Friends.
Next from the press: LAW AND LIFE OF ROME (LONDON, 1967)
So much toil for the author, but still a joy to read:
J.A.C. uses stories to teach, knows to give pleasure teaching;
Just ask: the Roman lawyer likes getting to the heart of each case.
LEGAL ADVOCACY IN THE ROMAN WORLD (LONDON, 1995)
Listen! Tongues for hire; the dock to defend.
There, a monumental triptych of permanent scholarship:
LEGAL ADVOCACY; LAW & LIFE; CONSILIUM PRINCIPIS.

Dear John, we wish you good health for many years to come,
Expert in law, expert in justice, both.

---

* By Guy Lee; English version by John Henderson.

CONTENTS

PREFACE

Editing a celebratory book for someone with as many friends as John Crook has ought to be easy; and as such things go, it was. I wish to thank the Managers of the Maitland Memorial Fund in the Faculty of Law in the University of Cambridge for a grant towards the project. At St. John's College, Cambridge, I wish to thank Prof. Malcolm Schofield, Mr. A.G. Lee, Mrs. Kathryn McKee and Mrs. Fiona Colbert. I wish to thank Dr. Mary Beard (Newnham College, Cambridge) and Prof. Samuel N.C. Lieu (Macquarie University) for support and advice. At the University of Auckland Dr. W.R. Barnes has given help well beyond the call of duty; and I also wish to thank Ms. Emily Baragwanath, Ms. Birgitte Kristoffersen and Ms. Jessica Priestley. All the contributors have met my requests and borne with my failings good-humouredly (Dr. John Henderson has had more to put up with than most). Finally, the encouragement and efficiency of Ms. Loes Schouten and Mr. Michiel Klein Swormink at Koninklijke Brill NV have made working on this book a constant pleasure.

CONTRIBUTORS

W.R. Barnes is Senior Lecturer in Classics and Ancient History, University of Auckland

Duncan Cloud is University Fellow in Ancient History in the University of Leicester

M.H. Hansen is Director of the Copenhagen Polis Centre under the Danish National Research Foundation

John Henderson is Reader in Latin Literature in the University of Cambridge, and Fellow of King's College, Cambridge

Keith Hopwood is Lecturer in Classics, University of Wales, Lampeter

David Johnston is an advocate and an honorary Professor of Law at the University of Edinburgh

Paul McKechnie is Senior Lecturer in Classics and Ancient History, University of Auckland

Kathryn McKee is Sub-Librarian of St. John's College, Cambridge

Paul Murgatroyd is Professor of Classics, McMaster University

Beryl Rawson is Professor Emerita of Classics, Australian National University

Joyce Reynolds is a retired Reader in Roman Historical Epigraphy, University of Cambridge, and Fellow of Newnham College, Cambridge

J.S. Sheldon is Master of the Lower School and a teacher of Classics and Sanskrit at Sydney Grammar School

A.M. Stone is Senior Lecturer in Ancient History, University of Sydney

R. Godfrey Tanner is Professor Emeritus of Classics, University of Newcastle, NSW

S.C. Todd is Reader in Classics, University of Manchester

Paul Weaver is Professor Emeritus of Classics, University of Tasmania, and Visiting Fellow, Australian National University

C.R. Whittaker is a retired Lecturer in Classics, University of Cambridge, and Fellow of Churchill College, Cambridge

Joseph Georg Wolf is Professor Emeritus of Roman Law, Universität Freiburg i. B.

INTRODUCTION

Paul McKechnie

1. A Challenge Accepted

In 1996 John Crook offered a challenge to the younger generation of scholars: to give an account of what the Roman characteristic he defines as "Thinking like a Lawyer" really consisted of. What he had in mind was an evaluative enterprise: in his words, "an estimation of the place of Roman law in general history as an intellectual phenomenon, a topic in the history of ideas . . . judged in terms of its significance in its own age."[1]

The article in which the challenge was issued was the distillation of a lecture given in Freiburg im Breisgau about the time when its author received a Freiburg honorary doctorate. John Crook, in his teaching career, kept up a measure of reserve about his outlook as classicist and historian. Conscientiously, he steered students to consider the merits of any or all of the theoretical frameworks for understanding history and society which were on offer in the twentieth century. He spoke to me enthusiastically of Max Weber, and of Keith Hopkins. At times, he might be provocative, as when he told me, "We [university teachers] are really part of the entertainment industry"; more often, he spoke almost wistfully about being without a grand unified theory by which to interpret everything. But in his Freiburg lecture he was unusually forthcoming. He spoke of a long-standing project aiming to integrate Roman legal and general history: ". . . some years ago it dawned on me," he said, "that . . . the legal historians were pursuing the legal history of Roman antiquity, but the general historians were making insufficient use of Roman law in their treatments of social and economic history."[2]

Not all the contributors to this book are of as young a generation as that which perhaps John Crook had in mind when he issued the challenge to take the next step in asking what Roman law can

[1] J.A. Crook 'Legal History and General History' *BICS* 41 (1996), 31–6 at 36.
[2] Crook 'Legal History and General History' (as in n. 1), 31.

tell us about Roman society; but all admire his work, both in large and in small. All are interested in the fundamental questions he raised in Freiburg. To choose just three: what kind of society develops techniques of procedural law as refined as those the Romans had? how good was the fit between what the law-sources tell us and what went on in society? and what relation was there between Roman and Greek legal principles? In this book, David Johnston, Paul Weaver and Joseph Georg Wolf offer chapters on differing facets of procedural law, in the courts and in official life, Keith Hopwood discusses legal prescription and social reality, and John Henderson and R. Godfrey Tanner approach the Greek/Roman interface from different angles.

Some of us might question the crookish assertion that the Athenians, though democratic, did not 'think like lawyers' (as for their having no jurisprudence, perhaps that is a matter of definition);[3] S.C. Todd's chapter, on questioning witnesses in Athenian courts, examines Athenian ways of thinking like a lawyer, and J.S. Sheldon considers how Athenians (or rather Herodotus, who was not quite Athenian), framed and comprehended a dynamic, long-lasting tradition which was foreign to them. M.H. Hansen's chapter broadens beyond Athens the issue of being a democrat.

"Thinking like a Lawyer", in the Freiburg lecture, was conceived as being near the heart of a wide-ranging exploration of the life as well as the law of Rome; and in a similar way this collection spreads into thought and literature as well as the prosaic "wie es eigentlich gewesen war" of Roman history. On being, and seeing, like a Roman, C.R. Whittaker discusses maps and the mental images behind them, while W.R. Barnes and P. Murgatroyd discuss the Virgilian texts the Romans habitually used 'to think with'. A series of contributions based on local studies or particular events concludes the book, with chapters by A.M. Stone on the *dignitas* of the Senate in 88 BC, Duncan Cloud on the consequences of the Pompeian tablets for understanding literary texts, Joyce Reynolds on bases of statues, paid for by women, in the baths at Aphrodisias, myself on the political motives behind Decius' and Valerian's persecutions of Christians, and finally Beryl Rawson on the route to Hades, smoothed by proper and legal regulation of undertakers at Puteoli.

---

[3] Crook 'Legal History and General History' (as in n. 1), 36; no jurisprudence, 33.

2. Celebrating a Colleague and Teacher

When he returned as a Research Fellow to St. John's College, Cambridge, where he had been an undergraduate (1939–41 and 1945–7), John Crook did not want to fail to hear when someone came to the door of his rooms. "If there is no reply to your knock," he wrote on a small card, "enter and knock on the door to your left." This card, initialled and dated "J.A.C. 1.10.51", stayed pinned to the door until some time in the mid-eighties. Perhaps it was removed to mark its owner's retirement from the Chair of Ancient History in 1984—but I speculate. I have failed to ascertain whether it is now in the College archives. The easy access the card implied was real, as I found myself in good times and bad, and as many others know. Behind 'the door to your left' was a very complete twentieth-century Cambridge don, who would teach anything undergraduates needed for the Tripos—though he did not mind saying what bored him, as I found when I offered him an essay about Epaminondas and fourth-century Thebes. As well as history, he taught Greek and Latin language with precision, subtlety and evident enjoyment—and there, as elsewhere, humour was always near the surface. "I set a prose once," he told me after explaining some howler of mine, "which began 'Abulhassan and his Moors . . .' One of the undergraduates started with Ἄβουλος δὲ καὶ οἱ Μῶροι . . ."

This book marks the fiftieth anniversary of the card's composition and display, and so also, first, the fiftieth anniversary of John Crook's Fellowship of St. John's, and secondly (within a few weeks), his own eightieth birthday, which falls on November 5, 2001. Before returning to Cambridge, he had spent a year at Balliol College, Oxford, as a research student, then three at the University of Reading, as an Assistant Lecturer from 1948 and Lecturer from 1949. In Cambridge, he was made a University Assistant Lecturer in Classics in 1953, advancing to Lecturer in 1955, and Reader in Roman History and Law in 1971. He became Professor of Ancient History in 1979, as successor to Moses Finley. In half a century at St. John's College, he fulfilled all the responsibilities which could be expected of a Fellow: Teaching Fellow from 1953 to 1984, Tutor from 1956 to 1964, Praelector from 1966 to 1971, President from 1971 to 1975.

Since his retirement in 1984, he has advanced to a remarkable 'second career', publishing enough to demand the whole working life of many an ordinarily productive colleague. *Legal Advocacy in the Roman*

World has perhaps been the outstanding work of this late period, though some might well point to his chapters in the *Cambridge Ancient History* as a model of their kind. The Crook Bibliography at the end of this volume illustrates the breadth of his published *oeuvre* since Reading days.

The colleagues and former students who have contributed show in their own diversity some of the breadth of John Crook's interests and friendships: people from John's and Cambridge, Britain and Europe, Canada, Australia and New Zealand. We are very glad to have the opportunity to present John Crook with this volume, as a mark of our esteem, and as a first attempt at answering his challenge to think like lawyers.

PECULIAR QUESTIONS

David Johnston

In *Law and Life of Rome*, John Crook discusses the economic significance of the *peculium* in Roman law.[1] The *peculium* was a fund of property owned by a slave's owner or a paterfamilias but entrusted to his slave or child. It could be made up of more or less any property: land; movable property; money; businesses; slaves (who might themselves have sub-*peculia*). It is quite clear that at least in high classical law the value of the *peculium* included the value of obligations owed to it. John Crook explains how the existence of the *peculium* "enabled the law to develop a series of rules making the slave an agent pledging his master's credit in dealings with third parties".[2] The way this worked within the framework of the law is that, whether or not the owner knew of or consented to his slave's or child's transaction, he could be sued as owner or paterfamilias up to but for no more than the value of the *peculium*.

The result is a type of limited liability. That is an interesting topic but not the one for discussion here.[3] The question for this essay is instead one which, although it is not raised in *Law and Life of Rome*, John Crook has asked me more than once. It is this: how did the Romans value the *peculium*? The question may sound a bit unexciting, but it is actually of great importance. It is obvious that, since much if not most trade was carried on using slaves as agents and intermediaries and most of them will have had *peculia*, the way in which the *peculium* was valued at the relevant date is critical. It made all the difference between recovering payment in full and recovering only a proportion or nothing. It is important that the law can produce a satisfactory solution in this situation.

There is a delicate balancing exercise to be carried out here: on the one hand, the only reason anybody would be willing to deal with a slave (who could not be sued personally) would be because

[1] *Law and Life of Rome* (London and Ithaca, NY, 1967), 188–9, 241.
[2] *Law and Life of Rome* 189.
[3] See my essay 'Limiting liability: Roman law and the civil law tradition' (1995) 70 *Chicago-Kent Law Review* 1515–38.

of his owner's liability based on the *peculium*; on the other, the whole point of the *peculium* regime was to introduce some form of limitation on the owner's liability. In short, for trade to work efficiently it is necessary for the owner to have some liability, but not too much. From the modern point of view the curiosity is not that there was a limitation on liability but that all the property belonged to the slave's owner, whether or not it was in the *peculium*. The difficulty in Roman law therefore lay in drawing the line between what was the property of Cassius (but in his slave Stichus's *peculium*) and what was the property of Cassius *simpliciter*. And the problem here, not least, is that owners ought surely to be free to dispose of their property as they see fit, and to arrange and rearrange their affairs so that property which was once in one *peculium* is now in another or in none at all.

Some rules or principles therefore need to be devised to determine when it can be said that a particular item of property is not within the *peculium* and when to say so involves stealing a march on a trading partner by reducing the slave's *peculium* and frustrating the trading partner's reasonable expectations as to creditworthiness. The remainder of this essay looks at the main issues that arise. The evidence, unfortunately, does not allow any dramatic conclusions to be drawn or a simple elegant answer to be given to John Crook's question.

The proper place to start is with the formula for the action. There is, however, no single free-standing action *de peculio*. Instead, the principal speciality about this type of action lay in the fact that in the final part of the formula the judge was instructed to pronounce judgment up to the amount in the *peculium*, which therefore represented a ceiling on the sum of the judgment. Consequently, the formulae for all contractual obligations could be modified from their ordinary form so as to proceed only up to the value of the *peculium*. Here is the formula for the action on the contract of deposit (*actio depositi*), limited to the *peculium* and reconstructed by Otto Lenel, together with a (non-literal) translation:[4]

> Quod Aulus Agerius apud Stichum, qui in Numerii Negidii potestate est, mensam argenteam deposuit, qua de re agitur quidquid ob eam rem Stichum, si liber esset ex iure Quiritium, Aulo Agerio dare facere oporteret ex fide bona, eius iudex Numerium Negidium Aulo Agerio

[4] O. Lenel, *Das Edictum Perpetuum* (3rd ed., Leipzig, 1927), 282.

dumtaxat de peculio et si quid dolo malo Numerii Negidii factum est quo minus peculii esset, vel si quid in rem Numerii Negidii inde versum est condemna, si non paret absolve.

Whereas AA deposited a silver table which is the subject of this action with Stichus, who is the power of NN, whatever Stichus ought, if he were free under civil law, to give to or do for AA as a matter of good faith, for so much let the judge condemn NN to AA up to the amount of the *peculium* plus anything which by the fraud of NN has been removed from the *peculium* or anything which has been turned from there to the benefit of NN; if it does not so appear let him absolve him.

The formula directs the judge's attention to three questions, so far as quantifying Aulus Agerius's claim is concerned: first, the amount in the *peculium*; second, the amount of any property which has been fraudulently removed by Numerius Negidius from the *peculium*; third, the amount of any benefit which has flowed to Numerius Negidius from the transaction. The last of these considerations is beyond the scope of this paper, although it is important to be aware of it as filling a gap which would otherwise exist. Regardless of the value of the *peculium*, if a creditor could prove that financial benefit had flowed to the owner (*in rem versum*) through the transaction in question, he was entitled to have recourse against the owner to the extent of that benefit. The result is that the value of the *peculium* was decisive only where it could not be proved that the owner had obtained a personal benefit from the transaction.

A further preliminary point of some importance is that the action based on the *peculium* was only one of a number of actions potentially available to the Roman creditor in relation to transactions entered into by slaves or dependent children. In particular, there were other legal remedies available to creditors and those who had dealings with a slave with the knowledge of his owner. So we are dealing here *ex hypothesi* only with cases where the owner did not at the time of the transaction know of or consent to it.[5] The result is that the limitation to the value of the *peculium* only came into operation if it was impossible to prove either knowledge or else direct financial advantage on the part of the owner. Where there was no question of knowledge or benefit, everything turned on valuing (i) what was in the *peculium*; and (ii) what had fraudulently been spirited out of it.

[5] Cf. Gai. 4.74.

To take the first point first. How did things get into and out of the *peculium*? A picture can be pieced together from a number of texts in the Digest.

Paul book 4 *Ad Sabinum*, *Dig.* 15.1.8:

> non statim quod dominus voluit ex re sua peculii esse peculium fecit, sed si tradidit aut cum apud eum esset pro tradito habuit. desiderat enim res naturalem dationem. contra autem simul atque noluit peculium servi desinit peculium esse.
>
> An owner cannot immediately make his property into *peculium* by mere intention but if he delivers it or holds it as delivered, for it requires an actual transfer. On the other hand, the *peculium* of a slave ceases to be *peculium* as soon as the owner wishes.

The doctrine that it is enough for the owner *nolle*, not to wish, that something be part of the *peculium* for it to cease to be so fits perfectly with the notion that it is a matter of complete freedom for an owner how he chooses to arrange his property. But where third parties are concerned, the doctrine is obviously problematic. The difficulty is that, if property can be removed from the *peculium* by mere *nolle*, then it is not obvious how, objectively, it can be maintained against an owner that property which he claims was not in the *peculium* actually was.

The question arises: would there be any objective evidence on which a creditor could rely to disprove the assertion that certain property was in fact not part of the *peculium*? The texts indicate the importance of accounts, *rationes*. In the definitions of *peculium* advanced by various jurists there emerges the key point that its accounts are kept separately from those for the rest of the owner's patrimony.[6]

Ulpian book 29 *Ad edictum*, *Dig.* 15.1.5.4:

> peculium autem Tubero quidem sic definit, ut Celsus libro sexto digestorum refert, quod servus domini permissu separatum a rationibus dominicis habet, deducto inde si quid domino debetur.
>
> Tubero, as Celsus reports him in book six of his *Digesta*, defines the *peculium* as what a slave with his owner's permission keeps separately from his owner's accounts, less anything owed to the owner.

Pomponius book 7 *Ad Sabinum*, *Dig.* 15.1.4pr.:

> peculii est non id cuius servus seorsum a domini rationem habuerit sed quod dominus ipse separaverit suam a servi rationem discernens . . .

[6] Cf. R.M. Thilo, *Der codex accepti et expensi im römischen Recht* (Göttingen, 1980), 137–9.

> What falls within the *peculium* is not what a slave keeps accounts for separately from his owner, but what the owner himself has separated, dividing his own accounts from those of his slave. . . .

On the face of it, therefore, a creditor could point to the accounts kept by the slave in order to demonstrate the owner's intention that a particular piece of property should be regarded as falling within the slave's *peculium*. Here it becomes necessary to distinguish between transactions between the slave and third parties and transactions between slave and slave-owner. So far as third-party transactions are concerned, although there appears to be no compelling evidence on the point, it seems likely that a judge would be entitled to conclude that a particular piece of property or a particular debt fell within the *peculium* if all the evidence—in particular the relevant accounts—suggested so, and the only contrary evidence was the owner's assertion. Even, however, if this was not possible on the evidence, it would be open to the judge on appropriate facts to conclude that, while the property could not actually be said to be in the *peculium*, the reason it was not was the owner's bad faith. This issue is discussed later.

Matters are more complicated where relations between slave and slave-owner are concerned. The fact that something is mentioned in the accounts does not necessarily mean much in itself. It is just a piece of evidence. The texts are quite clear that a debt is not created simply by being entered into the accounts: it is created only by a legal transaction which properly gives rise to indebtedness. That emerges from continuing the quotation from Pomponius from above, as well as from elsewhere.[7]

Pomponius book 7 *Ad Sabinum*:

> sed hoc ita verum puto, si debito servum liberare voluit dominus, ut etiamsi nuda voluntate remiserit dominus quod debuerit desinat servus debitor esse. si vero nomina ita fecerit dominus ut quasi debitorem se servo faceret cum re vera debitor non esset, contra puto: re enim non verbis peculium augendum est.

> I think this is true if the owner wished to release his slave from a debt, that by mere intention the owner may release the debt so that the slave ceases to be his debtor. On the other hand, it is the opposite if the owner has recorded debts so as to appear to be indebted to his slave when actually he is not: for the *peculium* is increased by facts not words.

[7] Pomp. 4 *Ad Q. Mucium*, *Dig.* 15.1.49.2; cf. Thilo, *op. cit.*, 147ff.

The conclusion therefore must be that a creditor could not tell, purely by requesting the slave's accounts, whether they accurately stated the value of the *peculium*. To be sure, he would have to seek further details about certain transactions in order to form a view as to whether indebtedness to the *peculium* was genuine or fictitious. This sounds a serious practical problem, but may on reflection have been of limited significance. Nowadays, it is worth bearing in mind, much the same difficulties can arise. The fact that debtors are shown in a company's balance sheet does not indicate that the debts will be recoverable. Trade involves risk. More significant, however, as a matter of Roman law, is that a Roman creditor would have been well advised to disregard entirely any apparent indebtedness to the *peculium* by the slave's owner or child's paterfamilias. The reason for this is simple: the paterfamilias or slave-owner was always entitled as a first charge against the *peculium*, and before its quantification in order to satisfy the claims of creditors, to deduct from the gross value of the *peculium* any debts the *peculium* owed to him. Consequently, before entering into a transaction with a slave or dependent child, a creditor ought always to have assessed the creditworthiness of the *peculium* net of these deductions, since under no circumstances would he be able to rely on notional indebtedness between slave and owner or father and son if a contract ended in litigation.

It seems reasonable therefore to conclude that, in valuing the *peculium*, a judge would have regard not just to the owner's or paterfamilias's own assertion as to what was in the *peculium* but also to the relevant *rationes*. Once items had been accepted as falling within the *peculium*, the question of valuing them would arise. This is not a matter on which there appears to be very much by way of evidence. The jurists were not greatly interested in such practicalities. But it is worth noting that it was not as simple as taking the book value of a debt: Scaevola indicates that, for the purpose of establishing an owner's liability, debts are to be included, but not invariably at book value,[8]

> since the expenses of recovery and the outcome of execution may be uncertain, and the time granted [for payment] to those found liable or for sale of their property if appropriate must be taken into account.

[8] Scaev. 2 *Quaest.*, *Dig.* 15.1.51: ". . . et sumptus in petendo et eventus exsecutionis possit esse incertus et cogitanda sit mora temporis quod datur iudicatis aut venditionis bonorum si id magis faciendum erit."

Accordingly, the conclusion for a person proposing to deal with a slave is that to reduce risk it would be important to inspect the accounts of the *peculium* and, in doing so, to apply suitable discounts to reflect the contingencies of recovery of indebtedness.

To turn to the second issue: property fraudulently removed from a *peculium*. The basics are set out by Ulpian:

Ulpian book 29 *Ad edictum*, *Dig.* 15.1.21pr.:

> summa cum ratione etiam hoc peculio praetor imputavit quod dolo malo domini factum est quo minus in peculio esset. sed dolum malum accipere debemus si ei ademit peculium: sed et si eum intricare peculium in necem creditorum passus est, Mela scribit dolo malo eius factum. sed et si quis cum suspicaretur alium secum acturum alio peculium avertat, dolo non caret. sed si alii solvit, non dubito de hoc quin non teneatur, quoniam creditori solvitur et licet creditori vigilare ad suum consequendum.

> With good reason the praetor also imputes to the *peculium* property which ceased to be in it as a result of the fraud of the owner. We must regard it as fraud if the owner takes away the *peculium*, and also if he allows the slave so to entangle the *peculium* as to prejudice the interests of creditors. If someone suspects he is going to be sued and diverts the *peculium* to someone else, he is fraudulent. But if he pays a creditor, I am in no doubt that he is not liable, since payment is made to a creditor and it is open to creditors to look out to obtain what is due to them.

The significance of the fraud provisions of the formula is not that property which left the *peculium* is brought back into it, but just that its value is taken into account in calculating the total extent of the owner's liability.[9] This is a liability based on *dolus*, fraud. From that two important points follow: first, that by analogy with the action *de dolo* the 'imputation' would extend only for one year from the date of the fraudulent act; and second, that *dolus*, that is a fraudulent intention on the part of the owner, would have to be proved. The requirement to prove fraud is always a serious restriction on a remedy. It is rather cold comfort that such tricks could not be played very often, and not more than once in relation to any particular trading partner. Among the jurists there is some (but not much) discussion of what would and would not amount to *dolus*.

Taking the slave's *peculium* away is something that was perfectly within the legitimate power of an owner or paterfamilias and might

[9] Cf. W.W. Buckland, *The Roman Law of Slavery* (Cambridge, 1908), 218–20.

indeed be perfectly innocuous: suppose, for example, that the slave had not been trading profitably and it was desired to let a different slave take over. As with any other remedy based on fraud, it would therefore be necessary to prove circumstances which showed that the removal of the *peculium* could not have been done for any legitimate reason but only for fraudulent purposes. This is a point which is taken for granted by the jurists, and there is therefore no substantial discussion of it either in connexion with the *peculium* or in connexion with fraud in general.

If even removal of the *peculium* imposed a burden of proof on the creditor which might in certain circumstances be difficult to discharge, allowing a slave so to entangle the *peculium* as to cause disadvantage to creditors must have been much more difficult to establish. As a concept 'allowing entanglement' is not altogether easy to understand. Nowadays the creation of multiple companies with cross-shareholdings but murky lines of association between one and another is the first resort of the scoundrel. Much the same may be what Mela had in mind. But how would it work? The most obvious manner of *intricare* would be to devise a *peculium* for a principal slave in which there were several other slaves each with his own sub-*peculium*. Ordinarily, the rule would be that a creditor could have recourse only with respect to the *peculium* of the slave with whom he had dealt: if he had had no dealings with the principal slave, then he could not have recourse against him, unless the principal slave knew of the transaction and could therefore be sued by another action.[10] But it is not easy to see how these perfectly legitimate means of containing liability could be proved to be fraudulent, except on rather exceptional facts. Although the way in which Ulpian describes *intricare* seems to suggest that it could take place at any time, rather than only after the relevant transaction had been entered into, there may be reason to doubt this. First, proof of fraudulent intent in relation to a general way of doing business rather than a specific transaction would be highly problematic. Second, as already mentioned, there were other remedies available for cases in which the owner or paterfamilias had authorized or simply knew of a particular transaction. The *peculium*-based liability had its main significance only when he did not. In general it follows that the owner's scope for fraudulent manipulation of the *peculium* would be restricted to the

[10] See e.g. Ulpian 28 *Ad edictum, Dig.* 14.1.1.19, and my essay 'Law and commercial life of Rome' (1997) 43 *Proceedings of the Cambridge philological society* 53–65.

period between the transaction and the time of being sued.[11]

To sum up. The evidence allows only tentative conclusions to be drawn. It is clear that there were distinct weaknesses in the system for suing in reliance upon a *peculium*. This is not altogether unexpected. There is no reason, after all, to assume that proof should have been easy. Gaius explains that, where he has another action by which he can recover in full, nobody will be so stupid as to put himself to the trouble of proving that the person with whom he dealt had a *peculium* and that his claim can be satisfied out of the amount in the *peculium*.[12]

None the less it would be wrong to draw the conclusion that the law was consciously designed so as to make it difficult to sue. That could not invariably be in the interests of any particular social group. Not even the jurists. The point is rather that liability *dumtaxat de peculio* was itself a break with the principle that a slave could not make his owner's position worse. As an exception to a well-established rule, it was bound to be interpreted in a manner which was restricted, even if a degree of inconvenience was the inevitable result. Some might conclude that this is but another illustration of the distant relationship of the jurists with real life and practice. But such a conclusion goes too far. There are two main reasons for saying so. First, by means of other remedies creditors were protected in the event that they could demonstrate that a slave-owner or paterfamilias knew of a transaction at the time it was concluded, or if they could demonstrate that he had derived benefit from it. The action based on the *peculium* was in a sense a last resort where neither of these was possible. Second, what was important was to depart from the principle that slaves could not bind their owners only so far as necessary to enable trade to work efficiently. Against the background of well-established principle, to expose a slave-owner or paterfamilias to unlimited liability where he knew nothing of the transactions in question would have been extreme. The *peculium* was a remarkable means of balancing the interests of those involved in trade, by imposing some liability but not too much. The contours of the action outlined in this essay are entirely consistent with that general philosophy.

[11] Cf. Paul 4 *Ad Plautium*, *Dig.* 15.1.47pr.

[12] Gai. 4.74: ". . . sed nemo tam stultus erit, ut qui aliqua illarum actionum sine dubio solidum consequi possit, vel in difficultatem se deducat probandi habere peculium eum cum quo contraxerit exque eo peculio posse sibi satisfieri vel id quod persequitur in rem patris dominive versum esse."

DIEM DIFFINDERE: DIE VERTAGUNG IM URTEILSTERMIN NACH DER *LEX IRNITANA**

Joseph Georg Wolf

1. Einführung

1.1 *Zur diei diffissio*

Konnte der Urteilsrichter den Prozeß nicht vor Ablauf des Gerichtstages mit einem Urteilsspruch beenden, mußte er ihn vertagen. Das Mittel war die *diei diffissio*, die 'Spaltung' oder 'Zerteilung des Tages'.[1] Die *diei diffissio* war schon den XII Tafeln bekannt, die nach gut beglaubigter Überlieferung verfügten, daß der Tag, der für das Urteilsgericht vorgesehen war, ohne weiteres 'zerteilt' sein sollte, wenn 'schwere Erkrankung' oder ein 'Gerichtstermin mit einem Fremden' den *iudex* oder eine Streitpartei hinderte, zur Verhandlung zu erscheinen;[2] vermutlich aber war sie sehr viel älter. Denn die 'Spaltung des Tages' als Mittel der Vertagung ist ein typisches Produkt der Pontifikaljurisprudenz:[3] eine gezielte Neuerung, die den überkommenen Rechtszustand scheinbar bewahrt, in Wahrheit aber überwindet. Wie die alte *mancipatio* an der Unveräußerlichkeit der Hauskinder, Sklaven und Arbeitstiere der bäuerlichen Wirtschaft festhält und sie zugleich aufgibt,

---

[1] *Diffissio* erst bei Gell. 14.2.1, offenbar aus einem der augusteischen Prozessgesetze von 17 v. Chr. sowie aus 'Erläuterungen' des Masurius Sabinus. *Diffindere* dagegen seit den XII Tafeln (s. A. 2); das Simplex *findere* seit Plautus. *Diffindere* <*dis findere*: zer-spalten, zer-teilen.

[2] XII T. 2.2: Bruns 20; FIRA I 31; *Roman Statutes* II 623—alle mit (den) Quellen, u. a. Ulp. *Dig.* 2.11.2.3; Iul. *Dig.* 42.1.60. Vgl. außerdem Kaser/Hackl 116.

[3] Oder denn der auguralen Disziplin, vgl. U. Manthe, 'Stilistische Gemeinsamkeiten in den Fachsprachen der Juristen und Auguren der römischen Republik', in: K. Zimmermann (Hrsg.), *Der Stilbegriff in den Altertumswissenschaften* (Rostock 1993), 69ff. Ein *augurium oblativum*, ein unerbetenes Zeichen der Gottheit, konnte den Tag 'spalten'; der 'abgespaltene' Teil des Tages war dann *nefas* und damit der Magistrat gezwungen, den schon begonnenen staatlichen Akt abzubrechen und am nächsten Tag vorzunehmen: Liv. 9.38.15/39.1: "Papirius C. Iunium Bubulcum magistrum equitum dixit; atque ei legem curiatam de imperio ferenti triste omen diem diffidit. . . . Dictator postero die auspiciis repetitis pertulit legem". Vgl. G. Wissowa, *Religion und Kultus der Römer* (2. Aufl. 1912), 531.

sozusagen die Veräußerung des Unveräußerlichen bewirkt,[4] so bewirkt die *diei diffissio* die Teilung des Unteilbaren, indem sie die Bindung des Urteilsgerichts an den vorbestimmten Gerichtstag dem Begriffe nach bewahrt, in der Wirklichkeit aber aufgibt.

Nach Zwölftafelrecht war sie vermutlich aber auch schon dem *iudex* zur Verfügung, der den Prozeß nicht am gleichen Tage mit einem Urteil abschließen konnte.[5] Direkte Zeugnisse haben wir freilich erst für den klassischen Formularprozeß. Gellius berichtet, daß er sich *ex ipsa lege Iulia*[6] sowie aus Masurius Sabinus und den Kommentaren anderer Juristen über *dierum diffissiones* belehrt[7] und daß er, als Urteilsrichter, auch selbst einmal den Tag 'zerteilt' habe, weil er Bedenken hatte, nach der Beweislage zu entscheiden.[8] Und aus dem Pomponius-Zitat einer Juristenschrift, von der wenig mehr als dieses Textstück auf einem Papyrus[9] überliefert ist, wissen wir, daß der *iudex*, der die Vertagung versäumte, das Urteil nicht nachholen konnte und dem Kläger haftete. Bis vor kurzem waren das die Nachrichten, über die wir verfügten. Durch den Fund der Bronzetafeln von Irni, deren größte Attraktion freilich das *intertium* ist,[10] wurden unerwartet aber auch sie aufgestockt.

Gellius belehrte sich über *dierum diffissiones*. Mit dem Plural kann er auf die verschiedenen Gründe anspielen, die dem *iudex* die Vertagung gestatteten.[11] Die *diffissiones* können aber auch die beiden Modi der 'Spaltung des Gerichtstages' sein, die wir unterscheiden müssen: die Vertagung *ipsa lege* und die Vertagung durch den Urteilsrichter. Beide sind für das 1. und 2. Jh. und damit auch für die Epoche der flavischen Stadtrechte Spaniens sicher belegt.[12]

---

[4] J.G. Wolf, 'Funktion und Struktur der Mancipatio', in Michel Humbert/Yan Thomas (Hrsg.) *Mélanges de droit romain et d'histoire ancienne: hommage à la mémoire de André Magdelain* (Paris 1998), 509f., 515f.

[5] Bethmann-Hollweg II, 591.

[6] Vermutlich aus der *Lex Iulia iudiciorum privatorum*, jedenfalls aber aus einem der beiden augusteischen Prozeßgesetze (Gai 4.30) von 17 v. Chr., die nach neuerer Meinung beide *iudicia privata* betrafen: Kaser/Hackl 161 mit A. 71.

[7] *N.A.* 14.2.1.

[8] *N.A.* 14.2.11.

[9] P. Ant. I 22, recto, col. II, 5–10 (ed. C.H. Roberts, London 1950).

[10] J.G. Wolf, 'Intertium' m. Lit.

[11] S. unten nach A. 61.

[12] Die *ipsa lege* insb. durch Ulp. *Dig.* 2.11.2.3 und Iul. *Dig.* 42.2.60; die durch den Urteilsrichter eben durch Gellius und den Papyrus.

1.2 *Zur Lex Irnitana*

Von den 97 Kapiteln, die das Stadtrecht von Irni zählte, handeln 9 Kapitel von der ordentlichen Zivilgerichtsbarkeit in Irni, von ihrer Verfassung und dem Rechtsgang. Es sind die Kapitel 84 bis 92, die auf den Tafeln IX und X mit 217 Zeilen 4 Kolumnen füllen.[13] Das Konzept dieser Kapitelfolge ist plausibel, Notwendigkeit und Abfolge der Regeln sind einsichtig.[14] Zuweisung und Definition der Gerichtsbarkeit eröffnen die Sektion (Kap. 84).[15] Die Verpflichtung des Magistrats, das Jurisdiktionsedikt des Statthalters, soweit es für ihn in Betracht kommt, öffentlich anzuschlagen und nach dessen Maßgabe zu judizieren, schließt sich folgerecht an (Kap. 85). In einem zweiten Block folgen die Regeln über Erstellung und öffentlichen Anschlag der Richterliste sowie deren Verbindlichkeit für den Magistrat (Kap. 86); über die Auswahl eines Richters aus dieser Liste, über seine Ernennung oder die eines listenfremden Richters sowie die Verpflichtung des ernannten Richters, seines Amtes zu walten und ein Urteil zu sprechen (Kap. 87); ferner über die Auswahl und Einsetzung von Rekuperatoren und ihre Urteilspflicht (Kap. 88); sowie schließlich über die Zuständigkeit des Einzelrichters und des Rekuperatorengerichts, die sich nach der stadtrömischen Praxis richten soll (Kap. 89).[16] Die Rechtssätze der noch folgenden drei Kapitel gehen über das Verfahren nach Einsetzung des Urteilsgerichts. Während Kap. 90 ausschließlich *de intertium dando* handelt, also von der Anberaumung eines Termins für das Urteilsgericht durch den Magistrat,[17] wird in Kap. 91 für eine Reihe von Prozeßhandlungen und die Folgen ihrer Versäumnis

---

[13] Vgl. Fernández/Del Amo 60, 66, 97–105; auch Gonzáles 147ff. Die Lex Irnitana war bekanntlich auf 10 annähernd gleich großen, etwa 90 cm. breiten und 57 cm. hohen Bronzetafeln eingeschlagen. Die Tafeln waren in 3 Kolumnen von durchschnittlich 53 Zeilen untergliedert. Von den 10 Tafeln hat der Fund von 1981 bekanntlich 6 an den Tag gebracht, die 3., 5. und die vier letzten Tafeln 7 bis 10.

[14] Zur Kapitelfolge: Simshäuser 170, auch schon *SZ* 107 (1990), 555f.; Rodger 76ff. Zur Notwendigkeit der Vorschriften: Der Gegenstand der Vorschriften, die nicht selbst (wie die der Kap. 89 und 91) auf den stadtrömischen Prozeß verweisen, konnte nicht durch Verweisung geregelt werden. Das liegt für die Vorschriften der Kap. 84, 85, 86 auf der Hand, gilt aber, wenn ich recht sehe, auch für die der Kap. 87, 88 und 92. Die Regelung der *datio intertii* in Kap. 90 ist umso auffallender, als für die *denuntiatio intertii* in Kap. 91 auf die Prozeßpraxis in Rom verwiesen wird. Die *in ius vocatio* etwa oder das *vadimonium* sind offenbar darum völlig ausgespart, weil sie im Edikt geregelt waren. All das bedarf noch der näheren Untersuchung.

[15] J.G. Wolf, 'Iurisdictio' 29–61 m. Lit.

[16] J.G. Wolf, 'Iurisdictio' 35ff. m. Lit.; G. Zanon, *SDHI* 58 (1992), 323 A. 60.

[17] J.G. Wolf, 'Intertium' bei II. und V.

auf das stadtrömische Prozeßrecht verwiesen—auch für die *diei diffisio*. Zuletzt, in Kap. 92, werden die Tage bestimmt, an denen das Urteilsgericht nicht oder nur mit Einverständnis aller Beteiligten verhandeln darf.[18]

Die Rechtssätze dieser Kapitel sind ihrer sprachlichen Form nach ganz überwiegend Gebote oder Verbote; sie richten sich an die Duumvirn, die Urteilsrichter oder auch die Streitparteien und gebieten oder verbieten ihnen ein bestimmtes Verhalten.[19] Ausnahmen sind die Vorschriften der Kap. 84 und 91. Der Satz, aus dem Kap. 84 besteht, fordert von keiner Person ein bestimmtes Verhalten, sondern gewährt dem Duumvir (und anhangsweise auch dem Ädil) eine beschränkte Gerichtsbarkeit in Zivilsachen. Sie wird ihm für Klagen gewährt, die auf dem Territorium der Stadt Bürger und Einwohner gegeneinander anstrengen und deren Streitwert allenfalls 1000 Sesterzen beträgt, ausgenommen eine Reihe teils durch allgemeine Merkmale, teils individuell bestimmter Klagen, von denen der Duumvir einige wiederum gewähren kann, wenn beide Streitparteien es wollen.[20] Kap. 91 enthält dagegen eine Verweisungsnorm—eigentümlicherweise in zwei Versionen. Ihr wenden wir uns jetzt zu.

---

[18] Durchweg wird auch noch Kap. 93 dem Abschnitt über die Zivilgerichtsbarkeit zugerechnet. Ich bin dessen nicht mehr so sicher wie in 'Iurisdictio' 29. Entscheidend wäre, daß *inter se iure civili agere* nicht auch rechtsgeschäftliches Handeln einschließt, sondern hier nur prozessuales meint—was der Zusammenhang nahe legen könnte; vgl. etwa Gonzáles 237 und Lamberti 369.

[19] In Kap. 86 etwa wird dem Duumvir geboten, die *iudices* für die Richterliste auszuwählen, sie auf drei Kurien zu verteilen, die Liste ihrer Namen bei seinem Tribunal anzuschlagen und nur einen Listenrichter einzusetzen, es sei denn, daß die Parteien sich auf einen listenfremden Richter verständigt haben. Die Gebotsnormen sind oft zugleich Organisationsnormen, wie etwa die Anweisung, eine Richterliste zu erstellen. Eine Untersuchung der Normtechnik der Munizipalgesetze steht noch aus; sie wäre von allgemeinem Interesse.

[20] All das wird in einem einzigen Satz zum Ausdruck gebracht, der zwar grammatisch streng komponiert, mit seinen zahlreichen Ausnahmen und Gegenausnahmen aber so überladen ist, daß wohl auch der Bürger von Irni seine Mühe hatte, ihn zu verstehen. Sollte Zweck des Publikationsgebots in Kap. 95 auch Belehrung der Bürgerschaft gewesen sein, so scheiterte diese Absicht vermutlich an der weithin schwer durchschaubaren sprachlichen Form des Gesetzes.

2. Das Kap. 91 der Lex Irnitana

2.1 *Der Text*

Der Text ist durch manche Nachlässigkeit des Graveurs, gelegentlich bis zur Unverständlichkeit, entstellt.[21] In der folgenden Wiedergabe sind diese Mängel angezeigt und versuchsweise behoben.[22] Die Markierung einiger Satzteile (durch Kursivdruck) sollen der leichteren Orientierung dienen.

X A 42 R(ubrica). Quo iure intertium denuntietur, dies diffindatur diffi-
43 ‹s›susve sit, res iudicetur, lis iudici[i] damni sit, res in iudi-
44 cio esse desinat.
45 Quacumque de re priuata iudices arbitri in eo municipio da-
46 ti subditi addictiue h(ac) l(ege) erunt, *is*[23] *iudicibus arbitris et is*
47 quos inter ii iudices arbitrive dati subditi addictive
48 h(ac) l(ege) erunt, de ea re intertium aduersario iudici arbitro-
49 ve in biduo proximo denuntiandi, diem diffindendi, dies
50 diffissos[24] iurandi, antequam iudicent, iudicandi litem ae-
51 stumandi, per quos dies et ubi ex h(ac) l(ege) licebit oportebit, et si
52 neque dies diffi‹s›sus neque iudicatum fuerit, uti lis iudi-
53 ci arbitrove damni sit, et si intra it[25] tempus, quod legis Iuli-
54 ae, quae de iudici‹i›s privatis proxime lata est, kapite XII
X B 1 senatusve consultis [[. .d et kaput]][26] ad it[27] kaput legis pertinen-
2 tibus conpr‹e›hensum est, iudicatum non sit, uti res in iudi-
3 cio non sit, *siremps lex* [r itque][28] *esto* atque[29] uti esset si eam rem
4 in urbe Roma praetor p(opuli) R(omani) inter cives Romanos iudicari iussisset

---

[21] Fernández/Del Amo 65ff.

[22] Die Wiedergabe beruht auf der Transskription von Fernández (103, 105), kontrolliert an den ihr beigegebenen Abbildungen der Tafel X (102, 104), und folgt durchweg J.G. Wolf, 'Intertium' bei A. 16. Sie geht weithin mit Lamberti 362ff. überein, deren Edition auch die Konjekturen der älteren Ausgaben verzeichnet.

[23] Hier wie oft (auch am Ende der Zeile) für *iis*, vgl. Kap. 92 X B 27.

[24] DIFFISI, *aes.*

[25] Für *id.*

[26] Radiert; *e* in *et* unsicher, *i* jedoch ausgeschlossen.

[27] Für *id*, und noch einmal in Zeile X B 17.

[28] LEX·R·ITQUE·ESTO, *aes; i* in *itque* vermutlich über einem radierten Buchstaben. Vgl. Z.18: *ius esto; Lex Rubria* cap. XXI tab. II 10f. und 40f.: "siremps lex res ius caussaque . . . esto". Lamberti 364 liest statt ITQUE *etque* und verbessert in *lex resque esto.*

[29] ADQUEM, *aes.*

5 et de e(a) r(e), ex ‹quacumque›[30] lege rogatione[m] quocumque plebis scito iudicia pri-
6 vata in urbe Roma fient, agi, fieri, denuntiari, diem diffin[[den]]-[31]
7 di, diem diffi‹s›sum esse, iudicari, litem iudici damni esse, rem in
8 iudicio non esse oporteret, praeter quam quod per alios dies
9 et alio loco h(ac) l(ege) denuntiari, rem iudicari, diem diffindi opor-
10 tebit. *Itaque iis omnibus*, de ea re et in eos dies in quos ex h(ac) l(ege) lice-
11 bit, denuntiandi intra it municipium et mille passus ab eo mu-
12 nicipio, aut ubi pacti erunt, diem diffi‹n›dendi, iudicandi in foro
13 eius municipi aut ubi pacti erunt, dum intra fines eius munici-
14 pi, utique ex [h]isdem causis dies diffinda[n]tur, diffi‹s›sus sit,
15 utique, si neque diffissum[32] e lege neque iudicatum sit per quos di-
16 es quoque loco ex h(ac) l(ege) iudicari licebit oportebit, iudici arbitro
17 lis damni sit, utique, si intra it tempus quod supra conpr‹e›hensum
18 est iudicatum non sit, res in iudicio non sit.[33] *‹sirempsn› ius esto* ‹atque› uti ‹esset› si ‹eam rem in urbe Roma praetor p(opuli) R(omani) inter› cives Ro-
19 manos ‹iudicari› iussisse‹t› ibique d(e) e(a) r(e) iudicium fieri oporteret ex [lege roga-
20 tione plebisve scitis] quacumque lege rogatione quocumque
21 plebis scito iudicia ‹privata›[34] in urbe Roma fieri oportebit, praeter quam
22 quod per alios dies et alio loco ex hac lege denuntiari, rem-
23 que iudicari, diemque diffindi oportebit. Quaeque ita acta
24 erunt ea iusta rataque sunto.

2.2 *Aufbau und Struktur des Textes*

Der Text besteht aus zwei Sätzen, die beide demselben Schema folgen und nur im Einzelnen von einander abweichen. Ihr Gegenstand ist ein und dieselbe Verweisung auf das stadtrömische Prozeßrecht. Die Differenzen erschweren indessen ihr Verständnis und sind die Ursache kontroverser Erklärungen. Es empfiehlt sich darum eine aufgliedernde Darstellung des Textes, die seine Struktur anschaulich macht.[35]

---

[30] Siehe Z. 19/20: *ex . . . quacumque lege.*

[31] Radiert.

[32] Ursprünglich DIFFINSUM, vom Graveur verbessert in DIFFISSUM: die 1. Haste des N radiert, die 2. verändert in S.

[33] Das Folgende, wie Rodger 84 vorschlägt, ergänzt nach Z. 3 f. González 179 ergänzt: "‹siremps lex› ius ‹causaque› esto ‹atque› uti si ‹praetor populi Romani inter› cives Romanos ‹iudicari› iussisse‹t›"; Lamberti 364: "ius ‹resque› esto uti ‹esset› si ‹praetor populi Romani› cives Romanos iussisse‹t›".

[34] Siehe Z. 5/6: *iudicia privata.*

[35] Vgl. Rodger 84: "its structure is somewhat daunting".

Rubrica. Quo iure intertium denuntietur,
dies diffindatur diffissusve sit,
res iudicetur,
lis iudici damni sit,
res in iudicio esse desinat.

Quacumque de re priuata iudices arbitri in eo municipio dati subditi addictiue hac lege erunt, *iis iudicibus arbitrisue et iis*, quos inter ii iudices arbitriue dati subditi addictiue hac lege erunt,

de ea re

intertium aduersario iudici arbitroue in biduo proximo denuntiandi,
diem diffindendi,
dies diffissos iurandi, antequam iudicent,
iudicandi litem aestumandi, per quos dies et ubi ex hac lege licebit oportebit,

et *si* neque dies diffissus neque iudicatum fuerit,
uti lis iudici arbitroue damni sit,
et *si* intra it tempus, quod legis Iuliae, quae de iudiciis priuatis proxime lata est,
kapite XII senatusue consultis ad id kaput legis pertinentibus conprehensum est, iudicatum non sit,
uti res in iudicio non sit,

siremps lex esto
atque uti esset
si eam rem in urbe Roma praetor populi Romani inter ciues Romanos iudicari *iussisset*
et *de ea re,* ex quacumque lege rogatione quocumque plebis scito iudicia priuata in urbe Roma fient,
agi,
fieri,
denuntiari,
diem diffindi, diem diffissum esse,
iudicari,
litem iudici damni esse,
rem in iudicio non esse *oporteret,*
praeter quam quod per alios dies et alio loco hac lege
denuntiari,
rem iudicari,
diem diffindi *oportebit.*

Itaque
iis omnibus,
de ea re et in eos dies in quos ex hac lege licebit,
denuntiandi intra id municipium et mille passus ab eo municipio, aut ubi pacti erunt,
diem diffindendi,
iudicandi in foro eius municipi aut ubi pacti erunt, dum intra fines eius municipi,

utique ex isdem causis dies diffindatur, diffissus sit,

utique, *si* neque diffissum e lege neque iudicatum sit
per quos dies quoque loco ex hac lege iudicari licebit oportebit,
iudici arbitroue lis damni sit,
utique, *si* intra id tempus quod supra conprehensum est, iudicatum non sit,
res in iudicio non sit,

siremps ius esto
atque uti esset
si eam rem in urbe Roma praetor populi Romani inter ciues Romanos iudicari *iussisset*
ibique *de ea re*
iudicium fieri *oporteret*
ex quacumque lege rogatione quocumque plebis scito iudicia priuata in urbe Roma fieri oportebit,
praeter quam quod per alios dies et alio loco ex hac lege
denuntiari,
remque iudicari,
diemque diffindi *oportebit.*

Quaeque ita acta erunt ea iusta rataque sunto.

2.3 *Die beiden Versionen*

2.3.1 *Die Grundstruktur der beiden Versionen*

Für den *iudex* und die Streitparteien einer in Irni anhängigen Rechtssache soll im Verfahren *apud iudicem* gelten, was gelten würde, wenn diese Rechtssache in Rom *inter cives Romanos* anhängig wäre.[36] Das Gesetz erklärt nicht offen, daß auch in Irni gelten soll, was in Rom gilt, sondern kleidet die Verweisung in die Form einer Fiktion. Den beiden Sätzen, aus denen der Text besteht, entsprechen zwei Teile, in die das Kapitel zerfällt. Mit *itaque* (X B 10) stellt sich der zweite Teil als Nutzanwendung des ersten Teils dar. Von einer Nutzanwendung oder Folgerung kann indessen kaum die Rede sein.[37] Für dieselben prozessualen Tatbestände verweist wie der erste auch der zweite Teil auf das stadtrömische Prozeßrecht. Für das benannte

[36] Vgl. Rodger 84f.; Simshäuser 175.

[37] *Itaque* hat seine ursprüngliche Bedeutung 'und so, so auch' nie völlig verloren. Crawford bei González 198 übersetzt denn auch "and so". Ich glaube nicht, daß es hier diese Bedeutung hat; vgl. Lamberti 365: 'pertanto'. Vgl. im übrigen R. Kühner/C. Stegmann, *Ausführliche Grammatik der lateinischen Sprache. Satzlehre* (4. Aufl. 1962) II, 131.

Prozeßhandeln vom *intertium denuntiare* des Klägers bis zum *iudicare* des Richters sowie für die Folgen seiner Säumnis wird die Geltung des stadtrömischen Prozeßrechts mithin zweimal angeordnet, wird in zwei Versionen seine Geltung auch in Irni vorgeschrieben.

2.3.2 *Abweichungen ohne sachliche Bedeutung*

Die Abweichungen im Einzelnen sind allerdings vielfältig. Zweimal werden umständliche Definitionen des ersten Teils durch zusammenfassende Begriffe raumsparend ersetzt: durch "iis omnibus" (X B 10) die einleitende Definition der Betroffenen "quacumque de re priuata iudices arbitri in eo municipio dati subditi addictiue hac lege erunt, iis iudicibus arbitris et iis quos inter ii iudices arbitrive dati subditi addictive hac lege erunt" (X A 45–48); und durch "iudicium fieri" (X B 19) kurz und bündig die spezifizierende Liste "agi, fieri, denuntiari, diem diffindi, diem diffissum esse, iudicari, litem iudici damni esse, rem in iudicio non esse" (X B 6–8). Die Klausel "id tempus quod supra conprehensum est" im dritten *utique*-Satz der zweiten Version (X B 17/18) nimmt auf die erste Version ausdrücklich Bezug, obwohl dort die Frist auch nicht genannt, sondern wiederum auf die *Lex Iulia de iudiciis privatis* verwiesen wird (X A 53—X B 2). Diese Abweichungen sind indessen ohne sachlichen Belang. Sie beweisen aber, daß der zweite Teil dem ersten nachgeschrieben worden ist, und schließen gleichzeitig aus, daß er ihn ersetzen sollte. Sonst übrigens hätte auch bei *denuntiandi* (X B 11) nicht *intertium* ausgespart werden können, dessen Ergänzung nur aus dem ersten Teil möglich ist. Bemerkenswert bleibt, daß mit "iudicium fieri" (X B 19) gegen das traditionelle Prinzip der Deutlichkeit von den einzelnen erforderlichen oder möglichen Prozeßhandlungen im Verfahren *apud iudicem* abstrahiert wird—vermutlich aber auch nur darum, weil sie in der ersten Version einzeln aufgelistet sind. Ohne sachliche Bedeutung sind auch die Umstellungen in den bedingten Konsekutivsätzen. Statt "et si neque dies diffissus neque iudicatum fuerit, uti lis iudici arbitrove damni sit" (X A 51–53) bevorzugt der zweite Teil "utique si neque si neque diffissum . . . neque iudicatum sit . . . iudici arbitrove lis damni sit" (X B 15–17). Diese invertierte Wortstellung rückt mit *utique* die Rechtsfolge an die ausgezeichnetste Stelle des Konsekutivsatzes und die Bedingung an die mittlere unbedeutendere.

2.3.3 *Zusätzliche Vorschriften in der zweiten Version*
Anders die Zusätze zum *intertium denuntiare* des Klägers und zum *iudicare* des Richters. Während die erste Version "intertium adversario iudici arbitrove in biduo proximo denuntiandi" hat (X A 48/49), heißt es in der zweiten "denuntiandi intra id municipium et mille passus ab eo municipio aut ubi pacti erunt" (X B 1/12); und während dort "iudicandi litem aestumandi per quos dies et ubi ex hac lege licebit oportebit" steht (X A 50/51), hat die zweite Version "iudicandi in foro eius municipi aut ubi pacti erunt dum intra fines municipi" (X B 12–14).

Kap. 90 handelt *de intertium dando*, von der Erteilung eines Termins für das Urteilsgericht durch den Magistrat. Hier, in Kap. 91, lesen wir in der ersten Version, daß der Kläger das ihm erteilte *intertium* Urteilsrichter und Prozeßgegner *in biduo proximo* anzeigen muß. Für diesen Tatbestand sollen dieselben Regeln gelten, die in Rom für die *denuntiatio intertii* gelten. Die Mitteilung der näheren Umstände war überflüssig, wenn auch im stadtrömischen Prozeß der Gerichtstag dem Urteilsrichter und dem Prozeßgegner *in biduo proximo* angezeigt werden mußte. Gleichwohl wird man nicht ohne weiteres den Gegenschluß ziehen—auch wenn die zweite Version ihn nahe legt. Hier nämlich ist nicht von Urteilsrichter und Prozeßgegner und Befristung die Rede, hier vielmehr lesen wir, wo die *denuntiatio* erfolgen muß: am vereinbarten Orte, in Irni selbst oder im Umkreis der Stadt, innerhalb der ersten Meile. Auch wenn in Rom Entsprechendes galt,[38] konnte diese Beschränkung nicht durch Verweisung geregelt werden.[39] Mit der Ortsbestimmung, die das Munizipalgesetz nur hier trifft, ist demnach in die Verweisungsnorm eine Gebotsvorschrift eingefügt.

Sie ist keineswegs die einzige. Dasselbe nämlich haben wir beim *iudicare* des Urteilsrichters. Hier wird in der zweiten Version bestimmt, wo er urteilen und erkennen muß: auf dem Forum von Irni oder an vereinbartem Ort, allerdings auf Gemeindegebiet. Auch diese Beschränkung konnte nicht durch Verweisung auf die stadtrömische Praxis geregelt werden, und auch sie trifft das Munizipalgesetz nur hier. Mit dieser Ortsbestimmung wird die erste Version insofern korrigiert, als die Klausel ". . . et ubi ex hac lege licebit oportebit (sc.

---

[38] Entsprechendes galt bekanntlich für die Begrenzung der Amtsführung *domi*. Vgl. auch Gai. 4. 104.

[39] Darum werden von den für anwendbar erklärten stadtrömischen Rechtsregeln auch die über Zeit und Ort in beiden Versionen ausgenommen: "praeter quam quod" etc. (X B 8–10 und 21–23).

iudicare litem aestumare)" ins Leere ging. Auf die erste Hälfte dieses Zusatzes, "per quos dies . . . ex hac lege licebit oportebit" (X A 51), antwortet dagegen Kap. 92. Dieser Verweis findet sich denn auch in der zweiten Version wieder: dem Katalog der Prozeßhandlungen vorangestellt (X B 10/11: "de ea re et in eos dies in quos ex hac lege licebit"), gilt er hier nicht mehr nur für das *iudicare*,[40] sondern auch für das *intertium denuntiare*[41] und *diem diffindere*.[42]

Diese Änderungen gegenüber dem ersten Teil folgen unverkennbar einem einheitlichen Konzept. Offenbar ging es vor allem um die Ortsbestimmung für die *denuntiatio intertii* und das Urteilsgericht. Konnten wir schon feststellen, daß die zweite Version der ersten nachgeschrieben ist, und ausschließen, daß sie die erste ersetzen sollte, so sehen wir jetzt auch ihren Anlaß: die Einfügung dieser Ortsbestimmungen und vielleicht auch der Kalendervorschrift (X B 10/11).[43] Damit stellt sich die zweite Version als Ergänzung der ersten dar.[44] Statt die Verweisungsnorm mit den Ortsbestimmungen und der Kalendervorschrift aufzufüllen, zog man es vor, die Verweisungsnorm zu verdoppeln und die neuen Vorschriften in die zweite Version einzurücken. Die Verdoppelung selbst war unschädlich, und offenbar wurde sie auch nicht als irritierend empfunden. Sie bot zugleich Gelegenheit, die beiden *utique*-Sätze leicht und rhetorisch wirkungsvoll abzuändern und einen dritten Konsekutivsatz (X B 14) hinzuzufügen. Andererseits konnte das Simile als lediglich der Ergänzung dienendes Doppel durch Zusammenfassung umfangreicher Definitionen und Listen, leicht zu ergänzender oder unschädlicher Auslassungen sowie direkter Verweise auf die erste Version spürbar verkürzt werden. Schließlich ist zu vermuten, daß die zweite Version nicht gleichzeitig mit der ersten entstanden, sondern später hinzugefügt worden

---

[40] Für *iudicia* vorgesehen sind in Irni alle Tage, für die das Gesetz Urteilsgerichte nicht untersagt. Die Tage, die es mit und ohne Vorbehalt für Urteilsgerichte ausschließt, bestimmt es in Kap. 92; dazu J.G. Wolf, 'Intertium' nach A. 100.

[41] In Kap. 92 X B 46–50 verbietet die Irnitana, dem Prozeßgegner und dem Urteilsrichter das *intertium* auf einen Ferialtag (mit der üblichen Ausnahme) anzuzeigen; dazu J.G. Wolf, 'Intertium' bei A. 126 und nach A. 141. Rodger 85 bezieht die Klausel "in eos dies in quos ex hac lege licebit" nur auf *denuntiandi*. Indessen lautet der Text "de ea re et in eos dies", etc.

[42] Es versteht sich, daß auch die Fortsetzung des Gerichtstages nur für einen Kalendertag angesetzt werden konnte, der für *iudicia* vorgesehen war, vgl. A. 40 und 41.

[43] Die Fiktionsklauseln "siremps lex/ius esto atque uti esset" (X B 3 und 18) sind beide schlecht erhalten und liefern darum kein Kriterium, vgl. oben A. 27 und 32.

[44] Zutreffend schon Rodger 85: "both parts of the chapter must be read cumulatively".

ist. Wenn diese Beobachtungen zutreffen, wäre in der *Lex Irnitana* auch eine zweite Textschicht identifiziert.[45]

2.4 *Die syntaktische Stellung der Konsekutivsätze*

Inhalt der Konsekutivsätze (eingeleitet mit *et*... *uti* im ersten, mit *utique* im zweiten Teil) sind Folgerungen aus der Verweisung "siremps lex/ius esto atque uti esset", etc. Konsekutive Nebensätze werden dem Hauptsatz, aus dem sich die Folgerung ergibt, regelmäßig nachgestellt. In unseren Verweisungsvorschriften stehen sie vor dem Hauptsatz. Vermutlich soll ihre Bedeutsamkeit hervorgehoben werden, der die logische Stellung der Konsekutivsätze nach der Fiktion und der Ausnahme ("praeter quam quod... oportebit") allerdings nicht gerecht würde.

2.5 *Zwischenergebnis*

Als ein Zwischenergebnis können wir zusammenfassen: Kap. 91 verweist für das Verfahren *apud iudicem* auf das stadtrömische Prozeßrecht. Die Verweisung in der Form der Fiktion geschieht in zwei strukturell gleichen und weithin auch gleichlautenden Versionen, die zwar nur im Einzelnen, aber vielfach von einander abweichen. Die beiden Versionen widersprechen sich nicht; die zweite, zweckmäßig verkürzte Version ist vielmehr als ergänzendes Doppel nachträglich der ersten hinzugefügt worden. Anlaß dieser eigentümlichen Überarbeitung der Verweisungsnorm war die Einfügung neuer Detailvorschriften. In beiden Versionen sind die konsekutiven Nebensätze mit den Folgerungen aus der Verweisung der Verweisung selbst vorangestellt sind.

3. Die Vertagung durch den Urteilsrichter

3.1 *Vorbemerkung*

Nach den Angaben der Rubrik verfügt Kap. 91: "nach welchen Rechtsvorschriften das *intertium* angezeigt werden soll, der Gerichtstag zerteilt werden soll oder zerteilt worden sein soll, die Streitsache

[45] Die Rede ist nicht von einer zweiten Textschicht der Irnitana, weil vorerst nicht auszuschließen ist, daß die Bearbeitung auf die Verweisungsnorm beschränkt und auch vor der Herstellung der Irnitana erfolgt ist. Zu einem vermutlich jüngeren Zusatz in der ersten Version s. unten bei A. 60, und zur Vermutung einer zweiten Textschicht in Kap. 84 J.G. Wolf, 'Iurisdictio' 32 A. 28 und 52 f. unter VI.3.

entschieden werden soll, der Prozeß dem Richter zum Schaden und die Streitsache nicht mehr Gegenstand des Prozesses sein soll" (X A 42–4). Die Vorschriften, auf die verwiesen wird, gelten nur für den *iudex*[46] und die Streitparteien: "is iudicibus arbitris et is quos inter ii iudices arbitrive dati erunt . . . lex esto" (X A 46–8 / X B 3) sowie "iis omnibus . . . ius esto" (X B 10/18). Das *intertium denuntiare* obliegt dem Kläger,[47] das *iudicare* dem *iudex*; und wie Gellius berichtet und der Papyrus bekräftigt,[48] ist auch die allfällige Vertagung des Verfahrens seine Sache.[49] Das schließt nicht aus, daß die Verweisung auch für die Vertagung *ipsa lege* gilt; denn die Klausel *diem diffindendi* deckt auch diesen Modus der *diei diffissio*.[50] Da jedenfalls für die Vertagung durch den *iudex* auf das stadtrömische Prozeßrecht verwiesen wird,[51] versuchen wir zunächst, die Verweisungsnorm unter dieser Voraussetzung unserem Verständnis zu erschließen.

3.2 Diffindi *und* diffissus esse

Im Programm der Rubrik sind *dies diffindatur* und *diffissus sit* durch enklitisches *-ve* disjunktiv miteinander verbunden.[52] Darum ist anzunehmen, daß auch die asyndetisch nebeneinander gestellten Satzteile *diem diffindi diem diffissum esse* (in der ersten Version, im Katalog des Bedingungssatzes der Fiktion: X B 6/7), und *dies diffindatur diffissus sit* (in der zweiten Version, im ersten *utique*-Satz: X B 14), im selben

[46] Und das heißt auch: nur für den Einzelrichter; für Verfahren vor Rekuperatoren gilt die Verweisungsnorm nicht; vgl. Rodger 84; auch Simshäuser 198ff.—Der Einfachheit halber vernachlässigen wir den *arbiter* und sprechen immer nur vom *iudex*.

[47] J.G. Wolf, 'Intertium' nach A. 141.

[48] Siehe oben A. 8 und 9.

[49] Darüber besteht nahezu Einigkeit. Nach Giménez Candela wurde die *diffissio* vom *iudex* 'betrieben' (39), mußte aber vom Magistrat 'bestätigt' (35) werden. Zutreffend in seiner Rez. schon Burdese, *SDHI* 57 (1991), 451. Unklar Kaser/Hackl 356f., 358. Nicht eindeutig auch González 235 zu Zeile 50/51: "*diem diffindere* no doubt refers to postponement by agreement, *dies diffissos iurare* to the invocation of one of the reasons which actually entitled a party to a postponement"; vermutlich aber geht er von der Zuständigkeit des Richters aus, vgl. Rodger 86.

[50] Die "distinzione tra diffissio, operante ope legis, e diffissio che richiedeva un intervento del iudice", klar getroffen von G. Zanon, *SDHI* 58 (1992), 317 A. 38, und A. Burdese, *SDHI* 57 (1991), 451f., wird weithin vernachlässigt, vgl. nur Kaser/Hackl 116, 356ff.

[51] A. Burdese, *SDHI* 57 (1991), 452.

[52] Daß die Partikel *-ve* nur kopulative Bedeutung hat, ist nach dem Zusammenhang auszuschließen, ebenso daß *-ve* für *-que* steht; vgl. Crawford bei González 197; Lamberti 363 vernachlässigt *diffissus sit.* Zum willkürlichen Austausch von *-ve* und *-que* vgl. M.W. Frederiksen, 'The Republican Municipal Laws: Errors and Drafts', *JRS* 55 (1965), 188 mit Hinweis auf Paul *Dig.* 50.60.63pr. und weit. Lit. in A. 32.

Verhältnis miteinander verbunden und demnach Paare sind.[53] Wir entnehmen also der Rubrik, daß Kap. 91 bestimmt, nach welchen Rechtsvorschriften

vertagt werden soll oder
vertagt worden sein soll;

der ersten Version unserer Norm, daß in Irni die Gesetzeslage ebenso sein soll, wie sie wäre, wenn der Prozeß in Rom stattfände und in diesem Prozeß

vertagt werden müßte oder
vertagt worden sein müßte;

und dem ersten Konsekutivsatz der zweiten Version, daß infolgedessen in Irni aus denselben Gründen wie in Rom

vertagt wird oder
vertagt worden ist.

Wenn der Urteilsrichter den *dies iudicii* 'zerteilt', ist der Gerichtstag im Rückblick, im Zeitpunkt seiner Fortsetzung 'zerteilt worden'. Das stadtrömische Prozeßrecht sah für beide Phasen, für die Vertagung selbst wie für die Fortsetzung der Verhandlung Regeln vor.[54] Auf diese Regeln wird in beiden Versionen gleichlautend *diem diffindendi* verwiesen: "im Hinblick auf die Zerteilung des Gerichtstages", oder mit einem bürokratischen Ausdruck: "betreffs Vertagung" (X A 49 und X B 12). Die Beschreibung der Prozeßhandlung, für die auf das stadtrömische Recht verwiesen wird, differenziert mithin nicht wie die Regelung, auf die verwiesen wird, zwischen der *diei diffissio* und der Fortsetzung des *dies iudicii* in einem neuen Termin, sondern begreift mit *diem diffindere* den gesamten Regelungskomplex.

---

[53] Disjunktive Konjunktionen werden eher selten weggelassen, doch fehlt es nicht an Beispielen, auch nicht in unserem Text: *iudices arbitri/arbitrive*: X A 45–49, 52/53, X B 16. Vgl. Kühner/Stegmann (o. A. 37) II 152, auch W. Kalb, *Das Juristenlatein* (2. Aufl. 1888, Neudr. 1961) 37 A. 1 i. f. (38), dessen Erklärung auf unseren Fall allerdings nicht zutrifft.

[54] A. Burdese, *SDHI* 57 (1991), 452, vermutet dagegen, daß *dies diffindatur* auf die Vertagung durch den *iudex* und *dies diffissus sit* auf die Vertagung *ipso iure* gemünzt sei. Indessen mußte der Urteilsrichter *dies diffissos iurare* und nach Burdese selbst diesen Schwur nur dann leisten, wenn er selbst vertagt hatte. Ähnlich erklärt Metzger 144ff. *diem diffindere* als 'prospective adjournment', *dies diffissos iurare* als 'retrospective adjournment': der Eid sei nur erforderlich gewesen bei unvorhergesehener, und das heißt ja wohl *ipsa lege* eintretender *diei diffissio*.

3.3 *Der Eid und die stadtrömischen Vorschriften*

Die stadtrömischen Vorschriften sind anzuwenden, wenn der Gerichtstag 'zerteilt wird', und sie sind anzuwenden, wenn der Gerichtstag 'zerteilt worden ist'. Daß die Vertagung durch den *iudex* geregelt werden mußte, versteht sich. Was aber blieb noch zu regeln, wenn der *iudex* das Urteilsgericht vertagt hatte? Unsere Verweisungsnorm hält selbst die Antwort bereit: Hatte der Urteilsrichter den Gerichtstag 'zerteilt', dann mußte er nach der Unterbrechung, wenn der 'zerteilte' Gerichtstag am folgenden oder an einem späteren Kalendertag fortgesetzt wurde, beeiden, daß der Gerichtstag 'zerteilt' worden war. Das ist im Folgenden auszuführen.

Während in der zweiten Version unserer Verweisungsnorm für die drei Tatbestände "intertium denuntiare, diem diffindere, iudicare" (X B 11–14) auf die stadtrömischen Vorschriften verwiesen wird, sind es in der ersten Version vier: "intertium denuntiare, diem diffindere, dies diffissos iurare, iudicare" (X A 48–51). Von dem Eid, "daß der Tag zerteilt worden ist", hören wir hier zum ersten Mal. Wer ihn leistet, sagt das Gesetz nicht—so wie es auch nicht sagt, wer das *intertium* anzeigt oder den Tag 'zerteilt'. Indessen wird der Eid geschworen, 'bevor sie urteilen': "dies diffissos iurandi, antequam iudicent" (A X 49/50). Danach können auch nur sie, die Urteilsrichter, es sein, die den Eid leisten.[55] Auch der Zeitpunkt des Eides läßt sich erschließen: Schwört der *iudex* den Eid, bevor er urteilt, und nimmt er auf seinen Eid, daß der Gerichtstag geteilt worden ist, dann leistete er ihn offenbar nach der Unterbrechung, in der wieder aufgenommenen Verhandlung.[56]

Den vier Tatbeständen "intertium denuntiandi, diem diffindendi, dies diffissos iurandi, iudicandi litem aestumandi" (X A 48–51) antworten im Katalog der Fiktion "denuntiari, diem diffindi, diem diffissum esse, iudicari" (X B 6/7). Während dort auf *diem diffindendi, dies diffissos iurandi* folgt, folgt hier auf *diem diffindi, diem diffissum esse.*

---

[55] Auch darüber besteht Einigkeit: D'Ors 45; Rodger 86f.; Lamberti 194 und schon *Labeo* 36 (1990), 254; Metzger 144 A. 4.

[56] Rodger 86f.; Metzger 145. Anders D'Ors 44f.: die *diffissio* sei in zwei Schritten erfolgt; zunächst habe der *iudex* die Verhandlung vertagt und dann, in einem zweiten Akt, aber noch vor der Unterbrechung, den Grund der Vertagung beschworen, die erst damit wirksam geworden sei. Wieder anders F. Lamberti, *Labeo* 36 (1990), 254: der Schwur sei ein promissorischer Eid gewesen, mit dem der *iudex* bei der Vertagung versprochen habe, zu dem von ihm festgesetzten Zeitpunkt wieder zu erscheinen.

Bei *denuntiari* ist *intertium* ausgespart,[57] weil dessen Ergänzung nicht zweifelhaft sein konnte. Sowenig aber *denuntiari* statt *intertium* hätte ausgespart werden können, sowenig kann *iurari* bei *diem diffissum esse* ausgespart worden sein.[58] Bleibt es danach bei *diem diffissum esse,* so dürfen wir vermuten, daß die stadtrömischen Vorschriften, die Anwendung fanden, wenn der Gerichtstag "zerteilt worden war", den Eid regelten, mit dem der *iudex* beschwor, "daß der Gerichtstag zerteilt worden ist".

3.4 *Die* dies diffissos iurandi-*Klausel: ein späterer Zusatz*

Vergleichen wir jetzt die beiden Tatbestandslisten, für die auf das stadtrömische Recht verwiesen wird, so ist nicht mehr zu übersehen, daß in der ersten Version die Klausel "dies diffissos iurandi, antequam iudicent" (X A 49/50) durch zweierlei aus dem Rahmen fällt: durch den Plural und das subjektlose *antequam iudicent. Dies diffissos iurandi* ist ein schwerer Stilbruch, besonders hart nach *diem diffindendi*, durch nichts gerechtfertigt und im ganzen Kapitel ohne Parallele.[59] Das Subjekt *iudices* ist zwar ohne weiteres zu ergänzen, seine Auslassung gleichwohl ebenso irritierend wie das aktivische Prädikat. Nach ihrer sprachlichen Form ist die Klausel ein Fremdkörper im Text der Verweisungsnorm; neben *diem diffindendi* ist sie auch nicht erforderlich. Vermutlich ist sie ein späterer, für uns allerdings höchst aufschlußreicher Zusatz.[60] Durch ihn ist uns der Eid bekannt und die Verweisungsnorm verständlicher geworden.

3.5 *Eidesthema und Vertagungsgründe*

Nach der Unterbrechung der Verhandlung, in der Fortsetzung des Gerichtstages, bevor er das Urteil fällte, beschwor der *iudex*, daß der Gerichtstag 'zerteilt' worden ist. 'Zerteilt', das heißt: 'wirksam zerteilt'.

---

[57] Wie auch X B 11 bei *denuntiandi* und X B 22 bei *denuntiari*.

[58] Anders allerdings Metzger 143ff.; er glaubt darum, daß die Klauselpaare durchgehend die Alternative "dividing or swearing" beschrieben.

[59] Ich sehe auch keine andere Nachlässigkeit dieser Art. Darum ist es unwahrscheinlich, daß diese "inelegant mingling of singular and plural" bei der Abfassung des Kapitels unterlaufen ist; zur 'Vermischung' von Singular und Plural in den republikanischen Munizipalgesetzen vgl. Frederiksen (o. A. 52) 192 bei A. 51.

[60] Er ist vermutlich jünger als die zweite Version unserer Verweisungsnorm, die dann nicht erst bei der Herstellung der Irnitana angefertigt worden sein kann; vgl. o. A. 45.

Die *diffissio* war wirksam und der Gerichtstag 'zerteilt', wenn die Vertagung aus anerkanntem Grunde erfolgt war. Der *iudex* nahm mithin auf seinen Eid, daß er die *diffissio* verfügt hatte, daß er sie aus gutem Grunde verfügt hatte und daß dieser Grund wirklich gegeben war.[61]

Den beiden ersten *utique*-Sätzen der zweiten Version entnehmen wir, daß es mehrere Gründe gab (X B 14) und diese Gründe in einem Gesetz aufgeführt waren (X B 15).[62] Das Gesetz war mit aller Wahrscheinlichkeit die *Lex Iulia iudiciorum privatorum*;[63] die Vertagungsgründe, die sie anerkannte, sind uns dagegen nicht überliefert. *Morbus sonticus* sowie *status dies cum hoste* sind von ihnen zu unterscheiden;[64] hinderten sie den Urteilsrichter oder eine Streitpartei, im angezeigten Termin zu erscheinen, war der Gerichtstag *ipso iure* 'zerteilt'.[65] Die XII Tafeln räumten dem Urteilsgericht nur einen Tag ein; konnte bis Sonnenuntergang das Urteil nicht gesprochen werden, mußte der Gerichtstag 'zerteilt' werden, wenn es überhaupt noch sollte gesprochen werden können.[66] In der späten Republik war es zur Gewohnheit geworden, die Verhandlung auf einen zweiten und dritten Termin auszudehnen.[67] Als Cicero *pro Caecina* plädierte, hatten die Rekuperatoren "wegen der unklaren und zweifelhaften Rechtslage" schon zweimal zu urteilen gezögert;[68] und zweihundert Jahre später vertagt Gellius gegen den Rat von Freunden und Experten das Urteilsgericht, weil er Bedenken hat, nach der Beweislage zu entscheiden.[69] Ein Grund, das Urteilsgericht zu vertagen, und sicher auch der am häufigsten bemühte Grund, muß danach die Überzeugung des Urteilsrichters gewesen sein, daß der Rechtsstreit noch nicht entscheidungsreif

[61] Rodger 86f.; A. Burdese, *SDHI* 57 (1991), 451, 452; G. Zanon, *SDHI* 58 (1992), 317 A. 38. Anders F. Lamberti, *Labeo* 36 (1990), 254, vgl. oben A. 56.

[62] *'E lege'* ist gegenüber der ersten Version ein Zusatz.

[63] Aus der sich Gellius (*N.A.* 14.2.1) über *dierum diffissiones* belehrte (siehe o. bei A. 7) und die in unserer Überweisungsnorm für die Befristung des Urteilsgerichts angeführt wird (X A 53/54); vgl. unten bei A. 75 und vor allem D. Johnston, 'Three Thoughts on Roman Private Law and the Lex Irnitana', *JRS* 77 (1987), 62–3; außerdem Metzger 98; Kaser/Hackl 357.

[64] Was häufig nicht geschieht, vgl. nur Metzger 94ff. oder Kaser/Hackl 356f.

[65] S. oben A. 2 und unten bei A. 99.

[66] Vgl. unten nach A. 75.

[67] Worüber Cic. *Caec.* 4–7, vermutlich aus taktischen Gründen, beredte Klage führt. Vgl. Bethmann-Hollweg II 591.

[68] Cic. *Caec.* 6, stellt es freilich so dar, als wäre gerade nicht die "unklare und zweifelhafte Rechtslage" Anlaß der Vertagungen gewesen.

[69] *N.A.* 14.2.11.

war[70]—weil etwa geschwätzige Einlassungen der Parteien und überlange Plädoyers den Tag erschöpften.[71]

3.6 *Si neque diffissum neque iudicatum sit*

3.6.1 *Die Haftung des Urteilsrichters*

Der Richter, der weder vertagte noch urteilte, hängte sich den Prozeß selbst an: er haftete dem Kläger auf Schadensersatz.[72] Wir kennen diese Vorschrift schon aus dem Pomponius-Zitat des Papyrus Antinoopolis 1.22; es lautet (recto, col. ii):[73]

5 . . . . Item Pomp(onius) scr(ibit), si fal-
6 so t(utore) a(uctore) m(inus)[74] fuerit diffisus
7 dies, ed(ictum) q(ui)d(em) cessare, et iudi-
8 cem, q(ui)a neq(ue) diffidit neq(ue)
8 s(ententi)am dixit, litem suam fe-
9 [cisse videri].

Die Ähnlichkeit mit Formulierungen der Irnitana ("dies diffissus fuerit; neque . . . neque": X A 52 und X B 15) läßt vermuten, daß beide Texte dieselbe Quelle zitieren, was dann wieder nur die *Lex Iulia iudiciorum privatorum* gewesen sein kann.[75]

---

[70] Donat. ad Terent. *Eun.* 331 (= 2.3.39) "'liquet': Et est verbum iuris quo utebantur iudices, cum amplius pronuntiabant". Sen. *Epist.* 65.15: "Aut fer sententiam aut, quod facilius in eiusmodi rebus est, nega tibi liquere et nos reverti iube" (wenn *reverti* nicht 'umkehren, weggehen' bedeutet).

[71] Anschaulich Cic. *Quinct.* 34: "(Hortensius) a me postulat ne dicendo tempus absumam, queritur priore patrono causam defendente numquam perorari potuisse"; *Tull.* 6: "Unum hoc abs te . . . pervelim impetrare . . . ut ita tibi multum temporis ad dicendum sumas ut his aliquid ad iudicandum relinquas. Namque antea non defensionis tuae modus, sed nox tibi finem dicendi fecit."

[72] Weil das Urteil nicht mehr gesprochen werden konnte und damit die allfällige Verurteilung des Beklagten ausgeschlossen war; vgl. insb. A. Burdese, *SDHI* 57 (1991), 453; Giménez Candela 41ff.; Kaser/Hackl 196 m. weit. Lit.

[73] In der Transskription des Herausgebers C.H. Roberts, *The Antinoopolis Papyri* I (1950), 50, der T. Giménez Candela, 'Una Revision de Pap. Ant. 22', *FS D'Ors* (1987), I 562, fast uneingeschränkt zustimmt. Zur Entscheidung des Pomponius s. F. de Zulueta bei Roberts 48f.; Giménez Candela, FS D'Ors (1987), I 565ff., insb. 569f. m. weit. Lit.; Lamberti 194f. und *Labeo* 36 (1990), 228ff.; Metzger 129ff.

[74] Giménez Candela; anders Roberts: *m(ale)*.

[75] Auch wenn sie die Rechtsfolge unterschiedlich beschreiben: mit "uti lis iudici . . . damni sit" die Irnitana, mit "iudicem . . . litem suam fecisse videri" der Papyrus; vgl. A. Burdese, *SDHI* 57 (1991), 453; Simshäuser 177.

3.6.2 *Der Endtermin für Urteil und Vertagung*

Die Haftungsvorschrift setzt für Urteil und Vertagung einen gemeinsamen Endtermin voraus:[76] War bis zu diesem Zeitpunkt weder das Urteil gesprochen noch der Gerichtstag 'zerteilt' worden, konnte das Urteil nicht mehr gesprochen werden. Der Zeitpunkt war notorisch. Er war so selbstverständlich, daß er nicht mehr eigens erwähnt wurde. Weder nennt ihn die Irnitana, noch nennt Pomponius ihn.

Seit den XII Tafeln war dieser 'äußerste Zeitpunkt' der Sonnenuntergang. Cicero bezeugt uns die Fortgeltung dieser Regel in der ausgehenden Republik,[77] und wenn sie für den klassischen Formularprozeß in Zweifel gezogen wurde,[78] so liefern inzwischen Pomponius-Zitat und Irnitana mit der Sanktionsnorm ein fast zwingendes Indiz. Die neuen Quellen waren allerdings auch Anlaß, die Regel überhaupt zu leugnen und ein anderes Verständnis des Zwölftafelsatzes vorzuschlagen. Mitsamt seinem Kontext lautet er:

> XII Tafeln 1.6–9[79]
> (6) Rem ubi pacunt ora‹n›to. Ni pacunt, in comitio aut in foro. (7) Ante meridiem caussam coiciunto. Com peroranto ambo praesentes. (8) Post meridiem praesenti litem addicito. (9) Si ambo praesentes, sol occasus suprema tempestas esto.

Während der Tag des Urteilsgerichts durch die *comperendinatio*, später durch die *datio intertii* festgelegt wurde,[80] regelten diese Sätze Ort und zeitlichen Ablauf der Verhandlung.[81] Die Vorschriften können etwa übersetzt werden: "Sie (die Streitparteien) sollen die Streitsache an dem Ort verhandeln, den sie vereinbaren. Treffen sie keine Vereinbarung, auf dem Komitium oder dem Forum. (7) Vor der Mittagsstunde sollen sie den Streitfall vortragen. Sie sollen miteinander streitig

[76] Gewunden Kaser/Hackl 357f.

[77] S. oben A. 68.

[78] F.L. v. Keller, *Der römische Civilprozess und die Actionen* (6. Ausg. 1883), 337f.

[79] Der konventionellen Ordnung dieser Sätze (Bruns[7] 19; *Roman Statutes* II 594) ist der Vorschlag G. Nicosias, *Il processo privato romano, II. La regolamentazione decemvirale* (1986) vorzuziehen.; vgl. J.G. Wolf, 'Die *manumissio vindicta* und der Freiheitsprozeß. Ein Rekonstruktionsversuch', in O. Behrends/M. Diesselhorst (Hrsg.), *Libertas. Grundrechtliche und rechtsstaatliche Gewährungen in Antike und Gegenwart* (1991) 88/89 A. 118; dort auch zu *ora‹n›to* in l. 6; zu *sol occasus* G. Radke, *Archaisches Latein* (1981), 131, 133.

[80] Zu *intertium* und *comperendinatio* vgl. J.G. Wolf, 'Intertium' nach A. 175.

[81] Die heute vielleicht noch überwiegende Meinung bezieht wegen *litem addicito* in 1.8 die Sätze auf das noch ungeteilte Verfahren vor dem Magistrat, vgl. J.G. Wolf (o. A. 79) 88/89 A. 118.

verhandeln bei Anwesenheit beider. (8) Nach der Mittagsstunde soll er (der Urteilsrichter) dem Anwesenden den Rechtsstreit zusprechen. (9) Wenn beide anwesend sind, soll der Sonnenuntergang der äußerste Zeitpunkt sein."[82] Wie *tempus* ist auch *tempestas* sowohl 'Zeitpunkt' wie 'Zeitabschnitt'. Im Zwölftafelsatz 1.9 ist *suprema tempestas* immer und zu Recht als Zeitpunkt verstanden worden: als der Zeitpunkt, bis zu dem das Urteil gesprochen sein mußte.

3.6.3 *Die* suprema tempestas: *ein Zeitpunkt*

Gegen diese Interpretation hat jüngst Ernest Metzger den Nachweis versucht,[83] daß die *suprema tempestas* kein Zeitpunkt, sondern vielmehr ein Zeitabschnitt, eine Tageszeit sei. Sie sei nicht der 'äußerste Zeitpunkt' für das Urteil, sondern vielmehr die 'letzte Tageszeit', zu der noch verhandelt werden könne. Der Satz verbiete, die Verhandlung in die Nacht hinein fortzusetzen. Aus diesem Grunde habe die Verhandlung bei Sonnenuntergang vertagt werden müssen.[84] Vielleicht sei die Vertagung bei Sonnenuntergang sogar ohne weiteres eingetreten und habe vom *iudex* nur verfügt werden müssen, wenn er vor Sonnenuntergang vertagen wollte. Dabei sei er, jedenfalls im späteren Formularprozeß, und obwohl auch das klassische Recht Vertagungsgründe vorsah, nicht an sie gebunden gewesen. Wie die *suprema tempestas* nicht der 'äußerste Zeitpunkt' für das Urteil, so sei die *diei diffissio* auch nicht die fiktive Zerteilung des Gerichtstages, sondern einfach die Unterbrechung der Verhandlung zur Fortsetzung am nächsten oder einem späteren Kalendertag. Eine dem *dies diffissus* ähnliche Erscheinung, die auch seine Bezeichnung erklären könne, sei der *dies intercisus* des Festkalenders, dessen erste und letzte Stunde der profanen Verwendung entzogen waren. Schließlich: die *diffissio* sei nicht nur *diffissio*, mit ihr vielmehr stets die Verfügung eines neuen Termins verbunden gewesen. Erst sie erkläre die Haftung des Urteilsrichters, "si neque dies diffissus neque iudicatum fuerit". Habe er nämlich versäumt, einen neuen Termin zu bestimmen, so sei nicht vertagt, und weil er auch nur in einem neuen Termin hätte urteilen

---

[82] Für *litem addicere*, wie sich aus dem Zusammenhang ergibt. Unrichtig Metzger 109: ". . . sunset shall be the latest time for proceeding".

[83] Metzger 91ff.

[84] Metzger 113: "If 'latest time of day' is the correct meaning of *suprema tempestas*, then table 1.9 is not limiting trials to one day's duration, but imposing the less rigorous rule that trials should not take place at night, that they must adjourn at sunset."

können, also auch nicht geurteilt worden.[85] Mit dieser Hypothese verschafft sich Metzger den Endtermin, den die Haftungsvorschrift voraussetzt, kompensiert er mithin seine Interpretation der *suprema tempestas* als 'letzte Tageszeit'.[86]

Gegen den Beifall der Kritik[87] halte ich Metzgers Abhandlung jedenfalls in diesem Punkte für verfehlt. Er argumentiert,[88] daß in drei der fünf Texte,[89] die den Zwölftafelsatz zitieren, nach dem Verständnis des Autors *suprema tempestas* die 'letzte Tageszeit' sei.[90] Das ist richtig und besonders deutlich bei Censorinus, dem Grammatiker des 3. Jhs. n. Chr. Nach seiner Darstellung war *suprema* der letzte Tagesabschnitt vor Sonnenuntergang, glaubten aber auch viele, *suprema* sei die Tageszeit nach Sonnenuntergang, "quia est in XII tabulis scriptum sic: 'solis occasus suprema tempestas esto' ". Das elliptische *suprema* ist ersichtlich die *suprema tempestas* des Zwölftafelsatzes, seine Verwendung als Bezeichnung der Tageszeit vor oder nach Sonnenuntergang aber nicht durch ihn gedeckt. Denn wie *meridies* ist *sol occasus* ein Zeitpunkt,[91] der auch nicht dadurch zu einem Zeitabschnitt wird, daß ihn die XII Tafeln zum 'äußersten Zeitpunkt' für den Urteilsspruch bestimmen. Wie es dazu kommen konnte, daß die Späteren unter *suprema* die 'letzte Tageszeit' vor oder nach Sonnenuntergang verstanden, liegt aber gleichfalls auf der Hand.

---

[85] Metzger 138: "Thus if 'divide the day' means not simply 'adjourn' but 'postpone', or more specifically, 'adjourn and reconvene at an appointed time', the two conditions for liability in the papyrus fragment and in the *lex Irnitana* are perfectly appropriate: a judge's failure to give judgment would not be assessed until the time for reconvening has passed."

[86] Vgl. o. nach A. 75.

[87] J. Crook, *Cambridge Law Journal* 57 (1998), 414; K. Hackl, *SZ* 116 (1999), 387; A. Lintott, *JRS* 89 (1999), 27.

[88] Metzger 112ff.

[89] Varro 1.1.6.5 und 7.51; Censorinus, *De die natali* (ed. Jahn 1845) 23–4, und Macrob. *Sat.* 1.3.14. Der Haupttext ist Gell. 17.2.10; hinzu kommen Fest. 305 M. und Plin. *N.H.* 7.60.212.

[90] Was, wie sich verstehen sollte, keinen Beweis für die Bedeutung von *suprema tempestas* in den XII Tafeln macht.

[91] Zu *meridies* vgl. Varro 1.1.6.4; Censor. 23 und 24; Plin. *N.H.* 7.60.212: "XII tabulis ortus tantum et occasus nominantur, post aliquot annos adiectus est et meridies, accenso consulum id pronuntiante, cum a curia inter Rostra et Graecostasin prospexisset solem; a columna Maenia ad carcerem inclinato sidere supremam pronunciavit, sed hoc serenis tantum diebus, usque ad primum Punicum bellum". Wie *meridies* ist *suprema* hier noch Zeitpunkt. *Rostra* und *Graecostasis* werden in das 5. Jh. v. Chr. datiert, die *columna Maenia* wurde 338 v. Chr. errichtet; vgl. F. Coarelli, *Il foro romano, I Periodo arcaico* (1983), 138ff.; auch J. Marquardt, *Das Privatleben der Römer* (2. Aufl. 1886, Nachdr. 1964), I 254ff.

Nimmt man wie Censorinus und die anderen von Metzger angeführten Gewährsleute, Varro und Macrobius, den Zwölftafelsatz aus seinem Zusammenhang heraus, so ist nicht mehr ersichtlich, daß er den Sonnenuntergang als 'äußersten Zeitpunkt' für den Urteilsspruch bestimmte; isoliert scheint er vielmehr den Sonnenuntergang zum 'äußersten Zeitpunkt' des Tages zu erklären. Um Zweifel an dieser Bedeutung auszuschließen, hat Varro auch keine Bedenken, den überlieferten Wortlaut zu verfälschen.[92] War aber die *suprema tempestas* der 'äußerste Zeitpunkt' des Tages, so lag es allerdings nahe, die angrenzende 'Tageszeit' als die 'äußerste' oder 'letzte' zu bezeichnen. Die unterschiedlichen Vorstellungen über ihr Verhältnis zum Sonnenuntergang belegen zum Überfluß, daß *suprema* nicht die angestammte, sondern eine abgeleitete oder geliehene Bezeichnung des einen oder des anderen Zeitabschnitts ist.

3.7 *Die Funktion des Eides*

War der Gerichtstag ordnungsgemäß vom Magistrat erteilt und vom Kläger sowohl dem Urteilsrichter wie dem Prozeßgegner angezeigt worden, mußte das Urteil bis Sonnenuntergang gesprochen werden. War es bis Sonnenuntergang nicht gesprochen, konnte es auch nicht mehr gesprochen werden, es sei denn, daß der *iudex* die Verhandlung vertagt, den Gerichtstag 'zerteilt' hatte. War nicht oder nicht wirksam vertagt worden, war der Prozeß gescheitert, war das Urteil, das gleichwohl noch gefällt wurde, ohne jeden Belang. Der Eid, daß die *diffissio* erfolgt sei, den der *iudex*, bevor er urteilte, leisten mußte, sicherte mithin den Bestand des Urteils. Er war, seiner Natur nach, kein absolut wirkender Bestandsschutz; er konnte natürlich falsch sein. Aber die Gewähr, die er bot, war hoch. Einmal war die Behauptung, daß der Gerichtstag 'zerteilt' worden ist, in praxi kaum, nämlich nur durch den Nachweis eines die Vertagung ausschließenden positiven Tatbestands zu widerlegen. Zum andern gab die Sanktion des Meineids der beschworenen Behauptung Dignität und Glaubwürdigkeit. Da

---

[92] Varro 1.1.7.51: "Naevius: 'patrem suum supremum optumum appellat.' supremum ab superrumo dictum: itaque duodecim tabulis dicunt: 'solis occasu diei suprema tempestas esto.' libri augurum pro tempestate tempestutem dicunt supremum augurii tempus". Der Ablativ *solis occasu* (= nach Sonnenuntergang!) und das hinzugefügte *diei* markieren die Umdeutung. Der Schlußsatz ("Die *libri augurum* nennen anstelle von *tempestas* den letzten Zeitpunkt für ein Augurium *tempestus*.") entspricht XII T. 1.9, kann aber auch 'varronisch' gelesen werden. Außerdem Varro 1.1.6.5: "suprema summum diei, id ab superrimo. hoc tempus XII tabulae dicunt occasum esse solis".

nach den Eidesformeln auch der Lex Irnitana[93] nicht nur bei Iupiter und den Penaten und den verstorbenen und vergötterten Kaisern, sondern auch beim Genius des regierenden Kaisers geschworen wurde, drohte bei Meineid die Anklage wegen *crimen maiestatis.* Wir halten fest: Der Eid des *iudex* schloß praktisch aus, das Urteil mit der Behauptung anzugreifen, daß die Verhandlung nicht ordnungsgemäß vertagt worden sei.

Der Eid, daß die Verhandlung vertagt worden ist, sicherte mit dem Bestand des Urteils zugleich Identität und Kontinuität des Urteilsgerichts; denn er schloß auch den Einwand aus, die Verhandlung, in der das Urteil erging, sei nicht die Fortsetzung des 'zerteilten' Gerichtstags gewesen; das Verfahren folglich nicht mit dem identisch, für das der Magistrat den Gerichtstag erteilt hat. Für den *iudex* selbst schließlich bewirkte der Eid in praxi den Ausschluß drohender Haftung:[94] zwar hatte er nicht, wie das Gesetz vorsah, an dem Tag, den der Magistrat mit der *datio intertii* als Gerichtstag erteilt hatte, vor Sonnenuntergang geurteilt; aber wie sein Eid fast unangreifbar bekräftigte, hatte er den Gerichtstag vor Sonnenuntergang 'zerteilt'. Bei wiederholter Vertagung muß Entsprechendes gegolten haben.

3.8 *Der Termin zur Fortsetzung des Gerichtstages*

Diei diffissio ist der Wortbedeutung nach nur die 'Spaltung' oder 'Zerteilung des Gerichtstages'. 'Zerteilt' aber wurde er, um am nächsten oder einem späteren Kalendertag fortgesetzt zu werden. Wann er fortgesetzt werden sollte, mußte bestimmt werden. Der Gerichtstag wurde vom Magistrat durch Dekret erteilt, auf Antrag und auf den beantragten Kalendertag.[95] Es ist nicht ausgeschlossen, aber ganz unwahrscheinlich, daß er auch den Termin zur Fortsetzung des Gerichtstages gewähren mußte;[96] denn es ging ja nicht um einen neuen *dies iudicii*, sondern um Vertagung im erteilten Urteilstermin.

[93] Vgl. Kap. 25 III B 21–24; Kap. 26 III B 41–43; Kap. 59 VII A 3–5; Kap. 73 VIII B 37–39; Kap. 79 VIII C 54–57.

[94] Lamberti 193ff. und *Labeo* 36 (1990), 253ff. stellt diesen Gesichtspunkt in den Vordergrund.

[95] J.G. Wolf, 'Intertium' nach A. 112.

[96] So allerdings Kaser/Hackl 357f. für den Fall, daß "die Verhandlung zum vorgesehenen Termin aus anerkanntem Grund nicht stattfinden" kann, offenbar aber auch für die "Vertagung, wenn die Parteivorträge die Zeit erschöpft haben" (358); auch G. Zanon, *SDHI* 58 (1992), 318 bei A. 40: daß nur der Magistrat den *iudex* ersetzen konnte, ist kein Argument.

Wenn der *iudex* den Gerichtstag 'zerteilen' konnte und im Fortsetzungstermin die *diffissio* beschwören mußte, dann war es mit aller Wahrscheinlichkeit auch seine Sache, den neuen Termin zu bestimmen.[97] Der Magistrat mußte das *intertium* auf den vom Kläger benannten Tag erteilen; für den *iudex* ist dagegen anzunehmen, daß er über den Fortsetzungstermin unabhängig von der Zustimmung der Streitparteien entscheiden konnte. Eingeengt war er nur durch den Bestand des Urteilsgerichts, das in Irni 18 Monate nach seiner Einsetzung erlosch; bei Ablauf dieser Frist mußte das Urteil gesprochen sein; nach ihrem Ablauf war die Streitsache nicht mehr, wie die Irnitana es ausdrückt, *in iudicio*.[98]

3.9 *Zusammenfassung*

Wir fassen zusammen, was wir der Verweisungsvorschrift des Kap. 91 über die Vertagung des Urteilsgerichts durch den Urteilsrichter entnommen haben. Die Vertagung war ein komplexer rechtlicher Vorgang, in dem das Gesetz sozusagen zwei Phasen unterscheidet: die *diei diffissio* selbst, ihre Verfügung durch den *iudex*, also ihre Vornahme, und die Beeidung der *diei diffissio*, auch durch den *iudex*, nach der Unterbrechung, in der Fortsetzung des Gerichtstages. Für beide Phasen wird auf das stadtrömische Recht verwiesen, das mithin beide Rechtsakte regelte, die eigentliche Vertagung und ihre Beeidung. Die Vertagung war an Gründe gebunden, die ein Gesetz vorsah, vermutlich die *Lex Iulia iudiciorum privatorum*. Die Gründe kennen wir nicht, erschließen aber, daß offenbar häufig vertagt wurde, weil der Rechtsstreit noch nicht entscheidungsreif war. Nach wie vor galt der Zwölftafelsatz, daß am Gerichtstag, den inzwischen der Magistrat mit der *datio intertii* erteilte, das Urteil bis Sonnenuntergang gesprochen sein mußte; wurde die *suprema tempestas* verfehlt, konnte es nicht mehr gesprochen werden, es sei denn, daß der *iudex* den Gerichtstag 'zerteilt' hatte. Hatte er auch die Vertagung versäumt, haftete er dem Kläger auf Schadensersatz. Alles spricht dafür, daß der Urteilsrichter mit der *diffissio* zugleich den Termin für die Fortsetzung des Gerichtstages verfügte. In diesem Termin mußte er, bevor er urteilte, beeiden, daß der *dies iudicii* wirksam 'zerteilt' worden ist. Der Eid sicherte neben

---

[97] A. Burdese, *SDHI* 57 (1991), 451; Lamberti 194f. und *Labeo* 36 (1990), 254.
[98] Vgl. nur Kaser/Hackl 352f., auch 358 A. 34.

Identität und Kontinuität des Urteilsgerichts den Bestand des Urteils und bewirkte in praxi für den *iudex* den Ausschluß drohender Haftung.

4. Die Vertagung *ipsa lege*

4.1 *Der Sachverhalt*

Die XII Tafeln verfügten, daß der *dies iudicii* ohne weiteres 'gespalten' sein sollte, wenn 'schwere Erkrankung' oder ein 'Gerichtstermin mit einem Fremden' den Urteilsrichter oder eine Prozeßpartei hinderte, im Termin zu erscheinen.[99] Für den *morbus sonticus* bezeugen Julian und Ulpian die Fortgeltung dieses Satzes im klassischen Formularprozeß.[100] Wir haben uns also für die Zeit der flavischen Stadtrechte Spaniens vorzustellen, daß der Gerichtstag, den der Magistrat mit der *datio intertii* erteilt und den der Kläger *iudex* und Beklagtem 'denunziert' hatte, *ipso iure* 'zerteilt' war, wenn einer von ihnen wegen 'schwerer Erkrankung' am Gerichtstag nicht zur Verhandlung erschien.[101] Die Geltung unserer Verweisungsnorm auch für diese Sachverhalte wird durchweg nicht in Frage gestellt.[102]

4.2 *Die Terminologie der Verweisungsnorm*

Nach ihrer Ausdrucksweise beschränkt sie sich nicht auf die Vertagung durch den Urteilsrichter. Die Passiva *dies diffindatur diffissusve sit* oder *diem diffindi diem diffissum esse* oder das Gerundium *diem diffindendi* können gleichermaßen von der Vertagung *ope legis* gebraucht sein. Kriterien können darum nur die Tatbestände sein, für die auf das stadtrömische Recht verwiesen wird, oder der Gegenstand der Regeln, auf die verwiesen wird—soweit diese Tatbestände und Regeln denn greifbar sind. Die *lex*, die wie in Rom, so auch in Irni gelten soll (X B 3), "wenn vertagt werden muß oder vertagt worden sein muß" (X B 6/7), kann eben das Gesetz sein, das die *diei diffissio* verfügt: das Zwölftafelgesetz oder die *Lex Iulia iudiciorum privatorum*, die vermutlich dessen Verfügung erneuert hat und weitere Vertagungsgründe hinzugefügt haben

[99] S. oben A. 2.

[100] Iul. *Dig.* 42.1.60, Ulp. *Dig.* 2.11.2.3.

[101] Unvereinbar mit der Überlieferung Kaser/Hackl 357: auch in diesem Fall habe der Magistrat die Vertagung verfügen müssen. Davon zu trennen ist die Frage, wer nach der *ipso iure* eintretenden *diei diffissio* den Termin für die Fortsetzung des Gerichtstages bestimmte; s. unten bei A. 106.

[102] Kaser/Hackl 356ff.; G. Zanon, *SDHI* 58 (1992), 317 A. 38.

könnte.[103] "Aus denselben Gründen" wie in Rom kann dann auch in Irni *ipsa lege* "vertagt werden oder vertagt worden sein" (X B 14).

4.3 *Die Funktion des Eides*

Nicht so glatt liegen die Dinge beim Eid. Giorgia Zanon vermutet, das Gesetz habe den Eid des *iudex* nur für den Fall vorgesehen, daß er selbst die Vertagung verfügt hatte, nicht also auch für den Fall der Vertagung *ipsa lege.*[104] Für diesen Vorschlag ließe sich anführen, daß die Vertagung durch das Gesetz nicht in der Verantwortung des *iudex* lag; gegen ihn aber auch einwenden, daß der *iudex*, wenn er selbst die *diei diffissio* verursacht hatte, durch eben den Eid außer Zweifel stellen konnte, daß ihn keine Verantwortung traf: daß die *diffissio* von Gesetzes wegen eingetreten und nicht, weil er ohne zureichenden Grund die Verhandlung nicht wahrgenommen hätte, von ihm die Vertagung versäumt worden war.[105] Hat der *iudex* selbst die *diei diffissio* verursacht, so ist also gut denkbar, daß er nach der Unterbrechung, in der Fortsetzung des *ipso iure* 'zerteilten' Gerichtstages (in der nunmehr die Verhandlung beginnen konnte) den Vertagungsgrund beschwören mußte, etwa die 'schwere Erkrankung', die ihn gehindert hatte, am angezeigten *dies iudicii* zur Verhandlung zu erscheinen. Nicht anders als im Fall der von ihm verfügten *diffissio* konnte er hier auf seinen Eid nehmen, daß der Vertagungsgrund, nämlich der Tatbestand, an den das Gesetz die *diffissio* knüpfte, wirklich gegeben war; und nicht anders als dort sicherte als dann der Eid den Bestand des Urteils und schloß zugleich für den *iudex* die drohende Haftung aus; war er nämlich ohne zureichenden Grund ausgeblieben, "war weder vertagt noch geurteilt worden". Der Eid wäre allerdings überflüssig gewesen, wenn, wie vielfach angenommen wird,[106] den Termin zur Fortsetzung des 'zerteilten' Gerichtstages

[103] Kaser/Hackl 116, 357. Zur Anschauung vgl. den Katalog der Gründe, die nach der *Lex Ursonensis*, Kap. 95, col. 2, Z. 19ff. und 28ff. den Magistrat und ebenso (was leicht übersehen wird, vgl. nur Kaser/Hackl 116 A. 13) den Privatmann entschuldigen, der vor Rekuperatoren für den *populus* eine Mult einklagen will und im angesetzten Termin nicht erscheint, vgl. Crawford, in *Roman Statutes* I 442. Wie erinnerlich gilt die Verweisungsnorm des Kap. 91 nur für Verfahren vor dem Einzelrichter, vgl. o. A. 46.

[104] *SDHI* 58 (1992), 317 A. 38; s. auch schon A. Burdese, *SDHI* 57 (1991), 452.

[105] Cicero verwendet in den Atticus-Briefen zweimal *morbum iurare* (1.10 [1].1; 12.12 [13].2) in der Bedeutung: die erwartete Teilnahme an einer öffentlichen Veranstaltung (einmal an der Bewerbung um das Konsulat, das andere Mal an einem Bankett des Augurnkollegiums) mit Entschuldigung absagen; vgl. Metzger 144 A. 5.

[106] Kaser/Hackl 357 mit Gewährsleuten in A. 22.

nicht der *iudex* selbst, sondern der Magistrat bestimmt hätte; seine Aufgabe wäre es dann gewesen, die Vertagung zu prüfen. Gegen seine Zuständigkeit spricht indessen, daß der *dies iudicii*, den er erteilt hat, keineswegs aufgehoben war und erneut erteilt werden mußte, sondern eben nur 'zerteilt' war; und daß die *diei diffissio*, wo nicht das Gesetz sie verfügte, in der Kompetenz des *iudex* lag.

Ist dagegen eine Prozeßpartei am angezeigten *dies iudicii* nicht zur Verhandlung erschienen, wird in aller Regel gegen sie ein Versäumnisurteil ergangen sein.[107] Dieses Urteil war aber nichtig, wenn die Prozeßpartei wegen 'schwerer Erkrankung' ausgeblieben war; dann nämlich war der Gerichtstag 'zerteilt' und damit die Verhandlung ausgesetzt. Machte die ausgebliebene Partei mit dem Vertagungsgrund die Nichtigkeit des Urteils geltend, indem sie die Fortsetzung des 'zerteilten' Gerichtstags verlangte, mußte sie den Vertagungsgrund beweisen, also ihre 'schwere Erkrankung' zur Überzeugung des Richters bringen. Denn sein *officium* erlaubte dem *iudex*, einen Termin zur Fortsetzung des *dies iudicii* nur dann zu bestimmen, und verpflichtete ihn dann freilich auch, wenn er sich überzeugt hatte, daß ein Vertagungsgrund gegeben und darum der Gerichtstag 'gespalten' und das Versäumnisurteil nichtig war. Er konnte in diesem Fall zwar nur beschwören, daß nach seiner Überzeugung der gesetzliche Vertagungstatbestand vorgelegen habe. Das aber mochte auch genügen. Nehmen wir die Irnitana beim Wort, so war Eidesthema, "daß der Gerichtstag zerteilt worden ist" (X A 49/50). Und diesen Eid konnte er auch leisten, wenn er von der 'schweren Erkrankung' der ausgebliebenen Prozeßpartei lediglich berichtet und überzeugt war. Auch hier sicherte der Eid den Bestand des nach nunmehr streitiger Verhandlung ergangenen Urteils. Denn nur bei eingetretener Vertagung war das Versäumnisurteil nichtig und der Weg für ein streitiges Urteil frei. Haftung, weil "weder vertagt noch geurteilt worden war", drohte in dieser Konstellation dem *iudex* freilich nicht.

Ziehen wir die Summe, so spricht viel dafür, daß die Verweisungsnorm des Kap. 91 nicht nur für die *diffissio* durch den Urteilsrichter, sondern auch für die von Gesetzes wegen eintretende Vertagung galt. Es wäre auch nicht einzusehen, wenn die Irnitana *diem diffendendi*, 'wegen der Spaltung des Gerichtstages', auf das stadtrömische Prozeßrecht verweist und die gesetzliche *diei diffissio* nicht einschlösse.

107 Kaser/Hackl 374.

CONSILIUM PRAESIDIS: ADVISING GOVERNORS*

Paul Weaver

Governors were the focal point of the administrative structure in the provinces of the early Roman empire. They were mostly senior senators in status. Yet, despite the detail involved in many of their duties and the comparatively short duration of their term in office, which in practice in some provinces was barely as long as twelve months, they generally lacked specific training or previous detailed knowledge of their province. How did they manage? What local infrastructure was there to assist them? Who were their advisers and in what form did these give advice?

To advise a magistrate in his jurisdictional functions, the characteristic Roman vehicle was the *consilium*, a panel of assessors chosen by him at his own discretion. Their advice was not binding and he alone was responsible for making decisions.[1] This procedure was used not only by Roman magistrates from the emperor (with the *consilium principis*) downwards, but also in the domestic sphere by the head of the household in exercising his jurisdiction as *paterfamilias*.[2] Provincial governors, who all exercised full civil and criminal jurisdiction, were

* The following special abbreviations are used:

Eck	= Werner Eck, *Senatoren von Vespasian bis Hadrian* (Munich, 1970)
Millar (1)	= Fergus Millar, *The Emperor in the Roman World* (London, 1977)
Millar (2)	= Fergus Millar, *A Study of Cassius Dio* (Oxford, 1964)
Mommsen	= Th. Mommsen, *Römisches Staatsrecht*[3] (Leipzig, 1887; repr. 1963)
Pflaum	= H.-G. Pflaum, 'Le consilium du préfet d'Egypte. Sa composition' (with E. Balogh), *Scripta Varia* 2. 250ff. = *RHDFE* 30, 1952, 117–24
Schérer	= J. Schérer, *P. Fouad Ier* 3 (1939) 45ff.
Sherwin-White	= A.N. Sherwin-White, *The Letters of Pliny. A Historical and Social Commentary* (Oxford, 1966)
Syme	= R. Syme, *Roman Papers* I & II (Oxford, 1979)
Talbert	= R. Talbert, 'Pliny the Younger as governor of Bithynia-Pontus' in *Studies in Latin Literature and Roman History* II, ed. C. Deroux (Brussels, 1980) 412–35
Thomasson	= B.E. Thomasson, *Laterculi Praesidum* I (Gothenburg, 1984)
Vidman	= L. Vidman, *Etude sur la correspondance de Pline le Jeune avec Trajan* (Prague, 1960)

1 See Mommsen 1. 307–19.

2 E.g. Valerius Maximus 5.8.2, 9.1.

no exception. They drew on members of their own staff and available Roman citizens of standing, provided that, at least from the early Severan period, they were not in their own province of origin.[3]

There were three categories of governor:

1. Proconsuls in the proconsular or so-called 'senatorial' provinces, such as Asia and Africa;
2. Legates (*legati Augusti pro praetore*) in the 'imperial' provinces, such as Syria and Gallia Lugdunensis;
3. Praesidial *procuratores* or *praefecti*, who governed minor provinces, such as Noricum, and Iudaea, but which also included the important province of Egypt.

Those in the first two categories were senators of senior standing, while those in the third were senior equestrians, to be distinguished from equestrian procurators who were the chief financial officials in other provinces.

What differences can be detected in practice, as well as in juristic terms, between these categories of governor, and what light, if any, do the answers shed on how the Roman system of provincial administration worked? The following is a preliminary excursion into the field.

1

First, a brief description of the overall structure of the imperial administration. There are four main institutional elements involved in the central administration of the early empire: (1) the emperor; (2) the senatorial aristocracy; (3) the equestrian hierarchy; (4) the slave-freedman service of the *familia Caesaris*. All of the last three, within the limits of their own career paths, are separately and directly responsible to the emperor, by whom, with the exception of the proconsuls and *their* legates and quaestors in the proconsular provinces, they are appointed and from whom they receive their instructions. Direct interaction between these three subordinate elements or sectors is manipulated, without being fully controlled, by the emperor to produce a relationship that is efficient and harmonious rather than uncooperative and discordant.

[3] Cf. Mommsen 318 n. 3.

According to this model, it would be normal for interaction to occur between two elements in the structure, in particular between the emperor and any one of the others. Hence the regular forms of written and oral communication from and to the emperor by way of instructions (*mandata*), letters, responses to questions, requests, reports and so on[4] to governors, both in proconsular and imperial provinces, and to his procurators, both equestrian and freedman, wherever they were.

Interest and problems centre on the interaction of the various sectors with each other, apart from the emperor, that is between senatorial governors and equestrian financial procurators, between equestrian and freedman procurators, and between officials of senatorial and freedman status. Delicate questions of authority and responsibility, and of limits in practice to the use of powers formally held, frequently arose in a system where each branch had a separate line of communication up to the emperor. A further complication is the relationship within the senatorial sector between the different legates in imperial provinces, all of whom are directly appointed by the emperor. Every emperor had his favourites, could change his mind, or simply wish to put down individuals, usually senatorial governors, if they proved inefficient or incompetent, or to replace those who threatened to become too powerful. Thus Ulpian, although he repeats more than once in the *De officio proconsulis* and elsewhere that the proconsul has the most complete judicial authority in his province and one that is greater than anyone except the emperor, immediately qualifies this in one passage with the warning that, of course, if there should be a case involving the financial interests of the *fiscus*, which is the concern of the emperor's procurator, the proconsul would do better to keep out of it.[5] Other restrictions on the governor's powers are hinted at by Ulpian, as when the status of an accused is such that he is not subject to the governor's jurisdiction, or if the accused is absent in another province on state business; and he gives a stern warning that a governor is personally

[4] See Millar (1) 313–36.

[5] *Dig.* 1.16.9pr. "nec quicquam est in provincia quod non per ipsum expediatur. Sane si fiscalis pecuniaria causa sit, quae ad procuratorem principis respicit, melius fecerit si abstineat." Add *Dig.* 48.6.6 (Ulpian), the case of Domitius Silvanus' freeborn son who was alleged to have been flogged and tortured, where the emperor Pius wrote to the proconsul: "Gemine carissime, velim audias eum", a request to which the proconsul was bound to accede.

liable under the *lex Iulia de vi* for physical mistreatment of *cives Romani*.[6] Consider the careful treatment of Paul while imprisoned at Caesarea by Felix and Festus, governors of Judaea.[7]

The way was therefore open for the emperor to intervene in the working relationship between the governor and the procurator or procurators responsible for the financial administration of a province. This was so whether the governor was a *legatus Augusti pro praetore* in an imperial province or a proconsul in a proconsular province. The emperor could intervene directly by instructions to his procurator(s) or indirectly by rescript to the governor on matters involving the imperial treasury.[8]

It was not uncommon, therefore, for the emperor to be involved at a given time with two of the other three sectors of his administration. Less common, and thus of considerable interest, are those occasions on which all four elements of the system are engaged together. A well-known example of this occurred under Nero in the aftermath of the suppression of Boudicca's revolt in Britain in AD 60.[9] In the row between the eminent senatorial governor Suetonius Paullinus and the equestrian procurator Iulius Classicianus, the mission of the imperial freedman Polyclitus sent by Nero to sort them out is quite extraordinary, as are the conduct of the procurator Classicianus and the rhetorical language used by Tacitus to describe the affair. In brief, this is *not* a paradigm of how the administration operated under normal conditions.

2

More instructive is an example involving Pliny the Younger during the second year of his governorship of Bithynia-Pontus *c.* AD 111–113. *Letter* 10. 84 is Trajan's response to a petition (10. 83) from the peo-

[6] *Dig.* 48.5.16(15).4 (Ulpian, on punishing adulteries) "nisi sit ea persona quae ad praesidis cognitionem non pertinet"; "qui in alia provincia rei publicae causa absunt". 48.6.7 "lege Iulia de vi publica tenetur qui, cum imperium potestatemve haberet, civem Romanum adversus provocationem (contrary to his right of appeal) necaverit verberaverit iusseritve quid fieri aut quid in collum iniecerit ut torqueatur."

[7] *NT Acts* 24.22–7; 25.1ff.; cf. 22.25–9.

[8] *Dig.* 49, Title 14 (*De iure fisci*) records many such imperial decisions.

[9] The primary source is Tacitus *Ann.* 14.38–9; cf. Cassius Dio 62.2.3. For the date, see R. Syme *Tacitus* (Oxford, 1958), 763ff. Additional arguments on the basis of the procuratorial appointments can also be made to support dating the rebellion to 60, not 61, *pace* Tacitus *Ann.* 14.29.

ple of Nicaea who are claiming the right to the property of citizens of Nicaea who die intestate, a right which they say was granted by Augustus. Trajan writes to Pliny:

> Nicaeensibus . . . debebis vacare, contractis omnibus personis ad idem negotium pertinentibus, adhibitis Virdio Gemellino et Epimacho liberto meo procuratoribus, ut, aestimatis etiam iis quae contra dicuntur, quod optimum credideritis, statuatis.
>
> You must give the Nicaeans a hearing, when you have brought together all the parties concerned in the matter, having invited (summoned?) the procurators Virdius Gemellinus and my freedman Epimachus to be present, so that, after assessing the arguments on both sides, you (three) can make a decision as to what you believe is best.

Thus, in the inelegant but concise and lucid administrative style favoured by Trajan. Whoever did the drafting, it is clear that the substantive reply came from the emperor himself. Note the requirement of cooperation between the different orders of officials and the assumption that they will be on good enough terms to work fruitfully together. The emperor's advice, which Pliny is obliged to follow (*debebis*), is quite precise, naming particular officials and their status ("adhibitis Virdio Gemellino et Epimacho liberto meo procuratoribus"). Why this particular group on this occasion? It is possible that others in addition to these two could be included at the governor's discretion. Trajan, however, does *not* name one whom we might have expected to be included if he was available. This is Servilius Pudens, a *legatus* and therefore of senatorial rank, who had arrived in the province late, some two months after Pliny, to the latter's great relief, as he puts it in the most tersely succinct letter of his correspondence, which has the air of a formal routine report.[10] That was about nine months before the date of the present letter (10.84). There is little reason to doubt that he had come to serve as an assistant legate in the province, appointed by Trajan, not by Pliny. His full title would have been *legatus Augusti.* He is not mentioned again in Pliny's plentiful correspondence with Trajan.[11] This reticence on Pliny's part deserves further consideration.

---

[10] 10.25: "Servilius Pudens legatus, domine, VIII kal. Decembres Nicomediam venit meque longae expectationis sollicitudine liberavit."

[11] See Vidman 62. E.G. Hardy's view (*Commentary* ad loc.) that Pudens was a 'normal' legate of the kind assigned to assist provincial governors in administrative and jurisdictional matters is correct, but not his assumption that he was a *legatus propraetore*, i.e. with delegated *imperium*, or that his function was that of an *adsessor*

Previous governors of Bithynia, as proconsuls, had had *legati* on their staff to assist them,[12] chosen by the governor with senatorial approval. Pliny's position as governor, however, was not that of proconsul, but as *legatus Augusti pro praetore*, albeit *consulari potestate*.[13] Pudens could not have been Pliny's appointment, on the long-standing principle that 'legatus non potest delegare'.[14] Subordinate legates of an imperial legate, such as Pliny, would be appointed by the emperor. The role of Pudens would have been mainly confined to civil jurisdiction, where the governor would need most relief from routine duties, and as a *legatus iuridicus* he would have possessed a lesser than full propraetorian *imperium* without capital jurisdiction (*imperium mixtum*).[15]

But, as Pliny's senior ranking assistant, he could be expected to take his place on the governor's *consilium*, if that is what it was, especially on a matter of such importance that the emperor himself had become involved and asked the governor to summon one.[16] Trajan may have felt there was no need to remind his governor of this. Perhaps Pudens was too far away on duty in Pontus—but so might either of the procurators have been—or perhaps the normal composition of the governor's *consilium* in imperial provinces differed in this respect from that in proconsular provinces. The fact that assis-

to Pliny. He confuses the status of the province, now under the emperor's control and governed by the emperor's legate, who did not have the power to delegate *imperium*, with the previous status of Bithynia-Pontus as a proconsular province in which the proconsul could delegate his *imperium* to his assistant legate. Talbert, 422, justifiably remarks that Pliny's staff are mentioned surprisingly little throughout the correspondence.

[12] 10.31.5: "iussu proconsulum legatorumve".

[13] *CIL* 5.5262 = *ILS* 2927. Pliny's "consularis potestas", although exceptional in the record for a governor of an imperial province, does not appear to have given him extra powers beyond those normally held and exercised by such imperial legates. For reasons of status, this would have entitled him to six lictors, as had been entitled the proconsuls who had preceded him as governor, rather than only five, as was normal for *legati Augusti pr. pr.* Despite much that has been written on the "special" nature of Pliny's mission (e.g. Vidman 42ff.; Talbert 412ff.), in practice it boils down to very little (see Millar [1] 325f., G. Burton, *JRS* 65 [1975], 92).

[14] *Dig.* 1.21.5pr. (Paulus): "mandatam sibi iurisdictionem mandare alteri non posse manifestum est." 2.1.5 (Julian): "more maiorum ita comparatum est ut is demum iurisdictionem mandare possit qui eam suo iure non alieno beneficio habet."

[15] *Dig.* 2.1.3 (Ulpian): "imperium aut merum aut mixtum est. merum est habere gladii potestatem ad animadvertendum facinorosos homines, quod etiam potestas appellatur. Mixtum est imperium, cui etiam iurisdictio inest, quo in danda bonorum possessione consistit." Cf. 1.21.1 (Paulus): 'mandata iurisdictione privato, etiam imperium quod non est merum videtur mandari, quia iurisdictio sine modica coercitione nulla est." See Sherwin-White 594f.

[16] Cf. *CIL* 10.7852 = *ILS* 5947, and Section 5 below.

tant *legati* in imperial provinces were appointed by the emperor and derived their *imperium*, however limited, directly from him[17] placed them in a somewhat different relationship to the governor in their province from that which obtained in proconsular provinces, where *legati* derived their jurisdictional authority from the proconsul himself. In the latter case they had propraetorian *imperium* delegated by the governor who was proconsul, and appeal from their jurisdiction was to the governor, not directly to the emperor.[18] In imperial provinces *legati iuridici* did not have propraetorian *imperium* at all,[19] which was restricted to the governor (*legatus Augusti pro praetore*), and appeal from their decisions would strictly speaking have to go, not to the governor, but back to the emperor from whom they had received their mandated jurisdiction.[20]

As regards membership of the governor's *consilium*, personal choice would play a paramount role. Certain restrictions applied to those who were resident in their home province.[21] The governor, whether proconsul or *legatus Augusti pr. pr.*, would bring with him his own hand-picked staff of friends and advisers (*comites*), including those specially selected for their expertise in the law (*adsessores*), who were paid a salary for their services.[22] But the legate of a proconsul was also in a different position from the assistant legate of an imperial governor in the following respect: he was chosen by the proconsul himself,[23] and could thus be, and often was, a close relative or friend

---

[17] *Mixtum imperium*, in the phrase of Ulpian (*Dig.* 2.1.3 [above, n. 15]).

[18] For the propraetorian *imperium* of *legati proconsulis*: *ILS* 1026 (7–8) ". . . leg. pro pr. provinciae Ponti et Bithyniae proconsulatu patris sui . . ."; 5947 (23): "M. Iulius Romulus leg. pro pr." (Sardinia); cf. 981, 1029, 1045, 1080, 1095, 1102, 1110, 1141, 1168, etc. Appeal: *Dig.* 49.3.2 (Venuleius Saturninus): "appellari a legatis proconsul potest".

[19] Apparent exceptions, e.g. *ILS* 1062: "[T. Statilio] Maximo . . . iuridico pr. pr. utriusque Pannoniae", are based on misapprehension of the status of the *legati* involved. At the time Maximus held this appointment (136/7), Pannonia was governed by Aelius Caesar with proconsular *imperium*; cf. Dessau ad loc.

[20] The process of appeal from *legati iuridici* is not clear in practice. The legal sources, when discussing appeals, where they do not refer specifically to proconsuls, regularly use the term *praeses* or *praeses provinciae*, which can include proconsuls as well as *legati Caesaris* and *procuratores Caesaris*, e.g. *Dig.* 49.1.21pr. and 1; 1.26. Cf. Mommsen 2.268.

[21] Mommsen 1.318 and n. 3.

[22] *Dig.* 1, Title 22 (*De officio adsessorum*); 22.4 refers specifically to the salary of *comites* of a *legatus Caesaris*. Cf. Mommsen 2.245f.

[23] Governors of consular standing (i.e. of the provinces of Asia and Africa), however, needed the emperor's approval if they chose as their legates senators who were themselves ex-consuls (Cassius Dio 53.14.7).

of the proconsul.[24] The term of his appointment was dependent on that of the proconsul. He was thus a natural choice as adviser and, given his extensive jurisdictional duties, would be most likely to head the proconsul's *consilium* when called upon to serve in matters of major concern.

The working relationship between the governor of an imperial province and his assistant legate, on the other hand, was different. The assistant was not the personal choice of the governor, though the latter's wishes may have been taken into account by the emperor in making the appointment; their terms of office did not necessarily coincide;[25] and although one had a lesser *imperium* than the other, officially they both would have borne the title *legatus Augusti*, indicating their separate appointment by and ultimate responsibility to the emperor. Although hard evidence in the form of examples is sparse, it would be no surprise *not* to find assistant *legati* acting as the personal advisers of imperial governors as members of their *consilia*. It would be a different matter if an assistant *legatus* or a *procurator Augusti* were called upon by the emperor to conduct a joint enquiry or make a joint determination. In such cases, however, it is likely that imperial financial interests were somehow involved and that it was the imperial procurator or procurators who were called upon to participate.

On the relations between a governor, an assistant legate and the emperor, from legal sources we know more about proconsular than imperial provinces. Particularly relevant is the *Digest*, Book 1, Title 16, *De officio proconsulis et legati*. The proconsul has the free discretion to delegate or not delegate jurisdiction; likewise he may withdraw such delegated functions, but not without first consulting the emperor (6.6.1). On the other hand, legates should not consult the emperor, but their own proconsul, and the latter will be obliged to reply to matters raised by legates (6.6.2). The proconsul is not to let his legate leave the province before himself (10.1). If a matter arises which

---

[24] E.g. *ILS* 1026: "proconsulatu patris sui"; 1061 "proconsulis patris sui". Cf. Eck 46f.

[25] Pudens arrived in Bithynia at least two months after Pliny (see above, n. 10). Was he simply dilatory in setting out or was his late arrival due to some delay in finalizing his appointment? It remains to be demonstrated that assistant *legati* in imperial provinces, including *legati legionis*, routinely entered and left their province at the same time as the governor, as did the proconsular legates. *Dig.* 1.16.10.1 (Ulpian), quoted by Sherwin-White 595, at the end of his commentary on Pliny 10.25, refers to *legati proconsulis*, not to assistant *legati* in imperial provinces.

calls for severe punishment, the legate must refer it back to the proconsul's jurisdiction; for he does not have the right to inflict the death penalty, imprisonment or severe flogging (11). Legates of a proconsul have no jurisdiction in their own right ("nihil proprium habent"), but only what has been delegated to them by the proconsul (13). (So much for the legate's propraetorian *imperium*!) It is difficult, however, to agree with Sherwin-White[26] that the title *legatus pro praetore* borne by the legates of proconsuls must be honorary and not technical. Status was undoubtedly involved, but *imperium*, however limited in practice, is also clearly implied.[27] The addition of *pro praetore* to the title of equivalent officials in imperial provinces, including legionary commanders (*legati legionis*), is avoided, except for the governor himself.

3

Is the procedure, then, outlined in Pliny 10.84 mentioned above, that of the governor's *consilium*, as it is generally assumed to be?[28]

> . . . contractis omnibus personis ad id negotium pertinentibus, adhibitis Virdio Gemellino et Epimacho liberto meo procuratoribus, ut . . . quod optimum credideritis, statuatis.

The verb *adhibere* in the passive, especially the past participle, is regularly used in the sense of being invited or summoned to join a superior official's *consilium*, sometimes without the actual word 'consilium'.[29] But if that were the case in this instance, apart from the decision being that of the governor Pliny himself, one would expect the final verb *statuatis* to reflect this by being in the singular, not plural. The second person singular is indeed used earlier in the sentence in the main verb *debebis*. Trajan, or whoever drafted the letter, has given a different (and significant) emphasis by a twofold use

---

[26] *Roman Society and Roman Law in the New Testament* (Oxford, 1963), 4 n. 1.
[27] Cf. the title *quaestor pr(o) pr(aetore)*, e.g. *ILS* 5947, also in proconsular provinces only.
[28] E.g. Sherwin-White 680.
[29] For examples: *Oxford Latin Dictionary* 1.40, s.v. *adhibeo* §5; *TLL* 1.643, s.v. I.6. Cf. Pliny *Letters* 5.1.5; 6.11.1 and 15.3–4. On two occasions when invited to join the emperor's *consilium*, Pliny does not use the more technical word *adhibitus* but a more forceful variation: 4.22.1 *in consilium adsumptus*; 6.31.1 *evocatus in consilium* (but ib. 13 *adhibebamur . . . cenae*).

of the second person *plural*—*credideritis*, *statuatis*—with which the letter concludes. This at least implies a joint decision in which all three officials are involved and for which they all are to share responsibility.[30] Where a magistrate summons his *consilium*, the decision is regularly expressed in the singular; e.g. Valerius Maximus 5.8.2: "adhibito consilio . . . damnavit", id. 8.3, 9.1; cf. *NT Acts* 25.12: ὁ Φῆστος (procurator-governor of Judaea) συλλαλήσας μετὰ τοῦ συμβουλίου ἀπεκρίθη . . . In inscriptions, the phrase "cum consilio collocutus", often abbreviated as "c. c. c.", followed by a verb in the singular, is standard, e.g. *CIL* 2.4125: "L. Novius Rufus, legatus Aug. pr. pr. c. c. c. . . . recitavit"; cf. 6.266; 10.3334; *ILAfr.* 591 = *AE* 1921, 38. The phrase *ex consilii sententia*, used in reaching a verdict and pronouncing sentence, does not imply a joint decision, much less joint responsibility for a decision. The magistrate is not obliged to follow the advice of his *consilium*, but only to listen to it; cf. Pliny *Letters* 5.1.5; 6.31.12.

Does *adhibitis* in *Letter* 10.84 above have overtones of 'invited' (as to dinner, 6.31.13) or 'summoned' (as to a superior's *consilium*)? That is, does a governor in practice normally direct imperial procurators to do what he wishes, or do they operate independently of the governor on instructions from the emperor? Other evidence in Pliny's correspondence with Trajan tends to support the latter. The allocation of troops by the governor to the procurator Virdius Gemellinus comes on the orders of Trajan, and also referred to Trajan for confirmation is the request for more troops by the imperial freedman Maximus ("libertus et procurator tuus"), who the governor discovered had already taken over those allocated to Gemellinus as (and that?) he was off on a special mission to Paphlagonia.[31] The language of the letters in general reflects the procurators' working relationship with the emperor and with each other, not with the governor.[32] The freedman Maximus, while working closely with his equestrian colleague in the role of assistant (*quem adiuvat*), can also operate on his own.

---

[30] On the composition and procedures of a governor's *consilium*, see especially Mommsen 1.314–19; also De Ruggiero, *Diz. Epig.* 2.609ff.; Liebenam, *RE* 4.915ff.; Pflaum 250f.

[31] 10.27: "Maximus libertus et procurator tuus domine, praeter decem beneficiarios quos adsignari a me Gemellino iussisti, sibi quoque confirmat necesse esse milites <sex. hos> interim, sicut inveneram, in ministerio eius relinquendos existimavi. . . . in futurum, quid servari velis, rogo rescribas."

[32] E.g. 10.28: "Maximum libertum meum", "Virdio Gemellino procuratore meo, quem [Maximus] adiuvat"; cf. 10.27: "Maximus libertus et procurator tuus".

Even more of a surprise for the governor was another imperial freedman, Lycormas, on another mission about which Pliny seems even less well informed (10.63 and 67). Lycormas is not called *procurator* by Pliny in either letter, simply *libertus tuus*. There is no mention of the equestrian procurator. Lycormas may therefore have been on a special assignment in the Crimean Bosporus and not a regular official of the provincial administration of Bithynia-Pontus at all. The tone of the imperial freedman's letter to the senatorial governor is quite brusque.[33] Pliny nevertheless reports the request to Trajan and gives reasons for not complying. He does not treat Lycormas as one of his own staff responsible to him.

If this reflects the formal relationship between officials of different status in the various sectors of the provincial administration and their separate links with the emperor, what of the relationship *within* the senatorial sector between governors and their assistant legates? Is there a significant difference between proconsular and imperial provinces in the role played by assistant legates in the process of advising and consulting their governor corresponding to the difference in their legal position and the circumstances of their appointment? The evidence, while not extensive, is diverse.[34]

4

First, we should consider the usage of a literary source, the early third-century consular historian Cassius Dio. He was himself an experienced administrator at the highest level—much more so than another

[33] 10.63: "scripsit mihi, domine, Lycormas libertus tuus ut, si qua legatio a Bosporo venisset urbem petitura, usque in adventum suum retineretur." For commentary, see Sherwin-White 648ff.

[34] One passage in the *Digest* mentions *consilium* in connection with a governor's delegated jurisdiction: 1.21.2pr. (Ulpian) "mandata iurisdictione a praeside, consilium non potest exercere is cui mandata." The translation in *The Digest of Justinian*, ed. A. Watson (Philadelphia, 1985) ad loc. by MacCormick is as follows: "When jurisdiction is delegated by a governor, his counselling functions cannot be carried out by the delegate." The phrase *consilium exercere* is rare. In this passage *exercere* is taken to be the equivalent of *adhibere* (cf. *TLL* 5.2.1376.76). This appears to mean that the legate of a provincial governor, including one in an imperial province, cannot exercise the governor's authority to summon his (i.e. the governor's) *consilium*. It is difficult to see why he should want to, unless the governor was incapacitated. Does it mean that he cannot summon a *consilium* of his own? Or even that he is prevented from sitting on or heading another's *consilium*, including the governor's own? In at least one proconsular province, that was patently not the case: *CIL* 10.7852 = *ILS* 5947 (see Section 5 below).

consular historian, Tacitus. In between his two consulships (*cos. suff.* 205/6 and *cos. II ord.* 229), Dio had personal experience as governor of both a proconsular and two imperial provinces (*procos. Africae* 223; *legatus Augusti pr. pr. Dalmatiae* 224–6; *legatus Augusti pr. pr. Pannoniae Superioris* 226–8).[35] To put it no higher, he was not insensitive to the niceties, at least in his time, of provincial administrative terminology and function.

Dio consistently uses different terms for assistant legates in proconsular and imperial provinces. His regular term for *legati proconsulis* is πάρεδρος (cf. *adsessor*), as in 53.14.7: τοὺς δὲ δὴ παρέδρους αὐτὸς ἕκαστος ἑαυτῷ αἱρεῖται ("each [proconsul] chooses his own assistants"); cf. ib. 5: καὶ οἱ παρεδρεύοντες τοῖς τὸ κῦρος τῆς ἀρχῆς ἔχουσιν ("and the [senators] assisting those who have the supreme authority [i.e. the proconsuls]"). The reason he gives (ib. 6) for calling them πάρεδροι and not πρεσβευταί, the normal Greek equivalent for *legati*, is that he is having regard to their function (πρὸς τὴν πρᾶξιν), not their name (οὐ πρὸς τὸ ὄνομα): οὕτω γὰρ ἂν ὀρθῶς αὐτούς, οὐ πρὸς τὸ ὄνομα ἀλλὰ πρὸς τὴν πρᾶξιν, ὥσπερ εἶπον, καλέσαιμι, ἐπεὶ οἵ γε ἄλλοι πρεσβευτὰς καὶ τούτους ἑλληνίζοντες ὀνομάζουσιν ("for this would be the correct way for me to call them, having regard not to their title but to their function, as I have said, although others call them by their Greek name 'representatives' [= *legati*])." Cf. 55.27.6: τῷ παρέδρῳ αὐτοῦ, ὃν πρεσβευτήν, ὥσπερ εἶπον, καλοῦμεν ("[instructions were given] to his assistant, whom, as I have said, we call a 'representative'"), referring to the legate of the proconsul of Achaea in AD 6. Other passages where Dio uses πάρεδρος (cf. παρεδρεύειν) as the equivalent of *legatus proconsulis* are 57.14.4 (Crete, AD 15), 60.25.6 (during the reign of Claudius), 72.5.4 (Achaea and Asia, *c.* 161–7).[36] In one passage, 72.11.3–4, he carefully distinguishes between a proconsul's legate and an assistant legate to the same person when governor in an imperial province. When Victorinus was governor of Germany (τῆς Γερμανίας . . . ἄρχων) under Commodus, his assistant legate is called τὸν ὑποστράτηγον, whereas later when he was governor (proconsul) of Africa, a legate of his there is ἕνα τῶν παρέδρων. In Dio, ὑποστράτηγος, ὑποστρατηγεῖν τινι, are the regular terms applied to a

[35] For the dates, see Millar (2) 23.

[36] Millar (2) 95 states that Dio is concerned at 53.14.5 with the Greek rendering of the Latin *adsessor*; he is in fact explaining why he prefers to use the term πάρεδρος rather than πρεσβευτής for the Latin *legatus* (*proconsulis*).

legatus legionis and, under the empire, for those *duces comitesque* who accompanied the *emperor* on campaign.[37]

These passages indicate clearly that Dio perceived (and felt that it needed emphasizing) a difference of function between the subordinate legates in the two types of province—to proconsuls they were 'assistants/assessors' (πάρεδροι), with the implication that they regularly sat on the proconsul's *consilium*, but in imperial provinces, in relation to governors who were πρεσβευταὶ καὶ ἀντιστράτηγοι, they were 'representatives' (πρεσβευταί) of the emperor and, where appropriate, were viewed primarily in their military function as subordinate commanders (ὑποστράτηγοι). This corresponds to Dio's associating the titles of proconsuls with peaceful duties and those of imperial governors more with warfare than civil jurisdiction (53.13.6). It does not, of course, show that an assistant imperial *legatus* did not or could not be summoned to sit on the *consilium* of his superior, the *legatus Augusti pro praetore*, but it does leave open the possibility that this was not normal practice, in the absence of instructions from the emperor.

5

Next, some documentary evidence on governors' *consilia* and their membership. Examples, both in the inscriptions and the papyri, are scarce. First, three inscriptions from the early imperial period:[38]

(1) *CIL* 10.7852 = *ILS* 5947 (Sardinia, AD 69)—a decree of L. Helvius Agrippa, proconsul of Sardinia, who in March 69 investigated a long-running territorial dispute between the Patulcenses and the recalcitrant Gallilenses.[39] It concludes (lines 23–7) with a list of the proconsul's *consilium*:

---

[37] E.g., in addition to 72.11.3–4 above, 60.20.3; 62.23.6; 74.6.2; 78.21.2; 79.7.1. See G. Vrind, *De Cassii Dionis vocabulis quae ad ius publicum pertinent* (Leiden 1923, repr. 1971), 88–92. For the use of πάρεδρος = *adsessor* in its usual sense of "adviser", ib. 91 n. 206. Dio appears to have no special term for *legati iuridici* in imperial provinces. He does not use the term which is regular in Greek inscriptions, viz. δικαιοδότης (but cf. 79.22.1: δικαιονόμος).

[38] For συμβούλιον = *consilium* in inscriptions of the republican period referring to *consilia* of the dictator Sulla, consuls and proconsuls during the period 139–74 BC: *SIG*^{3} 747.5f., 30, 58; 741.6; 684.11; *IGR* 4.290.

[39] See Mommsen, *Gesammelte Schriften* 5.337ff.

> In consilio fuerunt: M. Iulius Romulus leg(atus) pro pr(aetore), T. Atilius q(uaestor)/pro pr(aetore), M. Stertinius Rufus f(ilius), Sex. Aelius Modestus, P. Lucretius Clemens, M. Domitius/Vitalis, M. Lusius Fidus, M. Stertinius Rufus (followed by the names of eleven *signatores* as witnesses).

This comprises eight members, in order of status, headed by his assistant legate and his quaestor, the two most senior officials on his staff, and includes a father-and-son pair, the M. Stertinii Rufi, with the son, who need only be in his twenties, coming next in order after the senatorial legate and quaestor. If he is placed ahead of his father because he has already held a vigintivirate post and thus qualified to enter on a senatorial career by way of a quaestorship,[40] then his father would be of equestrian status, as should also be the four whose names precede him on the list.

(2) *AE* 1921, 38 = *ILAfr.* 591 (Aunobaris, Africa Proconsularis, 117–38)—also from a proconsular province—records a decree of a Marcellus, proconsul during the reign of Hadrian,[41] determining a boundary dispute between one Iulius Regillus and the Aunobaritani: "Marcellus procos. collocutus cum consilio decretum ex tabella recitavit . . ." (lines 6–8). On an adjacent stone, *AE* 1921, 39 = *ILAfr.* 592, are appended the names of ten persons who are apparently (but not specifically stated to be—the stone is incomplete at the top) members of his *consilium.* The names heading the existing list give no indication of high official rank or senatorial status, except that they all have *tria nomina* and are presumably Roman citizens:

> L. Iulius Catullinus, Q. Pompeius Primus, L. Sem/pronius Flaccus, Q. Cordius Clemens, M. Cladius Phil/ippus, L. Neratius Bassus, L. Marius Perpetuus scriba qu(a)es/torius, Sex. Serius Verus haruspex, L. Pomponius Cari/sianus scriba librarius, P. Papenius Salutaris/scriba librarius.

The only officials listed are four lower-grade staff of the proconsul or the quaestor—three *scribae* and one *haruspex*—who are placed last. The first six names may be those of equestrians. Ten is a common number for a *consilium.*[42] If this is in fact the *consilium* of a proconsul of Africa, it is at a surprisingly low level. It is just possible that

[40] Cf. Pflaum 119.

[41] He is perhaps M. Vitorius Marcellus *cos. suff.* 105; cf. Thomasson 390, Africa Proconsularis no. 159; R. Syme *ZPE* 37 (1980), 5ff.; but see also Eck 213 n. 412.

[42] Cf. Mommsen 1.318 n. 2.

they are the names of ten witnesses to the signing of the decree (cf. the eleven witnesses in [1] above).

(3) *SIG*³ 827 G = A. Plassard, *Fouilles de Delphes* III. 4, no. 290 (Delphi, 110–117), which records a boundary determination between the Ambrossii and the people of Delphi in the province of Achaea, carried out by C. Avidius Nigrinus *legatus Aug. pr. pr.*, perhaps as *corrector* and/or a consular legate replacing the proconsul when Achaea was governed for a time by imperial legate under Trajan.[43] As Nigrinus was *cos. suff.* 110, this would have to date from the period 110–17. Although the inscription is fragmentary, four names at the head of the *consilium* are listed, again without official titles:

> in consilio adfuerunt Q. Eppius, Fl(avius) Arrianus, C. Papius Habitus, T. Liv[ius?] [in consilio adfuerunt . . .]us Pollio, Q. Eppius, Fl. [Arrianus]' (id. no. 294).

The second name, Fl(avius) Arrianus, is of interest. If, as is probable, he is the historian Arrian, he must have been under thirty at the time he served on the *consilium* of a consular governor or *corrector*.[44] If he was proconsul of Baetica by c. 125,[45] only ten years after serving on the the staff of Nigrinus, one may conjecture that he already had a senatorial career in prospect, judging by his position close to the head of the latter's *consilium*. Again the impression is gained that persons of appropriate status might serve at quite a young age as advisers on the *consilia* of provincial governors, both proconsular and imperial.[46]

---

[43] See Syme 2.781–2; R. Talbert, *The Senate of Imperial Rome* (Princeton, 1984), 400. For the possibility that Nigrinus was sent to the province by Trajan as *corrector* during the governorship of a proconsul, see Eck 258; Thomasson 193 no. 24. He is not to be confused with his father Avidius Nigrinus who was governor of Achaea as proconsul under Domitian (Pliny 10.65–6); see Thomasson 192 no. 15, and for yet another Avidius, his uncle, as proconsul of Achaea in the same period, ib. no. 18.

[44] Cf. A.B. Bosworth, *CQ* 22 (1972), 184 n. 2. If Nigrinus was only of praetorian status, i.e. if the inscription dates from before 110, Arrian would presumably have been too young (twenty or under) to serve in the role. On Arrian, see Bosworth, *CQ* 22 (1972) 163–85; id., *A Historical Commentary on Arrian's History of Alexander* I (Oxford, 1980), 1f.; P.A. Stadter *Arrian of Nicomedia* (Chapel Hill, 1980), 7f., 194 n. 47.

[45] Bosworth, *Commentary* 2.

[46] A curiosity in this context is a group of three fragmentary curse tablets (*tabellae defixionum*) found in cinerary urns at Emporiae in Tarraconensis, dated to the reign of Vespasian (*AE* 1952, 122; G. Alföldy, *Fasti Hispanienses* 19f.). They contribute to

6

Finally, two papyri which record the names and composition of the *consilium* of the prefect of Egypt:

(4) *P. Fouad Ier* 3, no. 21 (AD 63).[47] The relevant lines are 4–9:

ἐν τῷ μεγάλῳ ἀτρίῳ. ἐπὶ βήματος, παρόντων ἐν συνβουλίῳ [N]ωρβ[α]νοῦ Πτολεμαίου δικαιοδότου καὶ πρὸς τῷ | [ἰδίῳ] λόγῳ, Ἀουιλλίου Κουαδράτου καὶ Τεννίου Οὐέτερος | [—]υ Ἀττικοῦ, Παπειρίου Πάστορος καὶ Βαιβίου Ἰουνκείνου | [χιλιά]ρχων, Ἰουλίου Λυσιμάχου, Κλαυδίου Ἡρακλείδου διοικητοῦ | [Κλαυ?]δίου Εὐκτήμονος, Κλαυδίου Σεκούνδου . . .

The *consilium* (συμβούλιον) is that of the prefect of Egypt, C. Caecina Tuscus, despite the fact that neither his name nor title appears on the papyrus. His decision concerning citizenship rights of some discharged soldiers is quoted verbatim in the first person singular at lines 11f. (εἶπον ὑμεῖν), 17 (ἔγραψα).[48] Cf. *P. Yale* 1528.15ff. . . . ἐν τῷ ἀτρείῳ | [κα]θημένου αὐτοῦ ἐπὶ τῷ βήματι. | Τοῦσκος εἶπεν ἡμεῖν . . . The similarity between the cases recorded in *P. Fouad Ier* 21 and *P. Yale* 1528 are striking—both are heard in the Great Atrium at Alexandria, the seat of the prefect's court, at about the same date, concerning the same questions involving the status and privileges of soldiers in Egypt; in both cases the nome *strategoi* are informed of the decision. Both decisions are clearly those of the prefect Tuscus, who is named in *P. Yale* 1528.17, and date from the same year and possibly the same group of hearings.

Heading the ten members of the *consilium* is Norbanus Ptolemaeus who, as both *iuridicus* (δικαιοδότης) and also *idiologus*, representing the

---

the provincial *fasti* of Tarrraconensis, but their value is otherwise problematic. Three imperial officials are listed on each tablet in order of seniority—the governor T. Aurelius Fulvus *legatus Augusti*, the assistant legate Rufus *legatus Augusti*, and the equestrian provincial procurator Maturus *pro(c)urator Augusti*—in connection with a legal determination of some kind involving two tribes in the north-east corner of the province, the Olossitani and the Indicetani. On all three tablets the word *consilium* occurs, referring separately to each of the three officials in such a way that it cannot be the *consilium* of the governor. It perhaps simply means the advice or opinion expressed by each, which in turn prompted malediction by the author of each tablet. With Pliny 10.84 in mind, if the legate Rufus here is a *iuridicus* (cf. Syme 1.389; 2.755), we may conjecture another joint investigation by the senior officials in different sectors of the administration to consider a civil dispute between parties in an imperial province.

[47] See esp. Schérer 45–7; Pflaum 250ff.

[48] Cf. the formula (ὁ δεῖνα) σκεψάμενος μετὰ τῶν ἐν τῷ συμβουλίῳ εἶπεν: e.g. *P. Oxy.* 2111.1.9–10; *P. Ryl.* 75.29; *P. Goodsp.* 29.10.

Special Account, was the senior equestrian official in Alexandria assisting the prefect in both legal and financial administration.[49] He is followed by five *tribuni militum*, senior officers of equestrian rank from the two legions stationed in Egypt, two from the *III Cyrenaica* and three from the *XXII Deiotariana*, as befitted the case under investigation.[50] There is a puzzle over the status of the procurator (διοικητής) Claudius Heracleides who appears as low as eighth out of ten, if the counsellors are listed in hierarchical order. This would be surprising if the office was at the equestrian level of *ducenarius* at this period, next in seniority to the *iuridicus* and *idiologus*.[51]

(5) *BGU* 288 (Fayum, AD 138–161), lines 14–15:

>]ι [κα]θημένων ἐν τῷ πραι | [τωρίῳ τοῦ κρατίστου ἡγ]εμόνος ἐ[ν] τῇ Θαισαρίου διαγνώ[σει] (followed by eight fragmentary lines containing sixteen names and possibly twenty in all).

Pflaum, in a careful reconstruction of the *consilium*,[52] posits from the fragments of *nomina* and *cognomina* a number of procurators and military tribunes at the head of the list. They do indeed have Latin *cognomina* (Crispus, Sestianus, Serenus), with the exception of a Iulius Epimachus (cf. Trajan's freedman procurator Epimachus in Pliny 10.84). Others who follow with Greek *cognomina* are lower in the hierarchy and could be prominent Alexandrians. Military matters need not be at stake—the case involves a certain Thaisarios, probably an Egyptian—even so, military officers may have served routinely as assessors on the prefect's *consilium*; but the inclusion of imperial procurators at equestrian level here is speculative.

7

From this brief survey, what conclusions can be drawn about the process of consultation and the lines of responsibility in the various kinds of province under the early empire? When groups of senior officials in a province were called together, who initiated such action and for what purposes, and who determined the composition of the group?

---

49 On the bureaucracy and administration of Roman Egypt in this period, see now A.K. Bowman, *CAH*² 10 (1996), 679ff.

50 Following Pflaum 252ff.

51 Cf. Schérer 47; Pflaum 256f.

52 Art. cit. 122f.

In the case of Pliny 10.84, the initiative for joint action (and the decision who was to be included) came clearly on instructions from the emperor. This was in response to a petition sent directly to the emperor by the representatives of a city within the province through the imperial postal system so that it would reach its intended destination as quickly and safely as possible. The emperor then laid down the procedure for a speedy resolution of the matter. But he did not simply refer it back to the governor for his decision alone. It was not a governor's normal *consilium*, but a conference of senior officials, including those responsible for the other sectors of administration in the province. The fact that both imperial procurators, equestrian and freedman, were required to sign off on the decision, makes it unlikely that the interests of the treasury in Rome were not involved in some way. Whether this was strictly the *aerarium* or the *fiscus* does not matter, as by this period in imperial provinces there is no sign of administrative personnel other than the emperor's own staff for supervising the collection of public revenues. But the case also involved the governor's civil jurisdiction over the cities of the province. Thus it is not left to the procurators alone to determine. Among the interested parties were no doubt those Nicaeans who were Roman citizens married to *peregrinae* who would stand to benefit from the Roman rather than Nicaean view of intestate succession. One of the main concerns of the *mandata* under which Pliny operated was the financial condition[53] of the cities. It would be significant, therefore, against the notion of his so-called 'special mission', if Pliny was *not* authorised to depart from normal practice in an imperial province, i.e. that the provincial procurator should at least share in administrative decisions in which a fiscal interest was involved.[54] In imperial provinces this procedure would lessen the potential for disagreement between

[53] 10.110, 111; see Sherwin-White 547f.

[54] Why Trajan required the senior *freedman* procurator to be brought in as well as the equestrian procurator, we can only speculate. Equestrian-freedman pairs of imperial procurators operating in tandem appear often enough in official documents. See, most recently, the example of Calpurnius Quintianus and Aelius Aug. lib. Amphigethes at Caesarea in Syria-Palaestina, on a papyrus published in 1974, supplemented by a recently published inscription from Caesarea (*P. Berol.* 21652 = *SB* 12.11043; W. Eck, *ZPE* 123 [1998], 249–55). The relationship between the two classes of procurators, termed 'collégialité inégale' by Pflaum, is a matter for a larger investigation; see G. Boulvert *Esclaves et Affranchis impériaux sous le Haut-Empire romain* (Naples, 1970), 392–409; Weaver *Familia Caesaris* (Cambridge, 1972), 278–81, with further references.

jurisdictions both deriving their mandate separately and directly from the emperor. Where there was uncertainty or lack of precedent, a direction from the emperor would be issued.

In proconsular provinces the situation was both more straightforward and more complicated. There the chief financial magistrate, the *quaestor*, senatorial in status, was directly subject to the *imperium* of the proconsular governor so that conflicts of jurisdiction could not arise. But the jurisdiction of the imperial patrimonial procurators in these provinces, although in theory confined to the imperial domains themselves, which happened to be most extensive in the senior proconsular provinces of Asia and Africa, in practice must have early on extended to matters not strictly financial within these limits and caused problems of demarcation with the quaestors and eventually, as imperial intervention in a province increased, with the proconsul himself. Witness the passage from Ulpian's *De officio proconsulis* (*Dig.* 1.16.9pr.) quoted above (n. 5) "Of course, if there should be a case involving the financial interests of the *fiscus*, which is the concern of the emperor's procurator, the proconsul would do better to keep out of it." It would be simplistic to assume that by the early third century this injunction applied only to cases strictly confined to imperial patrimonial property.

It is not unusual to find provincial procurators, at least of equestrian standing, acting in common with senatorial governors of both kinds of province, proconsular and imperial, in making decisions particularly on matters involving land, such as boundary disputes, whether or not the *fiscus* was directly involved,[55] just as it is normal to find procurators exercising their own jurisdiction alone.[56]

The position regarding subordinate officials of senatorial standing, i.e. *legati proconsulis* and *quaestores* in proconsular provinces, and *legati legionis* and *legati iuridici* in imperial provinces, is another matter. It is clear that proconsuls during the year in their province exercised direct authority over their subordinates and called them in for formal

[55] E.g. *OGIS* 538 = *IGR* 3.335, between Sagalassos and Tymbrianassos in Galatia (AD 54/55)—note the plural verb . . . ροθέτησαν. Cf. *Fouilles de Delphes* III. 4 (1970) nos. 287, 288 (AD 98, 99); *AE* 1939, 178 = *Syria* 20 (1939), 52f. (AD 102); *Dig.* 50.1.38.1 (AD 161–7): "idque excutere praesidem adhibito procuratore debere"; *CJ* 2.36 2 (AD 226): "procuratorem meum una cum praeside, praesente fisci patrono, adire vos debere".

[56] On procuratorial jurisdiction, see, for example, the extensive discussion in *Historia* 10 (1961), 116f. (Stockton); 11 (1962), 377f. (Seager); 13 (1964), 180–7 (Millar); 14 (1965), 362–7 (Millar); and *Latomus* 25 (1966), 461–89 (Brunt).

consultation, including them taking their place at the head of the proconsul's *consilium*. It is not clear that the same applied within imperial provinces. As far as the governor's *consilium* is concerned, the evidence is inconclusive. These need not have included senior officials, such as *legati*, but did include, amongst others of note, persons of junior age and status, provided they were Roman citizens, and those whose official position was that of salaried *adsessores* and *comites* of the governor or army officers. Assistant *legati* in these provinces exercised a jurisdiction of their own, delegated and circumscribed by the emperor, not the imperial governor. While we have as yet no details of a *consilium* of such *legati* or indeed of an equestrian praesidial *procurator*, these can be assumed to have consulted *consilia* of their own. Although the process of appeal from their decisions remains unclear, it is likely that such appeals and also serious cases requiring the exercise of full magisterial *imperium* were customarily referred to the governor to deal with in the course of his *conventus* circuit.

The position of the *praefectus Aegypti*, as often, was somewhat different. He alone had full judicial competence in all classes of cases, both civil and criminal. But while only the prefect was empowered to hold the *conventus*, which he must do in person, he could, and did, without reference to the emperor, at the time of the *conventus* directly delegate a large number of cases to be heard by his subordinate equestrian officials such as the *iuridicus*, the *idiologus* and the *dioiketes*, and at other times outside Alexandria to the *epistrategos*. It would be natural for these officials to serve also on the prefect's *consilium* when requested. In this respect the situation in Egypt was similar to that of a governor in a proconsular province.

ASPECTS OF VIOLENT CRIME IN THE ROMAN EMPIRE

Keith Hopwood

Professor Crook, in his article 'Legal History and General History',[1] comments on the difficulty of using Roman law as a source for Roman history: "The law is, after all, normative: it doesn't *des*cribe what has happened, it *pre*scribes what is supposed to happen."[2]

He then gives a characteristically sharp observation of his own, doubtless observed while walking from his rooms in St. John's College, Cambridge, of massed undergraduate cyclists breaking the one-way system along Trinity Street while the helpless police look on. Laws are complex enactments: that they are intended to prescribe or forbid a course of action makes them part of a process of change to, or accommodation within, local customs.[3] Legal anthropologists have animadverted on this process for many years: does the law change society or does society change the laws? An extreme example is the use of law to reform society. In 1926 Turkey, under Mustafa Kemal Atatürk, adopted the Swiss Civil Code.[4] The efficacy of this action has been much discussed: keen Kemalists see it as an act which "draws our people upwards to civilisation."[5] It is, of course, now a major arena of contestation between secularists and those proposing a return to the *sharia* of Islam.[6] The Swiss code has been keenly evaded and adhered to by different sectors of the population—and by the same people at different times. John Crook's anecdote nicely shows the ten-minute bursts of lawlessness in Cambridge carried out by people who are law-abiding for the remaining fifty minutes of the hour.

The effectiveness of a law depends on its enforceability. An unenforceable law is no law at all. But what about laws that are

[1] *BICS* 41 (1996), 31–6.

[2] Ibid. 34.

[3] Moore (1975), 8.

[4] Date in Hotham (1972), 140. Minimal discussion in Kinross (1964), 424; unmentioned in Mango (1999) and Zürcher (1993).

[5] Anonymous lawyer cited in Hotham (1972), 140.

[6] As I write, I notice that this week's *Times Higher Education Supplement* (30/3/01), p. 10, reports on the threatened closure of Fatih University in Ankara for "failing to comply with the principles of secularism".

partially-enforceable, perhaps for fifty minutes of every hour? It is highly unlikely that the majority of laws are fully enforceable: some people will break them and remain unapprehended, or there will be circumstances where the law is unenforceable through social pressures. It is better, therefore, to see (if one can) law as process in the sense of a set of circumstances that may lead to a certain result.[7] The result may be very different from that in the mind of the legislators, as is evident from Steven Runciman's anecdote about Metaxas' attempt to halt the deforestation of Greece by goats, through offering a reward for every goat killed. Greek peasants turned to goat-breeding to claim the rewards more easily.[8] The potentiality of the 'may' in the definition of process is always of importance when considering the achievement of any legislation.

Enforceability may be almost impossible when the law concerns sexual activity, particularly if that activity is carried out privately and between consenting parties. Unless one party accuses the other for an offence for which s/he is equally culpable, how might the misdemeanour become apparent? Yet states have throughout history had such laws on the statute books. It seems that at this point we have to consider law as part of 'ideology'.[9] The point is partially taken up by Lloyd:[10]

> No amount of positivist insistence that law and morals or policy are distinct can alter the fact that legal decisions are inevitably based on an ideology. It is therefore better to face up to this and make a conscious effort to recognise what are the operative values of one's society and develop the law accordingly, rather than attempt to treat all legal decisions as purely technical exercises in legal logic.

He goes on to examine the principle of 'caveat emptor' and, like Marxist scholars, he sets it in the context of capitalist ideology.[11] But this is only part of the problem. If, however, Lloyd sets legal decisions (to which we can add law-making) within the context of "the

[7] Definition adapted from Moore (1978), 42.

[8] Runciman (1991), 22.

[9] The definition of 'ideology' is contentious. For the purposes of this paper I take Plamenatz's definition: "a set of closely related beliefs and ideas, or even attitudes, characteristic of a group or community." (1970), 15. For a different view, see Larrain (1979), passim.

[10] (1964), 212–13.

[11] On Marxist approaches to contract, see Hirst (1979), ch. 5, and National Deviancy Conference (1979), passim.

operative values of one's society", then the laws themselves are an important historical source for the ideology of their time and the compromises legislators were forced to make with customs and established interest groups to ensure that the laws were enforceable: legal history becomes general history, and general history is richer if it takes legal history into account. The laws passed are an invaluable source for the ideology of their period: they may or may not tell us what people were doing; instead, they tell us what the ruling groups wanted people to be doing and what they wanted them not to do.

At this point one might object that common sense suggests that laws are a response to activities perceived as anti-social and are responses to challenges, not opening moves in themselves. This view fails to take into consideration semi-enforceable and partial legislation: on this view such enactments are utterly invalid. But let us consider a case the 'common-sense' view would consider crucial: the repetition of laws, which was common in the later Roman empire. A serious problem throughout the Roman empire was banditry. One way of dealing with the problem was to forbid the harbouring of bandits by citizens of the empire. Laws against this practice were passed in 374, 383, 391 and 400.[12] Was not the first law sufficient? Why were reiterations needed? Any 'logical' system would simply refer to its initial condemnation of the practice. Although these reiterations very roughly correspond to outbreaks in Isauria, the prohibitions are empire-wide, and it is surely more sensible to see in these laws the responses of different regimes on coming to power (the enactments would correspond to the reigns of Valentinian and Valens [374], Theodosius [383 and 391] and Arcadius and Honorius [400]). The repetition belongs to the ideological sphere rather than the juristic. Emperors had to show that they were opposed to banditry, and these laws were, in effect, calls to their supporters to follow them in this legitimating pursuit.

If, then, law is a form of ideology, it is a unique form by which the verbal formulation of a law is an attempt to transform society at large. To some extent, it is[13] like magic, in that a form of words is used to transform the outside world. Normally, ideology can be acquiesced in or resisted: law attempts to impose a new ideology or enforce an existing ideology on the populace. It is not just a system of ideas

[12] *CTh.* IX.29.1; IX.29.2; VII.18.7; VII.18.10.

[13] On this aspect of language, see Thomas (1971), 210–2, and de Romilly (1975).

and moral saws, but a form by which they are imposed. Again, we can go further and say that the formulation of these impositions reflects on the nature of society—legal history becomes general history.

One of the laws I shall be dealing with later[14] has been condemned by a recent author as 'slack'.[15] Slackness is only important if law is seen as a fully coherent system. In such a system, laws must be capable of one interpretation, provide absolute criteria for judging whether an action is felonious or not, and be capable of examination in the courtroom. Today, many hours are spent in ensuring such accuracy in the laws.[16] Ancient laws, which were probably *ad hoc*, did not have a need for systematisation. In the later Roman empire, such laws achieved heights of vagueness (for the legal purist) and fictional power. A law of 392 against banditry is worth analysing closely:[17]

> Per omnes regiones, in quibus fera et periculi sui nescia latronum fervet insania, probatissimi quique et destrictissimi defensores adsint disciplinae et cotidianis actibus praesint, qui non sinant crimina inpunitate coalescere.

This law concerns the activities of the *defensores civitatis*,[18] so the *defensores* mentioned in the text are a specific group of officials serving within the cities of the empire. Their prescribed activities take a narrative form here which conveys considerable ideological weight.

The opening clauses pose the problem to be faced: "In all those regions where the wild madness of bandits, careless of its danger, rages . . ." We are advised of a widespread problem, in this case, banditry, but it is described in expanded terms. These terms do not help the *defensores* to enforce the law, but give the government's view on the crime which suits the prevailing ideology of the time.[19] We hear that the madness of bandits is *fera* (wild/bestial) portraying not only the madness which the government sees as opposition, but looking forward, proleptically, to the punishment meted out to bandits.[20]

---

[14] *CTh.* IX.30.5.

[15] Honoré (1998), 224.

[16] Yet, vitally, some modern enactments do not envisage their modes of implementation. Government in Britain today lays responsibility for enforcement of its policies on delegated bodies, such as NHS Trusts, County Councils, Universities, etc, but does not assimilate them into its power structure by directly giving them the means to carry out the programme in question. In Higher Education today, the University for Industry (UfI) project is an example of this.

[17] *CTh.* I.29.8 (= *CJ.* I.55.6).

[18] On the *defensor* see Jones (1964), 144–6.

[19] For a contemporary example, see Amm. Marc. XIX.13.1–3.

[20] Hopwood (1983), 180; Coleman (1990).

Indeed, the crime is so wild as to be utterly careless of its own self-preservation and the ultimate irresponsibility.[21] The state is facing an attack by feckless beasts: what resources can it bring to bear? Before we are dismayed, the superlative *probatissimi quique* restores our confidence that the state has men of such proven integrity to call upon. Not only are they men of the greatest probity: they are *destrictissimi*—with their swords already unsheathed to bring order out of the threatened chaos. By now, we realise that these men are the *defensores civitatis* whom the government can conjure from the earth with a jussive subjunctive so embedded within a description of their virtues that it almost seems a throwaway. The achievements decreed for the *defensores* roll on: "adsint disciplinae et cotidianis actibus praesint." With so firm and rapid a response, what chance has a mere abstract (the madness of bandits) against our heroes? Finally, we hear that the *defensores* will take pre-emptive action not to allow crimes to build upon each other with impunity (where are the criminals?). The narrative pattern is all. We are not told how the *defensores* are to accomplish this feat. It is assumed that they will do this by the powers that they already have.

From a practical point of view, this legislation is redundant. It is seen as a sign of the "increasing obscurity" of the Roman legal process.[22] But that 'obscurity' reveals a changing pattern of legislation (or reglementation),[23] as the government relied on its prestige and status to secure obedience. The 'obscurity' also serves as a rallying point for the urban élites on whose support the government relied. As new legislation was published on notice boards in the cities, the committed would be heartened by its presence.

So far I have argued that legislation changes with society, and has a relation to society that is difficult to predict. How, then, are laws made? In a seminal study of modern legislation against drug-abuse in the US, Becker described a pressure group whom he called "moral entrepreneurs."[24] In the Roman empire, these would be the Emperor and his council or consistory. However, these bodies were open to canvassing from outside, as Corcoran's analysis of recipients in the Tetrarchic period attests.[25] Legislation was open to local influences:

[21] On the irresponsibility of banditry, see Libanius *Or.* 48.35–6.
[22] MacMullen (1962, reprinted 1990), esp. 70–1.
[23] The term is Moore's: (1978), 18.
[24] (1963), ch. 8.
[25] (1996), ch. 5.

as we shall see, the laws against possession of horses in Picenum, Apulia, Calabria, Bruttium and Lucania in the fourth century[26] imply that local landowners had informed the consistory of problems and that other groups intervened to modify the legislation in their own interests. We might, with de Robertis,[27] consider also an intervention by the *corpus suariorum* or swineherds' guild. These inferences hint at the range of moral entrepreneurs in the Roman empire.

With these points in mind, I want to study some Roman approaches to violent crime, starting with the *lex Iulia de vi*[28] and its associated problems of self-help, and finishing with these laws prohibiting the use of horses in southern Italy. We will see trends in Roman criminal law, disguised by the changing forms of legislation, but still common across four centuries.

1. Violence and Self-Defence

The *lex Iulia de vi* has been studied as a law granting appeal[29] or as a blanket disarmament of the inhabitants of the Roman empire.[30] Little thought has been given to the law as 'process'—how it was created, modified and interpreted in use. Here we need to consider social structures which were apparent to the drafters, but not to a modern reader. Legal history and general history become crucially intertwined. The same text has already been used in two discourses about the nature of the Principate. We must analyse its operation carefully.[31]

The law is preserved in the *Digest*[32] and there is an extensive commentary by Paul.[33] The law reads as follows:[34]

> Lege Iulia de vi publica tenetur, qui arma tela domi suae agrove inve villa praeter usum venationis vel itineris vel navigationis coegerit.

[26] *CTh.* IX.30.1–5.
[27] (1972), 206 n. 55.
[28] I do not split the lex into public and private sections.
[29] Garnsey (1966).
[30] MacMullen (1974), 35 n. 26. Criticised by Brunt (1975).
[31] This discussion builds on Hopwood (1989), 178–9.
[32] *Digest* 48.6.1–11.
[33] *Sent.* V.26.
[34] *Digest* 48.6.1.

This cannot have been intended to disarm the inhabitants of the empire: even in this first clause, there are exceptions made. Brunt has observed that the law as a *lex rogata* was originally confined to the Roman citizens dwelling in Italy.[35] He concedes that at some future date the law seems to have applied to all the inhabitants of the empire, but cannot be certain of the means by which this was achieved or the time-scale involved. If he is right, we need to imagine the spread of legislation to the provinces as a gradual, piecemeal process, and not a systematic imposition of legislation. Here, the question enters into the vexed area of 'Romanisation'.[36]

The legislation itself concerns not the holding of arms, but the collection of arms (*coegerit*).[37] At once there is a favoured group of people: those who have arms already. We cannot speculate on the prevalence of weapons among the citizens of the early empire, but we might well suggest that those in possession of arms were members of the aristocracies in Rome and elsewhere, bred to the use of arms. Even with this exception, further clauses make the carrying of weapons legitimate: they can be received by bequest (ancestral weapons suggest a well-off family), or they can be essential for the purposes of one's trade. The final clause, after dealing with attacks on houses (see below), concludes with the deflating statement:[38] "qui telum tutandae salutis suae causa gerunt, non videntur hominis occidendi causa portare".

The intention of the law does not seem to have been to disarm the inhabitants of Italy or the empire. The granting of the right to wayfarers to bear arms must surely have increased the dangers of travelling.[39] Travelling was dangerous enough anyway.[40] We hear of disappearances of an equestrian and a town-councillor,[41] and, although Roman law was very harsh on those who did not turn up to defend

---

[35] (1975), 273. It may, however, have been incorporated into some provincial edicts so that the inhabitants of individual provinces might have been brought under its jurisdiction.

[36] See, for example, the essays collected by Mattingly (1997); by Huskinson (2000); and by Hoff and Rotroff (1997).

[37] Thus Brunt (1975), 262.

[38] *Digest* 48.6.11.

[39] That danger increases as more people possess arms has been demonstrated by Hanawalt's study of homicide in medieval Oxford (1979).

[40] See, for example, Horace *Ep.* I.2.32; Martial VII.72.8; Columella *RR.* I.5.7; Juvenal X.22; Lib. *Or.* 34.76. The *locus classicus* is, of course, the man rescued by the 'good Samaritan' on the road from Jerusalem to Jericho, Luke 10.30.

[41] Pliny *Ep.* VI.25.

their cases, an acceptable excuse was capture by bandits.[42] Epictetus' hypothetical traveller faces a whole range of choices:[43] τίνι προσκατατάξας ἑαυτόν; τῷ δεῖνι, τῷ πλουσίῳ, τῷ ὑπατικῷ; The people chosen and their ranks are not accidental: τῷ δεῖνι (any Tom or Dick), τῷ πλουσίῳ (a local wealthy man, probably a town councillor) or, finally, τῷ ὑπατικῷ (the proconsul of the province). They might all provide a safe journey by means of their armed entourage. The ordinary citizen (τῷ δεῖνι) might have availed himself of arms by the *lex Iulia* described above; a rich man would have hangers-on, or even armed estate-guards (*saltuarii*/ὀροφύλακες)[44] who would ensure some sort of protection. The proconsul would, of course, have an army escort.

This passage makes it clear that the *lex Iulia* did not disarm the subjects of Rome. The statute seems to have concerned itself with the limiting of the use of arms within the empire. These reasons were: livelihood, hunting, travel or self-help. All are interconnected in that they all concern journeys outside the city-state. Those who hunt need weapons for the despatch of their prey and the means to secure access to any parts to which their quarry might try to escape. The wealthy man (τῷ πλουσίῳ) might well find the need to protect his person in the countryside as he prepared with his servants to kill their prey. Equally, the traveller, might find the need to protect himself when threatened in the mountains. All these are subsumed within the category of self-help. It is therefore useful to examine this overall category.

Although the use of force to acquire claimed goods led to the loss of a civil suit,[45] it was enjoined in cases of criminal damage from earliest times.[46] A relevant case is the 'Cnidian Chamber-Pot Incident' which had its summation by Augustus in 6 BC.[47] Here, the *princeps* is giving his verdict on a squabble which broke out among the curial class in Cnidus. One faction besieged a family in their house (we are not told whether this was a town-house or an estate-centre).[48] Weapons are not explicitly mentioned, but the attacks were μεθ'

[42] *Digest* 27.1.13.7.

[43] *Discourses*, IV.1.94.

[44] Robert (1949), 58.

[45] Robinson (1995), 30. This is the case mentioned by Professor Crook (1967) as 'piquant': I here supply the details.

[46] In the Law of the Twelve Tables: see footnote 57 below.

[47] S. Riccobono *et al.* (eds.) *Fontes iuris Romani anteiustiniani* (1940–3), vol. 3, no. 185 (= IGRRP IV.1031).

[48] On estate centres, see Hopwood (1986).

ὕβρεως καὶ τρόπῳ τινι πολιορκίας[49] which implies that the assailants had weapons. Those besieged, Euboulos and Tryphera, had the option of negotiation or fight. Augustus himself comments that they did not order their followers to kill their enemies. The *princeps* suggests that the anger felt by these defenders might not unjustifiably lead to murder (ὡς ἂν ὑπ' ὀργῆς οὐ[κ] ἀδίκου προήχθη(ι)).[50] The final outcome was that the besieged cast down excrement from chamber-pots onto the besiegers until one slave accidentally dropped the pot as well, and in so doing killed a leader of the besiegers. Augustus supports the besieged party and justifies the use of violence well beyond that they claimed, going so far as to hint that the murder of the assailants would have been justified in this case.

That this is the sort of violence the *lex Iulia* aimed to prevent is shown by the gloss on the law in the *Sententiae Pauli*:[51]

> Lege Iulia de vi privata tenetur, qui quem armatis hominibus possessione domo villa agrove deiecerit expugnaverit obsederit clauserit, idve ut fieret homines commodaverit locaverit conduxerit.

Here, the focus is on the nature of the affray, not the collection of arms in itself. The law therefore seems to be there to stop local small-scale leaders (not leaders of revolts, *pace* Brunt)[52] arming their followers to make a forcible conclusion to the tensions on town councils.[53] The importance of this for provincial peace is clear when we consider the reliance of Rome on local élites, formed as town councils, to govern the empire locally.[54] If the curial classes were split, whole territories might also split along factional lines and intervention might be necessary. The problem was that allowing the local élites to bear arms protected them against subversion from below, but allowed factions within the élite to arm against each other.

This is compounded when we turn to the problem of self-help. If all citizens have the right of self-defence and can bear arms, how does one determine which party is the aggressor? It is not immediately obvious to an arresting officer whether a man is armed for offensive work or his own self-protection. The hazardous nature of

---

[49] Lines 14–5.
[50] Line 22.
[51] V.26.3.
[52] (1975), 266–70.
[53] On such tensions, see Brown (1978), ch. 2.
[54] Lendon (1997), passim. See Goodman (1987) for the consequences of a breakdown of local government.

the environment and the presence of feuds among the élites make the issue more complicated. This is where *dolus* (now known as *mens rea*) comes to the fore.[55] The establishment of intention was vital.[56] Juridically, it was a matter for the courts to define: practically, it was the task of the arresting officer. At each stage of the process, the legitimacy may be reassigned. Each case has a history. Given the nature of our sources, the history of that process often eludes us.[57]

This was more than a procedural problem. Developed legal systems ensure that they enshrine the state's monopoly of violence, to which any challenges must be deemed illegitimate. If, however, the state concedes the principle of self-help, there will be difficulties in discerning which use of force is legitimate unless there is some overarching legal authority. In the Roman empire, that authority was the Emperor and, as in the case of the Cnidian Chamber-Pot Incident, he had the last word. However, this issue returns us to the status of law as process, and the temporary nature of some solutions to legal problems. Presumably, time had elapsed between the occurrence of the Chamber-Pot Incident itself and the decision to delegate the resolution of the incident beyond Cnidus. This delegation would be to the proconsul of Asia in the first instance, and thence to the *princeps*. There may have been several reasons for this deferral.

Firstly, there was the nature of the incident itself. Self-help had always been allowed by the Roman state to an individual in certain cases such as the right to repel a burglar on one's property by night,[58] or to a town as a corporate body if the decurions led them.[59] The former condition did not apply, as the besieged property had not yet been broken into, and it is unclear from Augustus' letter whether the besiegers intended to force an entrance. The high status of the parties to the dispute also precluded solution within the *boule* at Cnidus. Decision had to be deferred elsewhere.

A decision of this nature, ultimately, involves the labelling of parties: one as legitimate in his use of violence, the other illegitimate. Cnidus did not have the necessary authority locally to label the activities of one party as illegitimate. The illegitimate use of force was

---

[55] For a brief approach to the concept of *mens rea*, see Morris (1976), 43–6.

[56] *Coll. Mos. et Rom.* I.6.1–4; I.11.3–4.

[57] On the importance of process, see Bourdieu (1977).

[58] Aulus Gellius, *NA.* XI.18.7–9, preserving the Law of the XII Tables (Table VIII according to *FIRA* (second edition), 59).

[59] Charter of the colony of Urso (*FIRA* (second edition), 191 = *ILS* 6087).

seen in the Roman empire as a form of *latrocinium* (banditry).[60] Equally, however, *latrocinium* was used to denote illegitimate rule, at least from the time of Domitian onwards.[61] Throughout the usurpations of the third and fourth centuries AD, failed candidates for the throne were described as 'bandits.'[62]

We have seen that the labelling process was constantly deferred to a higher power: individuals using force would be considered by the council and the governor,[63] councillors by the governor and the Emperor. When emperors disagreed, where was the authority? That was a prize of the victor after the arbitration had been decided by arms. Hence St Augustine's famous comment "Remota itaque iustitia quid sunt regna nisi magna latrocinia? Quia et latrocinia quid sunt nisi parva regna?"[64]

If there was a succession crisis, St Augustine's paradox became more evident. This, surely, is why bandits had the exceptional legal status described by Shaw.[65] They were men who constantly lived by the kind of violence that had to be declared illegitimate if the Roman order[66] were to continue.

Consequently, it is a reflection of the ideology of the times that self-help was enjoined more and more on the inhabitants of the empire during the crisis of the third century and into the fourth. In 243 Gordian III granted anyone the right to resist an attacker even up to the point of killing him,[67] and in 391 Theodosius and his co-emperors redrafted the old law to allow people to kill intruders on their estates even if they were soldiers.[68]

These laws were not *cartes blanches* to the whole population. The clue lies in the word *praedia*. Estate-owners were given the right to

---

[60] The standard Roman definition of banditry is at *Digest* 50.16.118 (Pomponius): "Hostes hi sunt, qui nobis, aut quibus nos publice bellum decrevimus; ceteri latrones aut praedones sunt." All violence not subsumed under the title of *bellum* was, therefore, banditry.

[61] Pliny *Ep.* I.12.8 on the death of Q. Corellius Rufus who, despite severe terminal illness, wanted to outlive 'that bandit' (Domitian) by one day.

[62] See the pseudo-learned discussion at SHA *Firmus et al.* 2.2–3. For a modern discussion, see MacMullen (1963), 223–4.

[63] On the assize circuit, see Habicht (1975).

[64] *Civ. Dei* IV.4.

[65] (1984).

[66] For the expression, see MacMullen (1966).

[67] *CJ.* IX.16.2–3. The lethal response need no longer occur on the property of the attacked party.

[68] *CJ.* III.27.1.

defend themselves. We have seen that these men had kept estate guards at least since the first century AD. Now, at the turn of the fourth to the fifth century, they and their private forces were given the power to protect their holdings. On Christmas Day 409, the local police forces in the eastern empire were abolished as a threat to security.[69] Order was seen to lie in the hands of the local landlords—the 'rich'—to whose care Epictetus' traveller considered entrusting himself.

2. Rustling and the Use of Horses

A series of laws in the *Codex Theodosianus* have local application and refer to specific groups in society. They purport to concern the use of horses in certain regions of Italy in the middle to late fourth century AD. They seem, rather, at first sight, to be attempts to control rustling.[70]

Much of the evidence for rustling in the Roman empire is localised, though general rules are found.[71] Hadrian laid down harsh penalties for rustling in Baetica,[72] so the laws we shall be dealing with are nothing out of the ordinary in respect of their localised application. What is interesting for the legal historian is that the generally existing laws did not seem sufficient and so had to be strengthened by laws directed to local circumstances. Again, we are forced to consider what sort of 'system' the Roman criminal law was when such *ad hoc* legislation was seen as proper. Logically, the existing laws were sufficient. Consequently there was an ideological force behind this legislation, or perhaps special influence. Hadrian was himself from Baetica[73] and the exaggerated penalties may stem from his own frustration, or that of his friends, large-scale cattle raisers in Spain. All this is hypothesis, but speculation as to the process why laws are drafted is always useful, for it can make us aware of the 'moral entrepreneurs' behind the apparently solid façade of the law.

The first law, dated 30 September 364, is addressed to the praetorian prefect:[74]

[69] *CTh.* XII.14.1. For a discussion, see Hopwood (1999), 192–4.
[70] *CTh.* IX.30.1–5. The most recent treatment is by de Robertis (1972).
[71] *Digest* 17.14.2; *Sent. Pauli* 5.18.2; *Coll. Mos. et Rom.* 11.2.1.
[72] *Digest* 47.14.1.
[73] SHA *Hadr.* 1.1.
[74] *CTh.* IX.30.1.

> Exceptis senatoribus atque honoratis, sed et his, qui provincias administrant, veteranis etiam, qui sub armis militia functi sunt, et decurionibus ceteris omnibus per Picenam atque Flaminiam, nec non etiam et Apuliam et Calabriam, Brittios et Lucaniam atque Samnium habendi equi vel equi copiam praeclusam esse sancimus. ii vero, qui minime animos ab huius modi usurpatione deflectunt, abactorum supplicio teneantur.

Here, on the face of it, is an example of bad drafting. The initial ablative absolute should be the only exception, but we immediately move into "sed et his", a clause which extends to "et decurionibus". These exceptions are tacked on, regardless of style, to the first absolute phrase. The first third of the text consists of these exceptions. Nevertheless, sloppy thinking is permissible when an audience will accept the case because they are already predisposed to do so. The initial ablative absolute separates out the highest echelons of society, and the artificial extension of the clause tags on government agents, resident veterans and town councillors. The language groups together the classes of later Roman society accurately, by status. The interdiction of the possession or gathering of horses (a nice parallel to the *lex Iulia de vi*) is briskly dealt with. We then have the penalty, but delivered in a convoluted fashion. The use of horses by the groups who have not been exempted is a *usurpatio* and for that crime, they are to be treated as rustlers. The law seems to treat this usurpation of social status as equivalent to rustling: the temptation is to gloss it and state that those *humiliores* seen in possession of horses would be considered as having a felonious intent to rustle. This is, of course, correct in legal terms. The law, however, does not say that. It states that the usurpation is equivalent to rustling. The perceived social outrage has the same result as a modern interpretation, but the ideological thrust of the text is to cast a 'common sense' law against rustling in very different terms. The social groupings of southern Italy are solidly etched within this law effectively directed against rustlers. The aristocrats of the area were to be the 'men on horseback'.[75] Anyone who could not prove himself to be a *honestior* when caught with a horse was clearly in trouble.

The second text, dated a week later, is a response to a query from the Consular of Campania:[76]

---

[75] From the title of Finer (1962), and the appropriate title of the Evans' book *Hero on a Stolen Horse* (1977).

[76] *CTh.* IX.30.2.

> Ut omnes latronum conatus debilitati conquiescant, pastoribus rei nostrae, id est lanigerarum ovium pecudumque custodibus, nec non etiam procuratoribus et actoribus senatorum habendi equini pecoris licentiam denegamus . . .

Here, *abigeatus* is conflated with *latrocinium*, an easy elision in rural contexts.[77] However, we now have further status definitions also. The first law had banned all non-*honestiores* and non-imperial-office-holders from possessing horses, but what about their agents—the shepherds on imperial estates, and the procurators and factors of senators? On one level, as these men were tied to their patrons and were therefore likely to have been of good behaviour,[78] there should have been no difficulty in allowing them the necessary mobility; equally, if the military and senators were allowed to facilitate the administration of the area and the better use of their estates, particularly as they are described in the law as the guards of the flocks, the case for allowing these men access to the mobility gained from horses is clear.

The problem lay elsewhere. Rustling was big business. Resetting (fencing) stolen cattle needed large resources. Robinson drew attention to a Trajanic ruling[79] by which resetters suffered *relegatio*, and this led her to believe that the resetting of rustled cattle was an upper class crime.[80] A more explicit text comes from Ausonius (slightly later than these texts) who chides one of his friends:[81]

> an maiora gerens tota regione vagantes
> persequeris fures, qui te postremo timentes
> in partem praedamque vocant? Tu mitis et osor
> sanguinis humani condonas crimina nummis
> erroremque vocas pretiumque imponis abactis
> bubus et in partem scelerum de iudice transis?

Here, the landowner condones the crimes of his countrymen, and takes a 'cut' of the booty. It was not a great step from this to organise raids oneself, using that sense of honour that has always accrued to Mediterranean shepherds from the raid on the animal stocks of a rival.[82] We are back in the world of the factious town councillors of Cnidus.

---

[77] Cf. *MAMA* IV.297 where aggressive pasturing is described as λΩστε . . . α.
[78] Cf. Tac. *Hist.* I.4 on the differences between the 'tied' and 'sordid' plebs.
[79] *Digest* 47.14.3.3.
[80] (1995), 26.
[81] *Ep.* 13.22–7.
[82] See, for example, Herzfeld (1985), 29–33.

The third text comes from June of the following year (365). The opening sentences reprise the earlier legislation with the useful gloss "ut istis in locis equo vehi his tantummodo liceret, quos ab huius modi sceleris suspicione locus aut dignitas vindicavit."[83] Here the text generalises the attempted exceptions made earlier. It is again strikingly confirmatory both of the assumed pattern of reporting the crimes and of the social structure of the area that place or rank might remove a man from suspicion. Whatever the *honestiores* might be up to, *scelus* is an occupation confined to the *humiliores*.

The main thrust of this enactment, however, was to allow swineherds to use horses. We have seen earlier how de Robertis felt that this was by representation by the guild of swineherds. However, we have seen that these enactments represent a series of negotiations between the powers in the affected region (which might include such a group), and the central government, to create the kind of order acceptable to them.

The fourth law in the series merely allows Palatine officials the use of horses. The fifth comes from a generation later (1 December, 399). The area is still the south of Italy, and there is a blanket ban on shepherds having access to horses. However, there is an interesting rider: "Alioquin, si interdictus usus animalium vindicetur, conscios usurpationis huius seu dominos vel procuratores religationis poena retinebit."[84] In this text, it is assumed that shepherds who have taken horses contrary to their status (again, that word *usurpatio*) could only have done this with the connivance of their superiors. Again, there is the common sense view that shepherds could have obtained horses either by stealing them or being provided with them by masters who were encouraging their nefarious activities. The law might also point to the use of shepherds by local landowners (*domini*) and officials to indulge in violent feuding.[85]

These laws are consequently concerned with more than the interdiction of the use of horses: they are endeavouring to ensure rural security while honouring the status of the élite. Given the equivocal rôle of the élite in preserving rural order, the laws had to be constantly renegotiated. Here is an area where legal history and general history combine, and the social background is essential to the understanding of the texts.

---

[83] *CTh.* IX.30.3.

[84] *CTh.* IX.30.5.

[85] For rural insecurity in Italy at this time, see Symm. *Ep.* 2.22.

3. Conclusion

In the above case, it is clear whom the arresting agent must detain: the man who cannot prove his status to be mounted and who has thereby 'usurped' the privilege of the use of a horse. The arresting officers might be army, or local agents, or even agents of the local élite.[86] All these figures would be aware of local hierarchies, and spot someone who was 'out of place'.

What light, then, does this cast on the *lex Iulia de vi*? The *lex Iulia* also precluded the right to amass arms, but is hedged in with so many qualifications and escape-clauses that it cannot have functioned effectively on those terms. Just as the arresting officer had to make a decision concerning the status of a rider, so the arresting officer had to come to a similar decision about the motives of the man travelling with weapons. Ideas of respectability, appropriateness, and, of course, status would apply.[87] Both laws protect the status of that group known from the second century AD onwards as the *honestiores*. These are the men to whom Epictetus' imaginary traveller on the journey of life must turn: on their own terms and at their own level they offered protection to those who could or would pay the price.[88] The law, therefore, that became a system to which the whole empire was subjected was ultimately flexible enough to accommodate local power structures and discretionary enough to permit the traditional activities of the élite.

This flexibility was the consequence of negotiation and redrafting in the fourth century, and of suitable qualifications in the earlier legislation. All this suggests that the Roman criminal law was an organic growth and that the central government was prepared to have the law differentially or unevenly enforced. The police officers in Trinity Street have ancient forebears in discretion.

Epictetus' traveller finally turns to the emperor himself for security: however, the price is too great for a free philosopher and the risks connected with the ruler's fall overwhelmingly great. The emperor's rule, as St Augustine (and, indeed, Epictetus' contemporary, Favorinus)[89] had seen, was ultimately based on a monopoly of

[86] See Hopwood (1999) for the transformations that were occurring at the time.
[87] Hopwood (1989), 178–9.
[88] Hopwood (1999), 190.
[89] SHA *Hadr.* 15.12–13.

violence. Once that was challenged, the chaos of banditry threatened.[90] Laws concerning violence take us to the heart of the legitimacy of the Roman order, and it is my privilege to offer my thoughts on this problem to John Crook, who has been such a stimulus to an approach which, if he did not agree with, he always encouraged.

Bibliography

Becker, H.S. (1963) *Outsiders: Studies in the Sociology of Deviance*, New York, NY.

Bourdieu, P. (tr. R. Nice) (1977) *Outline of a Theory of Practice*, Cambridge.

Brown, P.R.L. (1978) *The Making of Late Antiquity*, Cambridge, Mass.

Brunt, P.A. (1975) 'Did Imperial Rome Disarm her Subjects?', *Phoenix* 29, 260–70.

Coleman, K.M. (1990) 'Fatal Charades: Roman Executions Staged as Mythological Enactments', *JRS* 80, 44–73.

Corcoran, S. (1996) *The Empire of the Tetrarchs: Imperial Pronouncements and Government AD 284–324*, Oxford.

Crook, J.A. (1967) *Law and Life of Rome*, London and Ithaca, NY.

——. (1996) 'Legal History and General History', *BICS* 41, 31–6.

Evans, H. and Evans, M. (1977) *Hero on a Stolen Horse: The Highwayman and his Brothers-in-Arms the Bandit and the Bushranger*, London.

Finer, S.E. (1962) *The Man on Horseback: the Role of the Military in Politics*, London.

Garnsey, P.D.A. (1966) 'The *Lex Iulia* and Appeal under the Empire', *JRS* 56, 167–89.

Goodman, M. (1987) *The Ruling Class of Judaea: The Origins of the Jewish Revolt against Rome AD 66–70*, Cambridge.

Habicht, C. (1975) 'New Evidence on the Province of Asia', *JRS* 65, 64–91.

Hanawalt, B.A. (1979) *Crime and Conflict in English Communities 1300–1348*, Cambridge, Mass.

Herzfeld, M. (1985) *The Poetics of Manhood: Contest and Identity in a Cretan Mountain Village*, Princeton, NJ.

Hirst, P. (1979) *On Law and Ideology*, London.

Hoff, M.C. and Rotroff, S.I. (eds.) (1997) *The Romanization of Athens*, Oxford.

Honoré, T. (1998) *Law in the Crisis of Empire 379–455 AD: the Theodosian Dynasty and its Quaestors*, Oxford.

Hopwood, K.R. (1983) 'Policing the Hinterland: Rough Cilicia and Isauria', in Mitchell, S. (ed.) *Armies and Frontiers in Roman and Byzantine Anatolia: Proceedings of a Conference Held at University College, Swansea in April 1981*, Oxford, 173–88.

——. (1986) 'Towers, Territories and Terror: How the East Was Held', in Freeman, P. and Kennedy, D. (eds.), *The Defence of the Roman and Byzantine East: Proceedings of a Colloquium Held at the University of Sheffield in April 1986*, Oxford, 343–56.

——. (1989) 'Bandits, Élites and Rural Order', in Wallace-Hadrill, A. (ed.), *Patronage in Ancient Society*, London, 171–88.

——. (1998) '"All That May Become a Man": the Bandit in the Ancient Novel' in Foxhall, L. and Salmon, J. (eds.), *When Men Were Men: Masculinity, Power and Identity in Classical Antiquity*, London, 195–204.

——. (1999) 'Bandits Between Grandees and the State: The Structure of Power in Roman Rough Cilicia', in Hopwood, K.R. (ed.), *Organised Crime in Antiquity*, London, 177–206.

[90] On the chaos of banditry, see Hopwood (1998).

Hotham, D. (1972) *The Turks*, London.
Huskinson, J. (ed.) (2000) *Experiencing Rome: Culture, Identity and Power in the Roman Empire*, London.
Jones, A.H.M. (1964) *The Later Roman Empire 284–602: a Social Economic and Administrative Survey*, Oxford.
Kinross, Lord (1964) *Atatürk: the Rebirth of a Nation*, London.
Larrain, J. (1979) *The Concept of Ideology*, London.
Lendon, J.E. (1997) *Empire of Honour: the Art of Government in the Roman World*, Oxford.
Lloyd, D. (1964) *The Idea of Law*, Harmondsworth.
MacMullen, R. (1963) 'The Roman Concept Robber-Pretender', *RIDA* 10, 223–4.
——. (1966) *Enemies of the Roman Order: Treason, Unrest and Alienation in the Empire*, Cambridge, Mass.
——. (1974) *Roman Social Relations, 50 BC to AD 284*, New Haven, Conn.
——. (1986) 'Judicial Savagery in the Roman Empire', *Chiron* 16, 43–62.
Mango, A. (1999) *Atatürk*, London.
Mattingly, D.J. (ed.) (1997) *Dialogues in Roman Imperialism: Power, Discourse and Discrepant Experience in the Roman Empire*, Portsmouth, RI.
Moore, S.F. (1978) *Law as Process: an Anthropological Approach*, London.
Morris, T. (1976) *Deviance and Control: the Secular Heresy*, London.
National Deviancy Conference/Conference of Socialist Economists (1979) *Capitalism and the Rule of Law: from Deviancy Theory to Marxism*, London.
Plamenatz, J. (1970) *Ideology*, London.
Robert, L. (1949) *Hellenica: Recueil d'Épigraphie, de Numismatique et d'Antiquités Grecques*, Paris.
Robertis, F.M. de (1972) 'Prosperità e Banditismo nella Puglia e nell'Italia Meridionale durante il Basso Impero', in *Studi di Storia Pugliese in Onore di Giuseppe Chiarelli*, Rome, 197–231.
Robinson, O.F. (1995) *The Criminal Law of Ancient Rome*, London.
Romilly, J. de (1975) *Magic and Rhetoric in Ancient Greece*, Cambridge, Mass.
Runciman, S. (1991) *A Traveller's Alphabet: Partial Memoirs*, London.
Thomas, K. (1971) *Religion and the Decline of Magic*, London.
Zürcher, E.J. (1993) *Turkey: a Modern History*, London.

MENTAL MAPS: SEEING LIKE A ROMAN[1]

C.R. Whittaker

Late on the evening of January 12th, 49 BC, Julius Caesar, accompanied by a few friends, jumped into a carriage in Ravenna, after borrowing some mules from a local baker, in order to travel to Rimini. It was to be a momentous journey, since by crossing the River Rubicon, where his army was awaiting his arrival, he would automatically trigger off the civil war that changed the course of history. The road he took was probably the *via Popilia* which joined the *via Aemilia* at Cesina, one of the great highways of Republican Italy. Yet somehow he lost the way and, after wandering about all night, at dawn a guide showed him the way back to the highway on foot by narrow paths.

In the dark, I suppose, anyone can get lost. But why should Caesar have needed a guide to get back on the road once it became light? The countryside north of the Rubicon is not difficult, and Caesar's party must have travelled the road often. The road, yes. But once off the main road, they needed to know the country, and for that they needed a map. The most important march in history nearly did not happen for want of a map, and Julius Caesar nearly missed his own moment in it.

1. Geography and chorography

I use the example to re-examine some questions about itineraries and maps in the Roman world. If even a meticulous military commander like Caesar possessed, at most, only an itinerary of his route, and if this fact passed without comment in the second century AD when Suetonius told the story,[2] what are we to conclude about

[1] A primitive, short version of this paper was tried out on an audience of medievalists in Parma. I am grateful now for the chance to improve it and to submit it to John for his approval—with the same trepidation as I felt many years ago while he was trying to turn me into a Roman historian.

[2] Suetonius *Caes.* 31.

Roman achievements in geography and cartography? How did they perceive the world and its ordering of space? And what, if anything, might this tell us about Roman concepts of frontiers and empire?

Briefly, for the sake of completeness, I begin with some banalities about the main streams of Roman spatial representations. Surveys of lands in their cosmic context (*geographia/ges periodos*) were well known to the Greeks, which the Romans regularly cited but hardly developed. By contrast were detailed descriptions of regions and places (*chorographia*), to which Romans and Romanized writers contributed with an enthusiasm engendered by an expanding empire.[3] To these two cultural rivers must be added the lesser stream of land survey (*agrimensio*). The skill of 'gnomonics', as Pliny calls it, also owed a debt to Greece, but developed as a peculiarly intense Roman technology to serve Roman law, administration and imperialism.[4]

Unfortunately it is never clear when either the Greek termination *-graphia* or the Latin equivalents *descripta* or *depicta* meant 'written' as opposed to 'pictorial' representations, nor how much written commentary accompanied pictorial maps, nor whether the distinction between geography and chorography was always strictly maintained. Vitruvius, for example, while almost certainly looking at a 'geographic' pictorial representation of the world, referred to physical features, such as rivers, "which are drawn and described (*picta itemque scripta*) by chorographers."[5] It is equally impossible to be sure, when the Elder Pliny referred to *situs depicti* apropos of Armenia or to the *forma* of Ethiopia contained in a military report, whether he meant pictorial maps or written descriptions.[6] But even if the language to describe them was ambiguous, the broad distinction between the two main categories was clear enough to Ptolemy in the second century AD—the one, he said, requiring a mathematician, the other an artist.[7]

From all these sources, however, the only *certain* map, in any sense that we would recognise it, to survive from antiquity is the celebrated Peutinger Table, although preserved in a medieval copy. The

---

[3] Levi 1964, 34; Nicolet 1988, 12–14.

[4] Pliny *NH* 2.187.

[5] *De arch.* 8.2.6.

[6] Compare Plautus *Poen.* 1114: "formam verbis depinxti"; or Cic. *De rep.* 2.29: "in sermone depinxerit". Although *forma* in Plautus's example means a woman's looks, the word can mean a 'shape', or even a diagram; Campbell 2000, 34.

[7] Ptol. *Geog.* I.1.

map is too well known and studied to need much description,[8] so I simply stress that, although it is a map which covers the whole world, it does not derive from the classical world map tradition of *geographia*. In spirit it is an itinerary map in the chorographic tradition, which in its present form is a parchment roll nearly seven metres long by 34 cm high, made up (originally, though one is lost) of 12 segments that cover 112,000 km of Roman roads, divided into 6,000 measured distances along which 555 vignettes depict towns, *mansiones* (inns), *mutationes* (post stations) and tourist sights.[9] The question is, why was this, the only map to reach us, an itinerary map? Was it by chance and atypical?[10] Or was it, as I believe, because itineraries dominated and infiltrated all the other categories of ancient representations and perceptions of space? This is not a novel idea. But, since it has been challenged recently, it needs restating more forcefully and elaborating.[11]

2. Geography and maps

Take the first category of world 'geographic' maps. The Greek schematic concepts of the inhabited *oikoumene* divided into three continents and the universal cosmos arranged into *climata* zones of latitude, although represented sometimes pictorially, were probably so only on miniatures, too small to show many physical or topographic features.[12] These sorts of global maps and 'scientific' studies, made famous in Alexandria by Eratosthenes and others, were often cited by Romans, from early authors such as Sallust, Virgil and Lucan to Macrobius and Orosius in the Later Empire. That in turn almost certainly influenced Isidore of Seville in the seventh century and the medieval fashion for miniature T-O maps and zonal *mappaemundi*. Although there is no evidence that any of the known illustrations

[8] Above all Levi 1967, Bosio 1983; and the codex illustrations in Weber 1976.

[9] The ms. is discussed by Miller 1916, xiii–xvii.

[10] As Dilke 1987, 120.

[11] A good survey of the whole mapping debate is in Brodersen 1995, ch. 1. The proposition I support is most importantly presented by Janni 1984, to whom it will obvious this paper owes a great deal. But recently challenged by Clarke 1999, 102–3.

[12] The two best known examples featuring Aristagoras in Sparta (Hdt. 5.49) and Strepsiades in Athens (Aristoph. *Clouds* 200ff.) are both cited in the context of philosophic, cosmographic originals.

derived from Roman originals, such maps are often found in medieval editions of classical authors and might have had classical proto-types.[13]

But while neither Strabo nor the Elder Pliny showed much interest in cosmic theories, despite paying them lip service,[14] it is plausible that the penchant in writers such as Caesar, Strabo or Tacitus, for comparing countries to geometric or natural shapes of triangles, cones, oak leaves, animal skins and so on, owed something to their pictorial representation on such cosmic maps.[15] The distortions of the size, shape and centrality of Europe compared to Asia or Africa in the continental divisions of cosmic maps both fed and fed on the Euro-centric and Romano-centric prejudices reflected in Roman mental mapping and Roman rhetoric.[16] It must have been this kind of map which Varro saw in the temple of Tellus, since Eratosthenes figures in the story—perhaps the same map later seen by Vitruvius, which led them both to exclaim on the good fortune of Italy's geographic location in the centre of the world.[17]

Such early cosmic projections coincided with Roman preoccupations with imperial rule, since, as Polybius saw, they were a means of contextualizing unknown places in the mind's eye.[18] A global setting was one reason why Strabo thought *geographia* was "relevant to the practice of provincial governors" by stressing "the whole *oikoumene* under one rule."[19] The symbolic significance of this sort of representation—sometimes probably focusing on relevant bits—was not lost on the father of the Gracchi, when he wanted to glorify his Sardinian campaign. And they served as emblems on the shields of mythical heroes. The inamorata of Propertius was not the last to feel closer to her lover by looking at a cosmic map.[20] Under the

---

[13] Woodward 1985, 511; Edson 1997, 11, 26–30, 40.

[14] Clarke 1999, 207–208; Pliny devotes only a few sections of Book II and Book VI to cosmography.

[15] Caes. *BG* 5.13, Strabo 4.199, Mela 3.6.50, Tac. *Agric.* 10. The prize for such shapely comparisons goes to Dionysius Periegetes, widely read in schools; Jacob 1981, 39–40.

[16] Not even Ptolemy was immune, and was enthusiastically vulgarized by Dionysius Periegetes; Jacob 1981, 37. Clarke 1999, 296, discusses the rhetorical tradition of praising cities through their geographic centrality.

[17] Varro *RR* 1.2.1–4, Vitruv. *De arch.* 8.2.6; the same map: Janvier 1994, 59. The same cosmographic context surrounds the 'painted worlds' on the *tabula* seen by Propertius from which, he says, he learnt about climates: *Eleg.* 4.3.39–40.

[18] Polyb. 3.36–38; Clarke 1999, 190.

[19] Strabo 1.1.16 (*tas praxeis hegemonikas* can, of course, refer to generals, also).

[20] Gracchus: Livy 41.28 (176 BC); Shields: Ovid *Met.* 5.185 (map of the Nile); 13.110 (the whole universe). Lover: Propertius *Eleg.* 4.3.35–40.

Empire, global views of the earth were ideal teaching aids for good citizens, but carrying a private copy of them ("depictum orbem terrae in membrana") was dangerous under a paranoid emperor.[21] What we can be sure about, however, is that this kind of map never served, nor was intended to serve, as a guide for travellers, generals or imperial councils.

Yet even the art of geographic representation was to some extent influenced by perceptions of chorographic space, particularly that associated with itineraries. When a soldier at Dura Europos needed a devise on his shield he crudely symbolized a snippet from an itinerary along the Black Sea coast.[22] Polybius's confused attempt to give a geometric orientation of Italy used the road from Marseille to the Alps as his base line.[23] The Cosmography of Ravenna described the Forth-Clyde neck in Britain by "the cities in Britain itself joined to each other by a straight line". Indeed, although it called itself a Cosmography, it had taken on many of the characteristics of the chorographic tradition[24]—something which I shall come on to discuss. If it is true that Agrippa's and Augustus's Map was the direct ancestor of medieval *mappaemundi*, like that now preserved at Hereford, it is clear from them that importance of locality was defined by places and roads, however small the global map.[25]

3. The domination of chorographic perceptions

If we now turn to chorography, geographic representation had little in common with what little we know about the great world map of Agrippa, set up by Augustus in the portico off the Via del Corso in Rome,[26] nor with any other monumental maps in the Later Empire, such as the teaching map at Autun in the fourth century or the map of Theodosius II in the fifth century.[27] In reality, we know little about

---

[21] Suet. *Dom.* 10; Jacob 1981, 56, on the *Periegesis* of Dionysius as a teaching aid.

[22] The notion that the Dura map was an actual itinerary is self-evidently implausible; Dilke 1985, 121–2; but Sherk 1974, 560, seems to assume it was functional; cf. below (note 57).

[23] Poly. 2.14.4–12: cf. F. Walbank, *A historical commentary on Polybius*, vol. I (Oxford, repr. 1970), *ad loc.*: "a very forced and schematic description."

[24] Dilleman 1975.

[25] Crone 1965; Woodward 1987, 292; Brodersen 1995, 273; Edson 1997, 142.

[26] Pliny *NH* 3.17; Nicolet 1988, 108; Zanker 1988, 141.

[27] Agrippa's Map: Pliny *NH* 3.17; the Autun map: *Pan.Lat.* IX(IV).21; Theodosius's map: Dicuil *De mens.* 5.4.

what these maps actually looked like, since we have to rely upon only brief references to their characteristics. If they were all intended as imperial propaganda, as seems likely, they cannot have been very detailed. Nevertheless, if Agrippa's Map was connected to the project initiated by Caesar and completed by Augustus, whereby distinguished geographers were sent out to bring back their findings from various parts of the world, then according to the *Cosmographia* of Julius Honorius they occupied themselves with collecting not cosmic projections but local, topographic details.[28] Many of the maps' features confirm that they were derived not from cosmological maps but from itineraries, of which I pick out three.

3.1

They were essentially routes linking spot points. Agrippa's Map marked key towns, such as Pasinou Charax on the Persian Gulf, Lixus in Africa, Arsinoe on the Red Sea or Chalcedon and Byzantium in Asia, at the same time providing dimensions which mostly appear to follow roads, including those Agrippa had helped to construct.[29] The later Autun map was to teach the young "the distances between every place (*spatia intervalla*) with its name."[30]

3.2

As we know from the Elder Pliny's account of Agrippa's Map, many details were transmitted not from the map itself but from the written *commentarii* that accompanied it. These were plausibly the origin of the topographic lists that have come down to us from the Later Empire, the *Divisio Orbis Terrarum* and the *Dimensuratio Provinciarum*.[31] However, Pliny's insistence on the visual purpose of Agrippa's Map—*orbis terrarum urbi spectandus*—makes it difficult to believe that there never was a map to go with the commentary, only an inscription.[32]

---

[28] Text in *Geog.Lat.Min.* pp. 21–23 (Riese); discussion in Brodersen 1995, 262–7.

[29] Pliny's references are collected by Dilke 1985, 44–52; Brodersen 1995, notes than the *loci* are coastal sites.

[30] Nicolet 1988, 112; Janni 1984, 62. The Autun map may be linked to the marble pillar or pilaster, now disappeared, reported to have had on one side a list of Italian cities along the *via Aemilia*. But another fragment of a written itinerary from Autun suggests more local information: *CIL* XIII 2681; see Miller 1916, lxxiv.

[31] Riese, *Geog.Lat.Min.* rev. ed. 1965; Nicolet 1988, 104–7; this may explain the reference to the *chorographia* of Augustus in the *DOT*.

[32] Argued by Brodersen 1995, 275–8, citing other passages where Pliny uses

Putting text and map together seems to have been the practice later. The two cartographers of Theodosius recorded that "one wrote while the other painted."[33] Medieval cartographers likewise regularly imposed a written text, often a chorographic list, onto *mappaemundi*.[34]

3.3

Finally, there is the method of demonstrating Roman dominance, and the relation between centre and periphery, as is implied by the maps' propaganda intent. This overlaps with what I noted earlier about global maps. The Antonine Itinerary and the Peutinger Table, both perhaps compiled in the fourth century from earlier itineraries and/or route maps, demonstrated power through the roads, the one focusing on Milan, the other on Rome. It is the roads on the sixth century mosaic map at Madaba which proclaim Jerusalem's importance in Palestine, as also in later *mappaemundi*. A place was comprehended by its routes.[35]

But the best evidence of the way that a Roman's sense of space and visual perspectives were shaped by the horizontal, linear movement of itineraries over land and sea is contained in Roman writers of history and geography. Maybe Polybius is a less than perfect example, since he was torn between his Greek instinct for geographic abstractions and his Roman readers' interest in itineraries—although even this latter day Odysseus (as he called himself) is famed for his descriptions of southern Gaul or central Greece through itineraries.[36] In Livy, however, we see how much Polybius's chorographic descriptions of *topos* and travel chimed with Roman horizontal perspectives in the famous scene when Hannibal looked out over the north Italian plain after crossing the Alps.[37] This is one of several similar landscapes described by Livy, despite his rare ventures into

spectare metaphorically; but metaphor does not rule out a literal sense, and at the most creates ambiguity.

[33] *dum scribit, pingit et alter*; Dicuil *De mens.* 5.4. The so-called *Divisio Orbis Terrarum Theodosiana* referred to in a manuscript of Leiden, similar to that of Ripoll, must be linked to this event as well as having links with Agrippa's Map through the *DOT* and *DP*; Dalché 1992.

[34] Woodward 1987, 326; Edson 1997, 135.

[35] Antonine Itinerary: Arnaud 1992; Madaba: Dilke 1985, Janni 1984, 125.

[36] The tensions are excellently discussed by Clarke 1999. Cf. Polyb. 3.39.8 and 34.12.12, the latter criticized by Strabo (8.8.5) for "following the chance route of a general."

[37] Polyb. 3.54; Livy 31.35.

spatial descriptions—the Romans' first view over the route into central Etruria from Mons Ciminus or Philip's view from Mons Haemus tracing his route to Italy. In an even rarer attempt to add dimensions to description, Livy measures the length and breadth of the conquest of L. Scipio against Antiochus by days' marches.[38]

Julius Caesar famously never once mentions a map in all his commentaries, which at the very least informs us about what his audience wanted (or did not). It is not impossible that he had a geographic miniature before him when he tried to give a global, bird's eye view of 'all Gaul' or the triangular projection of Britain—the same perhaps as that available to Strabo, although Strabo pointedly does not refer to any map when he cites the geography of Caesar's *Commentaries*.[39] But the distortions and lack of features, such as the peninsulas of Brittany and Cherbourg, show it was probably small and crude.[40] Much more prominent in the narrative is Caesar's description of Gaul as though 'looking' (*spectat* is his word) from Provence, or the way he recounts his advance by itineraries without orientation and with distances measured by marches. Again, like Livy, Caesar describes sites, such as Gergovia or Alesia, as though they were landscapes viewed horizontally by a general or an observer on the ground—"Before the town a plain stretches out . . ."—which at Gergovia is made more immediate by the conceit of pretending points from where one could not see.[41]

We know Strabo, although a Greek-speaking Roman provincial, was close to Augustan thinking and representations of empire, so much so that that some have exaggeratedly thought his geography was written to be a manual of Roman administration.[42] Hence he is interesting as an example of Roman sensibilities towards space.

---

[38] Livy 9.36; 40.21–22; 38.59; Girod 1974, 481–5.

[39] Caesar *BG* 1.1; 5.13. Strabo 4.1.1. Goudineau 1990, 321, reconstructs a map following Strabo's description but stresses that Caesar's Roman audience had no interest in precise topography. Dilke 1985, 102, discusses a not very convincing map supposedly engraved on a stone at Mauchamp (Aisne); cf. Brodersen 1995, 143–4.

[40] See Rambaud 1974, 114–16, for distortions (the Ardennes as 500 miles long instead of 175, etc.).

[41] Rambaud 1974, 121–3, but I doubt that Caesar must have had "une carte sommaire" (p. 119) for setting his winter quarters, since local guides were always available (e.g. *BG* 2.7). Compare Lucretius, *De re. nat.* 2.5–6, for viewing battles: "suave etiam belli certamina magna tueri/per campos instructa".

[42] Based on Strabo 1.1.16–17 (see above, note 19). Clarke 1999, 202, dismisses the idea. I am much indebted to this recent study of Strabo.

One only has to think of his chorographic perception of a country through descriptions of discrete *topoi*, rather than the spaces between them, which tend to be filled with tribal names; his firm outlook from the centrality of Rome; the explicit sense of journeying in his use of *periploi*, such as those of Ephorus, when he is organizing topographic material. There are many examples like "the voyage from Miletus to Heraclea, including the bays of the gulfs . . ." with its alternative land route; or the Black Sea coast itinerary from the mouth of the Danube to Byzantium.[43]

But the Elder Pliny is far and away the most informative Roman writer about contemporary spatial concepts, both in the evidence that he preserves and in his own way of seeing. He tells us, for example, that when Augustus commissioned the world geographer, Dionysius of Charax, to provide a 'full account' (*ad commentanda omnia*) before Gaius Caesar's eastern expedition, the result was a route, an excerpt of which is the *Parthian Stations*.[44] Like the other writers he has his global images and spatial preferences—Europe is larger than Asia and more desirable, Hispania Citerior is shaped like a wedge, and so on.[45] But by contrast with the meagre sections when he discusses cosmic mapping, the chorographic commentary occupies four full books (III–VI), much of it stemming from itineraries like those on Agrippa's Map or from *periploi* to which he had easy access as a naval officer.[46]

Again and again Pliny himself travels mentally with the ships or route marchers. In southern Gaul he follows the *via Domitia*, Italy is traced by "the line of the coast", Isidorus's dimensions for the Peloponnese, he says, are wrong because they do not follow the indented coast line, the distance from Dyrrhachium to Byzantium is overestimated by a third because he follows the *via Egnatia*, and from Byzantium to the delta of the Danube is likewise measured by hugging the coast.[47] The limits of the Roman Empire are probed and expanded by journeys, sometimes *inexplicabilis*, to the Troglodytes, to

---

[43] Rome: Clarke 1999, 216–17; Ephorus: 8.1.3; Miletus etc.: 14.1.9; the Black Sea: 7.6.1.

[44] Pliny *NH* 6.141.

[45] Pliny *NH* 3.5, 3.29.

[46] See the high opinion of P's information about the route to India held by Tchernia and De Romanis 1997—in contrast to that of Syme 1988b, 229: "a sorry and messy compilation."

[47] Pliny *NH* 3.31–35; 3.43; 4.9; 4.46; 4.78.

the Garamantes, to Ethiopia, in search of the source of the Nile or an eastern Eldorado.[48] Most spectacularly, two dimensions of the entire world are measured by the sum of the routes—*mensura currit duplici via*—which ends up doubling longitude over latitude.[49] Pliny's eye for description is that of the traveller who pauses to view the landscape stretching horizontally in front of him. The mountains of Thessaly "curve like a theatre and in the *cavea* in the foreground are seventy-five cities"; the gentle slopes of the Vale of Tempe "rise beyond human sight on either side".[50]

4. The agrimensores and Ptolemy

There is no need to spend much time over the *agrimensores*. The surprise is that, notwithstanding the importance of land surveys in the law and life of Rome, when it came to wider spatial perceptions Romans did not think like lawyers or land surveyors. As we have seen already, there was a certain built-in interest in geometric forms and projections at the level of cosmic mapping. But when it came to topography, it is very doubtful whether all those land cadasters that were recorded on *varias formas* of wood, bronze or parchment and kept as copies in a central records office in Rome were ever consolidated into master Ordnance Survey maps, not even in the case of Italy. A recent commentary on the *agrimensores*, for example, suggests that the *forma* for the settlements at Lucus Feroniae in Latium would have been difficult to locate on a map of all Italy.[51] The document called *expositio et ratio omnium formarum*, possibly written by Domitian's military surveyor, Balbus, has nothing to do with a general survey map, despite its title, and there is nothing in it to suggest that Balbus did any surveying for that purpose.[52]

It is far from clear from the writings we possess whether the surveying skills of the *mensores* were even used to map out roads and itineraries, although I think it probable. All that Balbus's text mentions is that he built two straight embankments for a road and mea-

[48] Pliny *NH* 5.34; 5.38; 6.181; 5.51; 6.160.
[49] Pliny *NH* 2.242–6.
[50] Pliny *NH* 4.30–31.
[51] Central office: Siculus Flaccus *De condic. agr.* 120.22–32 (Campbell); cf. the discussions in Campbell 2000, 343, 397.
[52] Campbell 2000, 204–15 and xxxix–xl.

sured the width of rivers or the height of hill forts to be stormed. But there are cases of the orientation of roads and the measurement of distances being made by dead reckoning which must have originated in the work of provincial surveyors. In Roman Britain, for example, Marinus of Tyre (Ptolemy's source) got hold of the correct dead reckoning distance between London and Chichester, even though the southern section of the actual road, Stane Street, had diverted from the true bearing.[53] How much that sort of 'gnomonic' thinking rubbed off onto Roman perceptions can perhaps be seen in the way Caesar described the battle of Alesia, in relation to a horizontal *kardo* and a perpendicular *decumanus*, as though the site had been centuriated.[54] But it is ironic, in the light of the example of the route between Ravenna and the Rubicon, with which I began, that this region of the Romagna has yielded some of the earliest evidence of centuriation, yet Caesar was still unable to figure out his route once off piste.[55]

On the other hand, it is easy to detect in the *agrimensores* affinities with the Romans' perception of space through itineraries. First, there is the obvious fact that the term *limites*, meaning road-balks between centuriated land, came to refer to the roads of the imperial frontiers. But then there is the similarity of topographic landscape and chorographic horizontal perspective shown in the miniature vignettes of towns which illustrate the medieval edition of the *corpus agrimensorum*, and which reappear in the medieval manuscripts of the *Notitia Dignitatum* of the Later Empire. They are almost certainly in some cases copies of Roman originals.[56] They also have close affinities with the vignettes of the Peutinger Table and before that with the crude vignettes appearing on the fragment of an itinerary painted on a soldier's shield in the third century which was discovered at Dura Europos.[57]

---

[53] Rivet 1974, 68, gives another example; cf. Trousset 1978, esp. 151–3, studying the frontier road in southern Tunisia using a cadaster orientation on Jebel Bou el Haneche some 200 km to the North-West.

[54] Rambaud 1974, 127, who goes so far as to believe the site may have been surveyed; cf. p. 113.

[55] Chouquer 1981, especially the plan on p. 854.

[56] Campbell 2000, xiv–xvi; Dilke 1971, 110–12, 126–32; Dilke 1987, 244; Alexander 1976, 17 (with other similarities in the figure of Rome personified); Levi and Trell 1964.

[57] It is not important to the argument here that the Dura fragment is thought by some not to be a genuine itinerary; cf. Brodersen 1995, 145–8, for references.

It would be strange in discussing Roman maps and mentality not to say something, however brief, about Ptolemy, since he represented the climax of Hellenistic studies in celestial projections and mathematical co-ordinates, which profoundly impressed the Middle Ages after the Byzantine rediscovery of his texts. From the introduction to his *Geography*, quoted earlier, it is clear that Ptolemy was obsessed with the divisions between geography and chorography and how to reconcile them in a world map without the usual distortions: "We propose to describe (*katagraphein*) our habitable earth, in order that the description may correspond as far as possible with the earth itself."[58] But whether or not Ptolemy actually produced a map or only a commentary and co-ordinates from which others could do so,[59] it is difficult to show that he had any direct influence on Roman civil or military thinking, or that he seriously influenced many Romans' image of the world. Their imagination thrived in human space not cosmic abstractions, and Ptolemy remained "a luxury for the few."[60]

Yet even in Ptolemy's geography one can detect the powerful effect of "information gained through travel" (*historia periodike*). His predecessor Marinus, he says, made extensive use of itineraries and *periploi*, like those of Septimius Flaccus or Julius Maternus in Africa, and he himself corrected Marinus's poor calculations from such records.[61] Müller, in his edition of Ptolemy's *Geography*, argued that, since long distances in the Antonine Itinerary and Ptolemy were often the same we can assume a common, itinerary source.[62] A particularly interesting example comes from Britain, which seems to confirm the theory that a linear vision of space on itineraries deformed the sense of triangulation.[63] Although Ptolemy's distances from London to Catterick and London to Binchester are roughly correct, the longitude of Binchester is so far wrong in a westerly direction that the two northern towns are placed about four times further apart than

---

[58] Ptol. *Geog.* 1.2—where he refers to several revisions of the *pinax* of his predecessor Marinus.

[59] The bibliography of the debate is listed in Dilke 1987, 207 n. 28. Most commentators subscribe to the view put forcefully by J. Fischer, that it is inconceivable P did not produce his own maps; summarized in the introduction to Stevenson (1991).

[60] Janni 1984, 73 (quoting Beazley); Edson 1997, 165; Crone 1975, 5; Jacob 1993, 85 and 473.

[61] Ptol. *Geog.* 1.2; 1.4; 1.7–8; 1.12; 1.17.

[62] Müller 1883–1901, I.141.

[63] See Janni 1984, discussed below.

they should be.[64] It makes me wonder whether the famous tilting flat of the north of Britain was really caused by an error of textual transmission rather than Ptolemy's own misconception derived from itinerary maps.

5. Itineraries in Roman life

The fact is that, despite the technical skills of the land surveyors in constructing roads and bridges, despite the existence of travelling sundials, and despite the familiarity of sailors with wind roses and steering across the open sea by use of the stars and an azimuth, none of this experience transmitted itself from practice to cartographic theory or multi-dimensional perception.[65] Notwithstanding exaggerated claims that ancient written sea itineraries (*periploi*) were ancestors of medieval portolans, we possess not a single reference to an ancient sea chart, and one only has to look at the portolan of Pietro Visconti in 1311 to see that we are now in a different world of ships with fixed rudders and sea compasses.[66]

If Roman perception of what we might call the 'real' world, as opposed to the cosmic world, was dominated by itineraries, it is not hard to see why. Itineraries, like the roads they documented, were the instruments of military conquest and provincial administration. Like the 'pacers' (*bematistai*) in the army of Alexander the Great, inscriptions record the presence of military *mensores* and chorographers in the Roman army, and our sources are full of descriptions of their routes.[67] Topography was limited mainly to the towns, *castra, castelli*, water points and food stores, the sort of *loci* that remain in the Antonine Itinerary and the Peutinger Table.[68] But that was all. It did not result in a general survey map. Vegetius in the fourth century, who said that a good commander should carry *itinera* both

---

[64] Rivet 1974, 74.

[65] Survey of roads, etc: Sherk 1974, 45; travelling sundials: Casson 1974, 176; open sea travel: Tchernia 1997, 257–8.

[66] Woodward 1985, 512; Janni 1984, 58–9; Edson 1997, 13.

[67] Alexander: Pliny, *NH* 6.61; inscriptions: *AE* 1947, 61; *CIL* VIII 12914; *IGRR* 1.1365; Roman sources collected by Sherk 1974.

[68] E.g. the *castra* on the route Aquincum-Crumero, *It.Ant.* 266; the *ala* stations on *It.Ant.* 254–6; Arnaud 1993, 36–37; water points: Pliny *NH* 6.51–2; vignettes for baths and inns on the PT, Levi and Trell 1964.

written (*adnotata*) and drawn (*picta*), refers only to set routes and short cuts, not to general features. Even the number of routes was limited. Ambrose tells us how rigidly an itinerary was imposed upon the soldier: "He goes out in the order which is prescribed . . . he completes his journey by the direct route . . . if he marches by another itinerary, he does not get his *annona*."[69]

The administrative function was similar. Although it is not now believed, as once, that the written Antonine Itinerary and the illustrated Peutinger Table are records of the actual travels of emperors nor routes of the imperial post (*cursus publicus*) and military supplies (*annona militaris*), elements of all these official functions are present in the documents.[70] For example, a *mansio Augusti in praetorio* is marked on the route between Ljubljana and the Danube; the term *mutationes* implies official changing of horses;[71] while legal and literary sources record the rigid itineraries both used and abused by the state for transport of tax supplies.[72] But although we possess records of individual imperial itineraries,[73] and plenty of evidence of private journeys by land and sea,[74] none of the extant itineraries and sea routes nor any literary source suggests that there was ever such a thing as an official, master map. We cannot prove even a state archive of official itineraries, although I find the idea plausible on the analogy of the archive for *formae* of land cadasters.[75]

In fact, it is doubtful whether the Antonine Itinerary or the Peutinger Table were even usable in their present form.[76] Both are late syntheses of numerous shorter, local itineraries, sometimes crudely fitted together with minor roads. They do not cover every part of

---

[69] *Exp.Ps.* CXVIII 5.2; cf. HA *Alex.* 47.

[70] *It.Ant.*: Arnaud 1992, contra Reed 1978; Peutinger Table: Dilke 1985, 115, is sceptical contra Levi 1967, 97.

[71] *It.Ant.* 260; Arnaud 1993, 33, thinks this is the relic of an earlier itinerary.

[72] Tacitus *Agr.* 19; *CTh.* XI.1.9; cf. Reed 1978, 243 for the probable location of *horrea* at Veldidina near Innsbruck as an explanation of its importance on the *It.Ant.*

[73] The journey of Hadrian (probably) in Cilicia was recorded on an inscription in Rome, *CIL* VI 5076; Syme 1988, 160; Alexander Severus published his route in advance by edict, HA *Alex.* 45.

[74] Notably the various *periploi* of which the best known is the *Periplous Maris Erythraei*, obviously written for traders.

[75] See below, n. 153. Miller 1916, lxvii, finds no evidence of official work in the *itinerarium maritimum* section of the *It.Ant.* Austin and Rankov 1995, 117, note that Arrian's *Periplus of the Euxine Sea* was not an official dispatch, but does refer (62.10) to a supplementary report (probably in Latin) sent to Hadrian.

[76] Janni 1984, 32; contra Casson 1974, 187, who compares the PT to a Michelin routier.

the empire systematically, although in some sectors, such as North Africa, they seem to draw upon a common source.[77] The local character of the underlying itineraries is shown when both documents record some distances in Gaul in leagues not miles, although the Antonine Itinerary sometimes confuses them, perhaps because milestones changed in the early third century.[78]

As with the official and military itineraries, so in private records it is the short, local and usually written itineraries of the earlier empire that have to be stressed, since this is what the evidence points to. The routes as we have them recorded are clearly not maps for travellers, but more like souvenirs of private voyages or monuments of local, civic pride. The four silver goblets found at Bagni di Vicarello (Lake Bracciano), dating from the Augustan period, have engraved upon them 106 stations between Gades and Rome travelling through North Italy, along the *via Aemilia* through Piacenza, Parma and Reggio. Although each one is slightly different, they were all dedicated at a sanctuary of Apollo, which implies a purpose other than cartography.[79] Vessels found in Britain, France and Spain decorated by the names of the forts of Hadrian's Wall must surely be personal souvenirs of soldiers in memory of the coldest days of their service, not guides for future conscripts.[80] I suspect that the private memento is also the explanation of the painted itinerary on a shield from Dura mentioned earlier.[81] More official looking are a series of pillars inscribed with itineraries that have been found at various towns in the Empire—Tongres in Belgium, Autun and Nîmes in France, Mainz in Germany, etc. But even though they record routes leading out of the town, possibly as far as Rome, and might conceivably have served as sign posts, they look more like advertisements of the city's importance, like those sign posts one find in airports saying 1,000 km to New York, 2,000 km to Delhi.[82]

---

[77] Arnaud 1993, 35; Dilke 1985, 125–8.
[78] Reed 1978, 234–5.
[79] Miller 1916, lxxi possibly belonging to a travelling businessman or his slaves, Dilke 1985, 123.
[80] Bibliography in Dilke 1985, 124.
[81] Cf. note 22.
[82] Miller 1916, lxxii–lxxv and Levi 1967, 28 provide the esssential bibliography.

6. Changes in the Later Empire

A change, however, took place in the Later Empire from the recording of single, shorter itineraries to composite itineraries and route maps. One reason for this change in cultural perspective was undoubtedly the vast increase in the numbers of travellers and the well known passion for travel which swept through late Roman society. Pilgrimage was not something new or unique to the later Empire. A study of Pausanias, the Greek 'religious tourist' in the second century AD, underlines pagan pilgrimage in his day as "a journey into one's identity in its topographic, cultural and spiritual resonances."[83] As we know from the non-stop attraction of festivals, ashrams and gurus in India, there is no greater stimulus than a combination of tourism and piety to take pilgrims on long distance journeys. But in the later Empire the urge became a passion.

The *Itinerarium Burdigalense* (or Bordeaux Itinerary) of AD 333 records the stages of an astonishing land journey, over 5,000 km from Bordeaux to Milan, Constantinople and Jerusalem, returning by sea and land via Brindisi, Rome and Milan, which lasted seven months. The itinerary is very much in the style of the Antonine Itinerary, a simple record of *mansiones* and *mutationes*, with only very brief tourist notes, mostly at holy sites—such as Tarsus, "where the apostle Paul lived", or Libissa, "the place where Hannibal was buried"—not unlike entries on the Peutinger Table.[84] The *Itinerarium Egeriae* in 381–4 is somewhat different, since it is not strictly an itinerary but the diary of Egeria, a noble lady who was probably a member of the imperial household of Theodosius I and travelled from Spain to Constantinople, from where she toured the holy sites of the Middle East, Egypt and Palestine. Her tour lasted three years and included voyages requiring heroic stamina, such as climbing Mount Sinai in the heat, *iubente deo*.[85] Both itineraries, however, codify the fashion for journeys as pious feats of asceticism and pilgrimage set by Helena, mother of Constantine, who travelled to Jerusalem in search of the true cross.

Although all this has been well studied, we need to note that between the Bordeaux Itinerary and the Itinerary of Egeria, that is,

---

[83] Elsner 1995, 128–35.
[84] *It.Burd.* 572 and 581.
[85] *It.Eger.* 3.2.

in the course of the fourth century, the fashion for religious tourism developed into a boom just at the same time that changes occurred in Roman mental mapping. The boom was encouraged by the pilgrimages of a succession of wealthy court ladies, most more pious than ascetic, who had an eye for publicity,[86] and by the increasing numbers of holy men and women whose fame attracted visitors.[87] Basil of Caesarea founded new bishoprics at the *mansiones* along the pilgrim itineraries between Ancyra and Tarsus, as well as encouraging the construction of hostels called 'basileias' and demanding tax exemptions for pilgrims.[88]

We can only guess at the size of the increased traffic. The impression we get is that it was considerable. Unlike the ascetic Egeria, the visit by the lady Poemenia to the holy hermit John in Egypt, was accompanied by an army of bishops, priests and servants, and such was local hostility to so many foreigners that at Nikiupolis a brawl resulted in several dead and a bishop being dumped in the river.[89] Poemenia was only one of many of the great and the good who made the 'Grand Tour' of the religious sites. The rich were assisted by local authorities and bishops who hoped for liberal patronage in return. Paula, for instance, who was Jerome's patron, was offered the use of the private *mansio* of the governor of Palestine, and the Younger Melania obtained a state warrant for the public *cursus* through her court connections.[90]

No small part of the religious traffic was caused by church administration and the ever increasing numbers of councils and bishops. Sometimes a delegation might include as many as 400 bishops plus a staff of priests and deacons. Summoned by imperial edict, they had the right to use the *cursus publicus*—described by Ammianus as "crowds of bishops scurrying backwards and forwards on public post-horses".[91] Such ecclesiastical transactions do not include unofficial travellers nor the couriers bearing the huge number of letters exchanged between men like Augustine, Jerome and Basil. Nor does it include

[86] For instance by Palladius, *Historia Lausiaca* and the *Vita Melaniae*.
[87] Cf. *It.Eger.* 17.1: in Mesopotamia *ad visendos sanctos monachos*.
[88] Basil, *Epp.* 94; 142–3; Gregory Naz. *Or.* 43.63 (= *PG* 36.577); Hunt 1982, 66.
[89] Palladius *H. Laus.* 35.
[90] *V.Mel.(Lat)* 52; Jerome *Ep.* 54.13; Casson 1974, 319; Hunt 1982, 183–6 and 229.
[91] Council of Arles (314): *data evectione publica*, *CSEL* 26.205; Ammianus Marcellinus 21.16.18; Casson 1974, 301–2.

all the many secular and religious personnel who illegally obtained state warrants for food and animals, and whose abuses fill the law codes. It comes as no surprise that the Council of Sardica complained that the *cursus publicus* was breaking down.[92] A law of AD 378 limited the number of horses that could be requisitioned at halts along the *cursus* to five per day (not to mention oxen and pack animals), which, given that there are over 400 *mutationes* marked on the Peutinger Table, suggests that travellers could have been numbered in tens of thousands.[93]

The poor did not have the advantages of the rich. But the foundation of churches and monasteries on the routes, including the provision of charitable *xenodocheia* or hospices, helped them to avoid some of the horrible *mansiones* that we know about and overlaid the itineraries with "a Christian pattern of travel and hospitality."[94] So much did this encourage travel that the Council of Nîmes in 396 protested that "many on the pretence of pilgrimage are running riot with the contributions of the Church", and the Council of Chalcedon subjected the poor to examination before granting them "letters of peace."[95] Egeria described the crowds at Jerusalem as 'mobs' (*turbae*); Gregory of Nazianzus declared himself unwilling to become a bishop of a small town on the pilgrim route because, "All is dust and noise and carriages; . . . all foreigners and travellers"; and Jerome complained of intolerable conditions from 'packed mobs.'[96] By the time the Anonymous Itinerary of Piacenza was composed in the sixth century there were two *xenodocheia* in Jerusalem for 1,200 men and women, plus more than 3,000 beds for the sick and *mensas innumerabiles*.[97]

The conversion of Constantine to Christianity, therefore, also radically transformed the world view of Romans. Travel made the world a smaller place. There was a new emphasis on the heroic journeys, both physical and spiritual, which were fused into one by the pilgrimage to Jerusalem. Christianity re-invented the classical *homo via-*

---

[92] Letters: Gorce 1929; abuses in the title *De cursu publico, angariis et parangariis*: *Cth.* VIII.5; Council of Sardica: *CSEL* 65.64.

[93] *CTh.* VIII.5.35.

[94] Hunt 1982, 62; Gorce 1929, 146ff.

[95] Council of Nîmes, canon 5 (*SChr.* 241.128); Council of Chalcedon, canon 11.

[96] *turbae: It.Eg.* 49.1; cf. Jerome *Ep.* 107.2; Gregory Naz. *De vita sua* 443–5 (= *PG* 37.1060); Jerome, *Ep.* 58.4.

[97] *Anon.Plac.It.* 23.

tor, such as Odysseus, who travelled for virtue. Aimless wandering without an itinerary became a metaphor for sin.[98] In the classical world long journeys were limited to marginal people—traders, wandering philosophers, outlaws, the antithesis of citizens. Augustine presents an image of the *perigrinatio animae* when he has a vision of the land of peace, seen from a high mountain, but he cannot reach it unless he keeps to the route guarded by the heavenly commander against fugitives and deserters.[99] The horizontal perspective of the traveller is the same as before but the boundaries had crumbled. International horizons were expanding under the impact of pilgrims like Egeria or monks from India, Persia, Ethiopia and the barbarian fringes, who "flock in from the four corners of the earth."[100]

7. Spatial perceptions and mental maps

It is fashionable to ask how ancient and medieval map makers perceived geographic space through their maps;[101] but less common to examine how their maps or itineraries shaped their perceptions. Both are equally important for understanding how Romans thought. The simplistic assumption that ancient and medieval cartographers were like us but more stupid misunderstands the cultural content of all maps.[102] Modern studies of mental maps find plotting of 'relative locations' and 'spatial preferences' more informative about movement and social behaviour than conventional maps.[103] It was the mind's eye which ancient chorographers stressed, since written texts—'la carte écrite'—created no less visible, spatial images than maps.[104] If anything, the written text was better as a visual aid. Diodorus's survey of Asia would enable readers to follow the history of Alexander's successors "with the whole topography and spaces set out *in front of their eyes*."[105]

Within the framework of the mental map the perception was shaped above all by the itinerary—the sense of linear movement

[98] Bowman 1983, but he wrongly ascribes this change to the Middle Ages.
[99] Augustine *Conf.* 7.1; Kuntz 1983.
[100] Jerome *Ep.* 107.2; cf. Turner 1978, 6–9; Hunt 1982, 245.
[101] For example, the recent publication of Edson 1997.
[102] Edson 1997, vii; Woodward 1985.
[103] Gould and White 1974, 15–19.
[104] Jacob 1992, 134 and 249; cf. Janni 1984, 74–8: "uno spazio visuto".
[105] Diod. 18.5.1.

between *loci* with visual pauses from fixed viewpoints. Pliny mentally envisaged the geography of the tribes along the Black Sea as an itinerary, even when passing from East to West by routes no Roman had actually travelled. "Let our imagination cross (*transcendat animus*)," he says, "the Ripaean mountains and proceed along the right bank of the ocean."[106] And that never seems to change. Orosius in the fifth century still visualizes the Christian world in terms of a journey with the pen—*stilo pervagabor*.[107] Written itineraries could be more easily memorized than maps, because they were sequential. That was why Cicero and Quintilian reversed the process and suggested orators should imagine itineraries to organize the memory: "a large number of *loci* . . . with short spaces between them."[108]

The horizontal perspective of the traveller is caught by the perspective of Roman paintings or reliefs. On the Palaestrina map mosaic of the Nile, for all its sixteenth century restorations, the panoramic view is preserved with a series of narrative vignettes rising from the foreground to the mountains of Ethiopia in the background.[109] The same, single line of vision typifies the pictures of villas in a formal garden landscape, a fashion which Pliny says (wrongly, as it happens) was the invention of the Augustan period. What is interesting about these paintings, which have been called 'cartographic spatial designs', is Pliny's characterization of them as "people going to the villas" or "with an access road"—space in movement along roads.[110] The formal, visual, landscape is echoed in his description of travel to Mt. Nympaeus in Phthiotis, "viewed for its garden design of nature"—*topiario naturae opere spectabilis*.[111] For such scenes of 'motion pictures' the base relief was an ideal vehicle. So, it is not surprising to find a modern commentator comparing the scenes on Trajan's column with cinema techniques of travelling and panoramic shots.[112] More to the point here, however, is the horizontal perspective of the *itineraria picta*, already noted in the vignettes of the Peutinger

[106] Pliny *NH* 6.33; P liked the flight of fancy, since in 4.94 he says, "Crossing the Ripaean mountains, we must coast along the shore of the northern ocean to the left until we come to Gades."

[107] Oros. *Hist. adv. pag.* 1.2.51.

[108] Quint. 11.2.21–2; Leach 1988, 75–8; cf. Jacob 1992, 57: "un dispositif mnémotechnique complexe jouant l'interaction de la vision de l'espace et du langage."

[109] Leach 1988, 911–93.

[110] Pliny *NH* 35.116–17; Leach 1988, 100.

[111] Pliny *NH* 4.29.

[112] Malissard 1974.

Table, which Vegetius says must be viewed by both the mind (*consilio mentis*) and the eye (*aspectu oculorum*).[113]

It would be wrong to claim that the horizontal view was the only way that Romans perceived space. There was also cosmic mental mapping. Eustathius, the Byzantine commentator of Dionysius Periegetes, imagines him like Daedalus flying over the world and looking down from above. The conceit of looking down from on high, like Icarus or Zeus, was common among geographers, Lucian tells us.[114] But these were geographic views of the world, valuable for conveying global descriptions and philosophic concepts of divine, rational order, "as though seeing it with one's own eyes", says Cicero.[115] Pliny found it a helpful way to convey a sense of the extensive oceans encircling the world, "as it were displayed to the eyes." And an anonymous Greek geographer went so far as to say, "Readers can contemplate the whole world *with the eyes of their mind*, without need of a map."[116]

But vertical perspective was of limited use in describing the real world of travellers or administrators, except in the often misleading attempt to describe the shape of a country. Dionysius was following the principles of cosmology derived from Ptolemy to give a global view of the world, but his work was also a *periegesis*—a guided voyage around it. It may be that his popularity in the schoolroom helps to explain the convergence of geography and chorography in the Later Empire—"so that what you perceive by your learning . . . you can see with your eyes", says Cassiodorus in recommending Dionysius to monks in the sixth century.[117]

8. Mental maps and mapping the mentality

By way of summing up, I see four ways in which itineraries and world maps, reflected, but also fashioned, the mental maps of antiquity.

---

[113] Veg. *Epit. rei milit.* 3.6; Levi (1981), 42.
[114] Lucian *Hist.Ver.* 26; cf. *Icaromen.* 11; Jacob 1981, 27–8.
[115] Cic. *De nat.deor.* 2.38.100.
[116] Pliny *NH* 2.170; GGM II. 494.5.
[117] Cassiod. *De instit.div.litt.* XXV, *cosmographia a monachis legenda*; Jacob 1981, 57–61.

8.1

First, space itself was defined by itineraries, since it was through itineraries that Romans actually experienced space, that is, by lines and not by shapes. This does not mean that Romans had no 'map consciousness'—only a 'utilitarian consciousness'.[118] As in their paintings, they had a different visual comprehension of space from ours. Their mapping sense was accurate for what was needed, even if other aspects were distorted.[119] In graphic form the Peutinger Table looks distorted because the information is hopelessly crowded into the space of a long parchment roll. But the movement was more important than the form. In that respect, therefore (and assuming most strip maps shared these characteristics), ancient maps reflected their function. But the function in its turn created the mental map. Ireland was believed to be North of Britain because it came after Britain on an itinerary.[120]

Polybius, Strabo, Caesar and others made use of geometric images drawn from cosmographs when wanting to give global descriptions of a country or an empire, and Polybius may even have attempted to apply the cosmologists' principle of triangulation. But if so, it has to be said he attempted it without much success, as though he was using distance to imagine a geometric shape, rather than the shape to calculate a distance.[121] There is not enough here, however, to persuade me that, when it came down to mental mapping on the ground, as it were, Romans ever viewed their localities and environment other as 'hodological space', the term adopted by Janni.[122]

This means, as Janni explains, that the relationship of locations was uni-dimensional, the route from A to B or A to C but not the area triangulated by the three points. Even if there were several itineraries in a region, sometimes side roads, too, running between major points, the points themselves were not imagined in a multi-

---

[118] Contra R.J.A. Talbert, *JRS* 77 (1987), 210–12. For Roman utilitarianism, see the introductory remarks of Chevallier (1974).

[119] Cf. Haynes 1980, 35.

[120] Ireland: "più in là lungo un percorso; Janni 1984, 102.

[121] Clarke 1999, 102–4, argues that Polybius "totally confounds" the notion that space was conceived only in linear terms. But in Polyb. 3.49 the comparison of the triangle Isere-Rhône-northern mountains (? Chartreuse Massif) with the Nile Delta is "absurd" (Walbank) and serves no geographical purpose. The triangulation of Italy in Polyb. 2.14 was incomprehensible to both Strabo (5.1.6) and modern commentators; see note 23.

[122] Adopting the term from Lewin 1951; Janni 1984, 13.

dimensional or geographic relationship. Relics of that can be found even in Ptolemy's co-ordinates, which were after all an attempt (even if a rare and esoteric one) to break out of the hodological straight-jacket.[123] Itineraries or maps could never have been used as guides across country, any more than one can use an underground map of London to walk around the city. That is why Caesar was lost when he left the route before the Rubicon. And that is why Roman maps are never mentioned in planning military strategy, being useful, according to Vegetius, only for the "distance between places" and the "quality of the road".[124]

8.2

Secondly, the essence of itineraries was space between topographic points—towns, *vici, mansiones,* and so on—which followed in linear succession. The mind focused not upon the continuity of the terrain but on the contiguity of the stops. The principle was the same as the rhetoric of *topographia*—"for the imagination can comprehend any region and in it create or construct . . . the site of a place."[125] It reflected the Roman political view of a world made up of a network of *civitates* and urban space, between which lay nothing except curiosities for the traveller—an historic battlefield, a bridge over a river.

This was the legacy Romans left to the Middle Ages. The 'Isidore Map' of the eighth century in the Vatican shows almost no detail except a large number of the letter "c" for *civitas.*[126] To turn off the route into space spelt danger (or, to the Christian, sin), the domain of the anti-citizen, the bandit. The horror of empty space was the worst of war against Celts and Germans, according to Strabo, since they fought "in pathless, deserted forests, making the uninformed Romans think that what was near was far away and keeping the roads hidden."[127] On the Peutinger Table blank spaces are filled with rubrics, such as, "Here scorpions are born".[128]

---

[123] See section 4 above.

[124] Vegetius *Epit. rei milit.* 3.6; Austin and Rankov 1995, 117–18.

[125] Auct. ad Herenn. 3.19.32: "cogitatio enim quamvis regionem potest amplecti et in eam situm loci cuiusdam . . . fabricari et architectari".

[126] Edson 1997, 63.

[127] Strabo 1.1.17.

[128] Levi 1967, 20–22, cites Plutarch on geographers who know nothing and say,

8.3

Thirdly, if all maps are controlled fiction which mediate specific views of the world, it is nevertheless impossible to tell which comes first in geographic perceptions and distortions, the imagination or the map. Italy, for example, was regularly given an almost due East-West orientation, even in Ptolemy. Pliny puts Genova, Rome and Campania on the same latitude. Vergil describes Carthage as opposite Rome. And this is how it appears on the Peutinger Table, parallel to the North African coast, and so close that Carthage looks nearer to Rome than it does to Naples. But was this because Africa, being the granary of Rome and a land of Roman estates, created a mental map of easy accessibility and, therefore, a spatial preference? Or was it because a *periplus* or an itinerary map stretched Europe out in such an orientation that it created the illusion that Africa was that close? We can detect the influence of a *periplus* when Procopius says that Sardinia lay between Rome and Carthage.[129] The Romans bequeathed this perception to the Middle Ages, since the *imago mundi* of Honorius of Autun in the twelfth century and the *mappamundi* of Matthew Paris in the thirteenth century continued to show the same orientation and relationship.

The illusion of the global centrality of Rome was created by the geographic theory of the continents and by chorographic itineraries, regardless of whether they were illustrated in map form or not—a typical example of the 'omphalos syndrome' employed by every imperial power. Europeans hardly noticed that the sixteenth century Mercator projections appeared to locate two thirds of the world's surface in high latitudes.[130] But in Rome it was by the network of roads in particular, and the names of places they united—what has been called in modern colonial history 'dispossession through naming'—that the relations between centre and periphery were illustrated, and which in turn enhanced the rhetoric of control.[131] The routes of the Antonine Itinerary represent the chains that linked the frontiers to the centre.

"Everything beyond is sandy desert with no water or full of wild animals or unexplored marsh."

[129] Vergil *Aen.* 1.13–14; Procop. *Bell. Vand.* 4.13.42; Janni 74–8; Dilke 1985, 116–17.

[130] Maps and power, discussed by Harley 1988.

[131] Gregory 1994, 171.

At the same time, however, such maps were cognitive interpretations, legitimations perhaps, following from practical perception. The discussion between Varro and his friends beside the map in the Temple of Tellus on the natural advantages of Rome's central position begins from the personal observations of those who had travelled: "vos qui multas perambulastis terras". From this standpoint it is easier to argue that Augustus believed he could conquer the East as quickly as he had the West, not because he was misled by distances on Agrippa's Map (which may be true), but because he, in common with all Romans, believed that Rome lay equidistant between the two poles.[132] The illusion created the mental map before the actual map fostered the illusion.

8.4

My last point is simply to reiterate what I said about the new perspectives created in the religious itineraries of the Later Empire, from which the Middle Ages again, and rather more obviously, received a legacy from Rome. No known composite written itinerary or painted map dates from earlier than the mid-fourth century and none ever functioned as a handbook for travellers. Earlier itineraries were short records of simple or single journey. The itinerary had therefore passed from the personal to the general, from the local to the universal—the beginning of a more complex sense of topographic relationships. The new mobility of the fourth and fifth century was filling in the gaps of space and time.

Both the Antonine Itinerary and the Peutinger Table show the influence of cosmographic geography on chorographic itineraries. The consolidated Antonine Itinerary is more interested in long distances than immediate travel—"neither utilitarian, nor administrative but cultural", a recent study concludes.[133] The Peutinger Table of itineraries also reflects the cosmic orthodoxy of the division of continents and the linking of the Caspian with the outer Ocean.[134] The cosmographic lists, the *Dimensuratio Provinciarum*, and the *Divisio Orbis Terrarum*, though believed to have an ancestry from Agrippa's

---

132 References to the earlier debate about Agrippa's Map are in Whittaker 1994, 14; cf. Isaac 1990, 403, for serious under-estimations of distances in the East.

133 Arnaud 1993, 46–9; he convincingly dates the *It.Ant.* to post-338.

134 Levi 1981, 139.

Map, were also late products. The Ravenna Cosmographer of the late sixth or seventh century, despite his "careless topography" was attempting the same task as the Antonine Itinerary in producing not an itinerary itself but a crude geography through itineraries.[135] Maps were becoming used not as guides but as historical records, not for actual travellers but for spiritual and mental *perigrinatio in stabilitate.*

There is a seamless continuity from the Antonine Itinerary and the Bordeaux Itinerary of the fourth century to the Anonymous of Piacenza in the sixth, the Ravenna Cosmographer in the seventh and Guido of Pisa in the twelfth. What happened in the Roman world we can perhaps begin to understand from what happened in France during the seventeenth and eighteenth century, although the analogy cannot be pressed in detail. In France perceptions of space changed, through the needs of centralized administration and through an increase in mobility, from the contiguity of 'places' to the continuity of territorial and political space. This is illustrated graphically by the remarkable maps of Nicolas Sanson in 1632, actually superimposing the itineraries of the *Guide de Chemins de France* upon a 'geographic' map of France.[136]

9. And the frontiers?

I asked at the beginning of this survey whether Roman perceptions of space might tell us anything about how they regarded frontiers. What is noticeable about the various Roman cartographic or chorographic sources I have quoted is the apparent absence of frontiers as limits to empire. The fragment of the Dura Map from a soldier's shield happens to include the route crossing the Danube between Istropolis and Tyra—that is, moving out of the Roman Empire into the territory of the Costoboci—without showing any landmark to signify a frontier. Pliny is the same. His description of the route from the Danube to the Crimean Bosphorus gives no hint of passing over a frontier. He does, it is true, elsewhere note boundaries of provinces, such as Numidia or Africa, but he gives us no sense that the journeys to the Troglodytes or the Garamantes were moving through

[135] Dillemann 1975; Rivet and Smith 1979, 185–215.

[136] Pelletier and Ozane 1995, 61; this is the theme of Nordman 1998, see esp. 511–27.

some formal frontier.[137] Strabo talks of tribes beyond the river lines of the advancing Roman armies, but I cannot find a trace of the idea of a limit in what he says, while by contrast he almost encourages the vision of an empire beyond the passage of Roman arms.[138]

If we move from the first century to a period when Roman military forts on the outskirts of empire took on a more permanent character, the image does not change. There are no boundary lines marked on Ptolemy's map, nor do frontiers appear in the vulgarized text of Dionysius Periegetes, derived from Ptolemy, which was on the reading list for monks in the sixth century recommended by Cassiodorus. Nor is there any mentions of limits or frontiers (as opposed to provincial boundaries) in the cosmographic lists, the *Divisio orbis terrarum* and the *Dimensuratio provinciarum*.[139] The Antonine Itinerary, which is essentially a catalogue of the communications within the administered provinces and not of the un-administered territories beyond, does happen to mention Hadrian's Wall, but as a point along roads which begin from posts twenty miles beyond it to the North.[140] On the Peutinger Table there are two points marked in the Syrian-Mesopotamian desert as *fines provinciarum*, similar to some inscribed boundary stones, but the general opinion is that these, too, record administrative boundaries, since they correspond to no known military positions.[141]

What interests me most, however, is the absence of any sense of passing through a barrier when moving beyond the territories under direct Roman administration. The only limit is the mental image of where the road ended, since the road brought order to the unknown. That was the point in Strabo's example of the Romans who were lost in Germany when they did not know where the road was. Beyond the end of the route all was "deserted and nameless", says Arrian.[142]

---

[137] Pliny *NH* 4.78; 5.22: *Numidiae finis*; 5.29: Africa, etc.

[138] Clarke 1999, 206, is non-committal about frontiers; but see Strabo 6.4.2 (Danube); 7.1.3–4 (Rhine and Elbe); 17.3.25 (provinces and land beyond waiting to be subdued); cf. Whittaker 1994, 26.

[139] Whittaker 1994, 14–16; Clarke 1991, 95–122.

[140] *It.Ant.* 71.464 (Cunz): "a limite, id est a vallo"; Bunbury 1879, 95, although he says the routes were "strictly within the limits of the Roman Empire".

[141] Whittaker 1994, 68 and n. 13 (pp. 286–7).

[142] Strabo 1.1.17; Arrian, *Peripl.* 20–2–3, cited by Austin and Rankov 1995, 112–13.

But the roads were constantly extended by probing outwards, as in Nero's praetorian expedition to Ethiopia or Aelius Gallus's venture into Arabia. Gaius Caesar's invasion of Parthia was planned on the base of the road to Kandahar described by Dionysius of Charax—one of the rare cases we know of chorographic intelligence acquired before an expedition. The probe at right angles to the military front is exactly the sense of *limites* used by Frontinus to describe Domitian's advance to "uncover the hiding places" of the Germans in AD 83, or by Velleius Paterculus to record Tiberius's offensive in Germany—*penetrat interius, aperit limites.*[143] In surveying terms it was like laying down a new *cardo* to the *decumanus* of the frontier road. That sense of a probing antenna was taken up by the term *praetensio* and *praetentura* in the later Empire, as is confirmed by an inscription along the road projecting out from the Jordanian front into the Wadi Sirhan.[144] The lateral boundaries of public imagination were the roads and rivers, like Britain's Stane Gate, Arabia's *via Traiana* or the great river highways of the Rhine and the Danube—the 'narratives' of travel. But they were not the frontiers.

There is no need to repeat what has been said about the military functions of the *mensores* in the surveying of the roads which were recorded on the itineraries. All I want to stress is that there is not the slightest evidence that they created composite military survey maps for the planning of strategic frontiers.[145] The *forma* of Ethiopia produced by the praetorians for Nero could have been no more than a crude sketch listing place names and distances, since they had no time for anything more.[146] It was probably typical of such military records. The only military duties Balbus records are immediate, practical tasks, such as laying out *rigores ordinati* for a road. Otherwise most evidence points to administrative activities like military allotments, sorting out land disputes, cadastrating land for tax purposes, or to civil engineering jobs like aqueducts.[147] There is nothing, in fact, to suggest the surveyors produced documents of strategic usefulness.

---

[143] Frontin. *Strat.* 1.3.10; cf. 1.5.10 (of Pericles): "limitem agere coepit, tamquam per eum erupturus". Vell. Pat. 2.120. See A. Passerini in De Ruggiero, *Dict. Antiqu.* s.v. 'limes'.

[144] Discussed with refs. in Whittaker 1994, 200–1.

[145] Campbell 2000, xl.

[146] Pliny *NH* 6.184, 12.18–19; Austin and Rankov 1995, 115.

[147] Campbell 2000, li–lii, who cites the famous inscription concerning the aqueduct at Saldae, in Algeria.

The most eloquent testimony of this is the silence of Frontinus, an aristocratic *agrimensor* 'manager' (that is, a writer but not a practician), who was also author of the *Strategemata*. In all the military 'stratagems' he never once mentions a map of any sort—not even where you might expect it; for example, when he discusses how to choose a site for battle, or how to select a rendezvous in retreat.[148] Nor is there any reference in Onosander's *Strategikos*, a Greek work dedicated to Q. Veranius, governor of Britain in AD 59, which became hugely influential at Byzantium. A general, he says, must know the stars (for time, however, not for orientation), he must have good guides, he must discuss matters with his staff. But not a word about a map.[149]

Not surprisingly, therefore, the recent, careful study of Roman strategic planning by Austin and Rankov concludes that, although emperors and generals must have mentally envisaged roads and coastlines for moving troops *within* the empire, this was, they say, "Much less so for the assessment of the limits of territory to be annexed or the predetermination of new frontier lines."[150] For information before tactical and strategic planning they relied on scouts. I assume that when Velleius Paterculus, a serving officer, spoke of Tiberius's *mira felicitas* in AD 4 by getting the fleet and the army to meet on the Elbe, he meant it was an exceptional event—although this was not the first visit to the Elbe by a Roman army or fleet. Stranger still, following the expedition, Velleius gives the distance between the Rhine and the Elbe as four hundred miles, when it should be about two hundred and fifty.[151] Even after three centuries of military contact, neither Septimius Severus in the third century, nor Julian in the fourth, had much idea of the geography of Mesopotamia.[152]

So, if there was consolidation of general mapping intelligence in the later Empire, as I have argued, it is nevertheless remarkably difficult to find evidence of it at an official or military operational level. Both the Antonine Itinerary and the Peutinger Table are thought to be unofficial initiatives, and there is no shred of evidence to prove any sort of government mapping office or officer at any

[148] Frontin. *Strat.* 2.2; 2.13; for F's status, see Campbell 2000, xviii; Cuomo 2000.
[149] Onos. *Strat.* 10.15; 39.2–3.
[150] Austin and Rankov 1995, 117.
[151] Vell. Pat. 2.106; I am baffled by the assertion of Syme 1988b, 242, that VP's figure is evidence of accurate intelligence.
[152] Isaac 1990, 402–7, with references to other examples.

period.[153] If there is little to show that mental mapping played any part in the planning of individual campaigns, the same is true *a fortiori* of the Grand Strategy of frontiers—that is, assuming we can even begin to talk of such a concept.[154] The perception of empire at that scale was mystical and ideological, as reflected in and created by the cosmologies of the day.

In sum, maps have the power to create 'imagined communities'.[155] Benedict Anderson's book with that title describes how the imposition of the Mercator Map on Siam by a colonial power in 1851 dramatically changed the social and political face of the country. Before that the comparisons with Rome are quite striking. Two types of maps, says Anderson, fashioned the imagination; the first vertical, cosmic maps of the Buddhists, used for spiritual journeys to heaven or hell; the second 'diagrammatic guides' for use in military campaigns and shipping, whose main feature was written-in notes. The perspective of the terrestrial map was entirely horizontal and never located in a larger geographic context. Space was viewed in terms of sacred capitals looking from the centre towards visible, outlying centres of population. As for frontiers, Anderson's study makes a point of underlining that, although rulers in Siam did sometimes set up some discontinuous boundary stones and markers, they were not regarded as limits. "They were understood horizontally, at eye-level, as extension points of royal power." Only after the imposition of a European map did the Thai think of boundaries as segments of a map-line. Before then boundaries did not define territorial power.

Bibliography

Alexander, J.J.G. 1976, 'The illustrated manuscripts of the Notitia Dignitatum', in R. Goodburn and P. Bartholomew (eds.), 1976, *Aspects of the Notitia Dignitatum*, (*BAR* 15), Oxford: 11–50.

Anderson, B. 1991, *Imagined communities*, rev. ed., London.

Arnaud, P. 1992, 'À propos d'un prétendu itineraire de Caracalla dans l'Itineraire d'Antonin', *BSAF*, 374–82.

[153] See above, note 75. Unofficial: Arnaud 1993, 34, contra Reed 1978. Austin and Rankov 1995, 140, suggest the possibility of maps archives at the central *scrinia* of the *ab epistulis*, but Talbert 1990/91, is rightly sceptical. Mommsen long ago pointed out (*Röm.Staatsrecht* 1047, anm. 1), that the *comes formarum* in the late Empire was in charge of aqueducts, not maps.

[154] Whittaker 1996.

[155] Anderson 1991, 170–83.

——. 1993, 'L'itineraire d'Antonin: un témoin de la littérature du Bas-Empire', *Geographia antica* 2, 33–49.
Austin, N.J.E. and N.B. Rankov 1995, *Exploratio: military and political intelligence in the Roman world from the second Punic War to the Battle of Adrianople*, London/New York.
Bosio, L. 1983, *La Tabula Peutingeriana, una descrizione pittorica del mondo antico*, Ravenna.
Bowman, L.R. (ed.) 1983, *Itinerarium: the idea of journey* (XV Int. Cong. Med. Stud., Kalamazoo, 1980), Salzburg.
——. 1983, '*Itinerarium: the shape of the metaphor*', in Bowman 1983: 3–33.
Brodersen, K. 1995, *Terra Incognita. Studien zur römischen Raumerfassung*, Zurich/New York.
Campbell, B. 2000, *The writings of the Roman land surveyors: introduction, text and commentary* (*JRS* Monograph 9), London.
Casson, L. 1974, *Travel in the ancient world*, London.
Chevallier, R. (ed.) 1974, *Littérature greco-romaine et géographie historique. Mélanges offerts à Roger Dion.* (*Caesarodunum* IXbis), Paris.
Chouquer, G. 1981, 'Les centuriations de Romagne orientale. Étude morphologique' *MEFRA* 93, 823–68.
Clarke, K. 1999, *Between geography and history*, Oxford.
Crone, G.R., 1975, *Maps and mapmakers: an introduction to the history of cartography* (5th ed.), Folkestone.
Cuomo, S. 2000, 'Divide and rule: Frontinus and Roman land-surveying', *Studies in the Hist. and Philos. of Science* 31, 189–202.
Dalché, P.G. 1992, 'Note sur la "carte de Théodose II" et sur la "mappaemonde de Théodulf d'Orléans"', *Geographia Antica*, 1, 91–108.
Dilke, O.A.W. 1971, *The Roman land surveyors: an introduction to the agrimensores*, Newton Abbot.
——. 1985, *Greek and Roman maps*, London.
——. 1987, 'Itineraries and geographical maps in the early and late Roman Empires' in Harley and Woodward, 1987: 234–257.
Dilleman, L. 1975, 'La carte routière de la Cosmographie de Ravenne', *BJ* 175, 165–170.
Edson, E. 1997, *Mapping time and space: how medieval mapmakers viewed their world*, London.
Elsner, J. 1995, *Art and the Roman viewer. The transformation of art from the pagan world to Christianity*, Cambridge.
Girod, R. 1974, 'Vision et répresentation géographique chez les anciens' in Chevallier 1974: 481–98.
Gorce, D. 1925, *Les voyages, l'hospitalité et le port des lettres dans le monde chrétien des IV e V siècles*, Wepion-sur-Meuse/Paris.
Goudineau, Chr. 1990, *César et la Gaule*, Paris.
Gould, P. and R. White 1974, *Mental maps*, Harmondsworth.
Gregory, D. 1994, *Geographical imaginations*, Oxford.
Harley, J.B. 1988, 'Maps, knowedge and power' in D. Cosgrove and S. Daniels (eds.) 1988, *The iconography of landscape*, Cambridge: 277–312.
Harley, J.B. and D. Woodward (eds.), 1987, *The history of cartography*, vol. I, *Cartography in prehistoric, ancient, and medieval Europe and the Mediterranean*, Chicago.
Harmand, L. 1974, 'Soldats et marchands aux prises avec l'universe atlantique' in Chevallier 1974: 247–55.
Harvey, P.D.A. 1987, 'Medieval maps: an introduction' in Harley and Woodward, 1987: 283–5.
Hayes, R.M. 1980, *Geographical images and mental maps*, London.
Hunt, E.D. 1982, *Holy land pilgrimage in the Later Roman Empire, AD 312–460*, Oxford.
Isaac, B. 1990, *The limits of empire*, Oxford.

Jacob, Chr. 1981, 'L'oeil et le mémoire: sur la Périégèse de la Terre habitée de Denyse' in Chr. Jacob and F. Lestringant (eds.), *Arts et légendes d'espace*, Paris: 23–97.
——. 1993, *L'empire des cartes. Approche théorique de la cartographie à travers l'histoire*, Paris.
Janni, P. 1984, *La mappa e il periplo: cartografia antica e spazio odologico*, Rome.
Janvier, Y. 1992, 'Vitruve et la géographie', *Geographia Antica*, 1, 49–78.
Kuntz, P.G., *Augustine's Confessions: archetype of a spiritual traveller*, in Bowman 1983: 34–53.
Leach, E.W. 1988, *The rhetoric of space: literary and artistic representation of landscape in Republican and Augustan Rome*, Princeton.
Levi, A. and M., 1964, *Itineraria picta. Contributo allo studio della Tabula Peutingeriana*, Roma.
——. 1981, 'Map projections and the Peutinger Table' in L. Casson (ed.) *Coins, culture and history in the ancient world*, Detroit: 139–48.
Levi, A.C. and B. Trell, 1964, 'An ancient tourist map', *Archaeology* 17, 227–36.
Malissard, A. 'L'espace sur la colonne trajane – essai d'étude filmique' in Chevallier 1974: 325–45.
Miller, K. 1916, *Itineraria romana*, Stuttgart.
Müller, C. *Ptolemaeus, Geographia*, 2 vols., Paris.
Nicolet, C. 1988, *L'inventaire du monde*, Paris.
Nordman, D. 1998, *Frontières de France*, Paris.
Pelletier M. and H. Ozane 1995, *Portraits de la France. Les cartes, témoins de l'histoire*, Paris.
Rambaud, M. 1974, 'L'espace dans le récit de César' in Chevallier (1974): 111–29.
Reed, N. 1978, 'Pattern and purpose in the Antonine Itinerary', *AJPh* 99, 228–54.
Rivet, A.L.F. and C. Smith 1979, *The place names of Roman Britain*, London.
Rivet, A.L.F. 1974, 'Some aspects of Ptolemy's geography of Britain' in Chevallier 1974: 55–81.
Sherk, R.K. 1974, 'Roman geographical exploration and military maps', *ANRW* II.1, 534–60.
Stevenson, E.L. 1991, *Claudius Ptolemy, the geographer*, New York (reprint of 1932).
Syme, R. 1988a, 'Journeys of Hadrian,' *ZPE* 73, 159–70.
——. 1988b, 'Military geography at Rome', *Class.Ant.* 7, 227–51.
Talbert, R.J.A. 1990/91, 'Rome's empire and beyond: the spatial aspect', *CahÉtAnc* 26, 215–23.
Tchernia, A. 1997, 'Winds and coins: from the supposed discovery of the monsoon to the denarii of Tiberius' in F. de Romanis and A. Tchernia, *Crossings: early Mediterranean contact with India*, New Delhi: 257–8.
Trousset, P. 1978, 'Les bornes du Bled Segui: nouveaux aperçus sur la centuriation romaine du Sud Tunisien', *Ant.Afr.* 12, 125–77.
Turner, V. and E. 1978, *Image and pilgrimage in Christian culture*, New York.
Weber, E. (ed.) 1976, *Tabula Peutingeriana: Codex Vindobonensis 324*, Graz.
Whittaker, C.R. 1994, *Frontiers of the Roman empire: a socio-economic study*, Baltimore.
——. 1996, 'Where are the frontiers now?' in D. Kennedy (ed.), *The Roman army in the East*, (*JRA Suppl.* 18), Ann Arbor: 25–42.
Woodward, D. 1985, 'Reality, symbolism, time, and space in medieval world maps', *Ann.Assoc.Amer.Geog.* 75, 510–21.
Zanker, P. 1988, *The power of images in the age of Augustus* (trans. A. Shapiro), Ann Arbor.

AENEID 6.826–35: HOMER AND CAESAR'S GALLIC COMMAND

W.R. Barnes

This paper as a whole is divided into three parts: the relation of *Aeneid* 6.826–35 to *Iliad* 7.279ff., the historical circumstances to which lines 834–5 refer, and the significance of that reference. In the *Aeneid* Anchises, identifying for Aeneas the souls of their descendants, points out Caesar and Pompey, who will fight a civil war; and in lines 832ff. he appeals to them not to fight.

> illae autem paribus quas fulgere cernis in armis,
> concordes animae nunc et dum nocte prementur,
> heu quantum inter se bellum, si lumina uitae
> attigerint, quantas acies stragemque ciebunt,
> aggeribus socer Alpinis atque arce Monoeci
> descendens, gener aduersis instructus Eois!
> ne, pueri, ne tanta animis adsuescite bella
> neu patriae ualidas in uiscera uertite uiris;
> tuque prior, tu parce, genus qui ducis Olympo,
> proice tela manu, sanguis meus!

In the *Iliad* the herald Idaios tells Hector and Ajax to stop fighting their duel.

> "μηκέτι, παῖδε φίλω, πολεμίζετε μηδὲ μάχεσθον.
> ἀμφοτέρω γὰρ σφῶϊ φιλεῖ νεφεληγερέτα Ζεύς,
> ἄμφω δ' αἰχμητά· τό γε δὴ καὶ ἴδμεν ἅπαντες·
> νὺξ δ' ἤδη τελέθει· ἀγαθὸν καὶ νυκτὶ πιθέσθαι."
> τὸν δ' ἀπαμειβόμενος προσέφη Τελαμώνιος Αἴας·
> "Ἰδαῖ', Ἕκτορι ταῦτα κελεύετε μυθήσασθαι·
> αὐτὸς γὰρ χάρμηι προκαλέσσατο πάντας ἀρίστους.
> ἀρχέτω· αὐτὰρ ἐγὼ μάλα πείσομαι, ἧι περ ἂν οὗτος."

Virgil's line 832, the first line of Anchises' appeal, was referred by Ursinus[1] to Homer's line 279, the first line of Idaios' appeal. Rightly; but if Virgil's general sense is the same as Homer's, "do not fight", his particular meaning is not I think what modern commentators

[1] *Virgilius collatione scriptorum Graecorum illustratus opera et industria Fulvii Ursini* (Antwerp, 1568), *ad loc.*

and translators say it is, "do not accustom your minds . . .".[2] The possessive epithet is not in the Latin. Servius observed that *adsuescite bella* is appropriate for the series of civil wars down to Actium: "iure dictum: ab ipsis enim quasi consuetudinem fecit populus Romanus bellorum civilium. septies enim gesta sunt: ter a Caesare . . . mortuo Caesare ab Augusto . . .". The idea is less appropriate for Caesar and Pompey alone in their war, which may have seemed in retrospect short enough as far as Pompey's death. Contemporaries saw the wars after Caesar's death as a continuation or repetition of Caesar's wars.[3] So, following "ab ipsis . . . quasi consuetudinem fecit populus Romanus", "do not accustom men's minds".[4] Line 832 refers to effects on the Roman people, like line 833;[5] as the perspective is historical the focus is national.

Virgil's allusion to Homer extends beyond line 832. Virgil's two imperative sentences in 832–3 can be referred to Homer's two imperative verbs in 279; Homer's verbs attracted critics' attention in antiquity because they express the same idea,[6] Virgil's sentences express different ideas. He alludes to the critics' interest in the question again, but perhaps in the Alexandrian manner contrarily, by using two nouns of the same sense in a pair of phrases, when Aeneas and Turnus would have engaged if night had not fallen, "ineant pugnas et proelia temptent", 11.912.[7] Then Anchises' appeal to Caesar and Pompey together not to fight (832–3) becomes an exhortation to Caesar to take the lead (834–5), as Idaios' appeal to Hector and Ajax to stop fighting (279–82) becomes Ajax' condition that Hector take the lead (283–6). In Virgil's "tuque prior, tu parce" (834) there is an echo in *parce* of Homer's ἀρχέτω (286), the word to which *prior* corresponds; as in *arma uirumque* (*Aen.* 1.1) from μῆνιν (*Il.* 1.1) and

[2] But cf. S. Farron, *Acta Classica* 23 (1980), 63, who translates "your minds", but argues for the interpretation I suggest.

[3] Hirt. *BG* 8, Praef. 2, Hor. *Epod.* 16.1–2 (see Mankin *ad loc.*), Virg. *G.* 1.489f.

[4] I take *adsuescite* as transitive: see *TLL* II 909, 25, 62, Norden on 832.

[5] The relation of *animis* to *uiscera* seems somewhat artificial, but that is not unique: cf. 12.950–1, *feruidus/frigore*.

[6] Gel. 13.25.18f., sch. Ar. *Ra.* 1159; the expression at *Ra.* 1159 is mentioned by Gellius in 7f. For another allusion to Homer here see J. Wills, *Repetition in Latin Poetry* (Oxford, 1996), 120 (but Heyne seems to refer only to Ursinus).

[7] Referred to *Il.* 7.279 by Ursinus *ad loc.*; 913–14/282. Virgil's *phrases* differ slightly in sense here also, an observation I owe to David West: see his translation, "they would have joined battle instantly and tried the fortunes of war."

ἄνδρα (*Od.* 1.1) the vowels of *arma* in the same place in the line echo the vowels in ἄνδρα, the word to which *uirum* corresponds.[8]

proice tela manu was referred by Germanus[9] to χειρὸς δ' ἔκβαλεν ἔγχος in *Il.* 14.419, in Hector's next great encounter with Ajax, when Hector, struck by Ajax with a rock, collapses, and lets his spear fall from his hand. χειρὸς δ' ἔκβαλεν ἔγχος has not much colour in itself; but it is unique in this shape and in this place in the verse. The line is not cited by later commentators, and is listed by Knauer in brackets as "Sicherlich von Vergil nicht bedacht".[10] But if more than one allusion to the duel in *Il.* 7 appears in 826–35 they make a context for an allusion to the encounter in *Il.* 14. "Subest vis quaedam verbo", according to Germanus; yes, if not the implication he suggests (see below).

Anchises gives Caesar two reasons to take the lead, one with each imperative, "parce, genus qui ducis Olympo", and "proice tela manu, sanguis meus".[11] They appeal to the origin of his descent on both sides; but the two phrases together may also carry an Homeric colouring. They resemble the naming pattern of διογενής and a patronymic or similar expression, which Homer uses conspicuously for Odysseus, διογενὲς Λαερτιάδη, but also for others,[12] including Ajax, Αἶαν διογενὲς Τελαμώνιε, at 9.644 and 11.465, and at 234 in this episode in some texts.[13] διογενής, "geleg. wörtl. genommen . . ., meist wohl nur allg. ehrender Epith. von Königen bzw. Heroen" (*LfrgE*), in conjunction with a patronymic was taken to refer particularly to descent: πατρόθεν ἐκ γενεῆς· ὡς ὅταν λέγῃ "διογενὲς Λαερτιάδη", τὸν πατέρα δηλοῖ, τὸ δὲ "διογενές" τὸν ἀρχηγὸν τοῦ γένους (schol. *Il.* 10.68 b, Erbse III 17, 67ff.; not cited in *LfrgE*).[14] Anchises' two reasons appeal to Caesar's dignity as Idaios gives Hector and Ajax two reasons in the confirmation of their dignity (280–1, to which he adds night as an external third

---

8 On such echoes see Wills (n. 6), 19f. (on *Aen.* 1.1: 25 n. 36).

9 *P. Virgilius Maro, et in eum Commentationes, et Paralipomena Germani Valentis Guelli, PP* (Antwerp, 1575), *ad loc.*

10 G.N. Knauer, *Die Aeneis und Homer* (Göttingen, 1964), Listen.

11 *genus qui ducis Olympo* and *sanguis meus* have been interpreted as reasons since Heyne; on *sanguis meus* see also J. Svennung, *Anredeformen* (Uppsala, 1958), §290 with §§ 268–9. For references to descent from the gods as a reason for accepting appeals see ἀντί τοί εἰμ' ἱκέταο, διοτρεφές, αἰδοίοιο, *Il.* 21.75; μνῆσαι πατρὸς σοῖο, θεοῖς ἐπιείκελ' Ἀχιλλεῦ, 24.486, with schol. c, Erbse V 601, 70ff.

12 Achilles (διογενὴς Πηλέως υἱός), Menelaus, and Eurypylus, once each.

13 7.234 is excluded by West.

14 τὸ μὲν Λαερτιάδη τὸν πατέρα δηλοῖ is suggested by Erbse.

reason, 282); Anchises' first reason invokes descent from Venus as Idaios' first reason confirms the love of Zeus for both.

Idaios' intervention can be seen already in Anchises' description and anticipation of Caesar and Pompey (826–31). Their war is postponed now by night, as Hector's and Ajax' duel is interrupted by night: "nunc et dum nocte prementur"/νὺξ δ' ἤδη τελέθει· ἀγαθὸν καὶ νυκτὶ πιθέσθαι. (827/282). *nunc* echoes νὺξ and corresponds in sense to ἤδη; *nocte prementur* echoes and corresponds in sense to νυκτὶ πιθέσθαι. The 'now' of *nunc* in 827 is not quite the same as that of ἤδη in 282, but is the same as that of νῦν and σήμερον in Hector's acceptance of the argument: νῦν μὲν παυσώμεθα μάχης καὶ δηϊοτῆτος/ σήμερον· ὕστερον αὖτε μαχησόμεθα, 290f.[15] There will be fighting/ fighting again, in the light/tomorrow, 828–9/291–3.[16] For the moment the future/present combatants are friends, 827/300–2.[17] Virgil's night, which has been explained by commentators with some care because it lies over a part of the underworld that has its own sun (640f.), can also be referred to Homer's night.

Other allusions to Hector and Ajax can be observed or in this context constructed in 826–31. For *paribus . . . in armis* (826) the commentators cite, rightly, Virgil's own reference to Pharsalus as well as Philippi in *G.* 1.489–90, "ergo inter sese paribus concurrere telis/ Romanas acies iterum videre Philippi".[18] One meaning of *paribus*, in the *Aeneid* as in the *Georgics*, is 'both Roman'; which in both poems implies a reason for not fighting. At the same time in the *Aeneid*, some have thought, "there may also be a notion of their equality as great generals";[19] I should say even "of their equality in dignity", for the ideas expressed in Lucan's "nec quemquam iam ferre potest Caesarve priorem/Pompeiusve parem" (1.125–6) had been expressed already at the time, for Pompey by Caesar, "neminem dignitate secum exaequari volebat" (*BC* 1.4.4), and for Caesar by himself, ἐγὼ μὲν ἐβουλόμην παρὰ τούτοις μᾶλλον ⟨ἂν⟩ εἶναι πρῶτος ἢ παρὰ Ῥωμαίοις

---

[15] On 291, suspected by some editors, see Kirk on 290–3. The sense of *iam* in Virgil's other use of *Il.* 7 in 11.913 (see above) is close to that of ἤδη in 282.

[16] On 293, athetized by Aristarchus, see Kirk on 290–3.

[17] See Kirk on 300–2 ("Hektor and Aias as '*good friends*'!"). In 827 the idea also carries Roman political content in *concordes* and an apparent reference to Camillus in 825: see P. Grimal, *REA* 56 (1954), 47; N.M. Horsfall, *Ancient Society* (Macquarie University), 12 (1982), 12.

[18] On Pharsalus and Philippi in *G.* 1.489–90 see Mynors *ad loc.*

[19] Conington on 826; Germanus cites 9.655, of equal ability in archery.

δεύτερος (of a poor community in the Alps, Plut. *Caes.* 11.4; cf. *Mor.* 206B), "difficilius se principem civitatis a primo ordine in secundum quam ex secundo in novissimum trudi" (Suet. *Jul.* 29.1). Idaios' second reason for Hector and Ajax to stop fighting is that both are, or have proved themselves to be, warriors, ἄμφω δ' αἰχμητά (281), that is, equal, as the scholia explain, ἴσους ἔφησεν αὐτούς, τὴν τοῦ Ἕκτορος ἧτταν ἐπικαλύπτων (Erbse II 273,30f.). The idea is a little strange as a reason for abandoning a combat; it is more in place in the context of games.[20] But *paribus . . . in armis* then shares one meaning with the *Georgics* ('both Roman') and another with the *Iliad* ('equal'), and, in the meaning it shares with the *Georgics*, the same rhetorical function with both ("you/they should not fight").

In 830–1 the Alps are the bulwark of Italy; the idea was familiar.[21] Cicero had compared Caesar's Gallic command with them as that bulwark, "cuius ego imperium, non Alpium vallum, contra ascensum transgressionemque Gallorum . . . obicio et oppono" (*Pis.* 81, cited by Henry). That may evoke from the Homeric background of 826–35 Ajax as ἕρκος Ἀχαιῶν in 3.229 and 6.5, and in this episode at 7.211, as he goes into combat with Hector; and even perhaps Ajax on the wall of the Greek camp in *Il.* 12.265ff., from which he goes to fight Hector in *Il.* 13 and 14.

I have analysed lines 832–5 first here, and have then gone back to 826–31, because Ursinus noticed the allusion in 832. H.-C. Günther separated 832–5 from 826–31 for other reasons; he argued, starting from the incomplete line 835, that Anchises' appeals in 832–5 were not written with the description and anticipation in 826–31, but were added by the poet later and left incomplete in line 835.[22] His reasons are not I think entirely convincing.[23] But the allusions to Homer's

[20] See G.S. Kirk in B. Fenik (ed.), *Homer. Tradition and Invention* (Leiden, 1978), 38f.

[21] At least since Cato; see Nisbet on Cic. *Pis.* 81.

[22] *Überlegungen zur Entstehung von Vergils Aeneis* (Göttingen, 1996), 42f.

[23] He suggests that (a) 835 (*sic*; rather 836) in content would follow better on 831 than on 835, (b) 832–5 is like 7.759–60 as additional details of a person in the form of an apostrophe (on 7.759–60, N. Horsfall, *RFIC* 125 [1997], 468), (c) the apostrophe diminishes the effect of the apostrophes in 841ff. But the content common to 826–31 and 836ff., which might be defined as the military power of the empire, is treated very differently between the two passages; 832–5, as adding to the description of a person or persons in the Parade, can be compared with 822–3 as moral comment; the apostrophe is appropriate in a context which is already at a high level of emotion in the exclamations of 828–9, and the apostrophes of 841ff.

duel, which appear in 826–31 as well as in 832–5, seem to be neither for the case nor against. Homer is less conspicuous in 826–31 than in 832–5 (which might suggest an argument that 826–31 were written with 832–5 already in view); but the idea that fighting is postponed now by night but will follow in the light is not incidental to 826–31. Caesar may evoke Ajax in his association with the Alps, and then evokes Hector in Anchises' appeal to him to act first. But he may even evoke Ajax again in Anchises' statement of his genealogy; and multiple reference in a character, which is everywhere in the *Aeneid*,[24] may be explained and interpreted in this context in other ways.[25] But if Günther is right Virgil has used Homer's episode in 826–31 and then returned to that episode later in 832–5; and similarly has alluded to *G.* 1.489–90 in 826 and has then returned to those lines later to complete as I shall suggest a double allusion in 835.

The circumstances in which Anchises makes his appeals differ from those in which Idaios intervenes; he is apparently not interrupting the war as Idaios interrupts the duel. The night at Troy comes during the duel; the night of the underworld is before the war. Caesar and Pompey have not yet been born. Anchises says they will fight;[26] but he might still attempt to stop them before they do fight. The moment in the poem suggests 'do not start to fight'. In the appeals themselves he is not, or not evidently, imagining himself forward in the future interrupting the war. *adsuescite bella* refers to the long series of wars that followed; *ne . . . adsuescite bella* might mean "do not continue to fight", but it might equally mean in that long perspective "do not start to fight [a war which will lead to others]". *parce* was interpreted by Servius as recommending Caesar's policy of clemency toward those on Pompey's side, that is, during and after the war: "Caesari dicit quem clementem circa Pompeianos legimus: cui vult tunc *ab Anchise* (SD) hoc esse mandatum". But after 832–3 it seems

are at another and already lower emotional level, that of formal variation in enumeration.

[24] J. Griffin in B. Gold (ed.), *Literary and Artistic Patronage in Ancient Rome* (Austin, 1982), 118ff., esp. 127ff.

[25] In the duel in the *Iliad* Hector was read as the loser, Ajax as the winner (see below); 'the collapse of distinctions that results from the play of literary models' (P. Hardie, *The epic successors of Virgil* [Cambridge, 1993], 34) may result here from the play of an historical event with a literary model (see also, on the effacement of differences between duellists, especially in civil war, Hardie 22ff.).

[26] The conditional form of *si lumina uitae/attigerint* is stressed by Farron (n. 2), 53f.

to mean not only "spare the Pompeians", but rather "spare your country", which he might say as well before the war.[27] So that Virgil's use of Homer in 826–35 does not imply that Anchises is interrupting the war. But his use of Ajax' condition may point to the circumstances he envisages.

Interpretations of Anchises' appeal to Caesar with reference to the events of the war start from one or the other of the two imperatives *parce* and *proice tela manu*. The use of *parce* with reference to Caesar's part in the war inevitably evokes the idea of his clemency. Norden suggested that Virgil's audience might think of his clemency after Thapsus; but to be first at that stage in the war would have been nothing more than to spare at all, even if he could anticipate more fighting. Caesar had announced the policy at the outset, and followed it through the war.[28] Austin and West point to Corfinium on 21 February 49, where Caesar spared Domitius, and quote his letter of 5 March to Oppius, in which he explains that clemency as his policy for the future.[29] Caesar in the letter compares himself not with Pompey, whom he rather says he wishes to conciliate, but with those who had fought past civil wars. Others may have made comparisons with Pompey for themselves.[30] But more particularly Caesar at Corfinium did not spare before Pompey when Pompey might have spared, or take a lead for Pompey to follow, but simply set a policy for himself. His action was not for Pompey as Hector's is for Ajax, in which Hector is to take the lead (ἀρχέτω), and Ajax, who as the other combatant might have acted, will then follow (αὐτὰρ ἐγὼ . . .).[31] And after *parce* there is then the second imperative, *proice tela manu*; and Caesar did nothing, at Corfinium or later in attempts at negotiations,[32] which Virgil might have described as laying down his arms, and as taking the lead in it.

---

27 Cf. Paratore on 834.

28 On the policy see S. Weinstock, *Divus Julius* (Oxford, 1971), 237ff., S. Rochlitz, *Das Bild Caesars in Ciceros "Orationes Caesarianae"* (Frankfurt am Main, 1993), 50ff.; Caesar does not use the word *clementia* himself (Weinstock, 236; Rochlitz, 43).

29 Cic. *Att.* 9.7C; Austin on 834, D. West in H.D. Jocelyn, H. Hurt (edd.), *Tria Lustra*, Liverpool Classical Papers No. 3 (Liverpool, 1993), 292f.; West had said in the same place "Anchises is clearly horrified at his kinsman's part in bringing about the civil war" (292), where I think "bringing about" is right.

30 So M. Treu, *MH* 5 (1948), 210ff., Weinstock (n. 28), 237; see also, for Cicero's views at the time, P. Brunt, *JRS* 76 (1986), 26ff.; Pompey as Sulla in Cic. *Att.* 9.10.6; 10.7.1.

31 The idea is perhaps audible in ἀρχέτω· αὐτὰρ ἐγὼ . . .

32 Caes. *BC* 1.24.4f.; 1.26.2ff.; 3.10; 15.6–19.8.

Before Corfinium Caesar had proposed to Pompey and the Senate through Roscius and L. Caesar that, among other arrangements, he himself should hand over the Gallic provinces (and necessarily their legions) to his successsors and Pompey should go to Spain (and necessarily again retain the forces there).[33] That was indeed laying down provinces and the forces in them, and first.[34] But when Pompey and the Senate made the condition that he withdraw from the places he had occupied he was not willing to withdraw while they had forces in Italy. He would not lay down those arms first; and in describing the terms of the response he represented it more generally as an attempt to have him give up his forces first (esp. *BC* 1.11.1).[35]

The other interpretation of Anchises' appeal to Caesar starts from *prior* and *proice tela manu.* In the most explicit statement of it, S. Farron rejected Servius' interpretation of *parce*:

> In lines 832–833 he dissuades them both from fighting the civil war. Then in 834–835, as a natural extension, he turns to Caesar and tells him to take the initiative in this. . . . Caesar is told that he should be the *first* (*prior*) to spare and disarm. This can apply only to the situation at the beginning of the war, not to clemency after it.[36]

Farron does not specify more particularly the circumstances in which they (or Caesar) might decide whether or not they (or he) would fight. I suggest not "at the beginning of the war" but "before the war"; that *prior* with *proice tela manu* alludes to the debate about Caesar's command in the Gauls and Illyricum that led to the war, and to a formulation of the question at issue from which *prior* has more point, both in a comparison of Caesar with Pompey and in Virgil's use of Homer.

---

[33] See K. Raaflaub, *Chiron* 5 (1975), 247–300; on the terms, 261ff.

[34] The legions in Illyricum are not mentioned, E. Rawson, *CAH*^{2} IX 428; but see Raaflaub (n. 33), 263 n. 69.

[35] On the Senate's response and Caesar's refusal, Raaflaub (n. 33), 271ff.; on the forces in Italy, 278f., 279f.

[36] (n. 2), 54; cf. 63f. So D.C. Feeney: "certainly Caesar was *clemens*, but only once he had begun the war; here Anchises is begging his descendant to lay down his arms first, before Pompey does", *PCPhS* 212 (1986), 12, and, quoting Feeney, E. Lefèvre in H.-P. Stahl (ed.), *Vergil's* Aeneid: *Augustan Epic and Political Context* (London, 1998), 108 with n. 57. R. Syme had already chosen this imperative of the two: "Virgil . . . made Aeneas' guide exhort Caesar to disarm before Pompeius", *The Roman Revolution* (Oxford, 1939), 317, and others after Syme have said that Virgil represents Caesar as responsible for the war.

By the year 50 Caesar's command was coming to an end, whether or not a date could be fixed in terms of law;[37] but Pompey's command in the Spains had been extended in 52 for five years.[38] When in 50 Caesar's enemies in the Senate renewed their attempts to remove him from his command the tribune Curio, and later Caesar in his own name, proposed that if Caesar was to lay down his command Pompey should lay down his also.[39] The question was implicitly or explicitly one of priority, whether Caesar should give up his forces while Pompey still had his. As Caelius saw it, "Caesari autem persuasum est se salvum esse non posse <si> ab exercitu recesserit; fert tamen illam condicionem, ut ambo exercitus tradant" (Cic. *Ad fam.* 8.14.2, Aug. 50). Velleius relates the question directly to the extension of Pompey's command (2.48.1). Caelius thought that the matter of the armies was one over which they would fight: "propositum est hoc de quo qui rerum potiuntur sunt dimicaturi".[40]

The question of priority is most explicit in the fuller narrative of Curio's opposition in Appian, *BC* 2.27.103–29.113. Curio first proposed that Pompey too should lay down his command (προσετίθει τὸ καὶ Πομπήιον ὁμοίως Καίσαρι ἀποθέσθαι τὰ ἔθνη καὶ τὸν στρατόν, 104), then, when it was objected that Pompey's time had not yet expired (⟨διὰ⟩ τὸ μήπω τὸν χρόνον ἐξήκειν τῷ Πομπηίῳ, 105),[41] that Caesar should not be replaced if Pompey were not replaced (μὴ χρῆναι μηδὲ Καίσαρι πέμπειν διαδόχους, εἰ μὴ καὶ Πομπηίῳ δοῖεν, 105). After Pompey in his illness had written to the Senate offering not to wait for the time fixed for his command (οὐκ ἀναμένων τοὺς χρόνους τοὺς ὡρισμένους, 107), Curio, pressing the offer, argued that Caesar should not be deprived of his army *before* Pompey himself had laid down his own

[37] See E.S. Gruen, *The Last Generation of the Roman Republic* (Berkeley, 1974), 492f., R. Seager, *Pompey. A Political Biography* (Oxford, 1979), 193ff.

[38] D.C. 40.44.2; 56.2; Plut. *Pomp.* 55.12 (four years); cf. Plut. *Caes.* 28.8, App. *BC* 2.24.92.

[39] Caelius in Cic. *Ad fam.* 8.14.2, Hirt. *BG* 8.52.4–5, Liv. *Per.* 109, Vell. 2.48.1, Plut. *Caes.* 30.1–2, *Pomp.* 58.3,5; 59.2, *Cat.Mi.* 51.4–5, *Ant.* 5.6 (on Plutarch's accounts see C.B.R. Pelling, *JHS* 100 [1980], 139f.), Suet. *Jul.* 29.2, App. *BC* 2.32.127–8 (on Appian's earlier narrative see below), D.C. 40.62.3; 41.1.4. On Caesar's letters see Pelling on Plut. *Ant.* 5.5.

[40] Cic. *Ad fam.* 8.14.2. In the same vein Seager says "[Curio's] move . . . perhaps did more than any other factor to bring about the confrontation between Pompeius and Caesar that led eventually to war", (n. 37), 155.

[41] A point of priority which Curio met in his response, that there would *not yet* be security if all did not lay down their commands: οὔπω τῇ πόλει τὴν εἰρήνην ἔσεσθαι βεβαίαν (105).

command (Κουρίων ... οὐχ ὑπισχνεῖσθαι δεῖν ἔφη μᾶλλον ἢ αὐτίκα ἀποθέσθαι οὐδ' ἐξοπλίζειν Καίσαρα τῆς στρατιᾶς, πρὶν καὶ αὐτὸν ἰδιωτεῦσαι, 110). He continued to argue that Pompey should lay down his command while Caesar still had his (εἰ μὴ νῦν σὺν φόβῳ τῷ Καίσαρος ἀποθοῖτο τὴν ἀρχήν ... 111). The Senate tended to favour Pompey; and some thought that it was not safe to dissolve Pompey's command *until* Caesar had *previously* laid down his arms (οἱ δὲ καὶ τῷ ὄντι οὐκ ἀσφαλὲς ἡγοῦντο διαλύειν τὴν ὑπὸ τῷ Πομπηίῳ δύναμιν, μέχρι πρότερον ἐκεῖνον ἀποθέσθαι, 112). Curio reversed the argument, maintaining that they must have Caesar against Pompey, or dissolve all commands (ὡς δέον ὑπάρχειν αὐτοῖς ἐπὶ τὸν Πομπήιον Καίσαρα, ἢ ὁμοῦ πάντας καταλύειν, 113). He then, Appian says, closed the session (113). Appian may be using a source contemporary with the events, even Pollio, a source, perhaps a principal source, for *BC* 2, who was in close association with Curio in the first months of the war.[42] Virgil need not be alluding to Pollio here for a fact of common knowledge;[43] but Appian's narrative demonstrates (if it were necessary) that the question of priority could be represented very explicitly as the point at issue in the debates about Caesar's command.

Confirmation that Virgil was taken to be referring to the question of Caesar's Gallic command can be found in Petronius' poem of the Civil War. The verb *proicere* is in common use for the laying down of arms.[44] But the use of it in the poem of the Civil War has the more point if it alludes to *proice tela manu* as a reference to the question of Caesar's command:

exuit omnes
quippe moras Caesar, uindictaeque actus amore
Gallica proiecit, ciuilia sustulit arma.
(122.141–3)

[42] Opinion on Appian's sources in *BC* is surveyed by W. Will in *Appian, Römische Geschichte II, Die Bürgerkriege*, tr. O. Veh (Stuttgart, 1989), 2–4, D. Magnino, *ANRW* II 34.1, 547–9; argument in detail by I. Hahn in G. Wirth (ed.), *Romanitas-Christianitas* (Berlin, 1982), 251–76. On Appian's preference for contemporary authority, Hahn, 265ff., 275f., and on Pollio in Book 2, 263f. with 260 n. 19; for some scepticism about Appian and Pollio, W. Steidle *H* 111 (1983), 402ff. On Pollio and Curio in the first months of the war see J. André, *La vie et l'oeuvre d'Asinius Pollion* (Paris, 1949), 13–15 and B. Haller, *C. Asinius Pollio als Politiker und zeitkritischer Historiker* (Diss. Münster, 1967), 23, 25–30. I am grateful to Tony Woodman for advice about Pollio.

[43] On Virgil and Pollio's *Histories* see L. Morgan, *JRS* 90 (2000), 51–69.

[44] *TLL* II 598, 69ff., X,2 1797, 7ff.

The lines that follow, which describe the Alps which Caesar was to cross, seem to allude to Virgil's reference to Hercules in *arce Monoeci* (144–6/830).

Anchises then is not imagining himself interrupting the war, as Idaios interrupts the duel, but is rather trying to prevent it. Virgil has introduced Homer's appeal and condition at an earlier moment in events. So Statius used Anchises' appeal to Caesar for attempts to forestall his own war, in an allusion running through two books. First in heaven, Jupiter to the gods as he starts the war: "vos, o superi, meus ordine sanguis,/ne pugnare odiis, neu me temptare precando/certetis", *Theb.* 3.239ff. (an ironic reversal of Anchises' purpose);[45] then at Argos, the seer Amphiaraus to the Argives: "proicite arma manu", 3.643; then at Thebes, a Bacchante to Eteocles: "tu peior, tu cede, nocens qui solus avita/gramina communemque petis defendere montem", 4.401f.

The debates about the Gallic command in 50 and early 49 have been seen already in some interpretations of lines in the Sibyl's account of those behind the walls of Tartarus, "uendidit hic auro patriam dominumque potentem/imposuit; fixit leges pretio atque refixit" (621–2). The lines have been reworked from Varius, Fragment 1 (Courtney), "uendidit hic Latium populis agrosque Quiritum/eripuit, fixit leges pretio atque refixit", which refers to Antony in his consulate. A case was once made for Antony in the *Aeneid* also, in which "uendidit hic auro patriam dominumque potentem/imposuit" was taken to refer to his tribunate, and the rest to his consulate.[46] The tribunate and the consulate are combined in a single sentence by Cicero in *Phil.* 2.47 ("ad haec enim quae in ciuili bello . . . fecit, et ad ea quae cotidie facit, festinat animus"); and he is said by Cicero to have sold his tribunate to Caesar and used it against the Senate's efforts to save the state on 1 January 49, 2.51 ("tum iste uenditum atque emancipatum tribunatum consiliis uestris opposuit").[47] Curio too is said, in a tradition that may have begun with Pollio, to have been bribed by Caesar;[48] and cases have been made, following Lucan and Servius, for him, at least in "vendidit hic auro

[45] On *meus ordine sanguis* here see Svennung (n. 11), §290.

[46] A. Weichert, *De Lucii Varii et Cassii Parmensis vita et carminibus* (Grimma, 1836), 104ff. (a second edition of arguments in *De Lucio Vario Poeta Commentatio III* [1831]).

[47] The same allegation in Plut. *Pomp.* 58.2; cf. Pelling on *Ant.* 5.2.

[48] See Pelling on Plut. *Ant.* 5.2.

patriam dominumque potentem/imposuit".[49] But these are not the only interpretations.[50] 621–2 are still rather more obscure than 834–5; and any argument from 621–2 to 834–5 risks circularity.

Lines 834–5 were called by Syme "this veiled rebuke".[51] If *adsuescite bella* refers to the whole series of civil wars, and *proice tela manu* refers to the debate about the Gallic command before the first war, and asks Caesar not even to start fighting that war, the term 'rebuke' may seem appropriate. But the veil of the passage as a whole is fairly heavy. *paribus . . . in armis*, not only of common nationality but also of equal standing in war, states a first balance; *socer* and *gener* strike another, which shares sorrow, or blame.[52] The war is a conflict of West and East, 830–1; the idea is emphasised by the initial assonance of *aggeribus, Alpinis, arce*, and then *adversis*. *Eois* qualifies *paribus* as 'both Roman'. But Caesar's Alps with more words are more suggestive than Pompey's Eastern forces. The Alps are here the bulwark of Italy; Cicero had compared Caesar's Gallic command itself with them as that bulwark, "cuius ego imperium, non Alpium vallum, contra ascensum transgressionemque Gallorum . . . obicio et oppono" (*Pis.* 81) (see above). Caesar may perhaps be assimilated to Ajax, ἕρκος Ἀχαιῶν (see above). His descent from the Alps is not necessarily an abandonment of that command; that was how Petronius was to put it when he alluded to these lines ("Gallica proiecit, ciuilia sustulit arma", 122.143). *arce Monoeci* alludes to Hercules, whose crossing was famous, and could be a paradigm (cf. D.H. 1.41–2). Caesar's re-enactment might be positive (cf. 801–3). He might also be constructed as Hannibal,[53] from Cicero's comparison of him taking towns

[49] See J.E.G. Zetzel, *TAPhA* 119 (1989), 271f. and n. 35, R. Thomas, *Virgil and the Augustan Reception* (Cambridge, 2001), 89–92. Zetzel decides for Curio in *hic* and Antony in *leges fixit pretio atque refixit*; Thomas is not explicit. The syntax and the very close structural similarity to Varius suggest that the lines refer to the one person.

[50] All of 621–2 refers to Antony in his consulate: Norden, *ad loc.* (*dominum . . . potentem* is Antony himself), H. Dahlmann, *Zu Fragmenten römischer Dichter*, AAWM 1982, 11, 24f. (*dominum . . . potentem* is Caesar). "uendidit hic auro patriam dominumque potentem/imposuit" refers to a type, the rest to the individual Antony: A.S. Hollis *CQ* n.s. 27 (1977), 188 (on the typical and the individual in Tartarus see Zetzel [n. 49], 264–72, esp. 269f. on 616f.).

[51] (n.36), 317.

[52] Sorrow: R.F. Dobbin, *CSCA* 14 (1995), 25, blame: Lefèvre (n. 36), 107f. On the larger context of the poem see F. Cairns, *Virgil's Augustan Epic* (Cambridge, 1989), 96ff.

[53] Briefly, Lefèvre (n. 36), 108.

in northern Italy with Hannibal (*Att.* 7.11.1), from Virgil's reference here to Hercules, whose example Hannibal had recalled in his march into Italy (Caesar's re-enactment then becomes negative), and from Lucan's and Petronius' later comparisons of Caesar with Hannibal, especially from Petronius' allusion to Virgil's Caesar's crossing in a context in which he will make the comparison of Caesar with Hannibal.[54] But if Caesar's crossing became a subject of the rhetorical schools with Hannibal's, as Norden concluded, Hannibal's itself as a subject may have been due to Livy, later than Virgil.[55]

Anchises' appeals in a forward perspective offer responsibility to Caesar, or urge it on him. He begins by appealing to Caesar and Pompey together (832–3), but then his appeal to Caesar alone (834–5) by its formal correspondence to the first appeal places the responsibility with Caesar. Two imperative verbs in the singular echo formally two imperative verbs in the plural; the anaphora of *tu* with a single verb repeats the anaphora of *ne* with a single verb; the sequence *prior, parce, proice,* continues in alliteration and thought *pueri* and *patriae. sanguis meus* strengthens the emotional claim of *pueri.*[56] The appeal honours his dignity. It echoes the hymnic style,[57] and it confirms his claims of divine descent;[58] it assimilates him to Aeneas. The appeal sets him above Pompey,[59] and corrects the implications of *paribus* (826). That word already sets him higher than Pompey had wanted; and Statius' allusion to the appeal in *tu peior, tu cede* (*Theb.* 4.401f., above) points to a reading of *prior* as implying 'superior', which was what Caesar himself had wanted.[60] It may also assimilate him to

---

[54] These ideas are discussed with reference to Petronius very usefully by C. Connors, *Petronius the Poet* (Cambridge, 1998), 125–30. In Petronius' poem "Caesar walked over the Alps in Hannibal's footsteps; Hannibal walked in Hercules', undoing his civilizing progress with war and destruction" (130); reading that sequence in the *Aeneid* is at least in part a matter of debate about theory.

[55] H. Stubbe, *Die Verseinlagen im Petron* (Leipzig, 1933), on 144ff. On the relation of Virgil to Livy see *EV* s.v. *Livio.*

[56] *pueri* from Anchises is already stronger than παῖδε φίλω from Idaios (279); *sanguis meus* uses the potential of παῖδε φίλω, which Idaios could not use with Hector and Ajax (see schol. *ad loc.*).

[57] On iteration of pronouns in hymnic style see Wills (n. 6), 82f., 361f.; cf. especially *Aen.* 7.41; 9.404 (from Wills).

[58] On Caesar's political use of his family's claims of origin see Weinstock (n. 28), 17f., 83ff., Farron (n. 2), 58ff., Dobbin (n. 52), 20f. Farron seems not to consider the tone and purpose of Anchises' appeal to them; cf. Dobbin 25.

[59] "Iam tum Iulium heroem vocat . . . voluit enim hac re indicare, Iulium illustriorem fore Pompeio", Cerda.

[60] See above on *par* and *prior* in Luc. 1.125–6.

Ajax, Αἶαν διογενὲς Τελαμώνιε (7.234, cf. 249; see above); as it refers to his descent from the gods it may set him at this moment above both Hector and Ajax, who were in their duel only loved by Zeus (7.280).[61] The phrases *genus qui ducis Olympo* and *sanguis meus* urge Caesar's dignity, which had been one of the principal reasons he asserted for fighting,[62] as a reason for not fighting; but they must honour his dignity to do so.[63] *parce* approves Caesar's policy of clemency in and after the civil war. Then *prior . . . /proice tela manu* takes the position that Caesar's opponents had taken in the debates that led to the war; and the relation between the two imperatives in the structure of the sentence, each with its own reason, conveys the implication that if Caesar had followed that policy of clemency before the war he would have laid down his command first. *proicere* may carry some irony here, amid common usage (see above), as the term which Caesar himself had used for his orders to the Pompeians he had trapped in the pursuit from Pharsalus.[64] And finally, after *paribus . . . in armis* in 826 has alluded to Pharsalus as well as Philippi in *G.* 1.489, *inter sese paribus concurrere telis*, now *tela* in 835 completes that allusion ("lay down the arms [that will be otherwise the arms] of Pharsalus and Philippi"). But all that remains within the veil of his dignity, which is the origin of his responsibility.

Hector in his duel with Ajax is a potentially subversive point of reference for Caesar in his war with Pompey. The criticism of the *Iliad* which survives in the scholia saw Hector as the inferior, Ajax as much the superior, in more than one respect.[65] Anchises' emphasis on Caesar's dignity, and perhaps a faint assimilation of Caesar to Ajax as well as Hector, suppresses much of that subversion; and if everyone knew that Hector had almost lost,[66] everyone also knew

[61] The difference between the standing of Achilles as one *born* from a god and that of Hector as one loved by Zeus is made explicit in *Il.* 24.55–61 and 64–70, at the conclusion of a theme that begins in the duel with Ajax (7.200–5, confirmed in 280; 22.167–76). On such hierarchies in *Il.* 20–24 see A.W.H. Adkins, *CPh* 70 (1975), 239ff.

[62] Cic. *Att.* 7.11.1; Gruen (n. 37), 492 with n. 151, 496 with n. 168.

[63] Cf. Dobbin (n. 52), 25.

[64] *BC* 3.98.1, cited by Conington on 835.

[65] See the scholia on (e.g.) 90 (Erbse II 243, 3ff.), 212 (265, 24ff.), 216, 217 (266, 46ff.), 284 (274, 41ff.); on Virgil's awareness of the criticism that survives in the scholia and elsewhere see T. Schmit-Neuerburg, *Vergils* Aeneis *und die antike Homerexegese* (Berlin, 1999), 16–18.

[66] *Il.* 7.307ff.; see the scholia on 307–12 in Erbse II 277, 27ff. So already on 276 (272, 17ff.), 281 (273, 30f.), 284 (274, 41ff.), 292 (275, 70ff.).

that Caesar had won. But it is worth noticing one suppression, and one more allusion.

The reasons that Anchises gives Caesar, *genus qui ducis Olympo* and *sanguis meus*, are more heroic than the reason Ajax gives Hector, αὐτὸς γὰρ χάρμηι προκαλέσσατο πάντας ἀρίστους (285),[67] and so set him above Hector. But if Anchises' reasons take the place of Ajax' reason, that raises the question of the reader's appropriate response to Virgil's omissions from his texts of reference, a question of presence in absence.[68] Virgil here does not simply omit Homer's idea, he introduces another in its place. But Anchises' appeal is one character's persuasion of another in their special relationship; persuasion has been his purpose from his opening with *pueri*.[69] The reader for whom Virgil has recalled both Ajax and Hector and the question of Caesar's command might therefore think beyond Anchises' purposes to Ajax' reason, which has some application to Caesar also.

Then *proice tela manu* in the context of Hector's duel with Ajax can be referred to χειρὸς δ' ἔκβαλεν ἔγχος, *Il.* 14.419. That phrase was cited by Germanus with "ut . . . complures arma proicerent, ac fugae simile iter videretur" (of forces in panic), Caes. *BC* 3.13.2, and with the expressions ῥίπτειν ὅπλα and ῥίψασπις; but it has no connotations of flight in *Il.* 14. Rather the loss of arms is a sign that the warrior is no longer a warrior, a sign of defeat (as in *Il.* 16.793ff. of Patroclus, where it undoes the arming of 16.130ff.). If *proice tela manu* alludes through that sign to anything for Caesar it is to the final event beyond the war. The text (whatever the reader supposes Anchises has in mind) urges Caesar to lay down his arms with that later (and consequential) loss of arms in view.

The passage as a whole in this reading of it may seem not to serve very well one of the dramatic functions of the Parade, which is to encourage Aeneas; or another, that the explanation of it to him should please Anchises. But reference to civil war inevitably strikes another note in this anticipation of Roman history, and at this length, fairly loudly.[70] The war, and Caesar's part in it, as catastrophes in

[67] The line explains 284 (γάρ); but ἀρχέτω in 286 is in conclusive asyndeton with 285 (Ameis-Hentze) and also repeats 284 in other terms.

[68] On such omissions see S. Morton Braund, R. Mayer (edd.), *amor: roma. Love in Latin Literature* (Cambridge, 1999), 67.

[69] 'vox blanditiarum', Cerda; cf. n. 56. On Anchises as a character with his own purposes see Thomas (n. 49), xviiif. and (e.g.) 53.

[70] This note, and others, were recognised already by Norden (p. 314); for the best account and a strong interpretation see Feeney (n. 36).

the achievements of Roman history, exemplify the Platonic and Pythagorean doctrines of the eschatology with which Anchises explains this vision, and, by implication, something of Roman history.[71] Future Romans will scarcely be exempt from the passions that attend the life of the soul in the body;[72] all souls have to be purged. "An anti-Caesarian construction" on lines 826–35 "would represent such a *volte-face*" from *Buc.* 9.46–50 and *G.* 1.466–92.[73] 'Anti-Caesarian' needs to be defined, in a range at least from Syme's 'veiled rebuke' to Farron's 'attack on Augustus' propaganda' through the person of "the man whom Vergil brands as a mass murderer".[74] (Then there would be the range from Anchises' appeal to Caesar to *dominum . . . potentem* [621], if that phrase could be referred to Caesar, whether in 50/49 or in 44).[75] Lines 834–5 do not refer to the same moment as *Buc.* 9.46–50 and *G.* 1.466–92; this need not be the same Caesar.[76] Or the same Virgil. The lines are in fact in accord with *Buc.* 9.46–50 (and *Buc.* 5) in associating Caesar with divinity. The passage does also attribute to Caesar a responsibility for the war (and the wars); but it is at that point that the passage is incomplete. To say so is not, I hope, cowardice; in the light of Günther's reconstruction of the place of such passages in Virgil's papers, and of Varius' editorial procedures, any reading of this piece of text in relation to the rest of the text should be provisional.[77]

Then there is Augustus, both outside the text and inside it, in the past the Octavian who had fought the later wars in Caesar's and Pompey's series, the first of them to avenge Caesar himself, and in the present *Diui filius.* Richard Thomas has recently argued that we should put a little distance between Virgil and Augustus, and between ourselves and Augustus.[78] I shall not offer to say what Augustus might have made of the passage. I draw attention instead to what may have been one of Horace's readings, with reference to Augustus:

---

[71] But not an end in the eschatology, Feeney (n. 36), 3f.

[72] Zetzel (n. 49), 282 .

[73] P.White, *Phoenix* 42 (1988), 351.

[74] Farron (n. 2), 53, 64.

[75] 50/49: Weichert (n. 46), Zetzel, Thomas (n. 49); 44: Dahlmann (n. 50).

[76] Cf. Dobbin (n. 52), 25.

[77] See Günther (n. 22), 63ff. On the relation of 827 to Camillus in 825 see Grimal, Horsfall (n. 17); and on *socer* and *gener* in the rest of the poem see Cairns (n. 52).

[78] (n. 49): Virgil and Augustus, 25–54, ourselves and Augustus, *passim.*

quaeque vos bobus veneratur albis
clarus Anchisae Venerisque sanguis,
impetret, bellante prior, iacentem
  lenis in hostem.
(*CS* 49–52)

In the context of the Aeneas legend here (37ff.), "bellante prior, iacentem/lenis in hostem" has been readily referred at least since Porphyrio to Virgil's *parcere subiectis et debellare superbos* (853).[79] Horace's idea is explained by Thomas as an Augustan appropriation of Virgil.[80] There may be more. *clarus Anchisae Venerisque sanguis* was referred to Virgil's *genus qui ducis Olympo* with *sanguis meus* (834–5) by Henry (*ad loc.*) for the double definition of Augustus' genealogy as well as the use of *sanguis*. If Horace's *prior*, of defeating the enemy, can be referred to Virgil's *prior*, of sparing the enemy without fighting at all, Horace might seem to have turned Anchises' exhortation to Aeneas in 853 against his exhortation to Caesar in 834f., even though the latter was for civil war.[81]

[79] The idea is older than Virgil, and common (E. Fraenkel, *Horace* [Oxford, 1957], 376). But see R. Merkelbach, *MH* 18 (1961), 97ff.; who refers Horace's treatment of the legend in the hymn to the whole of *Aen.* 6; and D. Feeney, *Literature and religion at Rome* (Cambridge, 1998), 36; who argues persuasively that this hymn for a Sibylline oracle's *ludi* "reanimates" Anchises' Sibylline exhortation (cf. Zetzel [n. 49], 278f. on Virgil and the *ludi*).

[80] (n. 49), 69ff.

[81] For another interpretation see M.C.J. Putnam, *Horace's* Carmen Saeculare (New Haven, 2000), 80; who seems to suggest that Horace is combining the two exhortations as expressions of the same principle of restraint. But Horace has transferred *prior* from sparing and laying down arms first to defeating the enemy. Horace's lines are evidently relevant to O. Zwierlein's attribution of 826–35 to the poet and declaimer Julius Montanus (*Die Ovid- und Vergil-Revision in Tiberischer Zeit I, Prolegomena* [Berlin, 1999], 116 ['deutlich nach Ovid']; see 591f.); but Zwierlein has not yet as far as I know published his argument in detail.

DIDO'S TREASURE AT TACITUS *ANNALS* 16.1–3

P. Murgatroyd

The story of Dido's treasure at *Annals* 16.1ff. has not received much scholarly comment, with the notable exception of D. Braund's 'Treasure-trove and Nero'.[1] To his interesting speculations there on what might have made Nero find the tale attractive, may be added its literary aspects; but the connection with the *Aeneid* has further significance than that. There are numerous thematic links (several of them striking) and some verbal similarities to the epic's lines on the queen,[2] and whether these Virgilian parallels were just taken over from his source(s) and exploited by Tacitus or developed to a greater or lesser extent by him,[3] they have real point and come together to form cutting condemnation of Nero and his world.

At *Annals* 16.1ff. Tacitus tells how Caesellius Bassus (Carthaginian by origin and mentally deranged) had a dream about buried treasure, took it as a promise of a certainty, went to Nero at Rome and told him that he had found on his estate a deep cave containing a large quantity of ancient gold bullion, speculating that Dido after fleeing from Tyre and founding Carthage had concealed this wealth, to prevent her people being corrupted, or hostile Numidian kings going to war with her for the treasure. Nero accepted the report without checking and sent ships to collect the gold quickly. Meanwhile he was praised by orators as a favourite of the gods (who supposedly produced the riches for him), his extravagance grew on the strength of this vain hope, and he squandered vast resources. Bassus, however, could not find the cave on his estate or nearby. Astonished that he had been deceived when none of his earlier dreams had

---

[1] In *Greece and Rome* 30.1 (1983), 65–9.

[2] For the presence of Virgil in Tacitus see e.g. B. Walker *The Annals of Tacitus: A Study in the Writing of History* (Manchester, 1952), 71–4; R. Syme *Tacitus* (Oxford, 1958), I 357f.; R.M. Ogilvie and I. Richmond *Cornelii Taciti De Vita Agricolae* (Oxford, 1967), 28; R.T. Baxter 'Virgil's Influence on Tacitus in Book 3 of the Histories', *Classical Philology* 66 (1971), 93–107; J. Bews 'Virgil, Tacitus, Tiberius and Germanicus', *PVS* 12 (1972–3), 35–48 and *Enciclopedia Virgiliana* V (Rome, 1990), s.v. *Tacito*.

[3] There is a much shorter version of the story with far fewer epic reverberations at Suetonius *Nero* 31.

proved false, he escaped his shame and danger by committing suicide (or some say that he was arrested and later released after his property had been confiscated in lieu of the treasure).

A quick summary of salient features in Virgil's lines on Dido will help elucidate the similarities in Tacitus. After Aeneas had been driven by the storm to the coast near Carthage, Venus (in disguise) met him and (at 1.338ff.) told him how in her home city of Tyre the ghost of Dido's husband (murdered by the king) had appeared to her in a dream, urging her to flee and showing her buried treasure (a mass of ancient silver and gold), and how she then (obviously believing the dream) had unearthed it, fled to north Africa with the wealth and founded Carthage amid warlike Libyans. Aeneas subsequently met and began an affair with Dido, after she had been driven mad with love[4] by Cupid, but had to leave her, briefly deceiving her by concealing his preparations for departure, and finally rowing off in haste.[5] The queen then committed suicide, demented by anguish.

Mention of Dido would automatically have made Tacitus' readers think of the famous lines on her in the *Aeneid*, and by way of clear reinforcement Dido's Virgilian epithet *Phoenissa*[6] occurs in *Annals* 16.1 (*Dido Phoenissam*). Then there are all the parallels. Like Dido, Bassus was Carthaginian, had a dream about buried treasure, consisting of a mass of ancient gold (*antiquo pondere* and *opes*, 16.1; cf. "veteris . . ./thesauros, ignotum argenti pondus et auri" and *opes*, *Aeneid* 1.358f., 364) and believed it; he was also mad, spoke to and got involved with a Roman leader (cf. the proto-Roman Aeneas) in an initially amicable but ultimately disastrous relationship and (in the account foregrounded by Tacitus) committed suicide largely because of that leader. Bassus also made a long journey (to Rome) and was deceived (by his dream). There seems to be an Aeneas at *Annals* 16.1ff. too—his descendant Nero.[7] As well as meeting with the Carthaginian, at first being friendly but finally being responsible for the Carthaginian's suicide (in the preferred version), the Roman

---

[4] *Aen.* 4.69, 78, 101 etc.

[5] *Aen.* 4.288ff., 573ff.

[6] In surviving Latin literature apart from *Annals* 16.1 the adjective is applied to Dido only at *Aen.* 1.670, 6.450 and (quoting Virgil) Servius on *Aen.* 1.664.

[7] Nero was also likened to his ancestor Aeneas in the lampoon mentioned by Suetonius (*Nero* 39): "quis negat Aeneae magna de stirpe Neronem?/sustulit hic matrem, sustulit ille patrem".

leader was told about Dido's flight from Tyre, founding of Carthage, wealth, warlike neighbours and dream of buried treasure, and he also got his ships rowing off quickly.[8]

The parallels are intriguing and bizarre and have a decidedly mock-solemn impact. A romantic and momentous episode of high drama and pathos from lofty epic (with divine involvement) re-appears as a shabby and ludicrous little incident (set squarely in the sordid human sphere), and in place of revered and illustrious heroic figures engaged in a great love affair we find one clown and mad-man taking in another in a scramble for loot—so degenerate and unheroic was Nero's world. There is also the black comedy of the absurd lunatic Bassus in the role of the noble and tragic queen Dido. The linking of Nero with Aeneas is even more grotesque and economically brings out many of Nero's failings by way of contrast, intimating how far short he fell of his eminent ancestor (who was renowned for *pietas*, put the good of his people before himself, was a genuine favourite of heaven, was a great warrior, with many moral qualties, had a loving relationship with his divine mother, and so on and so forth).

[8] There are other (less conspicuous but still possible) ties: at 16.1 for *inlusit . . . per vanitatem* cf. *Aen.* 1.352 *vana spe lusit amantem*, and for *Tyro profugam* cf. *Aen.* 1.340 *Tyria . . . urbe profecta*; so too Bassus' dream is called an *imago* (cf. *imago* of Sychaeus' ghost in Dido's dream at 1.353), he buys an interview with Nero (*aditum emercatus*; cf. the Carthaginians' purchase of land, *mercatique solum*, at 1.367), the cave in his dream may look to the cave in which Dido and Aeneas began their affair, and there is mention of lust for gold (*cupidine auri*; cf. *auri caecus amore* at 1.349); for *spe inani* at 16.3 compare *vana spe* at 1.352, and for Bassus' *pudor* in that chapter cf. Dido's feelings of shame at 4.550ff. and 596f.

DIRECT DEMOCRACY, ANCIENT AND MODERN

M.H. Hansen

In the beginning of 1990, during one hundred days, John Crook devoted all his time to translating my Danish account of Athenian fourth-century democracy into English. I spent the Lent term in Cambridge and we met every day in the morning and worked all day. John had prepared a rough translation of some five pages during the preceding evening. He dictated this version to me. I put it onto my portable computer (an Olivetti, i.e. the famous Ollie, whose invaluable assistance is acknowledged in the preface to the 1991 edition). In the evening I produced an annotated and finished version of the day's work while he prepared a draft of the next five pages, and so on, day by day. What is more, besides translating the book, he exposed all my views to criticism. Every day many problems had to be discussed. Not a single argument was accepted *prima facie*, and trying to persuade the Devil's advocate I often had to reformulate my argumentation or rethink my position. Thereby the English version became a better book than the Danish original. In our discussions we often touched on problems of modern democracy, which appeared in a new light when seen in an Athenian perspective. Thus, translating the first short chapter and repeatedly throughout our sessions we returned to the relation between ancient Athenian democracy and modern ideas about direct democracy. I promised John that, one day, I would treat these issues in more detail, and here is the obvious opportunity. John has spent so much of his life in Socratic discourse with his many pupils and friends whereby they have got a much better grasp of the problems they were trying to solve. Thus, he has indirectly left his mark on hundreds of books and articles about ancient history published during the last fifty years. Here is another one.[1]

Until Alexis de Tocqueville in 1835–40 published his *De la démocratie en Amérique* democracy was almost invariably taken to be direct

[1] The original version of the this paper was presented in Stockholm in September 1999 at a seminar about ancient Athenian democracy and our modern western democracies, arranged by the Swedish *Academy of Democracy*.

democracy practised in a small community, such as ancient Athens or eighteenth-century Basel,[2] and democracy and representation were seen as opposed forms of government.[3] In the wake of de Tocqueville's book the concept of democracy became rapidly connected with the concept of representation, and in 1842—before the abolition of slavery—the United States were praised as the "most perfect example of democracy".[4] Democracy without further qualification came to mean representative democracy, and direct democracy was from now on relegated to historical footnotes. During the last generation, however, the concept of direct democracy has re-appeared as a possible alternative to the prevailing form of representative democracy.

The case for replacing representative by direct democracy is based on a combination of four propositions: the first is the almost universal belief that democracy is a 'Good Thing'. The second is the proposition—often presented as a corollary of the first proposition—that maximum democracy equals optimum democracy. The third is the very plausible axiom that direct democracy is more democratic than representative democracy and thus constitutes maximum democracy. The fourth is the claim that modern technology has made a return to direct democracy possible.[5]

These propositions are, again, based on a number of beliefs which are invoked as justifications for direct democracy, ancient or modern. In my opinion at least five basic beliefs are involved, which I suggest here to call the five pillars of direct democracy. They are:

---

[2] *Encyclopædia Britannica* 1st edn. 1771, s.v. "*Democracy*: the same with a popular government, wherein the supreme power is lodged in the hands of the people: such were Rome and Athens; but as to our modern republics, Basil only excepted, their government comes nearer to aristocracy than democracy."

[3] As late as 1848 the new Swiss federal constitution treated democracy and representation as direct opposites: *Constitution de la confédération Suisse du 12 Septembre 1848.* The first really important political movement launched under the banner of democracy was Andrew Jackson's democratic party set up in 1828 (J. Roper, *Democracy and its Critics* [London 1989]).

[4] The concept of representative democracy made its first appearance in a letter from Alexander Hamilton of 1777 (to Gouverneur Morris, 19 May 1777); but it took a long time "for the concept of representation to be ingrafted upon the concept of democracy" (Th. Paine, *Rights of Man* [1792, republished Cambridge 1989], 170). That happened in consequence of A. de Tocqueville, *De la démocratie en Amérique* i–ii (Paris 1835–40). *Encyclopædia Britannica* 7th edn. 1842, s.v. *Democracy*: "the most perfect example of democracy is afforded by the United States of North America at the present day."

[5] *Four propositions about direct democracy*: (1) Democracy is a 'Good Thing': see J.J. Rousseau, *Du Contrat Social* (Amsterdam 1762), Book 3 Chapter 15; Barber (1998); Carson and Martin (1999), 39. (2) Maximum democracy = optimum democracy:

1. The belief that ordinary citizens are *intelligent* people who are capable of making sound decisions about themselves and their fellow citizens.[6]
2. The belief that ordinary citizens are prepared to *disregard their self-interest* in case of conflict with the national interest.[7]
3. The belief that ordinary citizens can be kept sufficiently *informed* about the issues at stake.[8]
4. The belief that ordinary citizens are *interested* in participating in political decision-making instead of delegating politics to professional representatives.[9]
5. The belief that rational decision-making can be conducted on an *amateur basis* if one distinguishes between the *expert knowledge* required to prepare and formulate the measures, and the *common sense* required to make a political choice between formulated alternatives.[10]

---

see, e.g., Barber (1984), especially 117–20, 131–2, 151. (3) Direct democracy = maximum democracy: see, e.g., Budge (1996), 190–2. (4) New technology has made a return to direct democracy possible: see, e.g., McLean (1989), 108–34, 171–2.

[6] Budge (1996), 188–90 presents "arguments and evidence which demonstrate that citizens in the mass are able to make policy-decisions which are not noticeably worse than those made by legislatures, if not somewhat better".

[7] Budge (1996), 109: "In the case of American States many individual results of individual initiatives (tax limitations, gun laws, harsh criminal penalties) can be satirized. However, there are always counter-examples where initiatives have supported public services against tax cuts, limited guns, upheld minority rights and protected the environment. Given the difficulty of saying what is 'objectively' good or bad, perhaps the safest ground for evaluation is to compare popular initiatives with what State legislatures have done. Here very little difference opens up". See also, e.g., Cronin (1989).

[8] Budge (1996), 60: "Participation also educates and expands citizens' capacities, which are not so limited anyway". 113: "there seems little in the copious survey evidence for the Unites States and Switzerland to suggest that electors are copiously under-informed in relevant respects compared to other political actors". See also Marcus and Hanson (1993).

[9] Budge (1996), 19: "If we extended the definition of participation to actively informing oneself and being attentive to politics, as participatory theorists would urge, the distinction between agreeable private pursuits with benefits and disagreeable political ones with costs would, however, almost totally disappear". 64: "after all participation can be pleasurable, and educational". Cf. 186–8.

[10] Budge (1996), 181: "Parliament would change into an advisory, investigative and debating committee informing popular discussion and voting, rather than substituting for it". 186: "Most will be recipients of information rather than active contributors, thus disappointing the highest hopes of participation". Today the crucial distinction between experts and politicians is acknowledged by all parliamentarians who, not being experts themselves, distinguish between the technical aspects of an issue (to be left to the experts) and the purely political aspects (to be decided by the elected representatives of the people). The interesting point is that parliamentarians hardly ever allow this distinction to be made in debates over whether political decisions should be made by referendum. In this case they prefer instead to

In the ongoing discussion of direct versus representative democracy a major problem is that today direct democracy is attested only at municipal level, for example in the New England town meetings[11] and in village assemblies in Bhutan.[12] It is also attested in federations at member state level, for example in some of the smaller Swiss cantons.[13] But it does not exist any longer anywhere as a form of government of a state. Admittedly, referendum is widely used in Switzerland, in Italy and in twenty-six of the states of the US, but even democratic states which allow some political decisions to be made by referendum are far removed from direct democracy in which every major political decision automatically has to be debated and voted on by the people.[14]

Consequently the five pillars of direct democracy have to be tested against historical evidence, and the only major well attested historical example of direct democracy is the type of democracy practised in the ancient Greek city-states from circa 500 BC down to the end of the Hellenistic period.

It is commonly, but erroneously, believed that the many hundred *polis* democracies were all direct, and in this respect different from modern indirect or representative democracy. We know that there was a type of Greek democracy in which the principal function of the popular assembly was to choose the magistrates and call them to account for their conduct in office, while all political decisions were taken by the elected magistrates. This is, if not necessarily representative, then at least indirect democracy.[15]

Most Greek democracies, however, were direct, and so was Athenian democracy, which, furthermore, is the only historical democracy for which we have sources enough to reconstruct its political institutions and democratic ideology.[16] Among modern champions of direct

---

emphasize the distinction between their own expert knowledge and the ignorance of ordinary citizens.

[11] Sly (1932); Mansbridge (1980).

[12] Vinding (1998).

[13] Kellenberger (1965); Carlen (1976). Until recently the cantonal popular assembly, the *Landsgemeinde*, existed in five cantons and half-cantons: Obwalden, Nidwalden, Appenzell Ausserrhoden, Appenzell Innerrhoden, and Glarus. During the last six years, however, the citizens have voted their assembly out of existence in Obwalden, Nidwalden and Appenzell Ausserrhoden.

[14] Gallagher and Uleri (1996); Budge (1996), 84–104.

[15] Arist. *Pol.* 1318b21–22, 28ff.; 1274a15–8; 1281b32–4; see Hansen (1999), 3.

[16] Hansen (1999), 1–2.

democracy there are two opposed assessments of Athenian democracy and its merits.

According to some theorists, ancient assembly democracy is essentially different from modern models of electronic democracy. Admittedly both are forms of direct democracy. But they are so different that next to nothing can been learned from studying the ancient form. These theorists usually take a negative view of Athenian democracy as, in fact, a disguised oligarchy. Modern direct democracy is not a return to something which once was, but, rather, the introduction of something completely new.[17]

Other theorists, however, hold that the Athenian example is a highly relevant historical example and that the methods to be used in modern direct democracy are adaptations to new technology of a political system which, essentially, was practised by the Athenians. There are, admittedly, major differences between ancient and modern direct democracy both in the form of debate and the way the vote is taken; nevertheless, some of the basic aspects of direct democracy are common to both forms.[18] Proponents of this more historical view of direct democracy tend to focus on the institutional and ideological aspects of Athenian democracy.[19] The fact that the Athenians excluded women and had slaves is, largely, irrelevant in this context—an obvious parallel is the American Declaration of Independence of 1776 and the American Constitution of 1787/9. We can

[17] E.g. Budge (1996), 16: "Clearly the Greek model is unworkable today and functioned badly in Athens too. It is hardly a means for extended participation either, given the exclusion of the large majority of the population from debate and voting". 26: "The phone-in, the televised debate, the casting of mass votes after debate, all opened up discussion to strata of the population which would never have got a look-in at Athens". No mention of Athens at all in Arterton (1987). Gallagher (1996), 234 concludes that even Liechtenstein (population: 29,000) is too large to be governed by Athenian-style direct democracy.

[18] McLean (1989), 158: "Could we reinvent Athenian democracy; more pedantically, some combination of democracy and demarchy that was at least as good as the Athenians'? It would have to be better in one regard: it must be workable in an entire population, and not restricted to free men." See also 5–12, 15–18, 28–9, 109, 127, 130–1, 158–9, 170–1. Fishkin (1991), 86–92; (1997), 18–26; 54–5; 80–1, 169. Carson and Martin (1999), 3–4, 31–3, 35, 40, 100, 104, 108, 116. Becker and Slaton (2000), 41.

[19] An important nineteenth-century evaluation of Athenian democracy can be found in J.S. Mill, *Considerations on Representative Government*: "Notwithstanding the defects of the social system and moral idea of antiquity, the practice of the dicastery and the ecclesia raised the intellectual standard of an average Athenian citizen far beyond anything of which there is yet an example in any other mass of men, ancient or modern."

appreciate the ideas and ideals advocated in these documents in spite of the fact that American women had no political rights before 1920, and that there was a large population of black slaves who were held neither to have been created equal, nor endowed by their Creator with inalienable rights such as life, liberty and the pursuit of happiness.

Thus, in spite of all the important differences between a small ancient city-state and a large, modern so-called territorial state, one important way of testing merits or draw-backs connected with direct democracy is to study the political system of ancient Athens from 507 BC, when Kleisthenes introduced *demokratia* in Athens, and 322 BC when this democracy was abolished in consequence of the Macedonian conquest of Athens.

The first thing to note is that what I call the five pillars of direct democracy were explicitly recognised by the Athenians as foundations of their political system:

1. The Athenians did believe in the intelligence and sound judgement of the ordinary citizen, and they put their belief to the test by letting all major political decisions be made by ordinary citizens either in the assembly (in which every citizen was entitled to speak and to vote) or in law courts and legislative committees manned with ordinary citizens (selected by lot for one day from a panel of 6000 citizens selected by lot for one year).[20]
2. Ancient critics of Athenian democracy, in particular Plato and Aristotle, claimed that the poor, always being in the majority in any political assembly, would avail themselves of any opportunity to soak the rich, especially by confiscation of property. That may have happened occasionally, but Athenian democrats took pride in stating that although the jurors in the democratic courts were sometimes tempted by irresponsible prosecutors to have a rich man convicted and his fortune confiscated, they almost always resisted the temptation and acquitted the defendant.[21]

[20] Dem. 3.15: "You have among you, Athenians, men competent to say the right thing, and you are the sharpest of all men to grasp the meaning of what is said, and you will at once be able to translate it into action, if only you do your duty" (transl. J.H. Vince). Cf. Eur. *Orestes* 917–22. See also Ober (1989), 158–60. On the degree of participation in Athens, see Hansen (1999), 313.

[21] Hyp. 3.33: ". . . that there is not in the world a single democracy or monarch or race more magnanimous than the Athenian people, and that it does not forsake those citizens who are maligned by others, whether singly or in numbers, but supports them. Let me give an instance. When Tisis of Agryle brought in an inven-

3. The Athenians believed that regular participation in the political institutions made the citizens sufficiently knowledgeable to make well-informed political decisions; and the democratic government at Athens was accompanied by publicity to a degree otherwise unheard of in past societies. Everything had to be publicized, either orally or in writing: assemblies were not only decision-making organs, they were the forum where many matters were brought to the notice of as many citizens as possible. It was a hallmark of democracy to have a written code of laws available to the public for inspection; and again and again in the inscriptions the formula is repeated that a proposal or decision is to be published so that it can be read by anyone who wishes.[22]
4. For many Greeks and most Athenians, political activity was a positive value and participation in the decision-making process an end in itself and not just a means to self-advancement, or to obtain some other advantage. According to Aristotle, man was a "political animal", i.e., the very stuff of human life at its most basic was involvement in social and political organization. It seems that the Athenians derived actual enjoyment from the formal play with complicated procedures like sortition, voting and debates in political assemblies. Accordingly the citizens' participation in the running of the political institutions was astonishing and unmatched in world history.[23]

---

tory of the estate of Euthykrates, amounting to more than sixty talents, on the grounds of its being public property, and again later promised to bring in an inventory of the estate of Philip and Nausikles saying that they had made their money from unregistered mines, this jury was so far from approving such a suggestion or coveting the property of others that they immediately disfranchised the man who tried to slander the accused and did not award him a fifth of the votes" (transl. J.O. Burrt). Plato and Aristotle hold that, in a democracy, the majority of poor will inevitably vote according to class interests and soak the minority of rich (Pl. *Resp.* 565A; Arist. *Pol.* 1304b20–4; 1320a4–6).

[22] Arist. *Pol.* 1281b3ff.: "For each individual among the many has a share of excellence and practical wisdom, and when they meet together, just as they become in a manner one man who has many feet and hands and senses, so too with regard to their character and thought. Hence the many are better judges than a single man of music and poetry; for some understand one part and some another, and among them they understand the whole" (transl. B. Jowett). Cf. Dem. 23.109. Political information brought to the attention of all citizens: Aeschin. 3.25, 32; Arist. *Ath. Pol.* 43.4; Eur. *Suppl.* 433–4.

[23] Thuc. 2.40.2: "Here each individual is interested not only in his own affairs but in the affairs of the state as well: even those who are mostly occupied with their own business are extremely well-informed on general politics—this is a peculiarity of ours: we do not say that a man who takes no interest in politics is a man

5. Although the Athenians supposed that every citizen would take an active part in the running of the democratic institutions, they also insisted that no citizen should be forced to engage in political activity at the top level. Political activity was divided into passive participation, that is listening and voting, and active participation, which included preparing proposals and taking an active part in political argument by speaking in the assembly and council and being an advocate in the popular courts. What the Athenians expected of the ordinary citizen was passive participation only, which demanded enough common sense to choose wisely between the proposals on offer, whereas active participation was left to those who might feel called to it. Democracy consisted in every citizen having the right to speak, *isegoria*, the genuine possibility to stand up and advise his fellow citizens; but the Athenians did not require or expect everyone to do so. Indeed, if every citizen had insisted on making use of his right to address his fellow citizens, Assembly-democracy would have broken down there and then. The Athenians presupposed a fundamental divide between leaders and followers, in this respect there is no distinction between ancient Athenian and modern representative democracy. And this divide is connected with the distinction between those who possess expert knowledge, that is the leaders, and those who possess enough common sense to listen to a debate and choose between the proposals submitted by the leaders.[24] The difference between

---

who minds his own business; we say he has no business here at all" (transl. Rex Warner). According to Aristotle man is a 'political animal' (*zoon politikon*, *Pol.* 1253a3). His purpose in life is to live an active political life (*bios politikos, Eth.* 1095b18ff.; *Pol.* 1325b16ff.) which is identical with being a citizen (*polites*) in a *polis*, and "citizens in the common sense of that term, are all who share in the civil life of ruling and being ruled in turn . . . and under an ideal constitution they must be those who are able and willing to rule and be ruled with a view to attaining a way of life according to goodness" (*Pol.* 1283b42–84a2).

[24] Thuc. 6.39.1: "I say, on the contrary, first that the word *demos*, or people, includes the whole state, oligarchy only a part; next, that if the best guardians of property are the rich, and the best counsellors the wise, none can hear and decide so well as the many; and that all these talents, severally and collectively, have their just place in a democracy" (transl. R. Crawley). Active participation not expected of ordinary citizens: Dem. 18.308; 19.99; 10.70–4; 22.30; Aeschin. 3.233; Eur. *Suppl.* 438–41. A philosophical formulation of the different levels of knowledge is found in Aristotle's *Politics* where he states that there are two forms of knowledge: one concerns how to make a thing, the other how to make use of a thing. It requires expert knowledge to build a house, but it requires common sense to choose a house that fits one's need. And it is not the cook but the guest who decides the quality of a meal (Arist. *Pol.* 1282a16–23).

> the Athenians and us is that in direct democracy the choice is between the proposals, and has to be made every other day, whereas, in a representative democracy, the only choice left to ordinary citizens is between the leaders, and the choice is offered the citizens only once every third or fourth or fifth year.

Moving from basic ideas to institutions there is a noticeable difference in how modern proponents of direct democracy use the Athenian example. Those who ignore Athenian democracy, or even take a fairly unfavourable view of it, tend to focus on the idea that all the people all the time must vote on all important political issues, and on how this can be done by electronic voting after the watching of political debates transmitted on TV. In a historical context the problems discussed are whether such a debate can replace a proper face-to-face debate in a public assembly like the Athenian, and whether electronic voting by millions of citizens can replace the direct voting by a show of hands taken among those who have listened to the debate.

These problems are certainly relevant, but we must not forget that direct decision-making in a popular assembly was only one aspect of ancient Athenian democracy. Other important aspects were: (a) the appointment of magistrates, jurors and legislators by the drawing of lots instead of by election; (b) a short term of office (usually a year) combined with a ban on iteration to ensure maximum rotation; (c) payment for political participation to make it possible for even poor citizens to exercise their political rights; and (d) the separation of initiative and decision, so that initiative and preparation of all bills was left to highly active and sometimes even semi-professional citizens in collaboration with a council which prepared all business for the popular assembly, whereas decision by vote was what was expected from the ordinary citizens.[25]

[25] Important aspects of Athenian democracy (apart from direct decision-making in a popular assembly) are: (a) the appointment of magistrates, jurors and legislators by the drawing of lots instead of election, see Hansen (1999), 197–9, 235–7, 308; (b) a short term of office (usually one year) combined with a ban on iteration to ensure maximum rotation, see Hansen (1999), 225–7; (c) payment for political participation to make it possible even for poor citizens to exercise their political rights, see Hansen (1999), 315–7; and (d) the separation of initiative and decision, so that initiative and preparation of all bills was left to highly active and sometimes even semi-professional citizens collaborating with members of the council of 500, whereas decision was what was expected from the ordinary citizens, see Hansen (1999), 71–2, 143–6, 306–7, 309, 312.

Those who really find inspiration by studying the Athenian political institutions are less interested in the face-to-face assembly democracy for which they have contemporary institutions to study, such as the New England town meeting or the Swiss Landsgemeinde. They focus instead on the other aspects, particularly selection by lot, for which the only modern parallel is the completely different modern jury. The extensive use of the lottery in democratic Athens is completely unknown today,[26] and if transformed to fit contemporary states and modern technology the analogy would be to have a small panel of citizens randomly selected from all citizens, but so few that they can carry on a debate, at least by telecommunication, and that they can be sufficiently informed about the political issues at hand. The idea is, then, to transform parliaments into preparatory and problem-formulating institutions whose proposals are to be voted on by deliberative and decision-making opinion poll panels, selected by lot from among all citizens. This form of popular rule is often called 'demarchy' instead of 'democracy', a term invented by John Burnheim.[27]

So sortition instead of election, rotation to ensure maximum participation, payment to stimulate participation, and the acknowledged distinction between active and passive participation are aspects of direct Athenian democracy which have recently been drawn into the debate about a return to direct democracy.

In *Democracy and Its Critics* Robert A. Dahl suggested one model democracy which incorporated such institutions:

> Suppose an advanced democratic country were to create a 'minipopulus' consisting of perhaps a thousand citizens randomly selected out of the entire demos. Its task would be to deliberate, for a year perhaps, on an issue and then to announce its choices. The members of a 'minipopulus' could 'meet' by telecommunications. . . . The judgment of a minipopulus would 'represent' the judgment of the demos. Its verdict would be the verdict of the demos itself.[28]

By far the most sophisticated and best tested version of this form of direct democracy, however, is the deliberative opinion poll as developed by, especially, James Fishkin: a couple of weeks before an elec-

[26] Elster (1989), 78–93; Carson and Martin (1999).
[27] Burnheim (1985), 9, 156–87; Carson and Martin (1999), 102–14. McLean uses 'demarchy' synonymously with what he calls 'statistical democracy' (1987), 157–61.
[28] Dahl (1989), 340.

tion or a referendum some three to five hundred randomly selected citizens are first provided with information about the issue at stake, then they are brought together to participate in a weekend of deliberation on the issue. During this session they debate with one another and listen to experts and political leaders to whom they can put questions and ask for further information. Both before and after the weekend a vote is taken. All experiments so far conducted in accordance with this method show that some panellists have changed their mind in the course of the debates and, especially, that a number of 'don't knows' have made up their mind. If the group of citizens is randomly selected and really represents a cross-section of the citizenry, the experiment indicates both how the people would decide the issue if they had to vote offhand without any information and interactive debate, and how they would vote if *all* citizens had had access to the same amount of information and exchange of views in a prolonged debate.[29] The difference between the first and the second vote reveals the importance of information and debate as key aspects of democracy.[30] By contrast with other models of demarchy, Fishkin does not envisage that it is left to the panel to decide the issue. The deliberative poll is intended to be a guideline for the electorate when, a few weeks later, all citizens have to vote.

Today the champions of modern direct democracy are in fact split between two models. One is the referendum model: to allow all citizens not only to elect their political leaders but also to decide a large number of key issues by direct vote, which can be conducted electronically.[31] The other is the demarchy model: to replace, or rather supplement, the elected legislators and their government with small panels of randomly selected citizens who can meet and debate the issues before they vote.

In both cases the decision is 'the voice of the people'. If a panel is enlarged from the circa 500 citizens used in most test polls to

[29] Fishkin (1991), 81–96; (1997), 161–228; Carson and Martin (1999), 87; Becker and Slaton (2000), 66–8; for a criticial view, see Merkle (1996).

[30] I am pretty sure that if Rousseau had experienced the deliberative polls he would say that the difference between the vote before and after represents the difference between 'la volonté de tous' and 'la volonté generale': see *Du Contrat Social* Book 2, Chapter 3.

[31] The first one to suggest a high number of electronically conducted referenda was Fuller (1971). A recent champion of this form of direct democracy is Budge (1996), 188 who imagines a total of circa fifty such referenda per year. See also Gallagher (1996), 240–50.

circa 3000, there is a very high probability that the panel will normally arrive at the same decision as that of a referendum with millions of voters (who had had the same information). The panel is, in fact, representative of the people in the true sense in which the elected legislators hardly ever are, especially if they take the view that they have been selected for their personal qualities and judgement and are not bound to vote as constituents think.

The advantage of referendums over deliberative opinion polls is that all citizens can participate in a referendum. The drawbacks are the absence of a face-to-face debate among all citizens, as well as the difficulty in keeping all citizens sufficiently informed about all the issues that have to be debated and voted on. Conversely, the advantage of deliberative opinion polls over referendums is that a 'minipopulus' of at most 1000 citizens can get access to all the necessary information, they can meet and debate, and they can devote the time and energy necessary to arrive at a rational decision. The drawback, on the other hand, is that only a minute fraction of the population gets an opportunity to be directly involved in the decision-making process. Even in small nations the possibility of being selected to serve on a panel is minimal.

I know of only one model of direct democracy which avoids the dilemma. Inspired by the Athenian example, and explicitly acknowledging his debt to ancient Athens, Marcus Schmidt, a Danish university teacher, has constructed a very interesting model of modern direct democracy which combines all the abovementioned features.[32]

His model democracy is organised along the following lines. Denmark has a resident population of five million of whom four million have political rights. Danes are full citizens for, on average, fifty-seven years, namely from when they come of age, at eighteen, until they die at, on average, seventy-five. 4,000,000 divided by 57 makes 70,000. Now, the idea is, on 1 January every year, to have 70,000 Danes selected by lot from among all the 4,000,000 adult Danes. These 70,000 constitute an Electronic Second Chamber and, using button-phones with pin-codes, they have to vote some 1000 times in a year on all major political decisions debated in the Danish

[32] Schmidt (1993). Marcus Schmidt is lecturer in marketing at University of Southern Denmark and he runs the largest Danish opinion poll institution with a carefully randomised panel of 1,500 persons. (*Gfk, Observa*). For a summary in English of Marcus Schmidt's model of direct democracy, see 'Institutionalizing Fair Democracy: the Theory of the Minipopulus' *Symposium/Futures* 33 (2001), 361–70.

Parliament. The following year another 70,000 electors are chosen by lot, and so on. The result is that almost every Danish citizen will be directly involved in the political decision-making process for one year by being a member of the Electronic Second Chamber. 70,000 Danes chosen at random is such a large number that the risk of their voting differently from the way 4,000,000 would have done is insignificant. All proposals debated in Parliament have to be submitted to the Electronic Chamber, both those passed and those rejected by the Parliament. Every political decision presupposes agreement between the Parliament and the Electronic Chamber. In the relatively few cases of disagreement between the Parliament and the Electronic Chamber, the issue has to be decided by a referendum involving the whole electorate of 4,000,000 persons. The Parliament will continue to prepare all bills and will be elected on a party-political basis just as before, so that there will be a division between initiative and preparation, left to professional elected politicians, and decision, shared by the Parliament and the Electronic Chamber. Of the 70,000 members of the Electronic Chamber, those who have a job will have a paid day off every week to study and debate the proposals on which they have to vote; all 70,000 will be sent the relevant material, and they will receive some compensation for their political participation. Every time they vote they will obtain a reduction in direct taxation amounting to the equivalent of £2, which means that the reduction in income tax comes to £2,000 in the course of the year they are members of the Electronic Chamber. The total costs of such a political system would come to 5 billion Danish kroner per year, or 2% of the state budget (in 1990).

Here direct popular vote on all major issues is combined with sortition, rotation, political pay and the co-operation between professional policy-makers in the parliament and amateur decision-makers in the electronic panel. Thus, all the five most prominent aspects of Athenian democracy are involved and the result is a model which, in my opinion, is a much improved version of the traditional forms of teledemocracy. Rotation and sortition, combined with a ban on iteration, ensures that all citizens for one year are actively involved in political decision-making. For the rest of their lives they have all the political rights they have today under representative democracy. On the other hand, it is feasible and not too expensive to give 70,000 persons sufficient time to keep themselves politically informed; political pay is an extra incitement, and it is possible to have a political debate, thereby precluding direct democracy from degenerating into a vulgar push-button democracy.

If such a kind of direct democracy is workable, it is supposed to have the following beneficial effects. (1) As a result of the increased importance of the decisions left to citizens, there will be increased participation. (2) Direct democracy will counteract corruption. (3) Lobbyism will have to come out in the open and can no longer be confined to the corridors. (4) The focus of politics will be issues instead of persons. (5) Political parties will play a less prominent role in politics. If, on the other hand, one of the pillars collapses, the whole building collapses too. If, e.g., only circa 20,000 out of the 70,000 members of Marcus Schmidt's 'minipopulus' are prepared to take their obligations seriously, it will thwart the whole idea of the reform.

So whether this form of democracy is inferior or superior to the prevailing form of representative democracy remains to be seen. It presupposes the veracity of the five propositions here called the five pillars of direct democracy. What matters in this specific context is that this and similar model democracies are indisputably based on institutions and principles borrowed from ancient Athens, and—as long as such a system is just a model—one important way of assessing its merits is an investigation of the merits or defects of the Athenian political system from Kleisthenes to Demosthenes.

Bibliography

Arterton, F. Chr. 1987, *Teledemocracy* (Washington, DC).
Barber, B. 1984, *Strong democracy. Participatory Politics for a New Age* (Berkeley and Los Angeles).
——. 1988, *A Passion for Democracy* (Princeton).
Becker, T. and Slaton, C.D. 2000, *The Future of Teledemocracy* (Westport, CT).
Budge, I. 1996, *The New Challenge of Direct Democracy* (Oxford).
Burnheim, J. 1985, *Is Democracy Possible?* (Berkeley).
Carlen, L. 1976, *Die Landsgemeinde in der Schweiz* (Sigmaringen).
Carson, L and Martin, B. 1999, *Random Selection in Politics* (Westport, CT).
Cronin, Th.E. 1989, *Direct Democracy: The Politics of Initiative, Referendum and Recall* (Cambridge, Mass.).
Dahl, R.A. 1989, *Democracy and Its Critics* (New Haven).
Elster, J. 1989, *Solominic Judgements* (Cambridge).
Fishkin, J.S. 1991, *Democracy and Deliberation* (New Haven).
——. 1997, *The Voice of the People* (New Haven), 2nd edn. with a new afterword (177–203). First edn. 1995.
Fuller, R.B. 1971, *No More Secondhand God* (Garden City, NY).
Gallagher, M. and Uleri, P.V. (eds.) 1996, *The Referendum Experience in Europe* (London).
Gallagher, M. 1996, 'Conclusion', in Gallagher and Uleri (eds.) 226–50.

Hansen, M.H. 1999, *The Athenian Democracy in the Age of Demosthenes* (2nd edn., Bristol). First edn. Oxford 1991 (Blackwell); editions in French (Les Belles Lettres 1993), German (Akademie Verlag 1995) and Polish (Wydawnictwo.DiG 1999).
Kellenberger, M. 1965, *Die Landsgemeinden der schweizerischen Kantone* (Winterthur).
Mansbridge, J.J. 1980, *Beyond Adversary Democracy* (New York).
Marcus G.E. and Hanson R.L. (eds.) 1993, *Reconsidering the Democratic Public* (University Park, Pa).
McLean, I. 1989, *Democracy and New Technology* (Oxford 1989).
Mill, J.S. 1861, *Considerations on Representative Government* (London).
Ober, J. 1989, *Mass and Elite in Democratic Athens* (Princeton).
Schmidt, M. 1993, *Direkte demokrati i Danmark. Om indførelsen af et elektronisk andetkammer* (København).
Sly, J.F. 1932, *Town Government in Massachusetts 1620–1930* (Cambridge, Mass.).
Vinding, M. 1998, *The Thakali. A Himalayan Ethnography* (London).

ADVOCACY, LOGOGRAPHY AND *ERÔTÊSIS* IN ATHENIAN LAWCOURTS[1]

S.C. Todd

1. Interrogation and Confrontation in Theory and Practice

Witnesses in classical Athenian lawcourts were not normally cross-questioned; instead, they seem to have presented their evidence, either orally or later in writing, without interruption.[2] Reading the speeches of the Attic Orators, this creates a somewhat static impression, with little of the interaction that we expect in major trials today between barrister and witness.[3] As with a Roman orator like Cicero, all that normally survives is a speech delivered on one side of the dispute, but whereas in a Ciceronian case we know that between the two *actiones* of the trial there was an interval for witnesses to be cross-examined, and there are indeed hints in some of Cicero's speeches of the ways in which he might discredit the opposition's witnesses,[4]

[1] Roger Brock, Tim Cornell, Malcolm Heath, Stephen Hodkinson, Asako Kurihara, Paul McKechnie and Lene Rubinstein have all generously contributed advice, encouragement, references or suggestions for this paper. My chief thanks, however, are to John Crook, for first inspiring my interest in legal history.

[2] The shift from oral to written evidence, probably soon after 380 BC, is discussed in §3 of this paper. In one earlier trial (Andok. 1.14, probably in 400 BC) a witness is examined in court by the defendant who has called him, but the questions are friendly rather than confrontational, and there is no evidence that the prosecution sought to cross-examine. This may simply represent an attempt by Andokides to vary the texture of what is a rather long speech, though the cheese-grater witness is similarly examined at Aristoph. *Wasps* 962–66 (but that could be for dramatic reasons). Leisi (1907: 112–14), coming from a civil-law perspective, sees the failure to interrogate witnesses as a fundamental weakness in the Athenian system of justice.

[3] The importance of cross-examination in a modern English trial can be seen from the fact that Du Cann devotes three of the twelve chapters of his *Art of the Advocate* wholly to this topic (Du Cann 1980: 95–143), and much of the rest of his book to it incidentally.

[4] Bonner (1922: 101) suggests that one reason why Athenian speeches are not often funny is that we lack the retorts of recalcitrant witnesses under cross-examination (for which see Du Cann 1980: e.g. 58–9). There may be some truth in this, but Cicero's vastly funnier speeches (which also lack cross-examination) deploy much of their humour when assassinating the characters of his opponents' witnesses: see e.g. Cic. *Pro Caecina* 28–30 (after cross-examination); *Pro Caelio* 61–70 (in advance).

such attacks on the credibility of opposing witnesses are rare in the Athenian orators, where the normal structure of the case was for each side to speak in turn, with each speaker during his speech presenting the testimony of witnesses to confirm his narrative as he chose, but without any opportunity for the opposition formally to challenge their testimony, at least during the trial.[5]

There was however one aspect of an Athenian trial which could give rise to interactive if not necessarily dramatic confrontation. Unlike witnesses, litigants at Athens could be cross-questioned by their opponents, and were apparently bound to answer such questions. The most famous example of cross-questioning (the Greek term is *erôtêsis*) occurs in Plato's *Apology*, where Sokrates interrogates his prosecutor Meletos at length, trapping him into self-contradiction. Admittedly this is a work of fiction, but Sokrates' statement that the law orders Meletos to answer (*Apology* 25d) is supported by the text of a statute quoted by Apollodoros in the course of his litigation against Phormion: "it is compulsory for both litigants to answer each other's questions, but they may not witness".[6] There is indeed some evidence that the obligation to answer the opponent's questions applied in preliminary proceedings also. The *anakrisis* (preliminary examination by the presiding official) is something about which we are not very well informed, but one of Isaios' clients, who is challenging the legitimacy of the self-styled children of Philoktemon's second marriage, claims that he had demanded at the *anakrisis* to know the identity of their mother, and that the Arkhon had "ordered them to reply according to the law".[7]

Against this background, the pattern of reference to *erôtêsis* in the Athenian orators and in the fourth-century rhetorical theorists is an interesting one. The *Rhetorica ad Alexandrum* (attributed in antiquity to

[5] Athenian litigants could declare their intention to challenge the testimony of opposing witnesses by prosecuting them by *dikê pseudomarturiôn*, but such a declaration took place at the end of the trial. The rare attempts in the speeches to impugn an opponent's witnesses are usually directed against the litigant who has allegedly suborned them (e.g. Isok. 18.57; Dem. 29.5), though occasionally a speaker chooses to represent one of his opponent's witnesses as the *éminence grise* behind the trial (e.g. Isaios 5.7–8; 9.23).

[6] τοῖν ἀντιδίκοιν ἐπάναγκες εἶναι ἀποκρίνασθαι ἀλλήλοις τὸ ἐρωτώμενον, μαρτυρεῖν δὲ μή (Dem. 46.10): the clause on *erôtêsis* is incidental to Apollodoros' argument, which concerns the ban on testifying.

[7] τοῦ ἄρχοντος κελεύοντος ἀποκρίνασθαι κατὰ τὸν νόμον (Isaios 6.12). On the *anakrisis*, see further §3 of this paper.

Aristotle, but now generally to Anaximenes) and Aristotle's own *Ars Rhetorica* both devote considerable attention to *erôtêsis*, which they both discuss towards the end of their treatises, but in very different ways. Anaximenes does so in §36, in a context explicitly concerned with lawcourt speeches, but in a way that suggests he is probably not talking about *erôtêsis* in our sense. This is a long chapter, and is split into two halves, discussing the ideal structure of prosecution and defence speeches respectively. It is worth noting that he locates *erôtêsis* among defence strategies (with no corresponding treatment in the prosecution half of the chapter), and that his analysis of *erôtêsis* immediately follows a discussion of how to respond to the prosecutor's anticipation of one's case (which does correspond to his earlier advice for the prosecutor on how best to anticipate the defendant).[8] The one-sidedness of this treatment of *erôtêsis* is striking, and so is the fact that each of his four examples takes the form of a single answer to a single question (three illustrating how to frame a factual excuse in the form "yes but", and the other one a formal denial drawing attention to a legal defence in the form "not I but the law"). Taken together, this suggests that the questions envisaged here are probably rhetorical rather than interactive: what is being discussed is not the cut-and-thrust of cross-examination, but rather how to construct your defence on the assumption that the totality of the prosecutor's case can be glossed in the form of a rhetorical question.

It should however be noted that there is one anecdote earlier in the treatise which does imply that Anaximenes is aware of possible interaction between participants in the trial, if not necessarily of cross-examination. This is told to illustrate his rather odd discussion of "stealing a testimony", which he glosses with the altercation: "Bear witness for me, Kallikles." "By the gods, not I, for I tried to prevent this man from doing that thing."[9] What seems to lie behind this exchange is the fact that in Athenian law only a witness could be prosecuted by *dikê pseudomarturiôn* for making a false statement, so the two interlocutors here are evidently colluding to enable the first speaker (presumably the prosecutor) to damage his opponent ("this

[8] *Rhet. ad Alex.* 36.1–30 (= 1441b30–1443b23) deals with prosecution speeches (including anticipation at 36.19–28 = 1443a7–1443b14); defence speeches are at 36.30–51 (= 1443b23–1445a29), with response to anticipation at 36.37–42 (= 1444a16–1444b7), and *erôtêsis* at 36.43–44 (= 1444b8–21).

[9] Μαρτύρησόν μοι, ὦ Καλλίκλεις (v.l. Λυσικλές). Μὰ τοὺς θεοὺς οὔκουν ἔγωγε· κωλύοντος γὰρ ἐμοῦ ταῦτα ἔπραξεν οὗτος (*Rhet. ad Alex.* 15.7 = 1432a5–7).

man") by exacting from Kallikles a damaging but non-actionable public declaration of the defendant's guilt. The rarity of personal names elsewhere in the treatise might suggest that this is a real case, though it could be objected that the nature of the anecdote requires a name, and there is indeed dispute in the manuscripts as to whether the name should be Kallikles or Lysikles.[10] The assumed setting is not stated, but for the trick to be effective it would presumably have to be sprung in court rather than at the *anakrisis* or before the arbitrator.

Aristotle's treatment, on the other hand, seems to envisage *erôtêsis* in our sense. Once again, it is found towards the end of the treatise,[11] and although the context does not distinguish structurally between lawcourt and non-lawcourt speeches, nevertheless his four examples are suggestive. Two of them relate explicitly to genuine or fictitious lawcourt speeches, though only one of these is an Athenian case (Sokrates' examination of Meletos in Plato's *Apology*: the other is the response to questions put forward by an anonymous Spartan on trial for his tenure of office as Ephor); but Athenian judicial proceedings are at least a possible setting for the other two (Sophokles' response to Peisander's interrogation about the Four Hundred, and Perikles' interrogation of Lampon on the Mysteries).[12] Each of these examples comprises a series of questions and answers, which clearly does imply interaction between interlocutors. They illustrate different ways of trapping your opponent into looking foolish, most commonly by the use of surprise, and they cover the topic from the perspective both of questioner and of respondent: whereas Perikles' and Sokrates' interrogations are recounted from the viewpoint of the questioner, those of Sophokles and of the Ephor are told to illustrate the trick of deflecting an anticipated final question.

---

[10] Other names in *Rhet. ad Alex.*: Lysitheides at 1.19 = 1422b22, Timotheos at 24.2 = 1435a14, Dion and Dionysios presented as exempla at 8.7 = 1429b15–17 (contrast Arist. *Rhet.*, which is full of named anecdotes).

[11] Arist. *Rhet.* 3.18.1–6 = 1418b40–1419b2.

[12] The most detailed discussion of the first of these is in Jameson (1972), who suggests a prosecution by Sophokles of Peisander with the latter attempting to implicate his prosecutor in the oligarchic coup, and accounts for Peisander's escape from Athens before conviction by suggesting a preliminary hearing e.g. before the Council, as was normal in *eisangelia* or impeachment. Carawan (1983: 216 n. 23) suggests the trial of Anaxagoras as a possible context in which Perikles might have opposed Lampon: this is attractive, though we have no direct evidence for Lampon's being the prosecutor in this case (Anaxagoras and Lampon do appear together as rationalistic versus religious interpreters of a prodigy at Plut. *Per.* 6).

The picture we get from the rhetorical theorists, therefore, is one in which litigants are expected to engage in altercations, ideally with their opponents. When we turn to the speeches of the Orators, however, confrontation of this type is notably rare. Leaving aside Sokrates' interrogation of Meletos in what is an explicitly fictitious speech,[13] there are only a few conclusive examples of *erôtêsis*. Lysias preserves two, in speech 12 *Against Eratosthenes* and speech 22 *Against the Grain-Dealers*, both of which contain a set of questions and answers within the body of the speech (12.25, 22.5), preceded by the summons to the opponent to "come forward" and face interrogation (12.24, 22.4). Slightly different is Lysias 13 *Against Agoratos*, where there are no questions or answers, but the speaker twice summons Agoratos to respond to a list of names that he is alleged to have denounced, and then asserts that he has admitted the second list: editors agree that the lemma *ERÔTÊSIS* should be inserted in the manuscript at the end of 13.30 and of 13.32. The fourth example is Isaios 11 *On the Property of Hagnias*, where Theopompos the speaker confronts his opponent with the text of the law on next-of-kin, simultaneously challenging him to answer a series of questions about his claimant's kinship to the deceased: no answers are recorded, but there are several hints that these are more than simply rhetorical questions: for instance the summons to come forward (11.4), the command to speak (11.5), and the subsequent reference to the opponent's inability to give a clear answer (11.6).

There are no other cases where *erôtêsis* can be shown to have taken place, though two passages seem to envisage the possibility. Demosthenes in speech 19 *On the False Embassy* challenges Aiskhines to refute the allegation that he has accepted bribes: we have again the demand to come forward and to answer (19.120), though the challenge is evidently not accepted, and interestingly there is no attempt to enforce it. Dem. 58 *Against Theokrines* envisages the possibility of interrogating the opponent about how he would have handled a hypothetical situation, but dismisses it on the grounds that he cannot be trusted to answer justly (*dikaiôs*, 58.45).

[13] There is further discussion at the end of this paper not only of Plato's *Apology*, but also of Xenophon's.

2. Confronting the Question

Faced with this discrepancy between the significant place given to *erôtêsis* by Aristotle and its apparent rarity in the Attic Orators, scholars have responded in several ways. The most recent treatment of the topic, by Carawan (1983), seeks to maximise the appearance of *erôtêsis* in the Orators, where he finds no fewer than fourteen examples. At least some of these, however, seem to be something rather different from *erôtêsis*; in others the questions may be rhetorical rather than real; and others are too fragmentary to allow secure interpretation. Andok. 1.101, for instance, refers to an imaginary cross-questioning that might have been conducted during the regime of the Thirty, but what is being envisaged here is surely *anakrisis* by a magistrate, not *erôtêsis* by an opposing litigant.[14] Similarly, Dem. 57.61 challenges "whoever wishes" (not necessarily Euboulides the opponent) to testify that the speaker is lying about Euboulides' voting record, but this is really a version of the challenge to use the speaker's time,[15] not to answer his questions. The boundary between rhetorical and real questions is more difficult to determine, but several of Carawan's passages contain no clear invitation to the opponent to respond.[16] Finally, no fewer than three of Carawan's passages are fragmentary: of these, the questions in Isaios *Against Hagnotheos* are hypothetical, and the reference may be to private accounting rather than law-court proceedings; Hypereides *Against Aristogeiton* looks more like a response to rhetorical questions posed in the opponent's speech; and Hypereides *On behalf of Kratinos* is explicitly not an invitation to step forward and answer questions.[17]

[14] The name Kharikles (one of the oligarchic extremists among the Thirty) is conclusive. The *anakrisis* (preliminary examination by presiding official) is discussed in §3 of this paper.

[15] For which see e.g. Andok. 1.23, 26, 55; Lys. 20.11; Dem. 18.139; 50.2.

[16] E.g. Dein. 1.83, on which see Worthington (1992: 260–1); Dem. 36.19; the string of questions in Dem. 18.61–71 (the vocative addressed to Aiskhines in §69 is not accompanied by any invitation to come forward and respond); and possibly Dem. 35.46–49 (where the phrase "just and according to law" at §49 seems to refer to the content of what Lakritos might say, rather than to any legal obligation to respond).

[17] The fragment reads ἀπόκριναί μοι, Ἑρμεία, ὥσπερ κάθῃ, which the Loeb translation renders as "Answer me, Hermeias, from your seat". I am not convinced by the translation of ὥσπερ κάθῃ, and we do not know Hermeias' relation to the case, but the reference to sitting rules out a formal *erôtêsis*.

A more traditional response would be to accept the discrepancy, but to explain it chronologically by suggesting that the procedure fell into disuse after the time of Lysias. This is the approach taken for instance by Bonner (1905: 57), who suggests as a possible reason for disuse the risk that the opponent might simply lie. Bonner highlights the care taken to guard against this in Lys. 13, where both sets of questions are prefaced by discussion of the possibility that Agoratos will deny responsibility.[18] If Bonner's hypothesis is accepted, *erôtêsis* would become one more example of the well-known fact that Aristotle's *Art of Rhetoric* is not a particularly close guide to Athenian forensic practice; it is notable, for instance, that the treatise contains far more quotations from epideictic speeches written for display (mainly those of Isokrates) than it does from the forensic corpus, and still more from Homer and the tragedians. There is however a problem with Bonner's thesis, in the shape of Isaios 11 (conventionally dated c. 360, though there is some dispute) and Demosthenes 19 (dated 343): the first of these speeches evidently does elicit some sort of response, while the second presumably has at least to envisage the possibility, which means that Bonner's putative disuse is neither sudden nor total.

I should at this stage acknowledge that I have no single and satisfactory alternative theory to put forward in place of those of Bonner and of Carawan. What follows therefore are some preliminary speculations. My justification for revisiting the topic inconclusively is that the Athenian Orators' substantial disregard for *erôtêsis* as legal practitioners—in marked contrast, as we have seen, to the apparent expectations of a theorist like Aristotle—may serve to highlight some of the more interesting differences between Athenian law and Roman law (and indeed most modern legal systems), in an area to which John Crook's own book on legal advocacy has recently drawn attention.[19] This is because the structure of the legal system at Athens puts considerable emphasis on the litigant as amateur, with the

[18] In addition, the second set is followed by a reading of a decree which the orator has evidently had ready to refute any such denial: a point which is explored in §3 of this paper.

[19] Crook (1995). In view of the long-running debate over whether and how far it is legitimate to describe as 'Greek law' the legal system reflected in the juridical papyri from Egypt, it is worth drawing attention to ch. 3 of Crook's book, which highlights the extensive (and from an Athenian historian's perspective very Roman) use of advocates in the papyri.

resulting absence of certain forms of legal professionalism (most notably jurists) and the invisibility of other forms (logographers or speech-writers). Ideally, an Athenian litigant was supposed to be his own narrator telling his own story, and this seems to have affected all sorts of relationships within the court-room: in particular, it means that the litigant himself is the prime narrator, rather than being one of the witnesses as tends to happen in systems where litigants are routinely represented by advocates.[20]

Amateurism was admittedly to some extent a legal fiction at Athens, for several reasons. Recent work by Rubinstein, for instance, has highlighted the extent to which extant speeches reveal the activity of teams of speakers, with *sunêgoroi* (lit. 'speakers alongside') operating alongside their litigants. There are indeed a few cases where the *sunêgoros* delivers the major speech, with or without a brief introduction in our texts by the litigant.[21] This indicates that the Athenians were capable of thinking like advocates, if not necessarily like lawyers. To the extent that the *sunêgoros* remains a "speaker alongside", however, rather than taking over the running of the case after the manner of a Roman advocate—the use of the term *patronus* to denote a Roman advocate is significant, because it implies a sense in which his political credibility is more at stake than that of his client[22]—this will not necessarily affect the assumed equation between orator-as-speaker (rather than litigant-as-witness) and narrator.

More significant in this respect is the question of logography, another aspect of covert professionalism. The assumption behind the Athenian legal system is that every citizen ought to be able to defend his interests, but the fact that not everybody is an equally skilled speaker led to the development of a system of ghost-writing, in which litigants would pay a professional orator to write a speech for them

[20] Hence perhaps the lack of interest in interrogating witnesses, on which see §1 above.

[21] On *sunêgoroi*, see Rubinstein (2000). Theomnestos the prosecutor seems to have delivered Dem. 59.1–15, leaving Apollodoros as *sunêgoros* (and probably author) to deliver §§16–126. Extant speeches delivered entirely by a *sunêgoros* include Lys. 13 and Dem. 36: we cannot always be sure whether the litigant himself delivered a separate (and presumably brief) introduction, but Dem. 36.1 is worded in such a way as to explain the situation if Phormion had not already done so.

[22] Cicero's emphasis on himself in the speeches he delivers as advocate (see e.g. *Pro Caelio* 6–14; *Pro Flacco* 1; and more generally on advocates *Pro Balbo* 1) may be partly the product of his self-conceit, but may also illustrate a broader difference between Roman and Athenian lawcourt oratory.

to learn off and perform.[23] The profession of logographer was necessarily secret, albeit perhaps an open secret, and the fact of having used one could be damaging, as at Dem. 32.31–2, where Demosthenes' uncle Demon has to defend himself against allegations that he has received help from his nephew. Anaximenes gives advice on how to respond to allegations either that you have learned off a written speech, or alternatively that you are a *sunêgoros* writing for money (*Rhet. ad Alex.* 36.37–42 = 1444a16–b7). Despite these aspects of professionalism, however, the amateur fiction nevertheless remained important. We should not assume, for instance, that the system will have been designed to benefit those litigants who chose to use logographers, a point to which we shall return.[24]

3. Preparation and Expertise: Some Preliminary Speculations

I begin this final section by returning briefly to Bonner's chronological hypothesis, in which *erôtêsis* fell into disuse after the end of Lysias' career in c. 380. It is, as we have seen, difficult to accept this as a complete or satisfactory analysis, because of the later cases in Isaios 11 and potentially in Dem. 19. Nevertheless, a revised version of this traditional model may be worth exploring further, because the period around 380 sees a number of changes in Athenian procedural law which may be relevant. The most notable of these concern the handling of evidence. The *Ath. Pol.* (written in the 330s or 320s BC) states that an official arbitrator was required if either party appealed against his judgment to seal all the testimonies, challenges, and laws submitted by both litigants in two *ekhinoi* or jars, one for each litigant.[25] This practice is referred to on several occasions in the Demosthenic corpus,[26] though not in earlier speeches, but logically it cannot have preceded the introduction of the rule that the

---

[23] This at least is the conventional view, for which see Usher (1976), in a powerful critique of the arguments of Dover (1968) that the extant speeches may reflect a greater degree of collaborative composition between logographer and client.

[24] See the discussion of Gomme's interpretation of evidence at the *anakrisis* in §3 of this paper.

[25] ἐμβαλόντες τὰς μαρτυρίας καὶ τὰς προκλήσεις καὶ τοὺς νόμους εἰς ἐχίνους, χωρὶς μὲν τὰς τοῦ διώκοντος χωρὶς δὲ τὰς τοῦ φεύγοντος, καὶ τούτους κατασημηνάμενοι (*Ath. Pol.* 53.2).

[26] Dem. 39.17; 45.8 (a document), 17, 58; 47.16; 48.48; 49.65; 54.27. It is difficult to establish a relative chronology, but none of the Demosthenic or Apollodoran corpus is likely to belong before the late 360s.

testimony of witnesses should be submitted in writing rather than orally, a shift which Calhoun (1919) plausibly located in 378/7.

The effect of this rule was clearly to prevent new evidence being submitted after the case had been heard by the arbitrator. It is important to note that only certain categories of case (certainly not public procedures, and of private *dikai* probably only those heard by the Forty) underwent official arbitration. Some scholars believe that the sealing of *ekhinoi* and the ban on new evidence applied also at the *anakrisis*,[27] but this is disputed. Earlier scholars tended to assume a positive answer, partly because of a failure to distinguish between different forms of preliminary procedure, but also because of assumptions about the purpose of the rule.[28] As Bonner (1905: 48) pointed out, however, there is no documentary evidence linking *ekhinoi* with the *anakrisis*, and for much of the twentieth century the scholarly consensus was negative, at least until Boegehold's 1982 publication of an *ekhinos*-lid recording the presence of several documents including a "*diamarturia* from the *anakrisis*", which Boegehold himself regarded as conclusive evidence for a positive answer, though other interpretations may be possible.[29]

The purpose of the rule against new evidence is less clear, and depends in part on the disputed question of where it applied. A minimalist view (particularly attractive if the rule applied narrowly to official arbitration) would see it as being designed simply to ensure that litigants took arbitration seriously and that the arbitrator's credibility was not undermined by the subsequent production of material unknown to him. A more far-reaching view (which tends to appeal to those who see it applying also at *anakrisis*) would be that the Athenians were looking to improve the quality and coherence of the evidence submitted at the trial. Gomme (1937: 73), for instance, argues that a litigant is entitled in advance of the trial to know more

---

[27] The preliminary hearing conducted by the presiding official, for which see §1 above.

[28] For simple conflation between arbitration and *anakrisis*, see e.g. Thalheim (1894: 2051), and cf. the discussion of Lipsius in n. 31 below. For an analysis based on assumptions about the purpose of the rule, see the discussion of Gomme (below).

[29] For his most recent view, see Boegehold (1995: 79–81). *Diamarturia* is the formal testimony of a witness, used to further or more often to block legal proceedings, normally on the grounds that the opponent's case is legally inadmissible. The possibility that this one could be a document from an earlier *anakrisis* (possibly even from a previous trial), sealed in the course of further proceedings before an official arbitrator, is explored in Todd (1993: 129).

than the bare outline of the evidence against him, presumably because he needs to prepare his speech. This may however be assuming too public a rôle for professionalism, because the rhetoric of amateurism that underlies Athenian justice could be held to mean that only a man who proposes to employ a logographer should be afraid of pleading his case extempore.[30]

Part of the problem here is that we simply do not know enough about what happened at the *anakrisis*, which makes it hard to determine its function within the structure of Athenian legal procedure. The reason for this is of course that extant speeches relate to trials rather than preliminary hearings. We do know that the verb *anakrinô* is used in the active of the presiding official, in the passive of the case, and in the middle of the litigants.[31] At first sight this might suggest that the presiding official was the only person entitled to put questions himself, and that the litigants would have to ask him to put their questions for them. We do have one clear case, however, in which questions were put by litigants to their opponents, and it is recounted in such a way as to imply that the latter were legally bound to answer.[32] One of the issues explored in Carawan's analysis of *erôtêsis* is whether each of the various surviving examples of interrogation represents a recapitulation of arguments that had already been rehearsed in preliminary proceedings, and to what extent some or others of them may confronting fresh areas of dispute, but our ignorance about the *anakrisis* means that there is considerable danger of circular argument here.

One question that might have been interesting to explore in this context is whether a litigant proposing to commission a logographer for his trial would normally expect to consult him in advance either of the *anakrisis* or of official arbitration, for advice on how best to

---

[30] Note Anaximenes' equation between those who use written speeches and those who pay for legal assistance (albeit from a *sunêgoros* rather than a logographer), cited at the end of §2 above.

[31] Harrison (1968–71.ii: 94–105 at 95 n. 1), in the course of what is still the best detailed survey of the *anakrisis*. Lipsius' analysis (1905–15.iii: 829–44) is weakened by a tendency to confuse the boundary between *anakrisis* and official arbitration. He claims for instance that the *anakrisis* of cases referred to official arbitrators would be conducted by the arbitrators themselves (Lispius 1905–15.iii: 835–6): this is based presumably on Isaios 5.32, where *anakrinô* is predicated of arbitrators, but in context these are clearly private arbitrators, so the verb must be being used in a non-technical sense.

[32] This is Isaios 6.12, quoted at n. 7 above, where the Arkhon "ordered them to reply according to the law".

present his case in these apparently less formal contexts. To my knowledge, we have no evidence for or against this, but it does provide a convenient transition back to one final perspective on our topic: that is, the relationship between *erôtêsis* and logography.[33] Of the five extant speeches with *erôtêseis* listed at the end of §1 of this paper,[34] both Lysias 12 and Demosthenes 19 are written as if to be delivered in person by Lysias and Demosthenes respectively. The other three are logographic, but in each case there is reason to regard the client as having more than average experience in public business: Isaios 11 is written for Theopompos, already the victor in a previous round of litigation over the property of Hagnias; the speaker of Lysias 22 is a member of the Council who claims to have been responsible for preventing the summary execution of the defendant grain-dealers by his intervention at a previous Council meeting; the evidence in Lysias 13 is more tenuous, but the anonymous speaker is delivering what from its length is clearly the main prosecution speech as *sunêgoros* for his cousin Dionysios who is the formal prosecutor and the brother of the deceased, and the most plausible reason for this is that he is simply a more experienced speaker. It is worth considering the possibility that *erôtêsis* was a risk worth taking (at least subject to reasonable precautions against surprise and the consequent need to extemporise) in cases where the speaker was either himself the orator or alternatively known by the orator to have at least a competent record in public performance.

In this context it is worth noting that the majority of the questions asked in the most fully-preserved *erôtêseis* are fairly leading, and the *erôtêseis* themselves fairly short.[35] We have of course only the orator's word for it that the opponents did reply in the way that appears in the manuscript,[36] but the narrow scope of the questions makes

---

[33] This point has been touched on by Carawan (1983: 222), who remarks that "logography did not put an end to extempore tactics", but does not systematically explore the logographic or non-logographic status of the speeches he analyses.

[34] Lys. 12, Lys. 22, Lys. 13, Isaios 11, and Dem. 19. (Dem. 58 can in this context be disregarded, because the speaker explicitly refrains from challenging his opponent to answer, whereas in Dem. 19 it would have presumably been possible for Aiskhines to accept the challenge.)

[35] Five questions-and-answers in Lys. 12.25, and four in Lys. 22.5. None of the questions or answers in either interrogation is longer than twenty words. (Contrast Plato's version of Sokrates and Meletos, below.)

[36] For a discussion of speeches which may have been 'improved' when the written version was disseminated after the trial, see Lämmli (1938: e.g. pp. 17–57 on Andok. 1 and Lys. 6, pp. 58–69 on Lys. 1, and pp. 69–73 on Lys. 24). See also

the preserved replies not implausible. Lysias 12, for instance, presents Eratosthenes with a series of straightforward factual alternatives (e.g. "Did you arrest Polemarkhos or not?") of a type that would probably be impossible for him to deny.[37] Eratosthenes does his best by claiming in response to two of the questions that he had carried out the arrest because he feared those in power, and that he had spoken against execution. Neither of these responses is likely to have come as much surprise either to the court or to Lysias,[38] who promptly seeks to establish a contradiction between them (12.27). Similarly in Lysias 22, for a metic to be asked "Are you a metic?" is hardly an opening question that admits a range of answers, and the next two questions are similarly directed.[39] Only the final question is in any sense open ("Tell me if you agree that you bought together more grain than fifty *phormoi*, which the law says is allowed"),[40] but given that the case has received some previous discussion in the Council, there is again good reason for Lysias to have been able to predict that the defence will be based on the claim that they had received orders to this effect from the public officials, and once again this response is made the basis of the next stage of the speech. In Isaios 11, on the other hand, only the questions are preserved: indeed only one question, taunting the opponent with his claimant's inability to claim any of the degrees of kinship to the deceased listed in the law that is being read out, though the question is interrupted by a carefully prepared parenthesis designed to leave him no scope for ambiguity e.g. by claiming to be the nephew not of the deceased but of the speaker. The questions here are framed in such a way that no

Dover (1968: 168–70) for an analysis of discrepancies between the *Embassy* and *Crown* speeches of Aiskhines and of Demosthenes, but the case against extensive post-trial revision of these speeches is argued strongly by Harris (1995: 10–11).

[37] Krentz (1984) argues for a much greater degree of trickery in this *erôtêsis*, but his reading rests on the identification of ambiguity not so much in Lysias' questions as in Eratosthenes' answers, in a way that would seem rather stupid for a defendant to do. For a more detailed rebuttal, see Sommerstein (1984).

[38] For the ways in which Athenian litigants might have been able to predict their opponents' arguments, see Dorjahn (1935).

[39] The second question presents what are hardly genuine alternatives ("is your aim in residing here as a metic to obey the laws of the city or to do whatever you please?"), and the third is equally directional ("do you accept that you deserve a death-sentence, if you violate the laws for which the penalty is death?").

[40] ἀπόκριναι δή μοι, εἰ ὁμολογεῖς πλείω σῖτον συμπρίασθαι πεντήκοντα φορμῶν, ὧν ὁ νόμος ἐξεῖναι κελεύει; (Lys. 22.5). There may be an ambiguity in the word *sumpriasthai* ('accumulate by buying', or 'buy as a cartel'), for which see Todd (1993: 318–19), though if so it is notable that the defendants make no protest.

credible answer can be given, and the exercise is in part a visual gambit designed to create a sense of conflict between the opponent and the law.

Taking these cases overall, there seems to be no great concern here to catch one's opponent on the hop, or to trick him into making an unguarded admission in the way that Aristotle advises. Rather, the primary concern is evidently to avoid giving the opponent enough rope to hang the speaker. Perhaps most interesting in this respect is the care taken in Lysias 13 to guard against upsets. As Bonner noted,[41] Lysias twice warns the jury in advance that Agoratos may try to deny responsibility. But he also follows the second interrogation by the assertion that even though Agoratos has admitted it, a decree of the assembly will nevertheless be read out as proof. This may suggest that alternative strategies have been prepared here, of the sort that would be fairly easy for a competent speaker to master and ought not to require him to extemporise: if Agoratos denies, produce the decree to refute him; if he admits it, produce it anyway with a marginally different introductory sentence; either way, you will retain the dramatic advantage of having appeared to confront him directly with his guilt, but with relatively little risk.

There does remain the question of how far our speeches are representative. We should beware of the possibility that trials of those without the resources to commission a logographer might have been more interactive, as well as the possibility already canvassed that aspects of our speeches may be literary fictions improved after the event. One obvious example of such literary fiction is of course Sokrates himself: so much so that not only Plato but also Xenophon constructed versions of the speech he ought to have delivered. Indeed, the fact that Xenophon's *Apology* also contains an *erôtêsis* (19–21), the content of which is wholly incompatible with Plato's, while obviously diminishing any confidence that we might be tempted to have in the veracity of either version, may nevertheless suggest that it was well-known that Sokrates really did cross-question Meletos (though it could simply mean that it would have been in character for him to do so). But the repeated statement by Plato's Sokrates that he ought to be allowed to conduct his defence in his own way[42] could imply a perception that *erôtêsis*—or at least *erôtêsis* that led to the

[41] Bonner (1905: 57), cited in §2 of this paper.
[42] Plato *Apology* 27b, alluding back to 17cd.

type of extended and confrontational interaction that we see uniquely in this speech[43]—was something which would not have been regarded as normal by an Athenian jury. Unless, of course, this is a case of literary fiction responding to a literary image of *erôtêsis* as manifested in the speeches of the orators.

Bibliography

Boegehold, A.L. (1982), 'A lid with dipinto', in *Studies in Attic Epigraphy, History and Topography, presented to E. Vanderpool* (= *Hesperia*, Suppl. 19), 1–6, Princeton.

——. (1995), *The Athenian Agora: results of excavations conducted by the American School of Classical Studies at Athens*, vol. XXVIII, *The Lawcourts at Athens: sites, buildings, equipment, procedure, and testimonia*, Princeton.

Bonner, R.J. (1905), *Evidence in Athenian Courts*, Chicago.

——. (1922), 'Wit and Humor in Athenian Courts', *CPhil*, 17: 97–103.

Calhoun, G.M. (1919), 'Oral and Written Pleading in Athenian Courts', *TAPA*, 50: 177–93.

Carawan, E.M. (1983), '*Erotesis*: interrogation in the courts of fourth-century Athens', *GRBS*, 24.3: 209–26.

Crook, J.A. (1995), *Legal Advocacy in the Roman World*, London.

Dorjahn, A.P. (1935), 'Anticipation of Arguments in Athenian Courts', *TAPA*, 66: 274–95.

Dover, K.J. (1968), *Lysias and the Corpus Lysiacum*, Berkeley and Los Angeles.

Du Cann, R. (1980), *The Art of the Advocate* 2nd edn., Harmondsworth.

Gomme, A.W. (1937 [originally published in *Classical Philology*, 1934]), 'The law of citizenship at Athens', repr. in and cited from *Essays in Greek History and Literature*, Oxford.

Harris, E.M. (1995), *Aeschines and Athenian Politics*, New York and Oxford.

Harrison, A.R.W. (1968–71), *The Law of Athens*. 2 vols.: vol. 1, *The family and property*; vol. 2, *Procedure*, Oxford.

Krentz, P. (1984), 'Was Eratosthenes Responsible for the Death of Polemarchos?', *Parola del Passato*, 39: 23–32.

Jameson, M.H. (1971), 'Sophocles and the Four Hundred', *Historia*, 20: 541–68

Lämmli, F. (1938), *Das attische Prozessverfahren in seiner Wirkung auf die Gerichtsrede*, Paderborn.

Leisi, E. (1907), *Der Zeuge im attischen Recht*, Frauenfeld.

Lipsius, J.H. (1905–15), *Das attische Recht und Rechtsverfahren*. 3 vols. in 4, Leipzig.

Rubinstein, L. (2000), *Litigation and Cooperation: Supporting Speakers in the Courts of Classical Athens* = *Historia Einzelschrift* 147, Wiesbaden.

Thalheim, Th. (1894), '*Anakrisis*', in *RE*, vol. 1.2, cols. 2050–1.

Sommerstein, A.H. (1984), 'The Murder of Polemarchos', *Parola del Passato*, 39: 370–2.

Todd, S.C. (1993), *The Shape of Athenian Law*, Oxford.

Usher, S. (1976), 'Lysias and His Clients', *GRBS*, 17.1: 31–40.

[43] There are nineteen questions-and-answers, and Sokrates is allowed up to 200 words at a time, with Meletos replying mainly in monosyllables and at times with considerable reluctance: typical of a Platonic dialogue.

HERODOTUS AND THE IRANIAN TRADITION

J.S. Sheldon

When Herodotus embarks on his sketch of Median history[1] he cites as his source some Persians whose aim is to tell the truth, not simply to eulogize Cyrus; he has, he claims, rejected at least three other accounts of which he is aware. As a native of Halicarnassus, Herodotus had access to learned Persians who would have been versed in the traditions, folklore and mythical history of their race as well as events of more recent times as passed on by what was almost certainly an oral tradition. Although records of the Old Persian language are preserved in cuneiform inscriptions, there is no evidence that the language was widely used in written form.[2] In all probability the written languages most commonly used in Persian administration were Elamite and later Aramaic.[3] It is reasonable therefore to assume that there was no written history of Median and Persian events in their own languages which could provide a detailed or accurate account such as Herodotus himself was compiling. On the other hand, it is likely that Herodotus' Persian informants would have known the early legends of the Iranian Kings which were passed down in a long oral

[1] Herodotus 1.95. See I.M. Diakonoff in *Cambridge History of Iran* (hereafter abbreviated as *CHI*) Vol. 2 (Cambridge, 1985), 89 n. 1, concluding that the information of Herodotus on the history of Iran, apart from personal observations, came from the accounts of Zopyrus, a Persian emigrant aristocrat, and from someone of the family of Harpagus, the Mede, whose descendants had settled in Lycia and so would have been neighbours of the Halicarnassian Herodotus.

[2] Ilya Gershevitch makes a convincing case for Persian illiteracy in 'Alloglottography of Old Persian' *Transactions of the Philological Society* 77 (1979), 114ff. Although this is in part an *argumentum ex silentio*, the total absence of clay tablets in OP script compared to the thousands in Elamite and Aramaic is striking. Concerning Cyrus's illiteracy the admittedly biased Babylonian Nabu-naid wrote on his memorial stele, "Cyrus did not know the imprint of the stylus, cuneiform writing on a clay tablet" (A.T. Olmstead *History of the Persian Empire* [Chicago and London, 1948], 54).

[3] For the use of Aramaic, see J.C. Greenfield in *CHI* Vol. 2, 698ff. Diakonoff in the same volume (114) argues for the existence of OP script in the seventh century, but there is no positive proof. The Ariaramnes gold tablet used by Olmstead (*History of the Persian Empire* [as in n. 2], 24) to argue for the earlier dating of OP is now regarded as spurious on linguistic grounds. See M. Schwartz in *CHI* Vol. 2, 684. The balance of probability is that the writing system was created specifically for the inscriptions by Darius I. See also J.M. Cook in *CHI* Vol. 2, 235.

tradition which only found written form in the early Sasanian period and which we read in the surviving Avesta.

It has been long recognized that Herodotus' account of Persian usages[4] contains important details which are confirmed by the Avesta. The paramount place given to the Supreme Being, *Ahura Mazda*, is shown by his reference to the worship of the whole circle of heaven as Zeus[5] and the contrast with Greek polytheism. The inconsistency we find in the Avesta between the virtual monotheism of Zarathustra's *Gathas* and the polytheism of the *Yashts*, which are hymns to individual nature gods reflecting the earlier nature worship of the Indo-Iranian peoples, is brought out clearly when Herodotus speaks of sacrifice to the sun, moon, earth, fire, water and winds.[6] To each of these we find major hymns addressed in the Zoroastrian liturgy. The great importance given to truth telling[7] is an accurate reflection of the basic virtue of truth or *asha* 'true order'[8] which in the Avesta is so constantly opposed to *drug* 'the lie' that the two concepts often seem to symbolize good and evil. Again Herodotus knows something about this when he tells us that the greatest crime among the Persians is lying.[9] Next to lying, he says, comes debt for the reason that the debtor is often forced to lie.[10]

Herodotus speaks of a law which prohibits the king from executing a man for one offence, and provides that he may only inflict just punishment when a reckoning has shown that the man's offences outweigh his misdeeds.[11] This is a fundamental tenet in Avestan theology which decides the fate of the soul after death. The pious Zoroastrian is advised never to neglect the opportunity to perform

---

[4] Herodotus 1.131ff. See W.W. How and J. Wells *A Commentary on Herodotus* Vol. 1 (Oxford, 1912) *ad loc.* and Appendix VIII; also James Darmesteter *Vendidad* in *Sacred Books of the East* Vol. 4 (Oxford, 1887), liiff. M. Schwartz in *CHI* Vol. 2, 693ff. has a useful discussion.

[5] For the importance of *Ahura Mazda* in the Elamite Persepolis Fortification Tablets and the equation with Zeus, see Schwartz in *CHI* Vol. 2, 688.

[6] *Hvar, Mah, Aramati, Atar, Apam Napat* and *Vata/Vayu* in Avestan.

[7] Herodotus 1.136.

[8] See Schwartz in *CHI* Vol. 2, 641–2.

[9] Herodotus 1.138.

[10] A similar idea appears in *Vendidad* 4.1, with which may be compared the famous references to 'Truth' and 'The Lie' in Darius' Behistun inscription; Schwartz in *CHI* Vol. 2, 685–6 notes "the echo of Gathic theology" in the way 'Lie' is treated as an independent active force in the inscriptions, where OP *drauga-* is the precise equivalent of Avestan *draoga- (drug-)*.

[11] Herodotus 1.137.

even the smallest good deed as it might, at the final reckoning, tip the scales in his favour and result in the salvation of his soul.[12] The practice of exposing the dead rather than burying them is based on the Zoroastrian belief in the sanctity of earth which must not be polluted by the decaying corpse, a thing of great evil in their eyes.[13] Herodotus comes close to the truth when he speaks of birds and dogs mangling the corpse before burial and even closer when he says that the Persians embalm corpses in wax before burial. The latter was no doubt inspired by the same desire to avoid desecration of the earth. The former confuses two things: the practice, still current among Parsees, of allowing the birds of the air to pick the flesh from the corpse and the ritual clearly set out in the Avesta[14] of bringing a dog, an animal of the 'good creation' in their scheme of things, to look upon the corpse immediately after death. This is to drive out the Corpse Fiend (Av. *drug nasu*).[15] It is also permitted for the dog to dismember the corpse. The *Vendidad* is largely concerned with rites of purification and again Herodotus is echoed by the Avesta when he refers to the reverence shown for rivers and the measures taken by the Persians to avoid polluting them.[16] Although Herodotus does not specifically refer to any aspect of Zoroastrian dualism[17] (*Ahura Mazda* opposed to *Ahriman*, the good and the evil creation,[18] etc.), he tells how the Magians kill every creature with their own hands except for dogs and men. The Magians to whom he refers are contemporary priests of the official Persian religion who by this

[12] This is embodied in later writings in the concept of *Hammistagan*, 'The Place of the Motionless Ones', which is a state in the afterlife where those whose good and evil deeds are exactly balanced remain until the resurrection of the body. Their punishment is only to endure cold or heat from changes in the atmosphere. See the Pahlavi *Arda Viraz Namag*, ch. 6.

[13] *Vendidad* 4.36–42 *et passim*. Schwartz, however, points out (in *CHI* Vol. 2, 696) that the *Vendidad* (more properly *Videvdat* lit. 'anti-daemonic law') shows the influence of the Magi, and the custom may be theirs rather than that of all Zoroastrians.

[14] *Vendidad* 7.3.

[15] Schwartz in *CHI* Vol. 2, 661, however, regards this as "a late Magian insertion".

[16] Herodotus 1.138.

[17] One of the points made by those who deny that Darius was a follower of Zarasthustra is the fact that he makes no reference to *Ahriman* despite many to *Ahura Mazda*. Given the nature of the inscriptions, the context for such a reference is not obvious and the argument is a weak one. See Darmesteter (ed.) *Vendidad* (as in n. 4), xliv.

[18] See Schwartz in *CHI* Vol. 2, 681 and *Yasna* 61.2.

time could be described as Mazdaean[19] if not also Zoroastrian.[20] He is wrong to restrict the ban to dogs and men: it should, of course, apply to all of the good creation; while, on the other hand, he is remarkably accurate in referring specifically to the extermination of ants, snakes, creeping and flying things and the importance given to this;[21] according to the *Vendidad* to kill the *krafstras*, evil creatures, is to atone for one's sins.[22]

It is not unreasonable to suppose that the relevant parts of the Avesta as we know it were part of the Persian liturgies and rituals practised in the time of Herodotus.[23] In his description of Persian sacrifice his slightly inaccurate reference to the Magian[24] who chants the song of the birth of the gods[25] most probably refer to the chanting of the *Yashts*. Where he speaks of them learning from the Assyrians to sacrifice to the 'heavenly' Aphrodite, he may be confusing this

---

[19] Gershevitch has argued for the introduction of the Zoroastrian calendar as early as 441 BCE. See Schwartz in *CHI* Vol. 2, 692ff. and the detailed discussion by Willy Hartner in *CHI* Vol. 2, 714ff.

[20] The date of Zarathustra is a matter of profound uncertainty. Experts in this field are divided between a very early date (c. 1400–1200 BCE) and a much later seventh- or sixth-century date. If the former is accepted, then *Kavi Vishtaspa*, the last of the *Kavi* chieftains, Zarathustra's convert and protagonist, belongs to legendary pre-history. With the later date (now more generally favoured) we bring Zarathustra close to the Achaemenian court, if we accept, as Olmstead and Schwartz do, that *Vishtaspa* is the historical Hystaspes, the father of Darius. Cf. A.R. Burn *Persia and the Greeks* (London, 1962) and H. Humbach and P.R. Ichaporia *Zamyad Yasht* (Wiesbaden, 1998).

[21] Herodotus 1.140.

[22] *Vendidad* 3.10, 14.5ff. See also Darmesteter (ed.) *Vendidad* (as in n. 4), lxxiii nn. 2–3 and Intro IV 35.

[23] See Darmesteter (ed.) *Vendidad* (as in n. 4), xliiff. See also Schwartz in *CHI* Vol. 2, 295.

[24] See Schwartz in *CHI* Vol. 2, 689 and 696–7. The Magi are one of the six Median tribes mentioned by Herodotus (1.125). Like the Levites, they seem to have provided a hereditary caste of priests. Darmesteter (ed.) *Vendidad* (as in n. 4), xlvff., argues that the Avesta was originally their sacred book and that their religion was not widespread, but restricted to their own caste. Ammianus Marcellinus (23.6) says that they were taught the magic science by King Hystaspes. This could be a veiled reference to the spread of Zoroastrianism from the court of *Vishtaspa*. The word *magav-* is restricted in OP to adjectival *magus*, an epithet of the usurper Gaumata, who, according to Darius' Behistun inscription, raised a rebellion and claimed to be Bardiya, son of Cyrus and brother of Cambyses. The name may be ethnic and without any religious significance in this context, although Darius claims to have re-built temples destroyed by Gaumata. For Herodotus, Bardiya is Smerdis, and Gaumata, also Smerdis, is one of two Magian brothers; the other is called Patizeithes (Oropastes, according to How and Wells, *Commentary on Herodotus* [as in n. 4] Vol. 1, 398). Patizeithes may well be a title: cf. Modern Persian *padishah*, 'prince'.

[25] Herodotus 1.132.

with the ancient worship of *Aredvi Sura Anaita*, the sacred river, to whom one of the *Yashts* is dedicated.[26] *Anahita* appears along with *Ahura Mazda* and *Mithra* in the inscription of Artaxerxes II (404–361 BCE) on his restored fortifications at Susa as well in his rebuilt apadana at Ecbatana.[27] In a later period still, Plutarch[28] associates her with Artemis.[29] Clement of Alexandria on the authority of Berosus[30] (who wrote about 260 BCE) adds that Artaxerxes 'erected statues to Venus-*Anahita* in Babylon, Susa and Ecbatana'. Greek vagueness about foreign deities has often been noted and such evidence must be treated with care.

To turn from these Avestan resonances in Herodotus to the account of early Iranian history given in the *Yashts* and elsewhere is, it seems, to draw a complete blank. Before the Avesta was known and understood by European scholars,[31] the only native source for the early rulers of Iran was the tenth century Persian national epic, the *Shahname* of Firdousi. The title means 'Book of Kings' and the subject matter deals with the history of Iran from the original establishment of the monarchy by *Hoshang* to the period following the Arab conquest. As the Avestan material became known, it was soon realised that within its hymns was enshrined the source for the mythic history of Iran handed down faithfully through many generations and receiving its final redaction in the *Shahname.* It was not difficult to recognise in *Hoshang* the *Haoshyanha* of the *Yashts* and further certain identifications quickly followed. One of the great heroes of Firdousi is *Jemshid*, whose name was traced through Pahlavi *Jam i shed* to *Yima-kshaeto*, King of the Golden Age, in the Avesta. In the excitement which followed these discoveries, attempts[32] were made to take things further and identify these figures with historical personages; for example, the great Persian hero *Feridun* was identified as Phraortes, the

---

[26] For a contrary view, see How and Wells, *Commentary on Herodotus* [as in n. 4] Vol. 1, 112–13.

[27] Olmstead, *History of the Persian Empire* [as in n. 2], 423.

[28] Plutarch *Artaxerxes* 23, quoted by Olmstead (*History of the Persian Empire* [as in n. 2], 471).

[29] See Darmesteter *Sacred Books of the East* Vol. 23 (Oxford, 1882), 53.

[30] A Babylonian scholar who wrote *Babyloniaka.*

[31] The first translation was that of Anquetil Du Perron into French published in Paris in 1771. It was thought by many at the time to be a forgery and the language was dismissed as a corrupt form of Sanskrit.

[32] E.g. Hammer in *Wiener Jahrbuch* 9, 10ff. referred to in Kreuzer-Baehr (*Herodoti Musae* [Leipzig, 1830]) in the note on Herodotus 1.96.

Median king of Herodotus's first dynasty.[33] None of these attributions has stood the test of time and such attempts at identification have long since been abandoned. In the Avesta the period of the mythical founders is followed by that of the *Kavis*,[34] of whom there are nine, the last being *Kavi Vishtaspa*. The *Shahname* carries the story into the Achaemenian period and beyond, but the Avesta closes its account with the patron of Zarasthustra.[35]

The learned Persians who provide Herodotus with information about their history would be likely to have known these legends as part of their inherited religion, and it would not be surprising if this knowledge coloured their account of it in some way. For the student of Herodotus and the Avesta it is tempting to explore the texts in the hope of finding such colouring. Christensen in his valuable study of the literary evidence for the early rulers of Iran, *Kayanides*, gives a timely warning that the history of the Deiocides and Cyrus as transmitted by the Greek historians is mixed with legends and that any attempt to use as evidence for it the lineage of early heroes found in the Avesta requires careful interpretation owing to the confusion of the legendary motifs. In particular, he warns that the identity of names is not sufficient to provide identity of persons.[36]

Herodotus opens his account of the Medes with reference to their revolt from the Assyrians.[37] Once they had cast off this yoke they used their newly won freedom to establish a monarchy. Herodotus names four kings of the Medes and attributes to the first of these the unification of the various tribes and the establishment of the kingdom. Assyrian cuneiform records present a much more complex situation in their descriptions of clashes with the various tribal chieftains in this region.[38] Towards the middle of the seventh century, however, a picture of a powerful and united Media emerges and Herodotus' account despite its over simplification contains much that is of value in piecing together the history of this obscure period. The

---

[33] Likewise, *Jemshid* is Deioces, father of Phraortes; *Kaikobad* (Av. *Kavi Kavata*) is Cyaxares, etc. In reality *Feridun* is the Persian form of Avestan *Thraetona*.

[34] For a full treatment of this subject, see A. Christensen, *Kayanides* (Copenhagen, 1931).

[35] See n. 20 above.

[36] A Christensen, *op. cit.*, 6–7.

[37] Herodotus 1.95.

[38] Diakonoff notes (*CHI* Vol. 2, 87) that "from Sargon's texts we know some fifty Median chieftains, most of them independent".

first of his kings has a father and a son called Phraortes. This name can be equated to Old Persian *Fravartish* which appears in the Behistun inscription as the name of a Median imposter who describes himself as *kshathrita* of the house of *Uvakshatra* (Cyaxares). Diakonoff[39] argues from this that the name Phraortes in Herodotus is based on a misunderstanding and that the second king should be called *Kshathrita*. This is also the view taken by Olmstead. I think it unlikely. The word *kshathrita*,[40] as Bartholomae[41] makes clear, means 'one possessed of kingship' and can therefore be translated in the inscription as 'I am a royal chief of the race of *Uvaxshatra*' and need not be a proper name at all. It should, however, be mentioned that a *Kashtariti* appears in Assyrian cuneiform as a leader of the Median rebels in the wars of c. 674–2,[42] and this gives some support to the renaming of the second king.[43] In any case for chronological reasons *Fravartish* of the inscription cannot be the second king, though he may have the same name, and may indeed be named after him.

Herodotus' third king, Cyaxares,[44] emerges clearly as an historical figure and can safely be equated to the *Uvakshatra* of the Behistun inscription, although the form of the name in Greek shows that such transliterations are approximate. The last of the four, Astyages, is equally authentic although there is no exact Old Persian equivalent for him.[45] **Arshtivaega* has been proposed and is certainly a possible name, though not actually attested. *Arshtibara* is a title 'spear bearer' which is applied in the Behistun inscription to *Gaubrava* (Gobryas) so that the name **Arshtivaega* may be either a title which at some point came to be used as a proper name, or otherwise a title which somewhere in the process of transmission came to be misunderstood as a proper name.

---

39 *Op. cit.*, 113ff.

40 Cf. Skt. *Kshatriya.*

41 C. Bartholomae *Altiranisches Wörterbuch* (Berlin and New York, 1979), 547.

42 Diakonoff, *CHI* Vol. 2, 114.

43 Diakonoff, *CHI* Vol. 2, 29. Although the chronology seems right, *Kashtariti* has a stronghold called Kar-Kashshi which Diakonoff says "probably meant 'colony of the Kassites'".

44 Similarly in Assyrian sources we read of a *Uaksatar* who paid Sargon tribute in 714 BCE and later attacked the Assyrian province of Harhar. Olmstead identifies him as Cyaxares I (*History of the Persian Empire* [as in n. 2], 23) to be distinguished from *Uvakhshatra*, the Cyaxares of Herodotus, whom Olmstead calls Cyaxares II.

45 He has been located in the Babylonian Nabu-naid annals as *Istuvagu* (see How and Wells *Commentary on Herodotus* [as in n. 4], 385).

There remains Herodotus' first king, whom he calls Deioces—and who for us belongs to legend rather than history, as there is no satisfactory evidence for him in Iranian or Assyrian sources. His name may, in fact, be a title of which the first element is *dahyu-*,[46] an important and well attested word for one of the tribal regions of primitive Iran.[47] In the Assyrian annals, the term for 'chief of township' (*bel ali*) is represented in Avestan *vispaiti-*, and with the increase in his importance, *dainhupaiti-*, which may point to some such title as **dahyauka*,[48] which could be the original of Deioces. It has been customary to equate Deioces with the *Dayaukka* mentioned in Assyrian sources, where he is a governor (*shaknu*) of the land of the Mannaeans exiled with his family to Syria by Sargon II in 715 BCE,[49] but, as Diakonoff puts it, 'his connection with the later Median dynasty, though possible, is not attested by any authentic sources'. There is, however, in the Avesta, a name *Dahaka*, which is close enough to Deioces to warrant investigation.

Like the other *Yashts*, the Hymn to *Aredvi* (*Aban Yasht* in Pahlavi) appears to contain ancient material possibly inherited from the Indo-Iranian period or shortly after along with accretions of later times. Among the latter may be counted a passage at the end which looks like an appendage and may indeed be a description of a statue of the type described by Berosus. Among the former, however, is the list of those who in early times offered sacrifice to *Aredvi*. Such a list is paralleled in a number of the other hymns and takes us back to this legendary period of Iranian history. According to this, the third and greatest king was *Yima* (Vedic *Yama*), whose long reign ended when he sinned and lost his divine glory (*kvaranah*).[50] His two daughters were carried off by a fiendish monster who was later slain by the next great king, *Thraetona*. This monster sometimes appears as a human king, but always as an evil one.[51] He is *Azis Dahaka* or, as a mortal, *Dahaka*.

---

[46] See H.W. Bailey 'Iranian Arya- and Daha-' in *Transactions of the Philological Society* 57 (1959), 110. In this masterly survey Bailey traverses the whole range of words connected with *daha-* in the Iranian languages. On the present subject he says "a perjorative word *dahaka* is used in the Avesta of the *azi-* 'serpent, dragon', conceived later of a mythical king called *dahak*".

[47] Diakonoff *CHI* Vol. 2, 91.

[48] Diakonoff *CHI* Vol. 2, 80.

[49] Diakonoff *CHI* Vol. 2, 90. Unlike the other governors mentioned, we do not know the name of his district; but it is possibly Messi.

[50] Yt. 19.33.

[51] As Darmesteter puts it, "when *Yima* was turned into an earthly king, *Azi* underwent the same fate".

In the *Arevdi* hymn *Dahaka* is one of those who offer sacrifice to her, but his prayer is not answered. The formulaic description of him is similar to that used a number of times in the Avesta.[52] Although he is called *Azis*, 'snake' or 'dragon', he is in human form in most of his appearances.[53] It is certain that the idea of the evil snake is an inheritance from the Indo-Iranian period, for in the Veda we hear constantly of the snake or dragon *Ahih* (the same word) who is the opponent of Indra and is slain by him.[54] *Azis Dahaka* is described in the extended formula[55] as having three mouths, three heads, six eyes and a thousand *yaoxsti*; the last word should, I think, be translated as 'ears' or 'connections' and not 'senses', as it usually is.[56] Here the Vedic parallel is unmistakable, for in two Rigvedic hymns[57] the three-headed, six-eyed fiend is killed by *Traitana* or *Trita Aptya*, son of the waters, just as *Azis Dahaka* is by *Thraetona*.[58] In the *Aredvi* hymn the locations of the sacrifices are mentioned and the fiend's sacrifice is described as being in the land of *Bawri*. Although this is the only occurrence of this place name in Avestan, it is plausibly translated as Babylon by analogy with the attested Old Persian form *babirav-*.[59]

---

[52] Yt. 5.29, Y. 9.8, Yt. 15.19.

[53] See Darmesteter *Sacred Books of the East* Vol. 23, 60 n. 2.

[54] The Elamite tradition knows a human-headed serpent under the form of which the god Humpan and possibly Inshushinak were identified by association and/or worship, see Diakonoff *CHI* Vol. 2, 8.

[55] Yt. 5.29, Y. 9.8.

[56] Darmesteter in his note on Yt. 10.82, where the phrase *hazangra.yaoxsti* is used to describe *Mithra*, connects it with the Persian root *nyosidan* (Pahlavi *niyokhsitan*), 'to hear' and adds "one might be inclined to translate 'a thousand ears' or 'a thousand hearings'." He rejects this, however, in favour of Neriosengh's Sanskrit translation *pranidhi* 'sense'. The Zand has at Y. 9.8 *hazar-wizostar* [*adadag pad gohrag*] 'with a thousand skills [unjust by nature]', which can hardly be relied on. The occurrences of the expression in the Hymn to *Mithra* are in contexts where the idea of hearing is paramount. He is actually described as *hazangra.gaesa*, 'a thousand eared' in that hymn and elsewhere. The words are similar enough for there to be some confusion. *Mithra* is also described as *baevaro.spasan*, 'possessed of ten thousand spies'. Formulas originally applying to *Mithra* may well have been applied to *Azis Dahaka* (and *vice versa*) in this fluid tradition.

[57] RV 1.158.5, RV 10.99.6.

[58] Darmesteter *Sacred Books of the East* Vol. 4, lxiii.

[59] It is curious that in this same yasht (Yt. 5.129) three similar words occur all in the appendage describing the statute. Two of them seem clearly to mean 'beaver, male and female', describing furs in which the goddess, or her statue, is clothed. The other is simply an adjective formed from these nouns. Bartholomae (*Altiranisches Wörterbuch* [as in n. 41], 925) rightly compares Sanskrit *babhrav-* which means 'ruddy brown' and is also used to describe an animal. Such a name could be suitable for the city of Babylon, which was famed for its baked brick walls.

In the *Ram Yasht*, *Azis Dahaka* appears among the familiar list of those who sacrificed to *Vayu*, god of the wind. This time he is set, like the other worshippers, "on a golden throne, under golden beams and a golden canopy with bundles of *baresma* and offerings of full boiling [milk] in his inaccessible palace of *Kvirinta*".[60] Zand exegesis locates the otherwise unknown *Kvirinta* in Babylon. The Pahlavi Greater *Bundahishn* calls the place *Kuling Dushit* or *Kurind Duzit*. In the 'Modern' Persian tradition (*Hamza*), this was *Kuleng Dis*, 'the fortress of the stork', since the palace was in the shape of a stork—an interpretation which, of course, may be based on a mistaken play of words.[61] Bartholomae[62] identifies it as a river, modern day Karind, on the heights of the Zagros Pass. There is little doubt, however, that the adjective *duzitam* is correctly translated as 'difficult of access'.

In these two passages *Azis Dahaka* is conceived of as an earthly king, despite his epithet 'three-mouthed'. His role as mythical dragon is clear in the *Haoma* hymn[63] which is part of the ancient liturgy surrounding the pressing of the sacred *haoma* plant to make the intoxicating drink known in the Vedic tradition as *Soma*. It would also seem likely that he is thought of as a dragon when he appears in the *Zamyad Yasht* as at one point he is described simply as *Azis*.[64] Nevertheless the part he plays there is that of those who have tried to seize the glory of kingship. Here, as elsewhere, *Azis Dahaka* appears amid the sequence of early Iranians beginning with the first man *Gaya Maretan* (lit. 'Earth Mortal') and continuing through *Yima* to the *Kavi* chieftains.

Is there anything here which might colour the account of the earliest Median King which Herodotus received from his learned Persian

---

[60] Trans. Darmesteter *Sacred Books of the East* Vol. 23, 253.

[61] There is a striking coincidence in the connection between Babylon and the stork in Aristophanes *Birds* 1141, where storks make bricks for the sky wall; parody of Herodotus' measurements for the city of Babylon (Herodotus 1.178) has long been seen in the neighbouring context; likewise the reference to the Pelargic (if it is not Pelasgic) Wall at *Birds* 832, suggesting 'storks' wall' (memorably translated by Rogers as 'storkade'!) is immediately followed by a reference to the 'Persian bird' which is, in fact, the cock, which had come to Greece from Persia by the late eighth century BCE Earlier (483) the cock is said to have been King of the Persians long before Darius, etc. In the Avesta, the cock is a chief of birds and has almost semi-divine status as *Sraosha-varez-* 'the Enforcer of Obedience' (*Vendidad* 18.14ff.).

[62] Bartholomae *Altiranisches Wörterbuch* [as in n. 41], 476.

[63] Y. 9.8.

[64] Yt. 19.47.

informants? Deioces was a clever man who was in love with power,[65] and so impressed his townsfolk with his ability to administer justice that they appointed him chief judge; his fame grew and people flocked from near and far to submit their cases to him. In order to induce Deioces to give up all his time to this business of justice the Median tribesmen made him leader, equipped him with a body guard and built for him "the great and mighty circle of walls within walls which are now called Agbatana" (Ecbatana). The hill fortress consisted of seven circles and each circle was of a different colour; from outermost they were white, black, purple, blue, orange, silver and gold.[66] The king then shut himself away in the fortress and refused to be seen by any but a chosen few. All matters for judgement were dealt with through agents, as the king did not wish people, especially his peers and those who had known him from early days, to see him. He wished them to believe that he was changed from what he had been. He remained strict in his administration of justice and had spies and eavesdroppers everywhere in his dominions. He reigned for fifty-three years.[67]

Whatever information Herodotus received has been coloured by his typically Greek view of kingship and tyranny. Herodotus tells us that Deioces was enamoured of power, and the way it changes him and makes him proud and inaccessible is in keeping with the suspicion of the ability of power to corrupt we find throughout Greek writing; at a later period, it became a *topos* in biographies of Alexander the Great. In describing the way Deioces was persuaded to be king, Herodotus tells how "the Medes were gathered together into the one place". Diakonoff says that "in Media of the seventh century BCE some intertribal connections survived within the limits of the Median tribal confederation as a whole, and according to a very credible report of Herotodus it was possible to hold tribal popular gatherings".[68] He quotes the Avestan word *hanjamana-* which means 'assembly'.

[65] Herodotus 1.196.

[66] Herodotus 1.198. The number seven recurs constantly. *Kay Us* (Av. *Kavi Usadan* or *Usan*), according to Pahlavi sources, also built a fortress of seven castles which may represent the seven *karshvars* or 'regions of the world' according to Zoroastrian cosmogony. In Babylonian temple building there are seven planetary colours which could be relevant here. For further on this see Schwartz in *CHI* Vol. 2, 92 and Christensen *op. cit.*, 81.

[67] Traditional chronology places his death about 650 BCE.

[68] Diakonoff, *CHI* Vol. 2, 91.

One can certainly equate this word to Old Persian *hangmata* 'together, complete' and with some probability to the place name Ecbatana.[69] The number seven is an especially significant one in the Mazdaean religion as it is the number of the divine heptad comprising *Ahura Mazda* and the six *Amesha Spentas*. The latter are personifications of qualities and the phrases describing them in the oldest part of the Avesta, the *Yasna Haptainhaiti* or 'Liturgy of the Seven Chapters', which along with the *Gathas* attributed to Zarathustra, is written in a slightly older East Iranian dialect than the rest.

The picture of *Dahaka* would be incomplete without reference to later writings which, as often, may contain quite ancient material otherwise lost to us. As a mortal king, *Dahaka* continues through the Iranian tradition into the *Shahnameh* of Firdousi. He is now *Zahhak*, and like Deioces, he comes from a good background, but not a royal one. He is a fine young man but comes under the power of the Evil One. Meanwhile *Jemshid* loses his royal power and when his people look for a new ruler they choose *Zahhak*, who is in fact an Arab. The snake motif also re-appears here; after his pact with the Evil One, *Zahhak* undergoes a change in his appearance, and two snakes grow out of his shoulders and remain as a hideous external sign of his interior corruption. In one of the ninth century Pahlavi texts the epithet *bevarasp* is applied to *Dahag*, as he is called there. This is taken to mean possessing 'ten thousand horses', but does not correspond to an adjective in the surviving Avesta. It is more likely, I think, that we are dealing with a distorted form of the attested Avestan *baevaro.spasan* which would mean 'possessing ten thousand spies', the king's 'eyes' and 'ears' so often mentioned, for example, in the Xenophon's *Cyropaedia*.

Deioces may or may not be an historical figure but, as described by Herodotus he is almost certainly a composite one.[70] His name is

---

[69] Gershevitch ('Alloglottography of Old Persian' [as in n. 2], 124ff.), who believes that the OP version of the Behistun inscription was a translation of the Elamite, explains that Elamite *kappaka*, 'mustered or collected', would be translated into OP as *hangmata*; in cuneiform transcription this would be indistinguishable from the name of the place *hagmata*[*na*], Ecbatana. He does not, however, mention a derivation of the place name from the past participle (Av. *hanjamana*), nor does Bartholomae *Altiranisches Wörterbuch* [as in n. 41], 1744.

[70] "We have a complicated and prolonged process compressed in naïve form within the field of activity and the lifetime of a single person, but nevertheless a true picture of a society on the eve of the institution of the state. Herodotus' description makes sense both typologically and chronologically." Diakonoff, *CHI* Vol. 2, 89.

probably derived from a title meaning 'lord of lands' and the other details about this first king of the Medes may contain elements taken from a number of leaders who contributed to the unification and establishment of the empire. That Herodotus' Persian sources have coloured this story with elements taken from a legendary Iranian king with a similar name **Dahauka/Dahaka* must remain a possibility. The inaccessibility of the king in his palace and the system of spies point in this direction, as well as a number of other details.[71]

Note

The Avestan and Pahlavi Sources

When the Achaemenian empire ended after conquest by Alexander (334–26 BCE), whatever existed of written and oral expression of its religion was threatened with extinction. During Seleucid rule (312–c. 141 BCE) and the subsequent empire of the Arsacid Parthians (c. 141 BCE to 224 CE) this remnant was conserved by the Zoroastrian communities in an oral tradition. As this was a time when local Iranian scripts based on the Aramaic alphabet were being developed, it is possible that some of it was conserved in written form as well. When the empire of the Sasanian Persians was established under Ardashir I (c. 224–240 CE), an attempt was made to revive the culture of the great age, and Zoroastrianism was elevated to the status of a national religion. In this and subsequent reigns, High Priests, such as Tansar and Kirder, collected the scattered religious material in oral and possibly written form, and codified it. The language of these people was Pahlavi, a middle Iranian development of the Persian found in the Achaemenian inscriptions. It was written in a highly ambiguous Aramaic script[72] containing only a limited number of consonants and employing many Aramaic ideograms. In order

[71] Herodotus is notoriously vague about the difference between Assyrians and Babylonians. If his sources knew and told him about *Dayaukka's* deportation by the Assyrian king, as well as *Dahaka's* palace in Babylon, there would be grounds for confusion. Herodotus, however, makes no reference to Babylon in this context and we are in the realm of shadow rather than substance. It may be remembered that the Avesta places *Dahaka's* unsuccessful appeal to *Aredvi* in Babylon and that in another passage he was listed among those who failed to seize the glory of kingship (Avestan *kvarenah*) see Yt. 19.49.

[72] *CHI* Vol. 2, 710–11 and K. Hoffmann and J. Narten, *Der Sasanidische Archetypus* (Wiesbaden, 1989).

to clarify the older inherited language of the sacred texts, a better alphabet, including all the vowels, was developed and it was in this form that the Avesta, as we know it, came to be written down probably in or before the reign of Khusrow I (531–579 CE). Native tradition asserts that this is not more than a quarter of the Great Avesta which had existed earlier. We rely upon the Pahlavi writers for much of our knowledge of the meaning of the Avesta, its history and background. There exist Pahlavi translations and commentaries which are called Zand. The incorrect use of the term Zand or Zend to describe the language of the Avesta is based on a misunderstanding of this word.[73] As well as this, much quotation from and discussion of earlier lost Avestan texts is found in the Pahlavi writings of the ninth century Zoroastrian clergy, especially in two important books, *Denkard* ('Acts of Religion') and *Bundahishn* ('Creation').

The antiquity of much of the Avesta is guaranteed by the closeness of its language to the language of the Vedas, and the reason for this is easily explained by reference to the early history of the people who called themselves *Arya.* They were a branch of the Indo-European tribes who are known to have been in the Iranian plateau in the first half of the second millennium BCE. Before those of them who later moved south and settled in India had separated, these people practised a nature worship which forms the basis of the Vedic Hymns and the *Yashts* of the Avesta. After the separation, the two groups developed their religions in different ways, though much remained common both in concept and expression. The sacred texts needed to be conserved without alteration as far as possible. The Indian tradition was fortunate to have the aid of writing from at least the seventh century BCE, so that the Vedic hymns are sung today in a form little altered from that time. The Iranian tradition was not so fortunate; it also suffered greatly from the disruption caused by foreign invasion and subjugation, culminating in the Arab conquest from the early seventh century CE. From then on it has survived in a thin but preciously guarded stream among the Parsees in India and the few Iranis left in the homeland.

[73] Mary Boyce (ed.), *Textual Sources for the Study of Zoroastrianism* (Manchester, 1984).

PHILOSOPHY, RHETORIC AND LEGAL ADVOCACY

R. Godfrey Tanner

In his outstanding recent study of Roman advocacy,[1] John Crook has exhibited the kind of fair-minded judgments, stated with wit and wisdom, which are familiar over many years to his friends, colleagues and pupils. Here I wish to explore briefly some issues related to his theme but not central to the argument of his study, and which therefore were not subjected to detailed analysis. The primary interest will be the relationship between philosophy and advocacy.

This is an issue which Cicero touches on: namely, whether an advocate can properly defend a client he believes to be guilty of the crime alleged. Cicero justifies the defending advocate in persisting with his brief because the great expert of the Middle Stoa, Panaetius of Rhodes, had declared that such conduct was ethically permissible.[2]

We must bear in mind the deep sympathy which that eminent Middle Stoic felt not merely for Platonism itself and the Old Academy as such, but also for the more sceptical New Academy under Carneades, who had believed that Absolute Truth was unknowable by men, and that both sides of any question therefore needed full and forceful presentation for those involved to achieve the most persuasive approximation to True Opinion, the nearest parallel to True Knowledge open to human minds.[3] Therefore both an advocate in court and a statesman speaking in council or assembly might strive by every argument to undermine the case which his opponents were advancing in order that the issues on both sides might be properly assessed so as to achieve the most just, reasonable and convincing decision on the question in hand.

We should remember that Carneades himself gave an example of his doctrine with an Athenian embassy in Rome during his visit in 156–5 BC, lecturing on one day with great eloquence in praise of justice, but defending injustice on the next with equal vehemence.[4]

---

[1] J.A. Crook, *Legal Advocacy in the Roman World* (London, 1995).
[2] Cicero *De officiis* 2.51.
[3] See Cicero *De republica* 3.5.
[4] Lactantius *Divine Institutes* 5.14.

His method of *disputatio in utramque partem* on this question was later adopted by Cicero himself in *De republica* 3. So a blend of New Academy scepticism with Middle Stoic principles largely underlay the Roman rationale for advocacy as a respectable and needful skill.

But what of the laws under which it functioned? This question brings us to jurisprudence. So here we must examine the impact of Stoic thought on Roman jurisprudence. As Roman rule extended round the Mediterranean it became necessary to render Roman law more adaptable to the Empire's multicultural bilingual civilization by embedding it in the concept of *ius gentium*—a natural law based on human behaviour patterns common to all known societies. Cicero subscribes to such a view of the Law of Nations in the famous passage of *De republica* 3 preserved by Lactantius.[5] The concept of Right Reason stated there has Stoic overtones. However, the issue of where Stoicism most impacted on jurisprudence is consequential to Stoic physics[6] rather than to Stoic ethics. In this system the whole cosmos is alive and conscious, and is seen as a *plenum* of interpenetrating energetic rational material called *pneuma* blending with inert matter to create tensional fields held in being by their pneumatic energy as it pulsated like magnetism, or the reciprocal mutual gravitation of earth and moon.[7] Thus it survived by repelling other such fields by pneumatic polarity, so that, although all such matter is deemed to be in contact, the self-conscious *pneuma* of the universal consciousness pulsates with perfect regularity to sustain life and cosmos. However, in many of the tensional fields embraced by the cosmos, pulse irregularities (described as πτοία or 'flutter') in the activity of their hegemonic *pneuma* would not affect the whole cosmic consciousness, but merely the particular entity; and such irregularities of their 'flutter' could shake to pieces these irregular tensional fields. At the dissolution of such fields as held rational *pneuma*, this substance could drift away with the collapse or death of the particular field or body itself, and float up to the level of the moon if its irregularities were missing or diminishing, and thus persist there until *ecpurosis*, the cyclic sublimation of energy into the cosmic fire of the universe.[8] Not being embodied in inert matter, no pneumatic fields

[5] Lactantius *Divine Institutes* 6.8.6–9.

[6] Samuel Sambursky, *Physics of the Stoics* (London, 1959), *passim*, but especially ch. 1. 'The Dynamic Continuum'.

[7] Sambursky, *op. cit.*, p. 42.

[8] Sambursky, *op. cit.*, p. 36.

could stretch themselves over such material to permit them to receive new sensory inputs, and they would remain with the last impressions before their death still dominant. This was the physical reason for permitting suicide. It allowed a Stoic *proficiens* to escape a painful fatal illness, or execution on a false charge, allowing him thus to die calm and self-possessed.[9]

Where irregularity was dominant, the *pneuma* of the defunct tensional field would not survive separately, but would be subsumed by cosmic *pneuma* once it dissolved. On the other hand, the more regular pneumatic pulse of the *proficiens*, though not yet wise and perfect, would remain locked in its past experience, and gain no new insights because it lacked the material frame on which to be stretched and to pulsate anew in response to new sense stimuli. But, aided by a happy life or a wise use of suicide, this *hegemonikon* could die in peace. The few wise souls in history, being perfectly in harmony with cosmic pulsation, would survive death as parts of the directive consciousness and activity of the cosmic *pneuma* of the world soul, adding strength to the cosmic energy and direction—perhaps as *daimones*—and as centres of wisdom or *daimones* they would automatically become inerrant and impeccable.[10] Natural law was thus identical with the spontaneous judgment of the truly wise—based on their pneumatic pulsations, which were in perpetual harmony with both cosmic mind and the creative energy. Nature's law was thus infallible, and expressed itself in physics and creation, as well as in judgments of the wise and the life cycle of entities.

It must not, however, be assumed that Stoic principles were the cause of the importance of jurisconsults in the Roman legal system. The great experts of earlier days, as de Zulueta remarks,[11] were the holders of the priestly offices in the State. But the opening of these offices to plebeians in 300 BC ended any tradition of understanding the law as a mystery passed on among aristocratic patrician families alone. The great *prudentes* of the late Republican era (such as Cicero's hero Scaevola the Augur, no doubt, or perhaps like Cato the Censor, who died in 149 BC), owed much to Greek ideas and rhetorical theory. As de Zulueta makes very clear regarding Roman

[9] Cicero *De finibus* 3.60–1; see also Diogenes Laertius 7.130.
[10] Marcus Aurelius *Meditations* 2.4.
[11] F. de Zulueta, 'The Science of Law' in C. Bailey (ed.) *The Legacy of Rome* (Oxford, 1923).

aristocratic traditions, "the republican *prudentes* merely represent the specialized ability of a great governing class . . . To this class jurisprudence was a branch of the art of government". It was to Cicero the "urbana militia respondendi, cavendi, scribendi". But Cicero himself was *advocatus*, not *prudens*, for there were few of the latter in that period, and in the early days most belonged to priestly colleges which performed rituals for the general welfare or practised divination by augury or other means.[12] As Ovid records, in the days of the monarchy, as men of later times believed, the kings had direct face to face dealings with the Gods, and King Numa called Jupiter himself by a spell to persuade him to end Rome's ruinous floods. Then when the God demanded human sacrifice, the king's wit caused Jove to accept the life of a fish in lieu of that of a man—a fish for the soul, and an onion for a human head.[13]

So the great heroes of early Rome were as much in tune with the universe as a Stoic *perfectus* could be, and therefore the small coterie of *prudentes* became very like those rare wise Stoics: if not *perfecti* then at least advanced *proficientes*. But sectarian adherence to the doctrines of the Stoa would not be required of men who were administrators rather than philosophers of the law in practice. While occasional instances occurred of *prudentes* who also acted as *advocati*, this was not a general practice, since *prudentes* usually advised citizens in the drafting of wills or contracts, and arranged legal compromises. Not normally pleading, they advised on issues of law and procedure where advocates were in doubt, as de Zulueta reminds us.

But now one must turn to the puzzles surrounding the place of rhetoric in legal education in Rome. Originally, it seems, as Cato advised, youths were taken by their fathers to Senate and *comitia*, as well as to the *quaestiones perpetuae*, or standing courts, to observe proceedings and hear debates. The influence of a speaker or pleader would depend on his status and personal character rather than upon the techniques of persuasion which he employed. But already after the war with Pyrrhus, Greek rhetoric and literature had begun to influence Roman public life. Finally, under the Flavians, Quintilian advocated teaching infants to speak Greek first by employing a Greek-

---

[12] De Zulueta, *op. cit.*, pp. 192–3. This was still the case with some in Cicero's youth, when he studied under that great *prudens*, Scaevola the Augur.

[13] Ovid *Fasti* 3.295–344.

speaking slave as nurse, thus making them bilingual.[14] But it remained a Roman aristocratic pose to assert contempt for Greek art and culture, and Cicero in the *Verrines* and elsewhere expresses his contempt for many aspects of Greek life, activity and aptitudes—a view at least most of his contemporaries seem to have at least affected to share, and which was still prevalent in Juvenal's satires.[15] Yet after delivering his first major speech *Pro Roscio Amerino*, Cicero retired from Sulla's Rome to study under Apollonius Molon, the great Rhodian orator, who later regarded him as his best pupil in public speaking.[16] Since Molon spoke no Latin, and had to be permitted to address the Senate in Greek when he came with the Rhodian embassy to Rome in 81 BC, it is clear that he must have considered young Cicero his best pupil in *Greek* oratory. Therefore, other young Romans who visited him must have been prepared to learn and practise in Greek, probably including Julius Caesar.[17] Further, the frequent Greek quotations and phrases in Cicero's letters to Roman friends tend to suggest that Quintilian's advice in *Institutio Oratoria* that a boy learn details of expression and style in Greek and Latin together reflects long-established educational usage rather than proposing an innovation. Again, in his tenth Book Quintilian lists the works that the adolescent prospective orator should read in both Greek and Latin, together with his judgment on their virtues and defects as models. Already in Book two he had recommended Livy and Cicero to be read as examples of the best narrative style when pupils were writing narrative exercises. And indeed the whole literary curriculum is designed to present models for emulation, rather than the cultivation of the reader's taste.

Clearly by Quintilian's day the practice of composition adopted by Lysias in writing speeches in character for his clients in Athens was being taught, as well as that of the declamation of such specimens with appropriate dramatic mannerisms. These methods were open to disaster if clumsily used, as Quintilian warns. His example in a case for fraud against an orphan boy's guardians, of the advocate, who arranged for his client the child to weep at a certain point in the narration which itemized the wicked dishonesty of his vile

---

[14] Quintilian *Inst. Orat.* 1.1112–14. Contrast with Plutarch *Cato* 23.
[15] ". . . omnia novit esuriens Graeculus . . ." (Juvenal *Satires* 3.78).
[16] Plutarch *Cicero* 4.
[17] Plutarch *Caesar* 3.

next of kin, fell flat, because the boy was told to weep when the *paedogogus* pinched him as a signal. But when the advocate asked the child "Why are you weeping?", he received the truthful reply, "Please, sir, the *paedogogus* is pinching me".[18] Understandably, this stage trick weakened an otherwise convincing case.

Another oddity which disturbs writers on ancient oratory is the material chosen for the topics of the pupils' *controversiae* or *suasoriae.* M.L. Clarke argues that the encounters with criminals and pirates such as Caesar had experienced reflected, first, the problems of navigation after the end of Athenian sea power in Greece, and secondly, under the Roman Republic the dominance of pirates in the Mediterranean after the collapse of Rhodian sea power until Pompey began effecting his measures.[19] John Crook, in a trenchant section of a chapter he graciously wrote in a *Festchrift* in my honour,[20] is doubtful that treating that type of material really prepared youths for advocacy, and this is probably true. Incidentally, Pompey could never have succeeded in resettling the pirates in empty cities in Asia if they had been criminals of the kind found now in Wormwood Scrubs. Probably piracy then had parallels with much modern white collar crime in the 1950s and 1960s, when companies were taken over by buyers who increased profits by paying off the defunct firm's often very dedicated executives at far less than their worth, and some of the victims took to corporate crime to provide for their families. As Rome took over kingdoms like Macedonia, Pergamon and Syria, local business often benefited from lower taxes, but there was neither place nor pay for the ex-officers of their defunct armies, or for the former royal civil service. Similarly, artists and craftsmen who had worked for royal courts now had no employer. Such factors explain the discipline of the pirates, and their beautifully decorated warships. Once they were given an empty city and vacant lands to settle and develop, these victims of ancient globalization returned to honest living, like Virgil's Corycian ex-pirate gardener outside Tarentum in *Georgics* 4.

From *Institutio Oratoria* 10.3 one may guess that the operation of *suasoriae* or *controversiae* in rhetorical training was designed thus because

[18] A slightly dramatised paraphrase of *Inst. Orat.* vi.i.41.

[19] See M.L. Clarke, *Rhetoric at Rome* (London, 1953).

[20] J.A. Crook, 'Once again the *controversiae* and Roman Law' in Kevin Lee, Chris Mackie and Harold Tarrant (eds.) *Multarum Artium Scientia* (Auckland, *Prudentia* Supplement, 1993), pp. 68–76. See further his *Legal Advocacy*, Excursus 3, pp. 163–7.

of Quintilian's belief that youths in their early teens should begin with the *rhetor* while still working with the *grammaticus* on literary texts of the kind recommended in his tenth Book. So Thucydides and Herodotus are there examined as Greek stylists, and particularly their manner of reporting speeches as possible models. Among Latin epic poets, Virgil wins the prize as second only to Homer in his art. Atacinus Varro is praised as a translator into Latin, but is not seen as a model rich enough in style to increase a boy's capacity to give a speech. While the author sees Ennius as grand but archaic, others are more useful to develop one's eloquence. In epic Ovid is criticized for his excessive ingenuity and taste for wanton themes. In satire Quintilian defends Lucilius from the strictures of Horace. Regarding elegy, the prize goes to Tibullus, "though some prefer Propertius", while, as models for iambic, Catullus and Horace rank first. The praise of Livy as a model, in 10.101, stresses that historian's agreeable narrative style, but above all his capacity to write striking speeches in the character of the personages to whom they are attributed. In oratory Quintilian's grand master was Cicero, though praise is given also to Calvus and Caesar. In his own day he singles out two models of good oratory, Domitius Afer in choice of words and every aspect of speaking is applauded, and Iulius Africanus for his vigour. The latter, however, is criticized as tending to be long-winded, and also censured somewhat for too ingenious play on etymologies.

The extent to which a youth's reading is expected to help his exercises in original speaking is immediately evident in the Elder Seneca's *Suasoriae*, of which the first is an imaginative reconstruction of a debate in Alexander's Privy Council as to whether the conqueror should seek to subdue all lands beyond the ocean then unknown. The question is left open. The *Controversiae*, designed for rather older lads of sixteen to eighteen or twenty, are illustrated by 1.2, where the youthful Seneca's friend Latro begins a discussion before his rhetoric teacher Marillus on the case of a priestess taken by pirates and sold to a pander to work as a harlot. Can she still be a priestess if she is in any sense unchaste? Supposing she slew a customer who refused to pay the brothel fee? The answer must be that she is unfit, even if she had not received him herself!

One question at once emerges from these examples: the likely impact reading philosophers would have on adolescents studying oratory. Here again the presumptions in *Institutio Oratoria* 10 are relevant. Quintilian (10.1.81) gives credit to Cicero for insisting that Plato was the master of exposition and persuasion, lifting his dialogues above the quality of ordinary prose by his divine and Homeric richness. Xenophon's writing is praised by Quintilian as agreeable and free of all affectation of style: work indeed worthy of the Graces themselves. Aristotle is saluted for his amazing combination of scientific understanding and literary output, as well as the variety of his interests, while Theophrastus deserves his Greek name, for his eloquence has elements of the divine. Stoic prose was briefer and colder, but powerful in argumentation. From all of this the conclusion is clear, the model for writing like conference minutes the themes of *suasoriae* and *controversiae* is really the dialogue method of Plato's philosophy applied to legal investigations or politics and policy making, and the controversial or bizarre subjects are chosen to retain the enthusiasm and attention of the young. Law cases of such a nature did occasionally occur, but as John Crook shows,[21] the routine taxation, contract, theft or assault cases are much more like lawyer's business. The rhetors' exercise books were intended for pupils' mental development, not simply specifically as legal training manuals. Rather, they point to advocacy's debt to philosophy.

This leads us back to the issue of jurisprudence. The end of trials by *comitia* courts and the creation of standing courts, or *quaestiones perpetuae*, led to the need for the *praetor urbanus* to direct panels of senators or equites chosen to sit as judges about their duties and the procedural rules by an Edict issued at the start of his year of office. Before long, most such *praetors* were content to reaffirm their predecessors' Edicts with occasional modifications to meet the needs of new laws of the *comitia*, or *senatus consulta*, or, under the Principate, *constitutiones principum*. In regard to non-Roman laws surviving in conquered provinces, the governor would recognise those of the cities or tribes in internal use, as was the custom in Sicily in the time of Verres and Cicero. But he would hold provincial courts for issues which involved Roman citizens or the interests of the Roman State, or citizens from different communities within the province when in dispute. We are getting back to the *ius gentium* concept in practice.

At this point it must be realized that *controversiae* were not merely

[21] See *Legal Advocacy* ch. 3, 'Advocacy in the Papyri', pp. 58–118.

based on philosophers' dialogues, but also on the praetorian edicts issued in Rome, or by governors of provinces, which gave *formulae* (from about 150 BC), whereby the praetor *in iure* with the parties determined what should be the matter at issue and what verdict should be given by the *iudex* appointed according to his decision regarding the evidence presented by the parties. In these matters the *responsa prudentium* regarding a question of law was often a matter of precedent and a *communis opinio* of the *prudentes* frequently settled the law on issues not covered by statute. Hadrian established a fixed Edict with the aid of his great jurist Salvius Julianus which certainly simplified some questions.[22]

The progressive grant of Roman franchise to subject peoples led both to new legal issues and the universalizing of Roman law, which culminated in the Edict of Caracalla in AD 214, extending Roman citizenship to all (or most) free inhabitants of the Empire.[23] One may suspect that Papinian, Severus' great jurist whom Caracalla executed on a dubious charge of conspiracy, was responsible for this *Constitutio Antoniniana*. Ulpian was another of the systematizers of the law who endeavoured to reduce the enormous inconsistencies which had arisen over the centuries. He was again an imperial official, who was murdered by soldiers whilst secretary to Alexander Severus in AD 222.

Nonetheless, the move of the seat of empire to Constantinople by Constantine the Great in AD 330 made legal reorganization essential, and this was carried out finally under Justinian, who was striving to re-unite the Empire, aided by his great jurist Tribonian.[24] Though essentially the *Code* and the *Novellae* are all proto-Byzantine, they did good service to Roman law in removing what de Zulueta calls "the tough core of *ius civile*", mainly the unfamiliar rules for inheritance and family law foisted on the newly enfranchised citizens by Caracalla's Edict. Again Christianity escapes from the age of persecution without receiving power to persecute pagans. Law has become a universal element in European culture, saluting the Cross but not really rejecting the Stoa.

The medieval revival of civil law in some of the new European nations shows that with Christianity it performed a vital and vital-

[22] See de Zulueta, *op. cit.*, p. 196.
[23] De Zulueta, *op. cit.*, p. 200.
[24] De Zulueta, *op. cit.*, p. 204.

izing role in later western civilization, and also gave birth to a parallel Church Canon Law. This tradition of law, which John Crook explains and defends both in *Law and Life of Rome* and in *Legal Advocacy in the Roman World* is not merely alive. It may well become yet stronger, influenced by European Union and globalization.[25]

[25] *Legal Advocacy*, p. 3.

PRO AND *ANTI*: THE *DIGNITAS* OF THE SENATE IN 88 BC

A.M. Stone

1

P. Sulpicius Rufus,[1] tribune of the plebs 88 BC, has won fame in history above all for his "anti-senate". This body of 600 *equites* is attested by Plutarch in his *Lives* of Marius (35.2) and Sulla (8.2). There are some difficulties in the record apart from the ἀντισύγκλητος itself. They can be resolved once the title and function of this armed retinue are clarified.

"What is the Latin for it?" asked Badian.[2] The right question, though he did not stay for an answer. Something like *aduersus* or *contra senatum* would be sufficient deterrent. But that was to overlook Greek practice in rendering Roman terms. *Antisynkletos* is no anomaly, but a simple example of a paradigm. ἀνθύπατος is *pro consule*; ἀντιστράτηγος is (whether or not always applied with legal exactitude) *pro praetore*; ἀντιταμίας is *pro quaestore*. The Greek *anti-* means "instead of", not "against". Clearly ἀντισύγκλητος is *pro senatu*.

Sulpicius had an equestrian retinue titled *pro senatu*.[3] Such a body, even when escorting the tribune in arms,[4] is not conceptualised as

[1] For the *cognomen*, Valerius Maximus 6.5.7; for his consequence, though nothing is said of *nobilitas*, Velleius Paterculus 2.18.5. Cf. D.R. Shackleton Bailey *Two Studies in Roman Nomenclature* 1st edn. (1976), 2nd edn. (1991), 84; originally reviewed by P. Harvey *AJP* 101 (1980), 119; E. Badian "The Clever and the Wise: Two Roman *cognomina* in context", *Vir Bonus Discendi Peritus: Studies in celebration of Otto Skutsch's eightieth birthday*, ed. N. Horsfall (1988), 6–7; M.J. Slagter *Transitio ad plebem* (1993), Diss. Bryn Mawr, 134–67.

[2] *Foreign Clientelae* (1958) 234, n. 1; again 'Quaestiones Variae' *Hist.* 18 (1969), 485 n. 110.

[3] A.W. Lintott came close to seeing this when he conjectured a mistranslation by Plutarch of something like "quos in consilium senatus vicem vocabat' ('The Tribunate of P. Sulpicius Rufus", *CQ* 21 [1971], 442 n. 3), but it was not his immediate concern to follow it further; A. Keaveney cites this with approval ("What Happened in 88?", *Eirene* 20 [1983], 55) among other approved possibilities like "gangster-slang"; effectively he still clings to the "anti-senate".

[4] The arms could be used, as (actually) against A. Sempronius Asellio (praetor 89), or (menacingly) in support of Q. Varius (tribune 90) (Appian *BC* 1.54; 1.37), but were chiefly symbolic of a state of emergency: cf. "Saga populus sumpsit" (Livy

a *praesidium* but as *consilium publicum* supplying that which the tribune felt he lacked in the constituted *senatus*: i.e. not merely a parade of *splendor* but *auctoritas*. It would be odd, therefore, if the 600 were in fact young sparks, whether the sons of senators or *equites Romani*.[5] Able-bodied youngsters of that class below the age of thirty were still required to officer the various armies in action throughout Italy in 88. Yet Plutarch writes νεανίσκοι, i.e. seems to be representing in Greek the Latin *adulescentuli*. But this cannot be right. It is necessary to start again.

The number 600 is significant. It refers to a defined group separate from the band or bodyguard of 3000 raised by Sulpicius. The officers of that bodyguard would not be a separate corps, and 600 of them would be too many; nor would such terms as pro-senator be applicable. 600 is the number of *equites* in the *comitia centuriata* who were not in the 1200 legionary cavalry, together making 18 centuries; 600 *equites* and various recognisable fractions of 600 were the building-blocks of various expedients for manning the criminal courts from C. Gracchus to the younger Drusus.[6] It is noteworthy that the most recent experiment, the *lex Plautia* of 89, had aspired to *concordia* by reducing the equestrian component to one-third, the lowest fraction for members of the order since before C. Gracchus.[7] A noble aim, but the corps of *equites* were angry men, not so easily set aside: in or after December 91 they had drawn daggers against tribunes of the plebs vetoing the *lex Varia*;[8] in 89 they had murdered

---

Per. 72); "Ob eam victoriam Romae saga posita sunt." (*ibid.* 73), of citizens not serving as soldiers in 91–90 BC. Cf. H. Strasburger's seminal discussion of Cicero's equestrian guard on 5th December 63. Again Plutarch (*Caesar* 8) portrays them as youngsters (*Concordia Ordinum* [1931], 39–40).

[5] Cf. A. Keaveney *Sulla, The Last Republican* (1982), 59; *Eirene* 20 (1983), 55.

[6] Livy *Per.* 60 (600 *equites*); *Lex Repetundarum* 14 (*FIRA* [ed. S. Riccobono]) enacts a panel of 450 for any one year; Appian *BC* 1.35 (for 300 *equites* to be empanelled with existing senators to make 600). See my forthcoming 'The Archaeology of the *Optimates*' in *Proceedings of the Conference Roman Crossings*, T.W. Hillard, K.E. Welch, F. Muecke edd.

[7] On the provisions of the *Lex Plautia* equalising three orders of *iudices*, Asconius *In Cornelianam* 79C. It broke the situation applying since C. Gracchus of equestrian control of the extortion-court and special *quaestiones*, briefly interrupted by an experiment in equal sharing under the *Lex Servilia* of Q. Servilius Caepio (consul 106). The scandalous conviction of P. Rutilius Rufus in 92 and the purge atmosphere of the *Quaestio Variana* in 90 cried out for jury-reform. M. Livius Drusus' quite different solution in 90 had never gone into effect. On *equites* and *iudices*, see in general P.A. Brunt *The Fall of the Roman Republic and Related Essays* (Oxford, 1988), chapters 3 and 4.

[8] Appian *BC* 1.37; Valerius Maximus 8.6.4.

the praetor A. Sempronius Asellio;[9] in the future they were to be a bulwark of Cinna's regime;[10] but in 88 they supplied Sulpicius not only with swords but with *auctoritas*.

It is now possible to revisit Plutarch's νεανίσκοι. If Sulpicius' armed and splendid retinue of *equites* was not designed for the basic thuggery which could be quite satisfactorily handled by the 3000 (*libertini*?), but rather to supply the *auctoritas* of the corps of (former) *iudices* as substitute for senatorial support, he needed mature men, not youths. Plutarch was not seized of this; he viewed it as a matter of street-credibility. His νεανίσκοι may be seen as a misunderstanding of *equestris iuuentus* or *equites iuniores*, i.e. men in their prime, and over 30 rather than under in the circumstances. They would be *equites* of judicial capacity.[11]

P. Sulpicius had a track-record in striking contrast with his activities as tribune in 88. He emerges into the light of history in 95 as prosecutor of C. Norbanus, the violent and seditious Marian tribune of 103, a prototype of his own later self.[12] In 91 he supported M. Livius Drusus in his tribunate "pro senatus auctoritate susceptus"[13] and as the most promising of the younger orators[14] he is portrayed by Cicero as a specially beloved companion of L. Crassus, most impressive of the senior orators.[15] The *principes* of Crassus' generation (including M. Scaurus *princeps senatus*)[16] invested the hopes

[9] Appian *BC* 1.54, Livy *Per*. 74; Valerius Maximus 9.7.4.

[10] Asconius *In or. in toga cand.* 89C: "Equester ordo pro Cinnanis partibus contra Sullam steterat multique pecunias abstulerant: ex quo saccularii erant appellati, atque ob eius rei inuidiam post Sullanam uictoriam erant interfecti."

[11] *Lex Repetundarum* 13 (*FIRA*): not less than 30 or more than 60 years of age and domiciled within one mile of Rome. They were perhaps only *iuuentus* in the sense of being entitled to parade *trabeati* at the *transuectio equitum* on the Ides of July (Livy 9.46.15; Valerius Maximus 2.2.9).

[12] Historically conceptualised in E. Badian "Caepio and Norbanus" (1957), *Studies in Greek and Roman History* (1964), 34–70.

[13] Cicero *De oratore* 1.24–5.

[14] Cicero *Brutus* 183, 201, 203–4; Cicero places him below his senior model L. Crassus (consul 95), the best in *his* generation, but implicitly ahead of his near equal C. Cotta (consul long after, in 75).

[15] In the comparison of the two orators who brought Roman eloquence into comparability with Greek (*Brutus* 138) Cicero places Crassus above M. Antonius (consul 99) in perfection (*Brutus* 143).

[16] Asconius *In Scaurianam* 21C: "Scaurus . . . M. quoque Drusum tribunum plebis cohortatus sit ut iudicia commutaret"; at 22C, Scaurus was put on trial for complicity with the (Drusan) Italian programme through the intervention of the younger Q. Servilius Caepio, his *inimicus*—and Drusus' (Pliny *NH* 33.1.20).

they had for their *dignitas* in another orator of promise, C. Cotta, standing for the tribunate of 90, and in Sulpicius, who was expected to be tribune next in the series in 89.[17] An organised succession to Drusus had been planned. The individualism rightly seen in the members of the Roman political class[18] was being subordinated to the urgent needs of their order and their *res publica.*

This much is well understood. The deaths of Crassus and Drusus and Scaurus, the exile of Cotta,[19] the absence of Sulpicius himself in the army in 90–89[20] changed much—but not, it seems, Sulpicius' political stance. A movement away from his friends and toward Marius during 90 and 89 is not an attractive hypothesis.[21] It is in contradiction of some most emphatic evidence of events that occurred when Cicero was eighteen and an interested observer with his friend Atticus, relative and friend of Sulpicius, of the unfolding tragedy of 88 BC. When Sulpicius became tribune in December 89 and Q. Pompeius Rufus became consul in January 88 they were still the closest of friends, living not only in affection (*amantissime*) but in what may be taken as *political* unity (*coniunctissime*).[22] The "capital hatred"

---

[17] *De oratore* 1.25.

[18] Notably, T.P. Wiseman 'Competition and Co-operation', in *Roman Political Life 90 BC–AD 69*, ed. T.P. Wiseman (1985), 3–19.

[19] L. Crassus' death shortly after the fictitious dialogue *De oratore* prompts a lament from Cicero within the work on the fates of the participants in it, which he associates with the conflagration of Italy, the unpopularity of the Senate and the prosecution of the leading citizens for treason under the *Lex Varia* (3.6–12, esp. 8).

[20] *Brutus* 304 (see n.28 below).

[21] Christian Meier makes Sulpicius' intention to resurrect equestrian power fundamental (*Respublica amissa* [1966], 217–8); E.S. Gruen *Roman Politics and the Criminal Courts* (1968), 223, 225–6, would have Sulpicius preparing the transfer to Marius on the basis of an existing friendship supposedly attested for 91 (*De oratore* 1.66): this passage merely argues that a trained orator can communicate the knowledge of experts better than they can; Marius is simply one of three experts hypothetically embarrassed by Sulpicius' eloquence. The anecdote presupposes nothing more than their being on speaking terms. J.G.F. Powell resolves the tension between Sulpicius' links with Marius and with his old friends by supposing that Q. Pompeius and Sulla need not have been anti-Marian either until violence developed in 88 ('The Tribune Sulpicius', *Hist.* 39 [1990], esp. 458–9). Q. Varius might not have lived.

[22] Cicero *De amicitia* 2. Cf. *Ad familiares* 6.9.1, where A. Caecina is commended as living *coniunctissime* with Cicero not only in the duties of friendship but in common studies. As between Pompeius and Sulpicius, conjunction must presuppose the campaign for the consulate in the one case and for the tribunate in the other; general affection is covered by *amantissime.* Cf. Cicero's *conjunction* with Pompey in personal and public affairs (*Ad Atticum* 1.19.7); Balbus' offer to *conjoin* Crassus with Pompey ("... ut cum Pompeio Crassum coniungeret") and to provide Cicero with a close *coniunctio* with Pompey, and with Caesar too if he wishes (*Att.* 2.3.3 and 4).

that Sulpicius conceived for Pompeius early in 88 was sudden and shocking to all, and involved a determination by Sulpicius to despoil *omni dignitate* those to whose *dignitas* he had once devoted his talents and passion, his hopes and theirs.[23]

Yet the evidence remaining reveals hostile acts by Sulpicius against his former friends, but nothing that they did to him which could justify such feelings in the first place. Sulpicius came to regard the consul Pompeius as no fit consul, the Roman Senate as no fit senate and the commander Sulla, equalled by no one but Cn. Pompeius Strabo in recent war service, as no fit commander. *Dignitas manquée* all round! Pompeius was deposed, the senate replaced, for Sulpicius at least, by an equestrian retinue, and Sulla deprived of his military command. For a short period Sulpicius, dissatisfied with all aspects of government, took control of Rome.[24] For an understanding of the turnaround of Sulpicius the background and record of another friend must be produced in evidence, another orator and idealist, as proud, fierce and ambitious as himself.

2

C. Iulius Caesar Strabo has been ill-served by his wit.[25] No doubt excellent in its time, it survives in various examples of repartee. But it has left one of the most gifted and active Roman politicians, a statesman who could take his cause to the streets, languishing under the dispiriting label of "humour"; it was already his pigeon-hole in Cicero's time, as we still see in *De oratore* 2.216–290.

The so-called First Triumvirate—and other political alliances—is conceptualised by Romans as *coniunctio*. Q. Pompeius and Sulpicius shared politics and policies in the eyes of the young Cicero and the Roman community.

[23] *De oratore* 1.25 (for the original commitment in 91); 3.11 (for its betrayal in Sulpicius' tribunate).

[24] Narrative accounts are extant (but not entirely compatible) in Appian *BC* 1.55–6; Plutarch *Marius* 35; *Sulla* 8. Though the text in the *Sulla* for Q. Pompeius' "deposition" is uncertain, the usual reading seems to be validated by the clear statement following that Sulla was not deprived of his consulate. Constitutionally a tribune could not make a consul not a consul, but prevented him from exercising his powers. Plutarch's report seems accurate in its reference to Sulpicius' stopping Pompeius ἐπάρχοντα, but technically loose in implying that Sulla *could* have been deprived of his consulate outright.

[25] On wit as Caesar's mark, E. Malcovati *Oratorum Romanorum Fragmenta*, 3rd edn. (1966), no. 73; 'Iulius' *RE* No. 135 (Diehl); and commonly at any casual mention.

And yet his introduction into the company of participants in the fictitious dialogue at *De oratore* 2.12ff. repays some consideration: the cultured half-brothers Q. Catulus (consul 102) and Caesar Strabo arrive at L. Crassus' villa unannounced, exchange wonted greetings *amicissime* and are eagerly quizzed for the latest political news. At 2.16 in a context of urbane banter Caesar makes mock-protest against his *familiaris* Sulpicius' being closer to or counting more with their revered Crassus than he does. This is to be taken with the just mentioned notice (2.12) that Catulus and Caesar arrived to find the ailing Crassus still in bed and Sulpicius sitting by his side. Of course, Cicero is not reporting a historical scene but applying the resources of art to a problem: how to convey the hierarchy of affection in this group of friends? It is done with psychological brilliance. Caesar and Sulpicius are rivals in their love of the dying Crassus. Caesar in this way is represented as a contender for the most serious consideration, Crassus serving here as central figure not only in oratory but in statesmanship.[26] His martyrdom to *res publica* is a known and awaited event in the dialogue, which is a fiction constructed, after all, around history.[27]

With the death of Crassus, the murder of Drusus and the outbreak of the *Bellum Italicum* their paths diverge. Sulpicius is not heard of during 90 BC, a year that would have demanded the attendance of Rome's first orator in his generation, had he been available. In 89 he was *legatus*.[28] It can be accepted that he was on military service from the end of 91 to well on in 89 when he was elected tri-

[26] L. Crassus is made to assert the supremacy of oratory among social and political arts (*De oratore* 1.29–34); Q. Mucius Scaevola the Augur (consul 117), father of Crassus' late wife, offers rebuttal on behalf of philosophy, religion, tradition, and other arts (*ibid.* 35–44). Crassus' larger development of the theme is responded to by M. Antonius. When Cicero (via Antonius) conceives a hypothetical intervention by the finest statesmen of them all, M. Scaurus *princeps senatus*, on behalf of *grauitas* and *consilium* as the bases of *auctoritas*, he characteristically subverts Crassus' (i.e. his own) line by having the imaginary Scaurus crush the loquacity of the orators by the look on his face (*ibid.* 214)! But, of course, it is the nature of oratory to keep talking, and that is what the company do.

[27] 3.1–12.

[28] *Brutus* 304; Cicero's argument for the dearth of orators in the Social War is enforced by C. Cotta's exile (*ibid.* 303), Hortensius' military service (*ibid.* 304), Antonius' absence (*ibid.*), C. Curio's silence (*ibid.* 305). If Sulpicius had been present and available at any time in 90–89, the fact would have to be registered as modifying the tenor of Cicero's argument; the reference to him as *legatus* may cover 90 as well.

bune of the plebs for 88. Caesar was detained in Rome during 90 by his duties as curule aedile, to which office he was elected before the fighting broke out. But *cura urbis* and liberal *munera* fell beneath the real needs of the time. The most significant notice of his activity is the almost daily *contiones* he addressed with carefully prepared speeches.[29] On what subject? There are two that would demand the talents of an engaged man of politics: the question of enfranchising the Italian allies; and the devastating operations of the *Quaestio Variana* as friend after friend of the absent Sulpicius and the present Caesar were hauled into a court manned by equestrian juries on charges of treasonable negotiations with the Italian allies leading to the current bitter, bloody war.[30] On both issues, which are of course really aspects of one issue, Caesar Strabo is known to have had views.

His brother L. Caesar (consul 90) was the author of the *lex Iulia* granting citizenship to those Italian *ciuitates* that wished to have it;[31] Lucius was also censor in the following year. Strabo addressed an oration to the censors of 89, i.e. to his brother and P. Crassus (consul 97), in which he movingly canvassed the state of Italy.[32] It is most likely, therefore, that some of his *contiones* of 90 will have been about the issue of allied citizenship under his brother's proposal; the

[29] *Brutus* 305: "C. etiam Iulius aedilis curulis cotidie fere accuratas contiones habebat." We have been alerted by Fergus Millar's work to the importance of *contiones* in Roman public life, above all in *The Crowd in Rome in the Late Republic* (1998). Caesar's presence in Rome does not negate the dearth of orators in Cicero's memory; cf. Caesar's damning lack of vehemence (*ibid.* 177), which is perhaps to be set against Cicero's betrayal of his youthful taste for strong meat: note his high enthusiasm for the admittedly rude genius of Q. Varius, C. Carbo, Cn. Pomponius (*ibid.* 305; cf. 207, 221 on Pomponius; 221 on Varius; *Orator* 213–4 on Carbo). The mediocrity of P. Antistius (*ibid.* 226) is modified by improvement (*ibid.* 308), and on one occasion clear superiority in argument to the mighty Sulpicius himself (226). Cicero's teeming brain and rich coverage are only unevenly disciplined by discrimination in this work.

[30] The prime case is that of C. Cotta, friend of both Caesar and Sulpicius; the relationship with Sulpicius (and Drusus) seems to amount to *conjunction* (*De oratore* 1.25); cf. n. 22 above. On Cotta's exile, balanced against Sulpicius' turnaround, *De oratore* 3.11; on its effect on the young Cicero's studious zeal, *Brutus* 305.

[31] Cicero *Pro Balbo* 21; backed by the Senate, Appian *BC* 1.49.

[32] Varro *RR* 1.7.10: "Caesar Vopiscus aedilicius, causam cum ageret apud censores, campos Roseae Italiae dixit esse sumen, in quo relicta pertica postridie non appareret propter herbam." *Prima facie* this is merely rhetoric on the fertility of a tract of land in dispute before a court. But this is not before a civil law court but before the censors; Caesar has been retained as *patronus*, not for his vehemence, but for his intellectual stature and/or his being brother to one of the censors. Though the details are elusive, the case would seem to have a broad and public dimension.

confinement of new citizens within a limited number of electorates (*tribus*) was not illiberal, nor regarded as such by the new citizens, until Sulpicius outbid this offer in 88.[33] It was originally a way of securing the assent of old citizens to a programme that might, if not channeled, swamp them.[34]

Caesar Strabo was also a courageous and effective opponent of the monstrous Q. Varius,[35] author of the *lex* that initiated a purge against those, above all the friends of the late Drusus, alleged to have conspired with and incited the secessionist allies.[36] Which cases Caesar was involved with is not known except one—Varius' own condemnation under his law early in 89. In 87 on Marius' re-entry of Rome with L. Cinna the expelled consul, Strabo was killed in expiation of *Varius*' death.[37] From this flows easy identification of Varius' backer, the ultimate organiser of Varius' equestrian support, the great man who valued Varius highly enough to avenge his death a little short of three years later, when so much more recent claims to vengeance had to be attended to: C. Marius himself.

In 90–89 B.C., therefore, it was Caesar Strabo who stood up to Marius' power and turned the tide: he was one of the few available to defend the accused; and since Antonius and Sulpicius were absent and Cotta exiled, he was the best;[38] he may have got some of them off; his attested public meetings cannot but have addressed the broader issues of Varius' violence and *backing*; he will have been among the *nobiles* who supported the *lex Plautia* which broke the equestrian con-

---

[33] On this Appian *BC* 1.49 *ad fin.*

[34] Cf. the structure of argument adopted by C. Fannius (consul 122) against C. Gracchus' proposal to extend citizenship (E. Malcovati *Oratorum Romanorum Fragmenta* 3rd edn. [1966], C. Fannius, p. 144, no. 3).

[35] Cicero *De oratore* 1.117: "uastum hominem atque foedum"; cf. Catiline's "uastus animus" (Sallust *BC* 5.5).

[36] Asconius *In Scaurianam* 22C; Valerius Maximus 8.6.4.

[37] Valerius Maximus (9.2.2) records his death through Marius' cruelty, though with his brother Lucius' consular and censorial titles wrongly attributed to him, as a sacrifice at Varius' tomb; he continues ". . . id enim malorum miserrimae tunc rei publicae deerat, ut Vario Caesar piaculo caderet." There is a clear differentiation between the branch of the Iulii Caesares victimised by Marius and their collaterals, Sextus (consul 91) and Gaius (praetor in uncertain year), brothers of Marius' wife. The future dictator exploited the Marian connection of his own branch but appropriated the oratory of Strabo (Suetonius *Iulius* 55.2).

[38] Not in Cicero's view (or memory?) in the *Brutus*; cf. n. 29 above. This is at odds with all other information, including Cicero's. Cicero may not have witnessed the condemnation of Varius. Caesar's oratorical effectiveness was not just street-power (cf. n. 40 below).

trol of the Varian *quaestio* and made it possible to accuse and convict Varius himself.[39] It is not difficult to discern in Caesar Strabo the uniquely subtle intelligence that constructed a charge against Varius under his own legislation. Varius, after all, had to cultivate connections with Italian allies in order to secure evidence of conspiracy by Roman nobles.[40]

Since Varius was able to remove tribunician obstruction with menaces,[41] any credible opponent must be credible on the streets. Caesar Strabo's friend Cn. Pomponius, tribune of the plebs 90, is attested as streetfighter against Sulpicius in 88;[42] the organisation, however, must have been put together when first needed: in the Varian times.[43]

---

[39] Asconius *In Cornelianam* 79C: "M. Plautius Silvanus tribunus plebis Cn. Pompeio Strabone L. Porcio Catone coss., secundo anno belli Italici cum equester ordo in iudiciis dominaretur, legem tulit *adiuuantibus nobilibus* . . ." The reference is to co-ordinated political activity presumably by continuing elements of the group around Drusus. *Nobiles/nobilitas* was to be the label of Sulla's party (e.g. Cicero *Pro Roscio Amerino*, esp. 135–42).

[40] Cicero *Brutus* 305: ". . . Q. Varius sua lege damnatus excesserat"; Valerius Maximus 8.6.4: ". . . sua (sc. Varii) lex eum domesticis laqueis constrictum absumpsit." That Varius' law would include clauses against seditious violence or usurpation of citizenship is highly unlikely: why frame a crime as though with oneself in mind? "*Domestic* nooses" do not work even in Valerius Maximus' ill-directed rhetoric as a description of what happened to Varius *after his departure from Rome*; they serve well, however, as a metaphor of entrapment by the adroit Caesar.

[41] Appian *BC* 1.37.

[42] Quintilian *Inst. Or.* 6.3.75: "C. Caesar Pomponio ostendenti uulnus ore exceptum in seditione Sulpiciana, quod is se passum pro Caesare pugnantem gloriabatur, 'numquam fugiens respexeris' inquit". Caesar's wit still coruscates in the midst of his defeat on the streets; in the absence of the *praenomen* I take Cnaeus the tribune of 90 BC to be the Pomponius in question here: as one of Varius' opponents in office in that year (Appian *BC* 1.37 envisages all Varius' colleagues as being against him; Valerius Maximus 8.6.4 "aduersus intercessionem collegarum" implies the same less distinctly; on another three known tribunes of 90, C. Curio, Q. Metellus Celer, and C. Carbo Arvina, active *optimates*, *Brutus* 305), and consequently as associate of the aedile Caesar in 90, he is most economically identified as Caesar's gang-leader in 88 (cf. n. 43). If the gangster and the tribune are relatives and collaborators, however, the substantive point of this note still holds good. It is difficult to take the tribune, and impossible to take the gang-leader, as belonging to those Pomponii who, like the young Titus (later Atticus), were closely aligned with Sulpicius in 88 (Cicero *De amicitia* 2)—though they may be related.

[43] Cn. Pomponius, popular orator (". . . lateribus pugnans, incitans animos, acer, acerbus, criminosus", Cicero *Brutus* 221) and tribune in 90, is an ideal nucleus for the construction of an effective physical resistance to Varius' power on the streets. Of the other known tribunes C. Curio was broken by the situation, Metellus Celer was lacklustre, Carbo Arvina showed real energy (*Brutus* 305), but may have been too principled for the work (Cicero *Ad familiares* 9.21.3). He was definitely on side, enough to be put to death by L. Junius Brutus (praetor 82) on the orders of the consul, the younger Marius, despite being cousin to the other consul Cn. Carbo.

There is evidence that Caesar had friends willing and able to supply him with slave-recruits for the army;[44] such persons could just as easily supply him with similar forces within the city. Caesar's resistance to Varius in 90 and his victory over him in 89 are not conceivable without a capacity for counter-violence. References to Caesar's *potentia* must be pragmatised in this context.[45] Varius did not long survive his conviction: whether Caesar was behind his savage death[46] or whether this could safely be left to the exiles' own initiative outside Rome has not come down to us. It was now possible for Caesar, having done great things in Rome, to spend some time in the army: here too, he was zealous to perform on a heroic scale.[47]

When Caesar announced his candidacy, not for the praetorship, but for the consulate, he was claiming what he had earned. He had assisted his brother in great matters of State; he had championed the extension of Roman citizenship only months after the total fail-

---

His denunciation of the younger Drusus in a *contio* as tribune of the plebs (*Orator* 213–4) is not to be interpreted as Marian or *popularis*: he appeals against Drusus (now dangerous to have known) to his father (tribune of the plebs 122, consul 112, censor 109), i.e. from the rash young *optimate* to the wise old *optimate*. As later in the case of P. Clodius after his tribunate in 58 until his death in 52, such a street- and locality-based organisation would tend to remain in being until decisively defeated. Thus it is proposed here that an organisation was constructed to resist Varius in 90, operated with great success in 89 and was defeated by Sulpicius' superior force in 88 and dissolved.

[44] Macrobius *Saturnalia* 1.11.32: "Bello sociali cohortium duodecim ex libertinis conscriptarum opera memorabilis uirtutis apparuit. C. Caesarem, cum milites in amissorum locum substitueret, seruos quoque ab amicis accepisse et eorum forti opera usum esse comperimus." B.R. Katz ("Caesar Strabo's Struggle for the Consulship—and More" *Rh.Mus.* 120 [1977], 58) may be accepted against T.J. Luce ("Marius and the Mithridatic Command" *Hist.* 19 [1970], n. 130). This is a reference to service in war. But friends like these would also be able to fund street-activity as well as contentious campaigns for the consulate.

[45] Cicero *Philippics* 11.11 (on L. Calpurnius Bestia's premature bid for the consulate in 43): "alter Caesar Vopiscus ille summo ingenio, summa potentia, qui ex aedilitate consulatum petit, soluatur legibus: quamquam leges eum non tenent propter eximiam, credo, dignitatem!" The *ingenium, potentia* and *dignitas* are here applied ironically to Bestia; the point of the ironic contrast, however, requires their genuine applicability to C. Caesar Strabo Vopiscus. Cf. Asconius *In Scaurianam* 25C: ". . . Gaius aedilicius quidem occisus est, sed *tantum* in ciuitate *potuit* ut causa belli ciuilis contentio eius cum Sulpicio tr. fuerit".

[46] The reference to punishment and torture (Cicero *De natura deorum* 3.81) cannot be official execution at Rome, since Varius had departed: Cicero's *excesserat* (*Brutus* 305) could only apply to death with the aid of an explanatory phrase or context (e.g. *Philippics* 2.12). By itself in Cicero *excedere* means 'to leave' (famously, *In Catilinam* 2.1). Marius made Caesar morally responsible (Valerius Maximus 9.2.2).

[47] Macrobius *Saturnalia* 1.11.32.

ure of his friend Drusus' programme. He had stood up for his friends and had entangled Varius in his own toils. Above all, he had helped cut back equestrian prominence and outmanoeuvred the great Marius. He had truly consular *dignitas* in terms of the Roman *hairesis*,[48] which must with all speed be confirmed by election to office.

3

The moment of Varius' exile was the time to conceive it, but not to implement it. Caesar's friends and rivals, including Sulpicius, were building up military repute; Caesar himself must seize the time before the war with the allies crumbled into a kind of peace—as it was largely to do by the end of 89; though sizable armies were still to be needed after that, the battles would be over for the time being. He was a man in a hurry. And yet the elections of 89 for one of the consulates of 88 are not a persuasive scenario.

Badian has shown how it could have been managed.[49] That is not the issue. Caesar was not to know that the elections for 88 would be postponed almost to the end of 89. A rational assessment earlier in the year of the situation and his chances would be called for—then and now:

[48] The young Scipio Aemilianus felt his own inadequacy in Roman eyes as being due to his neglect of the forum (Polybius 31.23.11).

[49] It is disturbing to the professional complacency of scholarship that the year in which Caesar Strabo sought to be consul has been in dispute without emergence of a consensus that would reinforce our commitment to dialectical progress. Nor do those who opt for a consulate in 88 and those who prefer a consulate in 87 necessarily agree each among themselves. The trail left by Photius from Diodorus Siculus (who must have *known*) has been beset by snares. The following are not exhaustive: E.S. Gruen "The *Lex Varia*", *JRS* 55 (1965), 72—in 88 for 87; E. Badian 'Quaestiones Variae' *Hist.* 18 (1969), 481–3—in 89 for 88; T.J. Luce "Marius and the Mithridatic Command", *Hist.* 19 (1970), 190–2—in 89 for 88; A.W. Lintott "The Tribunate of P. Sulpicius" *CQ* 21 (1971), 446–9—in 88 for 87; G.V. Sumner *The Orators in Cicero's Brutus* (1973) 105—accepts Badian and Luce, is unhappy about Lintott's reopening it; T.N. Mitchell "The *Volte-Face* of P. Sulpicius Rufus in 88 BC" *CP* 70 (1975), 197–204, esp. 201–2—in 88 for 87; B.R. Katz "Caesar Strabo's Struggle for the Consulship—and More" *Rh.Mus.* 120 (1977) 45–63—in 89 for 88; A. Keaveney "Sulla, Sulpicius and Caesar Strabo" *Lat.* 38 (1979), 451–460—in 89 for 88; J.G.F. Powell "The tribune Sulpicius" *Hist.* 39 (1990) 453—in 88 for 87. The very list tells a story; full discussion of the arguments is impossible here, and is perhaps best undertaken by a scholar without a vested interest.

1) Since both Caesar and L. Sulla were patricians, Caesar would have to campaign against Sulla. Another candidate, Q. Pompeius Rufus, was in *coitio* with Sulla. Sulla, moreover, had spent the war in high command and, apart from Cn. Pompeius Strabo, had done more than anyone militarily to win it. Could Sulla conceivably be displaced?
2) Since Caesar had done so much harm to Marius, support from that quarter was inconceivable. For what it is worth, moreover, a mediaeval epitome of Diodorus Siculus has Caesar basing his campaign on rivalry with Marius.[50] A consular campaign against Sulla without support from Marius was surely not on.
3) Caesar needed to be dispensed from the laws impeding his candidature for the consulate.[51] Would he wait till the end of 89 BC before seeking legislation for a campaign against the powerful *coitio* of Sulla and Q. Pompeius? Only if he had been promised the connivance of the consul conducting the election, Cn. Pompeius Strabo (consul 89), would he have the remotest chance. Of this there is no trace.[52]
4) But if Caesar was on a promise from Cn. Pompeius, it is Sulpicius the tribune who stopped him. In that case Sulla was the *direct* beneficiary of Sulpicius' intervention, and we should read of it as an exciting and morally problematic episode. We should be knee-deep in improving reflections about the mutability of human affections and fortune. Plutarch in his *Life of Sulla* is unaware of any impediment to the smooth election of Sulla with Q. Pompeius.[53]
5) Sulpicius' opposition to the candidacy of his friend Caesar on behalf of the alliance of his friend Q. Pompeius with Sulla for the consulate of 88 could hardly be represented by Cicero as a popular breeze that blew him further than he wished to go.[54] In terms

---

[50] Diodorus Siculus 37.2.12: Photius is manifestly inept (to the point of conflating the elder and the younger Marius), and yet it is hard to see what would lie behind any serious confusion here as to the structure of political rivalries. For chronology, of course, he is not to be held responsible.

[51] This is, admittedly, inferred from *Philippics* 11.11, strictly applying only to Bestia, the "parallel" case.

[52] Chr. Meier does, however, propose this (*Res publica amissa* [1966], p. 238 n. 187). After the death in battle of Cn. Pompeius' colleague L. Cato quite early in the year, there was no question at least who would be conducting the election. As to the *spes continuandi consulatus* in 88 (Velleius Paterculus 2.21.2), whatever the basis of this allegation against Cn. Pompeius, it came to nothing.

[53] 6.9–10.

[54] *De haruspicum responsis* 43: "Sulpicium ab optima causa profectum Gaioque Iulio

of the outcome it would be an optimate gale that deposited Sulla and Q. Pompeius—and their helmsman Sulpicius—safely in the consular harbour for which they had been heading all along. Mission accomplished! How could so successful an operation be the catalyst for Sulpicius' quarrel with his old friends, much less civil war? And yet Sulpicius' opposition to Caesar Strabo's consular campaign is so represented.[55]

Clearly Caesar stood forward early in 88 to claim one of the consulates of 87. In terms of the likely competition (Cn. Octavius and L. Cinna were the eventual winners; P. Servilius Vatia also stood)[56] Caesar's chances were good. But if the aged Marius were to stand in *coitio* with another candidate, the situation was otherwise. And the consuls Sulla and Q. Pompeius would look askance at *both* the candidature of Caesar Strabo *and* that of Marius, since Sulla might be displaced or recalled from the Mithridatic command at an early date by *either*. There is much more scope for popular breezes and misunderstandings. But this does not exhaust the complexities of the situation early in 88.

4

Caesar Strabo will have made his claim to early consideration for the presidential office of consul on the basis of public service. It was not merely military or oratorical or juristic performance that deserved the notice of the electorate but distinguished benefit to *res publica* in those capacities (*summa dignitas*). Caesar stepped forward, not as mere orator, but as destroyer of Q. Varius and *ipso facto* patron of his victims, whether specifically assisted by Caesar's efforts or now in exile. The emergence of Caesar's candidacy and a movement to recall

consulatum contra leges petenti resistentem longius quam uoluit popularis aura prouexit." The *optima causa* here is the *uera causa* of opposition to Strabo's extraordinary candidacy which Sulpicius shared with his colleague P. Antistius (*Brutus* 226). It is also to be identified with unspecified *bonae actiones* represented as the *beginnings* of Sulpicius' tribunician activity (Asconius *In Cornelianam* 64C).

[55] Asconius (25C) makes Caesar's contention with Sulpicius over the extra-legal campaign for the consulate the *causa belli ciuilis*; he makes Sulpicius' further progress from good to evil *actiones* the actual *initium bellorum ciuilium* (64C).

[56] Plutarch *Sulla* 10.3: the best resolution of a defective text.

exiles early in 88 should be taken as no coincidence. He was their man. And they were the ones he had not saved—yet.

That the exiles in question are primarily the persons condemned by the *quaestio* set up by Q. Varius should need no argument. It was those like L. Memmius,[57] L. Calpurnius Bestia,[58] and above all Sulpicius' friend C. Cotta,[59] once hoped-for successor to Drusus in the tribunate, whose plight concerned so many *optimates*; it was not about expelled Italians whose problems were now being solved anyway by other means.[60] A proposal was brought forward at this point recalling those who had not been permitted to plead their cause.[61] Since those who had come before the Varian *quaestio* had been "tried", it has been suggested that the proposal could not refer to these. But trials under mob-pressure would be polluted by that fact, at Rome as well as elsewhere. And variable pressure was applied: the accused Scaurus was actually acclaimed by the mob and his prosecution collapsed.[62] This very fact is an indicator of the vital role played by these mobs. The flexible M. Antonius[63] and the dogged and virtuous Q. Pompeius[64] were not convicted; others, many more than the few we are sure of, did not find favour; some will have anticipated their own conviction. The very fact that the term *ui eiecti* was later applied in another bill precisely to those who had been described as *quibus causam dicere non licuisset* in the first[65] should put

---

[57] Probably: accused (Sisenna frg. 44 apud *HRR* Peter), he may or may not be the Mummius (Achaicus!) in Appian *BC* 1.37. On the accused under the *Lex Varia*, see E.S. Gruen 'The *Lex Varia*', *JRS* 55 (1965), 59–73.

[58] Appian *BC* 1.37: he went into exile without pleading.

[59] Cicero *De oratore* 3.11; *Brutus* 303, 305; Appian *BC* 1.37: in the course of an impressive defence he openly attacked the *equites*, who supplied the jury, and left Rome before the *iudices* had voted. A published version was put out by L. Aelius Stilo (*Brutus* 205). Cotta maintained the philosophic *apatheia* of his uncle P. Rutilius Rufus, for whom he had spoken two years before, while his friends Caesar and Sulpicius were to turn to violence—eventually against each other.

[60] For argument that the exiles were Italian allies affected by the *Lex Licinia Mucia* of 95, see E. Badian 'Quaestiones Variae', *Hist.* 18 (1969), 487–90, reflecting E.S. Gruen's concerns ('The *Lex Varia*', *JRS* 55 [1965], 71–73), but not the pointlessness of further conjecture asserted by Gruen.

[61] *Ad Herennium* 2.45.

[62] Asconius *In Scaurianam* 22C; Valerius Maximus 3.7.8.

[63] Cicero *Tusculan Disputations* 2.57; Antonius absented himself from Rome in 90–89 (*Brutus* 304). He may not have been out of danger.

[64] Cicero *Brutus* 304. Pompeius stayed, perhaps at some risk, to pursue the consulate at the elections of 89. To what extent did he owe such security as he enjoyed in 90 to Caesar Strabo's organisation?

[65] *Ad Herennium* 2.45: the author is clear that despite an altered terminology, the

the identity of the exiles to rest: they were those who in one way or another were denied due process at trials held under the *lex Varia* in 90.

Here Q. Pompeius is moved into the spotlight. Like Sulpicius he was a friend of the exiles, and had indeed come just short of being one of them himself. It has been suggested attractively that Pompeius is the unknown proponent of the exiles' bill vetoed by Sulpicius and that this was the cause of the famous quarrel.[66] This must be dismissed on several considerations. 1) The quarrel is represented in our texts as Sulpicius' grievance against Pompeius; this scenario would tend rather to give Pompeius a grievance against Sulpicius. 2) Later in the year with Sulpicius dead and Caesar apparently neutralised, when Sulla and Pompeius were in full control at Rome, the recall of C. Cotta and the exiles was not carried through, and was still resisted by the consuls.[67] Cotta languished in exile till 82 and Sulla's second entry of Rome in arms. 3) A success for Caesar Strabo, reinforcing his claim to the consulate, was at no time in the interests of Sulla and his colleague and *adfinis* Pompeius, destabilising as it would do Sulla's military prospects. It is best to conclude that the first proposal to recall the exiles vetoed by Sulpicius was put up by one of the tribunes of 88 acting in Caesar's interest.

Sulpicius was still at one with the consuls of 88 in resisting Caesar's bid for the consulate: the rivalry of Sulpicius and Caesar and the anxieties of Sulla and Pompeius over Sulla's command gave edge to their proper and truly *optimate* opposition to any destabilisation of the *leges annales*. But Sulpicius' resistance could not rest on princi-

content (and therefore intention) of the law proposed by Sulpicius was substantively unchanged from that which he had vetoed. The author pardons him if there were circumstances dictating his word-play (like the change in Caesar's position after he had been driven from the streets?). It should be borne in mind that a book on rhetoric is not even likely to be a rhetorical book, and deserves all the consideration of a work of fact. The term *ui eiecti* echoes Cicero's "Cotta . . . eiectus est e ciuitate" (*De oratore* 3.11).

[66] R.G. Lewis "P. Sulpicius' law to recall exiles", *CQ* 48 (1998), esp. 199.

[67] Appian *BC* 1.63: the pressure on the consuls seems to have come mostly from the factional supporters of those who had been expelled as enemies by the Senate after Sulla and Pompeius returned to Rome in arms: the Aurelii Cottae are unlikely to have threatened assassination! But it would be difficult to frame legislation to restore their friends, the victims of the *Lex Varia*, and not their enemies the Marians: both could well be described as *quibus causam dicere non licuit* and as *ui eiecti*. Yet nothing was done for Rutilius Rufus, though he could have been covered under *ne quis iudicio publico circumueniatur*.

pled legality in the face of Caesar's power in the streets. Sulpicius must match him. His fellow-tribune P. Antistius, who was later to serve the regime (as cautiously as possible) in the "Marian" years of Cinna's continuous consulates,[68] acted with Sulpicius in arguing the case against Caesar's claim. Did he re-introduce Sulpicius to Marius? Certainly Sulpicius now organised gangs which defeated Caesar's in battle. Once Sulpicius was master of the streets of Rome, it was possible to take over himself the agenda of recalling the exiles relabelled as *ui eiecti.*

5

With Caesar Strabo eliminated from the equation, the issue of the Mithridatic command lay squarely between Sulla, the designated commander, and Marius, for whose revival Caesar's defeat was a catalyst. Sulpicius, without known street-activity in his past, had quite suddenly created a force that defeated Caesar's. Without positing too much at this stage of events, it is fair to say that the defeat of Caesar was pleasing to Marius and the equestrian former *iudices* and that they were prepared to think well of Sulpicius, who had achieved so much of what they wished. This is to put it at its minimum.

On the other side, Sulpicius' friends the consuls Q. Pompeius and Sulla were pleased enough to be rid of Caesar's campaign for the consulate of 87 and for the war in the East. Other leading senators will have felt differently: Caesar's brother Lucius (consul 90, censor 89) and his half-brother Q. Catulus (consul 102) would understandably not rejoice with Sulpicius in his victory on the streets. M. Antonius (consul 99, censor 97) had been prosecuted under the *lex Varia* and not convicted, though he spent some time away from Rome in 90–89.[69] P. Crassus (consul 97, censor 89) was colleague of L. Caesar in the censorship. All those who were opponents or potential vic-

---

[68] He was *iudex quaestionis* in 86 when he contracted a marriage-alliance with the young Pompeius, before him on a charge of receiving goods out of his father's peculation (Plutarch *Pompey* 4). Antistius was in good company with the consular and censor L. Marcius Philippus, the future consul Cn. Carbo and Q. Hortensius the orator in assisting the promising young man. It is interesting that Antistius was *aedilicius* still, not yet praetor, when he was put to death in 82 for Sullan sympathies (Velleius Paterculus 2.26; Appian *BC* 1.88). He may have over-calculated the risks and prospects at each stage.

[69] See n. 63.

tims of Q. Varius or close to them, all those who were among the *nobiles* who diminished equestrian participation in the courts through the *lex Plautia*, were at this time likely friends of Caesar Strabo and hostile to the organised *equites*—and Marius. They are the *principes* most likely to have supported the consul Sulla with *sententiae* when he entered Rome in arms shortly after this time. Certainly Marius thought so when he ordered the deaths of the above-mentioned four ex-consuls and Caesar Strabo on his re-entry into Rome at the end of 87.[70] These men will have been disinclined to support Sulpicius' further agenda in 88. Again, this is to put it at its minimum.

What support could Sulpicius still count on? L. Marcius Philippus (consul 91) had given hostile evidence against some of the Varian victims in 90,[71] including Q. Pompeius; he would be promoting the break up of Drusus' circle: the quarrel of Sulpicius and Caesar was grist to his mill. Why not Sulpicius versus Pompeius as the next step on Philippus' disintegrative agenda? Q. Mucius Scaevola, the Augur (consul 117) and L. Valerius Flaccus (consul 100, censor 97) had attested links with Marius.[72] And of course there was Sulpicius' close friend Q. Pompeius the consul still on board! So it was thought.

The chief plank in Sulpicius' platform needs no general discussion here. The proposal to enrol the new citizens in all thirty-five Roman electoral tribes was bold and statesmanlike.[73] In the present context three points need to be made: 1) the effect—and perhaps the intention—of the proposal was to outflank the Caesars, whose law conferred citizenship on the Italian *ciuitates* but restricted the weight of their vote; 2) on an acceptance of Cicero's claim that Sulpicius and the consul Q. Pompeius were politically *conjoined* down

[70] Appian *BC* 1.71–74; Livy *Per.* 80; Velleius Paterculus 2.22.

[71] Cicero *Brutus* 304. If Philippus (with or without others) were to support Sulpicius' proposal at this point, he would drive a wedge between Pompeius, against whom Philippus had given evidence like an accuser, and Pompeius' friend Sulpicius, who had to be delivered somehow to Marius. It is to be recalled that it was Philippus who as consul had threatened to seek an alternative source of *consilium publicum* in 91 (Cicero *De oratore* 3.2) and who at a later time improvised a delightful variation on the theme when he suggested sending out the young Pompey *pro consulibus* in 77 (Cicero *Pro Lege Manilia* 62). What Philippus did tactically, Sulpicius would do with moral passion.

[72] Scaevola's grand-daughter was married to Marius' son (Cicero *De oratore* 1.24 and 66; *Ad Atticum* 12.49.2) and Rutilius Rufus termed L. Valerius Flaccus (consul 100, censor 97) more servant than colleague to Marius (Plutarch *Marius* 28.5).

[73] G. De Sanctis must here be singled out *honoris causa* (*La guerra sociale* [1976] a fragment of his incomplete *Storia dei Romani*, 106–127, esp. 109–113).

to the moment of their quarrel,[74] Sulpicius counted on support from the consuls, Pompeius and his *adfinis* Sulla, in steering their joint programme through the senate; 3) the reform would make Marius master of the enlarged *comitia.*[75] Sulpicius could live with that. Neither his opponents in the Senate *nor his friends the consuls* could be expected to.

Caesar's bid for the consulate had exposed Marius' continuing lust for power and command. It had surfaced from time to time since 100 BC and had never really gone away.[76] When Sulpicius' proposal went to the Senate for a preliminary decree, it must have been coldly met by the Caesars and their set; but the consul Pompeius had no interest in pushing it through either, were it not for loyalty to his old friend. The great enterprise initiated by Drusus to bind all Italy in gratitude to the Senate would only culminate in Marius' gain and Sulla's loss. Pompeius could not do it: no senatorial decree was passed to endorse Sulpicius' law, and Sulpicius turned on Pompeius, turned on Sulla, and rejected the Senate as an appropriate source of *consilium publicum.* He had alternative friends lying in wait. He was still at heart an *optimate*; he could not set the sovereign People above all *auctoritas*;[77] he found it in the equestrian former *iudices* who consented to act *pro senatu*, to escort Sulpicius in all their *splendor* and to arm themselves against the consuls and Senate who had abdicated their

---

[74] *De amicitia* 2.

[75] Appian *BC* 1.55: the notices of Marius' motivation and the structural effect of the electoral distribution of the new citizens are intertwined with a narrative of the seduction of Sulpicius, which is retrospective defamation; cf. Plutarch *Marius* 35, and esp. *Sulla* 8.1; Velleius Paterculus 2.18.5–6 allows for a transformation from good to evil and gives Sulpicius, not Marius, the initiative. Our authors have worked from results to causes; Cicero *De haruspicum responsis* 43 outdoes all of them in subtlety and integrity in a sentence.

[76] T.J. Luce makes the case ("Marius and the Mithridatic Command" *Hist.* 19 [1970], 161–94), though he cannot be followed in every detail.

[77] Even in his latest manifestation, therefore, Sulpicius is not to be identified with the tradition of the Gracchi and Saturninus. There is no trace of popular sovereignty in his rhetoric or ideology. The old Roman citizens in the rural tribes are the one element, moreover, for which he does nothing. They are subsumed into a vast hegemonic scheme which reveals him as essentially true to Drusus' approach even in his 'Marian' phase.

[78] Sulla's baffled conservatism as master of Rome with full access to all the resources of *consilium publicum* in the later months of 88 tells the story. Appian's list of reforms (1.59) must be an anticipation of identical measures enacted by Sulla as dictator because Cinna as consul makes no attempt to reverse them; he seeks only to re-enact Sulpicius' law (here called Marius' plan) on citizenship prior to recalling the Marian exiles (1.64). And yet cancelling any measures passed by Sulla and Pompeius about senatorial *probouleusis* or tribunician power or centuriate voting would be a vital pre-requisite. (*Contra* A. Keaveney, with literature, "What Happened in

leadership. Sulpicius did have a point: what did the leading senators, the *principes ciuitatis*, plan to do instead?[78]

The tragedy of Sulpicius is as well known as the fate of *res publica* at the hands of Marius and Sulla. Q. Pompeius Rufus has been ignored. This good man was torn apart. As tribune in 99 with his colleague L. Cato (consul 89), he had taken the initiative to recall Q. Metellus Numidicus *before* it was politically feasible.[79] He was no time-server. As urban praetor he displayed a crabbed and truly Roman morality.[80] He had manfully and with limited resources of talent withstood and come safe out of a prosecution under the Varian law.[81] He had brought Sulla into the Drusan reformers' fold by marrying his promising and spirited son to Sulla's relentless and grasping daughter.[82] Now he became the victim of his old friend Sulpicius and the puppet of his new friend Sulla. His son lost his life to hirelings of his former friend.[83] He lent his *imperium* and *auctoritas* to Sulla's entry of Rome in arms;[84] what he had given to Sulla he lost himself. He became an object of pity to be somehow provided for.[85] In the last moments of his life he was the butt of a cruel charade enacted by soldiers at whose unmasking he saw not men of his own but Cn. Pompeius Strabo's.[86] He was too weak to be a martyr, though he may well have suffered more. For ourselves he is an object-lesson of the invidious ambiguity of the central position in a Münzerian cluster.

Two further measures of Sulpicius reflect his final position. The distribution of *libertini* through the 35 tribes[87] looks like a broadening of the civic body complementary to the similar distribution of Italian new citizens: as the Italians were to be participants in the

88?" *Eirene* 20 [1983], 71–3: it is, for example, astonishing that Sulla should have legislated an increase of 300 senators, a measure which "it is highly unlikely that Sulla had the time to actually put . . . into effect".)

[79] Orosius 5.17.11.

[80] Cicero *De oratore* 1.168; Valerius Maximus 3.5.2.

[81] Cicero *Brutus* 304. If Caesar Strabo supported Pompeius' defence, Pompeius' breach with him was another sacrifice to his alliance with Sulla. But this is conjecture.

[82] On the marriage, Appian *BC* 1.56; on Cornelia's conduct to her son, Valerius Maximus 4.2.7.

[83] Livy *Per.* 77; Velleius Paterculus 2.18; Plutarch *Sulla* 8.3.

[84] Appian *BC* 1.57–8.

[85] Appian *BC* 1.63.

[86] Appian *BC* 1.63; Valerius Maximus 9.7 Mil. Rom. 2; Livy *Per.* 77.

[87] Asconius *In Cornelianam* 64C; Livy *Per.* 77.

civic life of the Roman community without future restriction on behalf of old Romans, so would the inhabitants of the metropolis, the tradesmen, skilled craftsmen and professionals, of slave-origin. If it was wrong to confine Italians to eight or ten electoral tribes, it was similarly so to confine *libertini* to four. And yet if we consider the likely composition of Sulpicius' armed band, we may reflect that such a redistribution would upgrade it from muscle acting on the whole electorate to an actual presence in every voting unit.

Sulpicius' proposal to expel from the Senate members even minimally in debt was obviously vindictive.[88] It rendered senators liable to the most minute scrutiny and reflected on the *dignitas* of the order and every member of it. It was seriously vexatious. In a society in which monetary liquidity was low, persons with land and assets sufficient to cover liabilities might well be unable momentarily to meet demands at the best of times. They would be exposed to *moral* correlation at their expense with the members of an order that dealt in money: the *fides* and the *dignitas* of Sulpicius' *pro senatu, equites* domiciled in Rome, would overshadow those of senators. In 88, however, the situation was in practice even worse: the destruction and expense involved in the *Bellum Italicum* will have hit senators hard. The more zealous they were for *res publica* the more likely they were to have funded troops, released slaves, mortgaged property, exposed themselves to the oppression of those very *faeneratores* who had killed A. Sempronius Asellio and supported Sulpicius now. But above all, this exposure would apply to Caesar Strabo and his friends who had financed street-activity.[89] For precisely the same reason the once wealthy Sulpicius was found at his death to be deeply in debt himself.[90]

6

The return to Rome in arms of the consuls Sulla and Pompeius put an end to the activities of Sulpicius and Marius now in a close and frank alliance to control the public space of Rome. During the advance of Sulla's army the Senate sent orders to desist.[91] In doing

---

[88] Plutarch *Sulla* 8.2.

[89] Cf. n. 44.

[90] For his wealth, Velleius Paterculus 2.18.5; for his debts, Plutarch *Sulla* 8.2.

[91] Appian *BC* 1.57 refers to three sets of emissaries from the Senate and a fourth sent by Marius and Sulpicius as though from the Senate; at 57–59, Pompeius is

so it placed itself at the disposal of the tribune who had denied its *auctoritas*, infringed the *dignitas* of its members, intimidated the consuls, and suspended one of them from the exercise of his presidential office. The actions of the consuls, especially Sulla, on their return now reveal *their* perception of senatorial *indignitas*.

Sulla convened the Senate to a session at which he proposed that twelve Roman citizens, including Sulpicius tribune of the plebs, be judged *hostes*.[92] There was general unease about the proceedings, which is crystallised by the recorded words of the aged Q. Mucius Scaevola the Augur (consul 117), no other senator daring to oppose Sulla's will.[93] On being asked to speak, Scaevola refused to deliver a *sententia*,[94] i.e. to participate in a judgment on the civic *caput* of the named men. To him it was a breach of Roman civil rights. He went on to praise Marius as saviour and *ipso facto* not an enemy.[95] He was therefore willing to participate in a senatorial *praeiudicium*. He protested against the pressure exercised by Sulla's troops posted outside.[96] Implicitly Sulla's *praesidium* had simply replaced Sulpicius'.

It was the last voice of another era, an era that had quite recently been represented by the voices, clear and confident, of L. Crassus and M. Scaurus *princeps senatus*. The acquiescent silence of the leading senators at the meeting called by Sulla, *their liberator from Sulpicius'*

---

fully associated with his colleague's actions; Plutarch *Sulla* 9.2 covers all communications in advance by declaring the Senate subject to the orders of Marius and Sulpicius; his narrative ignores his protagonist's consular colleague.

92 Appian *BC* 1.60 specifies charges: sedition, making war on the consuls, summoning slaves to insurrection by the pronouncement of freedom, and gives the fullest list of names; Plutarch *Sulla* 10.1 has Sulla summon the Senate and secure a death-sentence—the rest is personal; Velleius Paterculus 2.19.1 has a charge of *nouae res* (equivalent to Appian's *stasis*) and adds confirmatory legislation of their *exilium* ('lege lata'); Cicero *Brutus* 168 (on Q. Rubrius Varro), Livy *Per.* 77, Valerius Maximus 3.8.5 and Florus 2.9.8 present the same three elements of the formula: *senatus*, *iudicare* and *hostes* (on this see R.A. Bauman 'The *hostis* declarations of 88 and 87 BC' *Ath.* 51 [1973], 270–93; cf. B.R. Katz 'The First Fruits of Sulla's March' *L'Ant.Class.* 44 [1975], 100–25; on the possible role of the enigmatic pontifex maximus Q. Mucius Scaevola [consul 95], cousin once removed (or more) to the Augur, see Bauman *Lawyers in Roman Republican Politics* [1983], 405ff.).

93 Valerius Maximus 3.8.5: "cuius (Sullae) uoluntati nullo obuiam ire audente."

94 *Ibid.*: ". . . solus Scaevola de hac re interrogatus sententiam dicere noluit."

95 *Ibid.*: ". . . numquam tamen efficies ut . . . Marium, a quo urbs et Italia conseruata est, hostem iudicem". A senatorial *praeiudicium* leaving the jury of a court still free to come to a different verdict was normal: e.g. the Senate's pronouncements in anticipation of Catiline's trial for *repetundae* in Africa (Asconius citing and commenting on Cicero *In toga candida* 85, 89C).

96 *Ibid.*: "'licet' inquit (Scaevola) 'mihi agmina militum, quibus curiam circumsedisti, ostentes . . .'"

oppression, is eery.[97] The older generation and its successors had been poignantly juxtaposed in love and reverence by Cicero's art in the dialogue *De oratore*, which is all about *government by talking*. The Republican commitment of the younger generation has in a few short years been transformed into something else: physical force which the teeming orators of the *Brutus* cannot quite disguise: they are so often *absent* now. The destined orators and statesmen, who were to re-enact in *conjunction* the mutual goodwill of L. Crassus, M. Antonius, M. Scaurus (near, though absent) and Q. Scaevola the Augur, had turned into victims of an inexorable process in which they were not quite innocent participants. Cicero celebrates the premature death of Crassus, which would forestall his witnessing the murder of Caesar Strabo, the exile of C. Cotta and the *indignity* inflicted on his own friends by P. Sulpicius before violent death took him too.[98] "Poena temeritatis non sine magno rei publicae malo constituta"[99] is surely the *hostis* declaration: it was the way Sulpicius went that was worst of all. It was not Sulla's "march on Rome" but what he did when he got there that foreboded public ill.

The defeated faction was not cowed at this time. They exerted pressure for the exiles' return and conspired against the consuls' lives: a tribune killed in 91, a praetor in 89, soon a consul. Appian defines them, male and female, by their wealth (*BC* 1.62). They are the equestrian alternative already astir to co-opt Cinna and bring back Marius (*ibid.* 64). And the courts? The age of *saccularii* had dawned:[100] but Sulla lived.

---

[97] Sulla's answer to senatorial emissaries requiring him to explain his advance on Rome was: 'To liberate the fatherland from tyrants' (Appian *BC* 1.57). Not only do we hear nothing of Scaevola the Pontifex or L. Marcius Philippus or L. Valerius Flaccus, statesmen for whom flexibility—and sometimes *concordia*—was a strong positive, but nothing of Marius' *inimici* either (cf. n. 70 above, and text), who should have been having a field-day.

[98] *De oratore* 3.9–12.

[99] *Ibid.* 11.

[100] See n. 10.

THE LAW IS NOT MOCKED: STRAIGHTENING OUT A CROOKED WILL (PHAEDRUS 4.5)

John Henderson

Introduction

This is not quite a paper about Roman law, neither is it quite a paper about the life of Rome. It is about a story written up for Romans, in Latin verse, at some point in the reign of Tiberius, a story which has Aesop turn up in Athens to trounce the best (legal) minds in the world at their own game. It's a long time since the story engaged (m)any minds, but where there's a will . . .[1]

The story comes to us sealed with matching distichs of prelude and valediction, telling us what to read, and what to make of it. But, mind, the promythium also opens the story to readers and enfolds us, too, while the epimythium pins each/every one of us to the hermeneutic aporias that lurk in any antithesis between consensual folly and solitary wit. For a start, the moment you see that common opinion, not to mention commonsense, has always been bound to agree that this fable is a cultural cliché, you'll be obliged to choose—am I a sheep if I don't find a different truth (perhaps, that culture is cliché; or—i.e.?—that truth arises in riddling difference, but decays in social exegesis . . .)? Pressurized decoding in a contest over conformity is a surefire way to make an audience join in and play too. A law of storytelling, here underlined in folklore about law.

I hope you'll see the point of, or a point in, setting Latin and English translation side by side: indeed I ought also to render into Attic (but I have examined Greek Composition with John Crook, and know better)—and perhaps you would enjoy La Fontaine's version as much as La Fontaine does:

> Une histoire des plus gentilles
> et qui pourra plaire au lecteur
>
> (*Fables* 2.20.5–6)[2]

---

[1] Henderson 1976: 134–46 foregathered cultural/linguistic data.

[2] Pinder 1869: 274 picked out 4.5 for commentary, avowing admiration: stuff meant for boys?

Let me preface the fable with my own cautionary moral. (Try stopping me.) If the tale is, like all tales, what each, or every, one of us makes of the tale—if that is what tales are, and what they are for, first and foremost, namely to lay on us quasi-distantiated provocations to contest or abide by power relations—, then this particular tale is (I propose at any level, across the range from collective affirmation to hermeneutic idiosyncrasy) not last or least about the impossibility of hiving off questions of law from the construal of life, in whatever Aesopian 'Athens' or Phaedrian 'Rome' our social context gives us to dwell in: the self-confuting irony of the mantra *iuris consultus abesto.*

Plus esse in uno saepe quam in turba boni
narratione posteris tradam breui.
  Quidam decedens tres reliquit filias,
unam formosam et oculis uenantem uiros,
at alteram lanificam et frugi rusticam,
deuotam uino tertiam et turpissimam.
  harum autem matrem fecit heredem senex
sub condicione totam ut fortunam tribus
aequaliter distribuat sed tali modo
ni data possideant aut fruantur, tum simul
habere res desierint quas acceperint
centena matri conferant sestertia.
  Athenas rumor implet. mater sedula
iuris peritos consulit, nemo expedit
quo pacto non possideant quod fuerit datum
fructumue capiant, deinde quae tulerint nihil
quanam ratione conferant pecuniam.
  postquam consumpta est temporis longi mora
nec testamenti potuit sensus colligi,
fidem aduocauit iure neglecto parens.
  seponit moechae uestem, mundum muliebrem,
lauationem argenteam, eunuchos, glabros,
lanificae agellos, pecora, uillam, operarios,
boues, iumenta et instrumentum rusticum,
potrici plenam antiquis apothecam cadis,
domum politam et delicatos hortulos.
  sic destinata dare cum uellet singulis
et approbaret populus qui illas nouerat,
Aesopus media subito in turba constitit,
"O si maneret condito sensus patri,
quam grauiter ferret quod uoluntatem suam
interpretari non potuissent Attici!"
  rogatus deinde soluit errorem omnium,
"Domum et ornamenta cum uenustis hortulis

et uina uetera date lanificae rusticae,
uestem, uniones, pedisequos et cetera
illi assignate uitam quae luxu trahit,
agros, bouile et pecora cum pastoribus
donate moechae.
nulla poterit perpeti
ut moribus quid teneat alienum suis.
deformis cultum uendet ut uinum paret,
agros abiciet moecha ut ornatus gerat,
at illa gaudens pecore et lanae dedita
quacumque summa tradet luxuriae domum.
sic nulla possidebit quod fuerit datum
et dictam matri conferent pecuniam
ex pretio rerum quae uendiderint singulae".
Ita quod multorum fugit imprudentiam
unius hominis repperit sollertia.

Not infrequently, there's more good in one man than in a crowd.
This I shall pass on to generations to come in a story that will not detain
you
long.
There was a man died leaving three daughters.
One was a good-looker, eyes locked onto all the guys;
while the other was into her woolwork, countrified and productive;
the third and last was a slave to the bottle, ghastliest of all.
Well, he made the girls' mother his heir, did the old man,
with the stipulation that she must share out among the trio
the whole inheritance equally, but in such a way that
they neither own nor have the benefit of what they are given;
next, as soon as
they were no longer in possession of what they received,
they must fetch their mother 100,000 sesterces apiece.
The talk fills Athens. Mother conscientiously
consults those versed in the law, but not one of them sorts out
on what basis the girls would not own what they were given
or have the benefit of it; let alone how, having come away with nothing,
they should then, on any scheme, fetch the money along.
After a lengthy interval of wasted delay
and no one managing to gather the thinking in the will,
the parent set the law aside and turned for help to equity.
She puts on one side for the slut the raiment, the toiletries,
bathroom silver, eunuchs, plucked pages;
for the one into textiles, the fields, livestock, farm, labourers,
oxen, draught animals, and farm implements;

for the boozer, the cellar-full of vintage casks,
spanking mansion, and dainty pleasure-gardens.
She was meaning to hand over the batches she had settled on like this,
and the people were backing her up, knowing the girls for what they were,
when Aesop suddenly showed up in the middle of the crowd:
"Good grief, if the father still kept thinking in the grave,
how crushed he would be about his will,
which Athenian wits couldn't manage to figure out!"
Pressed for an answer, he unravels what had thrown one and all:
"The mansion and trappings, with the luscious gardens and all,
and the old wines, you must give to her of the woolwork, the country cousin;
the raiment, pearls, train of attendants, et cetera,
put down for the one who drags her life in luxury;
fields, ox-pen, and stock complete with stockmen,
present to the slut.
None of them will manage to put up
with having what is foreign to her character.
The ugly one will sell the finery to get hold of wine;
the slut will get shot of the fields so she can doll herself up;
while the one who thrills over stock, slave to her precious wool,
will hand over the mansion of excess for any amount you come up with.
In this way not one of them will own what she was given,
and the money as stated they shall fetch to their mother
from the price paid for what they have each sold."
And so it was, that what escaped the dull wits of so many
was tracked down by the shrewdness of one man.[3]

1

The intro proclaims this a story about the long and short of stories and storytelling. It will be the second *longest* fable in Phaedrus (at least as his battered collection of five books of Aesopica in verse—upwards of 150, perhaps 200, tales—comes down to us).[4] Does it

[3] The text is tralatician (disputed: v. 15 *non* Pithou: *si non* PR^{GuVi}, *ni* Havet [cf. v. 10]; v. 22 *eunuchos, glabros* Havet: *eunuchos · glabros* PR^{Vi}, *eunuchos glabros* most editors; v. 38 *bouile* is my correction of *buuile* Havet: *utiles* PR^{GuVi}, *uites* Pithou, *et uillam* Bentley, *utilia* Ellis, et al.; v. 42 *gerat* Dressler: *paret* P [from v. 41], *imperet* Bothe, *ferat* Postgate (hesitantly); v. 44 *luxuriae domum* [*luxoriae d.* PR^{GuVi}]: *luxuriam domus* Postgate, *luxuriam et domum* Hare. See Henderson 2000: 245–6 for the references). The translation is mine.

[4] Henderson 1999.

need explicit recommendation because it flags and then flops?[5] Is that why we get epimythium as well as promythium, both pure and simple, both of them short but sweet? Or is the thinking that Phaedrus will overblow the fourfold repetition of the three characterisations of the three daughters and the problem of carving up and customizing the three shares of the estate destined for them because his storyline is '*about*' overplaying the simple testamentary kernel? In that case, he must *mean* to fill our ears with his triangular triplications in order to maximise the triumph of the one sage verdict over the many attempts by many would-be exegetes who have been stumped through many a dark hour.

So, the thought runs on, the tale projects power onto its coordinates of space, time, and language. Aesop appears 'suddenly' and speaks out straight and strong: we are told, not that his speaking *is* speaking, but instead that it is 'constitutive'—sets up on a sure basis, is unshakably secured, for good, by the steady stance of its author—and is set to dispel the unstable floundering of 'them all' (*constitit*, v. 29). Phaedrus 'fills' his poem with clamouring guesswork from the legal experts, 'not one of them' able to speak a word aloud (vv. 13–14).[6] All they can do is re-wind, and it takes "a lengthy interval of wasted delay" (v. 18) for the narrator to act out for us the irritating stalling which is the price of build-up toward the instantaneous intervention of the hero.

We can choose whether to see this version as taking far too long for our liking in order to communicate how excruciating the fix was, *in* the story, or else to thank Phaedrus for cutting a long story short like this, and letting us stay *out* of the fix. And it can dawn on any or all of us how much of storytelling is about baiting listeners, how many tales make a point of telling us that we're lucky not to be in them, how odd it is that we ever collude with the unfounded prevarication that we are not.[7]

Back in the story line, we are yet to reach the point where the 'many' become 'all'. As the preliminary localization of 'Athens' gives way to Aesop's scorn for 'Attic' wits (vv. 13, 32), the widow wins

[5] Cf. 3 *Prol.* 34, *breui docebo*, 3.7.1, *breuiter proloquar*, 3.10.59–60, *breuitate nimia quoniam quosdam offendimus* (the longest editorial, the longest beast-fable, and the longest poem of all), with Henderson 2000: 37, 41, 200 nn. 9, 11.

[6] On *rumor* in anecdotes, cf. esp. 5.7.29, *App.* 10.6, with Henderson 2000: 113, 123, 142, 228 n. 29.

[7] See Henderson 2000: index, s.v. storytelling, turning on the reader.

backing from the citizen body as such—a *populus* mocked as mere *turba* (vv. 28–9)—precisely so that the one-off sage can trounce 'everyone' (*omnium*, v. 33).[8] This public opinion is in full possession of all the relevant facts (*nouerat*, v. 28) but unable to handle the question (cf. *rogatus*, v. 33). Their collective responsibility—their role in this narration—should be to supplement (match, complete, model, convey, inculcate) 'mother-love'. They must stand in for their fellow and peer, preserve the structuring of one family configuration in the name of them all. They must vindicate the viability of society as an orderly system, authorised to write the past, through the interpretation of the present, onto the disposition of the future. But it takes the marginal outsider without standing or share in the city to (re-)constitute Athens, its fathers, mothers, families and fortunes. We would otherwise have no story, if family and families could sort themselves out . . .[9]

Here at the heart of Phaedrus' fable, the emphasis on 'all or nothing' city-state-wide totalization feeds into a telling extrapolation of the frame's promise of 'brevity': wherever we turn there will be more implied than stated, more to unpack than the narration will spell out, larger meanings than a few words suggest. Something (of greater dimensions, of more than ephemeral pertinence) is getting *said*, and it concerns 'everyone'. The story *names* 'Aesop' and 'Athens', and (or but) fastens upon one everyman, his wife and daughters. Yes, the story must function within the specified setting. But it exceeds its setting, too. It *is* a fable, and, besides, this is Aesop in Phaedrus' *Latin*, this Athens scans in *senarii*. The poem stages the oral intervention of the sage in that agora beneath the Acropolis; but it is written at Rome, when Athens was part of the Empire of Caesar Tiberius, and Aesop a transplanted figure of parables for the Latin West. It reads as a Roman fable—but is it then (not) about Athens, about Rome, or neither about Athens nor Rome, or the cultural translatability of 'Greece' through Rome?

[8] Aesop in Athens: 3.14.1–2, *quidam . . . Atticus/Aesopum*, Henderson 1976: 99, and 2000: 189–90 (on 1.2).

[9] Conversely, the law would boss domestic conflicts only when its own codes of honour failed: esp. Rei 1998: 99.

2

To be brief, Athens of fabulous yesteryear is where lessons of people power unmasked as mob incompetence were born, as the other side of the coin of Attic invention of democratic self-congratulation. On the other hand, triumph of 'the one' over 'the many' (vv. 48–9) is what collapse of the Roman Republic taught the imperial Rome of Caesar Augustus. Under his successor Tiberius, the rudiments of political thought (what matters most?) could align Athens with Rome as cities singing the same song—the (irredeemable) failure of Athenian demos mapping straight onto the (rectified) flawed forum of the Roman *populus*. The collected lore of the Greek street corner could be looted for the libraries of the Roman mansion, and our fable could be filched from the mythic iconoclasm of the rootless slave sage, whose move from the wings instantly turns the masters of western civilization into a rabble of dunces to right and to left (vv. 28–9). His poke at the pretensions of propertied culture could be conscripted by the literate establishment of the eternal superpower, and so it is that the folk-hero gets to be lip-synched by his caricature: Phaedrus.

The Roman fabulist was no Athenian, and, likely enough, no Greek ('Thracian', he tells those who take him at his word; but Roman slave names were a master's whim, no ethnic guarantee); but neither was he 'Phrygian', unlike Aesop, the Greek nowhereman (so Phaedrus, for what it may be worth, also takes care to point out to us).[10] What we know of this author—on the frail (?) basis of the heading of his main MS—is that Phaedrus was a former slave of the imperial palace: 'freedman of Augustus'.[11] We must guess what he is up to in Tiberius' Rome; what sort of a project these 'fables' could have meant or managed to be. Most obviously, this is relaxed entertainment branded as minor verse, and its literate readers will identify with their own stake in the serious business of safe conveyance of a considerable estate. Poetential subversion is easily recuperated without fuss, since these are silly somebody-elses, not Romans; since this is only one trivial, perhaps hum-drum, 'mini-story' in a miscellany of a couple of hundred; and since this narration insists on thrusting forward, as its reassuring spine, sponsorship of the 'thinking' of

[10] 3 *Prol.* 56; 52, cf. Henderson 2000: 88, 212 n. 67; 62, 79, 88, 208 n. 39.
[11] Henderson 1999: 308 n. 4.

the Father, as attested in his testament: *testamenti . . . sensus* (v. 19) ~ *sensus patri* (v. 30).[12]

Naturally, Aesopic fables are awash with demonstrations that tales which side with the powerful must court and expose anxiety, vulnerability, orientation toward the powerless; that is even part of their definition (as Phaedrus explained, or kidded, in his third Prologue).[13] So we should not altogether lose sight of the send-up of Attic 'haves' repetitiously relished by this narration. And not only is it unclear 'whose' story this is, but Phaedrus has at the start of this fourth book of fables just pressed the issue on every reader. He says he had meant to stick at Book III, and leave plenty for others to come (cf. 3 *Epil.* 11–7); but "how will they guess what I left out and give it their own individual moral and tone?" Phaedrus will deliver afficionadoes a fourth helping—"of what I dub 'Aesopian', not 'Aesop's', fables,/because he showed not too many, whereas I'm planting loads more,/working with the ancient format, but with fresh topics" (4 *Prol.* 1–7; 10–13).[14] It follows that we have been alerted to an abyssal impossibility if we try to decide whether a particular fable is 'Aesop's' or 'Aesopian'—whether it carries the distinctive print of Aesop or the hallmark of Phaedrus.

As it happens, Phaedrus experts judge 4.5 'Aesopian'.[15] It is enticing bait for 'either-or-ist' thinking, bent on discriminating between Athenian and Roman 'elements' in the fable's handling and cultural assumptions, especially in the area of Law. As if the fable is a problem (as if it just *is* a problem), as if this is the issue, and that is the way to its 'solution'.

3

To sketch out lines of argument, let us start from reasons why this can not be an Attic story. Athenians who died without sons did

---

[12] Cf. Jennings 2000: 58–82, 'Author(izing) the Hero', esp. 66, 'Who owns (folk) wisdom?'.

[13] Henderson 2000: esp. 2–3.

[14] The phrase *res nouae* can't entirely shed its usual sense of (political) 'revolution'.

[15] E.g. Perry 1965: xcv, n. 3, "obviously late and of Roman invention" (because Aesop is in Athens). Cf. Nøjgaard 1967: 2, 127. Guaglianone 1970–1 attempts a survey of Phaedrus' fables where quasi-legal proceedings appear, and suggests influence from Roman declamation: systemic slippage between script and intent made the testament a favourite scenario (Bonner [1977] 313–7).

indeed need to make their will known, and even made wills.[16] If a father without sons wanted to snub shameful daughters, his will would run into a wall of resistance, and risk being set aside in court, with the dirty washing bringing *real* shame on the family.[17] In any case, he could make no woman, not even his widow, his heir.[18] And the problem of 'marrying' daughters to estate could not even begin to arise in anything like the form envisaged in the story. Instead, this is where the (in)famous mechanism of the Athenian 'epiklerate' kicked in—and spawned deliberation, consternation, and (not least) litigation. The estate must pass through the daughters to those sons that they will bear to the closest patrilateral relatives that are now obliged to wed the girls. Somehow all the players must adjust to the disruption that buys continuity of the family substance and eventual retrieval of patriarchal succession. Distinctively Attic law to the rescue![19] If the tale is about looking for a way for a father to beat 'the system', then it can't work in Athens.

Or, rather, Phaedrus' effort is a *pis aller* that does drag in 'Athens', but only by transmogrifying it out of all recognition. By the same token, features of his poem which emphasise 'Rome' may be marking cultural translation, casual or designed, and serve to open the story to pertinence to Roman readers, via detour to Athens. Thus the currency of *centena sestertia* (v. 12) doesn't convict Phaedrus of abysmal failure to rustle up some authentic Attic drachs![20] Less superficially, perhaps, the 'legal' phrasing in the archaism (*ni*) and disjunctive precision of phrase *ni data possideant aut fruantur* (v. 10) colours the story 'Roman', and not *not* about Roman law.[21] But how

---

[16] Cf. Harrison 1968: 88, Lacey 1968: 88.

[17] Such daughters must inherit: Isaeus 3.42, Lacey 1968: 139–40. Such wills set aside: Ps.-Aristotle, *Problems* 29.3, Harrison 1968: esp. 151–3. In Roman fiction and fact alike, the *Querela inofficiosi testamenti* was a specially prolific generator of dispute: Berger 1953: 665, Champlin 1991: 115.

[18] Cf. Just 1989: esp. 95.

[19] Lacey 1968: esp. 139–40, MacDowell 1978: esp. 95–8. Scafuro 1997: 281–305, 'Disputes about *epikleroi*', shows how much manoeuverability could be found, 'behind closed doors', in the juggling of epiklerate along with other avenues, in particular adoption, so as to accommodate specific factors not necessarily excluding personal preferences; and shows how Roman theatre, and self-congratulatory modern criticism, dealt with its 'translatability'.

[20] The Roman round figure of 100,000 sesterces loudly advertises 'a fortune' (the traditional threshold for membership of the first class at the *Comitia Centuriata*): e.g. Catullus 23.26, Juvenal 1.92, Macrobius 2.4.61.

[21] *ni*: Ritschl 1868: esp. 625–6, Fordyce on Catullus 61.146. *possideant* and esp. *fruantur* make distinctively Roman noises: cf. Gardner 1986: 163, "The interests of

superficial, and how structural, is which feature? When Aesop reaches for the epitaph formula on 'sentience in the grave' (v. 30) to spank Athens, for example, it flags up bi-cultural valency across the Graeco-Roman divide.[22] If the mother's role in 4.5 is conceivable within the terms of Roman reality, as *heres fiduciaria* charged to see the estate does reach the children as it must and as *pater* ordains, the sticking-point is still that a chasm yawns where male family and friends would have to be, in whatever city.[23] If the Roman principle of joint 'universal succession' between heirs "ran counter to the natural desire of testators to leave the house to John and the best tea-set to Mary, and so on", then the story reads as a sardonic pseudo-plot to outwit the system.[24] But in that case, we know perfectly well that worrying how to give siblings 'equal' shares is not a Roman preserve, but precipitates cases and stories in every 'Athens' under the sun.[25] The aporia, clearly enough, is to tell apart 'surface detail' of Phaedrus' poem, and 'structural core' of Aesop's (putative) fable.

If we squeeze 4.5 for what *could* derive from a fable found in Phaedrus' usual Greek source of Aesopica, and so (arguably) at one remove from Greek folklore, we can point to the abstract 'story pattern' of consulted experts outdone by oddball Aesop, as found in (e.g.) 3.3, a story which *is* attested in Greek.[26] And of course the

---

children might be safeguarded by leaving their mother only the usufruct of the property, but it was not uncommon for the mother to be made an heir"; Saller 1994: 174, Johnston 1999: 47, on *Digest* 33.2, where *paterfamilias* leaves usufruct to his widow for life, but ownership to his children. McGinn 1998: 110–11 sketches how sensible Romans could take "the most practical course" and "leave . . . the mother a high degree of flexibility".

[22] E.g. Plato, *Menexenus* 248b, Sulpicius (Cicero) *Ad Familiares* 4.5.6, Lattimore 1942: 55–7, Lier 1903: 54–5.

[23] *Heres fiduciaria*: Crook 1967: 125, Daube 1969: 96, Champlin 1991: 121 and n. 67. On the whole topic of 'women in Roman succession': Crook 1986; and on Roman wills and widows in particular: Champlin 1991: 120–6. Pressing Phaedrus' Rome for topical salience would lead us to (e.g.) Dio 56.10.2, on the Augustan laws of 9 BCE that fine-tuned adjustment to the exclusion of élite women being instituted as an heir: Gardner 1986: 78; to Justin *Institutes* 2.23.1 (with Moyle's note ad loc.), on Augustan legislation binding the heir to transfer the estate just as directed by the will; etc. Certainly, the *condicio impossibilis* was a distinctive clause within testamentary law: Justin, *Institutes* 2.14.10, *pro non scripto habetur*. But the *problem* arises wherever people try to read a last will and testament.

[24] Crook 1967: 120.

[25] Equal shares: Saller 1994: 164; kinds of division among Roman children: Champlin 1991: 112. Even where primogeniture prevails, 'equalizing' shifts of palliation always lurk, infiltrating *those* systems: see below.

[26] Henderson 1976: 45–52, cf. Plutarch, *Banquet of Seven Sages* 3.149c.

theme of the baffling bequest did feature in Aesop as in any body of folklore:

> A dying farmer tells his three sons a treasure is buried among the vines. They dig over the whole vineyard but find nothing. So the vines yield a crop way more abundant and profitable than ever before, and they realise . . .
>
> (Aesopica 42 Perry)[27]

This 'parallel', however, raises the question of the 'punch line' (through its own self-denial). Speculating whether Aesop's 'solution' suits one city or language significantly better than the other (from our point of view, *an* other) leads us into a very tight hermeneutic circle. We'll wait longer than the story says Athens did before some shrewd sage comes along to excogitate a subtle Greek original which Phaedrus has failed to deliver into his dull-witted Latin! For there's precious little drollery about Phaedrus' Latin when the enigmatic stipulation is decoded: "sic nulla possidebit quod fuerit datum/et dictam matri conferent pecuniam/ex pretio rerum quae uendiderint singulae" (vv. 45–7). How is this a clever play on words, on concepts, or even on legal terminology, let alone one which would, or could not, go (back) into Greek satisfactorily?

4

No, it's not just my lousy 'translation' to blame. If the fable wants to show off verbal/discursive dexterity, we are still looking for its scornful 'Aesop' to save the day: even an expert can see that the lone parent is merely authorized to *violate* the stipulation of the will (its *condicio*, v. 8). She is not to put the provisions of the will into operation, to the best of her ability, but to set up its first provision, then stand well back, and wait for the second provision to eventuate, under its own momentum.

Once you let yourself think at all about any of these considerations, and that is, after all, what the suspenseful stage-business of the consultation sequences rather obliges you to do, it will be obvious that Aesop's solution is porous. It will only bite if the girls have the default clause imposed on them, *scilicet* they must live with what

---

[27] Cf. Aesopica 703 Perry (below), Grimm, *Kinderundhausmärchen* 124 (with Bolte-Polivka's commentary), etc., Lockwood 1921. Stories rarely specify a *written* testament.

they're given, or, *failing that*, sell up and forfeit the proceeds to mother. Now would a shrewd narrator (like you, like me) be content to leave slack in the system (like this)? . . .

Fortunately, this is not the only (mug's) game in storytelling town. Here is a parable which will make everyone wonder if anyone (else) gets it:

> There was once a Sufi who wanted to make sure that his disciples would, after his death, find the right teacher of the Way for them. He therefore, after the obligatory bequests laid down by law, left his disciples seventeen camels, with this order: "You will divide the camels among the three of you in the following proportions: the oldest shall have half, the middle in age one third, and the youngest shall have one ninth".
>
> . . . The disciples were. . . . amazed at such an inefficient disposition. . . . Some said . . ., others sought advice and then said . . .; others were told by a judge . . .; and yet others held that the will was null and void because its provisions could not be executed. . . . Everyone they tried failed, until they arrived at the door of . . . Hazrat Ali.
>
> He said: "This is your solution. I will add one camel to the number. Out of the eighteen camels you will give half—nine camels—to the oldest disciple. The second shall have a third of the total, which is six camels. The last disciple may have one ninth, which is two camels. That makes seventeen. One—my camel—is left over to be returned to me."
>
> This was how the disciples found the teacher for them.
>
> (Idries Shah 1974: 111)

Whatever *this* story is 'about', and of course I know it only in English translation (assuming that it is not the brainchild of Idries Shah), and of course I have no idea at all whether it gains anything or everything from being put (back?) into Sufi idiom or preferred language, nevertheless it proclaims unmistakable pride in its *arithmetic*! Yet it is, it says it is, an induction into the (Sufi) Way. Surely it must communicate shrewdness through a specific brand of lateral thinking? This may already be the first (most important?) step toward jumping the tracks of banal mundanity and into Sufism, I'm not sure (and would hardly say if I thought I was). Maybe the teaching is out to satirize the kinds of overinvestment in apportioning things to people (and vice versa) which keeps lawyers in demand (outside the Sufi Way). Perhaps our guru Hazrat Ali primarily cocks a snook at mentalities that are preoccupied with slicing up countable possessions and making sure all tallies to the last. If so, the story simulates, and so shares in, the diabolical computationality it means to sidestep and circumvent. Whereas, it may be, Aesopic Phaedrus just messes with our minds. He set us up to expect a neat twist from a brainteaser that will find a lawyer's crack, in a specimen of legal discourse, only to induct us into a quite different event. A 'Way' of his own. The 'shaggy dog story', no less. That abuse of story and telling, part and parcel of the (self-)satire of 'Aesop':

> By their father's will three sons inherited equal shares in a pear tree, a goat, and a mill.
>
> They put the problem of dividing the estate between them before the judge. Father had ordered that it be divided equally, so that none of them should have more of it than another. "How, then, do you propose to divide it?", he asked them.
>
> The eldest said, "I'll take all in the tree that is straight and crooked", the second, "I'll take all in the tree that is green and dry", the third, "I'll take the roots, trunk, and all the branches." "Then which of you will have the biggest share?" asked the judge, "I can't tell, any more than anybody else can. Let the whole tree go to the one who can answer this question."
>
> The goat? The goat was left to the son who prayed for it to grow the biggest. The sons prayed it might be so large as to drink the sea dry and still be only half-full, or so big that if all the linen, hemp and wool in the world were woven into one thin rope, it would not go right round the goat's shin, or so huge that he stretched to everywhere an eagle could see flying up to heaven and looking out beyond the four corners of the earth . . . "Which of you prayed for the largest goat? I can't tell, any more than any body else can," said the judge. "Let the goat go to the one of you who has prayed for the largest goat."
>
> The mill was left to the son that friends and neighbours thought the laziest and most good-for-nothing. The eldest said he'd stayed in bed for a year, while raindrops falling through a hole in the roof had gone in his ear so often that they had rotted his head and got through to the other ear: "I'm so lazy I didn't even turn my head." The next said if he had no food for a fortnight or a month he would be too lazy to stick anything in his mouth, "even if I was sat at table with a delicious feast in front of me." The youngest said that if he was dying of thirst and stood in water up to his chin, he would die before he bent his head down far enough "for even a single drop". The judge said "You don't know, nor do I, nor does anybody else, which of you is the laziest and most good-for-nothing."
>
> So the judge and the three brothers—[28]
>
> (Aesopica 703 Perry)

[28] —went their own ways without having come to any decision about the inheritance. (A précis of Steinhöwel, *Fabulae Extravagantes* 13.)

5

In short, Phaedrus' riddle hands us down neither law nor wit, whatever the appearances (the fable's smokescreen). But we're not done with it yet. Why would we pass up any chance to ungag the genre's mouthpiece, prankster Aesop?

The satirist in our midst. Here to spray misogynist mockery around for us, in whatever his chosen victim town of the day. No, he's not come to tinker with pretty paradox, but to rough up more defenceless dumb beasts. See how the girls' incorrigible natures are levelled: to the jaundiced eye, three daughters are rotten luck, and nothing will come of nothings. They are all stuck like it, one undifferentiated mess in triplicate, filed past us by narrator and hero alike:

> (i) First off, 'good looks' betoken 'bad looks', for we are to know, and enjoy knowing, that to label a female 'shapely' *is* to run the 'male gaze' over her body, and to call a girl a man-hunter is to stigmatize her as 'too male' (v. 4). This, it will turn out, was her one instant of attention. (ii) In this line-up, the traditional 'good girl', who sees to her spinning and weaving safe down on the farm away from wicked town, is a disappointing dud, maybe already stuck with all the connotations of 'rusticity' ('non-totty'); as the litany recurs, we'll find her a bore—no scandal, no variation, just the same old winding and snipping, snipping and winding . . . (vv. 5, 23, 35; but cf. 43 below).[29] (iii) Third and worst—'ugliest and foulest', and alliterating foully into the bargain, here is the drunk, to prove that with women what you see is what you got—and the suggestion of end-stress in the superlative tars her plain Jane predecessor's feathers into the bargain, besides mocking the uplift of a Cinderella or Cordelia, last and best (v. 6).
>
> Second time around, the ladies come in the same order: (i) has become a 'slut', no more, no less (*moechae*, v. 21: a hefty—Graeco-Roman—obscenity); no change out of (ii); (iii) is the only *potrix* in extant Latin Literature, so she *must* be beyond the pale (v. 25).[30]
>
> Enter Aesop, and he dutifully runs through (ii), then (iii), now dignified with the grander, anyhow wider, gloss as 'the one who drags her life in luxury', then (i), just 'slut' again (vv. 34–9).
>
> Finally, the sage leads, with (iii) as 'the ugly one', then (i) still simply 'slut', and finally (ii), given *her* (dubious) accolade, as 'the one who thrills over stock', as well as still 'slave to her precious wool' (vv. 41–4).

[29] Just the life, for the world's ideal wife: Treggiari 1991: 243 and esp. 111. As cultural a universal as female nature . . .

[30] Cf. *compotrix*, Sidonius, *Letters* 2.9.

Yes, the girls are carefully opposed: but only so that they can then be shuffled without compunction: in a word, 'equalized'. At the same time, together with all the variations on the phrases for the assignment and, ultimately, the disposal of the portions, and for the decoding of the riddle,[31] the itemized three-way split accumulates cumulations of types of property which intertwine with the girls. Not only is the equation of woman to real estate cemented into place by the natural necessity which calibrates personality and character with the plant and accessories ordained for the designs for life (vv. 21–6, 34–9, 41–4), but the stereotypes reach out to infect the aspirations of every *paterfamilias* on planet Plutocracy—the erotic life of things in the politics of materialist fetishism: "with her fog, her amphetamine, and her pearls"—Just Like a Woman, in three doses . . .[32]

6

But was that just the jester's heartlessness worn on Aesop's sleeve? I'll have one more go. As a determined effort to intimate that (even naughty-nasty) anecdotage 'about' law in the life of any city can see through the institutional structures themselves, let alone their preoccupying red tape (clean through to the infamous *nom et non du père*).

Suppose we watch closely the apparatus of power-and-knowledge interposed between absent Father and congregated Social Order. One-and-all and all-for-one must bond paternity with succession to property; but in that case how can a destabilizing flip from male to non-male ownership be prevented? The system that stands in for the will of the father must turn to its supplementary Other if the circle is to be squared. From an alternative universe, from outside

---

[31] *distribuat. . . . seponit. . . . destinata dare . . . date . . . assignate . . . donate*, vv. 9, 21, 27, 35, 39; *uendet . . . abiciet . . . quacumque summa tradet*, vv. 41, 42, 44; *expedit . . . colligi . . . interpretari . . . soluit . . . repperit*, vv. 14, 19, 32, 33, 49.

[32] Cf. *Digest* 33–34, Johnston 1999: 46–7 for snapshots of kinds of objects prized in wills, Champlin 1991: 123–4 for standard wifely property; the Roman will was their prize way to judge the living by rating them against self and each other in terms of the value of things (*ibid.* 17). Wyke 1994 explains how adornment ('feminization') of the female body stamps otherness and danger onto woman, and earns her abuse that masquerades as public-spirited policing. The reflex connection between women and property centred on the dowry, since the daughter's narrative is locked onto marriage; there are inevitable overtones in the listed luxuries of 4.5, cf. Henderson 1976 nn. *ad loc.*; cf. Mayor on Juvenal 1.75.

the proprieties of familial society, the system is to be re-founded as a mythic parable of female implosion, the truth of patrilineage.

No citizen ought to be caught voicing the derogation of its legitimate women, the daughters-who-will-marry-and mother the(ir) men, yet girls may never fully substitute for their brothers—for example, those sons that this safely distanced Lear never fathered. *Mater* is present to implement, not to supplant, the paternal fiat (a necessarily doomed project from within the patriarchal system, since conjugal equalization through the status of *parens* only threatens the predominance of the male). But she, no more than absent *pater*, could not without loss of face disown his offspring for failing to be male (vv. 13, 20, 30). Quite outside the community's laws, and driving the system from within, however, there appears the spokesman for the Law which permits the will of the Father to ordain (un)worthy successors, but on condition that they be prevented from displacing his authority, and held to doing his will.

In this sense, the sage ~~speaks~~ (speaks *indirectly*) for the father's indirect, but ~~stipulated~~, disqualification of those girls. And so it is that a family without a future, a surplus nuclear unit, is put at the disposal of teaching a lesson in the underlying dynamics that propelled each city through generation upon generation of citizens. At the price of public mockery of Father's own women, certified by mockery of the public, we harp on daughters, and inherit the joy materialised in gendered derision as the mainspring of patriarchal law . . .[33]

Conclusion

For fun or otherwise, Phaedrus' moral bids us see his tale within the frame of a 'legacy willed to the future' (*posteris tradam*, v. 2). And inheritance stories always reflexively image and enact the working of 'tradition'. Likewise, the written collection of tales 'hands down to tradition' and 'transfers into memorialised form' lasting parables of ephemeral narrative as cultural legacy (4. *Prol.* 6, *famae tradere*, 18–19, *uestras in chartas uerba transfertis mea,/dignaque longa iudicatis memoria*). Far from scorning traditional readings, and instead eliciting maverick difference in interpretation (vv. 48–9), it could strike anyone,

[33] A Lacanian Aesop . . .? Try Lacan as *our* 'Aesop'. (E.g. Lacan 1992: 167–78, on 'jouissance/Loi')

if not everybody, that this fable puts on display its funny business of encrypting atavistic theorems, confident that only the iconoclastic alien in us will ever notice. And so, both in the story and in its reading, the trick, the inanity, the law is . . . that everyone and no one gets exactly what's coming to them.

Bibliography

Berger, A. (1953) *Encyclopedic Dictionary of Roman Law (Transactions of the American Philosophical Society* 43.2), Philadelphia.

Bonner, S.F. (1977) *Education in Ancient Rome: from the Elder Cato to the Younger Pliny*, London.

Champlin, E. (1991) *Final Judgments: Duty and Emotion in Roman Wills 20 BC–AD 250*, Berkeley and Los Angeles.

Crook, J.A. (1967) *Law and Life of Rome*, London.

——. (1986) 'Women in Roman succession', in Rawson, B.M. (ed.) *The Family in Ancient Rome: New Perspectives*, 53–82, London.

Daube, D. (1969) *Roman Law: Linguistic, Social, and Philosophical Aspects*, Edinburgh

Gardner, J. (1986) *Women in Roman Law and Society*, London.

Guaglianone, A. (1970–1) 'Commento alla Favola IV 5 (poeta) e alle altre favole giudiziarie di Fedro', *Annali della Facoltà di Lettere e Filosofia, Università di Macerata, Rome III–IV*, 437–52.

Harrison, A.R.W. (1968) *The Law of Athens: the Family and Property*, Oxford.

Henderson, J. (1976) *Anecdote and Satire in Phaedrus: Commentary and Discussion*, Unpublished PhD Dissertation, University of Oxford.

——. (1999) 'Phaedrus' Fables: the original corpus', *Mnemosyne* 52, 308–29.

——. (2000) *Telling Tales on Caesar: Roman Stories from Phaedrus*, Oxford.

Idries Shah (1974) *Thinkers of the East*, Harmondsworth.

Jennings, V.J. (2000) *Representing Aesop*, Unpublished PhD Dissertation, University of Cambridge.

Johnston, D. (1999) *Roman Law in Context*, Cambridge.

Just, R. (1989) *Women in Athenian Law and Life*, London and New York.

Lacan, J. (1992) *The Seminar of Jacques Lacan, Book VII: The Ethics of Psychoanalysis 1959–60*, New York.

Lacey, W.K. (1968) *The Family in Ancient Greece*, London.

Lattimore, R. (1942) *Themes in Greek and Latin Epitaphs* (*Illinois Studies in Language and Literature* 28), Chicago.

Lier, B. (1903–4) '*Topica carminum sepulcralium Latinorum*', *Philologus* 62, 445–77, 563–603, 63. 54–64.

Lockwood, D.P. (1921) 'Post-mortem wit in folktale, literature and Roman law', *Transactions of the American Philological Association* 52, xvii–xviii.

MacDowell, D.M. (1978) *The Law in Classical Athens*, London.

McGinn, T.A.J. (1998) *Prostitution, Sexuality, and the Law in Ancient Rome*, Oxford.

Nøjgaard, M. (1967) *La Fable Antique. 2. Les Grands Fabulistes*, Copenhagen.

Perry, B.E. (ed.) (1965) *Babrius and Phaedrus*, Cambridge, Mass. and London.

Pinder, N. (1869) *Selections from the Less Known Latin Poets*, Oxford.

Rei, A. (1998) 'Villains, wives, and slaves in the comedies of Plautus', in Murnaghan, S. and S.R. Joshel (eds.) (1998) *Women & Slaves in Greco-Roman Culture*, 92–107, London and New York.

Ritschl, F. (1868) 'Plautinische Excurse XXIV *ne nei ni*', in *Opuscula Philologica* 2. 622–32, Leipzig.

Saller, R.P. (1994) *Patriarchy, Property and Death in the Roman Family*, Cambridge.
Scafuro, A.C. (1997) *The Forensic Stage: Settling Disputes in Graeco-Roman New Comedy*, Cambridge.
Treggiari, S. (1991) *Roman Marriage*: iusti coniuges *from the Time of Cicero to the Time of Ulpian*, Oxford.
Wyke, M. (1994) 'Woman in the mirror: the rhetoric of adornment in the Roman world', in Archer, L.J., S. Fischler, and M. Wyke (eds.) (1994) *Women in Ancient Societies*, 134–51, Basingstoke.

THE POMPEIAN TABLETS AND SOME LITERARY TEXTS

Duncan Cloud

In April 1959, workmen building the first section of the Autostrada del Sud south of Naples came across the remains of a building 600 metres south of Pompeii's Stabian gate in the locality of Murecine. The function of the building has, I think, never been definitively established;[1] in it was discovered a basket containing papyrus documents relating to the business of what was probably a finance house in Puteoli belonging to the Sulpicii. Some documents had been found in Herculaneum just before the Second World War and selectively published just after it,[2] but their full significance was not recognised until the publication of the much ampler collection from Pompeii. John Crook was among the first to recognise that the latter had been badly served by their original editors and to do something about it; furthermore, he was a pioneer in utilising them as an invaluable source of information on how Roman private law actually worked in Italy.[3] These papyri do have a further value; they can illuminate literary texts. As John Crook's friends know, he has a vast knowledge of Classical literature and it seemed to me an appropriate tribute to show how these papyri can be exploited to enhance our appreciation of some passages in Latin literature, particularly in

[1] G. Camodeca, *Tabulae Pompeianae Sulpiciorum* (Rome, 1999), I.11 and n. 2, thinks that it was "la sede di un *collegium*", though it might have been the headquarters of the finance house itself. See also J. Andreau, *Banking and Business in the Roman World* (tr. J. Lloyd) (Cambridge, 1999), 71–9, who adds the possibility that it was an inn.

[2] The four texts relevant to this essay were published by G. Pugliese Carratelli under the title '*Tabulae Herculanenses* I' and '*Tabulae Herculanenses* II' in *Parola del Passato* 1 (1946), 379–85 and 3 (1948), 165–84 and commented on by V. Arangio-Ruiz, 'Il Processo di Giusta' *ibid.* 3 (1948), 129–51 and 'Tavoletti ercolanesi', *BIDR* 62 (1959), 223–45 (= *Studi epigrafici e papirologici* [Naples, 1974] 327–44 and 552–70). For the provenance see F. Costabile, 'Nuove luci sul "processo di Giusta"', *St. Sanfilippo* (Milan, 1987), 7, 187–230; the papyri were discovered in the Casa del Bicentenario in 1937 (199 n. 20).

[3] Crook, 'Working Notes on some of the new Pompeii Tablets', *ZPE* 29 (1978), 229–39. For a full history of the editing of these tablets before the definitive edition of Camodeca cited in n. 1: see 15–16 of that work.

Augustan poetry. I will admit at once that the significance of the tablets for most of these examples has already been briefly noted by scholars of Roman law; it is the writers of commentaries on Roman literature who seem to have missed, partly or wholly, the importance for their work of these discoveries. I would also admit that this piece would have undoubtedly been improved, if it had received the *ultima lima* of the dedicatee.

I shall be concerned with a single institution which figures prominently in the Pompeii tablets, *vadimonium*, which corresponds roughly to English 'bail',[4] and with one basic form of it, the form that serves in effect as a summons on the defendant to appear before the magistrate, though, as we shall see, the procedure is not quite as simple as that. It may be a purely private arrangement between the parties and thus be extra-judicial, or it may be sanctioned by a magistrate; cases are bound to arise in a town like Puteoli where the finance house operated[5] when the parties will need to be certain that the *praefecti iure dicundo* are empowered to deal with their case; if they are, then a *praefectus* will sanction the *vadimonium* and it will in a sense be judicial.[6] However, whether the *vadimonium* was a purely private arrangement or had the backing of the magistrate, the structure of the *vadimonium* remained the same; consequently, there is no obvious way of telling one from the other and I shall lump them both together as summons to initial court proceedings *vadimonia*.[7] I

[4] 'Bail' is only roughly equivalent to *vadimonium*, because no money is paid down and because, at least in the form with which I shall be mainly concerned, it consists of a verbal contract between plaintiff and defendant that the latter will turn up at a certain date, time and place immediately prior to the two parties appearing before the magistrate in the first part (*in iure*) of a civil action. A sum is specified that the defendant will be liable to pay the plaintiff in the event of his non-appearance at the specified place. It is the plaintiff who is to receive the money, not some organ of the state.

[5] No-one has satisfactorily explained why documents relating to the activities of a finance house in Puteoli ended up in a basket in the outskirts of Pompeii some forty kilometres away.

[6] *Lex Irnitana* 84 gives a long list of cases which the magistrates of Irni in Southern Spain cannot try; it also fixes a financial ceiling (in that little community as low as 1000 sesterces). Otherwise, such cases are to be heard by the provincial governor. On the other hand, if both parties are agreed, the local magistrate can ignore these restrictions (lines 17–18). If similar rules applied in Puteoli, where the alternative would be the court of the urban praetor at Rome, then it is easy to envisage a large number of disputes where the plaintiff or both parties would seek the advice and/or permission of the prefect before proceeding further with their *vadimonia*.

[7] Naturally, when the parties are citizens living in Rome they have in any case to take their case to the urban praetor, and there will be less need for the magis-

shall not be concerned with other forms of *vadimonium* except incidentally.[8]

I give an example of one such *vadimonium*, TPSulp 3,[9] which is almost complete, apart from the names of the *signatores* which must have been in the original (*cp.* PSulp 15, a *vadimonium Romam*) and which (uniquely in the collection) contains a statement, italicized in my text, asserting that the sums mentioned in the *vadimonium* are less than the sum at issue in the dispute between the litigants. This is a working text, based on the *scriptura exterior* with the lacunae corrected from the *scriptura interior* which offers an almost identical text up to the word *nomine*. Apart from the name of the second consul, there are no problems with the remaining 19/20 words, derived from the *scriptura exterior* alone:[10]

> Vadimonium factum C. Sulpicio Fausto III nonas
> Iulias primas Puteolis in foro ante aram Augusti
> Hordionianam hora tertia; HS L *maioris summae rem in*
> *iudicium deducturus* et HS I depositi anuli arrae
> nomine stipulatus est L. Faenius Eumenes, spopondit
> C. Sulpicius Faustus. actum Puteolis V nonis Iuliis
> L. Vitellio L.*f.* [Mes]salla Poblicola cos.

---

trate to give his backing to the *vadimonium*. However, the joke in Plaut. *Aulularia* 37–40 implies that the praetor's backing for a *vadimonium* was sometimes requested; Euclio is so miserly that, when a kite swoops down and snatches away a morsel of food from the skinflint, he goes howling to the praetor to demand permission to impose a *vadimonium* upon the offending bird:

> Pulmentum pridem eripuit ei miluos
> homo ad praetorem deplorabundus venit;
> infit ibi postulare plorans, eiulans,
> ut sibi liceret miluom vadarier.

There would not be much of a joke if the praetor never authorised *vadimonia* for anything.

[8] We have copies in the Sulpicii archive of *vadimonia* to Rome where the local magistrates were unable to deal with the case themselves. *Lex Irn.* 84 and other epigraphic texts refer to *vadimonia* to the court of the provincial governor. A quite different sort of *vadimonium* appears in Gaius *Inst.* IV.184 where the magistrate cannot conclude his business *in iure* with the litigants before the end of the day and the defendant is bailed to reappear in court at a subsequent date and time. The decision is the magistrate's, not the plaintiff's; the *vadimonium* is fully judicial and constitutes an order from the magistrate, not just a permissive act on his part, as in the case of the 'judicial' summons-*vadimonia*.

[9] The enumeration is as in *Tabulae Pompeianae Sulpiciorum*, see n. 1.

[10] The name of the second *cos. suff.* is uncertain. I have given Camodeca's text, where *Messalla Poblicola* will be the writer's mistake for *Messala Vipstano Gallo*, probably Poblicola's brother.

On 3 July 48 AD L. Faenius Eumenes imposed a *vadimonium* on C. Sulpicius Faustus of 50,000 sesterces in cash and a ring worth 1000 sesterces if the latter failed to turn up in front of the Hordionian altar of Augustus in Puteoli at the third hour on 5 July. Eumenes intended to bring an *actio ex empto* against Faustus (TPSulp 2) but the parties eventually settled out of court (TPSulp 27, 4 September of the same year). A *vadimonium* was a verbal *stipulatio*, but naturally the parties would keep witnessed copies in case of argument about its contents.

In one important particular the discovery of these documents has altered our perception of the way in which summons-*vadimonium* worked. Hitherto the doctrine had been that *vadimonium* operated as a gentlemanly alternative to *in ius vocatio*. Instead of the plaintiff physically dragging the defendant from his home to court (*in ius vocatio* + *manus iniectio*) the latter stipulated that he would appear before the magistrate on a certain date at a certain time and if he failed to honour his promise he would be liable for the sum named in the stipulation.[11] But from these *vadimonia* it becomes clear that the defendant promised to meet the plaintiff not at the magistrate's tribunal but at a prominent statue, altar or building near the court.[12] Most of the *vadimonia* relating to legal proceedings in Puteoli were to the Hordionian altar of Augustus. The *vadimonia* to Rome are all to places in the Forum of Augustus, often specified in some detail, perhaps when the defendant did not know Rome and might try to plead that he had lost his way. TPSulp 19 is an extreme example; the

[11] See A. Fliniaux, *Le Vadimonium* (Paris, 1908), 104–5 for a good statement of this position.

[12] The one exception is in TH 13–14, a *vadimonium* to Rome where the parties agree to meet "Romae in foro August. ante tribunal praetoris urbani hora secunda." But as Camodeca remarks (*L'archivio puteolano dei Sulpicii*, [Naples, 1992], 50), *ante* is not the same as *ad*; the litigants arranged to meet in front of the court, not at it. In view of the explicit statement in this *vadimonium*, in the public domain since 1948, that at the time of the document (probably 75 AD) the praetor's tribunal was in the *forum Augusti* I do not understand why L. Richardson (*A New Topographical Dictionary of Ancient Rome*, [Baltimore, 1992], 160) denies that the *f.A.* was ever regularly used for legal business. The Pompeian *vadimonia Romam* go back to 40 AD (TPSulp 19, a *testatio sistendi Romae*). Suet. *Aug.* 29.1: "Fori extruendi causa fuit hominum et iudiciorum multitudo quae videbatur non sufficientibus duobus etiam tertio indigere." suggests that it had been from the start in Augustus' mind to move the praetor's tribunal there. See Camodeca 'Una nuova fonte sulla topografia del foro d'Augusto', *Athenaeum* 64 (1986), 505–8 and F. Castagnoli *Doxa* 3 (1950), 75 in 'Topografia di Roma antica', 54–89. V. Kockel, *Lexicon topographicum urbis Romae*, ed. E.M. Steinby, II, (Rome, 1995), 290, gets it right.

vadimonium is to "in front of the statue of Gracchus at the fourth column close to the steps."[13] *In ius vocatio* will have followed, for it was the only procedure available to get the defendant from the place of meeting to the magistrate's tribunal. What is more, Gaius (*Inst.* IV. 183), writing in the mid second century, writes of *i.i.v* as the standard way of getting a defendant to court: "In summa sciendum est eum qui cum aliquo consistere velit <*in ius vocare*> oportere, et eum qui vocatus fuerit, si non venerit, poenam ex edicto praetoris committere."[14] Yet the use of summons-*vadimonia* was also normal, to judge from their use by the freedmen of Pompeii and Herculaneum. Thus the only way of reconciling the testimony of the Pompeii tablets and that of Gaius is to suppose that *i.i.v.* followed the meeting of the two parties near the tribunal. It is not surprising that the sequence *vadimonium* followed by *in ius vocatio* has now become standard doctrine.[15]

This is the chief way in which our understanding of *vadimonium* has been altered by the discoveries at Murecine. However, it also seems likely that the sums of money or equivalents in objects of value were roughly the same as the sums at issue in the suit.[16] This would support a plausible solution to a problem raised by Horace *Sat.* I.9.35–37. In one respect the tablets have modified only slightly what the literary sources had already suggested: eleven out of the sixteen Pompeian *vadimonia* that still preserve the time for meeting

[13] ". . . In foro Augusto [ante] statuam Gracci [ad colum]nam quar[tam prox]ume gradus." This is actually from a fragmentary *tabula sistendi*, a document attested by witnesses that the defendant did turn up at the appointed place. Cp. TH 6 for similar precision in a *vadimonium Romam.*

[14] The supplement is certain, not only because of *qui vocatus est* but because of 184: "cum autem *in ius vocatus fuerit* adversarius neque eo die fuerit finiri potuerit negotium . . .", a clause that in any case assumes *i.i.v.* to be the normal form of summons.

[15] See M. Kaser and K. Hackl, *Das römische Zivilprozeßrecht* (Munich, 1996), 231.

[16] "Il suo importo nei nostri (*i.e.* those treated in his book on the archive of the Sulpicii) *vadimonia* stragiudiziali doveva di regola coincidere o comunque essere assai vicino alla stima del valore della lite" (Camodeca cited n. 1, 52 = book cited in n. 12, also 52). The *vadimonium* cited above is, as C. points out, particularly telling. If it was normal for a *vadimonium* to be for less than the sum at issue, why make a point of saying so in this document? The implication is the opposite; it was *unusual* for *vadimonia* to be for less than the sum at issue, at least in an *actio ex empto*, like that of Eumenes (TPSulp 2). Interestingly, the *actio ex empto* is not one of the only two actions, the *actio iudicati* and the *actio depensi* (*Inst.* IV.186), for which Gaius says bail is taken for a sum equal to, as opposed to half, that being claimed. No doubt it is for this reason that some scholars think that Gaius is more generally wrong about the sum stipulated in the *vadimonium.*

give the time as the third hour. The two literary references usually cited point to the fourth hour.[17] However, the tablets also give meeting-times at every hour between the first and the fifth and two at the ninth hour, one of which (TPSulp 19) is at Rome, as, interestingly, is the only one for the fourth hour (TPSulp 15). The Herculaneum tablets are for the second (TH 13–14), third (TH 15) and fifth hours (TH 6).

However, what we now know about the timings for the fulfilment of *vadimonia* does enrich the metaphor in Manilius I.244. Lines 242–244 read:

> Hanc (*sc.* partem, *region*) ubi ad occasus nostros sol aspicit actus,
> illic orta dies sopitas excitat urbes
> et cum luce refert operum *vadimonia* terris.

In Goold's 1977 Loeb translation: "When the sun reaches our occident and looks upon this lower world, there the dawn of day is rousing cities from slumber and is bringing to those lands with daylight the appointed round of work." Housman in his edition of Book I[18] glossed *operum vadimonia* as "negotia praestituto tempore obeundi necessitatem." As Housman and Goold by their translation and gloss respectively show, Manilius did not mean that everyone started work at dawn, but that some people started work at dawn and in the course of the day all had to perform different tasks at fixed times. So long as we supposed that people answered bail at the fourth hour, one element in the metaphor was missing, but now we know that answer to bail could be demanded at any time from the first hour (TPSulp 12) to the ninth (TPSulp 10 and 19), it is clear that

[17] The bore in Horace *Sat.* I.9 remembers when a quarter of the day has passed, *quarta iam parte diei/praeterita* (35–36), *i.e.* at the end of the third hour, that he must answer bail then (*tunc*). As for Martial VIII.67: his guest arrives before the fifth hour, much too early for dinner, "cum modo distulerint raucae vadimonia quartae", but meaning and text are uncertain. However, the poet does link *vadimonia* in some way with the fourth hour; though it is not at all clear whether *raucae . . . quartae* (*raucae* because "exercet raucos tertiae causidicos", *id.* IV.8.2) is nom. plural or gen. sing. and why praetor or litigant would want to postpone *vadimonia* as early as the fourth hour, if that is what *distulerint* means.

[18] M. Manilii *Astronomicon* liber primus, (London, 1903), 22. Manilius' use of the plural suggests that Housman is right about the meaning of *operum*. Scarcia's "gli impegni di lavoro" in his edition of Book I (Verona, 1990, 29) would require 'oper*is*', while Liuzzi's "l'impegno delle *fatiche*" (ed. Bks. I and II [Lecce, 1983], 33) is impressionistic.

vadimonial practice was a better metaphor for the round of work than we had thought.

However, it is chiefly because the parties to a *vadimonium* met at a place close to but not identical with the magistrate's tribunal that our commentaries on literary texts need revision. I will begin with a passage, well-known to romanists, from Cicero's *Pro Quinctio*. According to Cicero's disingenuous narrative, Naevius waits for Cicero's client, P. Quinctius, to be well on his way to visit his estates in Gaul before he summons his friends to witness that he has answered bail and Quinctius has not:

> (Naevius) pueros circum amicos dimittit, ipse suos necessarios ab atriis Liciniis et a faucibus macelli corrogat ut ad tabulam Sextiam sibi adsint hora secunda postridie. veniunt frequentes. testificatur iste *P. Quinctium non stetisse et stetisse se*; tabulae maxime signis hominum nobilium consignantur. disceditur.
>
> (*Quinct.* 25)

Now among the vadimonial documents from Pompeii are, as we have seen (n.13) a number of *testationes sistendi* (TPSulp 16–21). None is complete, but from the data provided we can construct the formula: consuls, date, place, name of party, time and a statement that the party had turned up, *stetit*, with a list of witnesses, *signatores*, to the fact (TPSulp 21). In Cicero's narrative we have a number of elements from this formula: time (*hora secunda*),[19] place (*ad tabulam Sextiam*), assertion that the party answered bail (*stetisse se* = *stetit*) and the list of witnesses. The consular year had been given in section 18 (*Scipione et Norbano coss.*).[20] Consequently it is now clear that the *tabula Sextia*, whatever it was, was the place from which *in ius vocatio* to the praetor's tribunal would begin. But for editors who supposed that *vadimonium* was a substitute for *i.i.v.* and that bail was to court, not some spot near the court—a reasonable view before the discovery of the tablets—there was, or should have been, a problem.

---

[19] If the function of the meeting *ad tabulam Sestiam* had been properly understood, scholars would have been less likely to think that the fourth hour was the normal time for answering bail.

[20] In sec. 24 Cicero gives the date of Quinctius' departure for Gaul (*xi Kal. Feb.*) but not the date of his non-appearance *ad tabulam Sextiam*. At sec. 57 Cicero does give it: *Idibus Feb.* Why then not give it here according to the formula? Perhaps because it was so soon after Quinctius' departure for Gaul as to arouse the suspicion in the judge that a reason for his choosing to go to Gaul at that precise moment was to evade answering to bail at an inconvenient time.

Kinsey in his generally admirable edition of the speech avoids it.[21] Pocock in his commentary on the *In Vatinium*[22] maintained that it was an outstation of the tribunal itself.[23] Pocock also maintained that the *tabula Sextia* was not, as was previously supposed, a bank but a picture, probably of C. Sextius Calvinus, awarded a triumph in 123 BC for his victory over Ligurians and Gauls; he was the founder of Aquae Sextiae. Pocock's suggestion provides a venue more in keeping with those mentioned in the tablets. To be sure there are no paintings of *triumphatores*, but there is a triumphal statue, of Cn. Sentius Saturninus, presumably set up because of his victories in Britain, mentioned only in Eutropius VII.13.2. On the other hand, nothing in the tablets attests a commercial meeting point. Moreover, Shackleton Bailey in his edition of Cicero's *Ad Familiares*[24] drew attention to *Schol. Bob.* (St. II. 147.23–6) commenting on the *tabula Valeria* mentioned in *in Vat.* 21 (the starting point for Pocock's Appendix). The scholiast says that the *tabula Valeria*, like the *tabula Sestia* "cuius meminit Pro Quintio", gave its name to the area; the name *tabula Valeria* was given to the place "ubi Valerius Maximus tabulam rerum ab se in Gallia prospere gestarum proposuerat ostentui vulgo." Now if the *tabula Valeria* was a picture of Valerius Maximus' victory over the Gauls, the *tabula Sestia* or *Sextia* ought to be a picture too, since it would be perverse of the scholiast to use the word *tabula* of two objects to be compared with one another to mean 'picture' in one case and 'bank' in the other. Of course, the scholiast could simply be wrong, as he is about the subject of the picture; for Pliny *NH*

[21] Adelaide, 1971. One might have expected discussion at 84–85 where he examines the nature of the *tabula Sextia* or 135, on sec. 61 where Cicero appears to mention a *vadimonium* followed by *in ius vocatio.*

[22] L.G. Pocock, *A commentary on Cicero* In Vatinium (London, 1929), Appendix V, 180–2.

[23] Arangio-Ruiz seems to have thought of the temple of Mars Ultor which figured in TH 15 as the stipulated meeting-place for the litigants as a cross between an outstation and a waiting-room. He referred to it as chosen "forse per evitare la difficoltà di ritrovarsi in mezzo alla folla che doveva formarsi davanti al tribunale stesso" (141) and described it as "un fervido centro di attività (oserei dire) paragiudiziale" ('Il processo di Giusta' 141–2, art. cited in n. 2), more of a waiting-room perhaps than an outstation. He cites Martial VII.51: Pompeius Auctus who "madens varioque togae limatus in usu" (5) "Ultoris prima Martis in aede sedet" (4), can recite all Martial's poetry, but only from the tenth hour onwards—"neque enim satis ante vacabit" (11). In fact, Auctus is a jurisconsult and advises his clients who have met at the temple as a result of their *vadimonia* at the temple.

[24] D.R. Shackleton Bailey, *Cicero: Epistulae ad Familiares* I (Cambridge, 1977), 287–8 on *ad Fam.* XIV.2.2.

XXXV.22 tells us that M' Valerius Maximus Messalla, consul of 263, was the first to set up a picture in a public place, in this case showing the victories over the Carthaginians and Hieron of Syracuse that earned him his triumph. However, as Shackleton Bailey points out, the scholiast's error may unwittingly indicate the kernel of truth behind his comment; Sextius earned his triumph for victories over the Gauls and the Scholiast has attached his source's comment on the *tabula Sextia* to the wrong *tabula*. In future, then, those who write commentaries on the *Pro Quinctio* can ditch the view that it was an outstation of the urban praetor's office;[25] it was almost certainly a picture in a portico near the praetor's tribunal where the parties to a *vadimonium* regularly met. Pocock and Shackleton Bailey provide a very plausible suggestion about the picture's subject matter.[26]

However, it is in connection with a group of three Augustan poetic texts that the Pompeian tablets are most interesting. All of them have some connection with the temple of Vesta. The most important of these is the ninth poem in Horace's first book of *Satires*.[27] The poem's ostensible theme is Horace's increasingly desperate attempt to get rid of the company of an insensitive arriviste who is bent on getting Horace to introduce him to the circle of Maecenas. However, the pest has been bailed to appear in court and the poem ends with the appearance of his opponent who hales him off to the magistrate.[28] For our purposes the key sections are:

[25] A view still to be found as an alternative in L. Richardson, *A New Topographical Dictionary of Ancient Rome* (Baltimore, 1992), 176; he further suggests that it might be a tablet with the Licinio-Sextian laws inscribed upon it.

[26] Roman lawyers examining the *Pro Quinctio* from the point of view of their special interests noted as long ago as 1985 (J.G. Wolf, 'Das sogenannte Ladungsvadimonium', *Satura Roberto Feenstra*, [Fribourg], 65 n. 38) the function of the *tabula Sextia* in terms of the *vadimonium* between Naevius and Quinctius, but they were not much concerned with the nature of the *tabula* and whether the Pompeian material could help us decide between the possible alternatives.

[27] I have written about this Satire in 'Satirists and the Law', *Satire and Society in Ancient Rome* (Exeter, 1989) ed. S.H.(M.) Braund 65–7. I agree with what I wrote then, but the present treatment is influenced by the subsequent papers of Henderson and Mazurek.

[28] N. Rudd, *The Satires of Horace* (Cambridge, 1962), reprinted with minor changes (Melksham, 1982), 74–85, and his earlier article, 'Horace's encounter with the bore', *Phoenix*, 15 (1961), 79–96 have not been bettered as traditional analyses of this poem. But for a more recent treatment see the pyrotechnics of J. Henderson, 'Be Alert: Horace, *Satires* 1.9', *Writing Down Rome* (Oxford, 1999), 202–227, a reworking of *PCPhS* 39 (1993), 67–93.

Ventum erat ad Vestae, quarta iam parte diei
praeterita, et casu tum respondere vadato
debebat; quod ni fecisset, perdere litem.
"si me amas" inquit "paulum hic ades." "inteream, si
aut valeo stare aut novi civilia iura:
et propero quo scis."

(35–40)

and

Casu venit obvius illi
adversarius et "quo tu turpissime?" magna
inclamat voce, et "licet antestari?" ego vero
oppono auriculam. rapit in ius: clamor utrimque,
undique concursus. sic me servavit Apollo.'

(74–78)

Many of the underlying themes are resumed in the final words: "sic me servavit Apollo." This sentence is an adaptation of *Il.* XX.443: τὸν δ' ἐξήρπαξεν 'Απόλλων. Apollo rescues Hector from Achilles, by shrouding him in a thick mist. Lucilius quoted this sentence in the original Greek; Horace, by translating it, is therefore both acknowledging Lucilius' prototypical status and implicitly rebuking him for including gobbets of Greek in Latin poetry, as he does quite explicitly in the following Satire (20–30). Finally, Apollo is patron of poets as well as lawyers and so the most suitable of rescuer deities.[29] Central to the narrative is the pest's decision to desert bail and follow Horace (35–42) as it provides the poem's conclusion, when the plaintiff catches up with him and drags him off to court (74–78). But on the theory of summons-*vadimonium* prevailing before the implications of the Pompeian material were understood, the law in the poem is absurd. Paratore was quite right to emphasize to his romanist readers that satire is not a genre in which to look for legal correctness and that, in real life, the poet by offering to act as witness to arrest might well have to appear in court at some stage in the legal pro-

[29] It seems to me that the recapitulation of so many of the themes of this satire is achieved at a certain cost: Apollo whisks away Hector, but the *adversarius* whisks away the pest, not Horace. Indeed, with his "*rapit* in ius" Horace points up the similarity between the plaintiff in this case and Apollo in that of Hector (*Il.* XX.443). So, as Porphyrio (on line 77) saw, the *adversarius* and no-one else is Horace's Apollo: "significat Horatius <se> sic liberatum ac recreatum, dum illum molestum adversarius rapit *Apollinem imitatus*." See further next note.

ceedings.[30] Apollo's rescue was thus only partial. However, as long as it was believed that *vadimonium* and *in ius vocatio* were *alternative* methods of summons, the final words would logically have to refer to a new or different prosecution. Yet, on the face of it, the pest is bailed, thinks it more advantageous in the long run to persuade Horace to introduce him to Maecenas than to win his case, and then encounters the plaintiff who drags him off to court in the manner prescribed by the Twelve Tables. We would have expected the latter to go to the urban praetor and ask for a writ of possession against the pest for deserting bail, not to institute what on the old theory have to be fresh proceedings.[31] However, since we now know that *vadimonium*, if used, preceded *in ius vocatio*, the bail of 35–42 and the *i.i.v.* of 74–78, are therefore connected. The pest's adversary, having located the would-be deserter of bail, does what he would have done if the pest waited for him at the temple of Vesta;[32] he takes him off to court. There may have been one difference; Pugliese

[30] In 'Ad Hor. *Serm.* I.9.35 e 74–78', *Synteleia Arangio-Ruiz* II edd. A. Guarino and L. Labruna (Naples, 1964), 828–48, especially the conclusion. The same point is made (independently?) in the one article known to me that takes some account of the Pompeian material (T. Mazurek, 'Self-parody and the law in Horace *Satires* 1.9', *Classical Journal* 93, (1997), 1–17). Mazurek suggests that Horace is ironic; his readers will know that his troubles are not over. This is plausible; I would however suggest that the Homeric image would work better if Horace's presence in court was not required immediately. Hector was saved from the wrath of Achilles only temporarily to meet his come-uppance later, and there is a curious observation in Ps. Acron—the formula addressed by the plaintiff to the witness whose ear he tweaked, "memento quod tu mihi in illa causa testis *eris*"—which may suggest (as it does to Paratore 835) that the same thing would happen to Horace, perhaps at the outset of the *apud iudicem* phase of the proceedings, the real *causa*. Mazurek's view that Plautine accounts of *antestatio* (*Curc.* 621–625; *Poen.* 1229–1233) apply to Horace and that he was obliged to accompany the litigants to the praetor's tribunal then and there is based on a couple of dubious assumptions, namely that Plautus is accurately representing Roman and not Athenian practice, and that if he is representing Roman practice c. 200 BC, that practice remained unchanged till 35 BC, even when *i.i.v.* followed *vadimonium*. Pugliese (cf. n. 33) is more convincing. Mazurek's notion that the reader is meant to think of Aristius Fuscus as the Apollo of the final word (an Apollo who fails Horace) is questionable, partly for the reason given in the previous note, and because he is such an unlikely deputy for the god of poetry, as a man whose literary interests are so obscure that the scholiasts do not know whether he composed comedies or tragedies or whether he was a *grammaticus*!

[31] Not unreasonably, in dismissing Pugliese's suggestion along these lines (*Il processo civile romano*, [Milan, 1963], 2.I.370 and 405–6), Paratore dubs it "più un' obbligatoria disperata scappatoia che non una soluzione chiara e indiscutibile" (842).

[32] Wolf, footnote cited in n. 26, and later romanists, have interpreted correctly the function of the temple in the poem's narrative.

plausibly suggested[33] that in the Rome of the late Republic and early Empire the plaintiff only resorted to *antestatio* and in the last resort *manus iniectio* when the defendant declined to go peacefully and continued to be recalcitrant, and that is what happened here.[34]

However, it is lines 35–40 that gain most from our new understanding of *vadimonium.* The pest is reminded by the sight of the temple of Vesta and the fact that the fourth hour has begun that as defendant to a lawsuit he was engaged on bail to meet the plaintiff there. "Si me amas . . . paulum hic ades" will bear its most obvious sense—"*Please* stay here for a little while" (so that the pest can chat up Horace a little longer and make his point about being a useful person, from Horace's point of view as well as his own, to introduce into Maecenas' circle). Horace mischievously misunderstands the pest to mean that he wants Horace to act as *advocatus* for him in court: "Damn it, my legs aren't up to standing around (either by the temple or in court) nor do I know any civil law." If commentators had realised that the pest was due to meet the plaintiff at the temple of Vesta, they would have understood *ades* in its basic sense as primary here. However, the legal overtones are there. As we have seen, Horace may have to turn up in court (*adesse*), but not as the pest's *advocatus* but as witness to arrest. This is a highly ambiguous poem; as Henderson has pointed out, Horace's own successful insinuation of himself into Maecenas' circle (if you cut out the cant) is not all that different from the pest's abortive scheme; Horace is to do for the pest what Virgil and Varius did for Horace (*Sat.* I.6.54–55). At one level, this poem (like I.6) is very indirect propaganda for Maecenas and his backer Octavian; the political group supporting Octavian may be short of *nobiles* but it scores on ethical standards.[35] On the other hand, the poem *has* to be capable of being read in a quite different way, has to be not only because Horace's *persona* is constantly self-deflating[36] but because Antony may end up on top

[33] *Op. cit.* (n. 31), 253–4.

[34] If Pugliese is right, then we could well see another layer of irony in the denouement. Horace (38–40) declines the pest's request that he stick with him, in the hope that the latter will put his lawsuit before his pursuit of the poet. But if he *had* stayed with the pest until the arrival of the *adversarius*, then *antestatio* would have been unnecessary and Horace could have slipped off, parting with the pest for ever!

[35] Ref. to I.M.Le M. duQuesnay, 'Horace and Maecenas', *Poetry and Politics in the Age of Augustus*, edd. A.J. Woodman and D. West (Cambridge, 1984), 19–58.

[36] Henderson *passim*, esp. 218–27.

and Horace cannot afford to be on the losing side twice. Thus Horace has selected a *persona* that is both safe and congenial.

There is one other point on which the tablets help a little. There is a tension between lines 35–37 and lines 74–78 in that, on the face of it, the first group of lines suggests that the pest is being bailed to reappear in court after postponement of proceedings, whereas the final scene describes the pest being haled off to his first appearance in court. Of the ancient scholiasts, Porphyrio saw clearly and Ps. Acron muddily that *antestatio* was part of *in ius vocatio*, the procedure dating from the Twelve Tables.[37] The notion that if the magistrate had to defer the completion of initial proceedings *in iure*, he expected a repetition of the meeting of the parties elsewhere and a repetition of *in ius vocatio* is mildly absurd. He requires the parties to return to court, not to the temple of Vesta, nor is it any longer in the particular interest of the plaintiff that defendant *should* turn up, since unless the defendant has a good excuse for absence, the plaintiff will win his case by default.[38] So the *adversarius* is haling the pest off to his first appearance before the praetor. One would therefore expect it to be the form of *i.i.v.* that normally followed bail, (but since the pest's behaviour was recalcitrant, a rougher than usual form). But lines 36–7 have suggested to some that the pest is being bailed to reappear for deferred proceedings *in iure* because he expects to lose his case, if he fails to answer his bail. In the case of failure to turn up for deferred *in iure* proceedings the pest would undoubtedly have lost his case, but in the case of failure to answer bail for first appearance in court, he would only be liable for the sum stipulated in the *vadimonium*, and that, in most actions, was thought to be half the sum at issue (Gaius *Inst.* IV.186). Now it may be that *fecisset* is the subjunctive of virtual *oratio obliqua* and represents what the pest thought or said to Horace, not the narrator's comment on the pest's situation, and the pest may be exaggerating, trying to extract sympathy from Horace or just plain ignorant. And, of course, the poet (who

[37] *Tab.* I.1 (= *Roman Statutes* [ed. M.H. Crawford, London, 1996], II.384–6, for text and notes).

[38] There is very little direct evidence about procedure in postponed *in iure* proceedings, but Gellius (VI.1.8–11) reports that Scipio Africanus ordered some soldiers "qui in iure apud eum stabant" to be bailed to appear before him in the citadel of the Spanish town he was intending to seize and "in arce eius oppidi ius dixit." In other words, Scipio ordered them to be bailed to reappear at the place where he was presiding over his court, not at some point near it.

is not, after all, writing a legal handbook), makes a better point if he suggests that the pest is even prepared to lose his lawsuit rather than miss an opportunity to join Maecenas' literary circle. However, as we have seen, the implication of TPSulp 3 is that *vadimonium* was normally for the sum at issue and if that was the case, then losing his bail money would have been the equivalent of losing his case.[39] Thus "debebat . . . perdere litem" is not far from the real state of affairs, even if legally inexact.

Finally, let us look at two passages in the elegists which suggest that until the construction of the *Forum Augusti* the temple of Vesta and its precincts were a favourite location for answering bail. The first is Propert. IV.2.55–58:

> Sed facias, divum Sator, ut Romana per aevum
> transeat ante meos turba togata pedes.
> Sex superant versus: te, qui ad vadimonia curris,
> non moror; haec spatiis ultima creta meis.

In this ætiological poem the god Vertumnus is giving an account of his functions, and is nearing the end of his course. Why should the person running to answer bail be running past the statue of Vertumnus in the *vicus Tuscus*? Because the temple of Vesta is only about 100 metres away and he does not want to be late. *Curris* prepares the reader for the metaphor in "haec spatiis ultima creta meis." Just as the litigant is on the last lap of his race to the temple, so Vertumnus is on the last lap of his poem. Moreover, it looks as if Romans dressed up to answer bail and attend court. A mysterious fragment of Novius refers to a *vadimoniosum vestimentum*,[40] and so there must been a garment appropriate for court attendance. Perhaps a toga? In that case the previous couplet, in which Vertumnus prays that Jupiter will grant that a Roman crowd, toga-clad, will eternally pass before his statue's feet, provides in *togata* a verbal link with the next.[41]

---

[39] In any case, the pest may have been involved in an *actio iudicati* or an *actio depensi*, where Gaius states that bail amounted to the sum at issue (*Inst.* IV.186).

[40] "Cur istuc vadimoniosum vestimentum vesceris?" (Frassinetti, *Atellanae Fabulae* 53 [Rome, 1967]). Nonius preserves the line as an example of *vescor* = *utor*, and it must therefore mean "why are you wearing that bail garment?"

[41] Since the toga is the garment of peace, this is also a prayer for peace. Vertumnus and his Etruscans assisted Romulus in his war with the Sabines (51–54); now he desires a peaceful Rome. If this analysis is correct, there is no need for the sort of transposition favoured by G.P. Goold in his 1990 Loeb edition, where he places 55–56 before 5–6.

My last passage is from Ovid *Amores* I.13.19–20:

> Atque eadem sponsum cultos ante Atria mittis,
> unius ut verbi grandia damna ferant.

In this poem the speaker criticizes Aurora; not only does she part lovers like himself and his mistress, but Dawn is unwelcome to many others. I have printed J.C. McKeown's text.[42] The couplet appears to mean: (the poet is addressing Aurora) "and it is you too who (*eadem*) who despatch smartly dressed persons in front of the Atria to act as sponsors, with the result that they sustain huge losses belonging to one word." The pentameter is taken to refer to the huge losses for which *sponsores* who are sureties for debtors are liable. This may be right, but what has "ante atria" to do with it? A very defective piece of Festus (448.33–37L) appears to place the Puteal Scribonianum "ante[a] atria" and on the basis of this Coarelli considers that the *atria* are the *atrium Regium* and the *atrium Vestae*.[43] On rather thin evidence the praetor's tribunal is supposed to have been next to the Puteal[44] and so "ante Atria" is taken to mean "into court." But this is as bizarre as suggesting that "in front of Westminster Abbey" could mean "in (the Houses of) Parliament". In fact, in front of the *Atrium Vestae* is not where one would expect to find a *sponsor* of the type mentioned in Horace *Sat.* II.6.23–26, a passage at the back of Ovid's mind. In that passage, the speaker is not on his way to assume his role as *sponsor*—he is that already—but to give legal effect to it in court. So what *are* the smartly dressed persons doing in front of the Atria? I would suggest as a possibility, and only as a possibility, that they are defendants answering their bail in front of the Atrium. As we have seen from TPSulp 3 the defendant answered 'spondeo' (*spopondit*) in accepting the stipulation, he met the plaintiff in front of a building near the court, and could sustain *grandia damna* if he lost his case. This explanation suffers from one difficulty analogous to that involved in the other, namely that he does not utter the word *spondeo* in front of the *atrium Vestae*; he uttered

[42] Ovid: *Amores* I (Liverpool, 1987), 158, and see his extensive note II (Leeds, 1989), 349.

[43] "Ante atria è un toponimo sicuramente da collegare con l'atrium Regium e con l'atrium Vestae", F. Coarelli, *Il Foro Romano* II (Rome, 1985), 171.

[44] Most convincingly Porphyrio on Hor. *Ep.* I.19.8, from whom Ps. Acron's note is probably derived. Also Ps. Acron on Hor *Sat.* II.6.35, but nowhere else. It must have been in that general area; cf. Coarelli, *op. cit.* in previous note 176ff.

it when he entered into bail and *responsum*, not *sponsum*, would be the *mot juste*. But Ovid needs *spondeo* to be uttered there in order to make the point of "unius . . . verbi." But, unlike the other explanation, mine does at least explain why the *culti* are *ante atria*, just where Ovid's readers would expect to find answerers to bail.

To sum up, the fact that the plaintiff bound the defendant to meet him at a point near the court, not at the court itself, explains the prominence of places other than the praetor's tribunal in literary texts involving bail. Indeed, it explains, at least in the Horace passage and possibly in the Ovid, why those places are mentioned at all.

A NEW INSCRIPTION FROM CARIAN APHRODISIAS

Joyce Reynolds

John Crook's generously available combination of learning, judgement, scepticism, and humour is a resource on which I have drawn for help very often over the years. I had hoped to be thanking him here with a new inscription bearing on the theme of law and life in the Roman world but I can find nothing in my collection with legal content that is suitable. If law is missing there, life is not; so I offer something which is exciting to me because very fresh; a text from Aphrodisias discovered early in 2001 in the unpublished notebooks of the French archaeologist André Boulanger[1] by Charlotte Roueché (another epigraphically-minded friend of John's, who is happy to be associated with this occasion). The stone carrying the text has not been observed since 1913 and neither photographs nor squeezes of it have come to light, so that it cannot be illustrated; but Boulanger was a good epigraphist whose reading we can accept with confidence, and the base itself is sufficiently described to be associated equally confidently with a number of others to make an interesting group.

The text was cut on a base of white marble (undoubtedly local), 0.65m. high and 0.485m. wide, with the first line on an upper moulding. The letters were 0.038m. high but are not otherwise described except as including a ligature of H and N in l.8. It was found in the East Court of the Hadrianic Baths, "in front of the last but one entry to the North Portico" but it is not at present clear whether this was near its original location.

ὑπὲρ Φλαβίας <u>scroll</u>	On behalf of Flavia
Ἀτταλίδος	Attalis

[1] French excavations undertaken by P. Gaudin in 1904 and 1905 included exploration of the Hadrianic Baths, see the report by G. Mendel in *CRAI* 1906, 178–84. Work was resumed in 1913 under the direction of A. Boulanger, who published an interim report in *CRAI* 1914, 46ff.; he had expected at least one more season there and never published the details of his finds. His epigraphic note-books passed into the hands of Prof. Louis Robert, and after his death Mme. Robert very kindly gave them to Charlotte Roueché, who is currently preparing their texts for inclusion in her projected computerised corpus of Aphrodisian inscriptions.

Αἰλιανῆς τῆς
ἑαυτοῦ γυ-
ναικὸς Τίτος
Φλάβιος 'Αθη-
ναγόρας 'Αγα-
θὸς τὴν καρυ-
ᾶτιν τῷ Δήμῳ

Aeliana
his wife
Titus
Flavius Athe-
nagoras Aga-
thus (gave) the
caryatid to the people.

A husband makes a donation to the city on behalf of his wife, whose name Aeliana suggests the possibility that her parents were recalling a connection (however indirect) with the emperor Hadrian. If that is so she can hardly have been of marriageable age before the later years of Hadrian's reign at the earliest. Flavia Attalis Aeliana has not as yet figured in any other Aphrodisian inscription, but her husband bears a name well known to us. A T. Flavius Athenagoras Agathus appears in a number of inscriptions as *procurator Augusti*, husband of a Sallustia Frontina of Roman senatorial rank and father of a son who entered the Roman Senate as well as of a daughter whose son did the same, rising to hold senatorial office, which has been dated under Commodus.[2] A recently published set of inscriptions of the first century AD gives his family background in a succession of ancestors whose public benefactions were considerable.[3] It is difficult, however, to identify him with the husband of the new inscription; if Flavia Attalis was his first wife who died young, his grandson by Sallustia Frontina could hardly have been old enough to hold the office attested for him as early as is supposed; and if she was a second wife, it is surprising that he is not described here as *procurator Augusti*. The basis for the dating of the grandson's career does not seem to me, at first sight anyway, to be quite secure, so that perhaps this argument could be overcome; but I incline to think that it is more likely that we have here the procurator's son at a comparatively early stage in his life before he entered the Senate. If so, there is still a difficulty, for in most of the inscriptions that we have for him, he is given his mother's *nomen* as well as his father's, appearing as T. Sallustius Flavius Athenagoras Agathus or T. Flavius Sallustius Athenagoras Agathus. I guess that he used his mother's

[2] *MAMA* VIII 517 with a correction in ll. 2–3 of the second column (where Σάνκτον is a misreading for Φλάβιον) gives the essential information, but there are a number of other texts.

[3] Joyce Reynolds 'The first known Aphrodisian to hold a procuratorship' in *Steine und Wege, Festschrift für Dieter Knibbe zum 65 Geburtstag* (Wien, 1999) 327–34.

nomen as a ploy to enhance his prestige, by proclaiming his link with his mother's senatorial family when seeking senatorial rank himself; so that we need not be too surprised if as a young man he appeared without it. But that is to embark on speculation well beyond the facts available. There might, I suppose, have been another member of the family who bore the same names as the procurator (which derive from traditions established in the family in the first century AD) and held no other Roman honours than the citizenship at any stage in his life. We must hope for new discoveries from Aphrodisias to clarify the point. What is certain is that this is a couple from the upper levels of the Aphrodisian governing class.

The base is clearly one of a number of similar ones that have been found in or near the Hadrianic Baths, mostly in the older unpublished excavation, but a few more recently.[4] Those known to me which have survived complete or more or less so are all moulded above on three sides, measure approximately 0.60m. in height and 0.60m. in width across the moulding (10–15cm. less across the face below it), and have a quite deep rectangular hole in the centre of the top surface for attaching a substantial item, probably a statue. The majority have an egg and dart moulding; but a quite substantial number have a plain one, on which a line of inscription (sometimes two) has been cut, as described on the base published here.

Apart from the present one, all for which enough of the text survives record a woman's name in the nominative case, often with titles indicating her membership of the élite group in the city,[5] usually, although not invariably, with her father's or husband's name and commonly with some title for him as well, and an indication that she has given an object too obvious to name to the Demos or to the Patris. The texts are not uniform—clearly each one was drafted individually by the donor or her agent—although the information given was substantially the same. On two of them,[6] a subsidiary text names a sculptor. That is why I have always thought that statues, rather than columns, stood on them.

[4] A few have been published, see Th. Reinach *REG* 19 (1906), nos. 28, 37, 69; G. Jacopi, *Mon. Ant.* 38 (1939), 225, no. 6; *MAMA* VIII 435 (very fragmentary).

[5] So High Priestess of Asia, High Priestess (of Aphrodisias), priestess of Aphrodite (in one case priestess for life).

[6] One is Reinach (as in n. 4), no. 69; see also M. Squarciapino, *La Scuola di Afrodisia* (Rome, 1943), catalogue no. 2, and *SEG* 40.296.

To my eye, the bases seem to be more or less uniform in two very closely similar series, one with egg and dart moulding, the other with plain moulding.[7] On the face of it therefore, they can be envisaged as placed side by side in a row (or two rows), their unmoulded backs presumably up against a wall which provided a back-drop for their statues. In the light of the new text we can make a provisional guess that the result was a row (or rows) of caryatids. Given the find-spots of the majority it is, I think a very probable hypothesis that they decorated some part of the Hadrianic Baths.

A striking feature of the Hadrianic Baths is that its quite grandiose decoration of sculptured marbles was given by a considerable number of donors who clearly acted cooperatively.[8] The goddess Aphrodite heads the subscription list, so to speak (her committee of *neopoioi* appears to have controlled a sizeable treasury); but the human donors recorded in the inscriptions have so far been all men. Now we seem to have a significant contribution by a group of women who also acted cooperatively, a feature for which it is not easy to find a parallel in other ancient buildings. It should be stressed, I think, that these women donors had the support of the male members in their families, their fathers or husbands, as the new text underlines; and it would be wrong to affirm that there is a women's initiative to be seen here. Rather perhaps the fact that a large Roman bath building would contain a section specifically for women might suggest to the leaders of public life, as they sought the funds that they needed, that its decoration was an appropriate purpose for which to attract and use women's money.

We now know that in the early years of Hadrian's reign (AD 124 and 125) Aphrodisias was negotiating with the emperor about its plans to build a new aqueduct (very possibly to be connected with those for the new baths) and the problem of funding it.[9] It is not clear that there had been any check to the city's prosperity, but there was certainly an increasing number of projects other than the building of utilities on which donors could spend their money; and we know from a letter of Antoninus Pius to Ephesus that the popularity of public entertainment might be thought to discourage more

[7] There are variations of a few centimetres in the measurements, but these are commonplace in the architecture of the city.

[8] Most of the texts are unpublished.

[9] Joyce Reynolds, 'New letters of Hadrian to Aphrodisias: trials, taxes, gladiators and an aqueduct', *JRA* 13 (2000) 5–20.

useful projects.[10] That had perhaps happened at Aphrodisias where a plan to divert to the fund for the aqueduct money normally spent by high priests on gladiatorial shows was associated with attempts to evade service as high priest. That is something of a context for the cooperation of a number of members of the governing class in the Hadrianic Baths, in which they can now be seen to have included their women.[11]

[10] J.H. Oliver, *Greek Constitutions of Early Roman Emperors from Inscriptions and Papyri* (Philadelphia, 1989), no. 138.

[11] I am particularly indebted to my nephew Bernard Reynolds without whom this note could not possibly have reached the editor in time.

ROMAN LAW AND THE LAWS OF THE MEDES AND PERSIANS: DECIUS' AND VALERIAN'S PERSECUTIONS OF CHRISTIANITY

Paul McKechnie

1. The Purpose of Decius' Edict

J.B. Rives has argued in 'The Decree of Decius and the Religion of Empire'[1] that by issuing the order in AD 249 that all inhabitants of the Roman empire should sacrifice to the gods, Decius (whether he knew it or not)[2] took a step on the long journey of transition from the ancient world to the middle ages. His edict was "in some ways the religious analogue to Caracalla's citizenship decree".[3] Religions of the Roman world were fundamentally local, but those of medieval Europe were universalizing.[4] Although local officials supervised the sacrifices Decius ordered, and those sacrifices might be made to gods worshipped in civic cults,[5] Rives holds that the edict "created a religious obligation between the individual and the empire", with the city functioning merely as the imperial administration's 'religious agent'. This, he argues, weakened the tradition of collective local cults, at the same time as strengthening the definitional boundaries of a religion of the Roman empire. As a result, the idea of Roman religion could be put forward more forcefully a few years later by Valerian, who decreed "that those who do not practise Roman religion ought to acknowledge Roman rites".[6] It was one of the ironies

[1] J.B. Rives 'The Decree of Decius and the Religion of Empire' *JRS* 89 (1999), 135–54.

[2] Rives 'Decree of Decius' (as in n. 1), 154 (and cf. 151, among other places).

[3] Rives 'Decree of Decius' (as in n. 1), 153.

[4] Rives 'Decree of Decius' (as in n. 1), 135.

[5] As Rives observes at 152 and n. 90, referring to sacrifices being directed to the Capitoline Triad at Carthage (Cyprian *De lapsis* 24 and *Epistles* 59.13.3), and the Nemeseis at Smyrna (*Martyrdom of Pionius* 6.3 and 7.2). *Libelli* (sacrifice-certificates) as preserved in Egypt follow a set wording, which does not specify to what deity or deities the sacrifices were made (John R. Knipfing 'The Libelli of the Decian Persecution' *Harvard Theological Review* 16 [1923], 345–90: at 346–7. Knipfing gives a version incorporating [in English] all attested elements of the standard wording).

[6] Rives 'Decree of Decius' (as in n. 1), 153; wording of decree from *Acta Cypriani* 1.

of history, Rives concludes, that Christianity—whose adherents suffered under Decius' edict—was later itself to become 'Roman religion', the defining religion of the Roman empire; but the reason why events took this turn may (he suggests) have been that the cult act of sacrifice—which Decius' edict enjoined—proved in the long term not to be a sufficiently strong element around which to build a unified religion.[7]

Some important questions are not addressed in Rives' presentation of his case. What about the Jews? Rives records what little there is to know—probably they were not required to sacrifice.[8] But why not? Rives contends that the primary purpose of Decius' edict was not to wipe Christianity out; and he favours emphasizing the edict's "positive goal of ensuring that everyone in the Empire, Christians included, perform a full and traditional sacrifice."[9] Well, everyone—but (apparently) Jews *excluded.* And yet they were an important minority. How did an exemption for Jews come to seem consistent with the overriding goal of the edict, if that goal was what Rives takes it to be?

And what about the issue of definition? Is it true that, as late as 249, empire-wide persecution of religious transgressors could not be undertaken until boundaries of the religion of empire had been set, in the form of the wording of new legislation?[10] That Christianity was illegal was not in doubt—in fact, early in the third century, Ulpian had collected the imperial rescripts laying down penalties for Christianity in his *De officio proconsulis.*[11] And well before Decius' time Christianity could be contrasted against *Roman* religion—as, for instance, in the *Martyrdom of the Scillitans.* Speratus, replying to the proconsul Saturninus' suggestion that he and his companions should "return to a right mind", outlines Christian moral values, prompting the proconsul to say:

[7] Rives 'Decree of Decius' (as in n. 1), 154.
[8] Rives 'Decree of Decius' (as in n. 1), 138 n. 16.
[9] Rives 'Decree of Decius' (as in n. 1), 142.
[10] Rives 'Decree of Decius' (as in n. 1), 153.
[11] Lactantius *Divine Institutes* 5.11.19 (cf. G.E.M. de Ste. Croix 'Why were the early Christians persecuted?' in M.I. Finley *Studies in Ancient Society* [London, 1974], 210–49 at 223–4; this article first published at *Past and Present* 26 [1963], 6–38). On Roman law as it affected Christians and Jews see also John Crook *Law and Life of Rome* (London and Ithaca, NY, 1967), 278–80.

> We also are religious people, and our religion is simple: we swear by the genius of our lord the emperor, and pray for his safety, as you also ought to do.

Later, passing sentence, the proconsul reads from a tablet:

> Whereas Speratus, Nartzalus, Cittinus, Donata, Vestia, Secunda and the rest have confessed that they live in accordance with the religious rites of the Christians, and, when an opportunity was given them of returning to the usage of the Romans, persevered in their obstinacy, it is our pleasure that they should suffer by the sword.

To the proconsul at Carthage in 180, then, *Roman* religion was not too fuzzy a concept to be applied in court. It was clear to him that the defendants were already (and in each individual case) under an obligation to the empire to "return to the usage of the Romans".[12]

What, also, about the *Constitutio Antoniniana*? Rives argues that Decius' edict was its 'religious analogue'—but did it need one? The extant fragment of it frames the emperor's decision in religious terms:[13]

> . . . I consider that in this way I can . . . render proper service to their [the immortal gods'] majesty . . . by bringing with me to the worship of the gods all who enter into the number of my people. Accordingly, I grant Roman citizenship to all aliens throughout the world . . .

A high-minded sentiment. Dio Cassius says Caracalla's real aim was to increase the tax take.[14] But even if so, the *Constitutio Antoniniana* recorded in writing the government's aspiration towards universalizing religion. The statute assumes that (only) being a Roman makes it possible to practise Roman religion, and so makes all free people into citizens. This legislated change accords conceptual priority to 'imperial' religion over 'local' religion: does it not indicate that central government had begun to subvert locally-based cults a generation before Decius?

Partial answers, at any rate, to these questions emerge from considering the nature of Roman legislation and legal precedent. An imperial edict might reiterate a long-standing principle and innovate (if at all) only by reminding officials to act against offenders: so

---

[12] The martyr-act does not record the martyrs' statuses, but the proconsul sentences them to death by beheading; this method of execution may indicate that they were Roman citizens.

[13] P. Giessen 40 col. 1.

[14] D.C. 77.9; cf. Fergus Millar *A Study of Cassius Dio* (Oxford, 1964), 152–3.

Decius, by legislating, was not necessarily stating a new religious principle. As for the Jews, precedent excusing them from polytheistic observance was substantial, and dated back hundreds of years. It had survived the destruction of the Jerusalem Temple, and two further Jewish wars; the ban against circumcision brought in by Hadrian had been rescinded under Antoninus Pius.[15] The *Constitutio Antoniniana*, for all its (professed) religious motivation, did not (it seems) legislate to change the religious conditions applying to Jews: indeed, Jews who were not already citizens received citizenship under it like everyone else. Similarly, Decius' edict did not seek to depart from precedent where the Jews were concerned.

So, as far as the statutory regulation of religion was concerned, Decius' edict was not innovative in quite the way Rives posits. It did not draw out hitherto unmentioned religious consequences of the *Constitutio Antoniniana* (since that law foregrounded religion anyway), it did not define a hitherto unexplained concept of 'Roman religion' (since 'Roman religion' was already understood), and it left intact the principal legally-established exception to the presumption that all Romans practised Roman religion.

All this indicates that the case Rives puts forward in his article cannot be accepted without important reservations. All the same, his basic proposal that the edict should be viewed from the perspective of traditional religion[16] is persuasive. He is not the first to suggest that instituting empire-wide persecution of Christians cannot have been the chief purpose of the legislation.[17] David S. Potter goes further and suggests that Decius may not even have been aware of Christianity as a problem; but he has probably underestimated Decius' general knowledge.[18] Christians were numerous enough for any emperor, even one who was (in Potter's phrase) 'quite stupid',[19] to

[15] SHA *Hadrian* 14.2 and *Digest* 48.8.11; cf. Amnon Linder (ed.) *The Jews in Roman Imperial Legislation* (Detroit and Jerusalem, 1987), 99–102.

[16] Rives 'Decree of Decius' (as in n. 1), 135.

[17] For a summary of views on whether Decius aimed to exterminate Christianity see Hans A. Pohlsander 'The Religious Policy of Decius' in *ANRW* II.16.3 (Berlin, 1986), 1826–42 at 1839–40.

[18] David S. Potter *Prophecy and History in the Crisis of the Roman Empire: a Historical Commentary on the Thirteenth Sibylline Oracle* (Oxford, 1990), 43. Rives, more plausibly, says ('Decree of Decius' [as in n. 1], 141) that "an emperor who required universal sacrifice in the mid-third century AD could hardly be oblivious of its implications for Christians."

[19] Potter *Prophecy and History* (as in n. 18), 41.

be aware that they existed and dissented from polytheism. And after his edict was passed, Decius took a personal part in enforcing it—G.W. Clarke seems to be right to argue that the emperor himself was the judge in the trial of Celerinus in Rome.[20] To Christians, of course, persecution looked like the main point. So Eusebius, little more than half a century later, read events in the context of the (mistaken) idea that Philip the Arab had been a Christian:[21] "Decius . . . on account of his enmity towards Philip, raised a persecution against the churches . . ."

The way the sacrificing-campaign worked indicates that it was primarily meant to capture divine blessings believed to be obtainable by practising Roman religion, and only secondarily to detect recalcitrant persons who ought to be punished. At Alexandria, the sacrifices took place in a public gathering, with individuals called forward by name to go through the necessary ceremony, and a large crowd in attendance;[22] Clarke is surely right to argue that the names did not come from census-rolls, in an attempt to summon all inhabitants individually, but were given in on the day to an official who then made a list, to save queuing.[23] Clarke also observes that one was not required to sacrifice in one's place of census registration—another compromise on the attempt to enforce universal coverage. Preserved *libelli* do not appear to have been issued to people whom it would have been easy to suspect of Christianity.[24] The inference must be that the sacrificing-campaign did not amount to a systematic inquiry into allegiance. Admittedly, bishops of the empire's main cities were attacked soon after the edict arrived (Fabian, bishop of Rome, being put to death on 20 January 250,[25] and Babylas, bishop of Antioch, four days later;[26] at Alexandria, the Prefect sent a soldier after Bishop Dionysius,[27]

---

[20] Cyprian *Epistles* 39.2.1 and G.W. Clarke 'Some Observations on the Persecution of Decius' *Antichthon* 3 (1969), 63–77 at 64.

[21] Eusebius *Ecclesiastical History* 6.39.1.

[22] Eusebius *Ecclesiastical History* 6.41.11.

[23] Clarke 'Some Observations' (as in n. 20), 71.

[24] Rives ('Decree of Decius' [as in n. 1], 141) is rightly unenthusiastic about suggestions that Aurelia Ammonous, daughter of Mystus, priestess of Petesouchos, the great, the mighty, the immortal, and priestess of the gods in the Moeris quarter (whose *libellus* is Knipfing no. 3, at Knipfing 'Libelli of the Decian Persecution' pp. 364–5), was a secret or former Christian, or had Christian relatives.

[25] Eusebius *Ecclesiastical History* 6.39.1.

[26] Eusebius *Ecclesiastical History* 6.39.4.

[27] Eusebius *Ecclesiastical History* 6.40.2.

and at Carthage Bishop Cyprian was declared an outlaw),[28] but this was only to be expected. Provincial officials knew that arresting bishops, or making them leave town, would help ensure compliance from their flocks.

So what benefit, not ordinarily obtained, did Decius hope to gain from the gods, or what particular motive impelled him to call for a campaign of sacrifice by everyone across the Roman empire? The guess sometimes hazarded that the whole thing was a (delayed) way of marking the millennium of Rome is not persuasive:[29] Rome's millennium was past and gone, and sufficiently celebrated, before Decius came to the throne. So if religious reinforcement of the principles behind the *Constitutio Antoniniana* was also not at issue, then what was? In this chapter I will draw attention to a possible political motive for Decius' edict, suggesting that on this occasion, and again under Valerian, strategic concerns provoked the demand by central government for a demonstration (directed to the gods) of religious unity.

2. Persian Aggression and Roman Weakness

Since Ardashir in 226 succeeded in taking over from the Parthian Arsacids, the Roman empire had had a new and militarily aggressive state as its eastern neighbour. Ardashir himself, Dio Cassius and Herodian say, claimed that the domains of the ancient Persian kings, as far as the sea separating Asia from Europe, were rightfully part of his realm.[30] In 232 Severus Alexander led a not very successful

---

[28] Cyprian *Letters* 66.4.1.

[29] Potter's explanation centres on this: "Decius . . . may have intended this act to reaffirm the *pax deorum*, and to reassure people throughout the empire that the empire was still secure after the passing of the millennium" (*Prophecy and History* [as in n. 18], 43).

[30] D.C. 80.4.1, saying that "he [Ardashir] accordingly became a source of fear to us"; Herodian 6.2.1–2. A.D. Lee (*Information and Frontiers: Roman Foreign Relations in Late Antiquity* [Cambridge, 1993], 21–2) does not think Ardashir would have known enough about the Achaemenid empire to speak in the terms Herodian records: he might be right if Persian tradition was Ardashir's only source of information. But Ardashir was probably not as isolated as that: it is likely that he had visitors from the Roman empire as informants. Plotinus, after all, went east with Gordian III's expedition, hoping to make contact with learned Persians and Indians (and he had difficulty getting back to Antioch after Gordian died: Porphyry *Life of Plotinus* 3). Others may have had more success, and been able to tell Ardashir about Darius and Xerxes.

Roman campaign against Ardashir,[31] but later in the 230s Carrhae and Nisibis were taken by the Persians, and held until recaptured under Gordian III in 242.[32] Potter suggests that a revolt in Africa, and perhaps a barbarian invasion across the Danube, may be reasons why the Romans did not move faster than they did to regain control of this Roman territory from Persia.[33] Unsettled conditions and weaker Roman control were also reflected in the brief restoration of the kingdom of Osrhoene under Abgar IX from 240–2: for most of the third century this territory was part of the province of Mesopotamia and Osrhoene, governed by an equestrian prefect.[34]

Between January and March 244, Gordian III died campaigning against Ardashir's successor Shapur I. A mound a few miles east of the Euphrates commemorated him.[35] Philip, who took over as emperor, got out of Gordian's Persian war, making a treaty on unfavourable terms. Potter concludes that the Romans paid 500,000 *aurei* to Shapur at once (with annual payments to follow), acquiesced in Shapur keeping Roman territory he had captured, and agreed not to help the king of Armenia against Persia.[36] After the 244 treaty, the eastern end of the Roman empire came under the command of Philip's brother, the Praetorian Prefect Julius Priscus, addressed as 'Prefect of Mesopotamia with consular standing' in a papyrus petition dated 28 August 245.[37] When he dealt with this petition, Julius Priscus was

---

[31] Herodian 6.5.1–6.6.

[32] Zonaras 12.18; George Syncellus p. 681 (= 443); cf. Potter *Prophecy and History* (as in n. 18), 190–6.

[33] Potter *Prophecy and History* (as in n. 18), 191–2.

[34] J. Teixidor 'Les derniers rois d'Edesse d'après deux nouveaux documents syriaques' *Zeitschrift für Papyrologie und Epigraphik* 76 (1989), 219–22, and Potter *Prophecy and History* (as in n. 18), 214.

[35] Ammianus Marcellinus 23.5.7, Eutropius *Breviarium* 9.2.3, Zosimus 3.14.2: Potter discusses the exact location of the mound at *Prophecy and History* [as in n. 18], 202–4: at 211 he attributes Gordian's death to a mutiny in his army, provoked by "a mismanaged attempt to invade Persia at the wrong time of year".

[36] Potter *Prophecy and History* (as in n. 18), 224–5: D. Oates (*Studies in the Ancient History of Northern Iraq* [Oxford, 1968], 82–9) noted the permanent destruction of a Roman fort at Ain Sinu, and suggested that the Romans abandoned the region between Singara and the Tigris after the 244 peace; and in the excavations of a fort at Kifrin on the lower Euphrates, the latest coins found were of Gordian III (E. Valtz *Kifrin, La Fortezza del Limes* [Turin, 1985], 112 and 120, and E. Valtz 'Kifrin, a fortress of the *limes* on the Euphrates' *Mesopotamia* 22 [1987], 81–9 at 88–9).

[37] Denis Feissel and Jean Gascou 'Documents d'archives romains inédits du moyen Euphrate (IIIe siècle après J.-C.)' *Comptes rendus de l'académie des inscriptions* 1989, 535–61, at 545–8.

conducting business at the Baths of Hadrian in Antioch—which may hint that it was difficult for him to take up residence in his province. Later, he had a grander title: he is described on a dedication from the later 240s as 'Rector of the Orient'.[38] Julius Priscus may have won back some territory for his brother (Zonaras says Philip soon broke his treaty with Persia, but in the Thirteenth Sibylline Oracle it looks as if the Persians were the aggressors—a version which may be more consistent with Julius Priscus trying in 245 to run the province of Mesopotamia from Antioch).[39] In an unpublished petition on papyrus, described by Denis Feissel and Jean Gascou (and from the same group of papyri as the one addressed to Julius Priscus), Rostamos from Birtha Okbanon in Mesopotamia asks officials to rule that Barsemaias must give up possession of a vineyard which Rostamos inherited from his father, but left six years ago to escape a Persian invasion.[40] This undated text may be connected with the frontier moving back in the Romans' favour in the mid-240s: the reason for the six-year interval may be that the vineyard had been in Persian-held territory from the time of the invasion to the time when the petition was filed.

But even if some vineyards were changing hands thanks to Julius Priscus' activities, there was no large-scale campaign in the 240s after Gordian III to reassert control of Roman territory up to its former eastern boundaries. So, by the time Decius was proclaimed emperor, in Pannonia,[41] there were areas inside the eastern frontier of his empire which had been under Persian occupation for almost a decade. Persian aggressive moves were more than 'razzias' (as Michael H. Dodgeon and Samuel N.C. Lieu call them):[42] Sassanid rulers wanted

[38] ILS 9005, from Philippopolis (Schuhba) in Arabia.

[39] Zonaras 12.19 says that "after a while, [Philip] put the agreement aside and got hold of the lands"; but *Sibylline Oracles* 13.27–31 says that ". . . there will briefly be an end to war, but not for long: when the wolf shall swear oaths to the dogs of gleaming teeth against the flock he will ravage, harming the wool-fleeced sheep, and he will break the oaths and then there will be lawless strife of arrogant kings . . ." It seems to be right to identify the dogs with the Romans and the wolf with Shapur (cf. Potter *Prophecy and History* [as in n. 18], 228).

[40] Feissel and Gascou 'Documents d'archives romains' (as in n. 37), no. 2, pp. 557–8.

[41] Zosimus 1.21.2; cf. A.R. Birley 'Decius Reconsidered' in Edward Frézouls and Hélène Jouffroy (eds.) *Les empereurs illyriens: Actes du colloque de Strasbourg (11–13 octobre 1990) organisé par le Centre de recherche sur l'Europe central et sud-orientale* (Strasbourg, AECR [Université des sciences humaines de Strasbourg. Contributions et travaux de l'institut d'histoire romaine, 8], 1998), 74.

[42] Michael H. Dodgeon and Samuel N.C. Lieu *The Roman Eastern Frontier and the Persian Wars AD 226–363* (London, 1991), 2.

to get and retain land for their empire, even if they did not really expect to carry out Ardashir's threat of taking all Asia as far as the Propontis from the Romans.

3. Persecution of non-Zoroastrians

At the court of Shapur I (242–272) there was a Zoroastrian clergyman called Kartir, and the king made his position "independent and authoritative over religious matters at court and in every province and place, and over the priesthood throughout the empire".[43] Kartir lived on into the reign of Vahram II (276–93), when his career-inscription at Naqsh-i-Rustam was composed and engraved. The inscription describes a Sassanid religious policy which (I will argue below) remained consistent under Ardashir and Shapur. I propose that Kartir's account of his activities amounts to a fair picture of what the Persians were doing in their realm in the 240s.

At the beginning of the text, Kartir records what he did with the broad-ranging powers the king gave him:[44]

> . . . at the command of Shapur, King of kings, and with the support of the yazads and the King of kings, religious services were multiplied in every province and place, and many Vahram Fires were founded. And many a priest became joyful and prosperous. And charters were sealed for many fires and priestly colleges, and much benefit reached Ohrmazd and the yazads, and there was much confusion for Ahriman and the devs . . .

Then he lists promotions and honours he received from Shapur's successors on the throne. Afterwards, he records the religious results of his policies:[45]

> . . . in every province and place of the whole empire the service of Ohrmazd and the yazads was exalted, and the Mazda-worshipping religion and its priests received much honour in the land. And the yazads, and fire and water and cattle, were greatly contented, and

[43] Inscription of Kartir on the Ka'aba of Zoroaster at Naqsh-i-Rustam (= KKZ), line 1: in M.L. Chaumont 'L'inscription de Kartir à la "Ka'bah de Zoroastre" (texte, traduction, commentaire)' *Journal Asiatique* 248 (1960), 339–80. Translation quoted from Mary Boyce (ed.) *Textual Sources for the Study of Zoroastrianism* (Manchester, 1984), 112.

[44] KKZ line 2.

[45] KKZ lines 6–10.

> Ahriman and the devs suffered great blows and harm. And the creed of Ahriman and the devs was driven out of the land and deprived of credence. And Jews and Buddhists and Brahmans and Aramaic and Greek-speaking Christians and Baptisers and Manichaeans were assailed in the land. And images were overthrown, and the dens of demons were (thus) destroyed, and the places and abodes of the yazads [i.e. fire temples] were established . . . And from the first I, Kartir, underwent much toil and trouble for the yazads and the rulers, and for my own soul's sake. And I caused many fires and priestly colleges to flourish in Iran, and also in non-Iranian lands. There were fires and priests in the non-Iranian lands which were reached by the armies of the King of kings. The provincial capital Antioch and the province of Syria, and the districts dependent on Syria; the provincial capital Tarsus and the province of Cilicia, and the districts dependent on Cilicia; the provincial capital Caesarea and the province of Cappadocia, and the districts dependent on Cappadocia, up to Pontus, and the province of Armenia, and Georgia and Albania and Balasagan, up to the 'Gate of the Alans'—these were plundered and burnt and laid waste by Shapur, King of kings, with his armies. There too, at the command of the King of kings, I reduced to order the priests and fires which were in those lands. And I did not allow harm to be done them, or captives made. And whoever had thus been made captive, him indeed I took and sent back to his own land. And I made the Mazda-worshipping religion and its good priests esteemed and honoured in the land. And heretics and harmful men, who being in the priesthood did not in their expositions further the Mazda-worshipping religion and the service of the yazads, them I punished and rebuked until through me they were amended. And I drew up many documents and charters for fires and priestly colleges. And with the support of the yazads and the King of kings, and by my act, many Vahram Fires were founded in the land of Iran, and many next-of-kin marriages were made, and many people who had not believed, became believers. And there were many who had held the religion of the devs, and by my act they abandoned the religion of the devs and accepted the religion of the yazads.

Summarizing a long career, Kartir groups related events rather than proceeding chronologically: he claims credit early in the inscription, for instance, for assailing Manichaeans—but Shapur I was not unsympathetic to Mani and his followers (Mani wrote the *Shapuragan* for him): it was Vahram I who had Mani tortured to death in prison, in 276. When Kartir writes of captured Roman territory, he lists one after another the furthest places Persian armies captured in their campaigns against the Roman empire. Many of the places mentioned were not held long: Antioch, for example, was captured by the

Persians in 252, but taken back by the Romans. As far as Zoroastrianism is concerned, Kartir makes a point of saying that he has supported establishment of sacred fires and priestly colleges both inside and outside Iran—and before listing the king's Roman conquests, he adds specifically that "There were fires and priests in the non-Iranian lands which were reached by the armies of the King of kings". These cult centres he has reorganized to reflect what he sees as the best up-to-date Zoroastrian practice: "There too, at the command of the King of kings, I reduced to order the priests and fires which were in those lands".

J. Duchesne-Guillemin, discussing Zoroastrian religion under the Sasanians, understands Kartir's career as one in which real political power came late: "Only under Shapur's successors," he writes,[46] "began Karder's promotion, which gave rise to the Mazdean hierarchy". Hormizd I, who came to the throne in 272, made Kartir, formerly an *ehrpat* ('master of knowledge', transliterated as *herbad* in Boyce's *Textual Sources*), into *magupat* ('Chief of magi': transliterated by Boyce as *mobad*). Duchesne-Guillemin goes on to discuss the influence Kartir may have had on the royal succession in the 270s, supporting as candidates for the throne first Vahram I (in 274) and then Vahram II (276–93), against their brother Narseh. But his interpretation, which minimizes Kartir's importance during Shapur's reign, is unsatisfactory. His late-career 'promotions' were a matter of giving new titles to a man who was already at the top. Kartir is mentioned by name in Shapur's inscription on the Ka'aba of Zarathustra at Naqsh-i-Rustam as receiving the same grant of animals and foods to be sacrificed on his behalf as other dignitaries who were not members of the royal family.[47] Kartir's nearby explanation of his own life's achievements fits this monumental context perfectly, and it is most natural to read it as implying that Kartir was an official of equal dignity with the others mentioned by Shapur: Hormizd the Chief Scribe, Naduk the Warden of the State Prison, Papak the Master of the Gate, and Mihrekhwast the Treasurer.

Furthermore, the hypothesis that Kartir was in post as 'Minister of Religion' from the 240s and throughout the years of Shapur's

---

[46] J. Duchesne-Guillemin 'Zoroastrian Religion', in Ehsan Yarshater (ed.) *Cambridge History of Iran* 3.2 (Cambridge, 1983), 866–908, at 880.

[47] See Boyce *Textual Sources* (as in n. 42), 111.

military conquests is attractive, on grounds of continuity of policy, because of the reforming religious outlook evident earlier in the *Letter of Tansar*.[48] In this letter Tansar, *herbad* in the time of Ardashir and in effect a predecessor of Kartir,[49] says that "Church and State were born of the one womb, joined together and never to be sundered". He goes on to explain to King Gushnasp the religious policies of Ardashir: imprisoning a religious dissident for a year (instead of putting him to death at once), and having "learned men . . . summon him at frequent intervals and advise him and lay arguments before him and destroy his doubts"; and closing dynastic fire temples set up by rival kings ("pure innovation, introduced by them without the authority of kings of old"). Ardashir and his minister Tansar acted against religious dissidents before Shapur ascended the throne. Kartir, therefore, probably came in to *continue* a policy of discouraging dissent against the official version of Zoroastrianism.

There was, then, an energetic decades-long campaign of pro-Zoroastrian reform in lands the Persians took over—and since the Persians took over and held territory inside the Roman empire, it must be assumed that areas formerly (and later) held by the Romans were subject to this campaign. Discouragement of non-Zoroastrian religions went along with Kartir's reform. When he says that "Ahriman and the devs suffered great blows and harm . . . the creed of Ahriman and the devs was driven out of the land and deprived of credence", he may be referring partly to non-Zoroastrian Persian religion, but that is not likely to be the only kind of religious deviance meant by "the creed of Ahriman and the devs". Greco-Roman deities, to a Zoroastrian, were 'devs', and their temples, where statues of them were kept, were 'dens of demons'. When Kartir says that "images were overthrown, and the dens of demons were (thus) destroyed", he probably means (among other things) that in his time, Greco-Roman temples and sanctuaries in Persian-occupied Roman territory were attacked. In fact, since 'the creed of Ahriman and the

[48] See Boyce *Textual Sources* (as in n. 42), 109–11. This letter is known from Ibn Isfandiyar's thirteenth-century *History of Tabaristan*. Boyce argues that the core of the letter as given by Ibn Isfandiyar is genuine, though she believes that it was revised in the sixth century, and that the *Vorlage* of Ibn Isfandiyar's Persian text was an Arabic version made in the ninth century.

[49] Duchesne-Guillemin ('Zoroastrian Religion' [as in n. 46], 877) comments on the simplicity of Tansar's title (*ehrpat/herbad*) and takes it as confirmation that at his date in Zoroastrianism "the idea of an ecclesiastical hierarchy was still to be born".

devs' is mentioned before (and separately from) the other religions opposed by Kartir (of Jews, Buddhists, Brahmans, and Aramaic- and Greek-speaking Christians), it is likely that Kartir saw polytheists (including Greco-Roman polytheists) as the most important and largest group among the enemies of Zoroastrianism.

4. Religion and the Defence of the Roman Empire

As it happens, the Thirteenth Sibylline Oracle, which distils the history of the Roman East in these years, refers in passing to 'desecrations of temples' (ἱεροσυλίαι) as one of the features of its 'uprising of the evil Persians'.[50] Since many other undesirable but ordinary events are listed in the same place (wars, battles, murders, famines, plagues, lightning, plundering) it would not be wise to insist that 'desecrations of temples' must be a reminiscence of Kartir's activities. But it may be: there is no reason to presume that ex-Roman territory was exempt from the actions Kartir says he took in 'non-Iranian lands' in general.

So, in the 240s, the Persians were doing their best to impose their reformed religion on Romans in the territories they were occupying. They were destroying temples, and discouraging Greco-Roman-style worship of local deities. Decius, with the normal Roman methods of intelligence-gathering at his disposal,[51] must have heard what was happening. Knowing that Roman religion was being persecuted would have give him in 249/50 a stronger motive than any so far suggested for his edict on sacrifice and the consequent persecution of Christians. The edict itself probably did not expound the emperor's political reasons for issuing it (such a reference might have required embarrassing admissions of defeats and loss of territory). Its overriding purpose was to co-ordinate an act of worship of Roman gods on the largest scale possible, by requiring every individual to make a sacrifice. Decius exempted Jews from sacrificing,[52] on the basis of

[50] *Thirteenth Sibylline Oracle* 12–13.

[51] A.D. Lee observes (*Information and Frontiers* [as in n. 30], 147) that the level of information available to Roman government about the Persians was high, by comparison with what could be found out about peoples across the northern frontier: it should be assumed that a good deal was known in the imperial palace about what was happening on the eastern frontier of the empire.

[52] Jacob Neusner argues ('Jews in Iran' in Ehsan Yarshater [ed.] *Cambridge History of Iran* III.2 [Cambridge, 1983], 909–23, at 913–5) that "of those 'opposed' by

long-standing precedent, but in the case of the Christians, acted consistently with normal practice as codified by Ulpian.[53] The aim was to obtain divine favour, or at least counteract any advantage the Persians might be obtaining from their gods as a result of Kartir's programme. Those who have argued that the sacrifices Decius ordered constituted a *supplicatio*, an act of worship serving to ask the gods for their help in the face of an urgent need, have a good case.[54] The sacrificing-campaign copied Kartir's methods: Kartir mobilized Iranians and conquered peoples to Zoroastrian observance, and Decius aimed to mobilize Romans to enact Roman rituals. His sacrificing-campaign was conceived as a religious solution to the (partly) religious problem of territory being lost to Persia, and Roman cults being persecuted by Zoroastrians in that lost territory. After all, no military solution could be contemplated in the short term. Decius, busy in 249 with a Gothic war,[55] had no opportunity to lead an army east to fight the Persians.

The fact that one quasi-universal act of worship was the point of Decius' edict explains why (although there was widespread anti-Christian action) other high-impact measures against Christians, such as confiscation of church property or a ban on Christian assemblies, were not enacted.[56] The once-for-all nature of the *supplicatio* is also the reason why persecution was not followed by ongoing action to discourage Christianity. If Decius knew how Tansar's and Kartir's reforms reasserted the centrality of the King of kings in Zoroastrian practice (closing fire-temples associated with other kings, re-educating clergy who preached ideas differing from the government view of Zoroastrian propriety), he did not go all the way to impose a Roman parallel: existing local cults were assumed to be satisfactory recipients of sacrifices. But Rives' observation that central government's

Kartir, it seems the Jews suffered least of all." Both sides seem to have thought that their aims could be achieved without (or without much) anti-Jewish action.

[53] Cf. n. 11 above.

[54] See Pohlsander 'Religious Policy of Decius' (as in n. 17), 1838, with references to others who have understood the sacrificing-campaign as a *supplicatio*: E. Liesering, N.H. Baynes, J. Vogt, J. Moreau, J. Molthagen. Rives, while acknowledging a similarity ('Decree of Decius' [as in n. 1], 150–1), does not think the decree mandated a *supplicatio*.

[55] Decius' campaigns are summarized by A.R. Birley in 'Decius Reconsidered' (as in n. 40), at 76–8.

[56] Observed e.g. by Rives ('Decree of Decius' [as in n. 1]), 142) and Pohlsander ('Religious Policy of Decius' [as in n. 17], 1839).

requirements were imposed in a novel way on the locally-based network of cults in the empire can, I suggest, be explained as arising from the Persian precedent. Shapur sought to strengthen his empire by uniting it behind Zoroastrianism, and persecuting dissidents (including ex-Romans in conquered territory)—so Decius decreed universal sacrifice in Greco-Roman cults in order to strengthen the Roman empire. Persian ministers attacked non-Zoroastrian religions, and Zoroastrian clergy who were inadequately supportive of the King of kings—so Decius attacked Christians who would not comply with his order to sacrifice.

In Valerian's persecution in 257–8 there were differences in the edict issued and the procedure followed. Sending persons accused of Christianity into exile was an option mentioned in the legislation: Cyprian was sent to Curubis, Dionysius of Alexandria to Cephro.[57] Christians were not allowed to meet, and access to Christian cemeteries was forbidden.[58] On this occasion, bringing Christians in line with Roman religion was the legislators' explicit purpose, as Cyprian was told at his trial.[59] In this respect, Valerian's persecution was more like Kartir's and Tansar's application of their requirement for religious uniformity than Decius' *supplicatio* had been: like Tansar, who arranged conversations with learned teachers for his imprisoned dissidents, Valerian aimed to secure *expressions* of conformity, rather than just get sacrifices made.

The decision to persecute was again connected with the politics of the eastern frontier. Valerian's accession to the throne (with his defeat in battle of Aemilius Aemilianus, who had defeated Trebonianus Gallus) came after the Persian capture of Antioch, and the new emperor, by moving his army east in 254, prompted a Persian withdrawal.[60] At first, then, he gave a military answer to the Persian question. He was not initially seen by Christians as hostile.[61] Things changed: Eusebius retells a story, which he has got from Dionysius of Alexandria, of the baneful influence on Valerian of Macrianus, "teacher and ruler of the synagogue of the Egyptian magicians" and

---

[57] *Proconsular Acta of St. Cyprian* 1; Eusebius *Ecclesiastical History* 7.11.10.

[58] Eusebius *Ecclesiastical History* 7.11.10.

[59] *Proconsular Acta of St. Cyprian* 1; cf. above, n. 6.

[60] In this paragraph I follow Potter's chronology: *Prophecy and History* (as in n. 18), 47–51.

[61] Eusebius *Ecclesiastical History* 7.10.2–3.

imperial Minister of Finance, who induced him to persecute.[62] It is possible that Valerian listened to Macrianus' views, since emperors routinely listened to high officials; but subsequent events suggest that renewed trouble on the eastern frontier was the factor which really provoked persecution of Christians. Dura Europos was attacked and fell in 257: by then, as in 249 under Decius, the emperor and his armies were tied down on the north-western frontiers, and the Persians could overrun under-defended eastern areas. Not until 259 could Valerian lead his army east, on the campaign which was to end when he was taken prisoner in battle by Shapur. The anti-Christian persecution of 257–8 filled the gap. It should be read as an attempt to respond to the Persians—who were forcing Romans to become Zoroastrians—with religious countermeasures, until circumstances permitted military action.

A case can be (and has been) made for seeing Decius personally as a man of traditional outlook who might on principle have favoured action against religious deviance;[63] but if Dionysius of Alexandria is right about the role of Macrianus in persuading Valerian to persecute, Valerian's background and initial assumptions may have been less conservative. In both cases, however, there is reason to think that the decision by central government to legislate for religious conformity was prompted both by the Persian threat to Roman territory and by knowledge of what the Persians were doing in lands they controlled. After the capture of Valerian in 260 things were different—not because the Persian threat had dissipated, but paradoxically because Roman authority was so much weaker in the east. Odaenathus of Palmyra and Callistus/Ballista were the defenders of Roman territory against Sassanid attacks after 260: and in their time they were neither directed by nor effectively accountable to central government. There is no reason to think they were anti-Christian. Paul of Samosata, bishop of Antioch in the 260s, simultaneously held appointment as a *ducenarius*[64]—a unique combination. I am not per-

[62] Eusebius *Ecclesiastical History* 7.10.4–6.

[63] See for instance Birley 'Decius Reconsidered' (as in n. 40), arguing that Decius may consciously have aimed to emulate republican Decii (78), noting that taking the name of Trajan may have given him ideas of how to deal with Christians (73), and drawing attention to the inscription from Cosa calling him *restitutor sacrorum et libertatis* (75, and C.I. Babcock 'An Inscription of Decius from Cosa' *American Journal of Philology* 83 [1962], 147–58).

[64] Eusebius *Ecclesiastical History* 6.30.8.

suaded by Fergus Millar's argument that Eusebius did not mean to be taken literally when he called Paul a *ducenarius*,[65] and I think he underestimates the impact on Antioch of the power of Odaenathus, Vaballathus and then Zenobia between 260 and 272.[66] To maintain their armies and expand the 'Palmyrene empire' as they did, they must have collected millions in revenue beyond their home area: it is reasonable to suppose that the procurator of Syria Coele (the post the Antioch-based *ducenarius* held)[67] was their man. Meanwhile in 261 Gallienus had issued his toleration rescript,[68] turning his back on attempts to fight the Persians with their own religious weapon, and coming to a policy more in line with the development of Roman governmental thinking on Christianity before Decius.

---

[65] Fergus Millar 'Paul of Samosata, Zenobia and Aurelian' *JRS* 61 [1971], 1–17 at 12–13).

[66] Millar 'Paul of Samosata' (as in n. 65), 9–10. The Antioch mint, as Millar points out (9), produced coins of Claudius II (268–70)—cf. K. Bittel 'Funde im östlichen Galatien: ein römischer Münzschatz von Devret' *Istanbuler Mitteilungen* 6 (1955), 27. Millar, however, seems to allow no middle ground between central government really being in charge, and the Palmyrene rulers being in open rebellion. Yet absence of central government (from the task of defending eastern provinces) created space for the Palmyrenes to expand their spheres of control, at the same time as tackling external threats. It may have suited these rulers to keep the situation ambiguous—for instance, by letting the mints go on making coinage showing the central rulers.

[67] Cf. Millar 'Paul of Samosata' (as in n. 65), 12.

[68] Eusebius *Ecclesiastical History* 7.13.

THE EXPRESS ROUTE TO HADES

Beryl Rawson

The orderly and proper disposal of the dead is a concern for any public administration, and this was particularly so in Roman Italy. In a generally warm climate, and in a culture where superstition and religious scruple were deeply embedded, there were reasons of hygiene, efficiency and religion behind the regulation of undertakers and associated matters. Legislation against arbitrary dumping of corpses, dung and other rubbish is known from several parts of Italy. At Puteoli a large marble inscription,[1] perhaps of the first half of the first century BCE, about the duties of a public undertaker, includes an injunction to bury corpses in the order in which they are reported to him, with two exceptions. The undertaker or his designated associate must provide the funerary services set down in the law in accordance with the order in which deaths are reported to him:

> . . . for the person who first reported a death, then for the others in accordance with the order in which they reported, unless the death reported is of a decurion or is a *funus aceruom*, for these must be given priority, but the order of the rest of the funerals should be maintained.[2]

Two categories of corpse which are to receive priority of burial, outside the order of reporting, are decurions (the town's councillors) and *funus aceruom*. Why were these groups awarded an express route, and why were they closely linked together (*funus decurion(is) funusue aceruom*)?

I take *aceruom* to be equivalent to *acerbum*, an equivalence attested

---

[1] *Année Epigraphique* (*AE*) 1971 no. 88. First published by Bove (1966); more recently discussed by Hinard (1995) and as part of a more extended discussion of graveyards and disposal of the dead in Bodel (1986 [1994]). The dating given here is that of Bodel. I am grateful to John Bodel for discussing aspects of this inscription with me. I also thank colleagues in the Ancient History Research Group at the Australian National University for discussion of an early version of this paper.

[2] II.19–23: ". . . ei qui primum denuntiauer(it) et deinceps reliquis ut quisq(ue) denuntiauer(it)—nisi si funus/decurion(is) funusue aceruom denuntiat(um) erit cui [*sic*] prima curand(a) erint, reliquor(um) autem fu/nerum ordo seruand(us)—omnes{q(ue)} res quae ex h(ac) l(ege) praestand(ae) erunt mitter(e) praeber(e)q(ue) quae praeb(endae erunt) d(ebeto)" (text as in Bodel (1986 [1994]).

elsewhere,[3] e.g. in the ablative in an epitaph (*CIL* 6.10097) for a boy who, from the grave, hopes that the passer-by will never experience grief, as his parents are now suffering, for such a death: *sic numquam doleas pro funere aceruo. Funus aceruom/acerbum* is an 'untimely death', literally a 'bitter' death. It occasionally refers to the person who is grieving for such a death (e.g. *CIL* 6.20462, where the parents as well as the dead child are *acerui*). In *CIL* 6.7574, a father's dedication for his daughter, the analogy with unripe fruit is made explicit; just as fruit picked too young, before its season, is unripe and bitter, so are early deaths bitter and especially lamentable:

> Our bodies are like apples hanging on a tree: they either fall when they are mature (*matura*) or come tumbling down too soon when they are unripe (*acerua*).

This phrase is often used of the premature deaths of the very young, although it sometimes refers to others who die before what might be judged their normal or natural time, e.g. young adults who predecease one or both of their parents.[4] Vergil uses it in the *Aeneid*, first of dead infants in the underworld (6.429) and then of the death of Pallas, a young man who has fallen in his first military battle (11.28). (The same line is used in each place: "abstulit atra dies et funere mersit acerbo".) Pallas' father, king Evander, refers to his son's death as *immatura mors* (11.166–7). In the underworld, those spirits competing to get to the Styx and aboard Charon's boat to make the crossing include mothers, husbands, heroes (implicitly those who fell in battle), children before puberty (*pueri innuptaeque puellae*), and young men cremated in the sight of their parents (6.305–40). Not all of these will be accepted by Charon. Only those who have had a proper burial will be allowed to cross, and even some of those will suffer on the other side and not reach Elysium. These include infants,

[3] It is an archaic and colloquial usage; but there are other linguistic irregularities in this inscription.

[4] Pliny (*Letters* 5.5.4) used the expression *acerba . . . et immatura mors* in the context of unfinished work, of a writer who has not fulfilled his potential, when a friend died—a mature man who had already achieved much but who was in the middle of an important writing project. The death of such men cannot help seeming sudden: "his nulla mors non repentina est, ut quae semper incohatum aliquid abrumpat". (I thank Michael White, of the University of Texas (Austin), for this reference.)

snatched from the breast, on the threshold of life and robbed of the sweetnesses of life, carried off by a black day and drowned in the bitterness of death:

infantumque animae flentes, in limine primo
quos dulcis uitae exsortis et ab ubere raptos
abstulit atra dies et funere mersit acerbo.

(6.427–9)

Seneca uses *funus acerbum* of children's deaths. In *On anger* (3.25.1) he observes that a poor man grieving for a lost child takes some comfort from seeing that the elite can suffer the same fate: *acerba funera* proceed out of grand houses as well as lowly ones. In a letter (122.10) castigating unnatural behaviour, he criticises those who turn night into day for their own entertainment: they are as good as dead, only a step from an untimely death ("quantulum enim a funere absunt et quidem acerbo?"), living as they do by the light of torches and wax tapers (associated with nocturnal funerals, especially children's).

The spirits of those who died 'before their time' (the *lemures*) were thought to wander restlessly at night and to need special attention from the living to appease them. In particular, those who died a violent death and remained unburied, e.g. those who drowned at sea or were murdered, suffered torment and could not cross the Styx in the underworld. They were condemned to wander for a hundred years before finding peace.[5] Sometimes their survivors set up cenotaphs which would preserve at least the name of the deceased and which would provide some sort of 'closure' to their existence. But until the body had itself been put to rest the spirits suffered and the living had reason to fear them.[6] These views would give a community good reason to give priority to the burial of the 'untimely dead' whenever such corpses were reported.[7] A general concern for proper

---

[5] *Aeneid* 6.325–330. The helpless unburied are *inops inhumataque turba*.

[6] Cf. Horace, *Epistles* 2.2.209, where the list of things to fear includes *nocturnos lemures*. Horace challenges his reader to claim that he laughs at (among other things) dreams, fears arising from magic, and the *lemures* which wander at night. The later commentator Porphyry explained that the *lemures* were the wandering shades of those "who died before their time (*ante diem*) and who were thus to be feared". Cicero, *On the laws* 2.57, refers to the earth (*gleba*) which must be thrown on bones to make a proper burial.

[7] The Puteoli inscription contains instructions, after the section on priority of burials, about prompt removal of the bodies of suicides-by-hanging and slaves (presumably slaves condemned to death for a crime). Roman pontifical law forbade the burial of those (*suspendiosi*) who took their own life *laqueo*: the rule for such a person was "ut qui laqueo uitam finisset, insepultus abiceretur" (Servius on *Aeneid*

funerary ritual and placation of the spirits of the dead is attributed to Numa, who is said to have put such matters under the supervision of the *pontifex* (*maximus*).[8]

The expression *acerbum* is attested for the deaths of the very young often enough for us to conclude that children must have been those most often given priority of burial according to this law. The use of the term in epitaphs, however, is wider. It is quite rare and is sometimes found in long, elaborate epitaphs (usually in verse), perhaps indicating a more literate section of the population. Of twenty-two examples (referring to twenty-four dead) from Rome, twenty-three persons are specified with an age, and of these twenty-three thirteen are aged twelve or under. The ages of the others range from fifteen to thirty-two. Of the sixteen for whom dedicators are known, thirteen dedications are by one or both parents (and a parent is mentioned in another), whose need to bury a son or daughter instead of being buried by them is against the expectations of nature and, in that sense, the deaths are premature. Spouses are involved in the two epitaphs without parents: a twenty-six-year-old woman is mourned by her husband (24243), and a thirty-two-year-old man is mourned by his wife and brother (9150). It may be that these marriages have not yet had time to produce children. The thirty-two-year-old was a slave who might well have been on the verge of receiving his freedom, having just passed the legal age of thirty and being an *arcarius*, a slave with considerable financial responsibility. When he died, however, he was still in the *potestas* of his master.[9]

In the inscriptions of Rome there are two examples of *acerbitas*, both of which are associated with premature death. In *CIL* 6.33696, Methe, probably a slave, is explicitly a child: she died at age thirteen, leaving *acerbitas* to those whose pet-child (*delicium*) she was. There are two names on an inscription on the left of the stone: Pomponia Gnoste and T. Vettulenus Hieronymus, who are probably the ded-

---

12.603). The law thus moves from those who must be buried promptly and in an orderly manner to those who could not be dignified with burial but whose bodies must be promptly removed, for reasons of public health, superstition, and status (slaves being property rather than persons). Why does the law specify "male or female slave" (*seruom seruamque*) but only *suspendiosum*?

[8] Livy 1.20.7. Numa's regulation of the state, especially religious matters, included not only ceremonies "sed iusta quoque funebria placandosque manes".

[9] Cf. Servius on *Aeneid* 11.143, below, for the parallel between a child *in potestate* and a slave.

icators of Methe's inscription. In a *columbarium* of the early imperial period, mother and father (unnamed) set up an epitaph, *sua acerbitate*, for the slave Eugenes (*CIL* 6.34271): as a *cubucularius* he could have carried out his job (as a bedroom attendant) at a young age.[10]

In Puteoli the term is almost absent from epitaphs, even though it is from there that the undertaker's instructions specify *funus acerbum* as one of the categories for priority of burial. Epitaphs to those who died younger than fourteen are not infrequent (about 140 out of almost 2000 inscriptions from Puteoli in *CIL* 10), but they are much simpler than most of those cited above. In only one (1784) is a form of *acerbum* used: the life of Gauia M. fil. Marciana had been cut off by an early death, *inmatura et acerba morte interceptae.* The age of the dead woman is not given but she is adult (she has a husband). She was from a distinguished family in Puteoli, and her epitaph was dedicated by her father, M. Gauius Puteolanus (a decurion), so she was almost certainly still *in patria potestate.* Other members of family are referred to, and she was given a public funeral (in 187 CE) because of their distinction and her own character.

In the table at the end of this chapter, details of the forms of *acerbum* used in epitaphs of Rome and Puteoli are summarised, to convey something of the flavour and context of the term. I have omitted the two uses of *uerbo acerbo* (*CIL* 6.7872, 23551), which clearly mean 'with a harsh word'; and the use of *acerbissimum* in the long, well-known inscription (*CIL* 6.1527) once referred to as the *laudatio Turiae.* In this long eulogy to a wife who had sacrificed much to save her husband during the triumviral period in the 40s–30s BCE, the husband refers to his *acerbissimum* experience because of Lepidus' treatment of the wife.

The phrase *mors immatura* is sometimes used, and its usage is consistent with the pattern of (*funus*) *acerbum.* For instance, an altar (probably not later than the Flavian period) attests the death first of the nine-year-old Successus and then of his mother Caesia Gemella, followed by a dedication by the boy's father Successus (*CIL* 6.26901). The father bemoans the fact that *mors immatura* has made him, as father, perform the duty which the son should have done for a parent: "quod fas parenti/facere debuit filius/mors immatura fecit/ut

[10] See Boulvert (1970: 30–31, 246–7) on the junior status of *cubicularii* compared with the *a cubiculo*, and their normally slave status, especially in the early imperial period.

faceret parens". There are other examples of unexpected and violent deaths which do not use the terms *acerbum* or *immatura* but which remind us of the uncertainty of life in urban centres in antiquity (and today) (Gunnella 1995).

Servius' commentary on *Aeneid* 11.143 (preparations for the burial of Pallas and the Arcadians' taking-up of funeral torches to greet Pallas' body) has several comments on nocturnal burials and the use of torches. Servius focusses on two aspects which might illuminate the privileged categories in the Puteoli undertaker's instructions: the relationship of magistrates and priests to death, and the nature of *funus acerbum*. His comments run thus:[11]

> It was the Roman tradition to hold funeral processions at night, by the light of torches, . . . because in a state bound by religious scruple they tried to prevent funerals crossing the path of either magistrates or priests, whose eyes should not be offended by another's death. . . . It was even more traditional for the funeral of those not yet adult (*inpuberes*) to be held by torchlight, to prevent the house being polluted by the death of non-adult offspring (*ne funere inmaturae subolis domus funestaretur*): this was especially the case for sons of men holding magistracies. Therefore Vergil has the body of Pallas accompanied by torches, being a premature death (*funus acerbum*) . . . Some authorities say that it was not considered right for the deaths of children under their father's authority ("de filiis qui in potestate patris sint") to be called *funus*, as those children have a slave's status in relation to their father, and if that were to happen the household (*familia*) would be polluted. So here the funeral of Pallas is, correctly, carried out by torchlight, as takes place for sons [i.e. sons *in potestate*]. Other (authorities), such as Varro and Verrius Flaccus, make this statement: if a *filius familias* dies beyond the city, freedmen and friends go to meet his body, which is brought into the city under cover of night by the light of tapers and torches. No one was invited to his funeral (*exsequiae*).

Varro and Verrius Flaccus were closest in time, of all commentators, to the Puteoli inscription, and they identify a lack of delay in funerals of *filii familias* which accords with the priority accorded to *funus acerbum* in the Puteoli document. Boyancé (1952) discusses the apotropaic function of torches at such funerals. Violent or premature deaths arouse fear, and nocturnal burials are a kind of precaution, to avoid pollution. The light of torches helps drive bad

[11] Servius' proposed etymologies are questionable, and are omitted in this translation; but his grasp of Roman tradition and ritual is usually taken to be sound.

spirits away. Scheid (1984) agrees with the apotropaic function of torches, but argues that this was fulfilled even when funerals in the daytime became more usual. They helped mark off the separate space of the dead from the living, and warned off those who might accidentally be polluted.

Servius had already identified *funus acerbum* as the death of children still in *potestas*, i.e. *filii familias*, in his commentary on *Aeneid* 3.64. In this passage Vergil was describing the proper funeral rites which Aeneas and his Trojans conferred on Polydorus, a young Trojan who had been murdered by his host, the king of Thrace. Aeneas heard Polydorus' voice complaining to him as Aeneas tried to pull pieces off a tree in Thrace to prepare an altar for a sacrifice. The Trojans decided to flee from the accursed and polluted place, but first they provided Polydorus with a proper tomb, in which his spirit was safely enclosed (*animamque sepulcro condimus*). An altar was crowned with dark wreaths, *caeruleis uittis*, and Servius associated this adjective with mourning: such wreaths were especially used *in acerbo funere*, when *filii familias* had died. 'The death of Polydorus, his being still as a boy (*puer*), was *acerbum*, and because he was of an age to have been still a *filius familias*.'

This interpretation of *funus acerbum* would give a concrete definition for an undertaker to use when assessing *funus aceruom*. In inscriptions and literature the term might be used more loosely, as the perception of what is 'premature' can be subjective; but an undertaker needs firm definitions or guidelines. It is unlikely that in a Roman legal context it would be left to the undertaker's discretion to judge what was a *funus aceruom* and thus which bodies would get priority of burial. *Filii familias* were the category intended, but on demographic probability these would be comparatively young, since adolescents and older sons and daughters were much less likely to have a *pater* alive.[12]

Néraudau (1987) contains the best previous discussion of *funus acerbum* of which I am aware. He too makes the association between young children and *filiifamilias* of any age,[13] but he refers only in

[12] Saller (1987) discusses the age at first marriage of Roman men, and the consequences of this—including the effects of *patria potestas*. He estimates, for example, that no more than 55% of fifteen-year-olds had a living father, compared with 85% for five-year-olds.

[13] Children are an age category, *filiifamilias* a status category, but both lack full

passing to the Puteoli inscription on undertakers' duties, and he does not comment on the association with decurions. Discussing mostly literary usage of *funus acerbum*, he argues for a development from the early Republic[14] to imperial times, when he identifies the emergence of sentimental values attached to children and childhood. Earlier, the unnaturalness of children's deaths involved pollution and thus their funerals were brief and nocturnal. Later, the unnaturalness caused demonstrative grieving and lamentation because display of feeling was now acceptable in the new climate of sentiment about children. But excessive display was still frowned on, as the child's legal status remained defective: it could claim no autonomy or civic achievement (and thus no *laudatio* could be offered). Néraudau does not, however, confront the question of whether an abbreviated funeral was considered appropriate for the young in the changed, imperial climate. Vergil does not describe Pallas' actual funeral, but the procession of the corpse from Aeneas' camp to the city of Pallas' father Evander is very grand, with all the trappings of a military hero (*Aeneid* 11.59–99, 139–49). Other examples suggest that by imperial times even children could have a splendid funeral and in daylight. The epitaph of the early second century for the six-year-old Marcianus claims that the whole neighbourhood poured out to watch his funeral procession and grieve for the loss of the young intellectual prodigy (*CIL* 6.7578).[15] Servius' commentary cites authorities of the period of the late Republic and the Augustan period (Varro and Verrius Flaccus) on how to deal with the body of a *filiusfamilias* who has died away from his home city: freedmen and friends go to meet the body, but there is to be no general invitation to the funeral. As Néraudau points out, Evander breaks this convention by rushing out to embrace his son's body (*Aeneid* 11.148–9).

The date of the Puteoli inscription was probably the first half of the first century BCE and would be consistent with the older principles and practices for the funerals of children and *filiifamilias*. Whether

civic autonomy and the death of either category is unnatural, i.e. against normal expectations or hopes.

[14] The earliest examples in literature are from Plautus, referring to the death of young soldiers (*Amphitruo* 190) and to the potential death of a young woman prostitute in her role of daughter to mother (*Asinaria* 595).

[15] ". . . quod tenerae aetati spes fallax apstulit annos." Even if there are elements of exaggeration in this epitaph for a young boy, the concept of such a funeral must be plausible to be engraved on a public monument. Further details of this epitaph in Rawson (1999).

undertakers were bound by the same rules for speedy burial of these in later periods is uncertain. The absence of the particular instruction about *funus acerbum* (and decurions) in any other of the known documents and texts about funerals suggests that these rules might have been less relevant later, but that is only an argument *ex silentio*. We have seen evidence that children's funerals could involve some display and visible grieving. There is ample evidence, in various media, for a changing attitude to children and childhood—or at least a changing manifestation of feeling, and greater visibility of children in these media—in the imperial period.[16] There is also a development towards 'heroisation', placing the good and the innocent in heaven rather than in some part of the underworld (however blessed).

A large, finely inscribed marble slab (*CIL* 6.21521) reflects this development. The epitaph, dedicated by Sex. Ossianius Sex. f. Com.[17] to his grandson M. Lucceius M. f., expounds the joy of the new life after death in greater detail, but also gives more detail of the horrors of the (more normal) fate in the underworld. In the first of three columns the grandfather tells of his grief that his grandson had been snatched away *praematura morte*, but then of his vision of Lucceius, larger than life, shining brightly in the sky and reassuring his *adfinis* that there is no need to weep for him, now that he has been translated to the stars of heaven and has become a god (*deus*). In the other two columns Lucceius tells of the dark and threatening places of the underworld which he has escaped and the opportunities for him now to choose whatever form of divinity he likes and a future which will be everlasting (not terminated by *tempus edax*). That such an epitaph contrasted with normal expectations is clear from the number of epitaphs which declare that the deceased is now only ashes. An epitaph from Pisaurum (*CIL* 11.6435) for the five-year-old Petronius Antigenes identifies his *domus aeterna* as the abominable sphere of Tartarus (*taetra Tartarei sidera*), where he must abandon all hope and fortune.[18]

---

[16] See, e.g., Rawson (1997a) on iconography and (1997b) on other art, inscriptions, papyri, law and literature.

[17] The stone is broken at this point, but it is not certain that Ossianius had a *cognomen*. Lucceius did not. The *CIL* editor thinks that the inscription could be Augustan. No age is given for the grandson, but on demographic probability and the reference to *tristi damnatam sorte iuuentam* the grandson can be taken to have died young.

[18] The epitaph to Lucceius is cited by Seston (1949) in his discussion of the bilin-

This new view of the fate of children is not widely attested in Roman Italy, but the evidence for the late second century and the third is sparse compared with that for the earlier imperial period. It seems to take us a long way from malevolent spirits and pollution. Perhaps the Puteoli regulations are a document only of their own period—and yet the continuing high rate of child mortality would still have been an incentive to deal quickly with many such deaths.

Servius' commentary on *Aeneid* 11.143, which gave us traditional views on *funus acerbum*, emphasised the threat of pollution to magistrates and priests. It might also offer a clue to the close conjunction of decurions and the untimely dead in the Puteoli document—a puzzling conjunction, and I know no discussion of this aspect, ancient or modern.[19] Nor do I know of other instances of this regulation elsewhere in Italy. Although regional variation must always be allowed for in Italy, other aspects of the Puteoli law are sufficiently like what is known of Roman funerary law to warrant the assumption that this was a fairly general Italian practice rather than a local peculiarity, at least for its Republican period.

Contact (physical or visual) with the dead was considered polluting, and Servius says that magistrates and priests particularly had to avoid such contact. As Bodel remarks (2000: 142), "the religious purity of their persons [magistrates and certain high priests] was intimately bound up with the welfare of the state". The problem of pollution applied even when the deceased was a close and beloved member of their family: the emperor Tiberius delivered the eulogy in 23 CE over his dead son Drusus on the *rostra*, but a veil covered the corpse to protect the eyes of Tiberius (*pontifex maximus*) from the sight (Seneca, *Consolation to Marcia* 15). Similar conventions must have applied when magistrates and priests officiated at other public funerals. Public funerals were voted for senators at Rome in both Republican and imperial periods,[20] so probably Italian town councils voted sim-

gual monument to the two-year-old Eutychos, found near Rome in 1935 and published in *AE* in 1945 (119) and further discussed by Boyancé (1952). In the sculpture on the monument the boy's horse is being drawn up to the heavens by an eagle. Part of the Greek text reassures Eutychos' father that he is not beneath the earth in Hades but has been taken up by Jupiter's eagle to join the stars. Eutychos is characterised as having known neither the bad nor the good of life: οὐ κακὸν οὐδὲ ἀγαθὸν γνοὺς βίος ὅττι φέρει.

[19] Modern discussion of other aspects of the Puteoli law: Bodel (1986 [1994], 2000); Hinard (1995).

[20] E.g. Cicero, *Philippics* 9.16–17, for Servius Sulpicius Rufus in 43 BCE, refer-

ilar honours—even if on a lesser scale—for their own members. In the imperial period public funerals were being voted for private individuals in Italian towns, even for women and children.[21]

The participation of senior officials in a funeral will have caused a suspension of public business, whether de facto or officially a *iustitium.* A *iustitium* was basically a suspension of business in the lawcourts, but, as we shall see, it could cover a wide range of activities. *Iustitia* recorded for the Republican period were associated with military emergencies. In 458 BCE, the *dictator* appointed to deal with Rome's war against Sabines and the Aequi declared a *iustitium* by which shops were closed throughout the city, all private business was suspended, and there was a military call-up of all able-bodied men (Livy 3.27). Similarly in 426 (Livy 4.31); and in 320 BCE, when news of the military disaster and disgrace at the Caudine Forks reached Rome (Livy 9.7.7–12), shops were closed, official business suspended in the Forum, and the garb of mourning was put on. On that occasion the consuls transacted no official business except the appointment of a *dictator* to hold the next elections. In 43 BCE, in the face of the crisis posed by Marcus Antonius' seizure of power in Cisalpine Gaul, Cicero urged the senate to declare a state of emergency (a *tumultus*): there should be a *iustitium*, military dress should be adopted, a levy should be held, and all exemptions from duty (*uacationes*) should be cancelled throughout Italy except for Gaul (Cicero, *Philippics* 5.31).

If decurions were accorded a public funeral, did this present problems for fellow-decurions, who would be expected to attend and perhaps officiate but who had to avoid pollution? Anyone attending a funeral had to undergo purification rites afterwards (Bodel 2000: 142). Attendance at a funeral and the process of purification were amongst the acceptable excuses in municipal law for not appearing at a scheduled legal case. For example, in the charter of Urso, in Spain, which was drawn up in the late 40s BCE, a magistrate could be excused on account of "a serious illness, an undertaking to appear

ring to precedents; Pliny, *Letters* 2.1, for Verginius Rufus in 97 CE, where the consul Tacitus gave the eulogy.

[21] E.g., as above, *CIL* 10.1784, for a distinguished woman from Puteoli; 10.680, a one-year-old from Surrentum (both of these from Campania); 5.4441, a six-year-old from Brixia; 5.337, a fourteen-year-old decurion from Parentium (both of these from northern Italy).

(in another court), a trial, a sacrifice, a funeral in his household, or purificatory rites".[22] After Augustus' death in 14 CE, Tiberius accompanied the body from Nola to Rome and was closely involved in funeral arrangements. This attracted pollution which might have kept him out of public business until after the funeral. In order to allow him to participate in the senate's first meeting after the death, the senate had to declare Tiberius formally free of pollution (Dio 56.31).

In the imperial period, the withdrawal of an individual from public business because of a family death became generalised to the whole community when the emperor died. The emperor's well-being was now identified with the welfare of the state. Thus *iustitia* could be declared if he or those close to him were in danger or died.[23]

The duration and extent of the *iustitium* would depend on the importance of the deceased. We know of *iustitia* in the imperial period for the time between the death and the burial. The deaths of Lucius and Gaius Caesar, in 2 and 4 CE, were especially serious because the young men were Augustus' adopted sons and his intended heirs. Municipal inscriptions preserve some of the detail of restrictions on religious, commercial and social life. Both Lucius and Gaius had been associated with Pisae, in the north-west of Italy, and the town voted similar honours to each of them.[24] Part of the text for Gaius runs (lines 20–37):

> From the day on which his death was announced until the day when his bones had been gathered and put to rest and the rites for his *manes* had been properly carried out, all should . . .,

followed by a long list of activities to be undertaken or forbidden, such as a required change of clothing; the closure of temples, baths and taverns; no banquets; matrons required to maintain a marginal form of mourning (*sublugere*). A fragmentary inscription from Cupra

[22] "morbus sonticus, uadimonium, iudicium, sacrificium, funus familiare feriaeue de(n)icales", *lex coloniae Genetiuae Iuliae* XCV.21–23, text and translation from *Roman Statutes*, ed. M.H. Crawford (1996), 1: 425–6. The same excuses were accepted from private citizens: XCV.32–34.

[23] Weinstock (1966) discusses the transformation of *inferiae* (sacrifice for the dead) into a public sacrifice for a member of the imperial family under Augustus, and the celebration of anniversaries of deaths of members of the imperial family. He sees a reflection of this ritual in Vergil, *Aeneid* 5.46ff., on the anniversary of the death of Anchises. Suspensions of public business similar to those detailed below were also associated with the anniversary of the death of C. Caesar.

[24] *CIL* 11.1420 (2 CE) for Lucius; *CIL* 11.1421 (4 CE) for Gaius.

Maritima, on the north-east coast of Italy, preserves the information that a *iustitium* had been declared at Rome in 4 CE until Gaius Caesar's bones had been placed in the mausoleum. Each of the young Caesars died in the provinces, so there would have been considerable delay between their actual death and the deposit of their bones in Augustus' tomb at Rome, but the record says that the *iustitium* lasted until the final act.

The accounts of Augustus' death and funeral (e.g. Dio 56.30–43, Tacitus, *Annals* 1.5–10, Suetonius, *Augustus* 100) do not give much detail of the *iustitium* declared on that occasion. We are told by Dio (56.43), however, that although women observed the prescribed year's mourning men observed it for only a few days. No doubt there had already been a fairly long delay since Augustus' death at Nola: the body had to be brought to Rome, with pauses at a number of towns along the way; it lay in the vestibule of his house on the Palatine while the Senate met and discussed several aspects; then there was the funeral procession and cremation, and Livia's five-day vigil at the pyre before Augustus' bones were gathered up and placed in his tomb. It is consistent with what we know of Tiberius that he would want to settle down to normal business as soon after that as possible; hence the tacit suspension of the *iustitium* by men in public life. When Livia died in 29, there was extensive mourning. Women were required to observe some form of mourning for a year, but Tiberius recognised the realities of political life and he was back at work almost immediately (Dio 58.2).

The popular Germanicus did not receive a public funeral when he died in the east in 19 CE, but when news of his death reached Rome there was, according to Tacitus (*Annals* 2.82.4), a spontaneous *iustitium*: the forums were deserted and houses shut. This unofficial suspension of public and private business lasted until after the burial of Germanicus, perhaps four months (Weinstock 1966); but then Tiberius stepped in and declared that the mourning and withdrawal from normal activities should end, on the grounds of the public good: Rome had to go on (Tacitus, *Annals* 3.6). The emperor Gaius, however, allowed a protracted *iustitium* for his favourite sister (and daughter of Germanicus) Drusilla when she died in 38. Religious, commercial and social life were severely restricted.[25]

---

[25] Philo (*Against Flaccus* 56) provides evidence that the *iustitium* extended to the

Citizens of lesser rank than the imperial family, whose death was honoured with a *iustitium*, could not have held up public business for such lengthy periods. One inscription from a municipal town (Capua) attests a suspension of legal business for one day ("uadimoniaque eius diei dif[ferantur]")[26] to allow the populace to turn out in force for the public funeral of a citizen whose military career had been followed by generous donations to the city. For decurions there was, as suggested above, the further dimension of official participation by a town's magistrates. Reasons of pollution and of public efficiency would create pressure to minimise the length of such a period. If the deceased decurion were himself a magistrate in office, his death could be seen as premature and a break in the natural order of things for not serving out his full term.

We thus have possible reasons for priority of burial for 'premature' deaths and those of decurions. But why the close coupling of the two? My best explanation at this moment is that each of these categories had the capacity to do harm (religious and practical) to the community if their burials were not carried out promptly and with all due attention.[27]

provinces, as he dates an attack on the Jews in Alexandria to when the workshops were closed as a sign of mourning for Drusilla. Dio (59.11.5) reports that in Rome Gaius cancelled the festivals which were then due to take place. Drusilla's *iustitium* may have lasted for three months, from June until her consecration in September.

[26] *CIL* 10.3903, a pronouncement by the *duouiri*, reporting a decree of the decurions.

[27] It is my hope that in laying out this problem, without a conclusive solution, this chapter will prompt John Crook to turn his attention to it. He is better equipped than anyone I know to throw light on such matters, and I am glad to be able to express here my warm appreciation of all his help and support over many years.

FORMS OF *ACERBUM* IN INSCRIPTIONS OF ROME AND PUTEOLI

All references are to *CIL* 6 except last entry, which is *CIL* 10.
y. = years; m. = months; d. = days; h. = hours.
S. = slave; Lib. = *libertus/-a*; Ingen. = *ingenuus/-a*; Eq. R. = *eques Romanus*
M. = male; F. = female.

Ref. no.	dedicatee	age	sex	status	dedicator(s)	epithets/other details
26680	Speratus	9 (?) m.	M.	S.?	*parentes*	An example of *mortis acerbae*. Vocabulary of pity, grief, weeping for his death.
14389	?	1y. 7m. 16d. 12h.	F.	S.?	Father, mother	Taken away *acerba morte. filiae karissimae.*
20462	Iulia C. fil. Felicitas	1y. 11m. 3d.	F.	Ingen.	*parentes*	*defuncto aceruo*; parents *similiter acerui et infelicissimi.*
28239	Hyparchus	4y.	M.	S.?	Mother and brother	(?)*uenit iniqua dies et acerbae* (sic) *terminis hora. alumnus.* Not permitted to survive *parentes*. Epitaph made *lachrimis acerbis.*
22397	Eparastus	4y. 18d.	M.	S.?	*parentes*	*funus acerdum* (sic). *filio dulcissimo.* Son left parents grieving.
19007	Geminia Agathe Mater	5y. 7m. 22d.	F.	Lib./ Ingen.	?	*mortis acerbus/eripuit Letus, teneramque ad Tartara duxit.* Plays on *signum*: *Mater nomen eram, mater non lege futura.* References to Fauentius, *nutritor plus quam genitor*; family members, incl. father who died earlier. Short life; played; loved by all; *ingenio docili, forma pulchra ac ueneranda*; looked more like boy than girl.
6189	Nice and Phoebe	7y. and 5(?)y.	F.	S.?	Father, mother	*arcula ace[rba tenet]. inmerito abductas. patria supplice voce iacent.*

Ref. no.	dedicatee	age	sex	status	dedicator(s)	epithets/other details
25128	?	8(?)y. 7m. 10d.	M.	?	*parentes* and friend	Snatched away by *Ditis acerba man*[*us*]. *doctus*. References to underworld and Clotho. *filio pientiss*[*imo*].
23818	L. Paquedius L. f. Ser. Ampliatus	8y.	M.	Ingen.	?	*subito ante oculos funera acerba dedi. aetate hic parua iaceo lacrimabile semper. infelix iaceo nunc cinis et lacrimae.*
24659	Hedone Pomponia	9y.	F.	Lib./ Ingen.	?	*me mors acerba . . . immatura abstulit. dulcissima, sua*[*uis*].
38721	Peculiaris	10(?)y.	M.	S.?	?	Was never *acerbus* to his family/associates (*suis*) except by his death.
9437	Pagus	12y. 9m. 13d. 8h.	M.	S.	?	*nunc funus acerbum et cinis in tumulis iacet et sine nomine corpus. dominus, delicium* of his *spes grata* of *parentes*; has abandoned them to long grief. Professional skill as jeweller.
10097	Ti. Claudius Esquilina Aug. (l.) Tiberinus	15(?)y.	M.	Lib.	Mother	Requests traveller to read epitaph: *sic numquam doleas pro funere aceruo. doctus.* Popular (actor?) with audiences. Now only ashes. Each *parens* scatters tears and flowers on his grave. Bound for Elysium: *ego ualle moror.*
30126	?	17(?)y.	M.	?	?	*adfluxit morte acerba.* A fatal day for his *parentes.*

Ref. no.	dedicatee	age	sex	status	dedicator(s)	epithets/other details
25703	Sabidia).l. Fusca	18y.	F.	Lib.	Father, mother, brother	Traveller requested to stop and read of *fata acerba.* Died in full flowering of youth. References to underworld.
1619	C. Iulius Seuerus and C. Iulius Gracilis	20y. 10m. 18(?)d. and 18y. 8m. 18(?)d.	M.	Eq. R.	*parentes*	Died in one accident, *quos mersit acerbo s . . . filiis dulcissimis. docti e gregi iuuenes.*
9199a	Zethus	20y.	M.	S.	Brother	*ossa . . . pia sunt sed acerba parenti Amphio.* Greets brothers and sisters. Steward of T. Vinius.
38425	P. Grattius Sp. f. Col. Celer	22y.	M.	Ingen.	?	Struck down *acerba morte nefanda.* Murdered: curse on murderer.
24243	Plaetoria Antiochis	26y. 3m. 24d. 10h.	F.	Lib./ Ingen.	Husband	She brought him no *dolor* except that of her *acerbissima mors. rarissimae feminae. castissimae, piissimae et de se optime meritae. dignissimae* (of his commemoration).
5508	?	28y.	F.	?	?	*funere acerbo.* Tomb holds her *iucundam, aeterno tempore.*
9150	Sulenius Parthenius Eurybatus	32y. 8m. ?d.	M.	S.	Brother, wife	*dulcissimus, acerbus, miser. anima innocens, dulcis omnibus suis et amicis acceptus. karissimo. arcarius.*
15837	Clodia C.l. Raphis	?	F.	Lib.	?	*pressit acerba dies.* Buried *prima aetate.*
10. 1784	Gauia M. fil. Marciana	?	F.	Ingen.	Father	*immatura et acerba morte interceptae.* Public funeral. Father (decurion) satisfied with honour in decurions' decree, paid for burial himself.

Bibliography

Bodel, J. (1986 [1994]) 'Graveyards and groves: a study of the *Lex Lucerina*' *American Journal of Ancient History*, 11: 1–133.

——. (2000) 'Dealing with the dead: undertakers, executioners and potter's fields in ancient Rome' in V.M. Hope and E. Marshall *Death and disease in the ancient city*, London and New York: Routledge, 128–51.

Boulvert, G. (1970) *Esclaves et affranchis impériaux sous le Haut-Empire romain. Rôle politique et administratif*, Napoli: Jovene.

Bove, L. (1966) 'Due nuove iscrizioni di Pozzuoli e Cuma' *Rendiconti dell'Accademia di Archeologia, Lettere e Belle Arti di Napoli*, 41: 207–39.

Boyancé, P. (1952) '*Funus acerbum*' *Revue des études anciennes*, 54: 275–89.

Crawford, M.H. (ed.) (1996) *Roman Statutes*, 2 vols. London: Institute of Classical Studies.

Gunnella, A. (1995) 'Morte improvvise e violente nelle iscrizioni latine' in F. Hinard (ed.) *La mort au quotidien dans le monde romain: actes du colloque organisé par l'Université de Paris IV*, Paris: de Boccard, 9–22.

Hinard, F. (1995) 'La "loi de Pouzzoles" et les pompes funèbres' in F. Hinard (ed.) *La mort au quotidien dans le monde romain: actes du colloque organisé par l'Université de Paris IV*, Paris: de Boccard, 205–12.

Kleiner, D. (1987) *Roman imperial funerary altars with portraits*, Rome: Bretschneider.

Néraudau, J.P. (1987) 'La loi, la coutume et le chagrin. Réflexions sur la mort des enfants' in F. Hinard (ed.) *La mort, les morts et l'au-delà dans le monde romain*, Université de Caen, 195–208.

Prieur, J. (1986) *La mort dans l'antiquité romaine*, Ouest-France: La Guerche-de-Bretagne.

Rawson, B. (1997a) 'The iconography of Roman childhood' in B. Rawson and P. Weaver (eds.) *The Roman family in Italy: status, sentiment, space*, Oxford: Clarendon Press, 205–32.

——. (1997b) 'Representations of Roman children and childhood' *Antichthon* 31: 74–95.

——. (1999) 'Education: the Romans and us' *Antichthon* 33: 81–98.

Saller, R.P. (1987) 'Men's age at marriage and its consequences in the Roman family' *Classical Philology* 82: 20–35.

Scheid, J. (1984) 'Contraria facere: renversements et déplacements dans les rites funéraires' *Annali del Istituto Universitario Orientale di Napoli (Sezione di Archeologia e Storia Antica)* 6: 117–139.

Seston, W. (1949) 'L'épitaphe d'Eutychos et l'héroisation par la pureté' *Hommages à Joseph Bidez et à Franz Cumont* (*Collection Latomus* II), Bruxelles: Latomus, 313–22.

Weinstock, S. (1966) 'The posthumous honours of Germanicus' in R. Chevallier (ed.) *Mélanges d'archéologie et d'histoire offerts à André Piganiol*, Paris: SEVPEN, vol. 2: 891–8.

JOHN CROOK: BIBLIOGRAPHY

Compilers: Paul McKechnie, Kathryn McKee and W.R. Barnes, with contributions from Duncan Cloud, David Johnston, Joyce Reynolds, A.M. Stone and Joseph Georg Wolf

Items are by John Crook as sole author except where noted otherwise.

1948 'A Metellus in Two Passages of Dio' *Classical Review* 62 (1948), 59–61

1951 'Titus and Berenice' *American Journal of Philology* 72 (1951), 162–75

1953 review of M.A. Levi (ed.) *C. Suetoni Tranquilli* Divus Augustus (Florence, 1951): *Journal of Roman Studies* 43 (1953), 229–30

1954 review of Walter Schmitthenner *Oktavian und das Testament Cäsars* (Munich, 1952): *Classical Review* n.s. 4 (1954), 152–4

1955 *Consilium Principis: Imperial Councils and Counsellors from Augustus to Diocletian* (Cambridge, CUP, 1955)

review of Heinrich Siber *Römisches Verfassungsrecht in geschichtlicher Entwicklung* (Lahr, 1952): *Journal of Roman Studies* 45 (1955), 167–8

review of C. Barini *Triumphalia: imprese ed onori militari durante l'impero romano* (Turin, 1952): *Journal of Roman Studies* 45 (1955), 238–9

review of Jean Béranger *Recherches sur l'aspect idéologique du principat* (Basel, 1955): *Classical Review* 5 (1955), 79–81

1956 review of R. Koebner (ed.) *Scripta Hierosolymitana vol. 1: Studies in Classics and Jewish Hellenism* (Jerusalem, 1954): *Journal of Roman Studies* 46 (1956), 174–5

review of Marcello Fortina *L'imperatore Tito* (Turin, 1955): *Classical Review* 6 (1956), 288–90

1957 A.H.M. Jones, P. Grierson and John Crook, 'The Authenticity of the *Testamentum S. Remigii*' *Revue Belge de philologie et d'histoire* 35 (1957), 356–73

'A Legal Point about Mark Antony's Will' *Journal of Roman Studies* 47 (1957), 36–8

'Suetonius *ab epistulis*' *Proceedings of the Cambridge Philological Society* 4 (1956–7), 18–22

review of David Daube *The Defence of Superior Orders in Roman Law* (Oxford, 1956): *Journal of Roman Studies* 47 (1957), 255–6

review of Martha W. Hoffman Lewis *The Official Priests of Rome under the Julio-Claudians* (Rome, 1955): *Classical Review* 7 (1957), 72–3

1958 review of Per Krarup *Rector rei publicae* (Copenhagen, 1956): *Classical Review* 8 (1958), 88–9

1959 review of L. Cerfaux and J. Tondriau *Un concurrent du christianisme: le culte des souverains dans la civilisation gréco-romaine* (Tournai, 1957): *Journal of Roman Studies* 49 (1959), 173–4

review of John Maurice Kelly *Princeps iudex: Eine Untersuchung zur Entwicklung und zu den Grundlagen der kaiserlichen Gerichtsbarkeit* (Weimar, 1957): *Classical Review* 9 (1959), 161–3

review of Clarence W. Mendell *Tacitus: The Man and His Work* (New Haven, 1957) and Ronald Syme *Tacitus* (Oxford, 1958): *Phoenix* 13 (1959), 38–41

1961 review of Jonas Palm *Rom, Römertum und Imperium in der griechischen Literatur der Kaiserzeit* (Lund, 1959): *Classical Review* 11 (1961), 68–9

review of Mason Hammond *The Antonine Monarchy* (Rome, 1959): *Classical Review* 11 (1961), 275–6

1962 'An Augustan Inscription in the Rijksmuseum at Leyden (SEG XVIII no. 555)' *Proceedings of the Cambridge Philological Society* 8 (1962), 23–9

1963 review of Albino Garzetti *L'impero da Tiberio agli Antonini* (Bologna, 1961): *Classical Review* 13 (1963), 207–10

review of Richard Koebner *Empire* (Cambridge, 1961): *Classical Review* 13 (1963), 122

Review of H.H. Huxley (ed.) *Carmina MCMLXIII: an anthology of Latin verses in the metres of lyric* (Manchester, 1963): *Eagle* 61 (1963), 53.

1964 review of Jochen Bleicken *Senatsgericht und Kaisergericht* (Göttingen, 1962): *Classical Review* 14 (1964), 196–8

review of A.N. Sherwin-White *Roman Society and Roman Law in the New Testament* (Oxford, 1963): *Classical Review* 14 (1964), 198–200

1965 'Patria Potestas' *Proceedings of the Classical Assocation* 62 (1965), 31–2

review of Antonio La Penna *Orazio e l'ideologia del principato* (Turin, 1963): *Classical Review* 15 (1965), 51–3

review of John Bishop *Nero: the Man and the Legend* (London, 1964): *Classical Review* 15 (1965), 364–5

1966 review of Blanche Parsi *Désignation et investiture de l'empereur romain (Ier et IIème siècles après J.-C.)* (Paris, 1963): *Journal of Roman Studies* 54 (1964), 202–3

review of Jean Gagé *Les classes sociales dans l'empire romain* (Paris, 1964): *Classical Review* 16 (1966), 100–2

review of G.W. Bowersock *Augustus and the Greek World* (Oxford, 1965): *Classical Review* 16 (1966), 220–2

1967 *Law and Life of Rome: Aspects of Greek and Roman Life* (Ithaca, Cornell University Press, and London, Thames and Hudson, 1967)

'A Study in Decoction' *Latomus* 26 (1967), 363–76

'Patria Potestas' *Classical Quarterly* 17 (1967), 113–22

'Gaius, *Institutes* I.84–86' *Classical Review* 17 (1967), 7–8

John Crook and Roy Stone, review of J.M. Kelly *Roman Litigation* (Oxford, 1966): *Classical Review* 17 (1967), 83–6

review of W. Kunkel *An Introduction to Roman Legal and Constitutional History* (Oxford, 1966): *Classical Review* 17 (1967), 201–5

review of G. Dobesch *Caesars Apotheose zu Lebzeiten und sein Ringen um den Königstitel* (Vienna, 1966): *Journal of Roman Studies* 57 (1967), 247

review of A.N. Sherwin-White *The Letters of Pliny: a Social and Historical Commentary* (Oxford, 1966): *Classical Review* 17 (1967), 311–4

1968 review of A.H.M. Jones *The Decline of the Ancient World* (London, Longmans, 1966) and S. Mazzarino *The End of the Ancient World* (London, 1966): *Journal of Roman Studies* 58 (1968), 251–3

review of J.P.V.D. Balsdon *Julius Caesar and Rome* (London, 1967): *Classical Review* 18 (1968), 214–5

review of E. Mary Smallwood *Documents illustrating the Principates of Gaius, Claudius and Nero* (Cambridge, 1967): *Classical Review* 18 (1968), 215–7

review of A.N. Sherwin-White *Fifty Letters of Pliny* (Oxford, 1967): *Classical Review* 18 (1968), 239

1969 'Commemoration of Benefactors Sermon' *Eagle* 63 (1969), 77–80

review of F. Millar *The Roman Empire and its Neighbours* (London, 1967): *Journal of Roman Studies* 59 (1969), 271–2

review of P.A. Brunt and J.M. Moore *Res gestae divi Augusti: with an Introduction and Commentary* (London, 1967): *Classical Review* 19 (1969), 59–60

review of Francesco della Corte *Suetonio, eques Romanus* (Florence, 1967): *Classical Review* 19 (1969), 62–3

review of Alan Watson *The Law of Persons in the Later Roman Republic* (Oxford, 1967): *Classical Review* 19 (1969), 88–90

1970 '*Strictum et aequum*: Law in the Time of Nero' *Irish Jurist* 5 (1970), 357–68
review of Regula Frei-Stolba *Untersuchungen zu den Wahlen in der römischen Kaiserzeit* (Zürich, 1967): *Classical Review* 20 (1970), 65–8
review of Alan Watson *The Law of Property in the Later Roman Republic* (Oxford, 1968): *Classical Review* 20 (1970), 359–61
review of David Daube *Roman Law: Linguistic, Social, and Philosophical Aspects* (Edinburgh, 1969): *Classical Review* 20 (1970), 361–3
1971 A.H.M. Jones and John Crook, P.Oxy. 2857, in G.M. Browne, J.D. Thomas, E.G. Turner and Marcia E. Weinstein (eds.) *Oxyrhynchus Papyri* 38 (nos. 2824–2877) (London, Egypt Exploration Society, 1971), 77–80
review of A.N. Sherwin-White *Racial Prejudice in Imperial Rome* (Cambridge, 1967): *Journal of Roman Studies* 61 (1971), 276
review of *Sympotica Franz Wieacker sexagenario Sachsbachwaldeni a suis libata* (Göttingen, 1970): *Classical Review* 21 (1971), 396–7
review of L.A. Thompson & J. Ferguson (eds.) *Africa in Classical Antiquity* (Ibadan, 1969): *Eagle* 64 (1971), 144.
1972 A.H.M. Jones *The Criminal Courts of the Roman Republic and Principate* (ed. John Crook) (Oxford, Blackwell, 1972)
review of Ronald Syme *Ten Studies in Tacitus* (Oxford, 1970): *Classical Review* 22 (1972), 221–2
review of H.U. Instinsky *Formalien im Briefwechsel des Plinius mit Kaiser Trajan* (Mainz, 1970): *Classical Review* 22 (1972), 222–3
review of Clarence W. Mendell *Tacitus: the Man and his Work* (London, 1970): *Classical Review* 22 (1972), 223
review of Peter Garnsey *Social Status and Legal Privilege in the Roman Empire* (Oxford, 1970): *Classical Review* 22 (1972), 238–42
review of Sir Ronald Syme *Emperors and Biography: Studies in the* Historia Augusta (Oxford, 1971): *Journal of Theological Studies* 23 (1972), 247–9
1973 'Intestacy in Roman Society' *Proceedings of the Cambridge Philological Society* 19 (1973), 38–44
1974 review of M. Humbert *Le remariage à Rome, étude d'histoire juridique et sociale* (Milan, 1972): *Journal of Roman Studies* 64 (1974), 234–5
review of Alan Watson *Roman Private Law around 200 BC* (Edinburgh, 1971): *Classical Review* 24 (1974), 239–40
review of Alan Watson *The Law of Succession in the Later Roman Republic* (Oxford, 1971): *Classical Review* 24 (1974), 240–3
review of A. Masi *Ricerche sulla 'res privata' del 'princeps'* (Milan, 1971): *Tijdschrift voor Rechtsgeschiednis* 42 (1974), 328–9
1975 *Consilium Principis: Imperial Councils and Counsellors from Augustus to Diocletian* (Cambridge, CUP, 1955): reprinted 1975
review of H.F. Jolowicz and Barry Nicholas *Historical Introduction to the Study of Roman Law*[3] (Cambridge, 1972): *Classical Review* 25 (1975), 66–9
review of A.N. Sherwin-White *The Roman Citizenship*[2] (Oxford, 1973): *Classical Review* 25 (1975), 282–3
review of Alan Rodger *Owners and Neighbours in Roman Law* (Oxford, 1972): *Classical Review* 25 (1975), 283–5
review of Giuliana Lanata *Gli atti dei martiri come documenti processuali* (Milan, 1973): *Classical Review* 25 (1975), 287–8
1976 *Law and Life of Rome: Aspects of Greek and Roman Life* (Ithaca, Cornell University Press, and London, Thames and Hudson, 1967): reprinted 1976
'*Sponsione provocare*: its Place in Roman Litigation' *Journal of Roman Studies* 66 (1976), 132–8
'Classical Roman Law and the Sale of Land' in M.I. Finley (ed.) *Studies in Roman Property* (Cambridge, CUP, 1976), 71–83

review of Alan Watson *Law Making in the Later Roman Republic* (Oxford, 1974): *Classical Review* 26 (1976), 85–6

review of D. Liebs *Die Klagenkonkurrenz im römischen Recht* (Göttingen, 1972): *Classical Review* 26 (1976), 135–6

review of R.A. Bauman *Impietas in principem* (Munich, 1974): *Tijdschrift voor Rechtsgeschiedenis* 44 (1976), 167–9

1977 *Law and Life of Rome: Aspects of Greek and Roman Life* (Ithaca, Cornell University Press, and London, Thames and Hudson, 1967): reprinted 1977

review of K.-H. Misera *Der Bereicherungsgedanke bei der Schenkung unter Ehegatten* (Cologne and Vienna, 1974): *Journal of Roman Studies* 67 (1977), 254

review of Jochen Bleicken *Lex publica: Gesetz und Recht in der römischen Republik* (Berlin, 1975): *Classical Review* 27 (1977), 49–51

review of H.J. Mette *Das römische Zivilrecht zu Beginn des Jahres 46 vor Christus* (Heidelberg, 1974): *Classical Review* 27 (1977), 129

review of Alan Watson (ed.) *Daube noster: Essays in Legal History for David Daube* (Edinburgh, 1974): *Classical Review* 27 (1977), 129–30

review of C. Nicolet *Le métier de citoyen dans la Rome républicaine*, (Paris, 1976): *Tijdschrift voor Rechtsgeschiednis* 45 (1977), 369–71

1978 *Law and Life of Rome: Aspects of Greek and Roman Life* (Ithaca, NY, Cornell University Press, and London, Thames and Hudson, 1967): reprinted 1978

'Working Notes on Some of the New Pompeii Tablets' *Zeitschrift für Papyrologie und Epigraphik* 29 (1978), 229–39

review of Bengt Thomasson *SPQR: senatores procuratoresque Romani nonnulli quorum cursus honorum munerumve post volumina Prosopographiae Imperii Romani edita aut innotuerunt aut melius noti sunt quomodo rei publicae operam dederint breviter illustravit Benedictus Thomae p.p* (Göteborg, 1975): *Classical Review* 28 (1978), 182–3

review of Fergus Millar *The Emperor in the Roman World* (London, 1977): *Classical Review* 28 (1978), 315–7

1979 review of M. Kaser *Über Verbotsgesetze und verbotswidrige Geschäfte im römischen Recht* (Vienna, 1977): *Journal of Roman Studies* 69 (1979), 201–2

review of A.A. Schiller *Roman Law: Mechanisms of Development* (The Hague, 1978): *Journal of Roman Studies* 69 (1979), 236

1980 review of C.P. Jones *The Roman world of Dio Chrystostom* (Cambridge, Mass., 1978): *University of Toronto Quarterly* 49 (1980), 400–401

1981 review of E. Badian (ed.) Ronald Syme *Roman Papers* (Oxford, 1979): *Classical Review* 31 (1981), 136

1983 'P. Turner 34' *Liverpool Classical Monthly* 8 (1983), 13–14

review of H.L.W. Nelson *Überlieferung, Aufbau und Stil von Gai Institutiones* (Leiden, 1981): *Journal of Roman Studies* 73 (1983), 212

review of B.W. Frier *Landlords and Tenants in Ancient Rome* (Princeton, 1980): *Journal of Roman Studies* 73 (1983), 213–4

review of G.E.M. de Ste. Croix *The Class Struggle in the Ancient Greek World* (London, 1981): *Classical Review* 33 (1983), 71–2

review of Jochen Bleicken *Zum Regierungsstil des römischen Kaisers: eine Antwort auf Fergus Millar* (Wiesbaden, 1982): *Classical Review* 33 (1983), 275–6

1984 *Law and Life of Rome: Aspects of Greek and Roman Life* (Ithaca, NY, Cornell University Press, and London, Thames and Hudson, 1967): reprinted 1984

'Lex Aquilia' Athenaeum 62 (1984), 67–77

'*Lex Plaetoria* (FIRA no. 3)' *Athenaeum* 62 (1984), 586–95

review of Alan Wardman *Religion and Statecraft among the Romans* (Baltimore, 1982): *Journal of Ecclesiastical History* 35 (1984), 143–4

review of Michael Crawford (ed.) *Sources for Ancient History* (Cambridge, 1983): *Antiquity* 58 (1984), 149

1985 '*Si parret* and a Joke in Petronius' in *Sodalitas: Scritti in onore di Antonio Guarino* vol. 3 (Naples, 1984–5), 1353–6

review of K. Visky *Spuren der Wirtschaftskrise der Kaiserzeit in den römischen Rechtsquellen* (Bonn and Budapest, 1983): *Classical Review* 35 (1985), 141–6

1986 '*Lex rivalicia* (FIRA I, no. 5)' *Athenaeum* 64 (1986), 45–53

'Women in Roman Succession' in Beryl Rawson (ed.) *The Family in Ancient Rome: New Perspectives* (London, Croom Helm, and Ithaca, NY, Cornell University Press, 1986), 56–82

'Feminine Inadequacy and the *senatusconsultum Velleianum*' in Beryl Rawson (ed.) *The Family in Ancient Rome: New Perspectives* (London, Croom Helm, and Ithaca, NY, Cornell University Press, 1986), 83–92

review of A. Giovannini *Consulare imperium* (Basel, 1983): *Journal of Roman Studies* 76 (1986), 286–8

Obituary of Jean-Bertrand Marie Barrère *Eagle* 71 (1986), 65–8

1987 '*Lex Cornelia de falsis*' *Athenaeum* 65 (1987), 163–71

'Was there a Doctrine of Manifest Guilt in Roman Criminal Law?' *Proceedings of the Cambridge Philological Society* 33 (1987), 38–52

John Crook, D.E.L. Johnston and P.G. Stein, '*Intertiumjagd* and the *lex Irnitana*: a Colloquium' *Zeitschrift für Papyrologie und Epigraphik* 70 (1987), 173–84

review of Marta Sordi *The Christians and the Roman Empire* (London, 1986): *Journal of Ecclesiastical History* 38 (1987), 625–6

1988 review of Max Kaser *Römische Rechtsquellen und angewandte Juristenmethode* (Vienna, Cologne and Graz, 1986): *Journal of Roman Studies* 78 (1988), 250–1

1989 Joseph Georg Wolf and John Crook, *Rechtsurkunden in Vulgärlatein aus den Jahren 37–39 n.Chr.* (Heidelberg, Abhandlungen der Heidelberger Akademie der Wissenschaften, 1989)

'A Negative Point about Mark Antony's Will' *L'antiquité classique* 58 (1989), 221–3

1990 '"His and Hers": What degree of financial responsibility did husband and wife have for the matrimonial home and their life in common, in a Roman marriage?' in Jean Andreau and Hinnerk Bruhns (eds.) *Parenté et stratégies familiales dans l'antiquité romaine: actes de la table ronde des 2–4 octobre 1986 (Paris, Maison des Sciences de l'homme)* (Paris, de Boccard, 1990 [= Collection de l'Ecole française de Rome, 129]), 153–72

review of P. Birks *New Perspectives in the Roman Law of Property: Essays for Barry Nicholas* (Oxford, 1989): *Classical Review* 40 (1990), 331–3

1991 *Law and Life of Rome: Aspects of Greek and Roman Life* (Ithaca, NY, Cornell University Press, and London, Thames and Hudson, 1967): reprinted 1991

Mogens Herman Hansen, *The Athenian Democracy in the Age of Demosthenes: Structure, Principles and Ideology* (translated by John Crook) (Oxford, and Cambridge, MA, Blackwell, 1991)

Obituary of John Ferguson (1921–1989) *Eagle* (1991), 39–41

1992 review of E. Champlin *Final Judgments: Duty and Emotion in Roman Wills 250 BC–AD 250* (Berkeley and Los Angeles, 1991): *Journal of Roman Studies* 82 (1992), 232–4

1993 'Once again the *controversiae* and Roman Law' in Kevin Lee, Chris Mackie and Harold Tarrant (eds.) *Multarum artium scientia: Festschrift for R. Godfrey Tanner* (Auckland, *Prudentia* Supplement, 1993), 68–76

John Crook and J.D. Cloud, 'Cicero *pro Vareno*: an Exposition and a Riposte' in H.D. Jocelyn (ed.) with H. Hurt *Tria Lustra* (Liverpool, 1993 [= *Liverpool Classical Papers* 3]), 169–80

'Babes, Sucklings, and Hugh Ashton's Tomb' *Eagle* (1993), 29–32

Obituary of Henry Dickinson Westlake *Eagle* (1993), 38–9

1994 John Crook, Andrew Lintott and Elizabeth Rawson (eds.), *Cambridge Ancient*

History IX²: the Last Age of the Roman Republic, 146–43 BC (Cambridge, CUP, 1994)
In this volume:
John Crook 'The Development of Roman Private Law', 531–63
John Crook, Andrew Lintott and Elizabeth Rawson 'Epilogue', 769–76
review of G. Camodeca *L'archivio puteolano dei Sulpicii* I (Naples, 1992): *Journal of Roman Studies* 84 (1994), 260–1
review of G.H. Guest *A Guest at Cambridge: Eagle* (1994), 56–9

1995 *Legal Advocacy in the Roman World* (Ithaca, NY, Cornell University Press, and London, Duckworth, 1995)
review of G. Crescimarone *Ecumene Augustea: una politica per il consenso* (Rome, 1993): *Journal of Roman Studies* 85 (1995), 286–7
review of E. Hermann-Otto *Ex ancilla natus: Untersuchungen zu den 'hausgeborenen' Sklaven und Sklavinnen im Westen des römischen Kaiserreiches* (Stuttgart, 1994): *Journal of Roman Studies* 85 (1995), 291–2

1996 Alan K. Bowman, Edward Champlin, Andrew Lintott (eds.), *Cambridge Ancient History X²: the Augustan Empire, 43 BC–AD 69* (Cambridge, CUP, 1996)
In this volume:
John Crook 'Political History 30 BC–AD 14', 70–112
John Crook 'Augustus: Power, Authority, Achievement', 113–146
M.H. Crawford (ed.), *Roman Statutes* (2 vols., London, 1996 [= *Bulletin of the Institute of Classical Studies* Supplement 64])
In volume II:
John Crook '41. Lex Aquilia', 723–6
John Crook '42. Lex Sulpicia', 727–8
John Crook '43. Leges de aquis', 729–30
John Crook '44. Lex Plaetoria', 731–2
John Crook and M.H. Crawford '47. Lex Cincia', 741–4
John Crook, M.H. Crawford and C.H. Williamson '63. Lex Quinctia', 793–800
'Legal History and General History' *Bulletin of the Institute of Classical Studies* 41 (1996), 31–6

1997 review of Karl Galinsky *Augustan Culture: an Interpretive Introduction* (Princeton, 1996): *Journal of Roman Studies* 87 (1997), 287–8
review of W.K. Lacey *Augustus and the Principate: the Evolution of the System* (Leeds, 1996): *Prudentia* 29.1 (1997), 78–81

1998 review of E. Metzger *A New Outline of The Roman Civil Trial* (Oxford, 1997) in *Cambridge Law Journal* 57 (1998), 413–15

1999 John Crook and J. Reynolds, 'The Cambridge Greek and Latin Book Club: a Brief Antiphonal Account, with an Appendix' in Christopher Stray (ed.) *Classics in 19th and 20th Century Cambridge: Curriculum, Culture and Community* (Cambridge, CUP, 1999 [= *Proceedings of the Cambridge Philological Society* Supplement 24]), 157–65

2000 John Crook, 'Three Hundred and Six Stakes', in Ulrich Manthe and Christoph Krampe (eds.) *Quaestiones Iuris, Festschrift für Joseph Georg Wolf zum 70. Geburtstag* (Berlin, Duncker and Humblot, 2000 [= Freiburger Rechtsgeschichtliche Abhandlungen, Neue Folge. Band 36]), 77–81.
Pernille Flensted-Jensen, Thomas Heine Nielsen and Lene Rubinstein (eds.), *Polis and Politics: Studies in Ancient Greek History Presented to Mogens Herman Hansen on his Sixtieth Birthday* (Copenhagen, Museum Tusculanum Press, 2000)
In this volume:
John Crook 'Introductory Flourish', 11–12.

INDEX

SUPPLEMENTS TO MNEMOSYNE

EDITED BY H. PINKSTER, H.S. VERSNEL, D.M. SCHENKEVELD, P. H. SCHRIJVERS AND S.R. SLINGS

Recent volumes in the series

149. VINOGRADOV, J.G.& S.D. KRYŽICKIJ (eds.). *Olbia.* Eine altgriechische Stadt im Nordwestlichen Schwarzmeerraum. 1995. ISBN 90 04 09677 9
150. MAURER, K. *Interpolation in Thucydides.* 1995. ISBN 90 04 10300 7
151. HORSFALL, N. (ed.) *A Companion to the Study of Virgil.* 1995 ISBN 90 04 09559 4
152. KNIGHT, V.H. *The Renewal of Epic.* Responses to Homer in the *Argonautica* of Apollonius. 1995. ISBN 90 04 10386 4
153. LUSCHNIG, C.A.E. *The Gorgon's Severed Head.* Studies of *Alcestis, Electra,* and *Phoenissae.* 1995. ISBN 90 04 10382 1
154. NAVARRO ANTOLÍN, F. (ed.). *Lygdamus.* Corpus Tibullianum III. 1-6: Lygdami elegiarum liber. Translated by J.J. Zoltowski. 1996. ISBN 90 04 10210 8
155. MATTHEWS, V.J. *Antimachus of Colophon.* Text and Commentary. 1996. ISBN 90 04 10468 2
156. TREISTER, M.Y. *The Role of Metals in Ancient Greek History.* 1996. ISBN 90 04 10473 9
157. WORTHINGTON, I. (ed.). *Voice into Text.* Orality and Literacy in Ancient Greece. 1996. ISBN 90 04 10431 3
158. WIJSMAN, H.J.W. *Valerius Flaccus,* Argonautica, *Book V.* A Commentary. 1996. ISBN 90 04 10506 9
159. SCHMELING, G. (ed.). *The Novel in the Ancient World.* 1996. ISBN 90 04 09630 2
160. SICKING, C.M.J. & P. STORK. *Two Studies in the Semantics of the Verb in Classical Greek.* 1996. ISBN 90 04 10460 7
161. KOVACS, D. *Euripidea Altera.* 1996. ISBN 90 04 10624 3
162. GERA, D. *Warrior Women.* The Anonymous Tractatus *De Mulieribus.* 1997. ISBN 90 04 10665 0
163. MORRIS, I. & B. POWELL (eds.). *A New Companion to Homer.* 1997. ISBN 90 04 09989 1
164. ORLIN, E.M. *Temples, Religion and Politics in the Roman Republic.* 1997.ISBN 90 04 10708 8
165. ALBRECHT, M. VON. *A History of Roman Literature.* From Livius Andronicus to Boethius with Special Regard to Its Influence on World Literature. 2 Vols.Revised by G.Schmeling and by the Author. Vol. 1: Translated with the Assistance of F. and K. Newman, Vol. 2: Translated with the Assitance of R.R. Caston and F.R. Schwartz. 1997. ISBN 90 04 10709 6 (Vol. 1), ISBN 90 04 10711 8 (Vol. 2), ISBN 90 04 10712 6 (Set)
166. DIJK, J.G.M. VAN. Αἶνοι, Λόγοι, Μῦθοι. Fables in Archaic, Classical, and Hellenistic Greek Literature. With a Study of the Theory and Terminology of the Genre. 1997. ISBN 90 04 10747 9
167. MAEHLER, H. (Hrsg.). *Die Lieder des Bakchylides.* Zweiter Teil: Die Dithyramben und Fragmente. Text, Übersetzung und Kommentar. 1997. ISBN 90 04 10671 5
168. DILTS, M. & G.A. KENNEDY (eds.). *Two Greek Rhetorical Treatises from the Roman Empire.* Introduction, Text, and Translation of the Arts of Rhetoric Attributed to Anonymous Seguerianus and to Apsines of Gadara. 1997. ISBN 90 04 10728 2
169. GÜNTHER, H.-C. *Quaestiones Propertianae.* 1997. ISBN 90 04 10793 2
170. HEINZE, T. (Hrsg.). *P. Ovidius Naso. Der* XII. *Heroidenbrief: Medea an Jason.* Einleitung, Text und Kommentar. Mit einer Beilage: Die Fragmente der Tragödie *Medea.* 1997. ISBN 90 04 10800 9

171. BAKKER, E.J. (ed.). *Grammar as Interpretation.* Greek Literature in its Linguistic Contexts. 1997. ISBN 90 04 10730 4
172. GRAINGER, J.D. *A Seleukid Prosopography and Gazetteer.* 1997. ISBN 90 04 10799 1
173. GERBER, D.E. (ed.). *A Companion to the Greek Lyric Poets.* 1997. ISBN 90 04 09944 1
174. SANDY, G. *The Greek World of Apuleius.* Apuleius and the Second Sophistic. 1997. ISBN 90 04 10821 1
175. ROSSUM-STEENBEEK, M. VAN. *Greek Readers' Digests?* Studies on a Selection of Subliterary Papyri. 1998. ISBN 90 04 10953 6
176. McMAHON, J.M. *Paralysin Cave.* Impotence, Perception, and Text in the *Satyrica* of Petronius. 1998. ISBN 90 04 10825 4
177. ISAAC, B. *The Near East under Roman Rule.* Selected Papers. 1998. ISBN 90 04 10736 3
178. KEEN, A.G. *Dynastic Lycia.* A Political History of the Lycians and Their Relations with Foreign Powers, c. 545-362 B.C. 1998. ISBN 90 04 10956 0
179. GEORGIADOU, A. & D.H.J. LARMOUR. *Lucian's Science Fiction Novel* True Histories. Interpretation and Commentary. 1998. ISBN 90 04 10667 7
180. GÜNTHER, H.-C. *Ein neuer metrischer Traktat und das Studium der pindarischen Metrik in der Philologie der Paläologenzeit.* 1998. ISBN 90 04 11008 9
181. HUNT, T.J. *A Textual History of Cicero's* Academici Libri. 1998. ISBN 90 04 10970 6
182. HAMEL, D. *Athenian Generals.* Military Authority in the Classical Period. 1998. ISBN 90 04 10900 5
183. WHITBY, M. (ed.). *The Propaganda of Power.* The Role of Panegyric in Late Antiquity. 1998. ISBN 90 04 10571 9
184. SCHRIER, O.J. *The* Poetics *of Aristotle and the* Tractatus Coislinianus. A Bibliography from about 900 till 1996. 1998. ISBN 90 04 11132 8
185. SICKING, C.M.J. *Distant Companions.* Selected Papers. 1998. ISBN 90 04 11054 2
186. P.H. SCHRIJVERS. *Lucrèce et les Sciences de la Vie.* 1999. ISBN 90 04 10230 2
187. BILLERBECK M. (Hrsg.). *Seneca.* Hercules Furens. Einleitung, Text, Übersetzung und Kommentar. 1999. ISBN 90 04 11245 6
188. MACKAY, E.A. (ed.). *Signs of Orality.* The Oral Tradition and Its Influence in the Greek and Roman World. 1999. ISBN 90 04 11273 1
189. ALBRECHT, M. VON. *Roman Epic.* An Interpretative Introduction. 1999. ISBN 90 04 11292 8
190. HOUT, M.P.J. VAN DEN. *A Commentary on the Letters of M. Cornelius Fronto.* 1999. ISBN 90 04 10957 9
191. KRAUS, C. SHUTTLEWORTH (ed.). *The Limits of Historiography.* Genre and Narrative in Ancient Historical Texts. 1999. ISBN 90 04 10670 7
192. LOMAS, K. & T. CORNELL. *Cities and Urbanisation in Ancient Italy.* ISBN 90 04 10808 4 *In preparation*
193. TSETSKHLADZE, G.R. (ed). *History of Greek Colonisation and Settlement Overseas.* 2 vols. ISBN 90 04 09843 7 *In preparation*
194. WOOD, S.E. *Imperial Women.* A Study in Public Images, 40 B.C. - A.D. 68. 1999. ISBN 90 04 11281 2
195. OPHUIJSEN, J.M. VAN & P. STORK. *Linguistics into Interpretation.* Speeches of War in Herodotus VII 5 & 8-18. 1999. ISBN 90 04 11455 6
196. TSETSKHLADZE, G.R. (ed.). *Ancient Greeks West and East.* 1999. ISBN 90 04 11190 5
197. PFEIJFFER, I.L. *Three Aeginetan Odes of Pindar.* A Commentary on *Nemean* V, *Nemean* III, & *Pythian* VIII. 1999. ISBN 90 04 11381 9
198. HORSFALL, N. *Virgil,* Aeneid *7.* A Commentary. 2000. ISBN 90 04 10842 4
199. IRBY-MASSIE, G.L. *Military Religion in Roman Britain.* 1999. ISBN 90 04 10848 3
200. GRAINGER, J.D. *The League of the Aitolians.* 1999. ISBN 90 04 10911 0
201. ADRADOS, F.R. *History of the Graeco-Roman Fable.* I: Introduction and from the Origins to the Hellenistic Age. Translated by L.A. Ray. Revised and Updated by the Au-thor and Gert-Jan van Dijk. 1999. ISBN 90 04 11454 8
202. GRAINGEr, J.D. *Aitolian Prosopographical Studies.* 2000. ISBN 90 04 11350 9
203. SOLOMON, J. *Ptolemy* Harmonics. Translation and Commentary. 2000. ISBN 90 04 115919

204. WIJSMAN, H.J.W. *Valerius Flaccus,* Argonautica, *Book VI.* A Commentary. 2000. ISBN 90 04 11718 0
205. MADER, G. *Josephus and the Politics of Historiography.* Apologetic and Impression Management in the *Bellum Judaicum.* 2000. ISBN 90 04 11446 7
206. NAUTA, R.R. *Poetry for Patrons.* Literary Communication in the Age of Domitian. 2001. ISBN 90 04 10885 8
207. ADRADOS, F.R. *History of the Graeco-Roman Fable.* II: The Fable during the Roman Empire and in the Middle Ages. Translated by L.A. Ray. Revised and Updated by the Author and Gert-Jan van Dijk. 2000. ISBN 90 04 11583 8
208. JAMES, A. & K. LEE. *A Commentary on Quintus of Smyrna,* Posthomerica V. 2000. ISBN 90 04 11594 3
209. DERDERIAN, K. *Leaving Words to Remember.* Greek Mourning and the Advent of Literacy. 2001. ISBN 90 04 11750 4
210. SHORROCK, R. *The Challenge of Epic.* Allusive Engagement in the *Dionysiaca* of Nonnus. 2001. ISBN 90 04 11795 4
211. SCHEIDEL, W. (ed.). *Debating Roman Demography.* 2001. ISBN 90 04 11525 0
212. KEULEN, A.J. *L. Annaeus Seneca* Troades. Introduction, Text and Commentary. 2001. ISBN 90 04 12004 1
213. MORTON, J. *The Role of the Physical Environment in Ancient Greek Seafaring.* 2001. ISBN 90 04 11717 2
214. GRAHAM, A.J. *Collected Papers on Greek Colonization.* 2001. ISBN 90 04 11634 6
215. GROSSARDT, P. *Die Erzählung von Meleagros.* Zur literarischen Entwicklung der kalydonischen Kultlegende 2001. ISBN 90 04 11952 3
216. ZAFIROPOULOS, C.A. *Ethics in Aesop's Fables: The* Augustana *Collection.* 2001. ISBN 90 04 11867 5
217. RENGAKOS, A. & T.D. Papanghelis (eds.). *A Companion to Apollonius Rhodius.* 2001. ISBN 90 04 11752 0
218. WATSON, J. *Speaking Volumes.* Orality and Literacy in the Greek and Roman World. 2001. ISBN 90 04 12049 1
219. MACLEOD, L. *Dolos and Dike in Sophokles' Elektra.* 2001. ISBN 90 04 11898 5
220. MCKINLEY, K.L. *Reading the Ovidian Heroine.* "Metamorphoses" Commentaries 1100-1618. 2001. ISBN 90 04 11796 2
221. REESON, J. *Ovid* Heroides *11, 13 and 14.* A Commentary. 2001. ISBN 90 04 12140 4
222. FRIED, M.N. & S. UNGURU. *Apollonius of Perga's Conica:* Text, Context, Subtext. 2001.
ISBN 90 04 11977 9
223. LIVINGSTONE, N. *A Commentary on Isocrates' Busiris.* 2001. ISBN 90 04 12143 9
224. LEVENE, D.S. & D.P. NELIS (eds.). *Clio and the Poets.* Augustan Poetry and the Traditions of Ancient Historiography. 2002. ISBN 90 04 11782 2
225. WOOTEN, C.W. *The Orator in Action and Theory in Greece and Rome.* 2001. ISBN 90 04 12213 3
226. GALÁN VIOQUE, G. *Martial, Book VII. A Commentary.* 2001. ISBN 90 04 12338 5
227. LEFÈVRE, E. *Die Unfähigkeit, sich zu erkennen: Sophokles' Tragödien.* 2001. ISBN 90 04 12322 9
228. SCHEIDEl, W. *Death on the Nile.* Disease and the Demography of Roman Egypt. 2001. ISBN 90 04 12323 7
229. SPANOUDAKIS, K. *Philitas of Cos.* 2002. ISBN 90 04 12428 4
230. WORTHINGTON, I. & J.M. FOLEY (eds.) *Epea and Grammata.* Oral and written Communication in Ancient Greece. 2002. ISBN 90 04 12455 1
231. MCKECHNIE, P. (ed.). *Thinking like a Lawyer.* Essays on Legal History and General History for John Crook on his Eightieth Birthday. 2002. ISBN 90 04 12474 8
232. GIBSON, R.K. & C. SHUTTLEWORTH KRAUS (eds.). *The Classical Commentary.* History, Practices, Theory. 2002. ISBN 90 04 12153 6